No Establishment of Religion

No Establishment of Religion

AMERICA'S ORIGINAL CONTRIBUTION TO RELIGIOUS LIBERTY

Edited by
T. Jeremy Gunn
and
John Witte, Jr.

OXFORD
UNIVERSITY PRESS

OXFORD
UNIVERSITY PRESS

Oxford University Press is a department of the University of Oxford.
It furthers the University's objective of excellence in research,
scholarship, and education by publishing worldwide.

Oxford   New York

Auckland   Cape Town   Dar es Salaam   Hong Kong   Karachi
Kuala Lumpur   Madrid   Melbourne   Mexico City   Nairobi
New Delhi   Shanghai   Taipei   Toronto

With offices in

Argentina   Austria   Brazil   Chile   Czech Republic   France   Greece
Guatemala   Hungary   Italy   Japan   Poland   Portugal   Singapore
South Korea   Switzerland   Thailand   Turkey   Ukraine   Vietnam

Oxford is a registered trade mark of Oxford University Press
in the UK and certain other countries.

Published in the United States of America
by Oxford University Press
198 Madison Avenue, New York, NY 10016

Library of Congress Cataloging-in-Publication Data
No establishment of religion : America's original contribution to religious liberty / edited by
T. Jeremy Gunn, John Witte, Jr.
p.   cm.
Includes bibliographical references (p.   ) and index.
ISBN 978-0-19-986039-5 (pbk. : alk. paper) — ISBN 978-0-19-986037-1 (hardcover : alk. paper)
1. United States—Religion—History. 2. United States. Constitution. 1st Amendment.
3. Freedom of religion—United States. 4. Church and state—United States.
I. Gunn, T. Jeremy (Thomas Jeremy) II. Witte, John, 1959–
BL2525.N6   2012
322'.10973—dc23   2011043410

1 3 5 7 9 8 6 4 2

Printed in the United States of America
on acid-free paper

{ CONTENTS }

127177

{ ACKNOWLEDGMENTS }

It has been a special privilege for me to collaborate on this volume with my distinguished colleague and friend, T. Jeremy Gunn. The idea for this volume emerged during Jeremy's tenure as director of the Program on Religion and Belief at the American Civil Liberties Union. There he kept encountering scholars on both the right and the left who exchanged partial accounts of the history of the First Amendment Establishment Clause. He also encountered advocates in both federal and state courts who seemed to have lost sight of the unique place of the no-establishment clause in the protection of religious liberty. This volume aims to deepen our understanding of the establishment clause in American history and our appreciation for its signature contribution to the modern understanding of religious liberty.

We have incurred a number of debts in the preparation of this volume, beyond the authors who have so generously shared their time and talents with us in its preparation. We would like to acknowledge that this work was supported in part by a generous contribution from the American Civil Liberties Union. We wish to emphasize, however, that the ACLU played no role in editing any of the work included in this volume. Accordingly, the views expressed in this volume are not intended to reflect the views of the ACLU and, in some instances, may disagree with positions taken by the ACLU.

We also wish to express our deep appreciation to our friends at the Henry Luce Foundation, particularly Michael Gilligan, Terry Lautz, and Toby Volkman. The Luce Foundation gave our Center for the Study of Law and Religion at Emory University a major grant for a project on "Law, Religion, and Human Rights," of which this volume is part and product. We wish to thank Ms. Amy Wheeler and Ms. Anita Mann of the Center for the Study of Law and Religion at Emory University for their expert administrative support of this project. We thank the Northern Illinois University Press and the *Utah Law Review* for their permission to reprint portions of the chapters by Mark McGarvie and Carl Esbeck. And we thank Emory law and religion students Justin Latterell, Andy Mayo, Jamie Schickler, and Judd Treeman for their excellent research assistance.

John Witte, Jr.
Emory University

{ LIST OF CONTRIBUTORS }

Thomas C. Berg is James L. Oberstar Professor of Law and Public Policy at the University of St. Thomas School of Law, Minnesota.

Derek Davis is Dean Emeritus of the College of Humanities and Dean Emeritus of the Graduate School of Arts and Sciences at the University of Mary Hardin-Baylor.

Daniel L. Dreisbach is Professor of Justice, Law and Society at American University.

Carl H. Esbeck is the R. B. Price Professor and Isabelle Wade & Paul C. Lyda Professor of Law, University of Missouri.

Paul A. Finkelman is currently the John Hope Franklin Visiting Professor of American Legal History at Duke University School of Law and also the President William McKinley Distinguished Professor of Law and Public Policy at Albany Law School.

Steven K. Green is Fred H. Paulus Professor of Law and Director of the Center for Religion, Law & Democracy at Williamette University College of Law.

Kent Greenawalt is University Professor, Columbia Law School.

T. Jeremy Gunn is Professor in the School of Humanities & Social Sciences, Al Akhawayn University, Morocco and Senior Fellow of the Center for the Study of Law and Religion at Emory University.

Ralph Ketcham is Professor Emeritus of History, Public Affairs, and Political Science and Maxwell Professor Emeritus of Citizenship and Public Affairs at Syracuse University.

David Little is T. J. Dermot Dunphy Professor Emeritus of the Practice in Religion, Ethnicity, and International Conflict at Harvard Divinity School.

Martin E. Marty is Fairfax M. Cone Distinguished Service Professor Emeritus at the University of Chicago and Senior Fellow at the Center for the Study of Law and Religion at Emory University.

Michael W. McConnell is Richard and Frances Mallery Professor of Law and Director of the Stanford Constitutional Law Center at Stanford Law School and Senior Fellow of the Hoover Institution, Stanford University.

Mark McGarvie is a lecturer in history and leadership studies and Director of Pre-Law Advising at the University of Richmond.

John Witte, Jr. is the Jonas Robitscher Professor of Law, Alonzo L. McDonald Family Foundation Distinguished Professor, and Director of the Center for the Study of Law and Religion, Emory University.

No Establishment of Religion

Introduction

John Witte, Jr.

Thomas Jefferson once described America's new constitutional guarantees of disestablishment and free exercise of religion as a "fair" and "novel experiment" in religious freedom.[1] These guarantees, set out in the new state and federal constitutions of 1776–1791, defied the millennium-old assumptions inherited from Western Europe—that one form of Christianity must be established in a community, and that the state must protect and support it against all other forms of faith. America would no longer suffer such governmental prescriptions and proscriptions of religion, Jefferson declared. All forms of Christianity had to stand on their own feet and on an equal footing with all other religions. Their survival and growth had to turn on the cogency of their word, not the coercion of the sword—on the faith of their members, not the force of the law.

America's new experiment in granting religious freedom to all and religious establishments to none was designed to end what James Madison called the Western "career of intolerance."[2] "In most of the Gov[ernment]s of the old world," Madison declared, "the legal establishment of a particular religion and without or with very little toleration of others, makes a pa[c]t of the political & civil organization." "[I]t was taken for granted that an exclusive & intolerant establishment was essential," and "that Religion could not be preserved without the support of Government, nor Government be supported with[ou]t an established Religion."[3] The main European powers that had colonized the Americas all had religious establishments—with Anglican establishments in England; Lutheran establishments in Germany and Scandinavia; Calvinist establishments in Scotland, the Netherlands, Switzerland, and Germany; and Catholic establishments in France, Spain, Portugal, and Italy.

Many founders laid the blame for the initial creation of these Western laws of religious establishment squarely on the first Christian Roman Emperor

Constantine in the fourth century. Seventeenth-century critics of religious establishment in England and America—John Milton, John Locke, Roger Williams, and William Penn—had already targeted Constantine as the culprit.[4] Roger Williams, for example, had written:

> [W]hen Constantine broke the bounds of this his own and God's edict, and [drew] the sword of civil power in suppressing other consciences for the [sake of] establishing the Christian [church.] [T]hen began the great mystery of the churches' sleep, [by which] the gardens of Christ's churches turned into the wilderness of National Religion, and the world (under Constantine's dominion) into the most unchristian Christendom. . . . There never was any National Religion good in this world but one [namely, ancient Israel], and since the desolation of that nation, there shall never be any National Religion good again.[5]

Such sentiments became increasingly commonplace in America after the Revolution of 1776. A New Hampshire conventioneer put it thusly in 1781:

> Who, sir, since that ever to be lamented era, when Constantine the great connected the church and the state together, has ever been able to fix an exact equipoise between the prerogatives of princes and claims of dignified priests. Visionaries have written about it, politicians have labored, but it is all in vain. The prince or priest must govern the whole. Priests when connected with the prince will sound the dread alarm, cry out infidel, infidel— the church, the church is in danger: and then lead armies under the banner of the cross, to exterminate heretics and massacre whole nations.[6]

A Massachusetts preacher echoed:

> No doubt, Constantine the Great, who first established [C]hristianity, had a good intention in the same; but all the darkness that has since overspread the Christian church, the exorbitant power of the popes and church of Rome, all the oceans of blood that have been shed in the contests about religion, between different sects of Christians, the almost total cessation of the progress of [C]hristianity, the rise of Mahometanism, the rise and spread of deism, the general contempt in which [C]hristianity is fallen; all may fairly be laid at the door of that establishment.[7]

James Madison wrote similarly against "Ecclesiastical Establishments":

> During almost fifteen centuries has the legal establishment of Christianity been on trial. What has been its fruits? More or less in all places, pride and indolence in the Clergy, ignorance or servility in the laity, in both, superstition, bigotry and persecution. . . . Torrents of blood have been spilt in the old world, by vain attempts of the secular arm, to extinguish Religious

discord, by proscribing all differences in Religious opinion. Time has at length revealed the True Remedy. . . . The American Theatre has exhibited proofs that equal and compleat liberty, if it does not wholly eradicate it, sufficiently destroys its malignant influence on the health and prosperity of the state.[8]

Anyone who was still not convinced could turn to Massachusetts jurist John Adams's massive three-volume *A Defense of the Constitutions of Government in the United States of America* (1788) for an exhaustive account of the "gory ecclesiastical or civil tyranny" of the Western tradition of religious establishments, and America's "glorious new experiment" of granting religious freedom for all and religious establishment to none. America has created something "strikingly original," Adams declared proudly.[9]

Some of the new American states came only gradually to this new understanding of disestablishment of religion. As both Michael McConnell and Mark McGarvie document in their opening chapters herein, seven of the original thirteen states still had forms of religious establishment at the time the First Amendment was being drafted in 1789. Massachusetts, Connecticut, and New Hampshire (along with the independent territories of Vermont and Maine that achieved statehood shortly thereafter) all retained what John Adams called their "mild and equitable" establishments of Puritan Congregationalism, although individual townships could go their own way.[10] After the American Revolution, Georgia, South Carolina, North Carolina, and Maryland replaced their exclusive Anglican establishments of colonial days with "multiple establishments" of "all denominations of Christian Protestants."[11] The four counties that comprised much of New York City still retained a soft Anglican establishment as well.

Though local practices varied in these establishment states, their governments still exercised some control over religious doctrine, governance, clergy, and other personnel. They still required church attendance of all citizens, albeit at a church of their choice. They still collected tithes for support of the church that the tithe-payer attended, and often gave state money, tax exemptions, and other privileges preferentially to one or some religions. They still obstructed the organization, education, and worship activities of dissenting churches, particularly Catholics and Quakers. They still used established church institutions and their clergy for birth, marriage, and death registries, for public education, poor relief, political rallies, and distribution of state literature. They still often administered religious test oaths for political officials, sometimes for lower officials and teachers, too. To be sure, these formal state establishments of religion, particularly the controversial practice of state funding and tax collections for religion, were eroding in support by 1789 when the First Amendment was being forged. These traditional state tithing provisions of state establishments of religion ended formally in 1833 when Massachusetts became the last state to abandon them. Yet many other vestiges of traditional establishments remained in place in many states thereafter.

Despite the remaining establishment practices, disestablishment movements were gaining support in the new states, especially as Baptist and other Evangelical advocates grew stronger and as Enlightenment arguments for disestablishment cut deeper into traditional establishment practices inherited from Europe and colonial America. By 1789, six of the original thirteen states had no establishment of religion. Rhode Island and Pennsylvania had never had establishments from the time of their founding. New Jersey, Delaware, and New York (except for the four counties that comprised New York City) had constitutionally abandoned their religious establishment shortly after the American Revolution. Virginia in 1786 passed its (ironically named) Act for the Establishment of Religious Freedom. And even in states that still maintained religious establishments—indeed, especially in these states— virtually all founders feared a national establishment of religion. Newspapers of the day were filled with hyperbolic projections of Anglican bishops, Presbyterian divines, and even the Catholic papacy presiding tyrannically over the vulnerable young nation. Such a national establishment of religion simply could not be allowed, even if state establishments of various types might be countenanced.

The term "establishment of religion" was an ambiguous phrase in eighteenth-century America. In the dictionaries and common parlance of the day to "establish" meant "to settle firmly," "to fix unalterably," "to settle in any privilege or possession," "to make firm," "to ratify," "to ordain," "to enact," "to set up," to "build firmly."[12] Such was the basic meaning of the term when used in the text of the 1787 Constitution: "We the people of the United States, in order to form a perfect union, to *establish* justice . . . do ordain and *establish* this Constitution" (preamble); Congress shall have power "[t]o *establish* an uniform rule of naturalization" and "[t]o *establish* post offices" (Art. I.8); governmental offices "shall be *established* by law" (Art. II.2); Congress may "ordain and *establish* . . . inferior courts" (Art. III.1); the ratification of nine states "shall be sufficient for the *establishment* of this Constitution" (Art. VI).[13]

Following this basic sense of the term, most American founders understood the establishment of religion to mean governmental actions to "settle," "fix," "define," "ordain," "enact," or "set up" the religion of the community—its religious doctrines and liturgies, its religious texts and traditions, its clergy and property. To most founders, the most notorious example of religious establishment in this sense was the established Anglican Church that prevailed in the American colonies until the 1776 revolution. According to the formal ecclesiastical law of the day,[14] the king was Supreme Head of the Church and Defender of the Faith. Together with Parliament, he mandated the Thirty-Nine Articles of Faith as the established doctrine, prescribed the Book of Common Prayer as the established liturgy, and made official the King James Version of the Bible. The king and his delegates vested, disciplined, and removed the clergy as political appointees, collecting tithes and taxes for their support and granting them privileges and immunities from civic duties. They instituted special criminal laws of blasphemy and sacrilege to protect the church's doctrine, liturgy, clergy, and property. They consigned all nonconformists to second-class status at best, officially tolerating only Protestants, but not Catholics and Jews, who would remain formally illegal in England until the Jewish and Catholic Emancipation Acts of the 1830s.

If "establishment of religion" meant anything to the founders, it meant at least this. No influential American founder writing from 1776 to 1800—even former Anglicans, who came to be called Episcopalians after 1789—defended this kind of traditional establishment law either for the national government or for any of the states. For many American founders, such an establishment of religion violated three other principles of religious freedom that they also championed: (1) liberty of conscience; (2) religious equality; and (3) separation of church and state.

For most founders, the movement to disestablish religion served, first, to protect the principle of liberty of conscience by foreclosing government from coercively prescribing mandatory forms of religious belief, doctrine, and practice. As both the original Delaware and Pennsylvania constitutions put it: "[N]o authority can or ought to be vested in, or assumed by any power whatever, that shall in any case interfere with, or in any manner controul, the right of conscience in the free exercise of religious worship."[15] Thomas Paine put forth this same argument:

> All religions are in their nature mild and benign, and united with principles of morality. They could not have made proselytes at first, by professing anything that was vicious, cruel, persecuting or immoral. . . . Persecution is not an original feature in any religion; but it is always the strongly marked feature of all law-religions, or religions established by law. Take away the law-establishment, and every religion reassumes its original benignity.[16]

The movement to disestablish religion served, second, to protect the principle of equality of all faiths before the law by preventing the government from singling out certain religious beliefs and bodies for preferential treatment. The problem for some founders was not so much government support of religion or its institutions; many founders thought religion was essential for cultivating virtue, maintaining order, and promoting good works in the community.[17] The real problem was preferential government support for one form of religion to the exclusion or deprecation of all others. Those policies could not be countenanced. This concept of no "preferential establishment" of religion came through repeatedly in state constitutional debates. In the Virginia Ratification Convention, for example, Madison and several other conventioneers said that they were seeking to "prevent the establishment of any one sect in prejudice to the rest."[18] A South

Carolina conventioneer likewise "oppose[d] the ideas of religious establishments; or of states giving preference to any religious denomination."[19] The New
Jersey Constitution provided "there shall be no establishment of any one religious sect . . . in preference to another."[20] Several state ratifying conventions suggested amendments to the U.S. Constitution that "no religious sect or society
ought to be favored or established by law in preference to others."[21]

The movement to disestablish religion served, third, to protect the basic
principle of separation of the offices and operations of church and state.
Disestablishment, in Jefferson's words, prohibited government "from intermeddling with religious institutions, their doctrines, discipline, or exercises."
It also kept government from "the power of effecting any uniformity of time or
matter among them. Fasting & prayer are religious exercises. The enjoining
them is an act of discipline. Every religious society has a right to determine for
itself the times for these exercises, & the objects proper for them, according to
their own peculiar tenets."[22] To allow such governmental meddling in the
internal affairs of religious bodies would inflate the competence of government. As Madison wrote, it "implies either that the Civil Magistrate is a competent judge of religious truth; or that he may employ religion as an engine of
civil policy. The first is an arrogant pretension falsified by the contradictory
opinions of rulers in all ages, and throughout the world, the second an unhallowed perversion of the means of salvation."[23]

A number of founders pressed this idea of separation of church and state
further by prohibiting not only governmental interference in religious bodies
but clerical participation in political office. Clerics who serve in government,
they argued, could use the threat of spiritual reprisal to force their congregants,
including fellow politicians who sat in their pews, to acquiesce in their political
positions. They would inevitably be conflicted over whose interests to represent and serve—the interests of their religious congregants or their political
constituents. Clerics who tried to serve both God and the state would be dis-
tracted from their fundamental callings of preaching and teaching, and
tempted to bend their religious messages toward political causes. These arguments for clerical exclusions led seven of the original thirteen states and several later states to ban ministers from serving in political office. These provisions
remained in place in a few states until the twentieth century before finally
being outlawed by the Supreme Court in *McDaniel v. Paty* (1978).

The American founders advocated the disestablishment of religion not only
because it violated the other religious liberty principles of liberty of conscience,
religious equality, and separation of church and state, but because religious
establishments simply no longer worked. Madison, for example, contrasted
the erosion of religion in establishment states with the flourishing of religion
in nonestablishment states of his day. In the Congregationalist establishment
states of New England and the south, he wrote, "[t]he old churches, built under
the establishment at the public expense, have in many instances gone to ruin,

or are in a very dilapidated state, owing chiefly to a transition desertion of the flocks to other worships." It had been "the universal opinion" in such states "that civil government could not stand without the prop of a religious establishment, and that the Christian religion itself, would perish if not supported by a legal provision for its clergy. The experience of Virginia [together with that of Rhode Island, Pennsylvania, New Jersey, and Delaware] conspicuously corroborates the disproof of both opinions. The civil government, though bereft of everything like an associated hierarchy, possesses the requisite stability and performs its functions with complete success; whilst the number, the industry, and the morality of the priesthood, & the devotion of the people have been manifestly increased by the total separation of the church from the state" and the complete disestablishment of religion.[24]

Similarly, John Leland, the fiery Baptist preacher, decried all establishments as "evil" and "harmful"—whether the Roman Empire's establishment of Christianity, the Ottoman Empire's establishment of Islam, Spain's establishment of Catholicism, New England's establishment of Puritan Congregationalism, or England and colonial America's establishment of Anglicanism. All such establishments are evil and harmful, Leland argued, first, because when "uninspired, fallible men make their own opinions tests of orthodoxy," then religion is stunted and stilted, "ignorance and superstition prevail, or persecution rages." Second, establishments are evil and harmful because "the minds of men are biased to embrace that religion which is favored and pampered by law, and thereby hypocrisy is nourished." Third, "establishments not only wean and alienate the affections of one from another," but they keep or drive nonconformists away from the state, taking their loyalty, work, and taxes with them and leaving dull anemic religions to propagate themselves or convert others by force. Fourth, "establishments metamorphose the church into a creature, and religion into a principle of state, which has a natural tendency to make men conclude that religion is nothing but a trick of state." Fifth, even in so-called Christian lands, "there are no two kingdoms and states that establish the same creed and formalities of faith." This brings neighbors and families into inevitable conflict and war, as European history has too often shown. Sixth, establishments merely cover for the insecurity and doubt of church leaders. Instead of having faith in the cogency of their views, they "dictate for others" and betray an "overfondness for a particular system" that becomes its own theological idol. And seventh, establishments cover the insecurity of politicians. "Rulers often fear that if they leave every man to think, speak, and worship as he pleases, that the whole cause [of statecraft] will be wrecked in diversity."[25]

Such sentiments eventually persuaded all the states to remove the most glaring features of traditional establishments—the state dictates of religious doctrine, liturgy, and canons, the overt state favoritism of one religion and bald discrimination against others. The question that remained controversial—in the eighteenth century as much as in our own—was whether more gentle and generic forms of state support for religion could be countenanced. Did disestablishment of religion prohibit governmental support for religion altogether, or did it simply require that such governmental support be distributed nonpreferentially among all religions? Did disestablishment require that government remove old Sabbath, blasphemy, marriage, and other laws grounded in religious teachings, or could those laws now be justified on grounds of tradition, morality, or utility? Did disestablishment mean removal of all religious texts and symbols from public documents and public lands, or all religious officials and ceremonies from political life, or could a democratic government reflect and represent these in ever more inclusive ways? Did disestablishment require states to abstain from all cooperation with religious bodies and officials in the governance of marriage, education, social welfare, and other social services, or could church and state still cooperate in these areas of "mixed jurisdiction"? Strong disestablishment advocates in the founding generation and thereafter, particularly those influenced by strict Baptist and Enlightenment liberal views, pressed for no religious aid, no religious laws, and no cooperation of church and state so much as possible. Others used arguments from civic republicanism and religious utility to argue for nonpreferential religious aid, maintenance of traditional religious morality, and generous cooperation between church and state.

The chapters in this volume take up the story from here, with Jeremy Gunn's sweeping introduction providing an excellent map of many of the main issues. In their opening chapters, David Little and Paul Finkelman analyze some of the prescient arguments and policies of disestablishment and religious freedom already in place in the seventeenth-century colonies of Rhode Island and New York. Rhode Island, David Little demonstrates, was the first American colony to operate without a formal religious establishment; it was inspired by the progressive theories of religious freedom advocated by its founder Roger Williams, a liberal Calvinist. New York, Paul Finkelman argues, was the first new state constitution to disestablish religion, inspired in no small part by its seventeenth-century experiment in religious pluralism with Jews, Quakers, Lutherans, Catholics, and Reformed Christians eventually living together in New Amsterdam, albeit after ample controversy. Not surprisingly, both these states became leading advocates of disestablishment after the American Revolution. The state of Virginia, Ralph Ketcham shows, though a bastion of established Anglicanism during the colonial era, quickly became a leader in the disestablishment campaign as well, under the masterful direction of Madison and Jefferson.

In later chapters Steven Green and Thomas Berg, echoing Jeremy Gunn's opening chapter, show how these state disestablishment practices became more culturally contested and constitutionally specific in the course of the nineteenth and early twentieth centuries. Protestant-Catholic rivalries, battles over aid to religious schools and charities, growing religious pluralism and antireligious and anti-immigrant animus were among the factors that prompted at least some states in the nineteenth century to insist upon a sharper separation of church and state and to adopt more stringent legal policies if not state constitutional provisions against government funding and support of religious causes, especially religious schools.

Although the new American states came more gradually and sporadically to a broader consensus on the meaning and method of disestablishment, the new national government committed itself to no establishment of religion early on. As Derek Davis's chapter shows, the Continental Congress of 1774–1789 legislated regularly on issues of religion, but already had begun to move toward greater religious freedom for the nation, if not disestablishment of religion. The U.S. Constitution, drafted in 1787, was largely silent on religion, except in prohibiting religious test oaths for federal office—a critical first step in the federal protection of religious freedom as Jeremy Gunn, Daniel Dreisbach, and Martin Marty each show in their chapters. More decisive in the national march toward disestablishment of religion was the First Amendment to the Constitution, drafted by the First Congress in 1789 and ratified by the states in 1791. It provided: "Congress shall make no law respecting an establishment of religion, or prohibiting the free exercise thereof."

The remaining chapters of the volume probe the original and evolving understanding of the First Amendment disestablishment guarantee in the first 150 years of the republic. The common foil for these chapters is the landmark Supreme Court case of *Everson v. Board of Education* (1947). This case incorporated the First Amendment establishment clause into the Fourteenth Amendment Due Process Clause, making it binding on state and local governments. More importantly for this book, *Everson* offered an account of the history and original intent of the Establishment Clause, which several later chapters in this volume expose for its inadequacies. "Among the stupendous powers of the Supreme Court," Mark DeWolfe Howe once wrote, "is the power not only to make history, but also to declare history."[26] In few areas of constitutional law outside the Establishment Clause has the Court's "declaration of history" proved so controversial.

In his chapter, Carl Esbeck sifts through the debates in the First Congress of 1789 and sorts out the most plausible original understandings of the key words *respecting, establishment,* and *religion* and the links between the no establishment and free exercise guarantees of the First Amendment. He also takes on directly various modern interpreters who regard the First Amendment establishment as a hearty endorsement of state establishments of religion, or a mere guarantee of freedom of conscience. He views the Establishment Clause as a jurisdictional limitation on the new federal government. Daniel Dreisbach continues the national story into the first decades of the nineteenth century, showing the continued dialectic between "separationist" and "accommodationist" interpretations and applications of the Establishment Clause, and the accepted discordance between federal laws and state laws on religious freedom.

These debates became more acute in the later nineteenth and early twentieth centuries, as Jeremy Gunn, Thomas Berg, and Steven Green all document, first at the state level, and then at the federal level, particularly as Congress sought repeatedly to develop a national law on religious liberty that would be binding on the states. Important in the last quarter of the nineteenth century was the battle over the proposed Blaine Amendment to the U.S. Constitution, which would have applied the First Amendment guarantees of no establishment and free exercise of religion to the states, and cut off government funding of religion. The federal Blaine Amendment narrowly failed passage, despite repeated efforts, but various states did adopt their own constitutional policies of no government funding of religion.

The penultimate chapter by Kent Greenawalt maps the range of hard interpretive issues that continue to this day to confront historians of the Establishment Clause and advocates of First Amendment freedoms. The closing chapter by Martin Marty sorts through the remaining myths and fictions of "Christian America" and "secular America." The no establishment clause, he argues, was not a rejection of religion and the church but a testimony to America's faith in religion and in the capacity of every peaceable religion to stand on its own once it was granted full freedom. This, Marty concludes, was the most original insight of the American founders about the nature of religion and government, faith and freedom.

The twelve distinguished chapter authors—selected for their diverse views— stake out strong and sometimes competing positions on what no establishment of religion meant to the American founders, and what it can and should mean for America today. Together, the authors hold up a wide canopy of responsible academic opinion on the genesis and genius of America's most original contribution to religious liberty. And together, they expose the fallacies of viewing America as either a Christian nation bent on perpetuating biblical ideals or a secular nation built with a high and impregnable wall of separation between church and state.

Notes

1. Saul K. Padover, ed., *The Complete Jefferson, Containing His Major Writings* (New York: Duell, Sloan & Pearce, 1943), 538, 673–76, 1147; P. L. Ford, ed., *The Works of Thomas Jefferson* (New York and London: G.P. Putnam's Son, 1904–1905), 11:7; Julian P. Boyd, ed., *The Papers of Thomas Jefferson*, (Princeton, NJ: Princeton University Press, 1950), 1:537–39.

2. James Madison, "Memorial and Remonstrance against Religious Assessments," in *The Papers of James Madison*, ed. W. T. Hutchinson et al. (Chicago: University of Chicago Press, 1962–1991), 8:298.

3. Letter to Rev. Adams (1833), in Daniel L. Dreisbach, *Religion and Politics in the Early Republic* (Louisville, KY; University of Kentucky Press, 1996), 117–21, at 118 (paragraph breaks omitted).

4. On Williams, see chapter 4 by David Little. See further examples in John Witte Jr., *The Reformation of Rights: Law, Religion, and Human Rights in Early Modern Calvinism* (Cambridge: Cambridge University Press, 2008), 226–48, and John Witte Jr. and Joel A. Nichols, *Religion and the American Constitutional Experiment*, 3rd ed. (Boulder, CO: Westview Press, 2011), 1–20.

5. Quoted in chapter 4 by David Little.

6. *New Hampshire Patriot*, July 23, 1781.

7. Elhanan Winchester, "A Century Sermon on the Glorious Revolution (1788)," in *Political Sermons of the American Founding Era, 1730–1805*, ed. Ellis Sandoz (Indianapolis, IN: Liberty Fund, 1991), 969, 989–90.

8. Madison, "Memorial and Remonstrance," secs. 8, 11. See also his Letter to William Bradford (January 24, 1774), in Madison, *Papers*, 1:537.

9. In *The Works of John Adams*, ed. C. F. Adams (Boston: Little, Brown, 1850–1856), vols. 4–6; see further John Adams, "A Dissertation on the Canon and Feudal Law (1774)," in ibid., 3:447, 451ff.

10. See sources and discussion in John Witte Jr., "'A Most Mild and Equitable Establishment of Religion': John Adams and the 1780 Massachusetts Constitution," *Journal of Church and State* 41 (1999): 213–52.

11. South Carolina Constitution (1778), Art. XXXVIII.

12. See entries under "establish" and "establishment" in John Andrews, *A Complete Dictionary of the English Language*, 4th ed. (Philadelphia: William Young, 1789); John Ash, *A New and Complete Dictionary of the English Language* (London: Edward and Charles Dilly, 1775); Samuel Johnson, *A Dictionary of the English Language*, 4th ed. (Philadelphia: William Young, 1773); William Perry, *The Royal Standard English Dictionary*, 1st Am. ed. (London: W. Strahan, J. and F. Rivington, 1788); Thomas Sheridan, *A Complete Dictionary of the English Language*, 2nd ed. (London: Charles Dilley, 1789).

13. See T. Jeremy Gunn, *A Standard for Repair: The Establishment Clause, Equality, and Natural Rights* (Buffalo, NY: Prometheus Books, 1992), 46–47, 71–73.

14. The best summary of the day was Richard Burn, *Ecclesiastical Law*, 4 vols., 3d ed. (London: A. Strahan, 1775).

15. Delaware Declaration of Rights (1776), sec. 3; Pennsylvania Declaration of Rights (1776), II.

16. Thomas Paine, *Rights of Man* (1791), in Philip B. Kurland and Ralph Lerner, eds., *The Founders' Constitution* (Chicago: University of Chicago Press, 1987), 5:95–96.

17. See chapter 9 by Daniel Dreisbach.

18. For Edmund Randolph, see Jonathan Elliot, ed., *The Debates in the Several State Conventions, on the Adoption of the Federal Constitution*, 2d ed. (Washington, DC: Printed for the Editor, 1836–1845), 3:208; see also ibid., 3:431. For Madison, see ibid., 3:330; for Zachariah Johnson, see ibid., 3:645–46.

19. Quoted in Chester J. Antieau, Arthur T. Downey, and Edward C. Roberts, *Freedom from Federal Establishment: Formation and Early History of the First Amendment Religion Clauses* (Washington, DC: Bruce Publishing, 1964), 106.

20. New Jersey Constitution (1776), Art. XIX.

21. Elliot, ed., *Debates*, 1:328, 334.

22. Thomas Jefferson, Letter to Rev. Samuel Miller (1808), in Kurland and Lerner, eds., *The Founders' Constitution*, 5:98–99.

23. Madison, "Memorial and Remonstrance," para. 5.

24. Letter to Robert Walsh (March 2, 1819), in Madison, *Writings*, 8:430–32 (spelling and punctuation modernized).

25. John Leland, "The Rights of Conscience Inalienable," in *The Writings of John Leland*, ed. L. F. Greene (New York: Arno Press, 1969), 179–92.

26. Mark DeWolfe Howe, *The Garden and the Wilderness* (Chicago: University of Chicago Press, 1965), 1.

1

The Separation of Church and State versus Religion in the Public Square

THE CONTESTED HISTORY OF THE ESTABLISHMENT CLAUSE

T. Jeremy Gunn

Foreign observers of the American legal system typically identify the United States as having a religion-friendly form of separation of church and state. From the early years of the nineteenth century, many—though certainly not all—outside observers praised this "American model" of separating church and state for its vigorous protection of the free exercise of religion while simultaneously excluding governmental involvement in religious activity. During most of the nineteenth century, and extending well into the twentieth, Americans themselves broadly agreed that one of the great contributions of the U.S. Constitution to religious freedom was its firm commitment to the doctrine of the separation of church and state. In 1878, a unanimous Supreme Court in *Reynolds v. United States* gave its official imprimatur by declaring, in the words of Thomas Jefferson, that the Constitution had established "a wall of separation between church and state."[1]

Seventy years later, in a sharply divided decision in *Everson v. Board of Education*, both the majority and dissenting opinions nevertheless agreed that "the wall of separation of church and state" should continue as the guiding touchstone for the constitutional relationship between religion and the government.[2] The majority and dissenting opinions in *Everson* also concurred that the meaning of the Establishment Clause could be found in its history. The *Everson* disagreement was not whether separation was the proper standard or whether history should be used to interpret it, but just how rigorously the doctrine should have been applied with regard to whether the state could subsidize student transportation to a parochial school.

Although *Everson* had merely reiterated the same term "separation of church and state" that had been commonplace in the United States for more than a century, it nevertheless provoked a reaction from a few influential scholars who began to challenge both the historical legitimacy of separation as a constitutional standard as well as its legal consequences.[3] A separate group of scholars and jurists responded favorably to the Court's use of the metaphor, and began publishing a stream of books and articles defending the separationist history of America.[4] During the following sixty years, a lively and often polemical debate ensued that ultimately was joined by scores of scholars arguing back and forth about the appropriateness of the wall metaphor, the term "separation of church and state," and the concept of separating the church from the state.

In the 1980s, the academic argument that had begun with a challenge to *Everson* spilled over into what would later be called the "culture wars."[5] Many associated with the so-called religious right began to argue that the term "separation of church and state" was not only a historical error, but that the Supreme Court had been involved in a deliberate attempt to impose un-American values on the Constitution. The most extreme denunciations of the term have come from persons who argue that the real origin of the term "separation of church and state" was in atheistic Soviet constitutions and not the American constitution, meaning that separationism should be opposed for being unpatriotic, un-American, pro-communist, and antireligious.[6] Whether those who make such extreme arguments are aware of their absurdity, cyberspace and popular debates are filled with denunciations of "the separation of church and state" because of its appearance in Soviet-era constitutions. They accuse secularists, liberals, and civil libertarians of using it as part of an evil effort to undermine religion in America.[7] This conspiratorial explanation is, of course, groundless. The terms "freedom of conscience" and "freedom of speech" similarly appeared in Soviet-era constitutions, but that would not seem to be a good reason for opposing those values in the United States. Moreover, the Soviet Union did not even exist in 1878 when the very conservative *Reynolds* court unanimously adopted "the wall of separation of church and state" as a guiding metaphor for interpreting the religion clauses of the Constitution.[8] Although these modern-day nativists do not trouble themselves with the accuracy of their claims, they do exemplify a rising public suspicion of the term.

The intellectual attack on the historical legitimacy of separation of church and state as a constitutional norm perhaps reached its zenith with the publication of Professor Philip Hamburger's book *Separation of Church and State* in 2002.[9] Hamburger went so far as to assert that the historical insertion of the term into American law had nothing to do with genuine religious liberty, but instead came into existence as an anti-Catholic code word that was deployed in the mid-nineteenth century by nativists, bigots, Know-Nothings, the Ku Klux Klan, liberals, and atheists. Hamburger even made an ad hominem attack against Justice Hugo Black, the author of the *Everson* majority opinion, by arguing that the justice's use of the term could be traced back to his own youthful association with the Ku Klux Klan. Rather than being a broadly accepted term, the book argues instead that the concept of the separation of church and state has a deeply tainted legacy. Hamburger's evidence and analysis will be challenged below.[10]

Coinciding with the mounting challenge to the term "separation of church and state," an alternative formulation has become increasingly prevalent. It stresses the legitimacy of the government's promotion of "religion in the public square." Although the term is particularly associated with a book by Richard John Neuhaus published in 1984, the underlying belief that the government properly may promote religion and religious values is not at all new.[11] Indeed, the belief that the government should promote religion might best be understood as having been *the* consensus opinion in America from the seventeenth century until the 1780s when it came under increasing attack.[12]

In many ways, the differing points of view that appear in this volume and that divide those who appeal to a "separation of church and state" from those who favor governmental support of "religion in the public square" echo the Virginia assessment controversy of the mid-1780s.[13] In 1785, Governor Patrick Henry of Virginia proposed a small three-pence general tax for the support of clergy, arguing that the government properly should be able to aid religion. In response, James Madison, in his famous *Memorial and Remonstrance* (1785), successfully argued that such aid to religion would constitute an impermissible "establishment." The Virginia legislature rejected Henry's requested financial aid to religion and adopted instead Thomas Jefferson's Virginia Statute for Religious Freedom. The same James Madison would later describe the U.S. Constitution as having established "mutual independence" and a "line of separation" between religion and the state.[14] The debate over whether the founders intended to separate religion from the state or whether they believed that the state could promote religion is one of the core disputes underlying the historical interpretations of the meaning of the Establishment Clause. Should the Constitution be understood to have adopted Henry's or Madison's understanding of the proper relationship between religion and the state? The *Everson* decision thus became a watershed in the interpretation of the Establishment Clause not because of any legal innovations, but because it launched an ongoing debate inside the United States about the validity of the doctrine of "separation of church and state" as well as the historical meaning of the Establishment Clause—of which this volume is but the most recent result.

The historical viability of the term "separation of church and state" is only one element of the larger controversy inside the United States that is now associated with the meaning of the Establishment Clause of the First Amendment, which reads: "Congress shall make no law respecting an establishment of religion." The meaning of these ten words, drafted in 1789 by the First Congress meeting in New York City, has been the subject of scores of Supreme Court opinions, hundreds of federal court decisions, thousands of academic articles, and tens of thousands of op-eds, letters to the editor, and campaign speeches. These words have been interpreted to allow (or forbid) actions such as: erecting Ten Commandments monuments, Latin crosses, crèches, or other religious displays on governmental property; financing by the state of trans-portation for children attending religious schools; providing tax-exempt status to churches and other religious institutions; allowing the phrase "one nation under God" in the Pledge of Allegiance; purchasing of textbooks by the state for religious schools; teachers praying with students in public schools; cele-brating religious events (such as Christmas) in public schools; and hiring by the government of legislative and military chaplains. These topics, which pro-voke heated controversy in public debates in the United States, resemble each other to the extent that they all involve, directly or indirectly, governmental support for religious activities, and their constitutionality is largely decided under the Establishment Clause.

The Establishment Clause of the First Amendment is, of course, only one of three provisions of the eighteenth-century Constitution that directly men-tions religion. The "No Religious Test" clause (Article VI section 3), as drafted in Philadelphia in 1787, provides that "*no religious test* shall ever be required as a qualification to any office or public trust under the United States" (emphasis added). The Free Exercise Clause of the First Amendment, which follows im-mediately after the Establishment Clause, was tied closely to it during its drafting history.[15] It provides that "Congress shall make no law . . . prohibiting the free exercise [of religion]." Although none of these clauses was adopted without controversy, the most volatile disputes have been concentrated on the Establishment Clause, which has generated the most serious historical in-quiry, legal analysis, and popular debate.

The Ideological Divide: The Separation of Church and State *versus* Governmental Promotion of Religion in the Public Square

Interpretations of the meaning of the Establishment Clause often fall into one of two broad ideological perspectives. The first favors the "separation of church and state" (or more properly *religion* and the state), whereas the second argues that the state may legitimately promote religion and religious morality in the public square. I will use *separationist* and *cooperationist* as shorthand terms to describe these two basic approaches.

It is important to note that separationists and cooperationists typically agree on several issues that often are overlooked. They largely agree that indi-viduals have the right to choose their own beliefs and to associate with others without governmental interference. They generally agree that individuals should be able to manifest their beliefs in public, again without interference by the government except in extreme cases. They further agree that the state should neither be able to select a preferred religion (or religions) nor provide financial or political aid to some religions while excluding others.

These important similarities do not, however, mean that there are not significant disagreements between the separationists and the cooperationists. They typically take divergent positions with regard to the questions whether the government should be able to promote religious symbols (Ten Commandments monuments, crèches, and Latin crosses), to sponsor religious activities (prayers and religious activities in public schools and legislative prayers), and to finance activities of religious organizations (including religious social service agencies and religious schools). Separationists typically oppose governmental promotion of these activities; cooperationists are more likely to favor them.

The cooperationist approach to government and religion largely prevailed in most of the original thirteen colonies up through the 1770s. But the tide began to turn toward a general consensus favoring the concept of separation of church and state during the Revolutionary War. As will be shown below, the term "separation of church and state" ultimately came to command overwhelming popular and intellectual support in the United States through much of the nineteenth and the first half of the twentieth centuries.[16]

The debate between the separationists and cooperationists has focused on two principal subjects: first, the philosophical (or ideological) differences regarding the role that the government should play in supporting religion, and second, the competing interpretations of American history that are relevant for discerning the meaning of the Establishment Clause. Cooperationists favor the active involvement of government in promoting religion and a morality-based politics and legal system. They take a stand against relativism and law that is devoid of reference to a higher source. Thus it may be appropriate, in their view, for the government to facilitate, finance, and encourage religion and religious activities. Cooperationists also have argued that attempts to forbid governmental officials from promoting religion in public schools or on governmental property is tantamount to hostility against religion.

Separationists typically argue that government encouragement of religion necessarily will result in preferences for some religions over others and that it impermissibly discriminates against nonbelievers. Such governmental involvement in religious questions is likely not only to corrupt religious groups by encouraging them to curry favor with governmental institutions, but also to promote an unseemly conflict among religious groups as they vie for governmental privileges and largesse. Such competition, separationists argue, ultimately compromises religious freedom while at the same time encouraging governmental officials to enhance their political power by obtaining support from influential religious communities.[17]

A second area of disagreement between separationists and cooperationists— and the one that is the focus both of this chapter and this volume as a

whole—is what history teaches about the proper interpretation of the Establishment Clause. This is not a debate about whether history should be used
to help explain the meaning of the clause, a position broadly shared. Unsurprisingly, scholars and citizens with differing philosophical values about the
appropriate role of the government in religious matters read their history differently. In brief, separationists, following in part the *Everson* court, tend to
emphasize the Virginia assessment controversy and Governor Henry's proposed tax to benefit religion, Madison's *Memorial and Remonstrance*, and the
adoption of the Virginia Statute for the Establishment of Religious Freedom,
as well as the influential role that both Madison and Jefferson subsequently
played in interpreting the meaning of the Establishment Clause.

Cooperationists tend to downplay the particular example of Virginia as
well as the importance of Jefferson and Madison's separationism. The two
former presidents' roles have been minimized for a variety of reasons ranging
from whether they represented a consensus viewpoint in the eighteenth century to whether they actually did approve of governmental promotion of religious activities in certain circumstances. Cooperationists generally see the
Everson decision as particularly misguided and its use of the example of Virginia as biased. They also tend to emphasize the importance of the support for
religious activities by governments from the 1770s through the nineteenth
century, including the hiring of legislative chaplains, donation of land grants
for religious institutions, issuance of prayer proclamations, and public statements by the founders—most famously in Washington's *Farewell Address*—to
show not only the importance of religion, but of governmental promotion of
religion and religious values.

Historical Errors in Interpreting Establishment Clause History

G. K. Chesterton famously described the United States as "a nation with the
soul of a church."[18] Regardless of whether this observation was designed to be
ironic or insightful, or both, Chesterton correctly identified a characteristic
that sets the United States apart from many other countries. Americans
typically—from the political left to the right—have an abiding reverence for
their Constitution. Thus when difficult questions arise regarding the proper
relationship between religion and the state, the historical meaning of constitutional passages will be examined to uncover the correct answer. The argument
is rarely made that a text written more than two hundred years earlier should
not be considered an appropriate guide for deciding how institutions of government ought to interact with religion today. Lawyers do not propose to
courts that the Constitution should not be taken seriously because it was
written by people who could not have anticipated the complexities of the
future. The Constitution remains the unquestioned beginning point. When

the text itself does not provide a needed answer, Americans look to the founders to help resolve disputes, as if their words and examples have a heightened authority. Washington, Madison, Jefferson, Hamilton, and Franklin are routinely invoked in debates as if they were fully competent to help resolve modern disagreements with their venerable advice. Statements by the founders are often cited as if they were "proof-texts" to refute an opponent's argument. Like Muslims who answer religious questions by referring to the example of the Prophet, Americans often believe that the founders' examples may be dispositive.

This tendency to treat the Constitution not simply as the primary legal text but as a revered one perhaps reaches its apex with questions raised by the Establishment Clause, for it is here that the nation with the soul of a church must sort out the relationship between religion and government. To the extent that the text itself leaves some ambiguity, the immediate recourse is to search history for the examples from the founders' generation that can best support the favored ideological position. The separationist *Everson* court was challenged by its cooperationist critics not for looking to the history of the founding generation to help explain the meaning of the text, but for focusing on the wrong historical examples and misinterpreting them. The importance of history for understanding the Establishment Clause has led those whose principal expertise is in jurisprudence to become historians as well as for historians to help structure legal arguments.[19]

Although there is no such thing as "objective" history, and all history necessarily is presented from a particular point of view, the tendency to present history as an argument is particularly strong with regard to interpretations of the meaning of the Establishment Clause. It is, therefore, important to look at historical claims related to the clause with an added degree of caution so as to assess whether the evidence is presented in as complete a context as possible as well as to ensure that the evidence and arguments are not driven disproportionately by biased viewpoints, however sincerely held. Because the history of the relationship among religion, politics, and law in the United States provides a sufficiently rich smorgasbord of personalities, practices, statutes, public and private letters, and indeed hypocrisy, historians can find almost anything they wish to consume. For this reason a few cautions are warranted.

Even if historians can never be entirely neutral, there nevertheless remains a striking difference between serious historical research undertaken from a particular viewpoint with a self-conscious recognition of one's own biases, versus an ideologically driven history that cherry-picks the evidence to support a theory and then twists or ignores inconvenient facts that contradict that viewpoint. Two of many recurring problems that arise in both separationist and cooperationist accounts of history are first, assuming that "establishment of religion" is a defined term whose meaning can be found in eighteenth-century America, and second, using quotations (or examples) out of their historical context as "proof-texts" to justify a particular interpretation of the correct meaning of the Establishment Clause.

Assuming That There Was a Defined Meaning of "Establishment of Religion" in the Eighteenth Century. Professor Michael McConnell, one of the most highly regarded commentators on the religion clauses of the First Amendment, begins his chapter in this volume by stating with regard to the term "establishment of religion" that "virtually every American—and certainly every educated lawyer or statesman—knew from experience what those words meant."[20] Noticeably, however, he does not quote any eighteenth-century lawyer or any statesman who defined "establishment of religion," and he similarly offers no evidence that "virtually every American" agreed with any definition at all. In reality, there was not a precise vocabulary on which to draw to explain with clarity what was and was not understood to be included within the rubric of an establishment of religion. In his chapter on the drafting history of the First Amendment religion clauses, Carl Esbeck shows to the contrary that the legislators attempted several different linguistic formulations for what was to become the Establishment Clause as they searched to find the words that best achieved their intent.[21] The debated options included that "no national religion be established," "no religion shall be established by law," "no religious doctrine shall be established by law," "religious establishments," "establish a religion," "establish a national religion," "no laws touching religion," "no law establishing religion," "no law establishing one religious sect," "establishing any religious sect," "establishing any particular denomination," and "establishing articles of faith"—until the final phrase "no law respecting an establishment of religion" was finally accepted. Thus the First Congress considered many alternate ways to express their intent rather than adopt a term that was widely shared or universally understood.

This is more than a quibble over the differences between the terms "establishment of religion" and "establish a religion." Between the 1770s and 1780s, variations of the root word *establish* were combined with religion in a variety of contexts. Although it is likely true that "almost everyone" would have agreed that the Church of England was an "established religion," there were disagreements about what else might constitute an establishment. Indeed, if we look carefully at eighteenth-century discussions, we see that the linking of the root words *establish* and *religion* did not identify any particular church-state arrangement, but that they were combined to form a term of opprobrium to disparage any disfavored church-state relationship. Like the words *inappropriate* and *unacceptable*, by at least the 1780s the term "establishment of religion" had become a pejorative.[22] Indeed, the last state constitution to use the term favorably was South Carolina's of 1778, which was replaced in 1790 when the Episcopalian Church was disestablished.

There are some interesting examples illustrating how the joining of the words *establishment* and *religion* did not create a term of art, but was used as part of a rhetorical attack. One useful illustration of this was the American response to the British Parliament's adoption of the Quebec Act in 1774.[23] The Act was designed to calm some of the religious conflicts within the predominantly Roman Catholic colony in Canada that had come under British control following the Treaty of Paris of 1763. Prior to that time, it was illegal for Roman Catholics living in England to hold political office or even to attend Catholic Holy Communion. In adopting the statute, the British Parliament liberalized the rights of Roman Catholics in Quebec and allowed them to practice their religion freely and to hold office in the colony, rights that would have been denied them had they moved to England. The Act itself declared:

> That his Majesty's Subjects, professing the Religion of the Church of Rome of and in the said Province of Quebec may have, hold, and enjoy, the free Exercise of the Religion of the Church of Rome, subject to the King's Supremacy . . . and that the Clergy of the said Church may hold, receive, and enjoy, their accustomed Dues and Rights, with respect to such Persons only as shall profess the said Religion.

By eighteenth-century standards, this is a remarkable document where a Protestant country recognized "the free Exercise of Religion" for Catholics and produced the first chink in the armor of the Corporation Act of 1661 that had disenfranchised Catholics in England a century earlier. Regardless of whether Parliament adopted this new law as a cynical ploy to curry favor with the French population in the Quebec colony in order to discourage them from joining with their increasingly revolutionary neighbors to the south, it constituted a victory for religious freedom.

When apprised of the terms of the Quebec Act, however, the First Continental Congress, meeting in Philadelphia, did not applaud the additional religious freedom granted to their beleaguered fellow colonials to the north, but denounced it as one of the infamous "intolerable acts." In fact, the Continental Congress criticized the British Parliament for having "*established*" the Roman Catholic Church in Quebec. On October 21, 1774, the Continental Congress resolved that "we think the Legislature of Great-Britain is not authorized by the constitution to establish a religion."[24] In what seems little more than disguised anti-Catholicism, the Congress declared:

> Nor can we suppress our astonishment that a British Parliament should ever consent to establish in that country a religion that has deluged your island in blood, and dispersed bigotry, persecution, murder and rebellion through every part of the world.[25]

By any reasonable reading, the Quebec Act did not actually "establish" Roman Catholicism—and yet this was exactly the term that the Continental Congress used to describe the first British law of the eighteenth century to grant Catholics the "free exercise of religion." It was not only the Continental Congress that used these words to denounce the Quebec Act. The colonial legislatures of South Carolina and Georgia did so as well, the latter calling it "little short of a full establishment to a religion."[26] The Reverend Ebenezer Baldwin, a New Light Congregationalist from (of all places) Danbury, Connecticut, decried the new law because it "establishes the popish religion."[27] Alexander Hamilton, a future author of the *Federalist Papers*, declared that with the Quebec Act "no reasonable impartial man will doubt, that the religion of the church of Rome is established in Canada."[28]

Other examples abound. In the 1785 Virginia assessment controversy, Madison's *Memorial and Remonstrance* repeatedly used the term *establishment* to condemn the three-penny tax designed to subsidize religious ministers. He condemned the tax:

6. Because the establishment proposed by the Bill is not requisite for the support of the Christian Religion. . . .
7. Because experience witnesseth that ecclesiastical establishments, instead of maintaining the purity and efficacy of Religion, have had a contrary operation. . . .
8. Because the establishment in question is not necessary for the support of Civil Government. . . .
9. Because the proposed establishment is a departure from that generous policy, which, offering an Asylum to the persecuted and oppressed of every Nation and Religion, promised a lustre to our country. . . .[29]

Even this small tax should be opposed, according to Madison's rhetoric, because it was an "establishment" that supported religion in a way that was both unnecessary and harmful for true religion while simultaneously undermining the state's important interests.

Other examples can be found in Massachusetts with regard to whether Congregationalism was "established" prior to 1833, as most (but not all) modern observers would agree. In the 1770s, Baptist preacher Isaac Backus and Rhode Island pastor Ezra Stiles (the future president of Yale College) denounced the Massachusetts "Standing Order" for being an "establishment," while Congregationalists John Adams and Charles Chauncey, among many others of their faith, insisted that it was not.[30] The word appeared to be understood by all as a pejorative term, with opponents of the Standing Order freely using it to criticize the Massachusetts arrangement while the supporters disputed the label. Thus, we look in vain for the eighteenth-century meaning of the term "establishment of religion," for it served more as a term of opprobrium to insult a disfavored church-state arrangement rather than as a term of art whose meaning was shared by everyone.

Citing Quotations and Examples without Providing the Appropriate Context. A second recurring error in both popular and sophisticated histories is the use of isolated quotations or historical examples to explain the founders' attitudes toward the relationship between church and state. One of the most frequent examples is taken from President George Washington's *Farewell Address* of 1796, which has been described as the "*locus classicus* of the notion that religion has a vital role to play in American civic life."[31] In the *Farewell Address*, published several months before the end of his second term, Washington expressed his valedictory observations to his fellow countrymen. Although known most widely for its recommendation to avoid "entangling alliances" abroad, it also made an important statement about religion at home. In one of the most frequently cited paragraphs in the Establishment Clause debates, Washington declared:

> Of all the dispositions and habits which lead to political prosperity, Religion and morality are indispensable supports. In vain would that man claim the tribute of Patriotism, who should labour to subvert these great Pillars of human happiness, these firmest props of the duties of Men and citizens. . . . And let us with caution indulge the supposition, that morality can be maintained without religion. Whatever may be conceded to the influence of refined education on minds of peculiar structure, reason and experience both forbid us to expect that National morality can prevail in exclusion of religious principle.[32]

This passage is repeatedly invoked as it were a straightforward proof that *the* founding father, and implicitly the Constitution, recognize both the importance of religion for the operation of society and that the government should play a role in supporting it. When these words are cited as evidence of the role the government should play, it is neither asked how Washington came to this understanding nor what evidence he possessed to reach this conclusion. Nor is it asked whether Washington's own personal religious practices were consistent with his public declarations. Nor are the ghostwriting roles played by James Madison and Alexander Hamilton considered as undermining in any way the prophetic vision of the Father of His Country. Rather, the words typically are quoted with the reverence due to a prophetic utterance expressing a self-evident truth. It is quoted as if it were a proof-text.[33]

And yet if the *Farewell Address* is to be taken as providing evidence on how the Establishment Clause should be understood, there is all the more reason to pay close attention to exactly what Washington specifically advocates rather than imagine what he might have meant. A careful reading of the *Farewell Address* does not support the common assumption that Washington believed that the government should promote religion. Although he does argue that religion is important, he does not suggest that is the responsibility of the government to promote it. Just as if Washington had touted the importance for society of parents loving their children, it would not follow that it becomes the role of government to love children or to pay parents to do so. The *Farewell Address* does not propose that the government should promote religious activities, religious symbols, or religious beliefs. Rather, to further his goal, Washington immediately proposed, in words typically omitted by those advocating political support for religion: "Promote then, as an object of primary importance, Institutions for the general diffusion of knowledge. In proportion as the structure of a government gives force to public opinion, it is essential that public opinion should be enlightened."[34] The *Farewell Address* did not advocate governmental support for religion, as is generally implied. Rather, it encouraged the development of institutions that would diffuse knowledge generally.

Another frequent example that is mistakenly used to suggest that the founding generation favored governmental support of religion was the Continental Congress's resolution on religion of October 12, 1778. The purpose clause of the resolution, which is the portion most frequently cited by proponents of governmental aid to religion, reads: "true religion and good morals are the only solid foundations of public liberty and happiness."[35] This introductory language may then be cited as evidence for the constitutionality of governmental financial support for religion, even though it was adopted more than a decade before the Bill of Rights was ratified.[36] What is more, the two specific resolutions themselves, rather than the general introductory language, are typically omitted, even though it is in the resolutions themselves where Congress explains exactly what it had in mind.

> *Resolved,* That it be, and it is hereby earnestly recommended to the several states, to take the most effectual measures for the encouragement thereof, and for the suppressing of theatrical entertainments, horse racing, gaming, and such other diversions as are productive of idleness, dissipation, and a general depravity of principles and manners.[37]

In this first resolution, Congress does not propose financial aid to religion, but encourages states to shut down theaters, horse racing, and gambling because they interfere with the war effort. The second resolution instructs army officers to ensure the compliance with "good and wholesome rules" against "prophaneness and vice, and the preservation of morals among the soldiers." Once again, Congress is not proposing "public financial support" for religion, but is trying to discourage drunkenness, betting, and cussing by the soldiers in the Continental Army.

The Separation of Church and State

Philip Hamburger's Recent Argument. It was in the context of the sixty-year-old academic challenge to *Everson*'s use of the "separation of church and state," the increasing popular hostility to the term, and the mounting prestige of the phrase "religion in the public square" that Professor Philip Hamburger launched a new salvo against separationism.[38] He, too, criticized *Everson* as "the foundation of subsequent establishment clause jurisprudence."[39] In a lengthy and deeply referenced volume, Hamburger argued not only that the separation of church and state was an inapt description of what the Constitution had accomplished, but that its prominence in American public discourse came not from any well-meaning but misguided effort by Jefferson in 1802 to summarize constitutional doctrine, but as a polemical term introduced into the nineteenth-century lexicon by anti-Catholic nativists, including the Know-Nothing political movement, the Ku Klux Klan, freethinkers, and atheists, as well as by conniving Republican politicians who promoted anti-Catholic sentiment to help them win in the elections of 1876. The common goal of the promoters of separation was to drive a wedge in the American population between Protestants and Catholics and thereby ostracize the latter. Rather than being an uncontroversial and descriptive term to be understood as synonymous with the American value of religious liberty, separation was in fact antithetical to respect for religious freedom, and it bears the taint of its bigoted past. Hamburger acknowledges that historically the term had earlier been used both by Baptists and by Jefferson, but then asserts that

> *the modern myth of separation* omits any discussion of nativist sentiment in America and, above all, omits any mention of the Ku Klux Klan. Yet nativists had popularized separation in America in the nineteenth century, and, during the first half of the twentieth, they continued to distinguish themselves as the leading proponents of this ideal.[40]

According to Hamburger, "[n]o nativist or Protestant organization more prominently supported the ideal of separation than the Revised Klan."[41] He quotes the Klan's Imperial Wizard, Hiram Wesley Evans, as praising Protestantism, Americanism, and the "separation of church and state" while at the same time Evans denounced Catholicism and the "inferior" races.[42] Hamburger even goes so far as to make an ad hominem attack on the author of the majority opinion in *Everson*, Justice Hugo L. Black, whose prior associations with the Ku Klux Klan are referenced to help explain the true underpinnings of *Everson*.[43]

But is Hamburger correct about the tainted legacy of separation of church and state? Several leading scholars of church-state relations, including Kent Greenawalt and John Witte who appear in this volume, have refuted much of Hamburger's thesis, even while acknowledging that separation of church and state was frequently used in the anti-Catholic tirades of the nineteenth century. They show that many nineteenth- and twentieth-century sources having no connection to anti-Catholic or nativist sentiments are filled with respect for the American constitutional value of separating church and state.[44] As will be shown below, Hamburger and those who challenge the deep American roots of separating church and state are fundamentally mistaken.

Theological Roots of Separation of Church and State. The concept of separating church and state has long and deep historical roots, as has been argued persuasively by my coeditor, John Witte Jr. Witte shows that the concept of separation of church and state is found ultimately in the Bible—in the Hebrew Bible's celebration of the wall of separation between the Temple and the commons of ancient Israel, and in St. Paul's literal talk in Ephesians 2:14 of "a wall of separation" between Christians and non-Christians interposed by the law of God. Such biblical passages were at the root of 1800 years of Western separationist theories—two ways, two cities, two powers, two swords, and two kingdoms, each yielding different understandings of how the institutions and offices of church and state were to relate. The American founders, writing in the decades before Thomas Jefferson's famous 1802 letter, drew from this tradition at least five distinct understandings of separation of church and state. They used the phrase to call for the protection of (1) the church from the state, (2) the state from the church, (3) the individual's conscience from the collusion of church and state, (4) the states from interference from the federal government in dealing with local religion, and (5) society and its members from unwelcome participation in and support for religion altogether.[45] The term "wall of separation" itself was first introduced into the American lexicon in the seventeenth century by the theologian Roger Williams, who first used the term with a modern, robust meaning as explained by David Little.[46]

Separation of Church and State in American Constitutional History. Even though the concept of separating the functions of church and state became increasingly accepted in the individual American states through the 1780s, the precise term "separation of church and state" itself was not used to describe the meaning of the First Amendment guarantees until 1802. On January 1 of that year, President Thomas Jefferson replied to a letter from the Baptists of Danbury, Connecticut, in which they had complained about religious discrimination against them and the establishment of the Congregational Church as the official religion of their state. Although recognizing that the Constitution gave the president no power to act on their behalf, they hoped that he might be able to provide some moral support for their plight. In response to their plea, Jefferson wrote:

> Believing with you that religion is a matter which lies solely between Man & his God, that he owes account to none other for his faith or his worship, that the legitimate powers of government reach actions only, & not opinions, I contemplate with sovereign reverence that act of the whole American people which declared that their legislature should make no law respecting an establishment of religion, or prohibiting the free exercise thereof, thus building a wall of separation between Church & State.[47]

Jefferson's letter to the Danbury Baptists did not claim to be introducing a new concept into American constitutional law, but appears instead to summarize the president's beliefs about what the U.S. Constitution already had accomplished.

Two decades later, following his tumultuous years in the presidency, James Madison wrote a letter that repeatedly advanced the *concept* of separating church and state as being consonant with the U.S. Constitution. In a friendly letter to a sympathetic clergyman, F. L. Schaeffer, Madison, crediting Martin Luther as an authority, argued that differentiating

> what is due to Caesar and what is due God, best promotes the discharge of both obligations. The experience of the United States is a happy disproof of the error so long rooted in the unenlightened minds of well-meaning Christians, as well as the corrupt hearts of persecuting usurpers, that without a legal incorporation of religious and civil policy, neither could be supported. A mutual independence is found most friendly to practical Religion, to social harmony, and to political prosperity.[48]

Ten years later, in the same year that Massachusetts disestablished its state religion, 1833, the Reverend Jasper Adams sent a copy of one of his recent sermons to the elderly James Madison as well as to Supreme Court Justice Joseph Story. Adams, the president of Charleston College, had written that "Christianity is the established religion of the nation, its institutions and usages are sustained by legal sanctions, and many of them are incorporated with the fundamental law of the country."[49] Adams criticized those who believe "that Christianity has no connexion with our civil Constitutions of government" because of "the absurd and dangerous consequences to which [such ideas] lead."[50]

Presumably hoping for a favorable response, the Reverend Adams sent his sermon to Madison and Story. Justice Story, who unlike Madison was not a participant in the drafting of the Constitution and the Bill of Rights, agreed with the conclusions contained in the sermon. Madison, however, disapproved.[51] Following a gracious note of appreciation to the preacher, Madison nevertheless made clear his disagreement with Adams's interpretation of the Constitution. He argued that it would be an error to have the state and religion "consolidated." Madison argued that religious freedom came to prevail as a direct consequence of the disestablishment of religion. Financial support for religion was indeed harmful for religion and for the state. Using the term "the line of separation," Madison admitted "that it may not be easy, in every possible case, to trace the line of separation between the rights of religion and the Civil authority with such distinctness as to avoid collisions & doubts on unessential points." However, the fact that it was not always easy to draw the line did not mean that the attempt should not be made or that the principle was incorrect.

Foreign Observers of American Separation. By the 1830s, the term "separation of church and state" was widely accepted as explaining the American approach and was understood to be a concept with which "everyone" agreed. The insightful French visitor to the United States, Alexis de Tocqueville, is widely applauded for having recognized the fundamental role that religion played in American civic life. In his visit to the United States in 1831, two years before Madison wrote to Adams, Tocqueville found that the positive role of religion came as a direct result of the separation of church and state. He reported that Americans

> all agreed with each other except about the details; all thought that the main reason for the quiet sway of religion over their country was the complete separation of church and state. I have no hesitation in stating that throughout my stay in America I met nobody, lay or cleric, who did not agree about that.[52]

Already in 1835, long before Hamburger's virulent nativists attacked Catholicism, Tocqueville, a Catholic, praised America's "complete separation of church and state" and the unanimity of Americans in support of it. In confirmation of his observation, one of the first American reviewers of *Democracy in America* agreed completely, stating that Tocqueville's claim about a widespread agreement on the value of the separation of church and state rests "on a correct estimate of the facts of the case as existing in this country."[53]

Other foreign visitors to the United States in the nineteenth century, both Catholics and non-Catholics, made observations similar to those of Tocqueville. The great Hungarian patriot and statesman Louis Kossuth wrote in 1852 that some countries are endangered by the "direct or indirect amalgamation of Church and State. [However,] of this danger, at least, the future of your country is free. [Your] institutions left no power to your government to interfere with the religion of your citizens."[54] Writing in 1862, Tocqueville's fellow Frenchman, the Count Agenor de Gasparin, declared that the United States had "proclaimed and loyally carried out the glorious principle of religious liberty" while at the same time adopting "another principle, much more contested among [the French], but which I believe destined also to make the tour of the world: the principle of separation of Church and State."[55] Gasparin's admiring American book reviewer, like Tocqueville's, praised the author and agreed with him. "He was led to see that the purity and efficiency of the Christian society [in America], the Church, [and then to] demand its entire separation from the political society, the state."[56] Another European count, the eccentric Pole Adam De Gurowski, concurred: "Religious liberty, the absolute separation of Church and State, has become realized in America far beyond the conception, and still more the execution, of a similar separation in any European Protestant country. This separation, and the political equality of all creeds, constitute one of the cardinal and salient traits of the American Community."[57]

One of the greatest theologians and religious scholars of nineteenth-century America was the Swiss-born and German-educated Philip Schaff, who first came to the United States in 1844 to teach at the German Reformed Theological Seminary at Mercersburg, Pennsylvania. Professor Hamburger cites an early work of Professor Schaff from the 1850s, arguing that he had an ambivalent attitude toward the doctrine of separation.[58] Not mentioned, however, is a work that Schaff wrote much later after having lived for several years in the United States, where he takes a strong position indeed: "We will only point in conclusion to the advantages of the separation of church and state over the other systems which have prevailed or still prevail in Europe. The American system secures full religious liberty."[59]

Republicans, Democrats, and the Election of 1876. During the second half of the nineteenth century, particularly in the wake of a new wave of Catholic immigration to the United States, many Republican politicians delivered anti-Catholic messages designed to curry favor with majority Protestants and to characterize the Democrats as the "un-American" party that favored immigrants over native-born Americans. In anticipation of the presidential election of 1876, James G. Blaine, a leading Republican candidate for president, proposed a constitutional amendment designed to prohibit both state governments and the federal government from providing tax funds for religious schools and other sectarian institutions.[60]

Hamburger and many others have described the Republicans' tactic of arguing for the "separation of church and state" as thinly disguised Catholic-baiting. Without condoning in any way the use of any code word to play on anti-Catholic sentiment, we nevertheless can ask *who else* in these debates used the term? The answer is easy: *pro-Catholic Democrats*—the opponents of those who are accused of having taken a special interest in promoting the term. The Democratic Party platform for the year 1876 endorsed "the total separation of church and State, for the sake alike of civil and religious freedom."[61] The principal legislative opponent of the Senate version of the Blaine amendment, Senator Lewis D. Bogy, a Democrat from Missouri, declared:

> We have heard much about religious freedom, and freedom of conscience, and *separation of church and state*. Who in this day and in this country would oppose either or any or all of these great ideas? Who in this country is in favor of uniting church and state? Who in this country or in this age of the world is opposed to religious freedom? . . . There would be no civil liberty without religious liberty. *There would be no liberty, according to modern ideas, without entire separation of church and state.*[62]

If Hamburger's theory were correct—that "separation of church and state" was a term developed by Republican bigots against Catholics—Democratic Senator Bogy's praise of the term makes no sense at all. If, however, the term had already been broadly accepted across the political and religious spectrum, as the evidence is increasingly showing, then Bogy's defense of both the term and concept is perfectly understandable.

Writing in the midst of the election year of 1876, J. Lewis Diman, a Brown University professor of history and political economy, did not identify the separation of church and state as a divisive term employed to ostracize Catholics, but as a common value that united all Americans and was fundamental to the American political system.

> We shall follow the most simple method if we fix our attention, at the outset, on the external features of our religious history; and, beyond question, the most characteristic of these is the entire separation that obtains, both in our Federal and State systems, between the ecclesiastical and the civil province. So heartily is this accepted, and so unhesitatingly is it maintained, that it ought, perhaps, to be regarded less as an external feature than as a fundamental maxim of our body politic.[63]

If separation was a code word used by Republicans against Catholics in the election of 1876, it seems that Democratic Senator Bogy was not the only one to miss it. One of the leading Catholic publications of the century, the *Catholic World*, published an article entitled "The Catholic Church in the United States, 1776–1876" in the middle of the electoral season and only one month before the constitutional amendment was debated in the House and Senate. The author offers a partial explanation of why so many Catholics in 1876 were Democrats: their admiration for Thomas Jefferson and his belief in separating church and state. "The state [according to Jefferson's theory], is a purely political organism, and *is not in any way concerned with religion*; and this soon came to be the prevailing sentiment in the Democratic party, whose acknowledged leader Jefferson was, which may explain why the great mass of the Catholics in this country have always voted with this party."[64] Moreover, Catholics in the United States "owe the freedom which they now enjoy to the operation of general laws [on religion]."[65] Far from feeling themselves to be the victims of a polemic, Catholics, like their fellow countrymen, embraced the concept, even in the dramatic year of 1876.[66] Far from being victims of Jefferson's anticlerical separationism, American Roman Catholics had joined the Democratic Party in part *because of* their belief in Jefferson's wall of separation.

Although Hamburger obviously recognizes that some Democrats had used the term favorably, including most obviously Presidents Madison, Jefferson, and Jackson, he does not mention President John Tyler, who, during his presidency in the 1840s, described the United States as having "adventured upon a great and noble experiment, which is believed to have been hazarded in the absence of all previous precedent—that of total separation of Church and State. No religious establishment *by law* exists among us. . . . The fruits are visible in the universal contentment which everywhere prevails."[67] The "separation of church and state" was not a term used exclusively by Republicans as a code word against Catholics: it also was used by Democrats, and indeed by Catholics as well. In other words, it was used across the political spectrum as a broadly and widely accepted term that was, as stated by Professor Diman, "a fundamental maxim of our body politic."

Theologians and Historians on the Separation of Church and State.
Some American theologians and historians who wrote about fourth-century
Christian history, when Constantine united church and state, found that their
own country had avoided the problems that Constantine unleashed. An October 1864 article in the *Princeton Review* found that the "amicable American
separation has thus far forestalled collision [between church and state]."[68] Six
years later another article also on the fourth century concurred: "it is conceded
by every enlightened mind, that *religious toleration*, the placing of all phases of
religious belief upon an equality—the separation of Church and state, and
freedom of conscience—are marks of progress, and ought to be found on the
statute-book of every free people."[69]

Historians and theologians approvingly, if sometimes questionably and
anachronistically, found forerunners of the separation of church and state in
early American religious history. Charles W. Elliott declared that Roger Williams "spoke for Liberty of Conscience and Worship, and for the separation of
Church and State."[70] A Quaker author credited Quakers: "Who more sturdily
fought the battle of religious freedom and political equality, and separation of
Church and State, than [George] Fox and [William] Penn."[71] Harvard President
Edward Everett was quoted as insisting: "We are indebted to [the Puritans] for
two great principles; one of which is the separation of Church and State."[72] The
former president of Yale College, the Reverend Theodore Dwight Woolsey, did
not go back as far as the Puritans, but equally praised the American constitutional innovation. Writing while president of the Evangelical Alliance, Woolsey declared: "The feeling of the country is now, and for the last generation or
two has been, that the true idea of government among us involves the entire
and absolute separation of Church and State, the complete liberty and exact
equality of all denominations of Christians."[73] The famous historian Samuel
Eliot Morison did not hesitate to refer to the 1818 law as one that brought about
"the separation of church and state in Connecticut."[74] President Woolsey, who
was from Connecticut and lived through the period of disestablishment,
observed that even though

> it provokes a smile to think that so small a change as that from the parish
> laws then existing to perfect freedom in supporting public worship should
> have awakened great alarm, we admire those strong religious convictions
> and energies which very soon converted the apprehended curse into a bless-
> ing. For that it was a blessing to religion [to separate the church and state]
> all unite in believing.[75]

Another observer who also knew the disestablished preachers of Connecticut
reached the same conclusion in 1844:

> I have been much in Connecticut during the last fifteen years, know many
> of the clergy, and have conversed much with them on the subject[.] Of the

200 or 300 once established ministers of that state, I am not aware of there being more than one Congregational minister in the state who would like to see the union of Church and State restored to it.[76]

In a later survey of disestablishment in New England, the famous historian George Bancroft triumphantly insisted that the "complete separation of the church and the state by the establishment of perfect religious equality was followed by the wonderful result, that the separation was approved of everywhere, always, and by all."[77] The year before *Democracy in America* appeared, the *Princeton Review* published an article that criticized the English system with its established church and praised the U.S. Constitution for launching the "experiment of separating the civil and ecclesiastical governments; and of leaving religion to provide for itself."[78]

Separationism and Catholicism. For American Catholics, the ostensible targets of Hamburger's nativists, the issue was more complicated than it was for the majority of Americans. Official Catholic doctrine in the nineteenth century sharply opposed the separation of church and state. In 1832, Pope Gregory XVI condemned those "who desire vehemently to separate the Church from the state."[79] When Pope Pius IX set out his *Syllabus of Errors* that criticized mistakes of contemporary society in 1864, one such error was the concept that "the Church ought to be separated from the State and the State from the Church."[80] In 1888, ten years after the U.S. Supreme Court praised "separation of church and state" as a correct interpretation of the Constitution in the *Reynolds* decision, Pope Leo XIII denounced "the fatal theory of the need of separation between Church and State," the "absurdity" of which was self-evident.[81] With such clear statements from Rome, we might have expected that American Catholics writing on the topic in the nineteenth century would overwhelmingly oppose separation.

What is remarkable, however, is that several Catholic authors went out of their way to praise the concept of separation of church and state even when they equivocated on the exact term itself. In 1865, the Paulist Fathers, whose mission was to proselytize the people of North America, began publishing the monthly journal *The Catholic World of General Literature and Science*. During the 1870s it published several articles about the relationship between church and state. Although *Catholic World* formally accepted the official condemnation of separation as stated in the *Syllabus of Errors*, several articles display some convoluted verbal gymnastics that formally repudiate the term *separation* and formally praise the term *union*, but that in fact argue in favor of the American system that separates church and state.

For example, in an article entitled "Church and State" (May 1870), the author describes the American approach to separation in highly favorable terms. "For ourselves personally, we are partial to our own American system, which . . . comes nearer to the realization of the *true union as well as distinction of church and state* than has heretofore or elsewhere been effected."[82] By keeping the church and state "distinct," as is done in the United States, the "true union" is permitted. This delicate dance that formally rejects the proscribed term but praises the American system continues. The state in America understands that it has "no spiritual competency, and cannot decide either for itself or for its citizens which is or is not the church that authoritatively represents the spiritual order."[83] This is, of course, a classic argument *for* separation: the state has no competence in spiritual matters, an argument emphasized by Madison in the *Memorial and Remonstrance*. The article concludes with striking praise in favor of the American system over the European system, where church and state are legally united, but where the unification ultimately resulted in conflicts between the two. "What seems to us to be needed [in Europe is] for the church to assert her *independence* of both [governments and popular majorities] so far as either attempts to control her in the free discharge of her functions as the church of God."[84]

Other *Catholic World* articles that described European events similarly approved of attempts to separate church and state. Catholics in Germany, at the Frankfurt Parliament (1848–1849), agreed with the resolution calling for "total separation of church and state."[85] France was criticized for *not* separating church and state (in the 1880s) because of parliament's wish to control the church (as revealed in an interview with a deputy of the French National Assembly).[86] Referring to the situation of Catholics in France, another article explained that the Church "is, undoubtedly, more free and independent where she is not subsidized by the state."[87]

Some *Catholic World* authors nevertheless avoided the complicated verbal dance and praised directly the separation of church and state, and even credited it for the religious freedom of Catholics in the United States. In "Religion in Our State Institutions," the author notes that if the state of New York, for example, had decided to establish a state church, it would not have been the Catholic Church, and that this would have led to discrimination. Rather than establish a religion, a

> complete freedom of religious profession and worship was proclaimed as being the only thing commensurate with complete civil liberty and . . . freedom of the individual which forms the corner-stone of the republic. *This really constitutes what is commonly described as the absolute separation of church and state, on which we are never weary of congratulating ourselves.* It is not that the state ignores the church (or churches), but that it recognizes it in the deepest sense, *as a power that has a province of its own*, in the direction of human life and thought, where the state may not enter—a province embracing all that is covered by the word religion. *This is set apart by the state*, voluntarily not blindly [which it may not] invade at any moment. *It is set apart forever.*[88]

Here we have unequivocal praise for the separation of church and state in perhaps the leading nineteenth-century American Catholic publication. Another Catholic writer criticized the established churches that had existed earlier in America and asserted that:

> The ablest lawyers in the country teach that *the fundamental idea of our civil government is that there shall be no interference of the state in church affairs. Absolute independence of the church; no interference of the state in religious matters*—such is the AMERICAN IDEA. . . . The framers of the Constitution were especially anxious to eschew church establishments or state religions.[89]

With the passage of time, Catholics and their publications became more comfortable in praising the separation of church and state that had been condemned by the Vatican. Father Edward McClynn was an Irish Catholic priest who transgressed church norms when he delivered a provocative public lecture in 1888 criticizing "the Pope in politics." In the United States, he declared, "we need no better union of Church and State than we have. *And what we call separation of Church and State is the best union*, where the Church will respect the rights of the country and the country will respect the liberty of all churches to teach their creeds. (Applause.)"[90]

In the 1930s, historians wrote about the Catholic contribution to the idea of the separation of church and state. Matthew Page Andrews was commissioned in 1935 by *The Catholic Historical Review* to write an article, which he entitled "Separation of Church and State in Maryland." Andrews found that Roman Catholics of seventeenth-century Maryland "applied the distinctively American principles of separation of Church and state and religious freedom for all."[91] Ultimately, in seventeenth-century Maryland, "the evidence of the establishment of religious freedom is overwhelming, whilst the absolute fact of the separation of Church and State in the Province of Maryland is positive and irrefutable."[92] One year earlier, a book by Andrews was favorably reviewed in *The Catholic Historical Review*. The review's author, Raymond Corrigan, SJ, admitted in the Catholic publication that there is a "naïve simplicity behind our blind partiality for 'the separation of church and state'" before declaring "Every American upholds the separation of Church and State for conditions as they exist in the United States, and should be ready to thank the founders of Maryland for this precious heritage."[93] In 1941, Catholic historian John J. Meng wrote another article for *The Catholic Historical Review* describing observations made by Catholics from France who, like Tocqueville, visited America in the nineteenth century. Many of them praised American laws that gave Catholics religious freedom, and several urged that France adopt laws separating church and state in order to enhance religious freedom in France.[94]

In the decade preceding Justice Black's 1947 opinion, Catholic writers and Catholic publications had warmly praised the separation of church and state as having benefited and protected their church in America.

Setting the Record Straight on Justice Black. Professor Hamburger makes an ad hominem attack on Justice Black by suggesting that his prior affiliation with the anti-Catholic Ku Klux Klan corrupted his views and thereby tainted *Everson* and its progeny. After citing the Klan's unsavory activities and after describing Black's personal association with the Klan, Hamburger tightens the noose: "Holding such views, which [were] 'anti-Catholic,' Black in 1947 led the Court to declare itself in favor of the 'separation of church and state.'"[95]

It is surprising and disappointing that a reputable scholar would suggest that Justice Black's *Everson* decision and the use of the term "separation of church and state" can be understood by reference to the specter of his prior association with the Ku Klux Klan. Although Black's earlier Klan affiliations are reprehensible and indefensible, it appears that the attempt to associate the Klan with the Court's acceptance of the concept of "separation of church and state" is little more than an accusation of guilt by association. Justice Black's prior affiliation with the Klan was, ultimately, utterly irrelevant to the Court's use of the term "separation of church and state" for five important reasons.

First, the "wall of separation of church and state" had been *unanimously* adopted by the Supreme Court as the governing metaphor for the religion clauses of the Constitution in the *Reynolds* case in 1878, seven years before Hugo Black was even born and more than thirty-five years before the Revised Klan came into existence. Moreover, as shown above, the term was broadly favored in American society before 1947, including by Catholics. Second, Black was only one of the nine justices on the *Everson* court who approved of the "wall of separation" metaphor—as both the majority and the dissenters accepted it. Third, the sole Roman Catholic then on the Court, Justice Frank Murphy, who had been raised as a devout Catholic, apparently failed to see any bias in the metaphor as he himself signed on to Black's majority opinion. The next prominent Roman Catholic on the Supreme Court, Justice William J. Brennan, also seems to have been unaware of the alleged anti-Catholic bias in the concept of separation of church and state as he, too, later became among its most stalwart champions. Fourth, as was shown in the preceding pages, prominent Catholic writers and scholars themselves had warmly praised the doctrine of separation of church and state from the mid-nineteenth century up to and including the decade of the 1940s when the *Everson* opinion was handed down.

Finally, it should be noted that Justice Black's majority opinion in *Everson* in fact *allowed the contested financial assistance to the Catholic students* that the dissenters would have denied. Thus the justice accused of harboring Klan-ish "anti-Catholic" bias, unlike the non-Klan member dissenters, supported the Catholic claim. Indeed, the opinion written by Justice Rutledge for the four dissenting justices was even more adamant than the majority opinion about the necessity of separating church and state. Whereas the majority and the dissenters in *Everson* disagreed as to whether it was constitutional for taxpayers to subsidize the transportation costs of parochial school students, they unanimously agreed that both the metaphor and the concept of separation between church and state were appropriate guides for helping to interpret the Establishment Clause. Although the justices obviously disagreed on how the metaphor and concept should be applied in the specific case, none of the *Everson* opinions rejects either of them.

Professor Hamburger found favorable references to the separation of church and state in the writings of nativists, anti-Catholics, and freethinkers because that is where he looked for them. The fact that he found such references in their tracts does not prove that they originated the concept any more than photographs showing Ku Klux Klan marchers carrying American flags proves that the Klan was responsible for introducing the Stars and Stripes to parades. A vast number of writers, quoted above, from Tocqueville, to the presidents of Harvard and Yale, to Catholics, to theologians, to historians, and to Democratic politicians, repeatedly spoke of the *unanimity* of Americans' praise for the concept of separation of church and state. Hamburger's sources do not prove his narrow claim. Rather, they support the broader claim by showing that *even* the Klan, bigots, and nativists are to be included as part of the "everyone" who accepted the concept.

Conclusion: Jefferson on Equality and Separation

Thomas Jefferson's pen played a key role in promoting two terms that are at the core of modern constitutional debates: "equality" and the "separation of church and state." Jefferson wrote perhaps the most famous and provocative words of the Declaration of Independence: "We hold these truths to be self-evident, that all men are created equal." It also was Jefferson who first used the term "separation of church and state" to describe the Constitution's approach to the relationship between religion and the government. Jefferson was, and continues to be, criticized for his own personal behavior and actions with regard to both of these concepts. The hypocrisy of a slaveholder declaring the self-evident truth that all men are created equal was not lost on his contemporaries, and it is the most enduring stain on his legacy. Jefferson also was, and is, subjected to personal attacks for his own attitudes toward religion and his arguably inconsistent and politically motivated treatment of religion during his governorship and presidency.

In "The Place of the Independent in Politics," James Russell Lowell described the U.S. Constitution as a "machine that would go of itself."[96] What Lowell found for the Constitution generally may apply with particularity to Jefferson's two ideas. In 1776, the United States was far from egalitarian. In many places Catholics were not permitted to vote or to hold public office. Slavery was enforced by law. Women could not participate in the political process. Wealth requirements were common for officeholders and voters. Despite each of these forms of discrimination, the idea of equality nevertheless captured the political and moral imagination and would not let go. Rather than wallowing in the entirely justifiable self-criticism of hypocrisy, the American legal system slowly and often erratically moved in the direction of promoting equality for its citizens. Although ultimate equality is indefinable and unachievable, Jefferson's words have served as a beacon urging movement in their direction. At each step of the ongoing constitutional process that gradually included races, religions, and gender into the political mainstream, it was Jefferson's phrase "all men are created equal" that drove the rhetoric—including when the word *men* itself came under attack. The ideal of equality continued "to go of itself" long after it was introduced into the highly inegalitarian world of 1776.

Although "the separation of church and state" is not a term whose legacy today glows with the same luster as "all men are created equal," it did so during the nineteenth century, as the evidence above reveals. Although the nineteenth century was not a golden age either for equality or for religious freedom, as the Civil War and anti-Catholic riots attest, it too witnessed a slow, halting, inconsistent, backsliding, stumbling, but ultimately positive movement toward a goal that could only dimly be perceived even by those with the greatest of foresight. The ultimate objective, of course, is not carving a word into stone or a metaphor into law, but achieving a society where all human beings are treated equally before the law and where the government's power is not deployed in favor of or against any religious belief.

Notes

1. Reynolds v. United States, 98 U.S. 145 (1878).

2. Everson v. Board of Education, 330 U.S. 1 (1947). The *Everson* opinions, both majority and dissenting, also agreed on two other issues that were largely uncontroversial at the time: applying the Establishment Clause to states (in addition to the federal government), and using history—particularly Virginia's history—as a principal tool to help explain that clause's meaning. The *Everson* court's decision to "incorporate" the Establishment Clause into the Fourteenth Amendment Due Process Clause, making it applicable to states as well as to the federal government, was not particularly surprising from a jurisprudential point of view in 1947 inasmuch as several other clauses of the Bill of Rights, including the Free Exercise Clause, had previously been incorporated. Moreover, by 1947, many state constitutions had adopted articles that specifically prohibited establishments of religion, often adopting the exact wording of the First Amendment. Thus, by the time *Everson* was decided, it was not particularly controversial to imagine that states, like the federal government, should be prohibited from establishing religions. See also chapter 10 by Steven Green and chapter 11 by Thomas Berg. In the 1876 debates in the Senate and House of Representatives over the so-called Blaine amendment, not one senator or representative argued that a state should be able to establish a religion if it so chose, the debate instead being whether the federal

government should be empowered to decide the question and whether it was a political impossibility that any state would ever consider establishing a religion. 4 *Congressional Record*, 5189 *passim* (August 4–14, 1876).

3. Prominent among the first generation of opponents to *Everson* were Mark DeWolfe Howe, John Courtney Murray, Edward S. Corwin, and Chester James Antieau. Included within this volume are several authors critical of *Everson* for reasons similar to these earlier scholars. See chapter 2 by Michael McConnell, chapter 9 by Daniel Dreisbach, and chapter 11 by Thomas Berg.

4. Early "separationists" included most famously Leo Pfeffer, Anson Phelps Stokes, and Leonard Levy.

5. For two early uses of the term "culture wars," see James Davison Hunter, *Culture Wars: The Struggle to Define America* (New York: Basic Books, 1991) and candidate Pat Buchanan's speech to the Republican National Convention in 1992.

6. According to the Reverend Pat Robertson:

Now when atheism came in under what used to be called the Soviet Union a new constitution was written, which said the state shall be separate from the church and the church from the school. In the United States of America people have tried to apply that phrase from the Soviet Constitution to the schooling of children in America. Both of these constitutions are wrong. There is nothing that should indicate that God Almighty should be separated from the government nor that Godly people should not hold office in government. . . . So there is nothing to indicate that there should be a separation.

The 700 Club, Christian Broadcasting Network, August 1, 1995 (reported in *Church & State* (April 1996), 11).

7. The Reverend Jerry Falwell argued that "Separation of Church and State has long been the battle cry of civil libertarians wishing to purge our glorious Christian heritage from our nation's history. Of course, the term never once appears in our Constitution and is a modern fabrication of discrimination." "Falwell Fax," April 10, 1998 (reported in *Church & State* (May, 1998), 18).

8. For religion in the Soviet constitutions, see generally Albert Boiter, "Law and Religion in the Soviet Union," *The American Journal of Comparative Law* 35, no. 1 (Winter, 1987): 97–126.

9. Philip Hamburger, *Separation of Church and State* (Cambridge, MA: Harvard University Press, 2002).

10. See below pp. 26–38.

11. Richard John Neuhaus, *The Naked Public Square* (Grand Rapids, MI: William B. Eerdmans, 1984). Neuhaus was a Lutheran priest who subsequently converted to Roman Catholicism. He argued that religious discourse was increasingly being excluded from the "public square" by secular elitists and intellectuals.

12. For Roger Williams's earlier challenge to the orthodoxy that the government should promote religion, see chapter 4 by David Little.

13. See chapter 6 by Ralph Ketcham.

14. See below p. 29.

15. See chapter 8 by Carl Esbeck.

16. For evidence of the widespread American acceptance of the term and concept of "separation of church and state" during the early years of the nineteenth century up through the 1940s, see below pp. 26–38.

17. One of the most influential statements of this separationist position is the famous *Memorial and Remonstrance* of James Madison. See chapter 6 by Ralph Ketcham and pp. 169–70 below.

18. G. K. Chesterton, *What I Saw in America* (London: Hodder and Stoughton Limited, 1922), 12.

19. Most of the authors in this collection have been involved directly or indirectly in drafting briefs to the U.S. Supreme Court in Establishment Clause cases.

20. See chapter 2 by Michael McConnell, p. 45.

21. See chapter 8 by Carl Esbeck.

22. For a more detailed explanation of this point, see T. Jeremy Gunn, *A Standard for Repair: The Establishment Clause, Equality, and Natural Rights* (New York: Garland, 1992). Another example to illustrate this point might be the use of the term *socialist* in twenty-first-century American political debates. When a disfavored piece of legislation is labeled as "socialist," the term is not being used in a technical manner to open a discussion about the merits of a political-economic system, but rather as a way of dismissing the proposal without further discussion.

23. An Act for Making More Effectual Provision for the Government of the Province of Quebec, in North America, 14 Geo. III c. 83 (U.K.) (1774). See further chapter 7 by Derek Davis.

24. Worthington C. Ford et al., eds., *Journals of the Continental Congress, 1774–1789*, 34 vols. (Washington, DC: U.S. Government Printing Office, 1904–1937), 1:83, 87–88.

25. Ibid.

26. See Gunn, *A Standard for Repair*, 75.

27. Ibid., 76.

28. Ibid., 77.

29. Gaillard Hunt, ed., *The Writings of James Madison*, 9 vols. (New York: G.P. Putnam's Sons, 1901), 2:183–91.

30. For the debates and arguments, see Gunn, *A Standard for Repair*, 88–95.

31. See chapter 7 by Michael McConnell, p. 59 and chapter 9 by Daniel Dreisbach, pp. 257–58.

32. George Washington, *Farewell Address*, in *The Writings of George Washington*, ed. John C. Fitzpatrick (Washington, DC: Government Printing Office, 1931–1944), 35:229.

33. A reader skeptical of these assertions need do no more than search the Internet generally or even American law review articles to determine whether my characterizations about the broad acceptance of this passage from the *Farewell Address* are correct.

34. Fitzpatrick, ed., *The Writings of George Washington*, 35:230.

35. *Journals of the Continental Congress*, 12:1001 (October 12, 1778).

36. Professor McConnell, for example, cites this quotation to conclude his section on "Public Financial Support" of religion, in which he argues that it was normal during the founding period for government to provide such support, thereby suggesting that "public financial support" of religion is appropriate because it supports "true religion" as a "solid foundation" of public liberty. See chapter 2 by Michael McConnell, p. 51.

37. *Journals of the Continental Congress*, 12:1001 (emphasis added).

38. See pp. 16–17 above.

39. Hamburger, *Separation of Church and State*, 3.

40. Ibid., 399 (emphasis added).

41. Ibid., 407.

42. Ironically, and without any apparent self-awareness, Hamburger's book has been particularly well received among Baptists from the Bible Belt who now argue that the "separation of church and state" is opposed to fundamental American values rather than being a direct inheritance of their own Baptist forebearers.

43. Hamburger, *Church and State*, 422–34, 462–63.

44. Kent Greenawalt, "History as Ideology: Philip Hamburger's *Separation of Church and State*," *California Law Review* 93 (2005): 367; John Witte Jr., "That Serpentine Wall of Separation," *Michigan Law Review* 101 (2003): 1869.

45. John Witte Jr., "Facts and Fictions about the History of Separation of Church and State," *Journal of Church and State* 48 (2006): 15–46.

46. See chapter 4 by David Little, especially pp. 104, 111–12, 121n7.

47. Thomas Jefferson, Letter to Messrs. Nehemiah Dodge, Ephraim Robbins, and Stephen S. Nelson, a Committee of the Danbury Baptist Association in the State of Connecticut (January 1, 1802), in Daniel L. Dreisbach, "Sowing Useful Truths and Principles: The Danbury Baptists, Thomas Jefferson, and the 'Wall of Separation,'" *Journal of Church and State* 39 (1997): 468. See also Saul K. Padover, *The Complete Jefferson* (Freeport, NY: Books for Libraries Press, 1943), 518–19.

48. James Madison to the Reverend F. L. Schaeffer (December 3, 1821), in *Letters and Other Writings of James Madison*, 4 vols. (Philadelphia: J.B. Lippincott, 1865), 3: 242–43.

49. Jasper Adams, *The Relation of Christianity to Civil Government in the United States: A Sermon*, 2d ed. (Charleston: A. E. Miller, 1833), 16.

50. Ibid., 17.

51. Hunt, *The Writings of James Madison*, 9: 487–88. There is some controversy about the version of the letter quoted by Hunt. The Library of Congress Manuscript Division has a draft of the letter in its archives, which can be seen at: http://memory.loc.gov/master/mss/mjm/23/1100/1175d.jpg.

52. Alexis de Tocqueville, *Democracy in America*, ed. J. P. Mayers and Max Lerner, trans. George Lawrence (New York: Harper & Row, 1969), 271–72.

53. Book review of *Democracy in America*, *North American Review* 43 (July 1836): 205.

54. Louis Kossuth, *The Future of Nations, In What Consists Its Security: A Lecture Delivered in New York, June 21, 1852* (New York: Fowler and Wells, 1854), 32.

55. Agenor de Gasparin, *The Uprising of a Great People: The United States in 1861* (London: S. Low, 1861), 63–64.

56. Review of books by Count Gasparin, *North American Review* (October 1862): 445.

57. Adam G. De Gurowski, *America and Europe* (New York: D. Appleton, 1857), 323.

58. Hamburger, *Separation of Church and State*, 272–73. In his 1855 work, Schaff states that the European assumption that state support is necessary for religion to survive "is practically refuted and utterly annihilated in the United States." Philip Schaff, *America: A Sketch of the Political, Social, and Religious Character of the United States of North America* (New York: Scribner, 1855), 87–88.

59. Philip Schaff, "Statecraft and Priestcraft," *North American Review* (November 1885): 442.

60. Explaining the full story of the so-called Blaine amendment debates goes beyond the subject of this chapter. It may be said, in brief, that James Blaine, a member of Congress and the former Speaker of the House, introduced his version of an amendment in December 1875. This proposed amendment has been widely interpreted as a cynical ploy to obtain favorable publicity for his presidential campaign. Blaine, however, lost interest in

his proposal, particularly after he failed to win his party's presidential nomination. As Congress moved toward recess in August 1876, the Democratic-controlled House of Representatives adopted overwhelmingly a revised version of the proposed amendment that had been drafted by the House Judiciary Committee. The Senate Judiciary Committee, controlled by Republicans, completely revised the House version, but narrowly failed to win the two-thirds majority vote required for a constitutional amendment. Blaine himself, who had in the interim resigned his House seat and had been appointed to the Senate, never participated in any of the debates that are generally associated with his name. He was the only senator not to vote on the Senate version. See further chapter 10 by Steven K. Green.

61. "Democratic National Convention Platform," *A Hand-book of Politics for 1876*, ed. by Edward McPherson (Washington, DC: Solomons and Chapman, 1876), 215.

62. 4 *Congressional Record* 5584 (August 14, 1876) (emphasis added).

63. J. Lewis Diman, "Religion in America," *North American Review* (January, 1876): 4.

64. "The Catholic Church in the United States: 1776–1876," *Catholic World* (July, 1876): 440–41(emphasis added).

65. Ibid., 441.

66. For further discussion of Catholicism and the separation of church and state, see below.

67. Letter from President John Tyler to Joseph Simpson (a "prominent Jew of Baltimore"), *William and Mary College Quarterly Historical Magazine* (July, 1904): 2.

68. "The Union of Church and State in the Nicene Age," *Princeton Review* (January 1864): 4.

69. "The Oecumenical Council," *Appleton's Journal of Popular Literature, Science and Art* (March 12, 1870): 301.

70. Charles W. Elliott, *The New England History*, 2 vols. (New York: Scribner, 1857), 1: 202.

71. Eli Kirk Price, *Memoir of Philip and Rachel Price* (Philadelphia: Eli K. Price and Philip M. Price, 1852), 172.

72. Flavel S. Mines, *A Presbyterian Clergyman Looking for the Church* (New York: General Protestant Episcopal Sunday School Union, 1853), 323.

73. Theodore Dwight Woolsey, *The Constitution and Government of the United States in Regard to Religion* (New York: Scribner, 1873), 4.

74. Samuel Eliot Morrison, Review of *Church and State in Massachusetts*, *New England Quarterly* (April 1931): 357.

75. Woolsey, *The Constitution and Government of the United States*, 5–6.

76. Robert Baird, *Religion in America* (New York: Harper and Bros., 1844), 115–16.

77. George Bancroft, *History of the United States*, 10 vols. (Boston: Little Brown and Company, 1866), 9: 277.

78. "The Church Establishment of England," *Princeton Review* (October 1834): 523–24.

79. *Mirari Vos*, August 15, 1832, para. 20.

80. *Syllabus of Errors*, 1864, para. 55.

81. *Libertas*, 1888, para. 18.

82. "Church and State," *Catholic World* (May 1870): 152.

83. Ibid., 156.

84. Ibid. (emphasis added).

85. "Prussia and the Church," *Catholic World* (March 1876): 788.

86. "Church and State in France," *Catholic World* (October, 1889): 16–17. The year 1889 was the one hundredth anniversary of the revolution. Church and state were separated by law in France in 1905.

87. "The French Radicals and the Concordat," *Catholic World* (October 1885): 135.

88. "Religion in Our State Institutions," *Catholic World* (April 1875), 1–2 (emphasis added).

89. "A National or a State Church," *Catholic World* (April 1874): 34 (italics added).

90. Edward McClynn, "The Pope in Politics: Dr. M'Glynn Talking to the Anti-Poverty People," in *The New York Times* (New York: The New York Times Company, 1888), 9 (emphasis added).

91. "Separation of Church and State in Maryland," *Catholic Historical Review* 21 (July 1935): 172.

92. Ibid., 176.

93. R. Corrigan, Book Review, *The Catholic Historical Review* 20 (July 1934): 199.

94. John J. Meng, "A Century of American Catholicism as Seen through French Eyes," *Catholic Historical Review* 27 (April 1941): 41, 42, 43, 45–47, 53, 57, 58.

95. Hamburger, *Separation of Church and State*, 463.

96. James Russell Lowell, *Political Essays* (Boston: Houghton, Mifflin and Co., 1888), 312.

2

Establishment at the Founding

Michael W. McConnell

It has been so long—about 175 years—since any state in the United States has had an established church that we have almost forgotten what it is. When the words "Congress shall make no law respecting an establishment of religion" were added to the Constitution, virtually every American—and certainly every educated lawyer or statesman—knew from experience what those words meant. The Church of England was established by law in Great Britain, nine of the thirteen colonies had established churches on the eve of the Revolution, and about half the states continued to have some form of official religious establishment when the First Amendment was adopted. Other Americans had firsthand experience of establishment of religion on the Continent—of the Lutheran establishments of Germany and Scandinavia, the Reformed establishment of Holland, or the Gallican Catholic establishment of France. Establishment of religion was a familiar institution in the founding era, and its pros and cons were hotly debated from Georgia to New Hampshire.

However, when the Supreme Court began to decide cases in the 1940s involving claims about an establishment of religion, the justices did not make a serious attempt to canvass the legal history of establishment—either in Europe, the American colonies, or the early American states—nor did they distinguish between the First Amendment and the various conflicts over establishment at the state level.[1] The justices focused instead on one event in one state—the rejection of Patrick Henry's Assessment Bill in Virginia in 1785 and the adoption of Thomas Jefferson's alternative Bill for the Establishment of Religious Freedom—on the assumption that "the provisions of the First Amendment . . . had the same objective and were intended to provide the same protection against governmental intrusion on religious liberty as the Virginia statute."[2]

This truncated view of history made the establishment question seem too easy. In the justices' account, a "large proportion of the early settlers of this country came here from Europe to escape the bondage of laws that compelled them to support and attend government-favored churches,"[3] and the transplantation of established churches to these shores "became so commonplace as to shock the freedom-loving colonials into a feeling of abhorrence,"[4] leading directly to the First Amendment. One would never know from the justices' careless description of history that no small number of the "freedom-loving colonials" considered official sanction for religion natural and essential, that the movement toward disestablishment was hotly contested by many patriotic and republican leaders, and that there were serious arguments—not mere "feelings of abhorrence"—on both sides of the issue. The justices never analyzed any of the books, essays, sermons, speeches, or judicial opinions setting forth the philosophical and political arguments *in favor* of an establishment of religion, and relied on only one, perhaps unrepresentative, example among the hundreds of arguments made *against* the establishment.

To be sure, the Virginia Assessment Controversy of 1784–1786 was an important and illuminating event.[5] But it was only one step in a series of legal developments moving from a formal, exclusive, and coercive state establishment to a system of equal religious freedom. It addressed only one of many issues raised by the establishment of religion. It took place in only one of many states that went through such a process; and it was not so much a debate about establishment as a debate about which of several possible arrangements should *replace* the "church by law established" in Virginia prior to the Revolution. To understand what an "establishment of religion" was and what disestablishment entailed, it is necessary to broaden our sights. It is difficult to know what the Framers of the First Amendment opposed if we do not know what those who favored establishment supported. We cannot understand the depth of the argument for disestablishment without understanding why reasonable men and women might have thought that establishment was necessary to republican government.

Nor did the Court give serious attention to the process of *disestablishment*: whether to the gradual dismantling of existing church establishments in the states or to the debates about the Establishment Clause at the federal level. Contrary to popular myth, the First Amendment did not disestablish anything. It prevented the newly formed federal government from establishing religion and from interfering in the religious establishments of the states.[6] The First Amendment thus preserved the status quo. Even at the state level, where disestablishment actually occurred, it was not a simple binary decision. The founding generation had to figure out what changes to make and what would take the place of the establishment. There were many plausible alternatives. Would they combine broad toleration with mild and noncoercive governmental support for religion, on the model still common in Western Europe? Would they create a secular public culture—a "republic of reason"—along the lines later followed in France? Would they introduce a pluralistic religious free-for-all? What would be the public function of religion, if any, in this new republic?

Unlike many modern Americans, most members of the founding generation believed deeply that some type of religious conviction was necessary for public virtue, and hence for republican government. What institutional forms would disestablished religion take, and how would this affect education, poor relief, public decorum, republicanism, and the inculcation of virtue?

The Law Constituting an Establishment of Religion

At the time of the founding, the period roughly from the beginnings of the American Revolution through the formative years of the new republic, the Church of England was the established church of the mother country, as it had been since the 1530s. Before American independence, the Church of England was established by law in the five southern colonies (Maryland through Georgia). It was also established, without explicit legislative authorization, in four counties of metropolitan New York. In Massachusetts, Connecticut, New Hampshire, and Vermont, localized establishments were formed where the majority within each town could select the minister and hence the religious denomination—usually but not always, Congregationalism (or "Puritanism"). The remaining colonies—Pennsylvania, Delaware, New Jersey, Rhode Island, and nonmetropolitan New York—had no official establishment of religion. Rhode Island, Pennsylvania, and Maryland were explicitly founded as havens for dissenters, though Maryland lost that status at the end of the 1600s.[7] Although the laws of these colonies would not pass full muster under modern notions of the separation of church and state—they all had religious tests for office, blasphemy laws, and the like—they were, by the standards of the day, religiously tolerant and pluralistic.

No single law created the established Church of England, though the Act of Supremacy and the Uniformity Acts passed in England in 1533 and 1534 formed the core. These laws were amplified by later Parliamentary and colonial legislation. When Thomas Jefferson began his legislative assault on the Virginia establishment in the early 1770s, his first step was to make a list of Acts of Parliament and the Virginia Assembly concerning religion. He found some twenty-three applicable English statutes (beginning in the days of Edward VI) and seventeen Virginia statutes (beginning in 1661).[8] Had he looked before those dates, he would have found many more. In 1661, when the religious laws of the colony had been systematically revised, the assembly members found that there had been "soe many alterations in the lawes, that the people knew not well what to obey nor the judge what to punish. . . ."[9]

Financial support from taxes was not a necessary hallmark of establishment. The Church of England did not receive a significant tax subsidy in England, though it did in the colonies. Even after dissenters were given the right of free exercise of religion and the Church of England lost its tax-supported status in Virginia, the Virginia Assembly continued to speak of it as the "church by law established."[10] To understand the meaning of the term *establishment,* therefore, we must examine the historical development of the established church from a variety of sources and times.

Establishment in England. In the mother country, the established Church of England had ancient roots. It stood in the shoes of the Roman Catholic Church, which had been literally the only church of the realm before the sixteenth century. Now under the rule of the monarch rather than the pope, the Church of England inherited much of the Catholic Church's property, its status, and many of its customary privileges. Every British monarch since 1520 has held the title Defender of the Faith, and has formally appointed the Archbishop of Canterbury and other high church officials. Parliament legislates the official scripture, liturgy, and dogma of the church. Most ecclesiastical legislation affecting the American colonists can be traced back to the reign of Elizabeth I, when the royal government consolidated its control over the national religion. The Act of Supremacy, originally passed under Henry VIII in 1534, and renewed in 1559, made the monarch the supreme head of the Church of England, and gave him or her "authority to reform and redress all errors, heresies, and abuses."[11] During the reign of Edward VI, Parliament enacted the Articles of Faith, which set forth the doctrinal tenets of the church, and the Book of Common Prayer, which prescribed the liturgy for religious worship. The Acts of Uniformity of 1559 and 1662 required all ministers to conform to these requirements, making the Church of England the sole institution for lawful public worship. Its purpose, as stated in the preamble to the 1662 version, was to effect "an universal agreement in the public worship of Almighty God."[12] The Test and Corporation Acts limited civil, military, ecclesiastical, and academic offices to participating members of the church. The Act against Papists and Conventicles prohibited unlicensed religious meetings; various penal acts punished dissenters for engaging in prohibited religious worship. Catholics and Puritans were particular targets, because both appeared to threaten the political legitimacy of the state. The flavor of this persecution is indicated by the titles of the laws: "An Act to prevent and avoid dangers which may grow by Popish Recusants,"[13] or "An Act to retain the Queen's majesties subjects in their due obedience."[14]

Establishment in the American Colonies. Established religion came to America's shores with the earliest colonists. It assumed two principal forms: an exclusive Anglican establishment in the southern states and a localized Puritan establishment in the New England states other than Rhode Island.[15] Although equally coercive, the Anglican and Puritan establishments were profoundly different in spirit: The New England establishments were based on the intense religious convictions of the people in the teeth of opposition from the mother country, whereas the Anglican establishments enjoyed the support of the mother country and were designed in part to foster loyalty and submission to governmental authorities. This is not meant to imply that the Anglican colonials or their clergy were insincere in their Christian belief, but only that their motives for immigration were less focused on religion, their religious commitments were less intense, and their religious institutions and beliefs were more closely aligned with that of the British state. These two forms persisted throughout the colonial period, and the New England form endured several generations longer.

Elements of the Establishment. An establishment of religion is the promotion and inculcation of a common set of beliefs through governmental authority. An establishment may be narrow (focused on a particular set of beliefs) or broad (encompassing a certain range of opinion), it may be more or less coercive, and it may be tolerant or intolerant of other views. During the period between initial settlement and ultimate disestablishment, American religious establishments moved from being narrow, coercive, and intolerant to being broad, relatively noncoercive, and tolerant. Although the laws constituting the establishment were ad hoc and unsystematic, they can be summarized in six categories: (1) control over doctrine, governance, and personnel of the church; (2) compulsory church attendance; (3) financial support; (4) prohibitions on worship in dissenting churches; (5) use of church institutions for public functions; and (6) restriction of political participation to members of the established church.

Governmental Control over the Doctrines, Structure, and Personnel of the State Church. Modern constitutional doctrine stresses the "advancement of religion" as the key element of establishment, but in the Anglican establishments of America, the central feature was control rather than advancement. As one historian of the Virginia establishment observed: "The ministers were generally under the control of a local oligarchy of hard-fisted and often ignorant squires, who were interested in keeping expenses down."[16] Even after churches lost any public financial support in Virginia, Maryland, and South Carolina, the state legislatures continued to exercise authority over them, including legislation addressing articles of faith. In Massachusetts, the leader of the Baptist opposition to establishment charged that the authorities were "assuming a power to govern religion, rather than being governed by it."[17] The two principal means of government control over the church were laws governing doctrine and the power to appoint prelates and clergy.

Mandatory Attendance at Religious Worship Services in the State Church. In England, from the time of Elizabeth I, those who "absent[ed] themselves from the divine worship in the established church" were subject to a fine of one shilling for a single absence and twenty pounds for a month's absence.[18] Similar laws compelling church attendance were enacted in colonial America. These laws were not just symbolic. In a study of grand jury presentments in Virginia between 1720 and 1750, missing church was the most common indicted offense in eleven of the twenty-two counties; it was the second most common offense

in seven others.[19] In New England, Baptists were regularly prosecuted for failure to baptize their children and for absence from the worship services of the
established Congregational churches.[20]

Public Financial Support. Churches cost money: for remuneration for the
minister, upkeep for the building, and support for the mission. In England, the
principal source of revenue for the church was income from land holdings,
most of them dating to before the Reformation. Edmund Burke, a penetrating
observer of the constitutional role of the Church of England,[21] explained that
this means of support was essential to the independence of the church and the
ability of the minister to perform his function. If he were dependent on
voluntary contributions, the minister would have to curry favor with the congregation, especially its wealthy members, and if he were dependent on Parliament, he would become a mouthpiece for the party in power. Beyond revenues
from property, tithes, and other minor earmarked fines, Parliament did not
appropriate general tax revenues for use by the Church of England, with the
exception of modest assistance to low-income clergy, denominated "Queen
Anne's Bounty." In the colonies, the established churches relied on essentially
the same sources of revenue—land grants and tithes—though tithes in America
were understood as taxes, rather than as a species of private property, thus
making them subject to repeal without seeming to confiscate property. After
the early period of colonial settlement, there were no appropriations from the
public treasury for religious uses, except for the educational or charitable functions of religious institutions, such as colleges or orphanages.

Land grants were among the most important privileges of the established
church. In New England, colonial governments granted public lands to
churches for meeting houses, parsonages, day schools, orphanages, and other
pious uses. In the Anglican colonies, counties were required to construct a
house of worship and a parsonage. In addition to revenues from land grants,
all nine of the American colonies with established churches imposed compulsory taxes for the support of churches and ministers. After an early experience
with voluntary support for religion, backed by the considerable force of community suasion, the General Court in the Massachusetts Bay colony voted in
1638 to tax all those who did not contribute voluntarily to the support of the
town minister. The typical arrangement in New England was to allow each
town to negotiate a salary with the minister, and to impose the level of taxes
necessary to comply with the contract. In Virginia, the legislature fixed the
salary of the parish minister at sixteen thousand pounds of tobacco per year,
plus glebe land and fees. Beyond that, the vestry was responsible for church
maintenance, poor relief, and other civil functions.

When the Revolution came, the churches divided. Loyalty to the Crown was
a central tenet of Anglican theology, and Anglican clergy were the leading Tory
opponents of Revolution. Puritans and their Reformed heirs and allies, by contrast, had long developed a theology of resistance to tyranny and especially to

the British monarchy. The Revolution was the final blow to the Anglican establishment. It made no sense to compel citizens to support a church that was doctrinally committed to royal supremacy and whose clergy were predominantly Tory in their politics. In every colony—now we may shift to the term "state"—with an Anglican establishment, the system of public financial support was suspended. But that did not mean that, as a matter of principle, Americans discarded the long-held view that religion was worthy of governmental support. In 1777, the Continental Congress chimed in that "true religion and good morals are the only solid foundations of public liberty and happiness."[22]

Prohibition of Religious Worship in Other Denominations. Throughout Western Europe, governments enforced restrictions on public religious worship outside of officially approved services. In pre-Elizabethan England, like most of Catholic Europe, the instruments of choice were heresy laws. Restrictions on public worship outside of the approved church were also common in Colonial America. Some of the colonies welcomed dissenters, either formally or de facto, as a means of promoting economic development or their founders' commitment to religious toleration. Georgia, North Carolina, and to some extent New Jersey were in the first category; Rhode Island, Pennsylvania, Delaware, and seventeenth-century Maryland were in the second.

Catholics were a common target of religious intolerance. The New England colonies (other than Rhode Island), South Carolina, and Georgia all maintained laws forbidding Catholic churches.[23] When it was reported that several Catholic priests had entered the colony of Virginia without specific statutory authorization, the governor ordered their arrest. It is also noteworthy that, under the pressure of war with France, the Virginia Assembly in 1756 enacted a law requiring all "Papists" to surrender their arms and ammunition.[24] This statute suggests a connection of sorts between our First and Second Amendments.

Use of the State Church for Civil Functions. An important but often forgotten aspect of the church establishment was the assignment of what would now be considered important civil functions, especially social welfare functions, to church authorities. At a time when local government offices were small and limited in function, the local church was a convenient tool for administration.[25] The state use of and cooperation with the church was an inheritance from England. In the seventeenth and eighteenth centuries, churchwardens, lay officials chosen annually by the church vestry, performed a mixture of civil and ecclesiastical functions in the mother country. This basic schema was transplanted to the colonies with an Anglican establishment, where the gentry-dominated system of courts and vestries reinforced the connection between church and state. In Virginia, these administrative functions continued even after the Declaration of Rights, and were gradually eliminated in the process of disestablishment.

In the early colonies, social welfare was rudimentary at best, and entirely entrusted to the church. The vestry was charged with "caring for the poor, the aged and infirm, the sick and insane, and for orphans and other homeless children."[26] Unlike in England, where workhouses were the backbone of the welfare system, in America orphans and children of the poor were generally apprenticed or indentured; failing that, the poor were generally assisted in their homes or boarded out. Churchwardens also provided medical care to the aged and infirm, and assumed the burial expenses of paupers. Like all church expenses, these functions were financed by taxes imposed on the general population, as well as by some private contributions. Because the Anglican Church bore the statutory responsibility for poor relief, this system greatly complicated the termination of compulsory religious taxes. For a few years after these had been suspended, Anglican vestries continued to exact taxes from the general population for support of these functions. No other church played this role in America.

In the colonial and early republican periods, there was no such thing as public education in the modern sense. Primary education was haphazard and informal, usually a combination of home education, apprenticeship, and rudimentary schools. Although some schooling was provided by (often itinerant) schoolmasters or in dame schools, most schools were taught or directed by the local minister. There was little or no state involvement in finance or control. Even when the state became more involved, there was no sharp distinction between public and private religious and secular schools, until well into the nineteenth century. The very term *public* meant only that schools were open to the general public; most of these were *private* in terms of ownership and control, and they charged fees, at least to those who could afford them. And there was no such thing as a secular school; all schools used curriculum that was imbued with religion. The *New England Primer*, of which some three million copies were printed, consisted largely of a hornbook and catechism.[27]

Even after the disestablishment of religion, most schools in the United States were conducted under religious auspices. Governmental financial support for education, especially in the more religiously diverse big cities, typically took the form of grants to private schools for the education of the poor, with the choice of schools left to the families involved. For example, in New York in 1805 there were schools conducted by Presbyterian, Episcopalian, Methodist, Quaker, and Dutch Reformed groups, as well as the "Free School Society," a nondenominational charitable group, with all receiving public support. Later these groups were joined by Baptists, Catholics, and Jews. Early federal aid, which typically took the form of land grants, went to private as well as public schools, including religious schools. Until 1864, education in the District of Columbia was provided entirely through private and semiprivate institutions, including denominational schools, partially at public expense.

By the Civil War, most northern and western states had established public school systems, and most ceased to support nonpublic education.[28] But public education was far from secular in character. In *Democracy in America*, based on his travels in the 1830s, Tocqueville reports that "[t]he greater part of education [in America] is entrusted to the clergy."[29] Most early school superintendents were Protestant clergymen.

Marriages and Public Records. In the Anglican colonies, such as Virginia, the settled minister, or "rector," had the responsibility by law to keep public records of births, burials, and marriages. If the minister failed in this duty, he was fined five hundred pounds of tobacco.[30] The principal purpose of these records was to ascertain the number of taxable units, or "titheables," in the parish and in the county. In England, marriages could be lawfully performed only by ministers of the Church of England. This authority was carried over to the Anglican colonies. The law expressly declared illegitimate the offspring of marriages performed by ministers outside the established church.

Perhaps the most "governmental" of all duties of church officials in Virginia was the obligation of the churchwardens to make biennial presentments to the county court of certain misdemeanors, including swearing, profanity, sabbath breaking, absence from church, drunkenness, fornication, adultery, and slander.

Limitation of Political Participation to Members of the State Church. A central feature of the establishment in England was the limitation of public office to members of the Church of England. The Test and Corporation Acts required that, in order to hold civil, military, academic, or municipal office, it was necessary to have taken communion in the established church within a certain period and to swear an oath against belief in transubstantiation, the Catholic doctrine that the bread and wine of communion are transformed into the body and blood of Christ.[31] The right to vote for members of Parliament was limited to those who would take an oath forswearing the "ecclesiastical or spiritual" authority of any foreign prince or prelate, the belief in transubstantiation, or the veneration of Mary or the saints.[32]

Similar restrictions on office-holding were also common in America. Most conspicuously, until adoption of the "Halfway Covenant" in 1662, Massachusetts limited full citizenship to those who supplied proof of a genuine conversion experience. In states where dissenters were successfully excluded, the issue would not arise. South Carolina presents a good example of the problem in more tolerant colonies. In the seventeenth century, many dissenters from the established Church of England had settled in South Carolina, and the colonial governors had mostly been dissenters—Quakers or Presbyterians. In 1704, the assembly enacted legislation on the model of the Test Acts, barring from the legislature any person who could not swear an oath that he took communion in the Church of England. This Act was said to be necessary "to quell all factions which so much disturb'd the peace of the Government."[33]

Religious restrictions on the right to vote were imposed in almost every colony.[34] Sometimes these were affirmative, such as extending the franchise only to members of the Protestant religion, the Church of England, or some other defined denomination. Sometimes they were negative, such as denying the franchise to Catholics, Jews, Quakers, or others. Catholics were the most frequently excluded group.

Even after Independence, every state other than Virginia restricted on religious grounds the right to hold office. Some excluded Catholics, some atheists, some non-Trinitarians, and some Jews. Four states, Georgia, New Jersey, New Hampshire, and South Carolina, simply limited the political office to "Protestants."[35] North Carolina excluded those who "den[ied] . . . the truth of the Protestant religion,"[36] opening a loophole under which a future Catholic governor served on the theory that although he did not affirm, neither did he "deny" that "truth."[37] Delaware required a belief in the Trinity.[38] Massachusetts merely limited public office to Christians, a liberal policy that inspired over sixty towns to protest against the inclusion of Catholics. Even Pennsylvania, which had no formal establishment, demanded that officeholders profess a belief in God and in the divine inspiration of the Old and New Testaments.[39]

Rationales for the Establishment

To understand the basis for religious establishment in political theory, we must distinguish between two different, almost antithetical rationales, which we may call the *theological* and the *political*. Establishment, under the theological rationale, is intended to glorify God, to save souls, and to ensure God's providence for the nation. Under the political rationale, the purpose of a religious establishment is to shape public opinion and character in a way favorable to the regime. One is based on the primacy of religion, the other on the utility of religion to the state.

Distinguishing Theological from Political Rationales. The theological rationale for establishment rested on confidence regarding religious truth. As Boston Puritan minister, John Cotton, wrote: "[T]he word of God in such things [religious fundamentals] is so clear, that [a person] *cannot but be convinced* in conscience of the dangerous error of his way, after once or twice admonition wisely and faithfully dispenses."[40] Thus, "[i]f such a man, after such admonition, shall still persist in the error of his way and be punished, he is not persecuted for cause of conscience, but for *sinning against his own conscience.*"[41] New England Puritans saw no inconsistency in arguing that magistrates had "no power against the laws, doctrines and religion of Christ" while asserting that they could use their power against those who teach false beliefs.[42] To use state power against Christ would be wrong; to use it to support Christ and his church was only right. In Nathaniel Ward's vigorous prose, "God doth no where in his word tolerate Christian States, to give Tolerations to such adversaries of his Truth, if they have power in their hands to suppresse them."[43] Under this way of thinking, use of government power with respect to religion is legitimate if, and only if, it is in support of the true religion.

The political rationale treated religion as a means for promoting the civic purposes of the state. It rested on the social utility rather than the truth of religion. Machiavelli, who called religion "the instrument necessary above all others for the maintenance of a civilized state," urged rulers to "foster and encourage" religion "even though they be convinced that it is quite fallacious."[44] Truth and social utility may, but need not, coincide.

In the English and American colonial traditions, both theological and political rationales were present, and frequently intermingled. Consider the official title of the British monarch: "[B]y the Grace of God, King of *England, Scotland, France* and *Ireland*, Defender of the Faith."[45] "Defender of the Faith," a title conferred by the pope in recognition of Henry VIII's opposition to the teachings of Martin Luther, represents the theological rationale. The king's job is to support and defend true religion. "By the Grace of God, King" represents the political rationale. If the people can be induced to believe that the king enjoys his power by the authority of God, a divine right of kings, they are more likely to be good monarchical subjects.

The theological rationale can be seen in the earliest colonial charters. There is good reason to suspect, however, that in most places and at most times, the political rationale was generally more influential, at least to those in command of the government. Religion is a key determinant of the values and virtues of a people, and the ability to shape values and virtues is useful to anyone who wishes to rule. This is particularly evident in the teachings of the Anglican Church, which emphasized that loyalty to the crown and obedience to the government are religious as well as civic obligations. One article of the Thirty-nine Articles of Faith of the Church of England affirmed the supremacy of the monarch in matters spiritual and temporal. The first provision of the 1604 Canons of the Church of England, which were carried over to the Anglican colonies, required ministers at least four times each year to deliver sermons teaching that the king "is the highest power under God."[46] This was to be done "purely and sincerely, (without any colour or dissimulation)."[47] In 1640, when civil war was looming in England, clergy were required on penalty of dismissal to "audibly read" this "explanation" of the royal power.

Theoretical Justifications for the English Establishment. In England, the monarch was the supreme head of the church; Parliament controlled the liturgy and articles of faith; the government appointed the bishops; government offices were confined to members of the church. This arrangement may fairly be called a union between church and state. But it was not a theocracy. Quite the contrary: The church did not control the government, but the government did control the church. The technical term for governmental control over the church in the

English tradition is *Erastianism*, so-called after the sixteenth-century Swiss-German theologian Thomas Erastus, whose polemics against the ecclesiastical power of excommunication contained the seeds of the notion that the civil authority must control the church.[48]

In the later sixteenth century, Richard Hooker, the most authoritative of the mainstream Anglican theorists (Locke reverentially called him "the judicious Hooker"), drew on biblical, scholastic, and common law sources to argue that no specific form of church government was required by scripture, and therefore the question of ecclesiastical authority must be determined by God-given reason and the long-standing practice of the nation. Hooker reasoned that authority over the church must be located in the whole body of the people of the church, and that the people had consented to the exercise of that authority by their constitutional institutions, namely, the king in Parliament. As one church historian put it, Hooker "made it clear that royal supremacy really meant the supremacy of that law which uttered the general consent of the nation itself."[49] Under the early Stuarts, however, Erastian theory shifted in the direction of the divine right of kings, in which the monarch was understood to have a divinely appointed prerogative to rule both church and state. This, coupled with increasing religious intolerance under Archbishop Laud, helped to bring on the English Civil War in the 1640s.

In the eighteenth century, the Whig-dominated Church of England became more latitudinarian in its practice and theology, and less intolerant of dissenters. A general principle of toleration or free exercise was hardly embraced, but Parliament came to recognize that denominations outside the Church of England could be sufficiently loyal and virtuous and should not be suppressed. First, Trinitarian Protestants (Presbyterians, Baptists, and Independents) petitioned for and received toleration; later the Unitarians sought and received similar treatment, though Jews and Catholics had to wait until the 1830s. Each petition was debated on its merits. After the Glorious Revolution in 1688 and the Hanoverian succession, the divine right of kings was understandably out of vogue, and the idea of a close "union" between church and state lost its appeal. Britain had evolved into a tolerant establishment, in which the state supported and controlled an official church but permitted a limited range of alternative faiths to worship publicly without penalty.

William Warburton, the Bishop of Gloucester and the leading eighteenth-century theorist of the Anglican establishment, argued that church and state were distinct and mutually independent, but allied in a joint enterprise of the governing of society.[50] The state needed the aid of the church to reinforce obedience to the laws and the performance of moral duties; the church needed the aid of the state for protection and financial support, in return for which it ceded its independence. Warburton's arguments were often borrowed by supporters of establishment in colonial America.[51]

In the colonial Virginia establishment prior to the Revolution, there was little debate over this rationale for the establishment. There were strenuous church-state disputes, to be sure, but with few exceptions the disputants took for granted the legitimacy of the religious establishment. Thus, Landon Carter, anticlerical though he was, could write of the "Necessity of Connection between the Religious and Civil Society,"[52] while Robert Carter Nicholas, a defender of the establishment, wrote in similar terms of "that necessary, that friendly and amiable Alliance between Church and State."[53] Church-state arguments in colonial Virginia were primarily over the locus of authority in the church—some contending that ministers should receive a dependable and adequate income so that they could exercise independence in their preaching, and others contending that lay control was necessary for the discipline of the clergy. No one seriously disputed the close relationship between government and the institutions of religion.

Post-Independence Justifications for American Establishments. In post-Independence America, the arguments for establishment took a republican cast. Observers then, and historians since, have stressed the close connection between republicanism, support for the cause of Independence, and the Reformed Protestantism of the colonies, especially in the antihierarchical form that it took after the First Great Awakening of 1720–1780. Anglicanism and Catholicism were associated with monarchism. Presbyterianism, Congregationalism, and Baptist ecclesiology were associated with republicanism and varying degrees of localism and federalism. Edmund Burke pointed to the religious sensibility of America as a leading explanation for the colonial unrest that later led to the Revolution:

> Religion, always a principle of energy, in this new people is no way worn out or impaired; and their mode of professing it is also one main cause of this free spirit. The people are protestants, and of that kind which is the most adverse to all implicit submission of mind and opinion. This is a persuasion not only favorable to liberty, but built upon it. . . . All protestantism, even the most cold and passive, is a sort of dissent. But the religion most prevalent in our northern colonies is a refinement on the principle of resistance: it is the dissidence of dissent, and the protestantism of the Protestant religion.[54]

Moreover, the Reformed Protestant emphasis on rectitude, sobriety, thrift, and virtue marched hand in hand with the civic republican virtue to which the new nation aspired.

During the years immediately preceding ratification of the First Amendment in 1791, interest in some form of official support for religion was on the rise. After the heady rush of public spiritedness that accompanied the American Revolution, many leaders became convinced that public virtue was seriously on the decline in the new nation. This conviction led in different directions: in some, it resulted in a loss of confidence in republicanism; in some it inspired development of a new science of politics that would rely on the clash of interests rather than on virtue as the wellspring of good government; and in some it stimulated efforts to reinvigorate institutions of local self-government through which Americans would learn to elevate the public good above their individual concerns. But a common reaction was to attribute the decline in public virtue to the paucity of public religious worship and teaching, which was the result of the collapse of the established church, especially in the South. Throughout the South, pulpits were empty and resources to attract a learned and able ministry were lacking. During the Revolution, Virginia lost half of its Anglican clergy, and Connecticut a third. Forty Virginia parishes were bereft of a minister. The Anglican clergy—now calling themselves "Protestant Episcopal"—informed the Virginia legislature that houses of worship were in short supply and "in a ruinous or ruined condition; and the clergy for the most part dead or driven away and their places unfilled."[55] They needed resources to rebuild. That is why, with only a few exceptions, every state witnessed a movement to institute or strengthen a religious establishment, albeit on broadly inclusive lines. The basic idea was to require everyone to contribute to the support of a church, but to allow them a certain degree of latitude in choosing which one to support. Such a system was adopted, at least in theory, in Georgia, Maryland, and most of New England, and was narrowly rejected in several states, most notably Virginia.

The birth of modern republican government is popularly associated with a rise of secularism, or at least a decline in reliance on religion for civic ends. But that did not seem so obvious to the founding generation. To their minds, republicanism both presupposed and demanded a degree of public virtue exceeding that required in monarchical regimes. In a monarchy, obedience to the laws could be enforced through the apparatus of coercion. In a republic, where the people are self-governing, it was generally thought that coercion had to be replaced, or at least supplemented, with a regard for the public good. Gordon Wood explains: "In a monarchy each man's desire to do what was right in his own eyes could be restrained by fear or force. In a republic, however, each man must somehow be persuaded to submerge his personal wants into the greater good of the whole."[56] Thus, although creation of the American republic went hand in hand with dismantling establishment of the pro-monarchical establishment of the Church of England, it stimulated concern for religion that would promote republican virtue. As Alexis de Tocqueville wrote:

> Despotism may be able to do without faith, but freedom cannot. Religion is much more needed in the republic they advocate than in the monarchy they attack, and in democratic republics most of all. How could society escape destruction if, when political ties are relaxed, moral ties are not tightened? And what can be done with a people master of itself if it is not subject to God?[57]

George Washington was thus articulating a common view when he stated in his Farewell Address: "Of all the dispositions and habits which lead to political prosperity, religion and morality are indispensable supports. . . . And let us with caution indulge the supposition that morality can be maintained without religion." He went on to say that a "refined education" might instill morality in minds of a "peculiar structure," but that experience and reason alike showed that this would not be sufficient for the society at large.[58] In a similar vein, Adams wrote that "religion and virtue are the only foundations not only of republicanism and of all free government but of social felicity under all governments and in all the combinations of human society."[59] John Witherspoon, the only minister to sign the Declaration of Independence and James Madison's professor at Princeton, wrote that "to promote religion is the best and most effectual way of making a virtuous and regular people."[60] Madison's uncle, also named James Madison, the first post-Independence Episcopal bishop in Virginia, declared that a free and republican society, "[d]estitute of that coercive power, which compels obedience to civil laws," was forced to depend even more upon virtue and thus on religion.[61] The Massachusetts Constitution of 1780 justified the compulsory support for religion by a similar invocation of social utility:

> [As the] happiness of a people and the good order and preservation of civil government essentially depend upon piety, religion, and morality, . . . [and that] these cannot be generally diffused through a community but by the institution of the public worship of God and of public instructions in piety, religion, and morality. . . .[62]

Advocates of the general assessment bill in Virginia offered much the same rationale: "Whereas the general diffusion of Christian knowledge hath a natural tendency to correct the morals of men, restrain their vices, and preserve the peace of society; which cannot be effected without a competent provision for learned teachers. . . ."[63]

As these speeches and documents illustrate, the official justification for governmental support for religion, by the 1780s, had ceased to have any real theological component. There was no mention of the need to glorify or worship God or to promote the salvation of members of the Commonwealth. There was only the civic justification that belief in religion would preserve the peace and good order of society by improving men's morals and restraining their vices. As the Presbytery of Hanover declared in a position statement favoring the general assessment bill in Virginia: "Religion as a spiritual system is not to be considered as an object of human legislation, but may in a civil view, as preserving the existence and promoting the happiness of society."[64] Indeed, Isaac Backus, a Baptist minister and leading advocate of disestablishment in Massachusetts, mocked the change in justification: "A little while ago," he said, the establishment was "for religion," but now it is said to be "for the good of *civil society*."[65]

The most thorough explanation of the rationale for religious establishment during the founding period was offered by Massachusetts Chief Justice Theophilus Parsons in the case of *Barnes v. First Parish* in 1810. Because Parsons was the principal architect of Article III, the religion section of the Massachusetts Constitution of 1780, there was no better person to set forth its purposes and to defend it against the disestablishmentarian attack. For his day in Massachusetts, Parsons was an advocate of an unusually broad freedom of religion. One of his first public causes was to oppose the proposed state constitution of 1778 for its failure to provide adequate protection for the rights of conscience. In particular, he protested the limitation of free exercise rights to Protestants "when in fact, that free exercise and enjoyment is the natural and uncontrollable right of every member of the State."[66] His defense of the Massachusetts establishment, therefore, should not be mistaken for a defense of religious intolerance.

Parsons began his opinion in *Barnes* on a civic note, observing the connection between the public good and the state of public morality:

> The object of a free civil government is the promotion and security of the happiness of the citizens. These effects cannot be produced, but by the knowledge and practice of our moral duties, which comprehend all the social and civil obligations of man to man, and of the citizen to the state. If the civil magistrate in any state could procure by his regulations a uniform practice of these duties, the government of that state would be perfect.[67]

This was an utterly conventional articulation of civic republican principle— standard fare for his day and time.

More challenging was his argument that "it is not enough for the magistrate to define the rights of the several citizens, as they are related to life, liberty, property, and reputation, and to punish those by whom they may be invaded."[68] This proposition directly contradicted Jefferson's dictum that "it is time enough for the rightful purposes of civil government for its officers to interfere when principles break out into overt acts against peace and good order."[69] In that opinion, Jefferson was not alone. Petitioners against the Virginia assessment bill from Montgomery County wrote:

> Cannot it be denied that civil laws are not sufficient? We conceive it cannot, especially where the minds of men are disposed to an Observance of what is right and an Observance of what is wrong. And we Conceive also that Ideas of right and wrong, may be derived merely from positive law, without seeking a higher original.[70]

Parsons offered two reasons law and subsequent punishment were not sufficient; these were based on the law's scope and its enforcement. First:

> Human laws cannot oblige to the performance of the duties of imperfect obligation; as the duties of charity and hospitality, benevolence and good

neighborhood; as the duties resulting from the relation of husband and wife, parent and child; of man to man, as children of a common parent; and of real patriotism, by influencing every citizen to love his country, and to obey all its laws. These are moral duties, flowing from the disposition of the heart, and not subject to the control of human legislation.[71]

Second:

> Neither can the laws prevent, by temporal punishment, secret offences, committed without witness, to gratify malice, revenge, or any other passion, by assailing the most important and most estimable rights of others. For human tribunals cannot proceed against any crimes, unless ascertained by evidence; and they are destitute of all power to prevent the commission of offences, unless by the feeble examples exhibited in the punishment of those who may be detected.[72]

Let us consider these arguments. Drawing on the distinction between law and morality, which he terms "perfect" and "imperfect" obligation, Parsons argued that society has a strong interest in behavior that, by its nature, is not susceptible to legal definition and enforcement. He gave a number of persuasive examples of "imperfect obligation[s]" that "flow[] from the disposition of the heart, and [are] not subject to the control of human legislation," including charity and hospitality, benevolence and neighborliness, familial responsibility, and patriotism. These are not merely "private" moral concerns; they affect the happiness of the community. Yet they cannot be legislated. If society wishes to influence its members to observe these imperfect obligations, it must attempt to inculcate the appropriate beliefs and habits. Moreover, he pointed out, even among those social duties that are susceptible to legal definition, the arm of the law falls short of full enforcement. He gave the example of acts committed in secret, without witnesses. Again, the remedy is to attempt to cultivate a spirit of obedience to the laws, as an alternative and auxiliary to coercion and after-the-fact punishment.

Seventeenth-century English philosopher Thomas Hobbes had claimed that "it is evident to the meanest capacity, that men's actions are derived from the opinions they have. . . ."[73] In effect, Hobbes argued, it is too late to seek to control human behavior after bad acts have already taken place. A wise ruler will attempt to shape the habits, inclinations, and character of the people. As Burke argued, "it is the right of government to attend much to opinions; because, as opinions soon combine with passions, even when they do not produce them, they have much influence on actions."[74] Let us be hardheaded about this: Who was right? Jefferson or Parsons?

The next step in Parsons's argument was that the best way for the government to inculcate the civic virtue needed for community happiness is to support religion. That is a far more troubling claim from our modern disestablishmentarian point of view. But throughout most of history, religious teaching has been one of the most powerful means of inculcation of ideas of morality. As Washington warned, "let us with caution indulge the supposition that morality can be maintained without religion."[75] If Washington is right, Parsons would argue, it is the province of government to be concerned about the public teachings of religion, from a civil, even if not a spiritual, point of view. In this, Parsons was not breaking new ground. For almost a century, the established church had been defended on the basis of its social utility.

But what about truth? Interestingly, Parsons' argument did not seem to rest on the truth of the doctrine being taught. The following passage is the only part of his opinion that even touches on the issue of truth:

> In selecting a religion, the people [of Massachusetts] were not exposed to the hazard of choosing a false and defective religious system. Christianity had long been promulgated, its pretensions and excellences well known, and its divine authority admitted. This religion was found to rest on the basis of immortal truth; to contain a system of morals adapted to man, in all possible ranks and conditions, situations and circumstances, by conforming to which he would be meliorated and improved in all the relations of human life; and to furnish the most efficacious sanctions, by bringing to light a future state of retribution.[76]

Christianity "had long been promulgated." Its "pretensions and excellences" were "well known." These words were carefully chosen. Parsons does not say that Christianity's pretensions were justified or that its excellences were truly excellent, only that these were "well known." The religion "was found"—by whom? on what basis? with what validity?—to "rest" on the basis of immortal truth. That is nothing more than a statement of sociological fact. In Massachusetts in 1780, the Christian religion had indeed been "found" to rest on immortal truth, but that is a far cry from saying that it was actually true. I do not mean to suggest that Parsons did not believe in the truth of the Christian religion; for all we know, Parsons was orthodox in his views and practices. But its truth was not a necessary element in his justification for the establishment. His was a political rationale: that religion should be established to serve the interests of society by inculcating ideas that promote the public interest.

In his *Barnes* opinion, Parsons also addressed what he considered to be the three principal "objections [that] have at times been made to this establishment": that taxing people for the support of religion is a violation of liberty of conscience, that it is unfair to force people to support religions with which they do not agree, and that it is "anti-christian for any state to avail itself of the maxims of Christianity, to support civil government."[77] Parsons responded that "the first objection seems to mistake a man's conscience for his money."[78] Liberty of conscience, he reasoned, is fully satisfied by the right to exercise one's own religious opinions and to refrain from attending any religious instruction of which one "conscientiously disapproves."[79] It does not include the right not to have one's tax dollars used to promote ideas one does not share. This is obviously contrary to the view taken by Jefferson and Madison that "to compel a man to furnish contributions of money for the propagation of opinions which he disbelieves is sinful and tyrannical."[80] But it bears strong resemblance to modern constitutional doctrine, which permits the government to extract money for promotion of the government's own messages (however abhorrent they may be to the taxpayer), as well as for controversial expenditures such as abortions or indecent or blasphemous art, to which some citizens have conscientious objections. Although the government may not force an individual to speak or to carry the government's message, it may force him to pay for it. To be sure, modern constitutional doctrine makes an exception for specifically *religious* governmental expenditures, but it is noteworthy that Jefferson and Madison drew no such line. For the most part, Parsons' distinction between requiring a person to engage in an objectionable activity and making her pay taxes for support of that activity, still seems to carry weight.

As for the second argument, Parsons argued that it is "wholly in mistake" to think that "it is intolerant to compel a man to pay for religious instruction, from which, as he does not hear it, he can derive no benefit."[81] The benefits derived from the inculcation of religious principles of virtue, Parsons noted, are not enjoyed so much by the listener as by the public at large. The object of the establishment is not to confer a benefit on those who wish to attend religious services, but to "form and cultivate reasonable and just habits and manners; by which every man's person and property are protected from outrage, and his personal and social enjoyments promoted and multiplied."[82] Even unbelievers receive this benefit: "From these effects every man derives the most important benefits; and whether he be, or be not, an auditor of any public teacher, he receives more solid and permanent advantages from this public instruction, than the administration of justice in courts of law can give him."[83] The argument is not dissimilar to the argument in favor of tax support of education: We all benefit when our fellow citizens are educated, even if we have no children in school.

The third argument to which Parsons responded is a religious objection: that it is "anti-christian" to use the Christian religion for state purposes. Parsons devoted many more words to this objection than to the others, but it is hard to escape the conclusion that his response to this is the weakest. The nub of his answer was that Christians should not object to having their religion used in this way because "from the genius and temper of this religion, and from the benevolent character of its Author, we must conclude that it is his intention that man should be benefitted by it in his civil and political relations."[84] Perhaps, but this is far from an obvious inference. Many would say— and in Parsons's day, many were saying—that it is an insult to God and an impious usurpation of the role of the church for the government to use religion for civil purposes and to presume to decide what religious truths should be taught to the people. As Elisha Williams, a Connecticut preacher and rector of Yale during the Great Awakening, put it: "[I]f Christ be Lord of the conscience, the sole King in his own kingdom, then it will follow, that all such as in any manner or degree assume the power of directing and governing the consciences of men, are justly chargeable with invading his rightful dominion."[85] Or, as James Madison put it in his *Memorial and Remonstrance*, for the state to "employ Religion as an engine of Civil policy . . . [is] an unhallowed perversion of the means of salvation."[86] Such arguments may have little *secular* force: Why should nonbelievers care whether the Christian religion is subjected to an "unhallowed perversion"? But they carried weight among Parsons's audience, and his response seems tepid and unconvincing. It is, indeed, a remarkable feature of the debates over establishment and disestablishment at the founding that the advocates of the establishment tended to offer secular justifications grounded in the social utility of religion, whereas the most prominent voices for disestablishment often focused more on the theological objections.

Conclusions

The establishment of religion thus commanded considerable support among Americans at the time of the founding. It had solid historical roots, it was linked in political theory to republicanism, and it was justified in terms of social utility rather than religious doctrine. Moreover, the First Amendment to the U.S. Constitution did not reject the idea of establishment. The amendment forbade "Congress" to enact any law "respecting an establishment of religion," meaning any law establishing religion at the federal level or affecting the establishment of religion at the state level. At this time, it was a real possibility that some of the states would choose to maintain a broadly inclusive establishment, and the amendment protected that state prerogative. Every state at the time with a bill of rights guaranteed full liberty of conscience or free exercise of religion, or both, but nearly half retained some sort of establishment. It was not until Reconstruction, and arguably not until incorporation of the Bill of Rights against the states, that disestablishment of religion became an essential element in the liberal conception of rights.

Even in the founding era, however, a principled liberal opposition to establishment was taking shape, mostly among dissident religious groups such as the Baptists and other heirs to the Great Awakening. Their argument against establishment of religion had a decidedly religious cast. It was a usurpation of spiritual authority for political bodies to purport to interpret the Scripture; conviction and conversion were the work of the Holy Spirit, not the legislature.

Moreover, they argued, government subvention would weaken religion and make it subservient to the state. Cutting the ties between government and institutional religion, they predicted, would create a more robust and energetic form of faith. And many observers of American history have concluded that disestablishment had precisely that effect. Tocqueville reported that religion was stronger in America than in any other country, and attributed this strength to the separation between church and state.[87] Madison similarly commented that "the number, the industry, and the morality of the Priesthood, & the devotion of the people have been manifestly increased by the total separation of the Church from the State."[88]

It is a mistake, therefore, to view the establishment of religion through the lens of modern preoccupations about whether political society is too infused with religiosity. Establishment was not really about religion; it was about government control over the formation of public opinion. And disestablishment was not an attempt to curtail the influence or prominence of religion in public life. It was to make religious practice free and independent, and therefore strong.

Notes

1. See McCollum v. Board of Education, 333 U.S. 203 (1948); Everson v. Board of Education, 330 U.S. 1 (1947).

2. *Everson*, 330 U.S. at 13.

3. Ibid. at 8.

4. Ibid.

5. See further chapter 6 by Ralph Ketcham.

6. See further chapter 8 by Carl Esbeck.

7. See further chapter 3 by Mark McGarvie, chapter 4 by David Little, and chapter 5 by Paul Finkelman.

8. Julian P. Boyd, ed., *The Papers of Thomas Jefferson*, 37 vols. (Princeton, NJ: Princeton University Press, 1950), 539–44.

9. William Waller Hening, *The Statutes at Large, Being a Collection of All the Laws in Virginia* (New York: R. & W. & G. Bartow, 1823), 2:41–42.

10. Mary Elizabeth Quinlivan, "Ideological Controversy over Religious Establishment in Revolutionary Virginia" (PhD diss., University of Wisconsin, 1971), 72–77.

11. Supremacy Act, 1534, 26 Hen. 8, c. 1 (Eng.), reprinted in Carl Stephenson and Frederick Marcham, eds., *Sources of English Constitutional History* (New York: Harper & Row, 1937), 1:311. As reenacted under Elizabeth I, the Act omitted the offensive phrase "supreme head," but did not diminish the monarch's power on any matters of substance. Act of Supremacy, 1559, 1 Eliz., c. 1 (Eng.), reprinted in ibid. 1:344–46.

12. Act of Uniformity, 1662, 14 Car. 2, c. 4 (Eng.), reprinted in Stephenson and Marcham, *Sources*, 1:543–46.

13. 1605–06, 3 Jam. 1, c. 5 (Eng.), reprinted in *Statutes of the Realm* (London: n.p. 1963), 4:1077.

14. 1581, 35 Eliz., c. 1 (Eng.), reprinted in Stephenson and Marcham, *Sources*, 1:354.

15. The term *Anglican* did not come into contemporaneous use until the eighteenth century, but I use it here as a shorthand for the Church of England prior to Independence. The term *Episcopalian* was sometimes used in reference to the Church of England prior to Independence, but I will reserve it to refer to the American successor to the Church of England after Independence. I will use the term *Puritan* to denote the congregational Reformed Protestantism of New England in the hundred or so years after settlement, and the term *Congregationalist* to denote the same church after the mid-1700s, when it had lost the theological and behavioral rigor that is associated with the term *Puritan*. I will use the term *Calvinist* or *Reformed* to encompass not only Puritans and Congregationalists, but Presbyterians, Dutch Reformed, Independents, and other denominations whose theology derives from the thoughts of John Calvin.

16. H. J. Eckenrode, *Separation of Church and State in Virginia* (Richmond, VA: Department of Archives and History, 1910), 13.

17. Isaac Backus, "Government and Liberty Described," in *Isaac Backus on Church, State, and Calvinism: Pamphlets 1754–1789*, ed. William G. McLoughlin (Cambridge, MA: Harvard University Press, 1968), 351.

18. William Blackstone, *Commentaries on the Laws of England* (Oxford: Clarendon Press, 1765), 4:51–52.

19. A. G. Roeber, *Faithful Magistrates and Republican Lawyers: Creators of Virginia Legal Culture, 1680–1810* (Chapel Hill: University of North Carolina Press, 1980), 141–42. Another study, based on records from Caroline County between 1740 and 1749, concluded that grand jury presentments for church nonattendance were "clearly routine," but not as common as those for some other crimes, such as charges of neglect against road surveyors. Rhys Isaac, "Religion and Authority: Problems of the Anglican Establishment in Virginia in the Era of the Great Awakening and the Parsons' Cause," *William & Mary Quarterly* 30 (1973): 4 n.2.

20. William G. McLoughlin, *New England Dissent 1630–1833: The Baptists and the Separation of Church and State* (Cambridge, MA: Harvard University Press, 1971), 15, 17.

21. I quote Burke at various points because he was the most interesting and persuasive defender of the established church in England at the time our First Amendment was being adopted. See further Michael W. McConnell, "Establishment and Toleration in Edmund Burke's 'Constitution of Freedom,'" 1996 *Supreme Court Review* 1005: 393, 432.

22. *Journals of the Continental Congress, 1774–1789* (Washington, DC: U.S. Government Printing Office, 1904–37), 12:1001.

23. See Sanford H. Cobb, *The Rise of Religious Liberty in America: A History* (New York: MacMillan, 1902) 123, 276, 420, 437.

24. Hening, *Statutes at Large*, 2:35.

25. A. Pierce Middleton, "The Colonial Virginia Parish," *Historical Magazine of the Protestant Episcopal Church* 40 (1971): 431, 444–45.

26. Ibid., 435.

27. Benjamin Harris, *The New England Primer*, ed. P. L. Ford (New York: Harper & Row, 1962).

28. See chapter 10 by Steven Green and chapter 11 by Thomas Berg.

29. Alexis de Tocqueville, *Democracy in America*, ed. J. P. Mayer (New York: Harper Perennial, 1969), 295.

30. Hening, *The Statutes At Large*, 54.

31. First Test Act, 1673, 25 Car. 2, c. 2 (Eng.), reprinted in Stephenson and Marcham, *Sources*, 1:555–56; Second Test Act, 1678, 30 Car. 2, st. 2, c. 1 (Eng.), reprinted in ibid., 1:556–57; Corporation Act, 1661, 13 Car. 2, st. 2, c. 1 (Eng.), reprinted in ibid., 1:542–43.

32. 6 Ann., c. 23 (1707) (Eng.), reprinted in Danby Pickering, *The Statutes at Large, from the Second to Eighth Year of Queen Anne* (London: Joseph Bentham, 1762–1807), 2:375–82.

33. John Wesley Brinsfield, *Religion and Politics in Colonial South Carolina* (Greenville, SC: Southern Historical Press, 1983), 23.

34. See Albert E. McKinley, *The Suffrage Franchise in the Thirteen English Colonies in America* (Philadelphia: University of Pennsylvania Press, 1905).

35. Chester James Antieau et al., *Freedom from Federal Establishment: Formation and Early History of the First Amendment Religion Clauses* (Milwaukee, WI: Bruce, 1964), 93–94.

36. Ibid., 109.

37. Ibid.

38. Ibid., 93.

39. For federal and later state developments, see chapter 9 by Daniel Dreisbach.

40. John Cotton, *The Bloody Tenent, Washed and Made White in the Bloud of the Lambe* (London: Matthew Symmons, 1647), 8.

41. Ibid.

42. Walter H. Bugess and John Robinson, *Pastor of the Pilgrim Fathers* (London: Williams & Norgate, 1920), 152–54.

43. Nathaniel Ward, *The Simple Cobbler of Aggawam in America*, ed. Lawrence C. Wroth (New York: Scholars' Facsimiles & Reprints, 1937), 3.

44. Niccolo Macchiavelli, *The Discourses*, ed. Bernard R. Crick, trans. Leslie J. Walker (New York: Penguin Books, 1970), 139, 143.

45. First Charter of Virginia, 1606, in *The Federal and State Constitutions, Colonial Charters, and Other Organic Laws of the United States*, 2nd ed., ed. Ben Perley Poore (Union, NJ: Lawbook Exchange, 2001), 2:1888–93.

46. *Bishops and Clergy of Canterbury Constitutions and Canons Ecclesiastical*, Canon 1 (1604).

47. Ibid.

48. See Weldon S. Crowley, "Erastianism in England to 1640," *Journal of Church and State* 32 (1990): 549; Weldon S. Crowley, "Erastianism in the Long Parliament, 1640–1646," *Journal of Church and State* 21 (1979): 45; Weldon S. Crowley, "Erastianism in the Westminster Assembly," *Journal of Church and State* 15 (1973): 49.

49. H. Hensley Henson, *Studies in English Religion in the Seventeenth Century* (London: John Murray, 1903), 144.

50. See William Warburton, *The Alliance Between Church and State* (London: Fletcher Gyles, 1736).

51. Quinlivan, "Ideological Controversy," 10–11, 37–39.

52. Ibid., 21.

53. Ibid., 34.

54. Edmund Burke, "Speech on Moving His Resolutions for Conciliation with the Colonies," in *Edmund Burke: Selected Writings and Speeches*, ed. Peter J. Stanlis (Garden City, NY: Anchor Books, 1963), 159–60.

55. Thomas E. Buckley, *Church and State in Revolutionary Virginia, 1776–1787* (Charlottesville: University of Virginia Press, 1977), 81.

56. Gordon S. Wood, *The Creation of the American Republic, 1776–1787* (Chapel Hill: University Press of North Carolina, 1969), 68.

57. Tocqueville, *Democracy in America*, 294.

58. George Washington, "Farewell Address" (1796), reprinted in Michael W. McConnell et al., *Religion and the Constitution*, 2nd ed. (New York: Aspen, 2002), 53–54.

59. "Letter from John Adams to Benjamin Rush" (August 28, 1811), in *The Spur of Fame: Dialogues of John Adams and Benjamin Rush, 1805–1813*, ed. John A. Schutz and Douglas Adair (San Marino, CA: Huntington Library, 1966), 192.

60. John Witherspoon, *Lectures on Moral Philosophy*, ed. Varnum Collins (Princeton, NJ: Princeton University Press, 1912), 110.

61. Nancy L. Rhoden, *Revolutionary Anglicanism: The Colonial Church of England Clergy during the American Revolution* (New York: New York University Press, 1999), 134.

62. Massachusetts Constitution of 1780, Article 3, reprinted in McConnell et al., *Religion and the Constitution*, 33–34.

63. "A Bill Establishing a Provision for Teachers of the Christian Religion" (December 24, 1784), reprinted in McConnell et al., *Religion and the Constitution*, 60.

64. William Henry Foote, *Sketches of Virginia: Historical and Biographical*, First Series (Richmond, VA: John Knox Press, 1966), 338.

65. Isaac Backus, "An Appeal to the Public for Religious Liberty," in *Isaac Backus*, 351.

66. McLoughlin, *New England Dissent*, 610–11.

67. *Barnes v. First Parish*, 6 Mass. 401, 404 (1810).

68. Ibid.

69. "A Bill to Establish Religious Freedom" (1786), reprinted in McConnell et al., *Religion and the Constitution*, 70.

70. "Petition from Inhabitants of Montgomery County to the Honorable Speaker and Gentlemen of the House of Delegates" (November 15, 1785), quoted in Quinlivan, "Ideological Controversy," 3.

71. *Barnes*, 6 Mass. at 404.

72. Ibid.

73. See Thomas Hobbes, *Leviathan* 2nd ed. (London: Ballantine Press, 1886), 228.

74. Edmund Burke, "Speech on the Petition of the Unitarian Society" (1792), in *Burke: Selected Writings*, 315.

75. Washington, "Farewell Address," 53–54.

76. *Barnes*, 6 Mass. at 406.

77. Ibid. at 408.

78. Ibid.

79. Ibid.

80. Jefferson, "Bill for Establishing Religious Freedom," 69–70.

81. *Barnes*, 6 Mass. at 409.

82. Ibid.

83. Ibid. at 410

84. Ibid.

85. Elisha Williams and Thomas Cushing, *The Essential Rights and Liberties of Protestants* (Boston: S. Kneeland and T. Green, 1744), reprinted in McConnell et al., *Religion and the Constitution*, 47–48.

86. "Memorial and Remonstrance against Religious Assessments from James Madison to the Honorable General Assembly of the Commonwealth of Virginia" (1785), reprinted in McConnell et al., *Religion and the Constitution*, 63, 65.

87. Tocqueville, *Democracy in America*, 271–77.

88. "Letter from James Madison to Robert Walsh" (March 2, 1819), in *The Writings of James Madison* 1808–1819, ed. Gaillard Hunt (New York: Putnam, 1908), 8:432.

3

Disestablishing Religion and Protecting Religious Liberty in State Laws and Constitutions (1776–1833)

Mark D. McGarvie

Disestablishment of religion, and the separation of church and state that resulted from it, did not occur by default. On the eve of the Revolution, eleven of the thirteen British-American colonies had established churches.[1] By the end of 1833, none of the states had an established church. The process of disestablishment occurred on a state-by-state basis over the course of over fifty years. In every state, disestablishment required positive action rooted in conceptions of improving republican society. As Americans of the twenty-first century think about the type of nation that the founders sought to create, they might well find instructive the positive steps taken by Americans from Maine to South Carolina during the Revolution and the early republic to disestablish religion. In the process of considering these steps, this chapter will explain how the separation of church and state came to be.[2]

Throughout this chapter, the separation of church and state will be presented as a process through which the founding generation moved religion from a matter of governmental (public) concern to a matter of individual (private) concern. The frequent use of the words *public* and *private* in the text conforms to the distinction between governmental and individual roles. Ironically, conservatives, who throughout most of America's history have been careful to circumscribe the role of government (public sphere) to protect individual rights and freedoms (private realm), have, in the current culture wars, seemingly intentionally confused the use and meaning of "public" and "private" when it comes to discussing the role of religion in society. The word *public* can, of course, mean "out in the open," as in a public debate or public concert. It also, however, can mean "pertaining to the government," as in "public sector." It is that latter meaning that applies throughout this text. The founders, in order to protect individual rights of conscience, limited government from addressing matters pertaining to religion. This action constituted a striking departure from the historical and contemporary patterns of Western society, and was taken in full appreciation of its meaning and significance despite considerable protest from minority dissenters.

The radical change wrought by the Revolution is understood in its contrast to the practices and assumptions that had governed for hundreds of years, not only in the colonies, but throughout Europe. Into the eighteenth century, Western societies assumed that a providential God aided them in matters both simple and profound, influencing events such as births, crop harvests, wars, and diseases. Just as important, governing officials recognized a value of religion within their societies in promoting order, discipline, and shared belief as a basis for moral and ethical judgment. Each of the thirteen colonies prior to the Revolution, regardless of its position on formal religious establishment, wrote and maintained laws respecting these two assumptions.[3] The absence of similar laws after the Revolution, and in fact the repeal and rejection of the colonial codes prescribing religion, indicate that by the late 1700s in America, those old assumptions were dying. As religion was reconsidered as a matter of individual conscience, it become less a matter of state (or public) concern.

Between 1776 and 1833, each state came to accept the preference for free exercise over state promotion of religion. Yet, many Americans throughout this period of tumultuous social as well as political transformation continued to advocate for public (governmental) endorsement and support of religion. These varied individuals, as different as Patrick Henry and Joseph Story, formed a significant, and often contentious, minority. The strength of these dissenting voices increased from the 1820s through the 1860s as American Christianity adopted an activist social gospel.[4] Yet, the positions of the Evangelical reformers of the antebellum era can neither be attributed to the founders nor used to rewrite the history of the early republic.

Colonial Religions Serve Social and Spiritual Functions

The significance of religious establishments in the American colonies cannot be measured only in the functional support provided by governments through church taxes and laws requiring church attendance. In sanctioning particular religious bodies, the colonies premised social order upon cultural homogeneity. More importantly, establishment promoted Christian values that came to permeate colonial laws and social norms. Protestant Christianity provided the ideological basis of the colonial American worldview, and colonial churches served as the institutional vehicles of its dissemination. Established churches further functioned to integrate Christian values, beliefs, and traditions with colonial social behavior. Through the practices of preaching, teaching, caring for the poor, and maintaining community records, churches built communities consistent with Protestant Christian values. In providing these community services, churches depended upon the support of civil governments. The symbiotic relationship between church and state that had existed in Europe persisted throughout English America in the colonial era.

In the cultural and religious maelstrom of seventeenth-century America, many prominent religious spokesmen argued for religious absolutism. This became a dominant perspective among New Englanders who established various forms of Puritan congregationalism. Meanwhile, religious establishments in the southern colonies are better understood as expressing the societal need for intellectual comfort and social integrity that could be provided by religion. Yet, in both New England and in the southern colonies, uniformity of belief strengthened the confidence of the early colonists and the bonds of their communities. In this context there was little room for tolerating deviance. As New England minister Nathaniel Ward stated: "He that is willing to tolerate any religion, or discrepant way of religion, besides his own, unless it be in matters indifferent, either doubts his own, or is not sincere in it."[5] In relying upon religion to build communities, colonists had little motivation to deviate from strict doctrinal positions. Spiritual error could not only fragment communities but bring the wrath of God upon them. Plagues, wars, fires, and droughts were frequently perceived by colonists as divine sanctions for communal sin.

In colonial America, though less than in Europe, the concept of community implicitly included acceptance of the existence of a social hierarchy in which the church played a key role. Ministers taught their adherents to obey the authorities and to assume their proper places in society. Calvinism accepted government as "an ordinance of God," proclaiming it the duty of governors to regulate the moral as well as the civil life of the citizenry.[6] Individual self-interest, including personal economic activity, had to be subordinated to the common good.[7] Civil governments relied upon the churches to imbue the people with sufficient piety to humbly defer to their betters and forgo personal gain for the sake of communal order. People were taught to accept the status God afforded them. In this context, laws readily subordinated individual desires or inclinations to Christian teachings and public concerns. Nearly all colonial communities proscribed wastefulness, idleness, and selfishness as much for their detrimental effects upon the community as for their violation of Jesus's moral exhortations.

Christian morality was infused into a variety of laws and social duties. Ministers from Massachusetts to South Carolina preached that God had created human society with rich and poor, and that the rich had an obligation to assist the poor. Many sermons explained the presence of the poor as a gift from God that allowed those at the top of the community to exhibit their Christian love. In addition, civil laws enforced this Christian duty. Throughout the colonies, people in need could make claims to their communities for aid. In New England, these requests were heard in town meetings; in New York and Virginia, they were put before the parish vestry. In all cases, the authorities called upon those with means to help those in need, invoking Christian duty in the process. The integration of church and state, Christian values and civic duties, is evident in all the colonies in their handling of poor relief.[8]

Throughout the colonies, law imposed duties upon the wealthy to privately support dependent workers, orphans, and the indigent. At a time when one's social position was believed to be derived from God rather than from one's own talent or effort, the wealthy more readily had to assume an obligation commensurate with their status so as to alleviate the sufferings of those beneath them. This charitable obligation, frequently written into law and institutionalized, reaffirmed colonial hierarchies. Colonial communities depended upon each group of people performing its sanctioned roles.

In New England, early civil magistrates perceived themselves as arms of God, enforcing his law through the enforcement of man's laws. Not only were biblical proscriptions on lying, idleness, and sexual license administered, but criminal penalties were imposed for failing to attend church or for engaging in such pursuits as playing cards, sports, or music, or for kissing one's wife on the Sabbath. In colonial Connecticut, the law required every home to have a Bible. Although governors in the South may have held more secular understandings of their authority, the laws they passed still evince a strong religious influence. In Virginia as well as in New England, criminal statutes called for the punishment of "sin" and prescribed public ceremonies so that the community could stand in witness to the criminal's punishment. The purpose of public punishment was to teach a lesson necessary to preserve communal order—to induce wayward sheep to return to the flock. The community itself acted in the process of preventing and punishing sin, exercising and encouraging a Christian pattern of redemption consisting of scorn, humiliation, and forgiveness.[9]

The churches did not limit their social goals to communal order. "From its earliest days, Christianity in America had a world-vision, a dream of a world won to Christ."[10] No religion offers itself to possible devotees as one of several possible truths. Religions profess to certainty in adherence to doctrines of absolute truth—at once gaining for believers both assurance of salvation after death and a moral code for behavior during life. This exclusionary absolutism, as much as the desire for social conformity, encouraged the establishment of religion throughout the colonies.

Colonial religious establishments took various forms. Colonists were characteristically required to support a church with tax payments, attend it for worship, and profess conformity in belief to its doctrines in order to vote or hold public office. Established churches alone could promulgate the creeds that could be taught in schools or perform wedding ceremonies and baptisms. In the later colonial period, established churches could more easily incorporate and gain the right to hold property.[11]

Yet, especially after the 1720s, the New England colonies generally permitted multiple establishments of Protestantism.[12] Typically the colonial legislatures compelled towns to maintain ministers and teachers of Protestant doctrine within their boundaries. Each town was free to select for itself the Protestant sect with which its minister would be affiliated. Although multiple establishments did increase the varieties of religious expression within the colony as a whole, the policy also helped to promote a town-by-town sense of homogeneity.

This modest religious pluralism of early eighteenth-century America did not indicate an unusually high degree of toleration. First, only Protestants benefited from the "liberality" of multiple establishment laws. Second, subtle differences in interpretation of scripture became the basis for discrimination among a proliferation of different sects, each offering its own particular doctrine. The flogging and hanging of Quakers as well as the banishment of dissenters led by Anne Hutchinson and Roger Williams have taken on legendary qualities in the story of early New England's Puritan establishment. However, during the seventeenth century, nearly all American colonies also enacted laws to deter deviant religious practices or beliefs. Laws enforcing religious conformity resulted in criminal prosecutions for blasphemy, heresy, sedition, contempt, passion, breaking of Sabbath day laws, or offering diverse new and dangerous opinions. These laws continued to be passed and enforced well into the eighteenth century. In 1703, South Carolina made blasphemy a crime, defining it as "defaming any person of the Trinity, denying the truths of Christianity, or denying the divine authority of the Bible." New York prosecuted a blasphemy case pursuant to an already-existent statute during that same year. Delaware brought a blasphemy suit in 1705, Maryland in 1710, and North Carolina in 1717. As late as 1757, Massachusetts found a farmer guilty of blasphemy for saying "God was a damned fool for ever making a woman" and sentenced him to a public whipping. During the Great Awakening, in an attempt to stifle the growth of evangelical dissenters, Connecticut passed a law prohibiting all itinerant preaching.[13]

Although colonial judges were strongly influenced by Christian doctrine in the performance of their functions, religious ministers in some colonies actually assumed the functional roles of magistrates, serving as an alternative to judges and lawyers. Several colonies, including Pennsylvania, Connecticut, New Jersey, and South Carolina, allowed defendants in civil or criminal suits to choose to have their cases heard by the clergy in the church or by a panel of arbitrators (frequently ministers) rather than in secular courts. These options presumed both the Christian influence upon colonial law and the communitarianism of the colonial era. A panel of five ministers, chosen to arbitrate a business dispute in 1675, counseled the disputants regarding the goals of the proceedings "that upon mutual forbearing and for guiding each other in love you may retain the spirit of unity of spirit in the bond of peace and returne to the enjoyment of communion with crist and one another in all his ordenances."[14]

Established churches served as essential components of community order and governance throughout colonial America. The Anglican (later the Episcopalian)

Church was established in Virginia by charter prior to the landing at James-town.[15] Church attendance and the maintenance of orthodoxy were compul-sory in Virginia as they were in New England. By the second half of the seventeenth century, elected vestry managed the parochial and local govern-ment affairs of the parishes, including census and recordkeeping, collecting religious taxes for the payment of the parish minister, and enforcing church discipline.[16] As in New England, laws recognized an integrated church and civil government to provide for Christian education, the proper care of chil-dren and the poor, and the preservation of social tranquility. The General Court "took cognizance of all causes whatsoever, both Ecclesiastical and civil, determining everything by the standard of Equity and good conscience."[17]

Ideological and Societal Changes Challenge Establishment

Contemporary Americans who view the American Revolution primarily as a means of effectuating political separation from England grossly minimize its radicalism and the extent of societal change it generated. The idea of self-government, expressed as republicanism during the founding era, derived from Enlightenment-era understandings of natural rights and liberties as vested in individuals.[18] The corporate communities that existed in both Europe and the colonies were challenged by new understandings that recognized the individual as the primary political, economic, and social actor. For most of the colonial era, conceptions of individual good, as well as individuals' desires, goals, and proclivities, were subordinated by law, custom, and morality to considerations for the good of the whole. The Revolution, relying upon repub-licanism as an expression of rights-oriented Enlightenment philosophy, trans-formed a communitarian society into an individualistic one.[19]

The Revolution, the ideology behind it, and the legal changes that it com-pelled altered nearly every facet of American life, including the roles of reli-gion and the churches in their new society. For hundreds of years in Europe and in America, religion had been regarded as a matter of public truth. Such a conception of religion posed few problems when a single state church, sup-ported by an economic and political elite, had the power to determine doc-trinal belief, ethical standards, and modes of religious devotion and practice. However, a society structured in such a hierarchical way required the popular acceptance of political and social inequality and the deference that it demanded. By the second half of the eighteenth century, the British colonists had largely ceased to accept that people were rightly unequal in legal stature or that any deference was appropriately due one's social betters.

During this same period, following the proliferation of sects spawned by the Great Awakening of the 1730–1740s and the tremendous growth of Deism, Unitarianism, and other liberal religious beliefs, uniformity in religious thought and practice gave way to tremendous religious diversity.[20] Many Americans began to distinguish matters of religion from scientific truths. Isaac Newton's laws of physics and gravity, and even Adam Smith's law of supply and demand, appeared verifiable in the natural world. Religion did not.

Many Americans considered the existence of God and the destiny of man after death to be unknowable. The laws of the newly independent states and nation could thus not prescribe roles based on faith rather than knowledge. During a debate on whether to require a Protestant test oath for state office-holding in North Carolina, delegate Jacob Henry argued, "the day, I trust, has long passed, when principles merely speculative were propagated by force."[21] James Madison expressed the same attitude in writing to his friend Thomas Jefferson concerning religious freedom: "I flatter myself [that] this country [has] extinguished forever the ambitious hope of making laws for the human mind."[22] Church membership and attendance fell to less than 5 percent during the founding era.[23]

In this intellectual context, Americans formed a new appreciation of religion as a matter of personal conscience rather than as a public truth.[24] Madison asserted this distinction in 1785 in writing: "The Religion then of every man must be left to the conviction and conscience of every man; and it is the right of every man to exercise it as these may dictate."[25] Once religion became a matter of individual belief, it was no longer the subject of public laws, but was now primarily a claim of individual freedom for all people. The key to protecting each person's freedom to believe in any or no religion, and the key to protecting the wide range of other individual freedoms recognized in the founding era, was the delineation of public and private spheres.

Social contract theory, which served as the basis for framing legitimate governments during and after the Revolution, presupposed the political equality of every individual. Each person, in the pre-political "state of nature," possesses equal rights and freedoms to pursue his or her own interests, hold property, satisfy desires, and be free from attacks or disturbances from others. Yet, without law or an administrative means of protecting these rights, they are at risk from the actions of people who would satisfy their own lusts, desires, or goals at the expense of the safety, security, property, or discretions of another. Therefore, in order to secure rights, people willingly sacrifice a very small amount of freedom to form a government, which is to function to protect all individuals in the maintenance of the rights they retain. By this reasoning, a public sphere, of very limited authority and extremely narrow scope, is created for the sole purpose of protecting the individual rights of the people. Perhaps no better summary of this theory exists than in Jefferson's second paragraph of the Declaration of Independence:

> We hold these Truths to be self-evident, that all Men are created equal, that they are endowed by their Creator with certain unalienable Rights, that

among these are Life, Liberty, and the Pursuit of Happiness—That to secure these Rights, Governments are instituted among Men, deriving their just Powers from the Consent of the Governed.[26]

Once Americans reconceived of religion as a matter of individual conscience, and of the primary role of government as helping to protect individuals in securing their individual rights, laws that established churches as public institutions or that required pronouncements of religious faith or belief as conditions to securing any political, civil, or economic rights were doomed. Various new state constitutions passed in the first decade after the Revolution offered the first dramatic break from the old colonial system. During the next decade, debates over religion at the Constitutional Convention and in the state ratifying sessions clarified the inconsistency between established religion and a government dedicated to the protection of individual rights and freedoms.[27] Yet, some New England states persisted with modified religious establishments well into the nineteenth century. Finally the Supreme Court of the United States, in its 1819 *Dartmouth College* case,[28] reaffirmed the heavy black line that American primary law had drawn between public and private spheres, and placed religion very squarely on the private side of that line.

Federal Constitutional Debates Clarify New Role for Religion in States

Although disestablishment occurred over time on a state-by-state basis, the debates concerning law and religion at the 1787 federal constitutional convention, as well as at the various state ratifying conventions, outline the ideological bases for separating church and state. Of central importance to understanding how every state would ultimately have to separate church and state are the debates over religion as a private matter to be protected from state action. These debates fit nicely into the growing ideological realization that all private actions required protection from the threats posed by the public sector. This sharp delineation of private and public spheres was not only innovative within America but within all of Western society. Legal protection of contracts, and ultimately of charters of incorporation as contracts protecting shareholder interests, served as the principal means of effectuating the new design for society.

Implicitly, law was reconceived in the Constitutional Convention—from supporting the social good through communitarian ideals consistent with Christian morality to serving ideals of individual liberty. A new understanding of "rights" provided the theoretical basis for a new type of law. Despite the relative absence of vituperative debate on the issue of religion during its drafting, the U.S. Constitution provided a radically new legal framework for religious institutions within American society. The new legal framework addressed two distinct but interrelated concerns: religious freedom and the separation of church and state.

The constitutional separation of church and state cannot be understood apart from the delineation of public and private institutions. Although colonial America paid little attention to this distinction in harnessing all available resources to address societal needs, the Constitution in Article 1, Section 10 provided for the independence of private institutions from public control. The Constitution effectively prohibited a governmental reliance upon private means to serve public ends. Ultimately, the constitutional separation of church and state derived less from the provisions addressing religion than from the broad liberal interpretation given the primary law by the Marshall Court in its exposition of the Contract Clause.

Chief Justice John Marshall's liberal understanding of the role of contracts in protecting individual liberty surprises some who see the Federalist judge as a defender of government power. His position indicates the breadth of Americans' acceptance of contract law principles as the primary means of transforming a hierarchical and communitarian society into one respecting equality and individual freedoms. In the early republic, contracts defined social relationships.[29] Contract law recognized the parties to a contract as equals, bound by law to perform their mutual obligations. It assumed that any potential party to a contract was reasonable, rational, and capable of making his own bargain. Community status, Christian brotherhood, and social deference became irrelevant in the enforcement of a wide range of social activities, ranging from the sale of goods and labor to marriage and military service. Moreover, contract law asserted its own system of morality. Performing one's contractual obligations, nothing more or less, established one as trustworthy. Frequently this morality was at odds with both Christian teachings and America's communitarian heritage.

The contrasting worldviews may best be illustrated by an example. Assume that a wealthy farmer was relaxing in a 1790 tavern having a beer with other local gentlemen when a poor drunk, a father of four young children, came into town leading his last cow. The cow was not a prime specimen, worth perhaps five dollars. Its owner wanted only to spend the afternoon with a bottle of whiskey, which cost two dollars. He asked the bar patrons if anyone would buy his cow. Receiving no offers, he encouraged interest by proposing the sale of the cow for only four dollars. Still there was no offer. Finally, the rich farmer, knowing the poor man's alcoholism and the price of a bottle of whiskey, offered two dollars for the cow. An agreement was reached, hands were shaken, and the money and cow exchanged. In the contract law of the 1790s, this agreement would be enforceable. The bargain was acceptable for having been struck between two legal equals who owed no duty to each other besides that embodied in their contract. The poor man's alcoholism and the needs of his family would be of no concern in the enforcement of the contract. In an earlier age, the transaction would most likely be invalidated under traditional under-standings of Protestant Christian morality, which proscribe taking advantage of a neighbor's weakness in order to enrich oneself while causing harm to that neighbor. In colonial America such a contract would most likely not have been enforced because of law's dependence upon Christian ethics and overriding concerns with community welfare. Equity, not contract law, would have pre-vailed.[30] In a colonial parish, where fair prices were set by community stan-dards rather than by market conditions, the wealthy assumed a duty to care for the poor, and moral imperatives discouraged excessive drinking and the poor care of children. Religion served as the basis of colonial moral values and of colonial law, but not of law in the early republic. This change constitutes per-haps the true radicalism of the Revolution.

State courts served as the primary vehicles by which contract law trans-formed American society. State court judges, who were predominately mem-bers of Jefferson's Republican Party, relied upon contract law principles to redesign a myriad of personal relationships and institutions.[31] At the same time, state legislators were using these same principles to reshape the role of churches in American society. Churches were quasi-public institutions during colonial times, but after the Revolution they had to adopt a corporate form and learn to behave as private institutions.

Disestablishment Occurs on a State-by-State Basis, Beginning during the Revolution

Immediately following the promulgation of the Declaration of Independence in 1776, the Continental Congress urged the newly independent states to so-lidify their political legitimacy through the drafting of new constitutions. An additional purpose—that of redesigning society to more closely conform to republican ideals—would also be served in this process. The Revolution sought to remove any existing social structures premised on patronage and privilege. Although social equality was not a goal, legal equality was. Eliminating artifi-cial hierarchies meant eviscerating the political power of established churches. Eleven states drafted constitutions during the Revolution, with the new consti-tutions serving as fundamental laws embodying revolutionary values. These constitutions became the first means by which Revolutionary-era govern-ments sought to disestablish colonial churches.[32]

The Revolutionary-era constitutions expressed the deep divisions then existing on issues of religion and represent a mixed legacy on the issue of dis-establishment. In no instance did early constitutional language determine the ultimate outcome of the disestablishment controversy within a state. Rather, the Revolutionary-era constitutions served as the first salvo in what would be nearly a fifty-year constitutional war to reshape America into a secular nation, in which civil institutions conformed to a new form of law that created its own morality and owed no deference to spirits or creatures deemed superior to man.[33] These early primary documents generally eliminated state support for religion and protected citizens from compelled religious behavior. However, during the war years, several states continued to condition full civil rights and political participation upon expressed Christian belief. As the Revolution was being fought, Americans were only just beginning to conceive of religion as a personal choice instead of a public truth, and of a republic in which personal rights and liberties were always threatened by any government that gained power at their expense.

Moreover, as churches in colonial America also had assumed primary responsibility for education and poor relief, expensive services that wartime state governments were woefully incapable of providing, total disestablishment would require a complete restructuring of institutional life in America. This did eventually occur, but it could not happen overnight. Americans during the Revolution considered themselves Christian people bound together by a shared morality. The state constitutions of the time generally depict those sentiments.

Presumably, disestablishment, in some states, should have been relatively easy. A majority of the non-slave population in North Carolina in 1776 did not attend church, the established Anglican Church was very weak, and the most dynamic religious sects were the Scottish Presbyterians and German Moravians in the western mountainous areas of the state. The 1776 constitution of North Carolina disestablished the Anglican Church, banned the clergy from holding office, and prohibited state support of any religion. It provided that:

> [N]o person, on any pretense whatsoever [shall] be compelled to attend any place of worship, contrary to his own faith or judgment, nor be obliged to pay, for the purchase of any glebe, or the building of any house of worship, or for the maintenance of any minister or ministry, contrary to what he believes right, or has voluntarily and personally engaged to perform; but all persons shall be at liberty to exercise their own mode of worship.[34]

Yet the same document provided that any person who denied the "being of God or the truth of the Protestant religion, or the divine authority of either of the Old or New Testaments" was incapable of holding public office.[35] North Carolinians disestablished Anglicanism, but remained committed to Christianity.

Further evidence of the difficulty states had in addressing conflicting goals is expressed in the 1776 Constitution of Maryland. In one section of this document, Maryland provided that no person could be forced "to maintain any particular place of worship or any particular ministry." This effectively ended Episcopalian supremacy but not religious establishment, for the constitution also provided: "Yet, the legislature may, in their [sic] discretion, lay a general and equal tax, for the support of the Christian religion; leaving to each individual the power of appointing the payment of money, collected from him, to the support of any particular place of worship or minister."[36] When the Maryland legislature attempted to act on this authority in 1780, the bill for multiple establishment encountered an early demise.

The mid-Atlantic states, in keeping with their histories of religious toleration, disestablished their churches in their Revolutionary-era constitutions. Reflecting the business orientation of these states, some constitutions focused as much on financial considerations as on rights. New Jersey in 1776 provided that no person would "ever be obliged to pay tithes, taxes, or any other rates, for the purpose of building or repairing any other church or churches, place or places of worship, or for the minister or ministry, contrary to what he believes to be right, or has deliberately or voluntarily engaged himself to perform."[37] Delaware prohibited any establishment of one sect over another and banned any "clergyman or preacher of the gospel of any denomination" from holding public office.[38]

Perhaps the most radical Revolutionary-era constitution was that written for Pennsylvania in 1776. The democratically conceived document provided for broad suffrage rights, a single popularly elected legislative body, annual elections, and even the popular election of military leaders and judges. Addressing religious freedom, Pennsylvania allowed that "No man ought or of right can be compelled to attend any religious worship, or erect or support any place of worship, or maintain any ministry, contrary to, or against, his own free will and consent."[39] The new government created by this constitution effectively destroyed the College of Philadelphia as a Tory and Anglican institution. However, Pennsylvania also embodied the ideological conflict inherent in American culture by requiring an oath of belief in God in order to vote. Pennsylvania deprived sectarian churches and church schools of previous political and economic support but desired to retain a Christian ethic among the citizenry.

New York not only disestablished the Anglican Church, but secured full religious liberty for its citizenry. Following the advice of the Continental Congress for each new state to draft its own constitution, the old Provincial Congress of New York convened on August 2, 1776, as delegates to the Convention of the Representatives of New York. Religious freedom was addressed in the opening pronouncement of a "day of fasting, humiliation, and prayer to Almighty God [for] his divine assistance in the organization and establishment of a form of government for the security and perpetuation of the civil and religious rights and liberties of mankind." The representatives appointed a committee of fourteen members to prepare a draft constitution ("plan of government"). This committee rejected a proposal for a multiple establishment raised by Presbyterian minister John Rodgers. Instead, the members proposed language providing that all people be free to exercise their own religious beliefs. This provision, expressed in Article 38, came before the representatives as a body in early 1777. John Jay spoke for those in attendance who feared the participation of Catholics in the republic so long as they professed belief in and devotion to the pope as God's agent on earth. Jay suspected that Catholics' allegiance to a foreign ruler limited their commitment to the republican principles of the new government. He suggested limiting religious freedom to practices not "inconsistent with the safety of the civil society." When this suggestion failed to garner sufficient support, he proposed that all Catholics be required to take an oath of allegiance to New York and its laws as superior to the orders of the pope. This too failed, but the representatives adopted the oath as necessary for all new immigrants, thereby limiting the likely immigration of new Catholics in the state without limiting the religious practices or beliefs of current residents.[40]

Several clergymen participating in the Convention supported the idea of religious freedom only so long as it did not imply that government would shun religion. J. H. Livingston, pastor of the Dutch Reformed Church in Albany, argued that the state must "promote religion in general" as well as "defend it from all persecution." Others led a movement for religious tests upon officeholders; one Presbyterian clergyman contended it was a generally acknowledged fact that Protestants made the best governors. This movement, like that led by Jay, failed to persuade the liberal representatives to put religious restrictions upon civil rights. In its new Constitution of 1777, Article 38, the State of New York provided:

> Whereas we are required by the benevolent principles of rational liberty, not only to expel civil tyranny, but also to guard against the spiritual oppression and intolerance, wherewith the bigotry & ambition of weak & wicked priests & princes have scourged mankind: This Convention doth further, in the name & by the authority of the good people of this State, ORDAIN, DETERMINE, & DECLARE, that the free exercise and enjoyment of religious profession and worship, without discrimination of preference, shall forever hereafter be allowed within this State to all mankind. Provided that the liberty of conscience hereby granted, shall not be so construed, as to excuse acts of licentiousness, or justify practices inconsistent with the peace or safety of the State.[41]

Little attention by the people of New York was given to the drafting of the Constitution. Most New Yorkers concerned themselves primarily with the war and their own sustenance. In order to escape discovery by the British, the convention representatives met secretly in various cities. The press did not even know the nature of their debates or the pace of progress of their task.[42]

Convention representatives expressed a desire to accomplish not only the legal task of disestablishment but to repudiate the establishment of the past years, which they regarded more as a de facto than de jure establishment. To make this clear the convention published a statement: "That all such parts of the said common law, and all such of the said statutes and acts aforesaid, or parts thereof, as may be construed to establish or maintain any particular denomination of Christians or their ministers . . . be and they hereby are, abrogated and rejected."[43]

Refusing to acknowledge that a state religion had ever been established, the representatives nonetheless rescinded all laws that could be construed as establishing a religion. Elsewhere in the Constitution, ministers of any religious faith were banned from holding state office. As unequivocal as the convention representatives were in separating religion from their new government, the early legislature of the state proceeded to attempt further to clarify and strengthen the constitutional provisions. In 1779 the legislature even passed a law sentencing Trinity Church minister Charles Inglis and his wife to death.[44] A subsequent proposal to seize the property of the church was comparatively mild.

The radicalism of Americans' thinking only increased during the war, and by its conclusion, the Revolution seemingly was fought not only against British authority, but against all forms of authority—including religious doctrines and church authorities. The hostility felt toward these authorities, even among a population that largely perceived itself as Christian, is evident in steps taken first in New York and later in Virginia to condemn church property as ill-gotten gains from unjust laws establishing the churches. This hostility was also evident in the prohibition on ministerial voting and office-holding in New York and Virginia.

Although the Anglican Church was not established in Georgia until 1758, the state had a history of public hostility toward dissenters. In the 1740s Jews and Moravians were persecuted to the extent that nearly all of these peoples fled the state or retreated to their own enclaves. Legislative requirements that college charters provide for Anglican presidents frustrated English itinerant preacher George Whitefield in his plans to build a college during the same time period. But the age of Revolution demonstrates the extent to which and how quickly values had changed. The constitution of Georgia in 1777 reflected the shift to secular humanism throughout much of Revolutionary-era America. Parishes with names such as St. Paul, St. George, Christ Church, and St. James were renamed Richmond, Burke, Chatham, and Liberty counties, respectively. The Georgia constitution, like those of Tennessee, Delaware, Kentucky, New York, and the Carolinas, prohibited clergymen of any denomination from holding office in the legislature. All persons were recognized as having "the free exercise of their religion; provided it be not repugnant to the peace and safety of the state." The only limits on religious freedom concerned secular order, not religious doctrine. Yet the Constitution did allow for the possibility of a legislative enactment creating a multiple establishment. Bills for this purpose were introduced in 1782 and 1784 but were quickly defeated.[45]

The Revolutionary-era constitutions evinced the difficulty that the drafters had in reconciling political liberty with a desire to preserve their Christian heritage. The mid-Atlantic states took the lead in eliminating public support for a preferred church, and in some cases, disestablished the churches completely. Yet, in many states, especially in the Northeast, the religious establishment succeeded not only in retaining its government support but in imposing test oaths and moral teachings upon the governing process. Significantly, the Revolutionary-era constitutions indicate a change in the thinking of many Americans. Reconceiving religious belief and practice as individual matters, even as rights, was the essential first step to entirely removing religion from the public sphere.

Separation of Church and State Conforms to Public/Private Distinction after the Revolutionary War

Following the Revolutionary War, the states had the luxury of rewriting their constitutions to conform better to social contract theory. Many of these later constitutions were drafted not by sitting legislatures but by conventions specifically called for that purpose and then ratified through popular consent expressed in voting. These constitutions reflect the rise in secular attitudes and conceptions of state power as limited by the rights of individuals to their own religious beliefs and practices. Distinguishing public and private realms was key to protecting individual rights.

Pennsylvania, in its 1790 constitution, eliminated its religious test for voting, providing that "every freeman of the age of twenty-one years, having resided in the state two years next before the election, and within that time paid a state or county tax . . . shall enjoy the rights of an election."[46] However, the state still required belief in "a God," whether Christian or not, and in some "future state of rewards and punishments" for a person to hold state office.[47] In its 1792 constitution, Delaware eliminated an oath for state officeholders that acknowledged belief in God, Jesus as his son, and the Bible as divine inspiration and in reasserting a right to religious freedom referred not to "God" but to a "Creator." Maryland, in 1795, exempted Quakers and others unable to take oaths, agnostics and atheists among them, from having to do so to hold office.[48]

South Carolina provides perhaps the best example of disestablishment in the postwar years. South Carolina, in which the established Anglican Church held considerable social and political prestige, moved to form its own independent government even before the Declaration of Independence resounded from Philadelphia. In March 1776, the new State of South Carolina (the second of the former colonies to take this action) issued its first constitution in conjunction with its own declaration of independence. The intent of the document was to establish a provisional government to address management of the war. The new government was less than democratic. Not only did it retain its closed and aristocratic cast, but civil rights, including the issue of religious freedom, were unaddressed. Oliver Hart had written to Henry Laurens of his hopes for religious reform days before the drafting of the constitution: "We hope to see liberty sit regent on the throne and flourish more than ever under the administration of such worthy patriots." His hopes were dashed when he saw the new plan of government. That spring, the dissenting clergy gathered under the direction of the Reverend William Tennant to plan for "securing an equality in religious privileges." Tennant was chosen to present the group's work, a petition for disestablishment, before the general assembly, a task he performed on September 11, 1776.[49]

His comments before the assembly reflected the priorities of dissenting ministers. The petition specifically objected to the establishment of one "particular denomination of Protestants in distinction from and preference to all other denominations." The ministers referred to the prejudicial treatment of one sect fomenting discord and a dangerous discontent within society. In closing, the petition called for a guarantee:

> That there never shall be any establishment of any one religious denomination or sect of Protestant Christians in this state by way of preference to another; that no Protestant inhabitant of this state by law be denied the enjoyment of any civil right merely on account of his religious principles, but that all Protestants demeaning themselves peaceably under the government established by the Constitution shall enjoy free and equal civil and religious privileges.[50]

If these provisions of the dissenters' petition were not adequately clear, Tennant's own comments left no room for confusion. He cited the inability of dissenting clergy "to marry their own people" and the unfair competition between the Anglicans, for whom "the law builds superb churches" and those denominations who must "build their own." Perhaps the most significant problem, he felt, was that the law allowed only one church to incorporate; it alone could hold property, sue in the court system, and collect alms and bequests. Tennant made certain the assembly understood that the dissenters did not wish the state's legislators to abstain from addressing religion, but only to stop favoring one sect over another: "The state may do anything for the support of religion without partiality to particular societies or imposition upon the rights of private judgment." Tennant championed the authority of the assembly to punish vice and encourage virtue.[51]

Disestablishment of the Anglican Church did not occur until the new constitution, adopted in March 1778, expanded upon the assembly's earlier action. The new South Carolina constitution declared that "The Christian Protestant religion [is] the established religion of this State." Furthermore, "no person shall, by law, be obliged to pay towards the maintenance and support of a religious worship that he does not freely join in, or has not voluntarily engaged to support." Yet all voters and officeholders were required to swear to their belief in "God, heaven, and hell" as understood in Protestant Christian doctrine.[52] Individual Episcopal congregations needed to reform themselves by incorporating as private independent bodies. For years afterward, they lacked a central organization, a bishop, and a diocese. Yet, once the anti-British feelings of the war years passed, Episcopal churches resumed significant roles in South Carolina society. The law may have made all churches equal, but Episcopalian members rendered their denomination socially superior. And, although the new document recognized due process protection and liberty of the press, religious freedom was limited to Protestant Christians.

By the 1780s in South Carolina, liberal exponents of Jeffersonian concepts of democracy began to question the restrictive nature of their own state constitution. Proposals for a constitutional convention started to appear in the press by the mid-1780s. In an editorial from September 7, 1786, the *Gazette of the State of South Carolina* argued that, though the war was won, "the American Revolution is just begun [as] the whole government must be made to conform to democratic principles." Many of the state's liberals found it especially discomforting that the constitution of 1778 had been adopted by legislative action without a convention. They tried in 1784, 1785, and 1787 to create a constitutional convention so as to have a document superior to the legislature and not subject to amendment through its proceedings alone. During these years the South Carolina House of Representatives actually passed bills to form a convention to create a constitution in greater conformity with "pure republican principles," but each time the Senate fought off the attack. Calls for a new state constitution focused primarily on republican theory and the need to protect civil rights. Republican concepts of political equality and freedom of conscience required a reconceptualization of South Carolina's social institutions.[53]

By 1787 complete religious freedom, requiring the abolition of the Protestant Christian establishment of 1778, had become a rallying point for the liberals. Unlike the disestablishment campaign of 1778, this crusade was carried out by those who premised their position on both the need of the government to recognize natural rights and the perception of religion as a matter of personal conscience. In this debate the liberals expressed significant distaste for all organized religion. At the climax of the debate, the *City Gazette* of Charleston published a letter from an American living in Paris: "France is indeed upon the eve of complete freedom; a new era is evidently approaching; political liberty in Europe must copy the example of America and will certainly be followed by a great and general change in many religious tenets of the present day, as soon as the empire of reason shall have established itself a little further over the minds of men." This writer found political freedom best expressed by those philosophers who sought to challenge religious beliefs that kept men subordinate not only to a god but inevitably to other men. These philosophers, "by drawing a distinct line of separation between spiritual and temporal concerns, have paved the way for universal peace, harmony, and good will among men."[54]

The contest in South Carolina pitted reason against revelation, liberty against piety, and legal equality against legal privilege. Evangelical clergymen, who had earlier fought establishment as preferencing the Episcopalians over all dissenting sects, recognized a need to clarify for their parishioners on which side of the battle line they were to stand. They chose to bind themselves to other Christians in opposing liberal reform. Methodist Bishop George Foster Pierce scorned those who rejected God's truth for one of man's own devise: "This specious, insinuating infidelity is distilling its poison under the patronage of science, education, and knowledge." The Rev. Thomas Reese wrote that God has "favored us" but "if we abuse the gifts of Providence, turn our liberty into licentiousness, and provoke the vengeance of Heaven by our daring impiety, and shocking immoralities, what can we expect, but that a righteous God will give us up to the fatal consequences of our own vices, and inflict upon us a punishment which we justly deserve." More liberal pastors found it more difficult openly to support a continued establishment. The Rev. Richard Furman, Oliver Hart's successor at the Charleston Baptist Church, remained silent on the disestablishment issue but advocated defeat of a companion provision that would prevent ministers from serving in a state office.[55]

In 1789 the legislature succumbed to calls for a new constitution. In February a South Carolina Senate committee was to meet with a delegation from the House of Representatives "to consider whether a convention of the people should not be called to consider and amend the Constitution of the State." In April the legislature decided to form the convention; the delegates would be chosen in a special election in October.[56] The election results indicated that broad disestablishment of religion would be a key concern at the convention.

The conceptual integration of disestablishment with a general expansion of civil rights was described in a series of letters to the *City Gazette* written by "The Reflector." In his first letter, he argued that the upcoming convention had the purpose "of correcting defects" in the existing constitution. The primary law of the state was to recognize that "freemen are all equal," regardless of their religious beliefs: "We expect the new constitution to be framed upon the principles of equal liberty and we charge you to guard our natural rights from invasion with the most jealous care . . . [and to] secure . . . [our] religious liberties." In a subsequent letter, the author expanded upon the concept of equal liberty, arguing that current constitutional tests of wealth and belief as prerequisites to voting rendered full enjoyment of the rights of citizenship conditional, and treated equals as unequals. The prescription of any religion should not be made upon any free man.[57]

The language used by "The Reflector" reinforces historian Edmund Morgan's assertion that republican liberties in the South were understood as assertions of equality among white free men and did not include black slaves.[58] There can be no mistaking the Reflector's use of "freemen" in instances in which writers in non-slave states would use "men" or even "people." The argument raised by the liberals in South Carolina in 1790 was that no free white man should be subject to the opinions or beliefs of another free white man—his equal. In acceptance of this argument, low-country elites and backcountry yahoos overcame class and regional distinctions to rewrite the state's primary law as an implicit protection of the interests and thoughts of white men.

This does not explain, however, the extra steps taken by the convention to ostracize the Christian churches and to secure the public sector from religious influences. The 1790 constitution abolished parishes (substituting counties for them), created a new state court system with exclusive jurisdiction over all legal matters in the state, provided for complete liberty of religious belief, and denied all clergymen the opportunity to hold state office.[59]

Disestablishment in South Carolina, as in all other states, involved much more than a change in the primary law or a revocation of the requirement that citizens support the churches. It involved the removal of the churches from their roles in public governance. In this change can be seen the importance of ideological debate to the disestablishment issue and the radical nature of the process. Liberal republican values came to replace Christian ethics in public institutions. Prior to 1790, churches in South Carolina had served as the public instruments of poor relief, recordkeeping, and to a lesser degree education. After the adoption of the new constitution, either government or private charities assumed these responsibilities. Wasting no time in implementing social change, the legislature of the state first addressed the issue of assisting the poor in 1791, passing a statute that provided for the election of county commissioners of the poor, as public employees, to assume the duties previously held by parish church wardens. These officials determined their counties' needs and set tax levies to respond to them. After 1800 the commissioners could force able-bodied recipients of poor relief to perform labor for the state in return for their benefits. Subsequent legislation allowed road commissioners to direct any state beneficiary to work on constructing and maintaining the state's highways.[60] From the perspective of the liberal ideology largely adopted by the Jeffersonian Republicans, it was irrational for the public to pay able-bodied people to do nothing.

The public programs started by South Carolina in the 1790s addressed pressing social problems. In 1794 the state created an Orphan House to shelter unemployable children, and in 1795 it created its first penitentiary. Appointees to public boards administered both facilities, which relied exclusively on state funding. The creation of new public institutions arose from a recognition that delegating responsibility to private entities not only continued archaic colonial practices, but entailed a loss of public control. Public control ensured that secular, rather than religious, values, priorities, and goals would inform the programs. As elsewhere, the need for secular public action arose in South Carolina primarily over the provision of education. Although the Jeffersonians generally abhorred the growth of government to address social needs, the one exception they recognized was education. The perpetuation of the republic depended upon an educated citizenry, and the state was required to recognize and perform its duties to secure its future. In 1797 Richard Beresford, a staunch Jeffersonian, published a pamphlet entitled "Aristocracy, the Bane of Liberty—Learning the Antidote," in which he urged his fellow citizens of South Carolina to support general or universal education. He contended that the state's "aristocracy" sought to retain power by keeping the mass of people ignorant. Beresford's pamphlet spawned a letter-writing campaign to the state's newspapers asking for public funding of "liberal and practical" education. These letters noted that republicanism required a citizenry able to support itself economically, independent of any community or institutional support. Republican education fostered an awareness of liberal political doctrine, building an appreciation of man's innate civil rights and the duty of government to protect them. Church schools could not be entrusted to meet these goals. The *Gazette* helped in this campaign in an editorial that noted the number of advertisements in the paper for lottery tickets sold by neighboring states to help fund their schools. The paper asked if South Carolinians wanted to continue to support other states' educational programs rather than their own and to contribute to the drain of talent from their state.[61]

In 1801 Governor Grayton proposed establishing a state college, which opened in Columbia four years later. However, it was 1811 before the Republican legislature could muster sufficient support to pass the first public education law in South Carolina. The legislation created at least one school in each of the state's forty-four election districts to teach "any white resident free of charge." But the state failed to fulfill the law's promise. Insufficient funds were raised even to pay the commissioners of education, much less to staff and maintain the schools.[62]

The public school movement succeeded primarily in generating a response from the churches. This response shows how churches had to adapt to their new roles as private institutions, outside the realm of governance. Threatened by the idea of public schools teaching "liberal and practical" knowledge, they responded by starting private schools of their own. In the second decade of the nineteenth century various churches opened Sunday schools. The Episcopal Church founded an educational organization in the summer of 1810 and thereafter adopted a uniform text written by the Rev. Frederick Dalcho entitled "The Evidence from Prophecy for the Truth of Christianity and the Divinity of Christ in a Course of Catechetical Instruction." The intent of the text was to teach that the Bible is absolute truth—a record of prophecy and fulfillment of Jesus as the Son of God. Dalcho preached that man was depraved by nature and that the combination of parental indulgence and secular education would encourage "children soon [to] betray their proneness to vanity and sin." The Presbyterian Synod of 1808 directed its member churches to establish grammar schools, a program only marginally successful even in the heavily Scottish Presbyterian Piedmont area. The Second Awakening in South Carolina resulted in the founding of numerous Christian outreach and educational societies, representing Baptists, Presbyterians, and Episcopalians. All of these efforts were attempts to combat the threat of secular education, and in the words of the Charter of the Columbia, South Carolina, Theological Seminary, to finally extinguish "the twilight of unenlightened reason." In a twist on the word describing the intellectual age in which the seminary was founded, its supporters asserted that "enlightenment" came both from and with religion. In all of these efforts, South Carolina churches utilized the corporate form to protect their funds and their message in a sometimes hostile environment.[63] In adoption of this form, churches recognized and conformed to their new role as private institutions outside the realm of governance, but free to dissent from and criticize public action.

Other states acted legislatively to further earlier steps taken toward disestablishment in the decades after the Revolution. New York's legislature took measures to attach church property and secure total freedom of conscience. As we saw, the wartime constitution of New York had disestablished the Anglican Church and protected freedom of conscience. By the 1780s, liberals demanded more.

After the judicial recognition of contract rights as superior to legislative enactment in the *Waddington* case of 1783, the New York legislature had little choice but to limit its disestablishment initiatives to comply with the prevailing contract law doctrine.[64] Unable to attach church property, the legislature forced the churches at least to reorganize along more liberal republican terms. In late 1784 the New York State legislature passed four laws asserting a new legal status for churches in the state. Each was enacted with near unanimous support and excited almost no attention in newspapers, sermons, or other forums of civic debate.[65] The Trinity Church Act "abrogated, abolished, annulled, repealed, and made void" the old charter of the Church created by the Crown, the Ministry Act of 1693, and all subsequent and other laws relating to the Anglican establishment or Trinity Church, the leading Anglican body in New York. The legislature found provisions of the 1697 charter "inconsistent with the spirit and letter of the Constitution of the State."[66] The purpose of these acts was to eliminate the legal monopoly that had been held by the Anglicans being the only churches able to incorporate. Under the new law, all sects could incorporate, and therefore hold property. The new law further repudiated any "pretentious claims . . . that the Episcopalian churches were [ever] established," an assertion that contributed to "the great vexation and disquiet of the good people of this state."[67] In the Church Incorporation Act, the legislature recited that under British rule and the presumed Anglican establishment "many charitable and well disposed persons have been prevented from contributing to the support of religion for want of proper persons authorized by law [that is, corporations] to take charge of their pious donations."[68] Accordingly, the law created a system of general incorporation for all religious bodies to follow. Trinity Church, and other churches in the state, chartered their institutions using this new corporate model.

As elsewhere in the new republic, the articulation of the legal model for religious institutions in New York did not resolve the ideological debate over the values and beliefs that would prevail in the society. Its ultimate resolution would now have to be reached in the context of a new legal design for social institutions. Churches were recreated as private institutions, protected by rights of incorporation. The legislature of New York, unable to interfere with private contract rights, would have to find new means of addressing public needs. By separating public and private institutions, the legislature implicitly separated state and church as well. Legal doctrine determined the form of church-state separation in New York, but legislative liberals committed to removing religion from government showed how use of the form could serve liberal principles.

King's College had been closed during the Revolution. In 1784 a group of moderates acting under the influence of the New York City mayor John Duane petitioned the legislature to issue a new charter to the school recognizing "that Liberality and that civil and religious freedom" won the war. The legislature went much further. Composed of representatives hoping to secure the principles of the Revolution, it created a new University of the State of New York, in which several campuses were united under a governing board of regents. The new university was to reflect the liberal attitudes of the state, being open to all residents and offering them a practical education to prepare them for business or political careers. The legislature also provided that, as a public institution, the school would no longer reflect religious sentiments. The original regents of the university included church delegates, but government officials and elected county representatives comprised the majority of the board. In 1787 the state legislature eliminated all clerical representation among the regents, banned chapel, and eliminated a religious requirement for the university president and test oaths for the faculty. It provided that "no professor shall be in anywise whatsoever accounted ineligible, for or by any reason of any religious tenet or tenets, that he may or shall profess, or be compelled by any bye law or otherwise to take any religious test oath whatsoever."[69]

Alexander Hamilton perceived the changes in New York State's institutions as paralleling those in the marketplace. Whether the issue was religion, education, or commerce, Hamilton sought to increase accessibility. In this, he acted surprisingly like his eventual antagonist, Thomas Jefferson. Their later disagreement must be seen as existing over means more than goals. When Hamilton wrote that "all monopolies, exclusions, and discriminations of traffick, are pernicious and absurd," he very well could have been writing on behalf of the man from Virginia.[70]

In both the substance and tone of the legislative enactments of the 1780s, the New York legislature evinced a hostility to the Anglican/Episcopalian Church and the use of state authority in furtherance of religious goals. However, the legislation is drafted in positive terms, granting all church bodies the right to incorporate. The common law rights to contract were specifically recognized as belonging to churches. These enactments presented state policy as a secular matter, unencumbered by the influences of the churches and their doctrines. Conforming to liberal property law concepts, churches were removed from their roles as public institutions and repositioned within civil society. However, implementing this policy was not easy. New Yorkers encountered a reaction from religious leaders who felt marginalized by the new state government. In addition, New Yorkers found it difficult to remove the churches from past roles without accepting a significant diminution in public services.

As early as 1773, New York appointed state overseers of the poor to supervise church wardens in attending to poor relief. By war's end, the role of the church was not only marginalized, but eliminated. In 1784, the parish, as a civic designation, was abolished and all laws calling for churches to use tax money in performance of public functions were repealed. Families were deemed primarily responsible for addressing personal needs, with counties assuming secondary responsibility. In the 1790s, new government agencies formed to construct highways, keep public records, provide aid to the poor, and collect taxes.[71]

Providing public education in New York proved to be even more difficult. Prior to the war, church-provided education dominated in New York as in the other colonies. This situation was untenable in a secular republic. Creation of a republican government brought with it a new recognition of societal dependence upon an educated citizenry holding republican roles. Governor Clinton's first address to the New York legislature in 1783 encouraged the creation of a state university system with the authority to form public schools for younger students. Yet, despite the best intentions of the governor and the legislature, New York struggled for thirty years to fund public education consistently. Education was left largely to private fee schools for the wealthy and private charity schools for common New Yorkers.[72]

The Mid-Atlantic states acted during the Revolution to disestablish their churches; in the South, disestablishment came during the constitutional era. Only in New England did the religious establishment hold political power throughout the constitutional era. Massachusetts, for at least two generations after the Revolution, created the political model that other New England states adopted. Ultimately, the U.S. Constitution, containing its sharp delineations of public and private spheres, would be used by the Supreme Court in a series of cases known as the "contract clause cases" to strike down state laws that encroached on private liberties expressed in contract. In order to protect rights, sometimes old policies had to change. Churches and other charities were found unable to hold property unless they existed as legal entities—and that required incorporation as private institutions.[73]

In 1815, the Jeffersonian Republicans in control of the governor's office and legislature in New Hampshire tried to take over Dartmouth College, a Congregational Church seminary, to transform it into a liberal university to teach the skills necessary for success in a capitalistic republic. Similar actions had previously been taken in many states without prompting litigation. However, in New Hampshire the church-affiliated school challenged the legislature's action in court. In 1819, the Supreme Court, in a pyrrhic victory for the church, prevented the takeover on the basis of the contract clause, holding the school's charter to be a contract. In the process, the court reminded all Americans of the heavy black line dividing public and private spheres and of the place of churches on the private side of that line. Subsequently, states stopped contributing support to church-affiliated schools and began instead to build secular state universities.[74]

Massachusetts resisted disestablishment and secularization longer than any other state. It held a constitutional convention in 1820, in which it considered eliminating a religious test oath for officeholders, state control of Harvard, and public support for religion. Just months after the *Dartmouth* decision precluded New Hampshire's interference with a private corporation serving that state's need in higher education, Massachusetts addressed whether it should fund a private institution controlled by the Unitarian Church or start a public school subject to the control of the state. Despite the clear legal precedent diminishing the state's rights to control a private religious school, Massachusetts voters rejected the chance to fund a state school and retained the test oath and an established church by a vote of twenty to eleven thousand. The issues were framed in terms of preserving the traditional "community" of the state. Religion was depicted as the glue that held society together and formed its values. An editorial asked "whether Infidels and Nothingarians shall enjoy the blessings of a government that derives its stability and equity from Christianity?"[75] This position stood in abject contradiction of liberal republican concepts of political equality. Yet, in 1820, it held sway in Massachusetts.

Although the voters in 1820 could reject the prevailing ideological and legal context, the court could not. Massachusetts churches faced a schism in the second and third decades of the nineteenth century, in which Congregational churches were being taken over by Unitarian ministers. Traditional Congregational doctrine conceived of a church as composed of its members, an autonomous political body united in pursuit of a godly society. The idea that a minister not of their liking could be imposed upon them was inconceivable to most Congregationalists. Yet this is precisely what happened after 1810. As traditional Congregationalists sought to leave these churches, the issue of ownership of property arose. In 1821, the Massachusetts Supreme Court, in a holding consistent with the *Dartmouth* case, ruled that only corporations could hold property, not amorphous societies of believers.[76] Unitarians, in control of the legally recognized charters, retained the churches and their funds as Congregationalists departed. Only in response to these court decisions did the citizens support disestablishment, putting all the churches on equal footing in 1833. Contract law succeeded where politics could not in overcoming public support of religion.

Conclusions

Americans, during the early republic, reconceived of religion as a private matter rather than a public truth. In state after state, until finally Massachusetts acted in 1833, religion was removed from the public sphere it once controlled and was placed instead in the private realm. The banning of test oaths; the securement of freedom of conscience; the restructuring of churches as corporations; the removal of churches from their earlier roles of providing poor relief, education, and recordkeeping; and the elimination of Christian teachings of doctrine and morals as the basis for law, education, and civic duty redesigned American society from a collection of Christian commonwealths in the early 1700s to a largely secular nation by the age of Jackson.

This process occurred largely at the state level. The religion clauses of the First Amendment did not protect religious freedom of individuals from state actions until the twentieth century. Yet, that does not mean that the separation of church and state was not conceived of and implemented during the founding era and in succeeding decades. The founders divided society into public and private realms and limited the scope and extent of public powers in order to protect private actions. The consideration of religion as a private matter, and of churches and other religious organizations as private corporations, was ultimately adopted by every state by 1833.

Americans sometimes focus undue attention on the radical libertarianism of Virginia in order to argue that the conceptions of religious freedom proposed by Jefferson and Madison are anomalistic. Yet, the same separation between church and state that Virginia sponsored in 1786 took place everywhere else by 1833, albeit without most of the language used in Virginia challenging religious belief. Contract law and its corporate law derivatives succeeded in accomplishing separation of church and state among the states even when the First Amendment could not.

Notes

1. There is considerable disagreement over the number of colonial establishments, much of it centered on whether a religious establishment was colony-wide or made on a county-by-county basis. Contributors to this volume differ on the number of colonial

religious establishments. I count eleven colonies in which religion was established by law in some places at some time prior to the Revolution. Only in Rhode Island and Pennsylvania do I find no evidence of formal religious establishment, though even in those colonies, religion largely influenced governmental action, including the laws and their enforcement.

2. Portions of this essay were previously published in Mark Douglas McGarvie, *One Nation Under Law: America's Early National Struggles to Separate Church and State* (DeKalb, Il: Northern Illinois University Press, 2004) and have been reprinted with the permission of the publisher.

3. See chapter 2 by Michael W. McConnell.

4. See chapter 9 by Daniel Dreisbach.

5. Nathaniel Ward, "The Simple Cobbler of Aggawam in America," in William P. Trent and Benjamin W. Wells, eds. *Colonial Prose and Poetry* (New York: Thomas Y. Crowell & Co., 1901), 1:2.

6. William G. McLoughlin, *Isaac Backus and the American Pietistic Tradition* (Boston: Little, Brown, & Co., 1967), 7.

7. Michael Zuckerman, "Holy Wars, Civil Wars: Religion and Economics in Nineteenth Century America," *Prospects* 16 (1991): 212, citing Stephen Foster, *Their Solitary Way: The Puritan Social Ethic in the First Century of Settlement in New England* (New Haven, CT: Yale University Press, 1971); Christopher F. Mooney, *Public Virtue: Law and the Social Character of Religion* (Notre Dame, IN: University of Notre Dame Press, 1986), 10–11; Stephen Innes, *Creating the Commonwealth: The Economic Culture of Puritan New England* (New York: W. W. Norton, 1995).

8. Robert A. Gross, "Giving in America: From Charity to Philanthropy," in *Charity, Philanthropy, and Civility in American History*, ed. Lawrence J. Friedman and Mark D. McGarvie (New York: Cambridge University Press, 2003), 33. See also Mark D. McGarvie and Elizabeth Mensch, "Law and Religion in Colonial America," in *Cambridge History of Law in America*, 3 vols., ed. Michael Grossberg and Christopher Tomlins (New York: Cambridge University Press, 2008), 1:324–64.

9. Richard W. Pointer, *Protestant Pluralism and the New York Experience: A Study of Eighteenth-Century Religious Diversity* (Indianapolis: Indiana University Press, 1988), 137; Lawrence M. Friedman, *Crime and Punishment in American History* (New York: Harper-Collins, 1993), 23–26, 32–37. See also Edwin Powers, *Crime and Punishment in Early Massachusetts, 1620–1692: A Documentary History* (Boston: Beacon Press, 1966); Louis B. Masur, *Rites of Execution: Capital Punishment and the Transformation of American Culture, 1776–1865* (New York: Oxford University Press, 1989).

10. Robert T. Handy, *A Christian America: Protestant Hopes and Historical Realities* (New York: Oxford University Press, 1969), 121; see also Sidney E. Mead, *The Old Religion in a Brave New World: The Jefferson Memorial Lectures* (Los Angeles: University of California Press, 1977), 2.

11. Leonard W. Levy, *The Establishment Clause: Religion and the First Amendment* (New York: Macmillan, 1986), 4–5.

12. See chapter 2 by Michael W. McConnell and chapter 4 by David Little.

13. Leonard Levy, *Blasphemy: Verbal Offense against the Sacred, from Moses to Salman Rushdie* (New York: A. A. Knopf, 1993), 238–66, esp. 264–66; Glenn T. Miller, *Religious Liberty in America: History and Prospects* (Philadelphia: Westminster Press, 1976), 46.

14. David Thomas Konig, *Law and Society in Puritan Massachusetts: Essex County, 1629–1692* (Chapel Hill: University of North Carolina Press, 1979), 104; Lawrence M. Friedman, *A History of American Law* (New York: Simon & Shuster, 1973), 45.

15. Marvin K. Singleton, "Colonial Virginia as the First Amendment Matrix: Henry, Madison, and the Assessment Establishment," in Robert S. Alley, *James Madison on Religious Liberty* (Buffalo, NY: Prometheus Books, 1985), 157–75, esp. 158.

16. Sidney E. Ahlstrom, *A Religious History of the American People* (New Haven, CT: Yale University Press, 1938), 188–92. See also Walter I. Trattner, *From Poor Law to Welfare State: A History of Social Welfare in America* (New York: Macmillan, 1989), 16; Robert W. Kelso, *The History of Public Poor Relief in Massachusetts, 1620–1920* (Montclair, NJ: Patterson Smith, 1969), 35–41; Roy M. Brown, *Public Poor Relief in North Carolina* (New York: Arno Press, 1976), 10–25; Edward Warren Capen, "The Historical Development of the Poor Law of Connecticut" (PhD diss. Columbia University, 1905), 22, 41–44, 59–63.

17. Robert Beverley, *The History and Present State of Virginia* (Chapel Hill: University of North Carolina Press, 1947), 255.

18. See Robert E. Shalhope, "Toward a Republican Synthesis: The Emergence of an Understanding of Republicanism in an American Historiography," *William and Mary Quarterly*, 3rd ser., no. 29 (1972): 49–80.

19. Gordon S. Wood, *The Radicalism of the American Revolution* (New York: Alfred A. Knopf, 1992), 96–97.

20. The Great Awakening is the subject of an extensive literature, but its role in spawning dissenting sects is developed in William G. McLoughlin, *New England Dissent, 1630–1833: The Baptists and the Separation of Church and State*, 2 vols. (Cambridge, MA: Harvard University Press, 1971); Patricia Bonomi, *Under the Cope of Heaven: Religion, Society, and Politics in Colonial America* (New York: Oxford University Press, 1986); Chris Beneke, *Beyond Toleration: The Religious Origins of American Pluralism* (New York: Oxford University Press, 2006). On the subsequent growth of Evangelism in the South, see Christine Leigh Heyrman, *Southern Cross: The Beginnings of the Bible Belt* (Chapel Hill: University of North Carolina Press, 1997). On the growth of Unitarianism, see J. D. Bowers, *Joseph Priestley and English Unitarianism in America* (University Park: Penn State University Press, 2007). On the growth of Deism and liberal religion, see Kerry S. Walters, *The American Deists: Voices of Reason and Dissent in the Early Republic* (Lawrence: University of Kansas Press, 1992); David L. Holmes, *The Faiths of the Founding Fathers* (New York: Oxford University Press, 2006).

21. Jacob Henry, "Speech in the North Carolina House of Democrats" (1809), in *Cornerstones of Religious Freedom in America*, ed. Joseph L. Blau (Boston: Beacon Press, 1949), 93.

22. James Madison, "Letter to Thomas Jefferson, January 22, 1786," in *The Writings of James Madison*, 9 vols, ed. Gaillard Hunt (New York: G.P. Putnam's Sons, 1900–1910), 2:216.

23. Some historians contend that only about 4 percent of American people belonged to a church in 1776. See Levy, *Blasphemy*, 268. However, there is considerable debate among historians as to whether statistics reflecting church membership and attendance of religious services constitute accurate indicia of religiosity. See Patricia Bonomi and Peter Eisenstadt, "Church Adherence in the Eighteenth-Century British American Colonies," *William and Mary Quarterly*, 3rd ser., 39–32 (1982): 247; Rodney Stark and Roger Finke, "American Religion in 1776: A Statistical Portrait," *Sociological Analysis* 49 (1988): 39–51.

24. The idea that new understandings of religion as a matter of personal conscience shaped church–state relations in the early republic is developed in McGarvie, *One Nation under Law*. See also Noah Feldman, *Divided by God: America's Church–State Problem and What We Should Do about It* (New York: Farrar, Straus, and Giroux, 2005), 12.

25. James Madison cited in John Witte Jr. and M. Christian Green, "The American Constitutional Experiment in Religious Human Rights: The Perennial Search for Principles," in *Religious Human Rights in Global Perspective: Legal Perspectives*, ed. Johan D. van der Vyver and John Witte Jr. (The Hague: Martinus Nijhoff, 1996), 517. Witte and Green argue that liberty of conscience is one of the essential principles that was embodied in the religion clauses of the First Amendment. See elaboration in John Witte Jr. and Joel A. Nichols, *Religion and the American Constitutional Experiment*, 3d ed. (Boulder, CO: Westview Press, 2011).

26. *The Declaration of Independence and the Constitution of the United States* (Washington, DC: U.S. Government Printing Office, 1956), 1.

27. See detailed treatment of these federal developments in chapter 8 by Carl Esbeck.

28. Trustees of Dartmouth College v. Woodward, 17 U.S. (4 Wheat) 518 (1819).

29. This concept enjoys tremendous popularity but is perhaps most strongly asserted by Jay Fligelman: "Central to the rationalist ideology of the American Revolution was the belief that in an ideal world all relationships would be contractual." See his *Prodigals and Pilgrims: The American Revolution against Patriarchal Authority* (New York: Cambridge University Press, 1982), 123.

30. This illustration is drawn from a reading of colonial and postrevolutionary case law. See McGarvie, *One Nation Under* Law, 210 fn. 4; Elizabeth V. Mensch, "The Colonial Origins of Liberal Property Rights," *Buffalo Law Review* 31 (1982): 703–4; Michael Grossberg, "Citizens and Families: A Jeffersonian Vision of Domestic Relations and Generational Change," in Gilreath, ed., *Education of a Citizen*, 3–27.

31. Christopher L. Tomlins, *Law, Labor, and Ideology in the Early American Republic* (Cambridge: Cambridge University Press, 1993); Michael Grossberg, *Governing the Hearth: Law and the Family in Nineteenth-Century America* (Chapel Hill: University of North Carolina Press, 1985).

32. Richard B. Bernstein, *Are We to Be a Nation? The Making of the Constitution* (Cambridge, MA: Harvard University Press, 1987), 43–80.

33. My argument here is predicated upon my understanding of *secularism* as a descriptor of observed behavior, not as a term defining a specific school of thought. As a term expressing a historian's judgment, it can be used to describe periods throughout American history during which religion, as a means of explaining and understanding the world, man, and nature, declined relative to preceding and subsequent periods. A different understanding of the term, referring to its use by historical actors in defining a particular school of thought, is very well developed in Feldman, *Divided by God*, 113–15, 129, 132.

34. Constitution of North Carolina, 1776, Art. XXXIV, in Benjamin Perley Poore, ed., *The Federal and State Constitutions, Colonial Charters, and Other Organic Laws of the United States*, 2d ed., 2 vols. (Union, NJ: The Lawbook Exchange, 2001), 2:1413–14.

35. Constitution of North Carolina, 1776, Art. XXXII, in Poore, *Constitutions*, 1413.

36. Constitution, of Maryland, 1776, Art. XXXIII, in Poore, *Constitutions*, 819.

37. Constitution of New Jersey, 1776, Art. XVIII, in Poore, *Constitutions*, 1313.

38. Constitution of Delaware, 1776, Art. 29, in Poore, *Constitutions*, 277–78.

39. Constitution of Pennsylvania, 1776, Art. II, in Poore, *Constitutions*, 1541.

40. Constitution of New York, 1777, in Poore, *Constitutions*, 1328–39; see also Pointer, *Protestant Pluralism*, 82.

41. Poore, *Constitutions*, 1338; see also Pratt, *Religion, Politics, and Diversity*, 114–15 (on Livingston); Anson P. Stokes and Leo F. Pfeffer, *Church and State in the United States*, rev. ed. (Boston: Beacon Press, 1967), 72–73. See further chapter 5 by Paul Finkelman.

42. Pratt, *Religion, Politics, and Diversity*, 54, 99.

43. Francis Newton Thorpe, ed., *The Federal and State Constitutions, Colonial Charters and Other Organic Laws of the State Territories and Colonies Now or Heretofore Forming the United States of America*, 7 vols. (Washington, DC: U.S. Government Printing Office, 1909), 5:2636.

44. Elizabeth Mensch, "Religion, Revival, and the Ruling Class: A Colonial History of Trinity Church," *Buffalo Law Review* 36 (1987): 472.

45. Ibid.; Georgia Constitution of 1777, Arts. IV, LVI, and LXII, in Poore, *Constitutions*, 378, 383; Franklin Hamlin Littell, *From State Church to Pluralism: A Protestant Interpretation of Religion in American History* (Chicago: Aldine, 1962), 15; Levy, *Establishment Clause*, 48 and Levy, *Constitutional Opinions: Aspects of the Bill of Rights* (New York: Oxford University Press, 1986), 159.

46. Pennsylvania Constitution of 1790, Art. III, sect. 1, in Poore, *Constitutions*, 1551–52.

47. Ibid., Art. IX, sect. 4, in Poore, *Constitutions*, 1554.

48. Amendment to the Maryland Constitution, Art. III, 1795, in ibid., 829.

49. Hart to Henry Laurens, March 19, 1776, Hart Papers; Clarke, *Southern Zion*, 132.

50. Tennant, "Writings," *South Carolina Historical Magazine* 61.4 (1960): 194–95 (all quotations).

51. Ibid., 194–97.

52. South Carolina Constitution 1778, Art. 28, Art. XXXIIII, in Poore, *Constitutions*, 1626–27.

53. Edgar, *South Carolina: A History*, 254.

54. "Extract of a Letter from an American Gentleman in France," October 14, 1789, *City Gazette* (Charleston, South Carolina), January 5, 1790. This could have been Thomas Jefferson.

55. Pierce quoted in Eugene Genovese and Elizabeth Fox Genovese, "Antebellum Southern Theologians," 31–40, at 32; Reese, "Essay"; Robert A. Baker and Paul J. Craven Jr., *Adventure in Faith: The First 300 Years of the First Baptist Church, Charleston, South Carolina* (Nashville, TN: Broadman Press, 1982), 206.

56. The *City Gazette or the Daily Advertiser* (Charleston, South Carolina), Saturday, February 21, 1789, 2 (quotation); "Report and Resolution No. 109," *Journals of the House of Representatives*, in *City Gazette or the Daily Advertiser* (Charleston, South Carolina), April 24, 1789, 4.

57. Letter entitled "The Reflector No. 1," addressed to the Printers of the *City Gazette*, in *City Gazette* (Charleston, South Carolina), April 5, 1790, 2; Letter entitled "The Reflector No. 2," addressed to the Printers of the *City Gazette*, April 9, 1790, 2.

58. Edmund S. Morgan, *American Slavery, American Freedom: The Ordeal of Colonial Virginia* (New York: W. W. Norton, 1975). An excellent updating of Morgan's thesis, including an analysis of gender as a historical determinant of the ideological construction, is Stephanie McCurry, *Masters of Small Worlds: Yeoman Households, Gender Relations, and the Political Culture of the Antebellum South Carolina Low Country* (New York: Oxford University Press, 1995).

59. Constitution of South Carolina 1790, Arts III, VIII, I. sec. 23, in Poore, *Constitutions,* 1628–34. See also James Lowell Underwood, *The Constitution of South Carolina,* 2 vols. (Columbia: University of South Carolina Press, 1989); Fletcher M. Green, *Constitutional Development in the South Atlantic States, 1776–1860; A Study in the Evolution of Democracy* (New York: De Capo Press, 1971).

60. Act No. 1500 of 1791, in South Carolina Statutes at Large, 5:175; Act No. 2344 of 1824, in South Carolina Statues at Large, 6:241, section 3.

61. John F. Thomason, *The Foundations of Public Schools in South Carolina* (Columbia, SC: State Co., 1925), 111–16, 167.

62. Ibid., 68, 6, 128–31.

63. Frederick Dalcho, "The Evidence from Prophecy for the Truth of Christianity and the Divinity of Christ in a Course of Catechetical Instruction" (undated, but published prior to 1819; now located at South Carolina Historical Society, Charleston).

64. Rutgers v. Waddington (N.Y. 1784). For a more complete explanation of the case and its effect on the condemnation of church property, see McGarvie, *One Nation under Law,* 111–17.

65. Pratt, *Religion, Politics, and Diversity,* 100.

66. *Laws of the State of New York, 1777–1801* (Albany, NY: State Publisher, 1886–1887), 1:647–49 (647).

67. Ibid., 1:661.

68. Ibid., 1:613.

69. Burrows and Wallace, *Gotham,* 238; *Laws of . . . New York,* 1:686–90.

70. Burrows and Wallace, *Gotham,* 274.

71. McGarvie, *One Nation under Law,* 117–19.

72. Ibid., 119–25.

73. See Trustees of Philadelphia Baptist Association v. Hart's Executors, 17 U.S. (4 Wheat) 1 (1819).

74. McGarvie, *One Nation under Law,* 152–89

75. *Boston Recorder,* September 16, 1820, 151.

76. Baker v. Fales, 16 Mass. 487 (1821), known as the Dedham case.

{ 4 }

Roger Williams and the Puritan Background of the Establishment Clause

David Little

Just over a hundred years ago, the Austrian legal scholar Georg Jellinek published a small, but important book on the American colonial origins of declarations of rights and their place in modern constitutional history.[1] The book contains two arresting conclusions. One is that "the idea of legally establishing inalienable, inherent and sacred rights of the individual is not of political but religious origin. What has been held to be a work of the [French] Revolution was in reality a fruit of the Reformation and its struggles."[2]

The second conclusion is even more daring. The "first apostle" of this radical rights doctrine, particularly as applied to the freedom of conscience, was not an eighteenth-century Frenchman, such as Lafayette, ardent supporter of the American Revolution and the French Declaration of the Rights of Man and Citizen. It was an earlier, more improbable person: the seventeenth-century Puritan outcast and founder of the Rhode Island colony Roger Williams (1603–1683?). "Driven by powerful and deep religious enthusiasm," says Jellinek, Williams "went into the wilderness in order to found a government of religious liberty."[3]

As to the first conclusion, Jellinek draws attention to seventeenth-century New England Puritans,[4] heirs of the Calvinist branch of the Protestant Reformation, and their "Plantation Covenants" or early constitutions that were imitated throughout the colonies.[5] A prominent feature, initiated by the New Englanders, was the inclusion of declarations of rights as part of a colony's founding document. Although there remained differences among them, eleven of the thirteen original states adopted constitutions between 1776 and 1789 that included declarations of rights while two of them retained their original colonial charters. Connecticut's was dated from 1662 and Rhode Island's from 1663, making these two documents, according to Jellinek, "the oldest written constitutions in the modern sense."[6]

Jellinek contends that it is the Puritan background that was decisive for the rise of modern constitutionalism in both the American and French cases. The U.S. Constitution, along with the Bill of Rights, was a direct consequence of the colonial experience,[7] and the French Declaration of the Rights of Man and Citizen was not, as hinted above, the product of the French Revolution or of Lafayette, Rousseau, or other French Enlightenment figures, but was also drawn, often word-for-word, from the declarations of rights of the American colonies.[8]

Above all, Jellinek contends that the early American documents were remarkable innovations. Although they selectively incorporated aspects of English common law, they were anything but carbon copies. "A deep cleft separates the American declarations from . . . English enactments," such as the Magna Carta (1215) and the Petition of Right (1628).

> The English statutes are far removed from any purpose to recognize general rights of man, and they have neither the power nor the intention to restrict the legislative agents or to establish principles for further legislation. According to English law, Parliament is omnipotent and all statutes enacted or confirmed by it are of equal value. . . . The American declarations, on the other hand, contain precepts which stand higher than the ordinary lawmaker. In the Union, as well as in the individual states, there are separate [arrangements] for ordinary and for constitutional legislation, and the judge watches over the observance of the constitutional limitations by the ordinary legislative power. . . . The declarations of rights even at the present day are interpreted by the Americans as practical protections of the minority.[9]

Subsequent scholarship has confirmed and expanded on Jellinek's first conclusion. According to a leading authority, the Charter of Massachussets Bay of 1629 "was not strictly a popular constitution, because it was in form and legal effect a royal grant, but in its practical operation after the transfer, it approximated a popular constitution more closely than any other instrument of government in actual use up to that time in America or elsewhere in modern times."[10]

To be sure, the process by which Puritan colonial thought and practice came to embrace the terms of modern constitutionalism was gradual and complex.[11] None of the founding documents of seventeenth-century Puritan New England manifested all of the characteristics of modern constitutionalism: (1) a written code understood as fundamental law antecedent to the government and based on a "self-conscious," "direct and express" act by "the people" whom the government is taken to represent; (2) attribution of political and legal authority, including limits on and division of power, such that any act of government outside the enumerated limits is an exercise of "power without right" and properly subject, if need be, to coercive restraint; (3) an independent judiciary responsible to interpret statutory law and to evaluate its constitutionality; and (4) the codification of a set of inalienable individual rights, whose enforcement is regarded as a critical condition of legitimate government.[12] However, some of these characteristics were present early on, at least incipiently, and their number expanded and grew more pronounced as time went by. The pattern of their development is important for understanding what came later. "[By adopting the U.S. Constitution] in the summer of 1787, Americans brought to completion the tradition of constitutional design they had begun more than a century and a half earlier."[13]

Central to that pattern of development were the religious and political predispositions the Puritans brought to the task of interpreting and implementing royal charters and other instruments that authorized their "errand to the wilderness." As with other colonial charters, the Massachusetts Bay charter granted the proprietors a certain amount of discretion in designing the form of government according to which their assigned territory would be administered.[14] However, Governor John Winthrop and the General Court[15] went well beyond the original wording, asserting that their charter permitted an astounding degree of political independence. As early as 1641, Massachusetts authorities refused help from the English Parliament because the colony might "then be subject to all such laws as [the Parliament] should make or at least such as [it] might impose upon us."[16] When in 1646 the authorities were criticized for considering themselves "rather a free state than a colony or corporation of England," they appeared to agree! Parliament might have authority in England, but "the highest authority here is in the general court, *both by our charter and by our own positive laws. . . . [O]ur allegiance binds us not to the laws of England any longer than we live in England.*"[17] Though the Puritans were slow to admit it, it was not a large step to the eventual replacement of the authority of the English crown, as well as of Parliament, with that of "the people" who inhabited the colonies.[18]

Something called the "Agreement of the Massachusetts Bay Company at Cambridge, England" (Cambridge Agreement), adopted on August 26, 1629, by the stockholders or "freemen" of the company before they sailed, helps to clarify the burgeoning commitments to constitutional self-government. The document served in effect to modify the Charter of Massachusetts Bay by transferring the government and the control of the charter to the colony. Moreover, it is a statement by the participants declaring their intention to establish a colony in accordance with principles they themselves consent to, and it emphasizes not the commercial purposes highlighted in the charter, but their mutual dedication to work for "Gods glory and the churches good."

The reactions of the Massachusetts Bay authorities and the sentiments contained in the Cambridge Agreement reflect a broader system of what one scholar calls "Puritan teachings on liberties of covenant and covenants of liberty [that] were one fertile seedbed out of which later American constitutionalism grew. Many of the basic constitutional ideas and institutions developed by the Puritans in the seventeenth century remained in place in the eighteenth century."[19] Some of the key ideas are well represented in the Mayflower Compact of 1620, adopted by the original Plymouth Pilgrims. Aspiring, they say, to "plant" a colony to the glory of God, the advancement of the Christian faith, and the honor of King and Country, they "solemnly and mutually in the presence of God and one another, covenant, and combine ourselves together into a civil body politic, for our better ordering and preservation, and . . . to enact, constitute, and frame just and equal laws, ordinances, acts, constitutions, offices from time to time, as shall be thought most meet and convenient for the general good of the colony."[20]

The Pilgrim Code of Laws, adopted a few years later, is another example. Having acknowledged the authority of the English King, the code declares the right of Plymouth colonists to "ordain, constitute, and enact" in such a way "that no act, imposition, law, or ordinance be made or imposed upon us at present, or to come but such as shall be imposed by consent of the body of associates and their representatives assembled, according to the free liberties of England."[21] Similarly, the Fundamental Orders of Connecticut of 1639 exhibits a strong sense of self-government based on a covenantal agreement. It lays out the institutions of government and law-making authority and provides for popular sovereignty expressed through majority rule. The document "clearly fulfills [some of] the functions of a constitution, though it is [known as] a compact."[22]

In particular, a strong Puritan disposition in favor of legal codes and publically recorded statutes, aimed at preventing magistrates from proceeding "according to their discretion," prevailed against staunch opposition by some leaders.[23] What is more, Puritans stood for a federal or covenantal structure of government in which both church and state, however closely combined, were divided into semiautonomous sub-bodies, each with its own internal, plural, and formally regulated structure, and all undergirded by a commitment to a set of fundamental individual rights. The state consisted of town governments, each with its own separate executive, legislative, and judicial authority, and all of them confederated into a broader colonial, and eventually state government.[24]

Finally, it was the colonists' specific experience with declarations of rights, and their unshakeable loyalty to them, that comprised a major reason for the eventual incorporation of the Bill of Rights into the U.S. Constitution in 1791. Although originally opposed to the addition of a declaration of rights, James Madison and other drafters changed their minds after they came to understand why the Constitution was at first resisted across the colonies. It was, said Madison, because "the great mass of people who opposed it, disliked it because it did not contain effectual provisions against the encroachment on particular rights, and those safeguards which they have been long accustomed to have interposed between them and the magistrate who exercises the sovereign power."[25] "Americans," says Jellinek, "could calmly [append a bill of rights to] their plan of government . . . because that government and the controlling laws had already long existed."[26]

There is also growing support for Jellinek's second conclusion that a seventeenth-century American Puritan, Roger Williams, rather than figures of the eighteenth century (whether French or American), provided the decisive inspiration for a doctrine of "inalienable, inherent and sacred rights of the individual," and, most especially, of a right to liberty of conscience.[27] In particular, Williams's fervently held belief in the right to liberty of conscience has led one scholar to assert that "the Nonestablishment Principle is a keystone of [Williams's] political career and is amply demonstrated in his writings."[28]

It is, indeed, the issue of the establishment of religion—whether or not the government might enforce by law one or more religions—that most divided Williams from other New England Puritans. Although many in the colonies believed that natural rights, including a right to "full liberty" of conscience, and a certain degree of separation of church and state, were central features of constitutional government, Williams's unconventional interpretations set him at odds with his fellows. The distinction between conscience and coercion entailed in his mind very radical consequences for the relations of church and state. For him, state power in matters of conscience ought to be much more restricted, and efforts to "establish by law" conscientiously held beliefs and practices had to be much more suspiciously regarded. Moreover, Williams propounded a more elaborate doctrine of the right to the liberty of conscience, including well-developed arguments from both religious and nonreligious premises,[29] than could be found anywhere else in the colonies.[30]

Finally, it has also become ever clearer, as Jellinek saw so acutely, that Williams's ideas laid the foundations for much of the thinking behind the adoption of the "religion clauses" of the First Amendment to the U.S. Constitution, and especially (for our purposes) of the Establishment Clause: "Congress shall make no law respecting an establishment of religion." For example, James Madison, a principal architect of the clause, advanced arguments against the establishment of religion, strongly following Williams's lead and focusing particularly on related questions of the greatest concern to Williams. One was guarding conscience by protecting minorities from majorities, as in allowing exemptions for conscience from generally applicable laws. Another was finding grounds for the liberty of conscience that are independent of religion in order to assure equal treatment of all citizens regardless of religious affiliation or belief.[31]

The Puritan Setting: Rights and Religion

Though the governing ideals and rules expressed in the Massachusetts Bay Charter and the Cambridge Agreement took time to evolve from corporation to commonwealth, and when completed amounted more to oligarchy than democracy—given the fear on the part of some of untrammeled popular control[32]—the Puritan authorities nevertheless "left out of their foundations two principles of government, the feudal and the hereditary, upon which democracy had always found it difficult to [develop]." Beyond that, the apprehensions about democracy of some leaders were partially counterbalanced by other leaders who affirmed the merits of elections as a necessary restraint on arbitrary government.[33] Also, of the greatest importance was the impulse in Massachusetts Bay and fellow colonies to adopt declarations of rights. Among other things, it bespoke significant movement toward drawing a distinction between the judicial and legislative aspects of lawmaking, and of confining the judicial function to the interpretation and enforcement of "a relatively stable corpus of statutory written law,"[34] including the bills of rights which for the inhabitants took on some of the characteristics of a constitution.[35]

The Massachusetts Body of Liberties (or "Liberties of the Massachusetts Colony in New England") was adopted into law by the General Court in 1641, and amounted to an exceptionally lengthy list of fundamental rights.[36] Its author, Nathaniel Ward (1578–1652), a prominent pastor and lawyer, incorporated provisions drawn from English statutes and precedents, but the Body of Liberties went well beyond those antecedents. The new code redefined and restructured the traditional rights of English subjects in the light of Puritan Christianity, adding modified portions of biblical law and some "daring rights proposals"[37] from left-wing English Puritan pamphleteers.

The document opens, significantly, by referring to "such liberties, immunities, and privileges" that "humanity, civility, and Christianity call for as due to every man in his place and proportion without impeachment or infringement," highlighting the several grounds, religious *and* natural, on which rights were believed to rest.[38] The author, Ward, makes the same point in a pamphlet written four years later, claiming that the enumerated rights are founded on a combination of "God's rule," experience, public deliberation, and the "light of nature." Underlying all these references, he says, is a universal set of moral "essentials," where, beyond local differences and variations in the form of government, "rule and reason will be found all one."[39] The tradition, originated by Massachusetts Bay, was particularly important in the proliferation of written rights guarantees in all the colonies by 1701, as well as in the elaboration of colonial declarations of rights in the 1770s and 1780s.[40]

There was, however, one part of the Body of Liberties that generated a particularly strong division of opinion: the rights pertaining to religious belief and practice, namely, section 95, articles 1 through 11, identified as "A Declaration of the Liberties the Lord Jesus hath given to the Churches." According to these articles, all members of the colony have "full liberty" to practice religion according to conscience, though only so long as they "be orthodox in judgment," and "every church has full liberty to elect church officers," "provided they be able, pious and orthodox."

The special conditions placed on religious rights, permitting free exercise but only in conformity with orthodox scriptural and doctrinal interpretation, points to what John Cotton himself called the "theocratic" character of the Massachusetts Bay Colony, namely, a state governed by officials regarded as being divinely guided.[41] This attitude led officials of the colony, such as John Winthrop, John Cotton, and Nathaniel Ward, to oppose ideas of religious toleration and liberty of conscience, ideas that had the effect, as Ward put it, of "hanging the Bible on the Devil's girdle," and, consequently, of undermining social order.[42]

Although leaders such as Cotton argued that church and state should not be "confounded," as they serve different ends and jurisdictions,[43] the two spheres should nevertheless be "close and compact and co-ordinate one to another,"[44] precisely so as to prevent the kind of heterodoxy in thought and practice and consequent disruption of social order that Nathanial Ward warned of. As one contemporary divine put it, "the interest of righteousness in the commonwealth and holiness in the churches are inseparable. The prosperity of church and commonwealth are twisted together. Break one cord, you weaken the other also."[45]

"Twisted together" church and state most certainly were. Although magistrates were precluded from holding church office, and church officials from holding civil office, only church members might vote in civil elections. In addition, churches and clergymen received direct public support through taxes and other donations, and religious beliefs and practices were extensively and harshly regulated by laws covering blasphemy, irreverence, profanity, idolatry, and "schismatic" activity. Ministers were regularly called upon to provide instruction on the pertinence of God's law to new legislation.[46]

It should be emphasized that government support for religion, as practiced by Massachusetts Bay, remained a significant factor in several states during and after the drafting and adoption of the U.S. Constitution. Vermont did not relinquish its system of establishment until 1807, Connecticut, until 1818, New Hampshire, until 1819, and Massachusetts, until 1833. Numerous other states, including Pennsylvania and Delaware, imposed religious tests for public office, which often excluded Catholics, Jews, and frequently atheists.[47] For example, all appointed and elected officials in Delaware were required to profess "faith in God the Father, and in Jesus Christ His only son, and in the Holy Ghost, one God blessed forever."[48] States also frequently enforced laws preferential to religion, following the Massachusetts model of mandating exposure to Calvinist doctrine in public schools, and of outlawing theatergoing, blasphemy, and disturbing the Sabbath.[49]

Roger Williams and the Nonestablishment Principle

Although it was widely shared throughout the colonies, by no means did all Puritans agree with the official Massachusetts Bay interpretation of the right of "full liberty" concerning religious belief and practice, or with the preference apparent in many of the colonies for one version or another of established religion. The task of articulating and mobilizing a staunchly opposing view fell principally to Roger Williams, who himself was in trouble with the Bay authorities almost from the time he first set foot in New England in 1631. Although Williams was widely reviled in seventeenth-century America, he was the first person on American soil to articulate fully the principles that ultimately would be embodied in the Constitution of 1787 ("no religious test" for public office) and the First Amendment to the Bill of Rights (forbidding Congress from enacting laws "respecting an establishment of religion" or interfering with the "free exercise of religion").

After being forced to move from one church to another because of his controversial views, Williams was indicted for continuing to oppose laws enforcing religion, as well as other official beliefs and practices he found offensive. These were such things as the assumption that colonial lands belonged to the English monarch and not, as he thought, to the Native Americans, or that the English flag was legitimate even though it prominently displayed a Christian cross at its center, thereby, in Williams's view, hopelessly confusing civil and spiritual spheres, or that public oaths should be required of unbelievers, who would thereby be compelled to hypocrisy. Predictably, Williams was found guilty as charged, and condemned to return to England for punishment. However, he eluded the authorities and, with the help of Narragansett Indians he had befriended earlier, found his way in 1636 to the territory that, under his leadership, would ultimately become the Rhode Island and Providence Plantation.

In 1643 Williams acquired a minimal patent for the towns of Providence, Portsmouth, and Newport from Parliament, which by 1647 was expanded into a fuller constitutional document that "gives us power to govern ourselves and such others as come among us, and [to establish] such a form of civil government as by the voluntary consent, etc., shall be found most suitable to our estate and condition."[50] In words less hesitant than the sentiments found in Massachusetts Bay, the document specifies without apology or reservation that the form of government will be "democraticall," which is to say, "a government held by the free and voluntary consent of all, or the greater part of the free inhabitants," assuring "each man's peaceable and quiet enjoyment of his lawful right and liberty." Then it continues in language largely reminiscent of the 1629 Charter of Massachusetts Bay and 1641 Body of Liberties to outline a representative political system together with legal institutions carefully regulated by due process, including extensive rights and liberties against arbitrary injury, trial, imprisonment, loss of property, and so on.[51]

Where the Rhode Island and Providence colony differed most sharply from Massachusetts Bay and other colonies was in the treatment of religion, a point articulated most eloquently in the Rhode Island and Providence Plantation Charter of 1663—promulgated thirty years after Williams first moved to Rhode

Island—that Williams and his associate, John Clarke, were able to acquire from King Charles II. It is this document, says Donald Lutz, that "served effectively as [a] colonial constitution and as [a] state constitution as well."[52] The charter commends the aspirations of the colonists "to hold forth a lively experiment, that a most flourishing civil state may stand and best be maintained . . . with the full liberty in religious concernments . . . and . . . in the free exercise and enjoyment of all . . . civil and religious rights." In a radical departure from Massachusetts Bay's traditional and circumscribed understanding of "full liberty," it then expresses a radically modern conception articulated in language that anticipates not only Jefferson's Act for the Establishment of Religious Freedom of 1786, but the U.S. Constitution.

> No person within said colony, at any time hereafter, shall be [in] any wise molested, punished, disquieted, or called into question, for any difference of opinion in matters of religion, and do not actually disturb the civil peace . . . but that all and every person and persons may . . . freely and fully have and enjoy . . . their own judgments and consciences in matters of religious concernments . . . they behaving themselves peaceably and quietly."[53]

Williams's whole approach can be summarized as a sustained and unrelenting assault on the idea of the legal establishment of religion, whether in its multiple historical guises, in the form it took in England, or in the various colonial versions Williams knew firsthand. For Williams, "freedom of religion" and "no establishment of religion" were concepts that were inextricably connected, and that ultimately were to become hallmarks of the U.S. Constitution. As later with Madison, a state "establishment of religion" is a violation of freedom of conscience and of the freedom of religion. Although states have the *power* to establish a religion they do not have the *right* to do so.

The titles of Williams's two best-known works, *The Bloody Tenent* (1644) and *The Bloody Tenent Yet More Bloody* (1652), epitomize what was for him the essential problem. The state's legal enforcement of religion, according to which people are punished for their conscientious convictions, opposes all that is right and holy, and, into the bargain, gives rise to violence and bloodshed. Williams supported this conclusion by several different arguments, though all of them were based on an age-old supposition about the difference between conscience and government that lay deep within the Christian tradition, and was developed in various directions by the Calvinist heritage in which he squarely stood.[54]

Drawing on Augustine (354–430), Thomas Aquinas (1225–1274), and others, John Calvin (1509–1564) previously had called attention to a sharp distinction between two forums or tribunals, the "internal forum" (conscience), and the "external forum" (civil authority).[55] The internal forum concerns personal, inward deliberation regarding fundamental belief and practice that is regulated by "spiritual power." The external forum concerns public deliberation regarding "outward behavior"—the needs of "the present life," such as food, clothing and the laws of social cooperation—that are regulated by the "power of the sword."[56] Calvin sometimes spoke of these as "two worlds" over which different kings and different laws have authority, requiring that they "always be examined separately."[57] The "outward" sphere of social order, underwritten by the threat of force, is clearly set apart from the sphere of conscience, and, as such, is delimited by it.

Calvin said as much in his commentary on Romans 13. The proper jurisdiction of a well-ordered government is defined exclusively by the "part of the law that refers to human society," or the second table of the Decalogue, whose basic principle, according to Calvin, is that "all individuals should preserve their rights." "There is no allusion at all [in Paul's discussion of political order] to the first table of the law, which deals with the worship of God."[58] Calvin stresses the same point elsewhere: Because "the whole of [Paul's] discussion concerns civil government[, those] who bear rule over . . . consciences attempt to establish their blasphemous tyranny . . . in vain."[59]

This, of course, was not *all* Calvin said. He occasionally contradicted himself: "No government," he says elsewhere, "can be happily established unless piety is the first concern; and those laws are preposterous which neglect God's right and provide only for men."[60] He solemnly pronounced that "civil government has as its appointed end, so long as we live [in the world], to cherish and protect the outward worship of God, to defend sound doctrine of piety and the position of the church"[61]—a principle he heartily favored in sixteenth-century Geneva.

As much as anything, this antinomy in Calvin's thought over the legal establishment of religion came to signify the basic division between Roger Williams and many of his fellow colonists. Williams embraced the first part, the liberal side, of Calvin's thought, and wholeheartedly rejected the second, the establishment side, whereas Massachusetts Bay affirmed and implemented the second part by playing down, if not entirely discarding, the first.

For Williams, there could be no two ways about it. Experience, reason, and religion all ultimately point the same way: The law of the sword—the indispensable instrument of the "external forum"—is not all-powerful. It must defer to and protect the law of the spirit: the law of reason, will, and affection that governs the "internal forum." When this rule is not observed, the historical lessons are clear. In Williams's words:

A most lamentably true experience of all the ages [is] that persecution for the cause of conscience has always proved pernicious. . . . He that reads the records of truth and time with an impartial eye shall find this to be the lance that has pierced the veins of kings and kingdoms, of saints and sinners, and filled the streams and rivers with their blood.[62]

A breach of civil peace [does not arise from] false and idolatrous practices [themselves, but from] the wrong and preposterous way of suppressing, preventing, and extinguishing such doctrines or practices by weapons of wrath and blood, whips, stocks, and imprisonment, banishment, and death by which men are commonly persuaded to convert heretics.[63]

Attempting to coerce conscience is to make a grievous mistake about how the mind works. For one thing, many of those who persecute conscience, including the Massachusetts Bay leaders, displayed an unseemly inconsistency by failing to apply to themselves charges they freely leveled against others. Ready to "cry out against persecution when they are under the hatches," such people are nevertheless ready "to persecute when they sit at the helm."[64] This tendency "to gross partiality," which "denies the principles of common justice" prompting people "to weigh out to the consciences of others what [is judged] not right to be weighed out to their own," is nothing more than "Machiavellianism," which makes a religion "but a cloak or stalking horse to [self-serving] policy and private ends."[65]

But a greater shortcoming would be to neglect the conceptual distinction between physical force and conscience. If one is attempting to regulate what Calvin called the "outward behavior" of human beings—to prevent them from taking what does not belong to them, or maiming or killing others to their own advantage—"cannons, . . . bullets, powder, muskets, swords, [and] pikes . . . are weapons effectual and [proportionate]."[66] Such weapons are appropriate because without them, physical harm or injury would occur. They are required for and capable of restraining action that is considered morally and legally illicit, and they may, if necessary, be effectively applied without or against the consent of the offender. It is precisely because the behavior in question is "outward" that it is under the jurisdiction of the "external forum," whose essential function is the administration of physical force. But things are different with the internal forum.

> To [try to] batter down [the strongholds of] false worship, heresy, schism, [spiritual] blindness or hardness [of heart] [and drive them] out of the soul and spirit, it is vain, improper, and unsuitable to bring those weapons which are used by persecutors—stocks, whips, prisons, swords, gibbets, stakes[.] ([W]here these seem to prevail with some cities and kingdoms, a stronger force sets up again what a weaker pulled down[.]) . . . [They are] never able to effect anything in the soul. . . . [B]ut against these spiritual strongholds in the souls of men, spiritual artillery and weapons are proper.[67]

According to the tradition in which Williams stood, the heart of the conscience is inward consent based on a conviction of truth and right. That is something that physical force, in and of itself, is incapable of producing. As a logical matter, force cannot compel belief because belief depends on reasons consisting of arguments and evidence. The threat of force, as in a case of robbery or rape, is not a reason in the proper sense because it lacks a valid justification. Thus, the only "weapons" suitably employed in the internal forum are "spiritual," namely, appeals and arguments subject to commonly understood normative standards, whose object is consensual or heartfelt agreement.

Accordingly, Williams's statement that physical weapons are unable to have any effect on the soul is basically a normative claim. He frequently asserts that "forcing of the conscience of any person" is equivalent to "spiritual" or "soul rape,"[68] implying that attempts to force conscience do in fact have consequences, and those consequences are invariably grave. Such attempts degrade or deform the conscience by inducing hypocrisy, narrow-mindedness, or self-betrayal precisely because they defy so completely the proper rules and procedures appropriate to the conduct of the internal forum. In a word, the use of force against conscience is a fundamental violation because of the nature of conscience itself.

This distinction is so powerful that it is understood, however dimly, even by highly disreputable people. "Do not even the most bloody popes and cardinals . . . put a difference between the crimes of murder, treason and adultery (for which although the offender repent, yet he suffers punishment) and the crimes of heresy, blasphemy, etc, which upon recantation and confession, are frequently remitted?"[69] In short, the idea is that the conscience—the internal forum, designed, as it is, to operate according to "the laws of the spirit"—must be respected as a special preserve free of direct forcible regulation, and any effort by the external forum to "invade" the internal forum is an atrocity against what Williams calls "the natural conscience and reason of all men."[70] This is the primary explanation, to his mind, of why "rivers of blood" predictably follow such "invasions." Wherever they "seem to prevail with some cities and kingdoms," it is because superior force succeeds temporarily in quieting opposition, though not in eliciting inward consent or eliminating potential resistance.

Along with references to experience and reason, Williams adds extensive appeals to Christian scripture, doctrine, and history. In one place, he writes that in shedding "the blood of so many hundred thousand of poor servants [of Jesus] by the civil powers of the world, pretending [thereby] to suppress blasphemies, heresies, idolatries, superstition, etc.," the persecutors of conscience are "lamentably guilty" of spilling the "most precious blood" of Jesus himself.[71] The decisive transgression took place

> when Constantine broke the bounds of this his own and God's edict, and [drew] the sword of civil power in suppressing other consciences for the [sake of] establishing the Christian [church.] [T]hen began the great mystery of the churches' sleep, [by which] the gardens of Christ's churches turned into the wilderness of National Religion, and the world (under Constantine's dominion) into the most unchristian Christendom. . . . There never was any National Religion good in this world but one [namely, ancient Israel], and

since the desolation of that nation, there shall never be any National Religion good again.[72]

This passage makes clear that Williams's famous image of the "wall of separation" between "the garden" and "the wilderness" does not mean, as Mark DeWolfe Howe has claimed,[73] that the wilderness is the civil state from which "the gardens of Christ's churches" must be walled off pure and undefiled, and with which the churches must have nothing whatsoever to do. Howe asserts erroneously that Williams favored a wall between the garden and the wilderness "not because he was fearful that without such a barrier the arm of the church would extend its reach. It was, rather, the dread of worldly corruptions which might consume the churches if sturdy fences against the wilderness [of the civil state] were not maintained."[74]

Rather, the wilderness Williams fears is the condition of an established religion where *both* church *and* state are mutually degraded and corrupted by failing to observe the critical distinction between the inward and outward forums. A state where there is no establishment—where conscience is free to exercise itself as it should—is, to be sure, a place in which "the gardens of Christ's churches" can exist as intended, but it is also a place in which the state can perform its duties as intended as well. It is such circumstances that exhibit the desirable degree of consonance and harmony between the religious and the civil organizations, thereby fulfilling the proper vocations of each.

Williams is simply reiterating—now in theological terms—the distinction between the inward and outward forums, directed by their different laws and sanctions, and tied to the key difference between the First and the Second Tables of the Decalogue, all of which Calvin had earlier emphasized. Indeed, Williams introduces his own discussion of the difference between the two tables, and its importance for governing, by referring enthusiastically to "that excellent servant of God, Calvin," and then by citing Calvin's comment limiting the jurisdiction of the civil government to the Second Table. At the same time, Williams is equally resolute in rejecting the "other side" of Calvin. That there is any value to the proposal that "Christ's ordinances and administrations of worship [should be] appointed . . . to a civil state, town or city, as [in] the instance of Geneva," Williams writes, "I confidently deny." [75]

Williams's notion of the details of the difference and the relations between church and state, and the theological interpretation of those details, are somewhat complicated, though he never strays very far from his nonestablishment position. He occasionally argues that scripture and history prove that "although the . . . church and the civil kingdom or government [properly understood] be not inconsistent, but . . . may stand together, yet they are independent,"[76] such that a political order may exist peacefully either without the presence of the church, or alongside churches that are divided from each other, so long as those divisions do not control the affairs of state.

Williams is frequently quite explicit in echoing one side of Calvin's thought to the effect that church and state are "two worlds" over which different kings and different laws have authority, requiring that they "always be examined separately."

> The civil nature of the magistrate we have proved to receive no addition of power from the magistrate's being Christian, no more than it receives diminution from his not being a Christian; even as the commonweal is a true commonweal although it have not heard of Christianity, and Christianity professed in it . . . makes it no more a commonweal, and Christianity taken away . . . makes it none the less a commonweal.[77]

Williams is confident that the ingredients for "civility," for a common life among people of different creeds, origins, and identities, are there ready to be put to use under the right conditions. A civil order based upon what has been called a "thin approach" to government, where citizens are able, singly or in groups, to pursue their own notions of the good so long as common rights and interests are not compromised, is largely compatible with Williams's view.

> Frequent experience in all parts of the world tells us that many thousands [of people] are far more peaceable subjects, more loving and helpful neighbors, and more true and fair dealers in civil interaction than many who account themselves to be the only religious people in the world.[78]

Utterances of this kind might lead us to think that, for Williams, church and state have, after all, very little to do with each other, and are indeed "two worlds" that must "always be examined separately." In fact, Williams does speak in one place of "divers sorts of goodness" wherein a subject or magistrate "may be a good subject, a good magistrate, in respect of civil or moral goodness," and wherever such virtue exists, "it is commendable and beautiful, though Godliness, which is infinitely more beautiful, be wanting."[79]

This way of putting things is certainly part of Williams's outlook, but it is by no means all there is. He also strongly favors a creative and constructive affinity between a civil authority liberated from religious control and what he believes to be the true message of the Christian Gospel. Although it is undoubtedly possible for secular regimes to organize themselves in peace and prosperity without Christian assistance, the proper Christian approach adds a significant layer of support and encouragement for a modern constitutional order, including the disestablishment of religion and the protection of the rights of free conscience. In short, the world needs all the help it can get in disabusing itself of the distortions of "national religion," and in thereby recovering its preexisting capacities for common civil and moral goodness. The Christian message, properly preached and practiced, may be of considerable auxiliary assistance. How else may we interpret the following passages?

There is a sword of civil justice, being of a material nature [designed] for the defense of persons, estates, families, liberties of a city or civil state, and the suppressing of uncivil or injurious persons or actions, which cannot, *now that it is under Christ, when all nations are merely civil*, extend to matters of the spirit and soul.[80]

I affirm that state policy and state necessity, which (for the peace of the state and the preventing of rivers of civil blood) [safeguards] the consciences of men, will be found to agree most punctually with the rules of the best politician that ever the world saw, the King of kings and Lord of lords.[81]

It would be impossible to read Williams's complete writings without appreciating his deep conviction, expressed repeatedly, that Christian scripture (properly interpreted) provides overwhelming evidence of the consonance between the Christian message and the legal disestablishment of religion.[82]

Beyond these reflections on the nonestablishment principle, Williams commented on two other related matters that came to exercise the thinking of Madison and other drafters of the U.S. Constitution a century later. One was the tension at the heart of modern constitutionalism over accommodating the interests of the majority with those of dissenting individuals and minorities. Williams was a political contractualist and therefore embraced the idea that "the will of the people is the supreme law," a concept fundamental to Calvinist constitutionalism. Such thinking underlay the several Rhode Island charters he obtained, or helped to obtain, first from the Parliament during the Interregnum, and later from Charles II after the Restoration.

The sovereign, original, and foundation of civil power lies in the people (who are the civil power as distinct from the government). If so, a people may erect and establish what form of government seems to them most meet for their civil condition. It is evident that such governments as are by them erected and established have no more power, nor for any longer time, than the civil power or people, consenting and agreeing, shall entrust them with. This is clear not only in reason, but in the experience of all commonweals, where the people are not deprived of their natural freedom by the power of tyrants.[83]

He goes on to emphasize, again in the spirit of (liberal) Calvinism, not only that "the very nature and essence of a civil magistrate" derives from "the people's choice and free consent," but also that it has as its *exclusive* purpose "the common-weal or safety of [the] people in their bodies and goods,"[84] or the adoption of "such civil laws [as] concern [their] common rights, peace, and safety,"[85] elsewhere characterized as "material civil nature,"[86] or concerns of the Second Table of the Decalogue.

Basic to Williams's approach is the protection of individual rights, including most prominently individual (and minority) rights of conscience. However important the people's will may be, whether expressed unanimously or by majority rule, a legitimate government—one not deprived of "natural freedom by the power of tyrants"—has an irreducible obligation to safeguard "any civil right or privilege" due a citizen simply as a human being ("as a man," in Williams's words),[87] or what he calls in another place, the "natural and civil rights and liberties" of all citizens.[88]

Although these fundamental rights apply to matters of property, political participation, and legal protection (as they did in Calvin's thought, as well as in Massachusetts Bay, Rhode Island, and other colonies), Williams's preoccupation, as we would expect, is with the special protection of the right of religious freedom or freedom of conscience. Williams denies to the state any authority "to govern the spiritual and Christian commonweal, the flock and church of Christ, to pull down or set up religion, to judge, determine, or punish in spiritual controversies,"[89] thereby insisting on a constitutional restriction on civil power and a protected space for the free exercise of conscience.

Once the principle of nonestablishment is accepted, the key remaining question, of course, is just where the proper line between the state and conscience is to be drawn. Williams is clear that in the face of a conflict between conscience and compelling state interest, such as public safety, peace, and common rights, conscience is expected to yield. For example, in all cases "wherein civility is wronged in [regard to] the bodies and goods of any," as in recorded instances of religiously sanctioned human sacrifice, "the civil sword is God's sword" "for suppressing such practices and appearances," including "the very principles" on which they rest.[90]

When the vital interests of the state are not at issue, Williams occasionally condones special exemptions from general laws for religious individuals and groups, even though he is not always entirely clear or consistent in the way he arrives at his conclusions. With some plausibility, he implies that because taxation pertains only to "outward" bodies and goods, religious activities and appurtenances, as something beyond the "merely civil," may be granted "immunity and freedom from tax and toll," perhaps endorsing, in keeping with subsequent American jurisprudence, a fitting limit on the civil control of religious affairs. Not too much can be made of the point, however, as Williams leaves the matter to the discretion of the civil authority.[91]

As to the question of the "seeming incivility" of Mary's virgin birth outside wedlock, he makes an impassioned plea for special exemption, in part, interestingly enough, on the basis of the principles of the administration of civil authority. He claims that it is beyond question that even "the most civil and the severest judge, upon due examination of the whole matter, might rationally and judiciously . . . have found [any] violence of civility, [or any] wrong to the bodies or goods of any."[92] Such reasoning opens the door, at least, to a claim Madison would later make in favor of religious exemptions from general laws unless the rights of others are violated or there is a substantial threat to public safety.[93]

At the same time, several of Williams's other judgments are harder to follow. In interpreting the aborted sacrifice of Isaac by Abraham, his claim that this, too, is a case of only "seeming incivility" is much less convincing, because a direct threat to bodily injury is obviously at stake.[94] Moreover, his assertions that the practicing of offensive patterns of dress and speech by certain religious groups, such as "the monstrous hair of women up[on] the heads of some men," or the use by Quakers of the familiar (and to Williams, contemptuous) "thou" in addressing superiors represented significant threats to public order and safety, and therefore should be outlawed, are controversial, at best.[95]

There is another example of special interest. It concerns Williams's response to the objection of some members of the Providence Plantation to a requirement of compulsory military service. Williams answers by employing a metaphor concerning the role and responsibility of a ship's captain. Under normal conditions, the captain has no right to tell the crew and passengers how or whether they should worship or how they should determine other matters of conscience. However, if the ship comes under attack, the captain is within his authority to command all hands to rally to the ship's defense. This is, it would appear, a simple matter of the necessary protection of the outward bodies and goods of the people on board, and is thus a consistent application of the basic principles of constitutional authority.[96] Williams's argument, unlike that of Madison a century later, does not make allowance for a constitutionally protected exemption of conscientious objection to military service. It is possible that those whom Williams was addressing were opposed not just to conscription but to the legitimacy of civil authority itself, in which case he was simply putting forward a general defense of civil government. However, it is also possible that in cases of conflict between an individual's conscientious objection to fighting and the "people's" compelling need to defend their common interest, Williams decided in favor of the latter. If so, Madison and Williams are simply at odds on this matter.

However, it is hard to be sure about Williams's settled position. In another place, where he again employs the metaphor of the role and responsibility of ship officials—this time, "the master and pilot," as he refers to them—Williams comes to a different conclusion with different implications for the constitutional division of powers and the exercise of conscience.[97] The special focus of the lengthy disquisition is on whether a prince, who happens to be on board, or the master and pilot of the ship, is the one or ones who have final responsibility for the ship's welfare. Williams answers that it is the master and pilot who have final authority, so that in a case where the prince commands one thing about how the ship shall be run or which course to take, and the ship's officials another, sailors "may lawfully disobey the prince, and obey the governor of the ship in the actions of the ship."

But Williams goes further: Should the officials "out of base fear and cowardice, or covetous desire of reward," acquiesce to the command of the prince "contrary to the rules of art and experience," and "the ship come in danger and perish, and the prince with it," the officials would be guilty of malfeasance and rightfully subject to punishment. The suggestion here is that the ship officials forfeited their authority by failing in their duty. Indeed, Williams states explicitly that the officials should be obeyed unless the commands "be in manifest error, wherein it is granted [that] *any passenger* may reprove" the officials (italics added). Williams's underlying point favors the right of groups *or individuals* to hold the actions of established authorities to account and to express (and apparently to act on) conscientious disagreement with their decisions, according to commonly accessible "rules of art and experience." Obviously, this line of thinking favors a quite expansive sphere of protection for individual conscience over and against governmental authority.

A last question related to the establishment of religion concerns the grounds of the "fundamental law" of a constitutional system. As with safeguarding individual and minority rights in face of "the will of the people," this issue was of intense concern to Williams.[98] If a particular religious point of view is the foundation of civil law, on what basis might nonbelievers be held accountable? It is true that Williams's fellow Puritans in Massachusetts Bay and elsewhere, had, like Calvin before them, invoked "humanity" and "civility," interpreted "in the light of nature" as providing grounds for their declarations of rights. As with Calvin, this was important for establishing universal liability; all human beings might justly be held to account for transgressing the law of their own nature, regardless of whether they had heard of and accepted Christianity.

The problem for Williams was that Calvin and many of his spiritual descendants went well beyond this standard. When they proceeded to claim that their version of "orthodox" Christianity was indispensable to the security and prosperity of the state, and that, therefore, citizens could legitimately be punished, not just for violating a moral code commonly accessible to human beings as such, but also for transgressing what they thought were the clear teachings of the "Lord Jesus," they caused a catastrophe for both religious and civil communities.

For Williams, the central tenet of the natural rights tradition was all-important: "from the beginning, the subjective idea of natural rights was not derived specifically from Christian revelation," "but from an understanding of human nature itself as rational, self-aware, and morally responsible."[99] That understanding lies behind the Rhode Island Charter of 1663, which Williams helped to design and obtain, when it assures citizens of "the free exercise and enjoyment of all their civil and religious rights," or of "their just rights and liberties." It also underlies Williams's own references to the "common rights" of citizens, or to "any civil right or privilege" due a person simply as a human being, or when he implies that these follow from what he calls a law "simply moral, civil, and natural." All such references suggest a well-developed belief in a natural right to conscience, taken to be antecedent to the government, and to warrant special protection in face of "the will of the people" that rests on foundations independent of Christian revelation or any other religious principle.[100] He underscores this commitment in one of his most ringing declarations concerning the nonreligious basis of civil authority. Political "power, might, or authority," he says, "is not religious, Christian, etc. but natural, humane and civil."[101]

> There is a moral virtue, a moral fidelity, ability and honesty, which other men (beside church members) are, by good nature and education, by good laws and good examples nourished and trained up in, that civil places of trust and credit need not be monopolized into the hands of church members (who sometimes are not fitted for them) and all others deprived and despoiled of their natural and civil rights and liberties.[102]

Williams registers these same sentiments in an early book he published on the language and ways of the Narragansett Indians whom he befriended in the process of settling Rhode Island.[103]

> Boast not, proud English, of thy birth and blood,
> Thy brother Indian is by birth as good.
> Of one blood God made him and thee and all,
> As wise, as fair, as strong, as personal.[104]

He writes this, despite making some very harsh comments about the religious beliefs and practices of the Narragansetts and other Native Americans he was able to observe. Indeed, what is especially interesting about his comments on the manners and morals of the Narragansetts is how much his assessment of them, and even of their final spiritual destiny, is affected by their degree of compliance, to Williams's mind, with the law that is "simply civil, moral, and natural."

> I have known them leave their house and mat
> To lodge a friend or stranger,
> When Jews and Christians oft have sent
> Christ Jesus to the manger.

> If nature's sons both wild and tame
> Humane and courteous be,
> How ill becomes it sons of God
> To want humanity.

> By nature, wrath's his portion, thine no more,
> Till grace his soul and thine in Christ restore.
> Make sure thy second birth, else thou shalt see
> Heaven ope to Indians wild, but shut to thee.[105]

Conclusions

With the help of recent scholarship, we have confirmed two important conclusions drawn a century ago by the Austrian legal scholar Georg Jellinek that provide the historical and conceptual background for the protection of religious freedom guaranteed by the Establishment Clause of the First Amendment to the U.S. Constitution.

The first conclusion, that the doctrine of legally enforceable individual rights taken to be essential to modern constitutions "is not of political but religious origin" has been verified with reference to the contributions of the Puritans of colonial New England. Drawing on their Calvinist heritage, and its commitment to the constitutional protection of civil rights and liberties, they expended considerable energy designing and implementing declarations of rights as an indispensable part of their civil covenants. Antedating by many years the French Declaration or the American Bill of Rights, these declarations prepared the groundwork for the later documents.

Jellinek's second conclusion—related to the first—has also been corroborated by examining Roger Williams's writings in the light of fresh scholarship. It is not to eighteenth-century figures (whether French or American) that we must look to find the distinctive source of this radical rights doctrine, but to a colonial Puritan, Roger Williams. We found that the principal difference between Williams and his fellows is conveniently summarized in reference to his opposition to the establishment of religion. He strenuously objected to the various forms of "National Religion" found not only in England and Continental Europe at the time but also in the other colonies, arguing that those arrangements profoundly misconstrued both the teachings of Christianity and of the "the light of nature." Only by recovering the proper balance between the inward and outward forums jointly prescribed by nature and the Christian tradition can truth and right prevail.

Williams's whole approach can be summarized as a sustained and unrelenting assault on the idea of the legal establishment of religion, whether in its multiple historical guises, or in the form it took in England, before, during, or after the Puritan Revolution, or in the various colonial versions Williams knew firsthand. For Williams, "freedom of religion" and "no establishment of religion" were concepts that were inextricably connected, and these concepts, which he shared with Madison, ultimately would become hallmarks of the U.S. Constitution. Both men agreed that a state "establishment of religion" is a violation of freedom of conscience and of the freedom of religion. Although states have the *power* to establish a religion they have no *right* to do so.

Notes

1. Georg Jellinek, *The Declaration of the Rights of Man and of Citizens: A Contribution to Constitutional History* (Westport, CT: Hyperion Press, 1979), first published in German in 1895

and in English in 1901. Trans. by Max Farrand, reprinted from an edition published by Henry Holt, 1901. Available online at http://files.libertyfund.org/files/1176/Jellinek_0162_EBk_v5.pdf.

2. Ibid., 77

3. Ibid.

4. Although Jellinek does not specifically include the founders of the Plymouth colony (1620), known as "Pilgrims," in his account, it is important to do so. Technically, Pilgrims were not Puritans, because they wished to separate themselves entirely from the Church of England, whereas Puritans, often very reluctantly, remained within the church the better to reform it. Still, the Pilgrims and Puritans shared a common theological and political outlook, and after the Massachusetts Bay colony was established in 1629, "very rapidly the distinction between the Massachusetts Puritans and the Plymouth Separatists lost its meaning, and the story of Plymouth became in large part that of Puritan New England." Francis J. Bremer, *The Puritan Experiment: New England Society from Bradford to Edwards* (Hanover, NH: University Press of New England, 1995), 36.

5. Jellinek, *Declaration*, 64ff. Jellinek does not claim the Puritans acted all on their own. He singles out the crucial contribution to the American experience of a radical English Puritan sect known as the Levellers. On their contributions, see A.S.P. Woodhouse, ed., *Puritanism and Liberty* (Chicago: University of Chicago Press, 1974), 357–67. See David D. Hall, *A Reforming People: Puritanism and the Transformation of Public Life in New England* (New York: Alfred Knopf, 2011) for abundant confirmation of "how close the colonists came to fulfilling the program of the Levellers, the most substantial and democratic of the groups that wanted to transform English politics and society" (p. xvi; cf. pp. 49–50, 124–26). Moreover, Hall's book provides compelling new evidence in favor of the critical contribution of colonial New England to the rise of modern constitutionalism (e.g., pp. 147–58).

6. Jellinek, *Declaration*, 22. See note 10 below.

7. Ibid., 85–89.

8. Ibid., ch. II, "Rousseau's 'Contrat Social' Was Not the Source of the [French] Declaration," and ch. V, "Comparison of the French and American Declarations."

9. Ibid., 46–47.

10. C. H. McIlwain, *Constitutionalism and Its Changing World* (Cambridge: Cambridge University Press, 1939), 241.

11. See Donald S. Lutz, *The Origins of American Constitutionalism* (Baton Rouge: Louisiana State University Press, 1988).

12. Charles Howard McIlwain, *Constitutionalism: Ancient and Modern* (Ithaca, NY: Cornell University Press, 1966), 9, 14, 21, 76, 81, 117, 139–40.

13. Lutz, *Origins of American Constitutionalism*, 5.

14. Ibid., 36.

15. The "General Court" is the traditional name for the Massachusetts legislature, a designation that has continued into the twenty-first century.

16. From *Winthrop's Journal*, cited in McIlwain, *Constitutionalism and Its Changing World*, 234.

17. Ibid., 235 (emphasis added).

18. Lutz, *Origins of American Constitutionalism*, 37.

19. John Witte Jr., *The Reformation of Rights: Law, Religion, and Human Rights in Early Modern Calvinism* (Cambridge: Cambridge University Press, 2007), 318.

20. The Mayflower Compact, in Williston Walker, *The Creeds and Platforms of Congregationalism* (Boston: Pilgrim Press, 1960), 92.

21. Cited in Lutz, *Origins of American Constitutionalism*, 40.

22. Ibid., 45.

23. Witte, *Reformation of Rights*, 316.

24. Ibid., 317.

25. Cited in Robert Allen Rutland, *The Birth of the Bill of Rights, 1776–1791* (Chapel Hill: University of North Carolina, 1955), 201.

26. Jellinek, *Declaration*, 89.

27. Several scholars have recently moved toward confirming Jellinek's original insights about Williams: Timothy Hall, *Separation of Church and State: Roger Williams and Religious Liberty* (Urbana: University of Illinois Press, 1998); Isaac Kranmick and R. Laurence Moore, *The Godless Constitution: A Moral Defense of the Secular State* (New York: Norton & Co., 1996, 2005); Martha C. Nussbaum, *Liberty of Conscience: In Defense of America's Tradition of Religious Equality* (New York: Basic Books, 2008); Sumner B. Twiss, "Roger Williams and Freedom of Conscience and Religion as a Natural Right," a paper delivered at a conference at Harvard Divinity School on November 13–14, 2009. Although the first three publications, especially Hall's and Nussbaum's, make especially valuable contributions to understanding the importance of Williams's thought in the American tradition, only Twiss's paper explicitly and systematically connects Williams's doctrine of liberty of conscience to the broader idea of natural rights, a connection Jellinek perceptively identified.

28. Nussbaum, *Liberty of Conscience*, 69.

29. By describing Williams as a man who founded a government of religious liberty because "he was driven by powerful and deep religious enthusiasm" (*Declaration*, 77), Jellinek obscures Williams's distinctly bifocal approach to justifying the right to religious liberty, according to which he supplied grounds that are *both* religious (scriptural/doctrinal) *and* nonreligious (rational/experiential).

30. Williams, of course, did not invent his approach to rights, including the rights of conscience, whether scripturally or naturally understood. He draws upon several traditions. One of them went back to John Calvin, and to the medieval and conciliar thinking on which Calvin drew. Another stemmed from sixteenth- and seventeenth-century Anabaptists and other "free-church" sectarians.

31. On Madison's views, see chapter 6 by Ralph Ketcham.

32. As one leader, John Cotton, put it: "If the people be governors, who shall be governed?" "A Letter from Mr. Cotton to Lord Say and Seal" (1636), in *Puritan Political Ideas, 1558–1794* ed. Edmund S. Morgan (Indianapolis, IN: Bobbs-Merrill Co., 1965), 163. Cf. John Winthrop's opposition to democracy, cited in Francis J. Bremer, *John Winthrop, America's Forgotten Founding Father* (Oxford: Oxford University Press, 2003), 355.

33. See Witte, *Reformation of Rights*, 317.

34. George L. Haskins, *Law and Authority in Early Massachusetts* (New York: Macmillan, 1960), 119–20.

35. Witte, *Reformation of Rights*, 287.

36. Morgan, *Puritan Political Ideas*, 171–97.

37. Witte, *Reformation of Rights*, 280.

38. Morgan, *Puritan Political Ideas*, 172–73. I have modernized and here and there "translated" some of the archaic words and forms of speech in the Body of Liberties, and in some of the subsequent citations from Puritan writings.

39. Nathaniel Ward, "The Simple Cobbler of Aggawam" (1647), in *The Puritans: A Sourcebook of Their Writings*, 2 vols., ed. Perry Miller and Thomas H. Johnson (New York: Harper Torchbook, 1963), 1:236.

40. Jellinek, *Declaration*, 24ff.

41. Cotton actually used the term to describe what in his mind is "the best form of government in the commonwealth, as well as the church." Morgan, *Puritan Political Ideas*, 163.

42. Miller and Johnson, *The Puritans*, 1:230.

43. Morgan, *Puritan Political Ideas*, 162–65.

44. Ibid., 163.

45. A statement by Urian Oakes, pastor and president of Harvard, cited by Witte, *Reformation of Rights*, 310.

46. I am drawing here on the excellent summary of the church–state arrangement in the Bay colony in Witte, *Reformation of Rights*, 310–12.

47. Nussbaum, *Liberty of Conscience*, 84–85.

48. Kramnick and Moore, *Godless Constitution*, 30. See further chapter 3 by Mark McGarvie.

49. Krannick and Moore, 119–20.

50. See G.B. Warden, "The Rhode Island Civil Code of 1647," in David D. Hall, John M. Murrin, and Thad W. Tate, eds., *Saints and Revolutionaries: Essays on Early American History* (New York: W.W. Norton & Co., 1984), pp. 138–151.

51. Acts and Orders of 1647 (Rhode Island) http://oll.libertyfund.org/index.php?option=com_content&task=view&id=1040S&;Itemid=264, p. 7.

52. Lutz, *Origins of American Constitutionalism*, 49. See note 10 above.

53. Charter of Rhode Island (1663) www.lonang.com/exlibris/organic/1663-cri.htm

54. Though Perry Miller did not always get Williams right, he is right on this point: "[Williams] remained to the end a stalwart Calvinist, believing firmly in predestination, reprobation, irresistible grace, and, above all, the perseverance of the saints." *Roger Williams: His Contribution to the American Tradition* (New York: Atheneum, 1953), 28.

55. Calvin, *Institutes of the Christian Religion*, 2 vols., ed. John T. McNeill, trans. Ford Battles (Philadelphia: Westminster Press, 1960), bk. 3, ch. xix, para. 15, 847–48; bk. 4, ch. x, para. 5, 1183.

56. Ibid., bk. 3, ch. xix, para. 15, 847.

57. Ibid.

58. Calvin, *Epistles of Paul the Apostle to the Romans and to the Thessalonians*, trans. Ross Mackenzie (Grand Rapids, MI: Wm. B. Eerdmans, 1976), ch. 13, v. 10, at p. 286.

59. Ibid., 283.

60. *Institutes*, bk. 4, ch. xx, para. 9.

61. Ibid., bk. iv, ch. xx, para. 2.

62. Roger Williams, *A Bloody Tenent of Persecution*, in *Complete Writings of Roger Williams*, 7 vols. (New York: Russell & Russell, 1963) 3:182. Citations from Williams are modernized for easier understanding.

63. Ibid., 3:80.

64. From Williams, *A Bloody Tenent*, cited in Miller, *Roger Williams*, 140.

65. Williams, *Bloody Tenent Yet More Bloody*, in Williams, *Complete Writings*, 3:498.

66. Ibid.

67. Williams, *Bloody Tenent*, in *Complete Writings*, 3:148–49. I have omitted passing references Williams makes to God's role in changing consciences because these are incidental to the more general conceptual point Williams affirms here and elsewhere concerning the implied distinction between reasons and causes I call attention to in the text.

68. Williams, *Bloody Tenent Yet More Bloody*, in *Complete Writings*, 4:325.

69. Ibid., 4:443.

70. Ibid.

71. Ibid., 4:494.

72. Ibid., 4:442. The reference to "ancient Israel" as the one exception to the nonestablishment principle underscores Williams's belief that the close interconnection of the religious and civil communities evident in the Old Testament was provisionally authorized by God "until Christ came." That arrangement was, as Williams says often, "a Nonesuch," or something never to be repeated.

73. Mark DeWolfe Howe, *The Garden and the Wilderness* (Chicago: University of Chicago Press, 1965).

74. Ibid., 6.

75. Williams, *Complete Writings*, 3:225.

76. Ibid., 3: 224–25.

77. Ibid., 3:355.

78. Williams, *Bloody Tenent Yet More Bloody*, in *Complete Writings*, 4:238.

79. Ibid., 4:246.

80. "Bloody Tenent," cited in Miller, *Roger Williams*, 133 (italics added).

81. Williams, *Complete Writings*, 3:179. In several places, Williams suggested a somewhat more positive role for the magistrate in regard to supporting the Christian Church. Once he said that a magistrate ought to "cherish (as a foster father) the Lord Jesus in his truth [and] in his saints, . . . and to countenance them even to the death," without Williams clarifying what he meant. He also referred to the obligation to protect Christians from civil violence and injury, but that would presumably apply to all religious groups (*Complete Writings*, 3:129). In another place, he again spoke without explaining further of countenancing and encouraging the church, though he added, again, a reference to protection from violence (which is a general obligation of the magistrate), and he immediately proceeds to condemn magistrates who encourage and protect only those religious groups "which they judge to be true and approve of," "not permitting other consciences than their own" (ibid., 3:280).

82. See, for example, James P. Byrd Jr., *The Challenges of Roger Williams: Religious Liberty, Violent Persecution and the Bible* (Macon, GA: Mercer University Press, 2002).

83. Williams, *The Bloody Tenent*, in *Complete Writings*, 3:249–50.

84. Ibid., 3:354.

85. Ibid., 3:366.

86. Ibid., 3:160.

87. Williams, *Bloody Tenent Yet More Bloody*, in *Complete Writings*, 4:414.

88. Ibid., 4:365.

89. Ibid., 3:366.

90. Williams, "The Examiner Defended," in *Complete Writings*, 7:243.

91. Williams, "Bloody Tenent," in *Complete Writings*, 3:252. See Nussbaum, *Liberty of Conscience*, 60, for confirmation of such an interpretation, though she criticizes him for not

stipulating that a tax exemption "should be given to all religions on the basis of some fair principle; here he sells his own ideas grievously short."

92. Williams, "The Examiner Defended," in *Complete Writings*, 7:245.

93. See note 37, above.

94. Ibid.

95. See Edmund S. Morgan, *Roger Williams: The Church and the State* (New York: Harcourt, Brace & World, 1967), 134–35.

96. Hall, *Separation of Church and State*, 46.

97. Williams, *Bloody Tenent*, in *Complete Writings*, 3:376–80.

98. This point has consistently been overlooked in part, I believe, because scholars either have underplayed the importance of the natural rights idea in Calvin's thought, which is such an important foundation of Williams's political outlook, or have failed to connect Williams to that tradition. For example, Brian Tierney, in an article on natural rights and religious freedom, claims incorrectly that Williams never used rights language. Brian Tierney, "Religious Rights: An Historical Perspective," in *Religious Human Rights in Global Perspective: Religious Perspectives*, ed. John Witte Jr. and Johan D. Van der Vyver (The Hague: Martinus Nijhoff, 1996), 42. John Witte in his *Reformation of Rights* largely ignores Williams; and Martha Nussbaum, in her otherwise forceful study of liberty of conscience in the American tradition, and of Williams's central place in that tradition, entirely overlooks the natural rights side of Williams's thought. Instead, she mistakenly traces the grounds of Williams's extra-religious appeals to Stoic thought. There is not the slightest evidence in Williams's writings that he paid any attention to the Stoics or other classical sources. His political thought is (liberal) Calvinist through and through. See David Little, "Calvin and Natural Rights," *Political Theology* 10(3) (2009): 411–30, and David Little, "Calvinism, Constitutionalism, and Religious Freedom: An American Dilemma" (forthcoming).

99. Brian Tierney, *The Idea of Natural Rights: Studies on Natural Rights, Natural Law, and Church Law, 1150–1625* (Grand Rapids, MI: Wm. B. Eerdmans, 1997), 76.

100. Sumner Twiss has elaborately and persuasively elucidated Williams's doctrine of natural rights in his brilliant paper, "Roger Williams and Freedom of Conscience and Religion as a Natural Right" (unpublished).

101. Williams, *Bloody Tenent*, in *Complete Writings*, 3:398.

102. Williams, *Bloody Tenent Yet More Bloody*, in *Complete Writings*, 4:365.

103. Williams, *A Key into the Language of America*. 1644; repr. ed. (Bedford, MA: Applewood Books, 1997), and excerpted in Miller, ed., *Roger Williams*.

104. Miller, ed., Roger Williams, 64.

105. Ibid., 62–64.

Toleration and Diversity in New Netherland and the Duke's Colony

THE ROOTS OF AMERICA'S FIRST DISESTABLISHMENT

Paul Finkelman*

In 1777, in the midst of the American Revolution, the newly created State of New York adopted its first constitution. Drafted mostly by John Jay, New York's first constitution is generally considered to be one of the best of the first American constitutions.[1] For scholars and citizens interested in religious liberty, the New York constitution stands out for two reasons. It was the only *new* state constitution to prohibit all state establishments of religion. Equally important, it was the only state constitution that *did not* include a religious test for office-holding.[2] This chapter explores the roots of this dramatic and truly revolutionary change in law.

New York's First Constitution and Religion

In 1684 the new royal governor, Thomas Dongan, arrived in New York. He was a practicing Catholic, appointed to govern a colony that was officially Anglican and British, with a plurality of settlers who were Calvinist and Dutch. Surveying his new domain, Governor Dongan reported to his superiors: "Here bee not many of the Church of England; [a] few Roman Catholicks; abundance of Quakers preachers men and women especially; Singing Quakers, Ranting Quakers; Sabbatarians; Antisabbatarians; Some Anabaptists; some Independents; some Jews; in short of all opinions there are some, and the most part none at all."[3] Dongan was charged with cementing the established Anglican Church, but in the end he would mostly fail.

New York would remain nominally Anglican until the Revolution, but it was mostly an establishment in name only. In 1777, while the Revolution raged with the outcome uncertain, New York became the first state to abandon any pretense of a religious establishment and the only revolutionary state that did not have a religious test for office-holding.[4] Recognizing the special needs of Quakers, the constitution provided them with alternatives for taking oaths and fulfilling their military obligations.[5]

Another clause banned clergymen from holding "any civil or military office or place within this State."[6] For New Yorkers, this was an important step toward religious freedom and disestablishment. In Great Britain, Anglican bishops sat in Parliament, and chancellors in equity were traditionally high clergy. New Yorkers understood that when clergymen held office, political liberty and religious liberty were threatened. They remembered that a keystone of the tyranny of King Charles I was his official religious intolerance and his use of the Church of England for political purposes. No reasonably educated American needed to be reminded that even before the regicide of Charles I in 1649, the Parliamentarians had justly beheaded the hated Archbishop William Laud, whose established church had been an arm of Stuart authoritarianism. Similarly, Americans recalled that King James II had tried to use a Catholic army to impose tyranny on the people of England, and to use the leading bishops in the realm (who also sat in Parliament) to subvert the liberties of Englishmen. The refusal of the bishops to support the king's attempt to undermine Parliament and the fundamental rights of Englishmen led to the *Case of the Seven Bishops* and then to the Glorious Revolution.[7] Although the bishops were the heroes at that moment, New Yorkers understood that the bishops of the established English church could easily use their power to threaten liberty. Indeed, from the perspective of revolutionaries who wrote the New York constitution, the Anglican support for the king in the ongoing struggle with Great Britain simply underscored the dangers of an established church. With this background, New York banned clergy from political office to help prevent a comingling of church and state.

The new state constitution's most important provision on religion began with a scathing attack on established churches, declaring that "benevolent principles of rational liberty" were required "not only to expel tyranny" but to "guard against that spiritual oppression and intolerance wherewith the bigotry and ambition of weak and wicked priests and princes have scourged mankind."[8] To prevent this, New York declared that "the free exercise and enjoyment of religious profession and worship, without discrimination or preference, shall forever hereafter be allowed, within this State, to all mankind."[9]

This clause is rightly seen as one of the most important statements of free exercise in the new nation. But, it is also a clear rejection of any sort of establishment. It equated an establishment of religion with "civil tyranny," "spiritual oppression," "intolerance," and "bigotry," while arguing that establishments led to "weak and wicked priests and princes" who "scourged mankind."[10] The reference to "priests" may have reflected prevailing fears of Catholicism, but more likely, the phrase was a direct reference to the Anglican priests such as

Archbishop Laud, who had been aligned with King Charles I, and the Anglican hierarchy aligned with King George III in opposition to the American Revolution.

More important than the clauses proclaiming religious liberty were the absent clauses. Unlike other state constitutions, New York's founding document had no religious tests for office-holding.[11] Nor was there any clause establishing a church or recognizing an official church, or indeed, any church.[12] In New York, separation was assumed as was political equality for people of all faiths. The ban on clergy officeholders, specific tolerance for Quakers, and condemnations of the "wicked priests and princes [who] have scourged mankind" reinforced this separation.

How did New York almost completely[13] avoid the religious discrimination and state establishments found in all of the other new states? What made it different from other states on political rights? Why was New York's position on free exercise so emphatic? The answers to these questions are rooted in the earliest history of New York, and the Dutch predecessor colony, New Netherland. To understand this history, we must begin by looking at the concept of toleration and establishment in Western Europe at the moment of North American settlement and then turn to the Dutch experience in New Netherland.

Religious Toleration in the Establishment World of the Seventeenth Century

At the beginning of the seventeenth century—the eve of British and Dutch settlement of the New World—virtually all European political leaders accepted the idea that religious diversity was dangerous to the stability of any government. Most Europeans believed that in any kingdom the ruler and the subjects should have the same religion. Political leaders and political theorists alike assumed that religious difference would inevitably lead to internal social conflict or even civil war and anarchy. The brutal wars of the sixteenth century certainly reinforced this idea. The Peace of Augsburg in 1555 reflected such theories, as it established the rule of *cuius regio, eius religio* (whose region, his religion). This rule allowed local rulers to decide the religion of their subjects. Some rulers allowed Jews or, in the Mediterranean area, Muslims, to live as subjugated residents but not citizens. A few places also allowed dissident Christians to reside, although usually in deeply circumscribed circumstances. Religious diversity among Christians was simply too dangerous for most jurisdictions. European leaders reaffirmed this principle in the Peace of Westphalia (1648), the treaty that ended the Thirty Years War.

In the seventeenth century the one great exception to this general rule was the Netherlands.[14] In the late sixteenth century the Netherlands began to emerge as the most tolerant nation in Europe. English separatists, who would eventually be known as the Pilgrims who settled the Plymouth Colony in 1620, initially found refuge in Leiden, Holland. By the 1620s, Amsterdam's Jews, although officially second-class citizens, "enjoyed virtual freedom of religion in all essential respects." Some Jews were actually granted citizenship. Roman Catholics were more despised than Jews in Holland, but nevertheless, despite the best efforts of the Dutch Reformed Church (Nederlandse Hervormde Kerk), "Roman Catholicism flourished in Amsterdam." By the 1630s "in practice the Roman Catholics had total religious freedom in Amsterdam" in terms of their actual practice, although "they could build no churches with towers in the public streets."[15]

Dutch toleration was not designed to undermine the established Dutch Reformed Church, and it did not, because the church in Holland was deeply entrenched and embraced the overwhelming majority of the population. Members of minority faiths were few in number, and were in no position to disrupt society. Some, such as the Jews and the Plymouth separatists, were simply grateful to have been given a place of refuge and had no interest in challenging existing church–state relations. Disestablishment was certainly not on anyone's mind in the early seventeenth century, even in the Netherlands. Almost all European leaders believed that if only one faith was practiced in a particular place, there was no need to think about separating religion from the state. At most, some people in Holland (and a few elsewhere) were beginning to argue for toleration, but even that was rare. This was before the appearance of John Milton's *Areopagitica* (1644) or John Locke's *Letter Concerning Toleration* (1689), which coupled at least limited religious toleration with disestablishment of religion. Religious toleration in Holland did not threaten the established church.[16]

This tolerance partially migrated to the New World along with the Dutch flag. In 1624, the same year the New Amsterdam settlement began, the Dutch West India Company (Westindische Compagnie—the WIC) also seized the Portuguese colony at Bahia, in Brazil. Six years later, the WIC seized Pernambuco, with its main city of Recife. Jews in Amsterdam helped finance these adventures in Brazil, and Jewish soldiers were heavily involved in the military operations that led to Dutch rule. Once the colony was in Dutch hands, the WIC guaranteed Jews freedom of religion in the privacy of their homes, and ordered that no Dutch official should "molest them or subject them to inquiries in matters of conscience."[17] By the mid-1640s there were 850 to 1,000 Jews in Dutch Brazil, and they constituted about half of the European population of Recife.[18] Thus, religious pluralism came to the Dutch New World early. However, the issues of tolerance and establishment were more complicated in the New Netherland colony, established the same year the WIC invaded Brazil.

The Dutch who arrived at Manhattan in 1624 were not seeking religious freedom. Nor did they hope to create any sort of idealistic city on a hill, as the Puritans would do years later in Massachusetts.[19] New Netherland was a purely commercial venture, sponsored by the private investors of the WIC. Settlement was necessary for economic success and the "Nineteen Directors" (the Heeren XIX) of the Company in Holland, wanted to have a harmonious colony. In addition to administrators, they arranged for clerics from the Dutch Reformed Church to provide for the spiritual needs and guidance of the settlers.

The WIC accepted the prevailing Western notion that an established church would aid in maintaining public order and help provide stability in the new community perched on the edge of their known world. At the same time, because Holland had greater religious freedom than anywhere else in the West, the leaders of the WIC understood the value of toleration and sometimes took advantage of it, as the involvement of large numbers of Jews in their adventure in Brazil illustrates. However, at first the New Netherland colony was far less cosmopolitan than the colony in Brazil. The WIC officials in Manhattan and at Fort Orange (now Albany, New York) hoped to establish a Dutch colony with a homogenous population of settlers who spoke the same language and attended the same church. In this way the organizers of the Dutch colony resembled the nearby British colonies in Virginia and Plymouth.

Early on, however, the leaders of the WIC in Holland began to stress the importance of tolerance, and in so doing, began to undermine the Dutch Reformed establishment in New Netherland. In 1638 the WIC declared that religion in New Netherland should "be taught and practiced" according to the same "confession and formalities of union" that were "publicly accepted" in Holland. This meant that the Dutch Reformed Church was the established church of the colony. But the WIC leaders also declared that this directive should be implemented "without . . . it being inferred from this that any person shall hereby in any wise be constrained or aggrieved in his conscience."[20] Significantly, at the time of this directive there were no known religious dissidents in the New Netherland colony.

Although the Heeren XIX in Amsterdam endorsed religious toleration, the New Netherland religious and secular authorities, especially under Director-General Petrus Stuyvesant, were not particularly tolerant of other faiths. They believed that religious toleration was dangerous to the stability of the colony. These Dutch Calvinists "interpreted a harmonious state to mean one in which the magistracy and church worked together to preserve doctrine and therefore civil unity. Conversely, they held that doctrinal diversity must necessarily lead to civil anarchy and disintegration of the state."[21] Theirs was a weak and underdeveloped colony, precariously sandwiched between French settlements to the north, powerful Indian tribes to the west, and strong English colonies to the east and south. "Because the colony was intended to be an efficient, disciplined trading center in a strange and unaccommodating wilderness, its leaders thought it essential to enforce existing social controls in a rigorous manner."[22]

The rulers of New Netherland naturally established the Dutch Reformed Church.

Initially, the colonial officials were able to sustain religious homogeneity. All of the first settlers were Dutch, and all were presumptively members of the Dutch Reformed Church. Although some probably only attended church when forced, none offered a different or dissenting view of religion. But the goal of homogeneity could not be maintained. Refugees, including the religiously oppressed, were more likely to move to the New World than were prosperous and contented Dutch citizens. Furthermore, the Dutch in Europe also undermined the intolerance of New Netherland. Despite persecution by the local authorities, members of other faiths moved to the colony in the 1640s and 1650s. The Heeren XIX usually allowed these outsiders to settle in the colony and granted them some religious freedom, often overruling the local colonial officials on these matters. Once they were allowed to live in the colony, these religious dissenters from the Dutch Reformed Church and other religious outsiders quickly sought other privileges, including citizenship and the right of public religious observance. When denied the latter right they appealed to authorities in Holland and sometimes practiced their religion in defiance of local authorities.

Thus, within a short time, the New Netherland colony became cosmopolitan, as people from much of the known world and practitioners of numerous faiths arrived. In particular, the presence of English Protestants, Jews, Quakers, and Lutherans led to pluralism that eventually undermined the established Dutch Reformed Church.

English Protestants

In 1640 a few Puritans from Massachusetts settled at Southampton, near the southeastern end of Long Island. Although encroaching on Dutch territory, they were so far from New Amsterdam that they posed no threat to the colony. In the next few years other English settlers drifted into the colony. Director-General Willem Kieft allowed these English dissenters to settle there, offering them not only religious freedom, but also "the liberty to appoint their own magistrates," subject to the approval of the Dutch leadership.[23] With Kieft's blessing Lady Deborah Moody, an Anabaptist, started a settlement on the southwestern tip of Long Island at Gravesend, in what is today Brooklyn. Moody opened her settlement to other dissenters, including Quakers. More famously, she allowed the radical Calvinist Anne Hutchinson, who had been expelled from Massachusetts, to move to what is now the Bronx, at Pelham Bay. Other English refugees settled in present-day Brooklyn, Queens, and farther out on Long Island. These refugees from New England orthodoxy tended to live by themselves in small villages and communities. They did not threaten Dutch hegemony or Dutch Reformed orthodoxy, while at the same time, they added much to the colony.[24]

Moreover, most were Calvinists, like the Dutch, although some, like Hutchinson, were extreme in their views and practices, and others like Lady Moody were even more radical in their beliefs. Thus, already in the early 1640s New Netherland accommodated a small number of non-Dutch Protestants because they would help populate the large and mostly empty colony.

The English Calvinist settlers were theologically close to the Dutch Reformed Church and posed no obvious threat to the colony's established orthodoxy. The non-Calvinists settled far from New Amsterdam, and thus were less threatening to the established church. Lady Moody's Anabaptist theology might have been troublesome, but as she had settled on the tip of what is now Brooklyn, she was well away from the center of New Netherland politics and culture. She was also quite circumspect in her religious practice, content to bother no one if no one bothered her. The more radical Anne Hutchinson might have been more problematic, but she was killed by Indians less than a year after she settled on Pelham Bay, which was also well away from the main settlement in New Amsterdam. More English settled at Flushing, Hempstead, and other places in what is today Queens and western Long Island. Although not challenging the established church, these outsiders nevertheless posed some threats to the nature of the Dutch Reformed establishment. Their very presence made New Netherland religiously diverse, and thus the established church did not have full control and authority over everyone in the colony. In addition, alternative religions, even those such as Puritanism that were compatible with the Dutch Reformed Church, offered competition to the established church. In Massachusetts Anne Hutchinson had proved that a charismatic voice from a different religious viewpoint could be dangerous to the established religious and political authorities. John Winthrop and the other Bay Colony leaders solved the problem of Hutchinson by expelling her.[25] Clearly, settlers who did not accept the official church were a potential threat to the establishment. In the 1650s some of these English settlements would become politically problematic for the Dutch authorities as they gave sanctuary to Quakers and undermined the Dutch Reformed establishment. In 1664 these English settlers would welcome the British seizure of the colony. But initially, in the 1640s, they were seen as isolated and innocuous. The presence of Lutherans, Jews, and Quakers was more problematic. By the time these immigrants arrived, Director-General Kieft had been removed in disgrace. His replacement was the most important colonial and longest-serving governor of New Netherland or New York: Petrus Stuyvesant.

Petrus Stuyvesant and the Non-Dutch Immigrants

Petrus Stuyvesant, the Director-General of the colony after 1646, was a professional soldier who had lost a limb fighting the Spanish. The peg-legged Director-General was "fiercely patriotic, fearless in battle, capable of towering rages, and an autocratic leader with a reputation for discipline and work."[26] The WIC sent him to the New World to bring order and stability to a teetering colony run by a company that was going bankrupt. He replaced Willem Kieft, who had nearly destroyed the colony in an unnecessary and costly Indian war. Stuyvesant "arrived in New Netherland at the colony's darkest hour, and he must have fancied himself something of a savior because from the moment he stepped ashore he became a whirlwind of activity, issuing proclamations, closing down brothels and taverns, and setting a new tone of optimism." The colonists never loved Stuyvesant, or even liked him; rather they "respected" and "feared" him. Despite his arrogance, narrow-mindedness, and authoritarianism, Stuyvesant was "the most capable man the Company had ever sent" to govern New Netherland.[27] His autocratic nature probably saved the colony from total chaos in the late 1640s and into the 1650s, but in the end his authoritarianism also undermined Dutch rule, so that the English takeover of the colony in 1664 would be accomplished without firing a shot. The English offered fair terms, and the burghers of New Amsterdam were quick to surrender their colony and their Director-General.

A towering figure in early American history and in the history of New York, Stuyvesant looms even larger in the history of American Jews, as I will note below. He was the first official to encounter the Jews, and the first to espouse an anti-Semitic response to them. He is, in a sense, an American Haman: He tried to do harm to the Jews and was stopped before he could complete his work.

However, Stuyvesant's response to the Jews must be put in a larger perspective. The WIC had sent him to run the colony and to rescue it from mismanagement and chaos. The son of a clergyman, Stuyvesant was an elder in the Dutch Reformed Church who "believed strongly in the Old World axiom that the combined forces of church and state were the best promoters of morality and social harmony."[28] Basically, he was opposed to the arrival of anyone who was not Dutch. Furthermore, he preferred that any Dutch who came to New Netherland be members of the Dutch Reformed Church. His attempts to expel the twenty-three Jewish refugees from Dutch Brazil in 1654, for which is he infamously known, must be seen in part as the actions of a political functionary trying to implement what he deeply believed were the policies best suited for the colony. His actions were colored by his strong devotion to the Dutch Reformed Church, his xenophobia, and his anti-Semitism. But Stuyvesant's anti-Semitism, although transparent and hateful, was in the end not particularly vicious, especially when compared to his response to other religious outsiders. He allowed the Jews to land in New Amsterdam, and while trying to get rid of them, he did not physically abuse them. Unlike the Lutherans, Quakers, and even some Puritans, he never jailed any Jews. His preferred method was "to require them in a friendly way to depart,"[29] which was far more gentle than throwing them in jail until he could put them on the next ship leaving his colony, which is how he later treated some Lutherans and Quakers. In the spring of 1655 he was preparing to place the Jews on ships to send them to Holland, but was still waiting for authorization to do so. By contrast, he did not even seek authorization to do this to some Lutherans and Quakers and jailed them while waiting to expel them.

Stuyvesant's response to the Recife Jews contrasts sharply with his response to the arrival of Quakers three years later. The Director-General tried to prevent Quakers from even landing in the colony, and when they secretly came ashore he jailed them under horrible conditions. The response of others in the Dutch colony to the presence of Jews, especially that of Dutch Reformed cleric Dominie Johannes Megapolensis, also reveals a nasty anti-Semitism that was directly tied to the public policy of the colony. Yet, even as Rev. Megapolensis wrote anti-Semitic tirades to his superiors in Holland, he also provided the Jews with charity through the winter of 1654–1655. The contradictions between the words of Stuyvesant and Megapolensis and their actions toward Jews, Lutherans, and Quakers underscore the complexity of religious liberty and establishment in New Netherland.

The Lutherans

The experience of the Lutherans in New Netherland illustrates the connection between toleration and establishment. The authorities in New Netherland vigorously opposed the presence of Lutherans because they threatened the Dutch Reformed establishment. Lutherans were eventually given some religious liberty in the colony, and their presence in fact did undermine the establishment.

In 1648 the Dutch began to encroach on the Swedish settlements to the south, and the final Dutch victory in 1655 extended New Netherland to present-day Wilmington, Delaware. Meanwhile, in 1649 Lutherans from Holland (where they had substantial religious freedom) began to drift into the colony.[30] In 1653, the year before the Jews arrived, the Dutch Lutherans in the colony asked for the right to import a minister and build a church. Local leaders of church and state opposed this request in an effort to protect the established church. The ministers emphatically argued that a Lutheran minister and church "would tend to the injury of our [Dutch Reformed] church, the diminution of hearers of the Word of God, and increase of dissensions." They feared it would "pave the way for other sects, so that in time our place [the New Netherland colony] would become the receptacle of all sorts of heretics and fanatics." They happily noted that Director-General Stuyvesant agreed that allowing a Lutheran minister and church would be "contrary to the first article of his commission," which required that he not allow "any other than the Reformed doctrine." The ministers reported that Stuyvesant was "zealous for the Reformed Religion" and "would rather relinquish his office than grant permission" for the Lutherans to have a minister or a church.[31] Toleration and establishment simply could not coexist, at least in the mind of Stuyvesant and the colony's Dutch Reformed ministers, Johannes Megapolensis and Samuel Drisius.

The Heeren XIX agreed with the Dutch Reformed clergy, resolving in February 1654 that no Lutheran ministers would be allowed in the colony.[32] Stuyvesant's opposition to the Lutherans did not end here, however. In 1655 he summarily expelled two Lutheran ministers from the recently captured colony at New Sweden (Delaware), although one who was too ill to travel was allowed to stay for the short term.[33] The subsequent treaty with Sweden ceding the territory to the Dutch allowed the remaining Swedes to keep this minister and openly practice their faith. But, what Stuyvesant had to allow in the old Swedish colony, because of the treaty, did not affect his rule in the rest of New Netherland.

In 1656 the Lutherans once again demanded a minister to serve the New Netherland colony, arguing that in Holland Lutherans were allowed to practice their faith openly. Stuyvesant responded by publishing a "placaat," which was the equivalent of an executive order or ordinance, against the Lutherans, and then jailing some of them.[34] The Heeren XIX reprimanded Stuyvesant for both acts. The WIC would not allow the Lutherans to have a church or a minister, but objected to their persecution. The Heeren XIX ordered Stuyvesant to "let them have free religious exercises in their houses."[35] Lutherans in Holland then directly petitioned the WIC for the right to have public worship and a minister in the colony, and in October the Lutherans in New Netherland petitioned Stuyvesant for the same right, claiming that the Directors of the WIC in Holland had allowed this. The authorities in New Amsterdam denied the request, reiterating that the Lutherans were only allowed private worship, and sent the petition to the Heeren XIX in Holland. The Lutherans in New Amsterdam argued that if their coreligionists in what had been New Sweden could have a minister, so should they. But, in March 1657 the Heeren XIX reaffirmed that the Lutherans could not have a church or a minister.[36] Significantly, at least three Lutherans were Directors of the WIC at this time, but they were unable to win the right to public worship for their coreligionists.

The leaders of the WIC understood, as did Stuyvesant and Rev. Megapolensis, that allowing a real Lutheran church in New Netherland would in fact undermine the Dutch Reformed establishment. This position illustrates how establishment required some religious suppression and significant denials of free exercise. The Dutch Reformed Church feared it could not maintain its power in the face of competition from nonestablished churches, such as the Lutherans.

The Lutherans were not satisfied, however, with worshipping at home without a preacher. They directly petitioned the States-General, Holland's legislature, for relief, but at the same time smuggled a minister, Rev. Johannes

Ernestus Gutwasser, from Holland into the New Netherland colony.[37] In response, in July, Revs. Megapolensis and Drisius petitioned the New Amsterdam government to prevent the Lutherans from having a minister and having full religious freedom. They warned that, if this happened, "the Papist, Mennonites, and others, would soon make similar claims. Thus we would soon become a Babel of confusion, instead of remaining a united and peaceful people. Indeed it would prove a plan of Satan to smother this infant, rising congregation, almost in its birth, or at least to obstruct the march of its truth in its progress."[38] The "rising congregation" was, of course, the Dutch Reformed Church in New Netherland. Significantly, while worrying about "a Babel of confusion," the Dutch Reformed ministers did not mention any threats from the city's small Jewish community. The real threats to the established church came from other Christians, especially Lutherans, Mennonites, Quakers, and Catholics.

New Amsterdam's officials responded quickly to the petition of the Dutch ministers concerning the Lutheran minister, Rev. Gutwasser. The mayor and aldermen ordered Rev. Gutwasser to appear before them to respond to the charges that he was secretly a Lutheran minister. He did not deny this. In fact, he "frankly answered, he had been sent on behalf of their [the Lutheran's] Consistory, to occupy the position of a preacher here, as far as it would be allowed." He also claimed that the Heeren XIX were sending a "letter of permit" to allow him to preach in New Netherland. The local officials explained these events to the WIC and expressed grave doubts that "the Hon. Directors would tolerate in this place any other doctrine, than the true Reformed Religion." The city officials ordered Rev. Gutwasser "not to hold public or private exercise" in New Amsterdam until they heard back from the Directors in Holland.[39]

In October Stuyvesant resolved the crisis by ordering Rev. Gutwasser to leave the colony immediately. The Lutherans and Gutwasser protested and petitioned, but to no avail. Having missed the opportunity to leave on his own, Gutwasser was arrested and summarily forced to sail back to Europe, or at least that is what was reported to the Directors of the WIC. In May 1658 the Heeren XIX confirmed that Stuyvesant had been correct in expelling Gutwasser: "That you have sent back here the Lutheran preacher is not contrary to, but rather in accordance with our good intentions." Significantly, in contrast to his treatment of Jews, which I discuss below, Stuyvesant did this without prior authorization of the WIC Directors in Amsterdam. Although the Directors approved what Stuyvesant did, they thought he "might have proceeded less vigorously." The Directors suggested that next time something like this happened, the Director-General should "use the least offensive, and most tolerant means" of removing an unwanted clergyman "so that people of other persuasions may not be deterred" from attending the Dutch Reformed Church, "but in time [might] be induced to listen and finally gained over."[40]

Meanwhile, Gutwasser had not actually left the colony, but had "concealed himself with a Lutheran farmer." In the summer of 1658 he was discovered. In reporting this to Stuyvesant, the Dutch Reformed ministers noted that the "perverseness" of the Lutherans had "led them to make false representations" to the government. Once again Stuyvesant took steps finally to remove Pastor Gutwasser, but the Lutherans protested that their spiritual leader was too ill to travel. The government granted him time to recover.[41] Meanwhile, Gutwasser continued to evade expulsion and to preach. Finally, in the spring of 1659 Stuyvesant had Gutwasser arrested and placed on a ship, which took him back to Holland.

In September the Dutch clerics reported that there was "now again quietness among the people" because the Lutherans were attending the Dutch Reformed Church. The established church was winning the battle, not with theological arguments, persuasive preaching, or Christian charity and benevolence, but with the tried-and-true method of established churches: force and repression. Revs. Megapolensis and Drisius worried that the Lutherans were still planning to try to bring a minister over. But for the moment, "imminent injury to this infant church" had "been averted" by the "vigilance and discretion of the Dutch ministers and the Director-General." In Holland the authorities of the Dutch Reformed Church reported that "The minister Gutwasser, has been put in jail and was sent to the Fatherland [Holland] with the first ships." The Assembly of the Church in Amsterdam "rejoiced in this."[42]

The crisis over Rev. Gutwasser had ended, and from the perspective of Stuyvesant and the Dutch Reformed Church this was cause for rejoicing. But the Lutherans did not go away. In 1660 Lutherans at Fort Orange (Albany) began to collect money to bring over a preacher. No Lutheran minister seems to have been brought over at this time, but the fear continued to rattle the Dutch clergy in the colony. Finally, in 1666 the new governor of what was by then the New York colony would grant Lutherans religious freedom and the right to have their own ministers.[43]

While Megapolensis and Drisius were battling the Lutherans and Gutwasser, they sent a very long letter to the religious authorities in Amsterdam, discussing the situation in New Amsterdam. They complained about the Lutheran pastor, and explained how they had petitioned the local government demanding his expulsion. They also complained about the Swedes in Delaware and the fact that the "Swedish Governor made a condition in his capitulation, they might retain one Lutheran preacher," which in fact they had. The Dutch clergy declared that this preacher was "a man of impious and scandalous habits, a wild, drunken, unmannerly clown, more inclined to look into the wine can than into the Bible." He would, they proclaimed, "prefer drinking brandy two hours to preaching one," and he often "wants to fight whomever he meets." The ministers also complained about Englishmen on Long Island, Mennonites who "reject the baptism of infants," and a "cobbler from Rhode

Island" who had come to preach "saying he had a commission from Christ." They worried about "Independents" and Presbyterians in some towns and Puritans in others. In a postscript they noted the arrival, in early August, of Quakers. The ministers at first thought the Quakers had all gone on to Rhode Island, "for that is the receptacle of all sorts of riff-raff people, and is nothing else than the sewer [*latrina*] of New England." But then they discovered that a few Quakers had secretly landed in New Netherland. Fortunately, the ministers reported these Quakers had been jailed and so they hoped "God will baffle the designs of the devil" and save the colony from "these machinations of Satan."[44]

While defeating the threat from the Lutherans, the leaders of the Dutch establishment were also fighting a second front against religious pluralism. This one probably did not really threaten the established Dutch church, except to the extent that any diversity threatens an establishment, and any precedent for diversity might be used by people of other faiths. This second front came from a tiny and virtually powerless group of Jews.[45]

The Jews

In 1654 twenty-three Jewish refugees from Recife arrived in New Amsterdam aboard a Dutch ship, the *St. Catrina*.[46] They had been part of the WIC settlement in Brazil and had fled when the Portuguese recaptured the colony. Most of these Jews in this colony escaped back to Holland, but those on the *St. Catrina* ended up in New Amsterdam. This first Jewish migration holds a special and iconic place in American Jewish history as the beginning of three-and-a-half centuries of Jewish transplantation to America. Almost immediately Director-General Stuyvesant and the leaders of the Dutch Reformed establishment tried to expel these Jews, but were thwarted by the Heeren XIX. In part this outcome resulted from the intervention of Jews in Amsterdam, but it probably was just as much a function of the WIC's own notions of both tolerance and the need for settlers. Eventually the Jews secured the right to stay, and although the Recife refugees did not particularly prosper—in fact most of them seem to have left the colony within a decade after their arrival—their subsequent coreligionists did prosper. Indeed, although the Puritans in Massachusetts Bay, with their established church, were never able to create a "New Jerusalem" for themselves, as their founding Governor John Winthrop had hoped, Jewish immigrants eventually accomplished that for themselves in the Golden Medina. The creation of this new Promised Land began in New Amsterdam in 1654.

The arrival of these Jews is also a key moment in the development of toleration—and the ultimate undermining of establishment—in New Netherland and later New York. Their arrival and their struggle to remain in the colony illustrates the complexity of allowing a diverse religious culture in the Dutch colony. When placed in the context of the earlier arrival of Lutherans and the later arrival of Quakers, the Jewish story tells us much about free exercise and establishment in this period.

The traditional story of the arrival of the first Jews is in part incorrect. The twenty-three refugees from Dutch Brazil were not in fact the first Jews in the colony. During the summer of 1654 "some Jews came from Holland" as merchants.[47] In late August of 1654, Jacob Barsimson[48] arrived in New Amsterdam on the *Peereboom* from Amsterdam. He paid seventy-two florins for his passage, which indicates that he did not come empty-handed. He may have been sent there by Jews in Holland to investigate the possibility of encouraging further Jewish emigration to New Netherland.[49] He is probably the first Jewish immigrant into what would become the United States, but it is possible that Asser Levy and Solomon Pietersen were also on this ship.[50] Alternatively, they may have come earlier, and thus would supplant Barsimson as the "first" Jew in the colony. The arrival of Barsimson, Levy, Pieterson, and perhaps other Jews before the Recife refugees is not simply of antiquarian interest—a search for the "first" Jew in what became the United States. Rather, the reaction to the arrival of Barsimson and the other Jews is important because it sheds light on how we understand Stuyvesant's response to the subsequent arrival of the Portuguese Jews.

Significantly, neither the civil officials in New Amsterdam nor the Dutch religious leaders seem to have been bothered by the trickling in of Dutch Jews in the summer of 1654. Their arrivals are matter-of-factly reported without any editorial comment or very much detail. From the records it is impossible to know how many Jews came before the twenty-three arrived from Recife, or even who all of them were. There are a number of complex reasons for this. Because these Jews were coming directly from Holland, they were not foreigners, even though from the perspective of Dutch Reformed establishment they followed a foreign faith. Barsimson apparently came at the behest of the Dutch West India Company, with a passport or some other papers "as one of a party of emigrants from Holland sent" by the Company.[51] It would have been politically inexpedient, or worse, for Director-General Stuyvesant to have challenged Barsimson's right to be there or even complained about his presence. This is also true for the Dutch Reformed clergy. They clearly believed that the presence of religious minorities in their community threatened their hegemony, but the clergymen were in no position to protest when non-Reformed immigrants came directly from Holland, especially if they came under the auspices of the WIC.

Even though he did not want Dutch Jews in his community, Stuyvesant must have known that Jews in Holland had relative religious freedom at this time. In the 1570s the Dutch Republic had established freedom of religious practice, and in 1585 the Dutch States General had invited Jewish merchants in

Antwerp to move to Amsterdam, where they were promised freedom. In the 1590s the Amsterdam city council granted citizenship to a few Sephardic merchants, even though citizenship was in theory only available to members of the Dutch Reformed Church. As one scholar recently noted, "It is likely that once these Portuguese immigrants settled in Amsterdam and shared their valuable trade connections with the Dutch merchants the authorities closed their eyes to the fact that they had really let in Jews."[52] These few Jewish citizens did not threaten the established church in Holland, but they did illustrate the importance of toleration in the Netherlands. At the time of Dutch settlement of the New World, Jews in Holland had established synagogues, burial grounds, schools, and rabbinical leadership. By the standards of the period, they had enormous religious freedom, despite their lack of political and legal equality. Amsterdam's eight hundred or so Jewish residents had three synagogues before the English Pilgrims migrated to Plymouth in 1620. In 1642 the Prince of Orange made an official state visit to the newly consecrated Portuguese Synagogue.[53] After the Peace of Munster (1648) Dutch authorities insisted (although with little success) that Dutch Jews should have the same rights as other Dutch citizens when doing business in Spain. They were allowed to be naturalized citizens, although they could not inherit citizenship, and, unlike almost everywhere else in Europe, they were allowed to attend universities. Barred from many professions, including the law, they were mostly merchants, physicians, and especially book publishers.[54] By 1630 Amsterdam would be "the chief centre of Hebrew printing for the entire Jewish world." In general, Dutch Jews would "play a larger role . . . in commerce, finance, colonial trade, intellectual life, and publishing. . . . than was possible before the 1790s in any other European country."[55] A few invested in the WIC. As Jacob Marcus observed, "As far as the Jew was concerned, in no place was the new age of tolerance better documented than Holland."[56] Thus, it would have been inappropriate—almost anti-Dutch—for the authorities in New Amsterdam to complain about the arrival of Barsimson and any other Dutch Jews in 1654.

The situation in New Amsterdam changed dramatically in early September 1654, with the arrival of the twenty-three Jewish refugees from Recife. We do not know whether these Jews went directly to New Amsterdam or came by a circuitous route that may have included an unplanned and unwanted stop in the Spanish Caribbean,[57] but by the time they arrived, they were virtually penniless and were sued for nonpayment of their passage. The spokesman for this group of "23 souls, big and little," was Solomon Pietersen, described in the record as "a Jew." Pietersen was not, however, one of the twenty-three refugees. Rather, he was one of the "first" Jews who came to New Amsterdam in the summer of 1654, before the arrival of the Recife refugees.[58]

Once these debts were finally settled the Jews had little to survive on. The Recife refugees immediately became dependent on the charity of the colonial government, the Dutch Reformed Church, and individual Dutch settlers. Rev.

Megapolensis "directed them to the Jewish merchants" who had arrived that summer. Megapolensis thought "it would have been proper, that they should have been supported by their own people." But, according to Megapolensis's account, the Dutch Jews in the colony "would not even lend them a few stivers," and thus he later reported, "they have been at our charge, so that we have had to spend several hundred guilders for their support." He complained that the Jews from Recife "came several times to my house, weeping and bemoaning their misery."[59]

It is not clear from Megapolensis's account if the "we" and "our" in this letter refers to the New Amsterdam government, the Dutch Reformed Church, or both. It is also not clear if Megapolensis personally gave them alms when they came "weeping" to his house or only gave them money from the church's coffers.[60] What is clear, however, is that Megapolensis thought the Jews to be an unnecessary burden on the community.

Compounding Megapolensis's complaints over the cost of supporting these Jews was his assumption that the refugees were planning to remain and develop a community. The twenty-three consisted of four families, including children who would presumably begin to make families of their own in the not-too-distant future. That the Jews wanted to stay in New Amsterdam made sense. They were homeless, stateless people. They had no place to return to, and no nation to protect them. As long as they could stay in New Amsterdam, they indicated they would.[61]

Rev. Megapolensis was not alone in this evaluation of the Jews. Within two weeks of their arrival, Director-General Stuyvesant wrote the WIC, asking permission to expel the Jews. Stuyvesant did not immediately write such a letter because he was apparently waiting to see what the Jewish refugees actually wanted. If they were only planning to stay for a short time, he was willing to offer them sanctuary, just as Rev. Megapolensis begrudgingly gave them food and other charity. But, when Stuyvesant found that "they would nearly all like to remain here," he acted to prevent this break in the high wall of Dutch establishment and hegemony in New Netherland. So, he sought permission from WIC officials "to require them in a friendly way to depart."[62] Stuyvesant offered three reasons for his position.

First, Stuyvesant suggested that the Jews were "very repugnant" to the colony's "magistrates." The source of this repugnancy is not entirely clear, although most likely their Jewishness and the fact that they were not Dutch was enough to make them "repugnant." Their poverty reinforced this view. However, even while worrying about their poverty, Stuyvesant claimed he feared their "customary usury and deceitful trading with the Christians."[63] This standard anti-Semitic canard was especially absurd in light of the actual circumstances of these immigrants. The newly arrived Portuguese Jews could hardly have been involved in moneylending or trading. On the contrary, they were money borrowers, having almost nothing of their own.

These comments, in the context of the previous Jewish immigration, also illustrate the apparent ambivalence of the New Netherland authorities toward Jews. Neither Stuyvesant nor anyone else in the community seems to have been bothered when the Dutch Jewish businessmen—who had come to participate in trade and might very well have become involved in moneylending— arrived earlier that summer. Their arrival did not lead to any anti-Semitic outbursts. Neither Stuyvesant nor Rev. Megapolensis was apparently concerned about Barsimson's business plans. Why then were the authorities in New Amsterdam concerned about the arrival of a few more Jews in September? The two other reasons Stuyvesant gave for wanting to expel these new Jews suggest the answer.

Stuyvesant noted that the church authorities feared that "owing to their present indigence they [the Portuguese Jews] might become a charge in the coming winter."[64] This seems to have been a major concern of both the religious and secular leaders of the colony. In this matter Stuyvesant's desire to force the Portuguese Jews to leave reflected the accepted seventeenth-century solution to the immigration of poor people: expulsion. Simply stated, Director-General Stuyvesant did not feel his colony should be held responsible for the maintenance of poor people from another country. It is likely he would have reacted the same way to indigent immigrants—whatever their religion—from anyplace in the world other than, perhaps, Holland.

Stuyvesant's third reason for wanting to get rid of the new Jews appears, at first glance, to be a classic example of anti-Semitism. On careful examination, however, Stuyvesant's position emerges as more complex. Stuyvesant concluded this portion of his letter to the authorities in Amsterdam with: "praying also most seriously in this connection, for ourselves as also for the general community of your worships, that the deceitful race—such hateful enemies and blasphemers of the name of Christ—not be allowed further to infect and trouble this new colony, to the dissatisfaction of your worships' most affectionate subjects."[65]

The phrases "deceitful race" and "hateful enemies" of Christ suggest the anti-Jewish attitudes of some Calvinists. However, dislike of Jews per se does not seem to have been Stuyvesant's main concern. Rather, he was worried that the Jews would "infect and trouble" the colony. In other words, Stuyvesant saw, correctly, that the presence of practitioners of any faith other than the Dutch Reformed threatened the colony's established church. Although anti-Semitic, Stuyvesant was also deeply concerned with the increasingly polyglot nature of the community. He objected to the Portuguese Jews not merely because they were Jews, but because they threatened the established church and the very Dutchness of the colony. The Jews were doubly dangerous because they threatened both religious and cultural establishments. This analysis is supported by an understanding of how most Europeans viewed ethnic and religious diversity and an examination of how Stuyvesant treated other non-Dutch or non-Calvinist immigrants.

The Jewish Struggle to Remain and the Dutch Establishment

When it became clear that the Recife Jews were planning to remain in New Netherland, both Stuyvesant and Megapolensis asked authorities in Holland to support their expulsion. Both saw this handful of Jews as a threat to the Dutch Reformed establishment in the colony. Megapolensis clearly disliked Jews, who, he believed, had "no other God than the unrighteous Mammon, and no other aim than to get possession of Christian property." He thought Jews were "godless rascals" and hoped authorities in Holland would order their expulsion. Significantly, however, after all of his anti-Semitic rants, Megapolensis did not ultimately make his case for expelling the Jews either on anti-Semitic or on theological grounds. Rather, he argued that if the Jews settled in the community it would be one more step on the road to ethnic and religious chaos that would undermine the established church. He noted "we have here Papists, Mennonites and Lutherans among the Dutch; also many Puritans or Independents, and many Atheists and various other servants of Baal among the English under this government, who conceal themselves under the name of Christians; it would create a still further confusion, if the obstinate and immovable Jews came to settle here."[66] This outburst is fascinating, because it is aimed as much at non-Jews as it is at Jews.

Stuyvesant's response was similar. Although the Recife Jews arrived in September 1654 to a cold welcome, they were allowed to disembark from their ship and initially given some alms. But when Stuyvesant realized these Jews planned to remain, he took steps to expel them. On September 22, 1654, Stuyvesant wrote the Directors of the Company, asking to be allowed to send the Recife Jews away.[67]

In January the Directors of the WIC received a long and detailed petition from a group of Jews in Amsterdam, who referred to themselves as "the merchants of the Portuguese Nation residing in this city [Amsterdam]." They complained that it had "come to their knowledge" that the Directors had "raise[d] obstacles to the giving of permits or passports to the Portuguese Jews to travel and to go to reside in New Netherland, which if persisted in will result to the great disadvantage of the Jewish nation." They also noted it could "be of no advantage to the general company but rather damaging." They reminded the Directors that many of the Portuguese Jews had "lost their possessions at Pernambuco," been oppressed by the Inquisition, and "have at all times been faithful and have striven to guard and maintain" the Dutch colonies in Brazil, "risking for that purpose their possessions and their blood." The petitioners noted that the English and French colonies in the New World were at this time welcoming the Portuguese Jews, and thus the Portuguese Jewish petitioners were perplexed as to why the Amsterdam Jews could not go to all the Dutch colonies. They also noted that some members of their community had been living in that city for "about sixty years" and many in their community were "born here and confirmed burghers." Thus they wondered why, as burghers of the city of Amsterdam, they were not allowed to move to the Dutch settlement.[68]

This was an impressive petition, arguing that politics, economics, foreign policy, loyalty, and fairness all favored Jewish immigration. So too did the reality that the New Netherland colony "needs people for its increase." Significantly, this petition said very little about the Jews from Recife. The Portuguese Jewish community was seeking permission to settle in New Netherland, not just for the twenty-three refugees from Brazil, but also for Jews in Holland who might move to the American colony. The Jewish merchants ended by asking the Heeren XIX to issue a resolution declaring that "the Jewish nation be permitted, together with other inhabitants, to travel, live and traffic there, and with them enjoy liberty on condition of contributing like others."[69]

In effect the petition of the Portuguese Jews was also an offer to help the WIC make New Netherland a success. It was a powerful argument. In April the company emphatically rejected Stuyvesant's request to expel the Jews.[70] The Heeren XIX were clearly unimpressed by Stuyvesant's letter and may have wondered what possessed the Director-General to expend so much energy and time on the arrival of a handful of Jews. Politely, but firmly, they informed him:

> We would have liked to agree to your wishes and request that the new territories should not be further invaded by people of the Jewish race, for we forsee from such immigration the same difficulties which you fear, but after having further weighed and considered the matter, we observe that it would be unreasonable and unfair, especially because of the considerable loss, sustained by the Jews in the taking of Brazil and also because of the large amount of capital, which they have invested in shares of this Company. After many consultations we have decided and resolved upon a certain petition made by said Portuguese Jews, that they shall have permission to sail to and trade in New Netherland and to live and remain there, provided the poor among them shall not become a burden to the Company or the community, but be supported by their own nation. You will govern yourself accordingly.[71]

As they had when the Lutherans arrived, and as they would when Quakers came to the colony, the Directors of the Company acknowledged Stuyvesant's fears that a polyglot community would be difficult. But, this was all they were willing to concede to their Director-General. In rejecting his request for permission to remove the Jews, the Directors reminded Stuyvesant of the important Jewish contributions to the settlements of the WIC in Brazil, pointing out that it would be "unreasonable and unfair, especially because of the considerable loss, sustained by the Jews" in Brazil for the company to now suddenly turn its back on the Jewish refugees from Recife. Morality dictated that the Jews be allowed to stay. So too did good policy, because the Jews had been loyal citizens, brave soldiers, and productive colonists for the Company.

The other reason the WIC Directors gave Stuyvesant was that the Jews had a "large amount of capital" invested in the Company.[72] In fact, only a very few Jews in Amsterdam were actual investors in the Company, and they had not invested much. The "large amount of capital" argument may have been a convenient answer to Stuyvesant, who surely understood that economic influence mattered for the Company. But the relatively small amount of Jewish investment in the Company could not have been decisive. However, Jews in Amsterdam, in addition to those who had invested in the Company, had also contacted the WIC on behalf of their coreligionists in New Amsterdam. That local influence, combined with the mere fact that there were Jewish stockholders, surely had some influence on the Directors of the WIC. Significantly, in this letter the Directors told Stuyvesant they were acting "upon a certain petition made by said Portuguese Jews." This was not a reference to the Jews already in New Netherland, but to the Jews in Holland, the "merchants of the Portuguese Nation" residing in Amsterdam. This petition of Jews in old Amsterdam concerning their own business interests helped determine the fate of the handful of Jews in New Amsterdam.

Finally, the Heeren XIX were influenced by the very practical matter that the WIC needed settlers in the colony. The Jews were there, and they were willing to stay there. They had been good settlers in Recife and the rest of Dutch Brazil. It would have been foolish to expel them from another WIC colony without a very compelling reason. The Heeren XIX knew that these Jews had been loyal residents of the WIC colony in Recife. From Stuyvesant's perspective they may have been foreigners, but from the perspective of the WIC, they were very much a known commodity. All of these reasons combined to frustrate Stuyvesant's goals. The Jews would stay and he would "govern" himself "accordingly." As the petition of the Jewish merchants noted, this was "a land that needs people for its increase."[73]

A year later the Company further strengthened its position on religious diversity. Stuyvesant had been complaining about the continuing presence of Jews, worrying that they would soon want their own house of worship. As with the controversy over the Lutheran minister, here the Directors of the Company could accede to one of the Director-General's demands, but they did so in such a way that could not have made Stuyvesant very happy. In March 1656 the Heeren XIX reaffirmed the "permission given to the *Jews*" to "enjoy" "civil and political rights" but not full religious freedom. They wrote:

> The permission given to the *Jews*, to go to *New-Netherland* and enjoy there the same privileges, as they have here, has been granted only as far as civil and political rights are concerned, without giving the said *Jews* a claim to the privilege of exercising their religion in a synagogue or at a gathering; as long therefore, as you receive no request for granting them this liberty of religious exercise, your considerations and anxiety about this matter, are premature

and when later something shall be said about it, you can do no better, than to refer them to us and await the necessary order.[74]

Thus, the Jews would remain. By this time, as noted above, both the civil and religious authorities were focusing on the dangers, as they saw them, from Lutherans. The Jews were clearly no longer a major annoyance. In addition, because the Jews were clearly outsiders, they did not threaten the established church in the same way that Lutherans did. It was unlikely that any member of the Dutch Reformed Church would suddenly abandon the established church to become Jewish. The Lutherans, however, posed such a threat. So too did other Christian faiths.

The Quakers in New Netherland

The Jews arrived in the midst of the established church's crusade against the Lutherans. Despite Stuyvesant's anti-Semitic outbursts, within a few years after their arrival the Jews were no longer very much on the minds of the authorities in New Amsterdam. The Lutheran problem and the secret arrival of Rev. Gutwasser had perplexed and bedeviled Stuyvesant and the ministers for much longer than the Jews. The Quakers would create an even greater challenge.

In the seventeenth century, Quakers were notorious for their opposition to most forms of political authority. With little exaggeration, one historian has argued that "As Bolsheviks were feared after the Russian Revolution of the twentieth century, so the very thought of Quakers frightened people of the seventeenth."[75] The Religions Society of Friends was founded by George Fox in 1652. The religion grew out of Puritanism and is an extreme example of "the relentless movement of the Puritan-Reformed impulse away from the hierarchical, sacramental, and objective Christianity of the Middle Ages towards various radical extremes in which intensely individualistic and spiritual motifs become predominant." Quaker teaching "undermined the establishment by minimizing the liturgical and teaching function of an ordained ministry, abandoning the idea of objective sacraments, and inspiring conduct which was attributed to the promptings of an inner voice. Most ominous of all to the authorities was the phenomenal missionary zeal which flowed from the Quaker conviction of the universality of the Holy Spirit's work."[76] The Friends became known as the "Quakers" because of their shaking or "quaking" while praying and giving sermons.

The description provided by the Dutch clerics of the arrival of a shipload of Quakers in New Amsterdam illustrates the consternation the Quakers could cause government officials. In early August 1657, a ship "having no flag" came into the harbor. This ship "fired no salute before the fort, as is usual with ships on their arrival." People in the colony "could not decide whether she was

Dutch, French, or English." When a government official boarded the ship, those on board "tendered him no honor or respect." When the ship's master came before Stuyvesant "he rendered him no respect, but stood still with his hat firm on his head, as if a goat." The ship was allowed to remain in the harbor for only one night.[77]

The Dutch ministers believed that after it was sent away, the ship went to Rhode Island—"the receptacle of all sorts of riff-raff people." As "all the cranks of New England" had moved there, the Dutch assumed these Quakers would do the same. However, before the ship left two Quaker women somehow managed to disembark and hide on Long Island among the English settlers, and "as soon as the ship had fairly departed, these began to quake and go into a frenzy, and cry out loudly in the middle of the street, that men should repent, for the day of the judgment was at hand." The two women were soon jailed. Other Quakers coming to New Netherland were expelled, jailed, and tortured.[78]

This was the beginning of the longest and most brutal religious suppression in the colony's history. Over the next six years, a number of Quakers were jailed, expelled, fined, placed at hard labor, and tortured for preaching in the colony. Non-Quakers were also jailed and fined for aiding or harboring Quakers.[79] The story provides a significant contrast to the treatment of the Recife Jews, who were not only allowed to disembark, but given charity when they landed.

This persecution proved futile. Each new persecution only strengthened the Quakers, especially in the English-speaking settlements on Long Island. The persecutions led some colonists to argue for religious toleration as a duty of Christian love. In the "Flushing Remonstrance" of 1658, thirty-one settlers, including the sheriff, called on Stuyvesant to stop levying heavy fines on people who harbored Quakers. The petitioners, who were mostly English, declared that "wee desire therefore in this case not to judge least wee be judged, neither to Condem, least wee bee Condemed, but rather let every man stand and fall on his own." They felt bound by God's law "to doe good unto all men," and thus, by Stuyvesant's decree, they were trapped between the law of God and that of man. Rather than persecute the Quakers, they would allow them freedom, because "if God justify who can Condem, and if God Condem there is none can justifye."[80] Stuyvesant not only rejected the petition, but arrested the leading petitioners for sedition.

Ultimately, officials in Holland ended the persecutions. The Heeren XIX told Stuyvesant that they too wished no Quakers had moved into the colony. But once in the colony, the Directors asserted "we doubt very much, whether we can proceed against them rigorously without diminishing the population and stopping immigration, which must be favored at a so tender stage of the country's existence."[81] In other words, the colony could not grow and prosper, and the investors with it, without tolerance.[82] The Directors told the Director-General to "shut your eyes" to the Quakers, and "not force people's consciences, but allow every one to have his own belief, as long as he behaves quietly and legally, gives no offence to his neighbors, and does not oppose the government." The Directors pointed out that this had been the practice in old Amsterdam "and consequently" the city had "often had a considerable influx of people." New Amsterdam too "would be benefitted by" this practice.[83]

Thus, as with the Lutherans and Jews, toleration once again won out over establishment. By 1660 the Dutch colony was a true polyglot, with Lutherans, Quakers, Jews, Catholics, Puritans, Anabaptists, and a number of other Protestants worshipping and threatening the established church. The final threat to the established church came from Anglicans, who arrived in 1664. Unlike the other non-Dutch Reformed settlers, these Anglicans were neither refugees nor defeated enemies. They were conquerors.

The Arrival of the English

In 1664 an English fleet seized New Amsterdam and, with it, the entire Dutch empire on the mainland of North America. New Netherland was renamed New York and New Amsterdam became New York City, after the colony's new proprietor, James, Duke of York. The Dutch city settlement at Fort Orange was renamed Albany, in honor of James's Scottish peerage, where James was the Duke of Albany. By 1664 there was growing toleration in England. Most Protestants had religious liberty. Catholics faced discrimination, but not persecution. Jews had been trickling into the country since the 1640s. The very fact that England had taken over a Dutch colony meant that a certain amount of religious toleration was necessary, because the overwhelming majority of the residents of the colony were not members of the Church of England. This also meant that no strong religious establishment could succeed in the colony.

In fact, the colony that James claimed was probably the most polyglot in the New World—with members of the Dutch Reformed Church; Lutherans from Holland and Sweden; French Calvinists; Presbyterians from the British Isles; Puritans, Separatists, Baptists, Anabaptists, Quakers, and a variety of other Protestant sects from England and elsewhere; and small numbers of Jews and Catholics. The only conspicuous absence was anyone who claimed membership in the Church of England.

Most of the residents of this new English colony were members of the Dutch Reformed Church. No official in the "Duke's Colony" ever contemplated expelling them or forcing them to accept the Church of England. This would have been impossible and impractical. Instead, the Duke and his deputies adopted an unusually tolerant policy on religious matters. The Articles of Capitulation, which the Dutch were compelled to sign, provided that the "Dutch here shall enjoy the liberty of their consciences in Divine Worship and church discipline."[84] What the Duke gave to the Dutch he also had to give to the Protestant dissenters living on Long Island. Initially, all towns in the colony were allowed to establish whatever church they wished. Minority faiths were granted the right to conduct meetings openly. In 1666 Lutherans gained the right, long denied under the Dutch, to build their own churches. In 1674 the Duke of York ordered his new governor, Edmund Andros, to "permitt all persons of what Religion soever, quietly to inhabitt wthin ye precincts of yor jurisdiccon, wthout giveing ym any disturbance or disquiet whatsoever, for or by reasons of their differring opinions in matter of Religion."[85] In 1683, the New York Assembly partially codified this tolerance in the colony's Charter of Liberties and Privileges, which declared:

> Noe person or persons which professe ffaith in God by Jesus Christ Shall at any time be any wayes molested punished disquieted or called in Question for any Difference in opinion or Matter of Religious Concernemnt . . . But that all and Every such person or persons may . . . at all times freely have and fully enjoy his or their Judgments or Consciencyes in matters of Religion throughout all the province.[86]

This charter did not separate church and state, but explicitly provided for government support for all Christian churches. Moreover, the colony's Jews were allowed to have their own house of worship, even though they clearly did not "professe ffaith in God by Jesus Christ." Although not given access to tax monies to support their teachers and clergymen, the Jews nevertheless had complete freedom of public worship, something the Dutch had denied them.[87]

Even without statutes and explicit protections of religion, no one seems to have been turned away from the colony for his or her religious beliefs. New York was already a commercial entrepôt and something of a melting pot. In 1678 Governor Andros reported to his superiors in London that he could find "Noe account" of "childrens births or christenings" because ministers had kept few records. Further complicating his attempts to take a complete census, Andros noted: "There are Religions of all sorts, one Church of England, severall Presbiterians and Independents, Quakers and Anabaptists, of serverall sects, some Jews. . . ."[88] A decade later Andros's successor, Governor Thomas Dongan, reported: "Here bee not many of the Church of England; [a] few Roman Catholicks; abundance of Quakers preachers men and women especially; Singing Quakers, Ranting Quakers; Sabbatarians; Antisabbatarians; Some Anabaptists; some Independents; some Jews; in short of all opinions there are some, and the most part none at all."[89]

At one level, the fears of Stuyvesant and the Dutch clerics had been realized. The colony they helped govern was no longer homogenous: It was a polyglot of religions and sects and ethnicities. But, it was on its way to becoming the most economically successful city in the New World.

Conclusion: The Struggle for Equality and the Defeat of Establishment

In many ways the Jewish experience in New Netherland sets the standard for understanding the conflict between religious freedom and religious establishment. It is hardly remarkable or surprising that the Jews in New Amsterdam faced anti-Semitism from the authorities. The Dutch Reformed clerics were deeply hostile to anyone who was not of their faith. Stuyvesant was not a tolerant man and not much given to reflection or philosophical musings. Indeed, his hot temper seems to have been one of his most famous traits. That he spouted anti-Semitic canards at the Jews, or made equally bigoted statements about Catholics, Lutherans, Quakers, Mennonites, and others seems to be exactly what we should have expected from him.

What is remarkable, however, is how the Jews in New Amsterdam were able to gain significant concessions from the Stuyvesant regime. These would not come all at once. Throughout the rest of the Dutch period, which would end in 1664, the Jews would have to petition the government, and then appeal to Amsterdam, for the right to own property, live where they wanted, have their own burial ground, have full access to business and trading opportunities, and even serve in the town guard like other burghers.[90] The Jews of New Amsterdam persisted in asserting their rights and participating in the community. They did not shy away from commerce and public life, but became actors in both phases of the community, and, in the process, put themselves into a position where they could claim the status of burghers.

As the Jews fought for and won concessions they created an atmosphere where religious toleration worked. By the end of the Dutch period persons of almost any religious faith were able to live in the colony. Catholics, Jews, Lutherans, and Quakers, among others, were allowed to hold their "superstitious" religious services—as the Dutch authorities called them—in private homes. The reason for this was not the desire to protect religion from government interference, which had motivated Roger Williams of Rhode Island.[91] This toleration was also not a function of Christian charity, love, or fear of God, although some in the colony thought it should be. Nor was toleration the result of an enlightenment philosophy that denied any role for the government in the saving of souls.

Toleration in New Netherland had almost no theory or philosophy behind it. It evolved out of the need to populate a frontier and encourage trade and commerce. Put simply, the Dutch West India Company valued worldly success above theology. For Petrus Stuyvesant "religion was an important instrument of social control," and the failure to exercise such control was "an invitation to an anarchy of contesting beliefs."[92] However, his superiors in Amsterdam understood that too much control of religion might lead to tyranny and would certainly discourage settlement. Lutherans, Jews, Quakers, Catholics, and others were allowed to settle and trade in the colony because they could make it grow and prosper. To put it another way, there was no need for a theoretical or philosophical defense of toleration because toleration—and a weakened established church—grew out of the practical reality that toleration had real economic benefits. This was the message the Dutch officials conveyed to Stuyvesant whenever he wanted to suppress religious minorities. Stuyvesant and other overly devout colonial officials were simply told to "shut your eyes" to persons of other religions, and let everyone in the colony go about his or her business. Indeed, business, not religion, was the purpose of the colony. Toleration stimulated growth and trade. And as the Merchants of the Portuguese nation had reminded the Directors of the WIC, "Yonder land is extensive and spacious. The more of loyal people that go to live there, the better it is." That was reason enough to allow persons of any faith to discreetly practice their religion and openly ply their trades.[93]

The Jews played a crucial role in the development of this economic and cultural polyglot, not just as businessmen and entrepreneurs, but as pioneers who helped successfully force the issue of toleration on the local government. In the process they helped undermine the Dutch Reformed establishment and later the Anglican establishment. In this sense, the story of the first Jews suggests a different moral for modern Americans than the traditional narrative. The Jews succeeded in the New World in part because of help from the Old, but also because in the New World they persistently demanded the right to be part of the polity, to build houses, participate in the economy, and stand guard at night like other burghers.[94] They also succeeded because the Directors of the WIC understood the value of hardworking immigrants who would help an empty colony grow. Finally, their success was directly tied to the future status of other minority groups. For these mid-seventeenth-century Jews, heterogeneity—what an early generation of historians called pluralism and what modern scholars call cultural diversity—was a blessing. The more diversity New Netherland had, the more the Jews (and Lutherans and Quakers) could prosper, and the more the colony could prosper.

Stuyvesant opposed Jews and Lutherans and Quakers and just about everyone else who was not Dutch who might come to his colony because he feared instability and chaos, and because he correctly understood that such diversity would undermine the Dutch Reformed establishment. He never understood that diversity could also lead to stability. Fortunately, Stuyvesant was defeated by Anabaptists, Puritans, Lutherans, Jews, Quakers, and other minority immigrants who persisted in helping the colony prosper in spite of its narrow-minded Director-General, and he was overruled by wiser leaders, in Amsterdam, who understood that in diversity there was strength.

In creating this diversity, the Lutherans, Jews, Quakers, and other outsiders not only made a place for themselves, but also undermined the Dutch Reformed establishment. The Dutch Reformed clerics and Director-General Stuyvesant predicted this would happen. But, economic necessity and the culture of tolerance in Holland overcame these concerns. Indeed, prosperity through diversity was in the end far more important than a strong established church. The English after 1664 fully understood this, and although they claimed to have an establishment, they did not. Well before the Revolution of 1776 the marriage of church and state in New York was collapsing. The 1777 Constitution simply affirmed the final divorce of what had already become a de facto separation.

Notes

*I am greatly indebted to Robert Emery, Mary Wood, Colleen Osteguy, and Robert Begg of the Albany Law School library for their extraordinary efforts in helping me with the development of this chapter. I also thank Gillian Berchowitz, Charles Gehring, Jonathan Sarna, and Lance Sussman for their helpful comments. The writing of this chapter was partially supported by a summer research grant from Albany Law School and a grant from the American Jewish Archives. I thank Kevin Proffitt and Dana Herman at the Archives for their help.

1. For a discussion of early state constitutions, see Melvin Urofsky and Paul Finkelman, *A March of Liberty: A Constitutional History of the United States*, 3d ed. (New York: Oxford University Press, 2011).

2. Virginia's constitution did not have a clause on requirements for office-holding, but it appears that earlier colonial rules on office-holding—including a confession of faith—remained in force during and after the Revolution, just as the established church continued in Virginia until after the Revolution.

3. "Governor Dongan's Report on the State of the Province," 1684, in *Ecclesiastical Records: State of New York*, 7 vols., ed. Hugh Hastings (Albany, NY: J.B. Lyon, State Printer, 1901–1916), 2:879–80; Douglas Greenberg, *Crime in the Colony of New York* (Ithaca, NY: Cornell University Press, 1978), 26; Edwin Scott Gaustad, *Historical Atlas of Religion in America* (New York: Harper and Row, 1962), 2.

4. Richard B. Saphire, "*Torasco v. Watkins* and *McDaniel v. Paty*," in *Religion and American Law: An Encyclopedia*, ed. Paul Finkelman (New York: Garland, 2000), 535–37.

5. New York Constitution, 1777, Article VII (property qualification for voting for members of the assembly); Article X (property qualification for voting for members of the Senate); Article XVII (property qualification for voting for the governor and qualification that the governor be a "wise and descreet freeholder of the State"); Article VIII (Quaker exemption from oath taking); Article Xl (Quaker exemption from military service).

6. Ibid., Article XXXIX. Modern legal theorists do not see bans on clergy office-holding to be protective of religious liberty, but the New York Constitution must be seen in the context of its time, set out in this chapter. On modern views of this issue see *McDaniel v. Paty*, 435 U.S. 618 (1978); for a discussion of this case see Richard B. Saphire, "*Torasco v. Watkins*," 535–37.

7. Steve Pincus, *1688: The First Modern Revolution* (New Haven, CT: Yale University Press, 2009) and William Gibson, *James II and the Trial of the Seven Bishops* (New York: Palgrave/Macmillan, 2009); Urofsky and Finkelman, *A March of Liberty*, chap. 1.

8. New York Constitution, 1777, Article XXXVIII.

9. Ibid.

10. Ibid.

11. Virginia's 1776 Constitution also had no religious tests for office-holding.

12. Virginia did not establish, or disestablish, a church in its 1776 document, but nevertheless the Anglican and then the Episcopalian church remained the established church in the state until after the Revolution. Virginia provided for religious freedom, but tied it to "Christian forbearance . . . toward each other." Virginia Bill of Rights, Sec. 16. Moreover, in the 1770s and 1780s there was massive and vicious official and legal persecution of Baptists and other dissenters in Virginia. See chapter 3 by Mark McGarvie and chapter 6 by Ralph Ketcham.

13. The final clause of the New York Constitution required immigrants seeking naturalization to "abjure and renounce all allegiance to all and every foreign king, prince, potentate, and State in all matters, ecclesiastical as well as civil." New York Constitution, 1777, Article XLII. This clause undermined the free exercise, presumably, of Anglican and Catholic immigrants seeking naturalization, by requiring them to "abjure and renounce" their allegiance to foreign bishops and the pope. This did not apply to people already in the state and those born there. It does not appear to have ever prevented the naturalization of any immigrant.

14. Ibid.

15. George L. Smith, *Religion and Trade in New Netherland: Dutch Origins and American Development* (Ithaca, NY: Cornell University Press, 1973), 98, 103.

16. See further chapter 1 by T. Jeremy Gunn.

17. Van Cleaf Bachman, *Peltries or Plantations: The Economic Policies of the Dutch West India Company in New Netherland, 1623–1639* (Baltimore, MD: Johns Hopkins University Press, 1969), 50–51; Rex H. Hudson, ed., *Brazil: A Country Study* (Washington, DC: Federal Research Division, Library of Congress, 1997), 22; Daniel M. Swetschinski, *Reluctant Cosmopolitans: The Portuguese Jews of Seventeenth Century Amsterdam* (London: The Littman Library of Jewish Civilization, 2000), 114; Lewis Samuel Feuer, *Spinoza and the Rise of Liberalism* (Boston: Beacon Press, 1958), 28; Jonathan Sarna, *American Judaism: A History* (New Haven, CT: Yale University Press, 2004), 6; I. S. Emmanuel, "New Light on Early American Jewry," *American Jewish Archives* 7 (1955): 5.

18. Swetschinski, *Reluctant Cosmopolitans*, 115.

19. See chapter 4 by David Little and chapter 2 by Michael McConnell.

20. Quoted in Henri and Barbara Van Der Zee, *A Sweet and Alien Land: The Story of Dutch New York* (New York: Viking Press, 1978), 91–282.

21. Smith, *Religion and Trade in New Netherland*, 64.

22. John Webb Pratt, *Religion, Politics, and Diversity: The Church-State Theme in New York History* (Ithaca, NY: Cornell University Press, 1967), 6.

23. Van Der Zee, *A Sweet and Alien Land*, 91–92.

24. Ibid.

25. And possibly arranging for her death as well. Many scholars argue that her death was not the result of random Indian–settler conflicts, but rather that the Indians who killed her had been put up to it by emissaries from Massachusetts, perhaps even with the support of Dutch authorities.

26. Oliver A. Rink, *Holland on the Hudson: An Economic and Social History of Dutch New York* (Ithaca, NY: Cornell University Press, 1986), 223.

27. Ibid., 225.

28. Patricia U. Bonomi, *Under the Cope of Heaven: Religion, Society, and Politics in Colonial America* (New York: Oxford University Press, 2003), 25.

29. Stuyvesant to the Amsterdam Chamber, September 22, 1654, reprinted in Samuel Oppenheim, *The Early History of the Jews in New York, 1654–1664: Some New Matter on the Subject* (New York: Publications of the American Jewish Historical Society 1909) [[hereinafter *Early History*], also published in *American Jewish Historical Society Journal* (*AJHSJ*) 18 (1909): 4–5.

30. Colonial Albany Social History Project at http://www.nysm.nysed.gov/albany/lutheran.html (accessed on September 18, 2008).

31. Revs. Megapolensis and Drisius to the Classis of Amsterdam, October 6, 1653, in *Ecclesiastical Records*, 1:317–18.

32. Classis of Amsterdam to Revs. Megapolensis and Drisius, February 23, 1654, in *Ecclesiastical Records*, 1:322–23.

33. Expulsion of Swedish Ministers from Delaware, September 25, 1655, in *Ecclesiastical Records*, 1:340.

34. The Directors to Stuyvesant, June 14, 1656, in Berthold Fernow, ed., *Documents Relating to the Colonial History of the State of New York*, o.s. (Albany, NY: Weed, Parsons, 1883), 14:351.

35. Ibid.

36. Petitions of the Lutherans to the Governor and Council, October 24, 1656; and letter from the Directors to Stuyvesant, April 7, 1657, in *Ecclesiastical Records*, 1:358–60, 372–73, 377–78.

37. The Classis of Amsterdam to the Consistory of New Netherland, May 25, 1657, in *Ecclesiastical Records*, 1:378–81. He is also called Goetwater in some of the letters.

38. Petition of Revs. Megapolensis and Drisius to the Burgomasters, etc. against Tolerating the Lutherans, July 6, 1657; Report of the Mayor and Aldermen of New Amsterdam Upon the Petition of the Ministers against Allowing Lutheran Service, July 14, 1657, in *Ecclesiastical Records*, 1:386–88; 388–90.

39. Petition, *supra* note 38; Record, *supra* note 38.

40. Remonstrance of the Inhabitants of Flushing, L.I. against the Law against Quakers, and various other documents relating to Quakers, in Fernow, ed., *Documents Relating to the Colonial History*, o.s., 14:402–9; Letter from the Directors to Stuyvesant, May 20, 1658, in Fernow, ed., *Documents Relating to the Colonial History*, o.s., 14:417–18.

41. Revs. Megapolensis and Drisius to the Director-General and Council of New Netherland, August 23, 1658 and Revs. Megapolensis and Drisius to the Classis of Amsterdam, September 24, 1658, in *Ecclesiastical Records*, 1:428–30, 432–36.

42. Revs. Megapolensis and Drisius to the Classis of Amsterdam, September 10, 1659, and Acts of the Classis of Amsterdam, November 3, 1659, in *Ecclesiastical Records*, 1:449–50, 454.

43. Rev. Gideon Schaats to the Classis of Amsterdam, September 22, 1660, in *Ecclesiastical Records*, 1:482–83 and response by the Classis, in *Ecclesiastical Records*, 504–5, 515–16. "Letter from the Governor in Regard to the Lutherans," October 13, 1666, in *Ecclesiastical Records*, 1:583.

44. Revs. Megapolensis and Drisius to the Classis of Amsterdam, August 5, 1657, in *Ecclesiastical Records*, 1:393–400.

45. Ibid.

46. The history of their arrival has been shrouded in legend and historical inaccuracies. For a discussion of this history, and a sorting out of the facts, see Paul Finkelman, "'A Land That Needs People for Its Increase': How the Jews Won the Right to Remain in New Netherland," in *New Essays in American Jewish History*, ed. Pamela S. Nadell, Jonathan D. Sarna, and Lance J. Sussman (Cincinnati, OH: American Jewish Archives of Hebrew Union College-Jewish Institute of Religion, 2010), 19–50, 488–96; see also Leo Hershkowitz, "New Amsterdam's Twenty-Three Jews—Myth or Reality," in *Hebrew and Bible in America: The First Two Centuries*, ed. Shalom Goldman (Hanover and London: Brandeis University Press and Dartmouth College, 1993), 171–81.

47. Rev. Johannes Megapolensis to the Classis of Amsterdam, March 18, 1655, in *Ecclesiastical Records*, 1:335–36. See also Oppenheim, *Early History*, 2.

48. Samuel Oppenheim, "More about Jacob Barsimson, The First Jewish Settler in New York," *Publications of the American Jewish Historical Society* 29 (1925): 39; Leo Hershkowitz, "Some Aspects of the New York Jewish Merchant and Community, 1654–820," *American Jewish Historical Quarterly* 66 (1976–1977): 10, and Leo Hershkowitz, "By Chance or Choice: Jews in New Amsterdam 1654," *AJA* 57 (2005): 1.

49. Oppenheim, *Early History*, 3; Oppenheim, "More about Jacob Barsimson," 41–42; Jacob Rader Marcus, *Early American Jewry: The Jews of New York, New England, and Canada, 1649–1794* (Philadelphia: The Jewish Publication Society of America, 1951), 24.

50. Leo Hershkowitz makes this argument in "By Chance or Choice," 1; Hershkowitz, "Myth or Reality," 171–81.

51. Oppenheim, "More about Jacob Barsimson," 39.

52. Karina Sonnenberg-Stern, *Emancipation and Poverty: The Ashkenazi Jews of Amsterdam, 1796–1850* (London: Macmillan, 2000), 27–28.

53. Saul S. Friedman, *Jews and the American Slave Trade* (New Brunswick, NJ: Transaction, 1998), 5; Karina Sonnenberg-Stern, *Emancipation and Poverty*, 28–29; C. R. Boxer, *The Dutch Seaborne Empire, 1600–1800* (New York: Alfred A. Knopf, 1965), 130; Feuer, *Spinoza and the Rise of Liberalism*, 7.

54. Information on this is found at the Jewish Museum of Amsterdam. See also http://www.jewishencyclopedia.com/view.jsp?artid=197&letter=N&search=Dutch%20Citizenship#578 and http://www.jewishencyclopedia.com/view.jsp?artid=248&letter=N&search=Dutch%20West%20Indies%20Company#737 accessed on September 18, 2008.

55. Jonathan Israel, "Introduction," in *Dutch Jewry: Its History and Secular Culture (1500–2000)*, ed. Jonathan Israel and Reinier Salverda (Leiden: Brill, 2002), 10.

56. Marcus, *Early American Jewry*, 14.

57. Hershkowitz, "By Chance or Choice," 4, argues they were delayed in Spanish Jamaica or possibly Spanish Cuba.

58. Berthold Fernow, ed., *The Records of New Amsterdam: From 1653 to 1674* (1897; repr., Baltimore, MD: Genealogical, 1976), 1:240, 241, 244, 249. This record provides some of the names of the Jews, including Abram Israel, Judicq de Mereda, David Israel, and Moses Ambrosius.

59. Rev. Johannes Megapolensis to the Classis of Amsterdam, March 18, 1655, in *Ecclesiastical Records*, 1:335–36.

60. Ibid.

61. As it turned out, most of these first Jews did not stay very long in New Amsterdam. Hershkowitz, "Myth or Reality," 171–81.

62. Stuyvesant to the Amsterdam Chamber, September 22, 1654, in Oppenheim, *Early History*, 4–5. Oppenheim provides only an extract of Stuyvesant's letter, and does not provide a source for this letter, indicating the extract was "recently found by the writer [Oppenheim] in a clearly written Dutch MS. of the period," ibid. at 4. This extract also appears in Jacob Marcus, *The Jew in the American World: A Source Book* (Detroit, MI: Wayne State University Press, 1995), 29, also without citation to a source.

63. Stuyvesant to the Amsterdam Chamber, *supra* note 62; Marcus, *supra* note 62.

64. Ibid.

65. Swetschinski, *Reluctant Cosmopolitans*, 51 notes that by the end of the seventeenth century Jews began to receive similar economic, social, and even political rights in Bordeaux and London.

66. Rev. John Megapolensis to the Classis of Amsterdam, October 6, 1654, in *Ecclesiastical Records*, 1:334–36. See also Van Der Zee, *A Sweet and Alien Land*, 290–91.

67. Stuyvesant to the Amsterdam Chamber, September 22, 1654, partially reprinted in Oppenheim, *Early History*, 4–5.

68. Petition to the Honorable Lords, Directors of the WIC, January 1655 in Oppenheim, *Early History*, 9.

69. Ibid.

70. Stuyvesant also sent three letters to the Directors on September 22, September 2, and October 27. Letter from the Directors at Amsterdam to the Director-General [Stuyvesant] and Council, April 26, 1655 in Gehring, ed., *NND* XII:48–49. The Directors of the W.I. Co., Dept. of *Amsterdam*, J. Bontemantel & Edward Man to Director [Petrus] Stuyvesant and Council in *New Netherland*, April 26, 1655 in Fernow, ed., *Documents Relating to the Colonial History*, o.s., 14:315.

71. Letter from the Directors at Amsterdam to the Director-General [Stuyvesant] and Council, April 26, 1655 in Gehring, ed., *NND* XII:48–49.

72. See Gehring, ed., *NND*, XII:48–49. Part of this translation is now in dispute. The traditional translation by Berthold Fernow, which the new Gehring edition confirms, and which has been repeated by almost all scholars, included this line: "and also because of the large amount of capital, which they have invested in shares of this Company." But more recently, the scholar Jaap Jacobs has argued that this line should actually be translated as "the large sums of money for which they are still indebted to the Company." See Jaap Jacobs, *New Netherland: A Dutch Colony in Seventeenth-Century America* (Leiden: Brill, 2005), 375–76. If Jacobs is correct, then my interpretation here is strengthened. However, there appears to be no consensus at the moment on this new translation, and even Jacobs admits that "the case for this completely different translation is not without weaknesses." He notes that there is "no other occurrence known" of interpreting the words as he does. Jacobs, *New Netherland*, 376.

73. Petition to the Honorable Lords, Directors of the WIC, January 1655 in Oppenheim, *Early History*, 9.

74. The Directors to Stuyvesant, March 13, 1656 in Fernow, ed., *Documents Relating to the Colonial History*, o.s., 14:341.

75. Pratt, *Religion, Politics, and Diversity*, 19.

76. Sydney E. Ahlstrom, *A Religious History of the American People*, 2 vols. (Garden City, NJ: Doubleday, 1975), 1:229, 230.

77. Revs. Johannes Megapolensis and Samuel Drisius to the Classis of Amsterdam, August 14, 1657, in *Ecclesiastical Records*, 1:399–400. Frederick J. Zwierlein, *Religion in New Netherland* (Rochester, NY: John P. Smith, 1910), 213–42.

78. Revs. Johannes Megapolensis and Samuel Drisius to the Classis of Amsterdam, *supra* note 77; Zwierlein, *supra* note 77.

79. In 1657 Dutch authorities in New Netherland tortured the Quaker Robert Hodgson in a variety of ways, including dragging him behind a horse cart, placing him in a vermin-filled dungeon, and severely whipping him and "chaining him to a wheelbarrow in the hot sun until he collapsed." He was later hung by his hands in a prison cell and "whipped until he was near death." After two days in solitary confinement, he was again whipped until near death. Hodgson's ordeal ended when Stuyvesant's own sister persuaded him to release Hodgson from prison and expel him from the colony. Smith, *Religion and Trade in New Netherland*, 223; Zwierlein, *Religion in New Netherland*, 213–46.

80. "Remonstrance of the Inhabitants of Flushing, L.I., against the Law against Quakers," January 1, 1658, in *Ecclesiastical Records*, 1:412–13.

81. Directors of the Dutch West India Company to Stuyvesant, April 16, 1663, in *Ecclesiastical Records*, 1:530.

82. Other evidence suggests that the actions of Stuyvesant were often in tension with the goal of the Directors to increase the population of the colony and to preserve basic liberties. For example, the Directors reprimanded Stuyvesant for inserting a clause "in the printed passports, given to freemen sailing from here [Holland] to *New-Netherland*" requiring "that they must remain there [New Netherland] for a certain number of years." The directors noted this was "offensive to many," "antagonistic to the liberty of free people," and "an obstacle to the increasing of the population." The letter to Stuyvesant ended: "You will govern yourself accordingly." Directors to Stuyvesant, July 30, 1654 in Fernow, *Documents Relating to the Colonial History*, o.s., 14:280. See also The Directors of the W.I. Co., Dept. of *Amsterdam*, David van Baerle, Edward Man. and Abr. Wilmerdonx to Director [Petrus] Stuyvesant and Council in *New Netherland*, March 13, 1656, ordering Stuyvesant to allow the ship *Scots* to sail "to and fro . . . because for the sake of increasing the population, trade and its freedom must not be hampered with, but ought to be relieved from all restrictions."

83. Directors of the Dutch West India Company to Stuyvesant, April 16, 1663, in *Ecclesiastical Records*, 1:530.

84. E. B. O'Callaghan, ed., *Documents Relative to the Colonial History of the State of New York*, 15 vols. (Albany, NY: Weed, Parsons, 1853–87), 2:251.

85. Pratt, *Religion, Politics and Diversity*, 26–35, 85. O'Callaghan, ed., *Documents*, 3:218.

86. *Colonial Laws of New York*, 1:115.

87. Jacob R. Marcus, *The Colonial American Jew, 1492–1776* (Detroit, MI: Wayne State University Press, 1970).

88. "Answer of Governor to Enquiries about New York," April 16, 1678, in *Ecclesiastical Records*, 1:709.

89. "Governor Dongan's Report on the State of the Province," 1684, in *Ecclesiastical Records*, 2:879–80.

90. Sarna, *American Judaism*, 9–10.

91. Paul Finkelman, "School Vouchers, Thomas Jefferson, Roger Williams, and Protecting the Faithful: Warnings from the Eighteenth Century and the Seventeenth Century on the Dangers of Establishments to Religious Communities," *Brigham Young University Law Review* (2008): 525; see further chapter 4 by David Little.

92. Pratt, *Religion, Politics, and Diversity*, 24.

93. Pratt argues that the failure to resolve the tension and contradiction between Stuyvesant and the West India Company officials undermined the Dutch colony. Ibid., 25. This may be true, although it seems unlikely that a consistent policy of either tolerance or repression would have prevented English seizure of the colony. Petition to the Honorable Lords, Directors of the WIC, January 1655, published in Samuel Oppenheim, *Early History*, 10.

94. Oppenheim, *Early History*, 9. See also Oppenheim, "More about Jacob Barsimson," 39; Leo Hershkowitz, "Some Aspects of the New York Jewish Merchant and Community, 1654–1820," *American Jewish Historical Quarterly* 66 (1976–1977): 10; Leon Hühner, "Asser Levy: A Noted Jewish Burgher of New Amsterdam," *American Jewish Historical Society Journal* 8 (1900): 99.

{ 6 }

James Madison, Thomas Jefferson, and the Meaning of "Establishment of Religion" in Eighteenth-Century Virginia

Ralph Ketcham

In its 170 years of existence before the era of the American Revolution, the English colony of Virginia had assumed the establishment of the Church of England on terms similar to those in effect in England. Parishes and clergy were supported by the state, and voices, meetings, and organizations deemed prejudicial to the effectiveness of the established churches could be punished and banned by public authority. Some liberal sentiment within the established church and the spread of dissenting religions in the colony, however, grew in ways that threatened the establishment. The established church appeared increasingly moribund compared to the dissenting and itinerant preachers themselves, newly invigorated by the Great Awakening of the 1740s. This trend, combined with the spread of Enlightenment ideals of freedom of conscience, and the experience of colonies such as Rhode Island and Pennsylvania with much broader freedom of religion, created a growing crisis in the public life of the colony of Virginia.

This chapter takes up the story of the rapid disestablishment of religion in Virginia, under the leadership of James Madison and Thomas Jefferson—from the more tentative provisions of the Virginia Bill of Rights in 1776 shaped in part by Madison to the powerful language of Thomas Jefferson's Act for the Establishment of Religious Freedom in 1786. This early experiment in disestablishment of religion proved to be a prescient example not only for later states in their efforts at disestablishment, but for the work of Madison and Jefferson in the federal government.

Madison and His Early Efforts to Disestablish Religion

The first two public matters that engaged the attention of the young James Madison were the harms that he believed were caused by religious establishments and the closely related issue of the infringement of religious freedom caused by the persecution of conscience. These two compelling issues not only prompted him to undertake serious study, but to soon thereafter engage in political action. As early as December 1773, at age twenty-three and at home in Orange, Virginia, after having graduated from the College of New Jersey at Princeton, he wrote to his college friend William Bradford and raised two "Queries." First, he asked, "Is an Ecclesiastical Establishment absolutely necessary to support civil society in a supream Government?" Second, "how far is it hurtful to a dependant State?" He asked Bradford to send books that would help him consider these questions.[1]

Two months after his first letter to Bradford, and after receiving word of the Boston Tea Party, Madison wrote again to his college friend not with a general "query" about "religious establishments," but instead with a specific condemnation of the role played by the Church of England as the established church in Virginia. He offered the harsh judgment that "if the Church of England had been the established and general Religion in all the Northern Colonies as it has been among us here, and [if] uninterrupted tranquility had prevailed throughout the Continent, it is clear to me that slavery and Subjection might and would have been gradually insinuated among us."[2] Madison was alert as always to the harms that religious establishments cause not only to individual rights but to society at large. "Union of Religious Sentiments," he continued, "begets a surprising confidence and Ecclesiastical Establishments tend to great ignorance and Corruption all of which facilitate the Execution of mischievous Projects." He then told Bradford sorrowfully "that Hell conceived principle of persecution rages among some [here] and to their eternal Infamy the Clergy can furnish their Quota of Imps for such business. This vexes me the most of anything whatever. There are at this [time] in the adjacent County not less than 5 or 6 well-meaning men in close Gaol for publishing their religious Sentiments which in the main are very orthodox. I have neither the patience to hear talk or think about anything relative to this matter, for I have squabbled and scolded abused and ridiculed so long about it, to so little purpose that I am without common patience. So I leave you to pity me and to pray for Liberty of Conscience to revive among us."[3] Thus Madison, as early as 1773, had already identified religious establishments in his home territory of Virginia as an enemy of the free exercise of religion and of freedom of conscience.

Madison's initial zeal to protect religious freedom came from his defense of the right of Christian clergymen to preach the gospel to willing listeners, a practice condemned by the religious establishment in Virginia. He had experienced himself at Princeton the importance of preaching without political restraint, and many of his classmates were at that very time attempting to engage in such practices as the American Revolution approached. He saw public preaching as a permissible and, equally important, civically useful effort on their part to bring an invigorated Christianity to southern colonies where the establishment of religion had made the religion close-minded and intolerant. To Madison, who had once looked at the ministry as the highest calling and who admired the open society that various nonestablished religions encouraged in the middle colonies, nothing was more absurd, unwise, and unjust than the spectacle of a moribund Anglican establishment using civil power to imprison "well-meaning men" who sought nothing more than their right to preach and thus (Madison believed) to likely improve civic life and public morality. "Zealous adherents to the Anglican Hierarchy," Madison told Bradford, did not have "that liberal catholic and equitable way of thinking as to the rights of Conscience, which is one of the Characteristics of a free people."[4] He congratulated Bradford on living in a land (Pennsylvania) that had "long felt the good effect of . . . religious as well as Civil Liberty. . . . I cannot help attributing those continual exertions of Genius which appear among you to the inspiration of Liberty and that love of Fame and Knowledge which always accompany it. Religious bondage shackles and debilitates the mind and unfits it for every noble enterprise, every expanded prospect."[5] Though Madison did not say it directly, the "noble enterprise" and "expanded prospect" for which he saw church establishment "unfitting" the mind was the emerging struggle for freedom from British oppression. This was an early expression of Madison's constant conviction that the most harmful effect of "established religion" (that is, compelled and formalized religion) was its suppression of the vital, useful energies that flowed from the unrestrained practice of religion in the public sphere—and eventually to the practice of citizenship in a self-governing society. Establishments of religion, he believed, were harmful both to individual freedoms and to public order.

In 1776, the Continental Congresses reconvened in Philadelphia at the same time that Madison himself was preparing to attend the first Virginia revolutionary convention in Williamsburg. The books he had earlier requested from Bradford in Philadelphia finally arrived: Adam Ferguson's *An Essay on the History of Civil Society* (1767), Joseph Priestley's *An Essay on the First Principles of Government, and on the Nature of Political, Civil, and Religious Liberty* (1768), and Philip Furneaux's *Essay on Toleration: With a Particular View to the Late Application of the Protestant Dissenting Ministers to Parliament, for Amending and Rendering Effectual the Act of the First of William and Mary, Commonly Called the Act of Toleration* (1773). Though Ferguson was no friend of revolution in America, his conclusion that the corruption in the Roman Empire derived in a significant way from the establishment of Christianity confirmed the revolutionary Madison's view of the harmful effects of church–state connection—in or outside of the British Empire. Madison also responded eagerly to Priestley's intent to set the honored writers of the English Whig tradition, especially John Locke, Algernon Sidney, and John Trenchard, "in a new or clearer point of light," especially their joining of political, civil, and religious liberty—an admirable "refresher course" for the young Virginian revolutionary.

The Virginia Convention of 1776, attended by the still-young James Madison, was notable for two reasons. First, it declared Virginia's independence from Great Britain and thereby placed itself in the position of being the first colony to break from the mother country. In so doing, it set a precedent that would be followed in rapid succession by the remaining twelve American colonies and the Continental Congress three months later on July 4, 1776. Second, it issued the Virginia Declaration of Rights, which created a New World precedent for governments and other political bodies to identify a broad range of core rights to which all human beings are entitled by the very fact that they are human beings. Not only was the Virginia Declaration of Rights a forerunner of the 1791 Bill of Rights of the U.S. Constitution, but it established a precedent that would eventually be adopted in many countries of the world.

Profiting from his scholarly reading and political engagement during the two years after he first raised his concerns with his classmate Bradford, Madison made important and far-reaching use of Furneaux's extension of the doctrine of religious liberty to its ultimate limit. Furneaux argued that a magistrate possessed no right whatsoever to restrain expressions of conscience because the concepts of establishment and of blasphemous libel incorrectly assumed that the good reputation and effect of religion required governmental support of an established religion. Thus Madison, like Furneaux, concluded that mere "toleration" of other sects was insufficient to protect religious freedom, and that establishments of religion themselves must be dismantled.

One of the major accomplishments of the convention attended by Madison was Virginia's 1776 Declaration of Rights pertaining to religion. Drafted principally by the elder George Mason (rather than the young James Madison), the final version as amended was sent to Philadelphia and published throughout the colonies and around the world. It expressed the general "tolerant" view of 1776 that made explicit reference to the divine at the same time that it emphasized "reason" as a means for understanding the divine. Article 16 of the Virginia Declaration provided: "That religion, or the duty we owe to our Creator, and the manner of discharging it, can be directed only by reason and conviction, not by force or violence; and therefore, that all men should enjoy the fullest toleration in the exercise of religion, according to the dictates of conscience, unpunished and unrestrained by the magistrate unless, under colour of religion, any man disturb the peace, the happiness, or the safety of society. And that it is the mutual duty of all to practice Christian forbearance, love and charity, toward each other."[6]

When the draft clause was first submitted to the whole of the Virginia Convention for consideration, Madison unsuccessfully attempted to persuade his fellow delegates to replace the "all men" phrase with the phrase "all men are equally entitled to the full and free exercise of it, according to the dictates of Conscience, and therefore that no man or class of men ought, on account of religion to be invested with peculiar emoluments or privileges; nor subjected to any penalties or disabilities unpunished and unrestrained unless under [etc.]." This substitute would have retained the clauses about restraint for reasons of public safety, and about the need to cultivate the practice of religious virtues. Madison sought to delete the invidious idea of "toleration," which Thomas Paine would later term "not the opposite of intolerance [or persecution] but . . . the counterfeit of it. Both are despotisms. The one assumes to itself the right of withholding liberty of conscience, the other of granting it."[7] Madison thus tried at the same time to broaden the "free exercise" concept and to retain and strengthen strictures on any efforts to enforce or establish civil power over religion or to impose civil restrictions because of profession (or lack of profession) of religion. As always, Madison had in mind to end government proscription of the belief and practice of religion, and to eliminate as much as possible the direct connection of church and state ("establishment") without upsetting religion's positive impact in the political realm.[8]

The final adopted version of Article 16 on religious freedom clearly reflected Madison's mature understanding: "That religion, or the duty which we owe our Creator, and the manner of discharging it, can be directed only by reason and conviction, not by force or violence; and therefore, all men are entitled to the free exercise of religion, according to the dictates of conscience; and that it is the mutual duty of all to practise Christian forbearance, love, and charity, toward each other."[9] George Bancroft called Madison's amendment of the religious liberty clause "the first achievement of the wisest civilian in Virginia."[10] Madison retained this fundamental view in 1785 and 1786 when he secured passage in Virginia of Jefferson's Act for Establishing Religious Freedom, in 1788 when he led the fight to ratify the U.S. Constitution, in 1789 when he introduced to the First Congress the Bill of Rights, in 1800 when he defended freedom of expression, in 1833 when he talked with Bancroft at Montpellier, and in everything he ever wrote on the subject of religion and politics.

Jefferson, Madison, and the Establishment of Religious Freedom in Virginia

The next prominent legislative effort to promote freedom of religion in Virginia came the following year, 1777, when Thomas Jefferson proposed the first draft of his bill for establishing religious freedom. By this time Jefferson had become famous for being the principal author of the American Declaration of Independence, drafted in Philadelphia at the same time that Madison was working on the Virginia Declaration of Rights in Williamsburg. Jefferson's own path to the drafting of what ultimately became the Virginia Act for Establishing Religious Freedom, adopted in 1786 while Jefferson was in Paris, depended intellectually on much the same broad Enlightenment philosophy that Madison had absorbed, though with less emphasis on the religion-validating Scottish "common sense" thought Madison had learned at Princeton and in his postgraduate study at Montpellier. Jefferson derived more from the freethinking, sometimes antireligious ideology seen in Bolingbroke, Thomas Paine, Joseph Priestley, and some French thinkers after Voltaire. In explaining his intentions in the second draft of the bill in 1779, for example, Jefferson noted that, although he depended on "principles which had, to a certain degree been enacted before" (evidently this meant Madison's phrasing in the Virginia Declaration of Rights of 1776), he wanted the new bill to be "drawn in all the latitude of reason and right." To this end, for example, he opposed an amendment to his bill that would have inserted the words "Jesus Christ" in the phrase "a departure from the plan of [insertion] the holy author of our religion." The insertion, Jefferson noted happily, "was rejected by a great majority, in proof that they [the legislature] meant to comprehend, within the mantle of its protection the Jew and the Gentile, the Christian and Mahometan, the Hindoo, and Infidel of every denomination."[11] Madison would also have opposed the insertion but with less emphasis that the Bill's "protection of opinion was meant to be universal" (Jefferson's phrase), and therefore especially designed to allow all individuals to believe or not believe as they pleased. Madison was always more attentive than Jefferson to the beneficial social and political effects of freedom of religion because of its general enhancement (so he believed) of a sense of justice and public spirit among citizens. He thought it significant that Pennsylvania and other middle and northern colonies with more freedom of religion had moved more earnestly toward the American Revolution than the southern colonies where firmer religious establishments prevailed.

Like many other delegates to the Continental Congress, Jefferson left Philadelphia after the Declaration of Independence in order to turn to legislative work in his home state. Jefferson wrote in his autobiography that, after drafting and signing the Declaration of Independence, "I knew that our legislation under the regal government had many very vicious points which urgently required reformation, and I thought I could be of more use in forwarding that work. I therefore retired from my seat in Congress on the 2d. of Sep[t 1776], resigned it, and took my place in the legislature of my state."[12] His intention, he later stated, was to form "a system by which every fibre would be eradicated of antient or future aristocracy, and a foundation laid for a government truly republican."[13] In moving from Philadelphia to Williamsburg, Jefferson sought to be in the most effective place not only to get rid of vicious principles and bad laws, but to enact wise and virtuous measures that would "republicanize" the laws of Virginia—an activist agenda that connected his signal achievements during the revolutionary decade between the Declaration of Independence in 1776 and the passage of the Bill for Religious Freedom in 1786.

Jefferson was one of the three principal reformers in Virginia, along with his former law teacher George Wythe and Edmund Pendleton, to replace or revise many of the laws enacted by Parliament in London. Four of the bills proposed in what became known as the "Revisal of the Laws 1776–1786" formed the core of the "system":

> The repeal of the law of entail would prevent the accumulation and per-petuation of wealth, in select families, and preserve the soil of the country from being daily more and more absorbed in mortmain. The abolition of primogeniture, and equal partition of inheritances, removed the feudal and unnatural distinctions which made one member of a family rich, and all the rest poor, substituting equal partition, the best of all Agrarian laws. The restoration of the rights of conscience relieved the people from taxation for the support of a religion not theirs; for the establishment was truly of the religion of the rich, the dissenting sects being entirely composed of the less wealthy people; and these, by the bill for a general education, would be qualified to understand their rights, to maintain them, and to exercise with intelligence their parts in self-government [this last bill not passed]; and all this would be effected, without the violation of a single natural right of any one individual citizen.[14]

For Jefferson, the overall reform of these laws aimed not only to assure natural rights to the people, but perhaps even more fundamentally, to prepare them "to exercise with intelligence their parts in self-government," first by providing them with the wherewithal to lead productive and responsible lives, then with the liberty of conscience to be free and open to engage their minds, and finally to complete their "qualification" for self-governing citizenship through a system of general education. For Jefferson, as for Madison, disestablishment of religion and liberty of conscience were always the most basic enterprises essential to the development of good citizenship.

The Virginia legislative reform committee, chaired by Jefferson in 1776, labored for three years. Some members worked on statutes carried over from English law before the establishment of government in the state of Virginia, some on laws passed in Virginia and in England between 1609 and 1776, and others on statutes needed anew to suit Virginia's status as part of a new, independent nation. Two members of the committee resigned or died. The remaining three, Jefferson, Wythe, and Pendleton, working partly together and sometimes independently, presented 126 bills to the General Assembly on June 18, 1779. The committee, exceedingly earnest, learned, and hardworking, had, under Jefferson's guidance, carefully divided up the drafting of the bills, making it uncertain sometimes exactly who drafted which bill.[15]

It is clear, however, that Jefferson drafted Bill No. 82 "for Establishing Religious Freedom," which was a newer version of the original draft bill of 1777. The need for the bill, even after the passage of Article 16 on religious freedom in the Virginia Declaration of Rights of 1776, arose, Jefferson noted, when the convention "proceeded to form on that declaration the ordinance of government, instead of taking up every principle declared in the bill of rights, and guarding it by legislative sanction, . . . passed over that which asserted our religious rights."[16] Thus, after 1776, and even after the introduction and publication of Bill No. 82 in 1779, various common law restrictions on religious freedom continued to exist including, for example, the right of a person to deny the "being of a God, or the Trinity, or assertions [that] there are more Gods than one." Severe civil penalties for religious offenses also existed under Virginia law, including prohibitions on public assembly, expulsions from the state, and denials of office-holding on religious grounds.[17] Jefferson wrote in 1782 that such was "a summary view of that religious slavery under which the people have been willing to remain," even after being able to make and live under their own laws. Ending this "slavery" was the purpose of the "Bill for Establishing Religious Freedom."[18] Divided into three sections, the Bill provides as follows:

Well aware that the opinions and belief of men depend not on their own will, but follow involuntarily the evidence proposed to their minds; that Almighty God hath created the mind free, and manifested his supreme will that free it shall remain by making it altogether insusceptible of restraint; that all attempts to influence it by temporal punishments, or burthens, or by civil incapacitations, tend only to beget habits of hypocrisy and meanness, and are a departure from the plan of the holy author of our religion, who being lord both of body and mind, yet choose not to propagate it by coercions on either, as was in his Almighty power to do, but to exalt it by its influence on reason alone; that the impious presumption of legislature and ruler, civil as well as ecclesiastical, who, being themselves but fallible and uninspired men, have assumed dominion over the faith of others, setting up their own opinions and modes of thinking as the only true and infallible, and as such endeavoring to impose them on others, hath established and maintained false religions over the greatest part of the world and through all time: That to compel a man to furnish contributions of money for the propagation of opinions which he disbelieves and abhors, is sinful and tyrannical; that even the forcing him to support this or that teacher of his own religious persuasion, is depriving him of the comfortable liberty of giving his contributions to the particular pastor whose morals he would make his pattern, and whose powers he feels most persuasive to righteousness; and is withdrawing from the ministry those temporary rewards, which proceeding from an approbation of their personal conduct, are an additional incitement to earnest and unremitting labours for the instruction of mankind; that our civil rights have no dependance on our religious opinions, any more than our opinions in physics or geometry; and therefore the proscribing any citizen as unworthy the public confidence by laying upon him an incapacity of being called to offices of trust or emolument, unless he profess or renounce this or that religious opinion, is depriving him injudiciously of those privileges and advantages to which, in common with his fellow-citizens, he has a natural right; that it tends also to corrupt the principles of that very religion it is meant to encourage, by bribing with a monopoly of worldly honours and emoluments, those who will externally profess and conform to it; that though indeed these are criminals who do not withstand such temptation, yet neither are those innocent who lay the bait in their way; that the opinions of men are not the object of civil government, nor under its jurisdiction; that to suffer the civil magistrate to intrude his powers into the field of opinion and to restrain the profession or propagation of principles on supposition of their ill tendency is a dangerous fallacy, which at once destroys all religious liberty, because he being of course judge of that tendency will make his opinions the rule of judgment, and approve or condemn the sentiments of others only as they shall square with or suffer from his own; that it is time enough for the rightful purposes of civil government for its officers to interfere when principles break out into overt acts against peace and good order; and finally, that truth is great and will prevail if left to herself; that she is the proper and sufficient antagonist to error, and has nothing to fear from the conflict unless by human interposition disarmed of her natural weapons, free argument and debate; errors ceasing to be dangerous when it is permitted freely to contradict them.

We the General Assembly of Virginia do enact that no man shall be compelled to frequent or support any religious worship, place, or ministry whatsoever, nor shall be enforced, restrained, molested, or burthened in his body or goods, or shall otherwise suffer, on account of his religious opinions or belief; but that all men shall be free to profess, and by argument to maintain, their opinions in matters of religion, and that the same shall in no wise diminish, enlarge, or affect their civil capacities.

And though we well know that this Assembly, elected by the people for their ordinary purposes of legislation only, have no power to restrain the acts of succeeding Assemblies, constituted with powers equal to our own, and that therefore to declare this act to be irrevocable would be of no effect in law; yet we are free to declare, and do declare, that the rights hereby asserted are of the natural rights of mankind, and that if any act shall be hereafter passed to repeal the present or to narrow its operations, such act will be an infringement of natural right.[19]

Madison, of course, was entirely pleased with the purpose and tenor of Jefferson's bill. By June 1779 and even more so by 1785, the two men had had ample opportunity to talk about the bill, and both saw it as a fulfillment of the Enlightenment ideals of natural rights, liberty of conscience, and civic improvement.

This would be the foundation of one of the most profound and important political friendships in American history. The changes, though mostly deletions, made in Jefferson's draft during the bill's slow and complicated legislative passages, reveal the different emphases in the thinking of the two men on religious freedom. The deletions in the first long phrase of the bill, for example—leaving only the simple statement that "Almighty God hath created the mind free," and then the deletion some lines later, of *"but to extend it by its influence on reason alone"*[20]—leave out philosophical assertions about how the human mind works and about the sole efficacy of reason. Jefferson favored this view of reason; Madison would not have objected to it, but would not have been inclined to emphasize it. More than Jefferson, Madison emphasized the good influence and public utility of the religious faith of many of his Princeton classmates, and he kept a place in his thinking for insights and beliefs that did not contradict but rather transcended reason alone.

One also can see the difference between the two men by noting Jefferson's enthusiasm for the writings of Thomas Paine and Joseph Priestley (free-thinking "atheists" in the polemics of the time) on the one hand, and Madison's admiration for two works that emphasized the social and political advantages of freedom of religion: Sir William Temple's *Observations upon United Provinces [of the Netherlands]* (1673), which extolled how religious freedom there had greatly stimulated the growth and prosperity of that state, and Voltaire's *Letters Concerning the English Nation* (1733),[21] which likewise saw England's greatness in the eighteenth century stemming from its religious toleration.[22] Although Madison was only mildly interested in the theologies involved, he was intensely attentive to the creative and vigorous societies nourished by religious freedom. Though both the Netherlands in the seventeenth century[23] and Great Britain in the eighteenth century had religious establishments, they were, compared to France, Spain, and indeed most other nations and empires of the world at the time, much less oppressive and intolerant and, in Madison's view, this greatly benefited them. Jefferson would not have disagreed, but would have emphasized—more than Madison—the philosophical issues.

In the early 1780s, after working with Jefferson in Williamsburg, Madison spent more than three years in the Continental Congress in Philadelphia where his main concern soon came to be strengthening the national government. While Madison worked in Philadelphia, Jefferson had become governor of Virginia. Barely escaping Cornwallis's army, which chased him from his home at Monticello, Jefferson moved with the state government to the Piedmont before suffering the great personal tragedy of the deaths of his wife and child. Thereafter he returned to join Madison in Congress, only to be promptly appointed to become the nation's minister to France. With England's recognition of American independence in 1783, and with his friend's departure for Paris by the fall of 1784, Madison returned to the Virginia legislature. Though separated by an ocean and hindered by irregular mail service, Madison and

Jefferson communicated frequently as the two men continued their earnest and like-minded attention to improving the principles and practices of self-government in Virginia and in the nation as a whole.

High on their common agenda was the enactment of Jefferson's pending "Bill for Establishing Freedom of Religion." It had suffered delay, efforts at amendment, and even attempts to set it aside entirely, as traditional forces from various religious persuasions sought to retain some establishment or state support for one or more religions. Many still accepted the old arguments that good government required the support of religion and that religion in turn needed government support to flourish. Repeating Madison's prerevolutionary arguments before leaving for France, Jefferson expressed his disgust with the obstruction and delays over his bill, and pointed to the fact that the experience of Pennsylvania and New York had disproved "the infallibility of establishments." Having "long subsisted without any establishment at all, . . . they flourish infinitely. Religion is well supported; of various kinds, indeed, but all good enough; sufficient to preserve peace and order." "Let us too give this experiment fair play, and get rid, while we may," he urged in 1782, "of those tyrannical laws"[24] that still oppressed Virginians and deprived their state of the civic benefits of freedom of religion.

In the fall of 1784, Madison was back in the Virginia legislature, now meeting in the new capital city of Richmond. One of his fellow legislators, the once-revolutionary firebrand Patrick Henry, led the forces favoring some kind of establishment or support of religion. Henry declaimed fervently that there had been "moral decay" in Virginia since disestablishment. Supported by petitions from tidewater counties where the establishment had been long entrenched, Henry introduced a new bill to support "Teachers of the Christian Religion" through a general tax assessment of three pence. Though the bill for a religious tax, as presented by Henry to the legislature, did not require citizens to support religions in which they did not believe, Madison still thought it "obnoxious on account of its dishonorable principle and dangerous tendency." He spoke earnestly against the bill, but sensing possible defeat at the hands of Henry's oratory and legislative skill, succeeded only in postponing final action on it until the next year.

Through the early months of 1785, Madison sensed a shift in popular opinion and was pleased that many people, including many religious groups in Virginia, seemed ready to oppose the pending legislation. In addition, Patrick Henry had since been elected governor and thus would be out of the legislature, "a circumstance very inauspicious to his offspring" there, Madison told Monroe.[25] Even some Episcopalians who favored more lay control of the church were uneasy that the assessment bill would strengthen the hand of the clergy who were expected under it to be the state-paid "Teachers of the Christian Religion." The Presbyterian clergy, fearful of lay opposition to the assessment and jealous of the advantage it might give the Episcopalians, began turning against their previous support of the bill. Baptists and Methodists, growing rapidly in the state, opposed this religious assessment in principle, and also well remembered their harsh treatment by the Anglican establishment before the Revolution, examples of which Madison had witnessed personally. Altogether it seemed to Madison that it might now be possible to not only defeat Henry's assessment bill but perhaps even pass Jefferson's Bill Establishing Religious Freedom.[26]

At his home at Montpelier in June 1785, Madison was pressed to draft a "Memorial and Remonstrance against Religious Assessments" that might circulate throughout the state encouraging people to send petitions to the session of the legislature that would be meeting that fall, as this was where the crucial votes would take place. To prepare his "Memorial," Madison turned once again to his books and papers on freedom of religion, a favored topic since his tentative questions about it to William Bradford twelve years earlier. He also had before him notes for the speeches he had delivered in the Virginia Assembly at the previous session, rehearsing his long-held views on the natural right of liberty of conscience and the dangers establishment of religion posed to both the vitality of religion and the responsible, moral conduct of the citizenry. The "Memorial and Remonstrance" identified fourteen reasons that he hoped would persuade the people and legislators of the assessment's violation of the natural and civic rights of freedom of religion and liberty of conscience:

1. Religious liberty was "in its nature an inalienable right . . . because the opinions of men, depending only upon the evidence contemplated by their own minds, cannot follow the dictates of other men. . . . Religion is wholly exempt from the cognizance" of civil society.
2. Because civil society itself has no right to interfere with religion, certainly the legislature, its creature, has no such right.
3. "It is proper to take alarm at the first experiment on our liberties. . . . Who does not see that the same authority which can establish Christianity, in exclusion of all other Religions, may establish with the same ease any particular sect of Christians, in exclusion of all other Sects?"
4. The free exercise of religion implies the right to believe in no religion at all, so even the most permissive tax to support religion might violate some consciences.
5. Civil magistrates can properly neither judge religious truth nor "employ Religion as an engine of Civil policy."
6. The Christian religion did not need civic support; it had often "existed and flourished, not only without the support of human laws, but in spite of every opposition from them."
7. "Ecclesiastical establishment," far from promoting religious purity and efficacy, had nearly always corrupted, stultified, and made it more bigoted.

8. The assessment, differed from "the Inquisition . . . only in degree," and would make Virginia no longer an asylum for the persecuted.
9. Good and useful citizens would be driven from the state or deterred from coming there by a religious tax.
10. Religious strife and dissention would be encouraged by laws touching on religion.
11. "The policy of the bill is adverse to the diffusion of the light of Christianity. . . . The bill with an ignoble and unchristian timidity would circumscribe it, with a wall of defence, against the encroachments of error."
12. An attempt to enforce a religious assessment obnoxious to many citizens would weaken respect for law and order generally.
13. Evidence was strong that a majority of the people opposed the assessment.
14. "Because, finally, the equal right of every citizen to the free exercise of his Religion according to the dictates of conscience is held by the same tenure with all our rights. If we recur to its origin, it is equally the gift of nature; if we weigh its importance, it cannot be less dear to us, if we consult the Declaration of those rights which pertain to the good people of Virginia, as the basis and foundation of Government, it is enumerated with equal solemnity, or rather studied emphasis. Either then, we must say, that the will of the Legislature is the only measure of their authority; and that in the plentitude of its authority, they may sweep away our fundamental rights; or, that they are bound to leave this particular right untouched and sacred: Either we may say, that they may control the freedom of the press, may abolish trial by jury, may swallow up the Executive and Judiciary Powers of the State; nay that they may despoil us of our very right of suffrage and erect themselves into an independent and hereditary assembly: or we must say, that they have no authority to enact into law the Bill now under consideration."[27]

Throughout the Memorial, Madison repeatedly used the word *establish* with reference to the three-pence tax, as if to underscore that even a small tax for the support of religious education qualified to make the law one that promoted an establishment of religion.

George Mason, who had been the principal author of the Virginia Declaration of Rights, arranged for the publication of the "Memorial and Remonstrance" (without indicating authorship) for distribution in northern Virginia, and George Nicholas circulated copies in central and western Virginia, all to encourage petitions to the legislature opposing the assessment bill. Of more than one hundred religious petitions submitted to the coming legislative session, only eleven supported assessment and ninety opposed it, thirteen of them using the language of the "Memorial and Remonstrance" to help express their opposition. A Presbyterian convention in August condemned the assessment bill and then even supported Jefferson's Bill, and a General Committee of Baptists opposed the religious tax. By the time the legislature met in October 1785, none of the supporters of religious assessment even thought it worthwhile to resurrect the bill for legislative enactment.

The tide having decisively shifted, Madison decided to include passage of Jefferson's Bill for the Establishment of Religious Freedom in the overall effort to pass the much-postponed reform of the laws that had been drafted years earlier. Under Madison's prodding, the legislature enacted thirty-five of the bills, but stalled and running out of time, in December it jumped ahead and took up Jefferson's Bill. Though there was "warm" opposition in the lower house, the bill passed essentially unchanged on December 17, 1785. In the Senate, opponents succeeded in deleting much of Jefferson's eloquent preamble, but a conference with the House restored the preamble fundamentally unmarred, and the bill received final enactment on January 19, 1786.

Reporting the news to Jefferson, Madison noted that though legislative maneuvering had "defaced the composition" to some degree, the enacting clauses especially had been passed unchanged: "I flatter myself," the legislator exalted to the author, that we "have in this country extinguished forever the ambitious hope of making laws for the human mind." Jefferson responded eleven months later that "it is honorable for us to have produced the first legislature who has had the courage to declare that the reason of man may be trusted with the formation of his own opinions." "[The Act] has been received with infinite approbation in Europe and propagated with enthusiasm," Jefferson wrote, and had been translated into French and Italian, and included in the *Encyclopédie méthodique* and other important publications. He was also pleased with the civic effects of the Act: it had "been the best evidence of the falsehood of those reports which stated us to be in anarchy."[28]

The drafting and passage of the Act for Establishing Religious Freedom clarified for Jefferson and especially Madison the meaning of the word *establishment* in their understanding of the place of religion in the realm of the political. They came to conclude that all establishments of religion—including the three-pence tax proposed in the Henry bill—violated religious liberty. They sought the total rejection of the time-honored precept that the good of both church and state required direct, statutory, and even financial support of some or all religious creeds or institutions, or required the diminishment or disadvantage of any other creed or institution. Hence, in language Madison later proposed for the "establishment clause" of the Federal Constitution, "the civil rights of none shall be abridged on account of religious belief or worship, nor shall any national religion be established."[29] Abridgment of civil rights on religious grounds both infringed the natural right of equal participation in self-government and denied to the polity the likely useful contribution of the citizen "better qualified" by the practice of liberty of conscience and free exercise of religion.

Madison and Jefferson believed that *all* establishments, whether in the states or by the federal governments, were violations of religious freedom. The establishment of "any national religion" similarly constrained important civic processes in that it would inhibit the growth of vigorous religious institutions that might contribute to "noble enterprises," as Madison believed had happened under freedom of religion in Pennsylvania before the Revolution. Establishment, in Jefferson's phrase, "beget[s] habits of hypocrisy and meanness," and in Madison's "shackles and debilitates the mind," all contrary to the idea and practice of good citizenship.[30] Unstated but unmistakably implicit is the proposition that friendly neutrality toward and even encouragement of religions that "enoble" and "expand" the mind (Madison's language in 1774) might be a worthy civic objective. Jefferson stated late in life (in 1822) that now that "the freedom of religious opinion, and its external divorce from the civil authority" had been vindicated in the nation, he even hoped "that the present generation will see Unitarianism become the general religion of the United States." Though he believed in only one God "as my reason tells me," Jefferson said, "I yield as freely to others that of believing in three, [since] . . . both religions . . . make honest men, and that is the only point society has a right to look to."[31] Put another way, Jefferson and Madison saw *establishment* as requiring the complete separation of church and state: formally, as institutions, as matters of law to avoid corruption and biases, but also because (again, especially Madison) religion had a useful and important role to play generally in the realm of the political.

Madison, Jefferson, and the Religious Freedom of the Nation

The views of the two men on the disestablishment of religion received further clarification in their discussion of the U.S. Constitution of 1787 and the possible addition of a bill of rights. Jefferson, seeing the new constitution in Paris and noting its lack of a bill of rights, wrote at once, in his usual sweeping style, "a bill of rights is what the people are entitled to against every government on earth, general or particular, and what no just government should refuse, or rest on inference." Madison agreed that natural rights should be protected, but believed that "parchment barriers" (words in constitutions or statutes) were not enough. In fact, he said, such constitutional measures could even be dangerous if they led to an unwarranted confidence that by themselves they would protect rights. It had been his experience in Virginia, notably in the sometimes strong public pressures in support of the religious assessments bill despite the Virginia Declaration of Rights, that he had "seen the Bill of Rights violated in every instance where it has been opposed to a popular current." There had also been, he added, "repeated violations of these parchment barriers . . . by overbearing majorities in every state."[32] Instead

Madison urged that rights would be better protected when the very structure of the government itself, depending on the people and, replete with checks and balances, would limit the intentions for and hinder the passage of oppressive acts.

Madison pointed out at the Virginia ratifying convention that freedom of religion in the United States "arises from the multiplicity of sects, which pervades America, and which is the best and only security for religious liberty in any society. For where there is such a variety of sects, there cannot be a majority of any one sect to oppress and persecute the rest. . . . The United States abound in such a variety of sects, that it is a strong security against religious persecution."[33] This was the case because the size and structure of the general government contained powerful implicit protection against sectarian or other impulses to establish religion or endanger liberty of conscience. Madison thus made the procedural defense of religious freedom part of his overall theory of preventing unjust or tyrannical measures through "the extent and proper structure of the Union," to include more factions that, along with checks and balances, would help prevent the domination of any one interest or party.[34]

Despite this "structural" argument that religious freedom was already protected from federal interference even before the adoption of the Bill of Rights, Madison agreed with Jefferson that there were two grounds, nonetheless, for adding a bill of rights to the new Constitution: "1. The political truths declared in that solemn manner acquire by degrees the character of fundamental maxims of free Government, and as they become incorporated with the National sentiment, counteract the impulses of interest and passion. 2. Although it be generally true . . . that the danger of oppression lies in the interested majorities of the people rather than the usurped acts of the Government, yet there may be occasions on which the evil may spring from the latter source; and on such, a bill of rights will be a good ground for an appeal to the sense of the community." The effectiveness depended on the work of the federal judiciary, which might, in Jefferson's words echoed by Madison, give a "legal check" through its "learning and integrity" to *"civium ardor prava jubentium"* ("the wayward zeal of the ruling citizens"). Most notable here is Madison's attention again to the uses of religious freedom and even the means of protecting it by understanding how the incorporation of "fundamental maxims of free Government . . . [in] the National sentiment" might improve the principles and practices of citizenship.[35]

After the ratification of the Constitution in 1789, Jefferson remained in France, now as ambassador for the new nation. There he observed the beginning of the French Revolution while Madison won election as a Representative from Virginia to the First Congress that would convene in New York City, the temporary capital of the new nation. The two political friends and allies nevertheless continued their joint efforts to implant the ideas of the Virginia Bill for Establishing Religious Freedom into the new federal constitution. During his campaign for Congress, Madison promised to sponsor a bill of rights. On June

8, 1789, he fulfilled that campaign pledge by introducing into the First Congress what became the first draft of the Bill of Rights. "The civil rights of none shall be abridged on account of religious belief or worship, nor shall any national religion be established, nor shall the full and equal rights of conscience be in any manner, or on any pretext, be infringed." "The people shall not be deprived or abridged in their right to speak, to write, or to publish their sentiments; and the freedom of the press, as one of the great bulwarks of liberty, shall be inviolable." "The people shall not be restrained from peaceably assembling and consulting for their common good; nor from applying to the Legislature by petitions, or remonstrances, for redress of their grievances."[36]

Though Madison's draft provision clearly sought to ensure individual rights, it is even clearer that he has in mind that the people must be protected and aided in their practice of deliberative citizenship. Hence they are not to be restrained in their right to vote, hold office, or speak because of their religion, nor is a national religion to be allowed that would stifle the cultivation of conscience or the deliberations associated with religious freedom. People must be able to express their "sentiments" on public affairs, just as a free press is a "great bulwark" undergirding the very existence of self-government. Finally, the right to assemble assures that the people can consult as part of the government for the common good, and to petition in order to engage with their government about their grievances. At the same time Madison revealed the particular meaning he gave to his opposition to "established religion": he meant that there could be no constitutional provisions or laws that constrain any kind of civic participation because of a person's religion (thus denying the people their probably useful place in public life, as for example, the long-standing denial of the ballot to Roman Catholics in England), nor could there be a national church supported and privileged to the detriment of other, in Madison's view, likely more vigorous, morally attuned free churches. As always, his emphasis was on the role of the rights—including the rights of religious freedom—in enhancing the public good.

As the proposals for a bill of rights passed through the House of Representatives, then the Senate, and finally a conference to resolve differences in the bills, Madison sought with only partial success to ward off changes that would alter the fundamental powers granted to the federal government in the Constitution, and especially that would weaken the guarantees of the newly added rights of the people. Both came up when a Connecticut Congressman said "he feared . . . that the words [of Madison's proposal] might be taken in such latitude as to be extremely hurtful to the cause of religion." This led to a motion (agreed to in the House) for substitute language in the religious freedom amendment: "Congress shall make no laws touching religion, or infringing the rights of conscience."[37] The intent was both to be explicit that the amendment should restrict only the federal government (hence "Congress shall make no laws"), and to prevent Congress from being able to interfere with existing state laws establishing religion (common in New England) or with similar laws that other states might choose to enact. Anti-Federalist sentiment in Congress was also still strong enough to defeat Madison's proposed addition to the bill of rights that "no state shall violate the equal rights of conscience, or freedom of the press, or the trial by jury in criminal cases"—"no state shall" was a red flag to state's rights proponents—but Madison was able otherwise to restore the stronger, clearer language of the basic amendment: "Congress shall make no law establishing religion, or to prevent the free exercise thereof, or to infringe the rights of conscience."[38]

Madison also helped defeat in the House other attempts to either eliminate the word *establishment* or weaken its scope, and he approved similar moves in the Senate to retain the strong, broad language. Though disappointed that his effort to extend the bill of rights protections to the states had failed, Madison was pleased with the final language that became part of the First Amendment. It did not basically depart from the intent of the public good, citizenship-enhancing language he had introduced to begin with—especially the broad meaning implicit in the word *establishment*. Although Madison's wish to use the federal Constitution to limit state establishments of religion did not succeed, this does not mean that he or others believed that state establishments were good. The federal Constitution similarly did not prevent the states from infringing upon other major rights, including freedom of speech, freedom of the press, or the right to peaceably assemble. The fact that the federal Constitution did not limit such state practices should not be understood to mean that state restrictions on these freedoms were acceptable from a perspective of the rights of the people.

Madison had explained again in introducing the amendments his deep political reasons for and understanding of the place of freedom of religion and other basic rights in the new American constitutional government. He told his legislative colleagues that "if we can make the Constitution better in the opinion of those who are opposed to it, without weakening its frame, or abridging its usefulness in the judgment of those who are attached to it, we act the part of wise and liberal men."[39] This would, he thought, help reconcile the tensions between liberty and majority rule deliberately present in the Constitution itself. He explained that

> the prescriptions in favor of liberty [i.e., the bill of rights] ought to be leveled against the quarter where the greatest danger lies, namely, that which possesses the highest prerogative of power. But this is not found in either the Executive or Legislative departments of Government, but in the body of the people, operating by the majority against the minority. It may be thought that all paper barriers against the power of the community are too weak to be worthy of attention; . . . yet as they [paper barriers; bills of rights] have a tendency to impress some degree of respect for them [natural rights], to

establish the public opinion in their favor, and rouse the attention of the whole community, it may be one means to control the majority from those acts to which it might be otherwise inclined.[40]

Freedom from established religion and liberty of conscience had basic roles to play in helping improve public opinion that in the long run was the only effective way to preserve a free, self-governing society. Madison's concern was: How could the nation organize its public life, enhance the quality of its citizenship, and improve the performance of its legislators and other leaders, and at the same time provide the strongest, most lasting protection to human rights?

Conclusion: Madison's Final Reflections

In retirement and nearly forty years after Madison and Jefferson had dealt with issues of establishment and liberty of conscience in Virginia and elsewhere, Madison had an opportunity to assess what had happened on the issues over his long lifetime. In response to inquiries about the status of religion in Virginia and the civil effects of religious freedom, he observed that there could be no doubt that

there has been an increase of religious instruction since the revolution. . . . The English church was originally the established religion. . . . Of other sects there were but few adherents, except for Presbyterians who predominated on the W. side of the Blue Mountains. A little time previous to the Revolutionary struggle the Baptists sprang up, and made a very rapid progress. Among the early acts of the Republican Legislature, were those abolishing the Religious establishment, and putting all Sects at full liberty and on a perfect level. At present the population is divided, with small exceptions, among Protestant Episcopalians, the Presbyterians, the Baptists & the Methodists. . . . The Old churches, built under the establishment at the public expense, have in many instances gone to ruin, or are in a very dilapidated state, owing chiefly to a desertion of the flocks to other worships. A few new ones have latterly been built particularly in the towns. Among the other sects, Meeting Houses have multiplied & continue to multiply; though in general they are of the plainest and cheapest sort. But neither the number nor the style of the Religious edifices is a true measure of the state of religion. Religious instruction is now diffused throughout the Community by preachers of every sect with almost equal zeal, tho' with very unequal acquirements; and at private houses & open stations and occasionally in such as are appropriated to Civil use, as well as buildings appropriated to that use. The qualifications of the Preachers, too among the new sects where there was the greatest deficiency, are understood to be improving. On a general comparison of the present & former times, the balance is certainly and vastly on the side of the present, as to the number of religious teachers, the zeal which actuates them, the purity of their lives, and the attendance of the people on their instructions. It was the Universal opinion of the Century preceding the last, that Civil Govt. could not stand without the prop of a Religious establishment, & that the Xn. Religion itself would perish if not supported by a legal provision for its Clergy. The experience of Virginia conspicuously corroborates the disproof of both opinions. The Civil Govt. tho' bereft of everything like an associated hierarchy possesses the requisite stability and performs its functions with complete success; Whilst the number, the industry, and the morality of the Priesthood, & the devotion of the people have been manifestly increased by the total separation of the Church from the State.[41]

In response to another inquiry three years later, Madison pointed out that the law giving a salary to congressional chaplains from public funds had passed without his "approbation"; he favored instead the payment of the chaplains by a "pittance from their own pockets" from members of "pious feelings."[42] In any case Madison thought that by 1822 the matter was not worth attending to; it illustrated, he thought, "the maxim of the law, *de minimis non curat* [do not bother with trifles]." Madison noted as well that while president he had issued "Executive Proclamations of fasts & festivals . . . [to] follow the example of predecessors." "But I was always careful," he added, "to make the Proclamations absolutely indiscriminate, and merely recommendatory; or rather mere *designations* of a day, on which all who thought proper might *unite* in consecrating it to religious purposes, according to their own faith & forms."[43] In looking historically at church–state relations in Europe, Madison explained that "it was the belief of all sects at one time that the establishment of Religion by law, was right and necessary; that the true religion ought to be established to the exclusion of every other; and that the only question to be decided was which was the true religion. The example of Holland proved that the toleration of sects, dissenting from the established sect, was safe and even useful."[44]

In every instance Madison bespoke his hostility to the idea of establishment in any form because of its harmful effect on vital religion and good government (both of which he favored), and because it was "useful" to the growth of a free, more republican society. For half a century, then, Madison held to the principles that he and Jefferson had implanted in the Virginia Act for Establishing Religious Freedom that "Almighty God hath created the mind free"; that "to suffer the civil magistrate to intrude his powers into the field of opposition and to restrain the propagation of principles on supposition of their ill tendency is a dangerous fallacy"; and "that all men shall be free to profess, and by argument to maintain, their opinions in matters of religion, and the same shall in no wise diminish, enlarge, or affect their civil capacities."[45]

Notes

1. William T. Hutchinson et al., eds., *The Papers of James Madison*, 17 vols. (Chicago: University of Chicago Press, 1962), 1:101–6.

2. Ibid.

3. Ibid.

4. Ibid.

5. Ibid.

6. Ibid., 1:175.

7. Thomas Paine, *The Rights of Man*, pt. 1, in *The Founders' Constitution*, 5 vols., ed. Philip B. Kurland and Ralph Lerner (Chicago: University of Chicago Press, 1987), 5:95–96.

8. Hutchinson et al., *Papers of James Madison*, 1:170–79.

9. Ibid., 1:175.

10. George Bancroft, *The History of the United States*, 6 vols. (New York: D. Appleton, 1883–1885), 4:416–17.

11. Julian P. Boyd et al., *The Papers of Thomas Jefferson*, 37 vols. (Princeton, NJ: Princeton University Press, 1950), 2:552.

12. Ibid.

13. Ibid.

14. Adrienne Koch and William Peden, eds., *The Life and Selected Writings of Thomas Jefferson* (New York: Modern Library, 1993), 49–50.

15. The long note by Julian P. Boyd in *Papers of Thomas Jefferson*, 2:305–24 tells with great precision and erudition the complicated story of the drafting, publication, and enactment or non-enactment of the 126 bills.

16. Boyd et al., *Papers of Thomas Jefferson*, 2:547–52.

17. Ibid.

18. Koch and Peden, *Writings of Thomas Jefferson*, 254.

19. Boyd et al., *Papers of Thomas Jefferson*, 2:545–49.

20. Ibid., 2:545, 552.

21. Also published as *Lettres Philosophiques* (Paris and Amsterdam: E. Lucas, 1734). Madison likely used the London edition of this work, published the prior year.

22. Ralph Ketcham, "Observing North Atlantic Polities, 1662–1840: Sir William Temple, Voltaire, and Alexis de Tocqueville," in *Connecting Cultures: The Netherlands in Five Centuries of Transatlantic Exchange*, ed. Rosemarijn Hoefte and Johanna C. Kardux (Amsterdam: Vrije Universiteit Press, 1994), 211–18.

23. See further chapter 5 by Paul Finkelman.

24. Koch and Peden, *Writings of Thomas Jefferson*, 296

25. Madison to Monroe, November 27, 1784, in Hutchinson et al., *Papers of James Madison*, 8:156–58

26. Lance Banning, "James Madison, the Statute for Religious Freedom, and the Crisis of Republican Convictions," in *The Virginia Statute of Religious Freedom*, ed. Merrill D. Peterson and Robert Vaughan (New York: Cambridge University Press, 1988) 114–18.

27. Hutchinson et al., *Papers of James Madison*, 8:295–306.

28. Ibid., 8:474.

29. James Madison, Speech in Congress, June 8, 1789, in ibid., 1:106. See further chapter 8 by Carl Esbeck.

30. Ibid., 1: 106

31. Thomas Jefferson, Letter to James Smith, December 8, 1822, in Koch and Peden, *Writings of Thomas Jefferson*, 642–43.

32. Hutchinson et al., *Papers of James Madison*, 11:297–300.

33. James Madison, Speech, June 12, 1788, in ibid., 11:132–33.

34. *Federalist* No. 10, in Clinton Rossiter, ed., *The Federalist Papers*, ed. Clinton Rossiter (New York: New American Library, 1961), 84.

35. Hutchinson et al., *Papers of James Madison*, 11:299–300.

36. Ibid., 12:98.

37. Ibid., 12:173–76.

38. Ibid. See detailed discussion of the First Congress's formulation of the First Amendment in chapter 8 by Carl Esbeck.

39. Hutchinson et al., *Papers of James Madison*, 11:299–300.

40. Andy G. Olree, "James Madison and Legislative Chaplains," *Northwestern University Law Review* 102 (2008), 177–81; Martha Nussbaum, *Liberty of Conscience: In Defense of America's Tradition of Religious Equality* (New York: Basic Books, 2008), 97–114.

41. Ralph Ketcham, ed., *Selected Writings of James Madison* (Indianapolis, IN: Hackett, 2006), 304–6.

42. Ibid.

43. Ibid.

44. Ibid., 306–7.

45. Ibid.

7

The Continental Congress and Emerging Ideas of Church–State Separation

Derek H. Davis

On January 20, 1775, in the British House of Lords, the illustrious Lord Chatham (William Pitt) delivered a remarkable speech. A former prime minister, Lord Chatham was an outspoken defender of the struggling colonists of America in their protracted controversy with the British king and parliament. He vindicated, in the fullest and clearest manner, the right of the colonists to refuse to be taxed without their consent. "The spirit," he said, "which now resists your taxation in America, is the same which formerly opposed loans, benevolences and ship money in England; the same spirit which called all England on its feet, and by its bill of rights vindicated the English Constitution, the same spirit which established the great, fundamental, essential maxim of your liberties, that *no subject of England shall be taxed but by his own consent.*" On this great principle, and in this cause, the American colonists, he added, "are immovably allied; it is the alliance of God and nature, immutable, eternal, fixed as the firmament of Heaven."[1]

At that same time, the Continental Congress, a rather impressive collection of colonial leaders, was in session in Philadelphia and had barely initiated those plans and purposes that only months later found expression in the great charter of the colonists' rights and liberties, the Declaration of Independence. Of this body of patriotic men, Lord Chatham made this memorable declaration:

> When your Lordships look at the papers transmitted to us from America; when you consider their decency, firmness, and wisdom, you can not but respect their cause, and wish to make it your own. For myself I must declare and avow, that in all my reading and observation—and it has been my favorite study, I have read Thucydides, and have studied and admired the master States of the world—that for solidity of reasoning, force of sagacity and wisdom of conclusion, under such a complication of difficult circumstances,

no nation or body of men can stand in preference to the General Congress assembled at Philadelphia.[2]

This was high eulogy, and from the lips of one so familiar with the great men of history, it was exalted praise. Naturally, Lord Chatham's assessment of the men of the Continental Congress would not have seemed to most Americans an exaggeration. Suddenly brought together to meet a pressing emergency, Congress's membership was made from the most thoughtful and talented men in the American colonies. And, the importance of the hour was recognized by these men who, as members of America's first national assembly, would set the course for the historic events centered on the formation and shaping of a new nation.

Perhaps it was John Adams who was most sensitive to the magnitude of the situation. "It has been the will of Heaven," he wrote in January 1776, "that we should be thrown into existence at a period when the greatest philosophers and lawgivers of antiquity would have wished to live. A period when [we have] an opportunity of beginning government anew from the foundation. . . . How few of the human race have ever had any opportunity of choosing a system of government for themselves and their children."[3]

The Continental Congress was the body of delegates that represented the common interests of first the colonies and then the states from 1774 to 1789. The first and second of these congresses, which assembled in September 1774 and May 1775, respectively, were called to meet a pressing emergency—potential war with Great Britain—and served only in an advisory capacity to the colonies because the congresses were extralegal bodies. Subsequent congresses, serving during and after the Revolutionary War, acted as the central government of the American union under the Articles of Confederation. The Continental Congress dissolved March 4, 1789, when it was superseded by the new government established under the U.S. Constitution.

Given the Congress's talented composition and the magnitude of the hour in which Congress was called to serve, one might be surprised that historians have often criticized the Continental Congress—particularly the inadequacies of the Articles of Confederation, which was indeed an awkward document that did not permit the national government to function efficiently. In retrospect, however, the Congress had many notable achievements: It declared independence from Great Britain, then successfully prosecuted the war and negotiated the peace. It also managed to carry on the routine administration of matters that were of mutual concern to the states, while allowing the states to maintain their sovereignty.

Religion and the Continental Congress

Rarely is the Continental Congress examined from the perspective of the role that religion played in its proceedings and official acts. Because the Congress operated free of any formal notions of church–state separation, its work was in fact frequently imbued with a profound religious spirit. The present study examines generally the ways in which religion influenced the work of the Congress and specifically its contributions to the competing merits of establishment and nonestablishment.

The religious dimensions of the work of the Continental Congress were in many ways a reflection of a culture dominated by Protestantism, but increasingly, at least among educated elites, influenced by Enlightenment rationalism. These competing perspectives contributed to different ideas about establishment among the founders.

It is important that we not read too much into the acts and proceedings of the Continental Congress in formulating state and national policy regarding religion in our own day. The era preceded formal ideas of church–state separation on a national scale. Some of the colonies had experimented with church-state separation insofar as they did not fund some churches over others, and separationist theories had been advanced since the days of Marsilius of Padua in the fourteenth century, but no nation had ever formally adopted a principle of church–state separation, as the United States was to do when it adopted the Constitution in 1787 and Bill of Rights in 1789. The members of the Continental Congress did not reflect systematically on the relationship between religion and the new nation that was gradually taking shape: They were consumed with prosecuting a war against Great Britain. Consideration of the role of religion in the new republic came later—after the colossal battle against the greatest military power on the globe. But the Congress did understandably enlist divine aid in its proceedings, encouraged the American people to do likewise, and generally operated with a profoundly religious outlook.

The American Constitution and Bill of Rights marked an important shift from the interdependence of the institutions of religion and government to their mutual independence. But it remains unclear how the founders sought to implement this new framework of independence. Would any advancement of religion by the federal government be permitted? Would the federal government have any authority to deal with religious questions arising in the states? To what extent would religious exercises be allowed in government circles? What were the meanings of the First Amendment's first sixteen words, enacted as part of the Bill or Rights in 1791: "Congress shall make no laws respecting an establishment of religion, or prohibiting the free exercise thereof"?[4]

The proceedings and official acts of the Continental Congress help discern the framers' intent with respect to the role of religion in the United States. The Constitution and Bill of Rights were not drafted in a vacuum, free from the influence of the nation's immediate history or of its leaders. They were written following a period in which the Continental Congress had served as the nation's first representative government and had confronted many difficult issues having to do with religion: the religious grounding of human government in general, the propriety of employing religious means for political ends, the meaning of religious liberty for American citizens, and the expenditure of government monies for religious ends. Moreover, of the fifty-five delegates to the Constitutional Convention, forty-two had served as members of at least one of the Continental Congresses.[5] They brought with them certain habits of thought and practices that would inevitably influence their thinking in drafting the documents that would determine policy and practice for many years to come. In short, examining the Continental Congress's record on religion sheds valuable light on the framers' original intentions.

Religion and the Continental Congress in Historical Context

Western political theory since the advent of the Christian era has been dominated by the belief that religion is central to a rightly ordered polity. Religion has usually been understood to have an ontological status that demands its formal recognition by the civil order. The inevitable result has been the struggle between "church" and "state" in which each has sought to dominate the other. The American constitutional system was a unique experiment in which this struggle was sought to be eliminated by making church and state essentially independent of one another. This experiment was attempted for reasons having to do with a mixture of expedience and principle, but the outcome was nevertheless unique in the history of Western civilization.

The Continental Congress, whose experience predated the experiment sanctioned by the Constitutional Convention, functioned essentially under traditional Western political theory, that is, on the belief that religion is central to a well-ordered polity. Yet the Continental Congress also began gradually to transition to a new theory that both religion and government might function best if constitutionally separated. So although the Continental Congress operated essentially with religion as an important support to its overall function, separationist elements can be detected as well. The Continental Congress frequently engaged in religious acts and legislated with respect to religious matters, but this troubled many of the framers, and seems to have influenced them to seek to separate more formally religion from American public life under the Constitution.

Politicians or Priests? Not only did the Continental Congress frequently pray and hear sermons as an assembled body, it also legislated on a wide range of religious themes such as sin, repentance, humiliation, divine service, morality, fasting, prayer, mourning, public worship, funerals, chaplains, and "true" religion. Sabbath recognition, moreover, was important enough that Congress declined to meet on Sundays except for rare special sessions.

The proclamations and official state papers of the Congress are, as Humphrey remarked, "so filled with Biblical phrases as to resemble Old Testament ecclesiastical documents."[6] The documents frequently invoke, as a sanction for their acts, the name of "God," "Nature's God," "Lord of Hosts," "His Goodness," "Providence," "Creator of All," "Great Governor of the World," "Supreme Judge of the Universe," "Supreme Disposer of All Events," "Jesus Christ," "Holy Ghost," and "Free Protestant Colonies." One document alone, Congress's Declaration of Rights of July 6, 1775, written to justify the use of arms against Great Britain, contained references to "the divine Author of our existence," "reverence for our great Creator," the "Divine favour towards us," and "those powers, which our beneficent Creator hath graciously bestowed on us," before closing with an expression of "humble confidence in the mercies of the supreme and impartial Judge and Ruler of the Universe."[7] Even the Declaration of Independence called upon God as a witness to Parliament's callous indifference to the colonists' rights. Indeed, from the opening to the final session of the Continental Congress, its assemblies were sometimes grounded in a fervent religiosity.

Catherine Albanese has likened the members of the Congress to a group of priests laboring on behalf of a new national church, "performing the functions appropriate to authority in an ecclesiastical situation: teaching and preaching, governing and celebrating."[8] As a collection of men who looked upon their congressional role as fundamentally political, the delegates probably would have had little appreciation for Albanese's depiction of them as "priests." Nevertheless, there can be no doubt that the Continental Congress frequently undertook its work in ways that made politics and religion close allies.

The religious dimension of Congress's work can be accounted for on at least three bases. First, although the Enlightenment in America by the 1770s had begun to make inroads into the traditional understanding of Christianity, the nation was still overwhelmingly biblically orthodox in its worldview, and the religious dimensions of civil government were in that day still generally taken for granted. These perspectives combined to produce within Congress a steady stream of Christian rhetoric that the Congress felt was appropriately related to its political function. Second, Congress's insistence on religious sanction was in part due to it having no specific legislative authority. Variously elected by colonial assemblies or by extralegal meetings, delegates to the Congress were aware of the absence of any clear legislative authority for the Congress and thus may have sought to remedy this deficiency by reliance upon a higher authority.[9] Third, and most important, the Congress was convened under the extraordinary circumstances surrounding the foreboding turn of events in the colonies' relationship to Great Britain. Independence and war were growing possibilities in 1774 when the First Continental Congress convened. The seriousness of the times, especially after war broke out, demanded, in the eyes of the congressional delegates, a reliance upon a higher authority for guidance and assistance. The presence of each of these factors can be seen in the various forms of religiosity demonstrated by the Congress in many of its acts and proceedings.

Prayer, Worship, and Other Religious Acts. Only one day after convening on September 5, 1774, Congress appointed a chaplain to lead prayer at its sessions.

Congress also appointed army chaplains and encouraged them to promote before the Continental Army the regular observance of Congress's designated days of colony-wide fast and thanksgiving. Each time one of its members died, Congress issued its standard resolution that its members "in a body, attend the funeral [at various Christian churches] . . . with a crape around the arm, and . . . continue in mourning for the space of one month."[10] When the war led to a scarcity of Bibles, a congressional committee recommended that they be imported from European nations other than the customary Britain because "the use of the Bible is so universal, and its importance so great."[11] Similarly, the Congress passed a resolution in 1782 praising the "pious and laudable" work of Robert Aitken, who had published an American edition of the Bible at a time when it was impossible to import any copies.

The Continental Congress not only engaged in public religious rituals, but sometimes encouraged all Americans in the pursuit of moral perfection as well. Soon after convening in 1774, believing God's favor in resolving the colonies' growing tensions with the mother country depended upon the morality of the people, Congress resolved to

> encourage frugality, economy, and industry, and promote agriculture, arts and the manufactures of this country, especially that of wool; and . . . discountenance and discourage every species of extravagance and dissipation, especially all horse-racing, and all kinds of gaming, cockfighting, exhibitions of shews, plays, and other expensive diversions and entertainments; and on the death of any relation or friend, none of us, or any of our families, will go into any further mourning-dress than a black crape or ribbon on the arm or hat, for gentlemen, and a black ribbon and necklace for ladies, and we will discontinue the giving of gloves and scarves at funerals.[12]

As inappropriate as this type of legislation might seem to the student of modern politics, it was actually somewhat common in the eighteenth century. Moreover, there is little doubt that the congressional delegates took the legislation seriously, for a year later, in 1775, when the Marquis de Lafayette invited the President of Congress to a play, Henry Laurens of South Carolina politely declined. Pressed by the marquis for an explanation, Laurens replied that because "Congress . . . passed a resolution, recommending to the several States to enact laws for the suppression of theatrical amusements, he could not possibly do himself the honor of waiting upon him to the play."[13]

There is evidence also that the American people took Congress's pronouncements with equal seriousness. The day that Congress had designated in July 1775 for its first fast day was observed in Philadelphia "with a decorum and solemnity never before seen on a Sabbath."[14] Almost a year later, on the eve of independence, a Philadelphia resident described his neighborhood on the May 17 fast day as "extremely quiet, observant and composed, in compliance with the resolve of the Honorable Congress."[15] Even three years later, on May

6, 1779, the same Philadelphian described his city as "very quiet" on a congressionally designated fast day.[16] Those who failed to observe the fasts were frowned upon by the faithful and often suspected of disloyalty to American interests.

Congress reserved Independence Hall for most of its official business but made collective worship in various churches a regular practice. It frequented Episcopalian, Lutheran, Presbyterian, and Congregational services during the war, and occasionally attended Catholic mass as a body.[17] After the victory over Cornwallis, Congress paraded in solemn procession to a Dutch Lutheran church to give thanks to God for America's great victory.[18]

In diplomatic correspondence, members of the Congress regularly employed religious language. In 1779, for example, the President of Congress, John Jay, concluded a letter to the king of France, Louis XVI, with a petition "That the Supreme Ruler of the universe may bestow all happiness on your Majesty is the prayer of your faithful and affectionate friends and allies."[19] John Hanson, President of Congress in 1782, opened his letter to the same king: "Among the many instances that Divine Providence has given us of his favor, we number the blessings he has bestowed on your Majesty's family and kingdom." And Hanson closed with: "We pray God, great, faithful, and beloved friend and ally, always to keep you in his holy protection."[20] Indeed, in formal written correspondence, even in communications between nations, religious language was nearly as routine as affixing a date or a signature.

The Clergy as Civil Servants. In spite of the prevalence of religious acts and religious language in Congress's work, however, it should be pointed out that those looked to by Americans as religious leaders, the clergy, were not unanimously thought to have a place of service as members of the Continental Congress. One might think that their religious training and outlook would be looked upon favorably by a Congress that employed religious language and engaged in religious acts so frequently. But many of the delegates perceived clergymen as having inherent limitations that made them unfit for civil service. John Adams, for example, writing to his wife on September 17, 1775, concerning the newly arrived delegates from Georgia, described the minister Dr. John Zubly as "too little acquainted with the world" and "too much loaded with Vanity" to be a good politician.[21] Adams's view that ministers were unqualified for public service was common in the founding era. Many of the colonies, and following independence, seven of the original states,[22] disqualified ministers from public office in an effort to assure the success of a new political experiment, the separation of church and state.[23]

Others thought the practice of excluding the clergy from political office to be opposed to liberty. Benjamin Rush, a delegate from Pennsylvania, saw no reason to distinguish ministers from any other citizens: "They had children, wives, and were community citizens like anyone else."[24] John Witherspoon, a Presbyterian from New Jersey and the only clergyman to sign the Declaration of Independence, was likewise opposed on the grounds that no good reason existed for limiting a minister's citizenship status. Later, James Madison argued that the disqualification violated "a fundamental principle of liberty by punishing a religious profession with the privation of a civil right."[25]

The significance of clergy disqualification as a founding era issue is that it reveals that many members of the Continental Congress, who generally held to traditional political theory upholding religion as essential to good government, made theoretical distinctions affirming that political service was essentially a civil rather than a religious function.

Preserving Religious Liberty. Notwithstanding concerns such as these, the Continental Congress from the beginning seems to have understood one of its main goals to be the preservation of colonial religious liberties in the face of English measures perceived as challenges to such liberties. This emphasis can perhaps be traced to June 17, 1774, when the Massachusetts legislature, on motion of Samuel Adams, issued an appeal for the convening of the First Continental Congress. Among the stated purposes was that the representatives of the colonies should devise measures "for the recovery and establishment of their just rights and liberties, civil and religious."[26]

The colonists believed that civil and religious liberties were completely interdependent. Massachusetts divine Charles Turner, in typical fashion, preached that "religious liberty is so blended with civil, that if one falls it is not expected that the other will continue."[27] The colonists' fear of the loss of "religious" liberties went beyond dislike of what many considered to be an excessive Anglican presence in the colonies. They also feared, probably unrealistically, that the Church of England would soon impose a colony-wide "establishment" and even appoint an American bishop to oversee it. The right to worship according to one's conscience was cherished by the colonists and became an emotionally charged issue in anti-British revolutionary rhetoric. Securing the right constitutionally came later—when the Constitution was drafted—but concern to preserve the natural right of religion was prominent in the Continental Congress

The creation of the Continental Congress and the performance of its tasks must always be evaluated in the context of the Revolutionary War. At stake for the Americans was not just their civil and religious liberties, but the freedom to order human government in such a way that might best protect those liberties, to the end that American liberties might never again be diminished and that the American way might become the standard for the rest of the world. Thomas Paine's *Common Sense* put it most succinctly: "The cause of America is in great measure the cause of all mankind. . . . We have it in our power to begin the world over again. A situation similar to the present has not happened since the days of Noah until now."[28] And as with *Common Sense*, these goals were generally seen in religious terms, as being ordered by Providence, which of course meant that God was on the side of the Americans and the war was something like a "rite of passage," a proving ground for Americans in which their readiness for what lay beyond the war was being tested.

Chaplaincies and Prayer Proclamations. The First Continental Congress assembled on September 5, 1774. The next day, Thomas Cushing of Massachusetts moved that the daily sessions be regularly opened with prayer. Formal objections were lodged by the orthodox Congregationalist from New York, John Jay, and by John Rutledge of South Carolina, on the ground that, "proper as the act would be," it was rendered impractical by the "diversity of religious sentiments represented in Congress."[29] Samuel Adams, also a Congregationalist, rose to speak in favor of the motion: "I am no bigot. I can hear a prayer from a man of piety and virtue, who is at the same time a friend of his country. I am a stranger in Philadelphia, but I have heard that Mr. Duche deserves that character; and therefore, I move that Mr. Duche, an Episcopalian clergyman, be desired to read prayers to the Congress tomorrow morning."[30]

Adams's motion carried without further discussion. The position of Jay and Rutledge should not go unappreciated, however. Their view represents the classic concern that governmental religious exercise, when there is no officially approved form of faith, will inevitably offend some and therefore should be avoided as an aspect of religious liberty. Adams's response represents the classic rebuttal: Governments should acknowledge God's sovereignty over all human affairs through prayer and other religious acts, regardless of who might be offended. The propriety of legislative prayers remains a lively issue today, as indicated by the fact that many federal and state legislators excuse themselves from chaplain-led prayers, not in protest of prayer per se, but of government-promulgated prayer.[31]

Days of Humiliation, Fasting, and Thanksgiving. Special fast days each spring and days of thanksgiving each fall were traditions of the New England colonies dating back to the seventeenth century. As colonial relations with the mother country increasingly deteriorated in the late 1760s and early 1770s, local communities as well as some of the southern colonies began to appoint special days of prayer and thanksgiving. In 1768 in the Massachusetts towns of Boston, Braintree, Charleston, and Lexington, for example, a day was observed as a special one of fasting and prayer in protest against the coming of British troops.

The idea of colonial fasts was introduced into the southern colonies in 1774. Thomas Jefferson recorded that he and several other members of the Virginia House of Burgesses, especially Patrick Henry and Richard Henry Lee, "were under conviction of the necessity of arousing our people from the lethargy into which they had fallen as to passing events; and thought that the appointment of a day of general fasting and prayer would be most likely to call up and alarm their attention."[32] The House of Burgesses appointed June 1 of that year as a day of fasting and prayer, and every member sent a copy of the resolution to the clergymen of his county. Jefferson described the observance as a "shock of electricity" that had a very positive effect on the people.[33] Other colonies followed suit.

It was the Continental Congress, however, that really unified the prayers of the people. It set July 20, 1775, as a day of humiliation and prayer for the restoration of the just civil and religious privileges of America, which was observed throughout the colonies. Thereafter, the Congress appointed a day in the spring for fasting, humiliation, and prayer, and a day in the autumn for thanksgiving. These were proclaimed by the governors of the states and were observed throughout the country. George Mason was convinced of their merit. As he wrote to Richard Henry Lee, "I have no objection to the Fast they have recommended; these solemnities, if properly observed, and not too often repeated, have a good effect upon the minds of the people."[34]

Although fast days and government proclamations of thanksgiving and prayer began during the early period of the Continental Congress, none was forthcoming from 1784 until 1789. Following the establishment of the new Constitution, fast days were never reinstated, although thanksgiving days were. Although one scholar has interpreted the end of thanksgiving and fast days as a sure sign that the Continental Congress's reliance upon God receded in its enjoyment of war success,[35] it is possible to see the end of the observance days only as the natural result of peace. The thanksgiving and fast days promulgated by the Continental Congress had been instituted as wartime events, so why should they not have been discontinued once the war was concluded? After the war, the Continental Congress never discontinued the practice of having its chaplain begin each daily session with prayer, and this would seem to be a better measure of whether the Continental Congress entered a period of spiritual declension after the war was concluded.

One might also argue that the fast days were not resumed after 1789 because the new Constitution removed religion beyond the purview of the federal government, but if that is true, why were thanksgiving days reinstated? The best explanation, again, seems to be that the fast days were essentially related to the war effort; when the war ended, so did the fast days. Days of national thanksgiving, however, which have continued off and on since the First Congress, are best explained as holdovers from the colonial period and as practices deemed substantially harmless by most governmental leaders under the new Constitution who sought to acknowledge God's authority over all things.[36]

It would be erroneous, however, to assume that the constitutionality of thanksgiving days has always been accepted without question. When, in the First Congress after the adoption of the Constitution, a resolution was offered in the House to request the president to "recommend to the people of the United States a day of public thanksgiving and prayer, to be observed by acknowledging with grateful hearts the many signal favours of Almighty God,"[37] objection was raised by at least two members. Thomas Burke of North Carolina, for example, thought that such an observance would be a "mimicking of European customs, where they made a mere mockery of thanksgivings."[38] Thomas Tucker of South Carolina suggested that "it is a business with which the Congress have nothing to do; it is a religious matter, and as such is proscribed to us. If a day of thanksgiving must take place, let it be done by the authorization of the several states."[39] Tucker's comment is of special interest because it occurred on the same day, September 25, 1789, that the wording of the First Amendment was approved by Congress. His view that a thanksgiving proclamation, as a "religious matter," was "proscribed" to Congress, strongly suggests that he understood the Establishment Clause, its meaning fresh on his mind, to prohibit Congress from engaging in religious acts.

To the objections of Burke and Tucker, however, Roger Sherman of Connecticut argued that not only was the practice of public thanksgiving a "laudable one," but one justified by scriptural precedents: "for instance the solemn thanksgivings and rejoicings that took place in the time of Solomon, after the building of the temple."[40] Elias Boudinot cited a more recent precedent: the thanksgiving days observed by "the late [Continental] Congress."[41] Sherman and Boudinot carried the resolution over the objections of Burke and Tucker, and on October 3, 1789, President Washington proclaimed a national day of thanksgiving, which he followed with several others during his administration.

Although Washington made every effort to frame his proclamations in language acceptable to all faiths, his successor, John Adams, called for Christian worship. Jefferson refused to issue any religious proclamations, believing that "the Constitution has precluded them."[42] James Madison, who sought a "perfect separation"[43] between religion and government, stated that "Religious proclamations by the Executive recommending thanksgivings and fasts are shoots from the same root with the legislative acts [of establishing chaplaincies]."[44] He regarded such proclamations as violating the Establishment Clause: "They seem," he wrote, "to imply and certainly nourish a *national* religion."[45] As president, however, Madison gave in to demands to proclaim days of thanksgiving, finding extenuating circumstances in the fact that he was president during the time a war was fought on American soil. Still, he used prayers that as far as possible were generic and nondiscriminatory.[46]

With one exception, Madison's successors followed his example and issued prayer and thanksgiving proclamations in nonsectarian language. The one exception was Andrew Jackson, who shared Jefferson's views and steadfastly refused to issue any thanksgiving proclamations because he thought he "might disturb the security which religion now enjoys in the country, in its complete separation from the political concerns of the General Government."[47] All of the presidents since Jackson have issued prayer proclamations, either annually or in connection with important or critical events, such as American entries into war. Moreover, in 1952 Congress passed a law providing for an annual National Day of Prayer, observed since, and which from 1988 has been observed on the first Thursday of each May.

Chaplaincies and Proclamations in Context. The appointment of legislative and military chaplains and the proclamation of national days of fasting, humiliation, and thanksgiving by the Continental Congress, although revealing the theistic, if not essentially Christian, worldview of the nation's earliest leaders, must be understood in an even broader historical context. These practices were not new; they had been commonplace in the colonies from the earliest days of American settlement.[48] They were so much a part of the fabric of American social life that hardly anyone noticed when the Continental Congress adopted the same ones. Furthermore, the adoption of these practices was in large measure precipitated by the special circumstances and demands of the Revolutionary War; in the case of the days of fasting and thanksgiving, their demise was coterminous with the war's end. Legislative chaplains, however, continued to serve in the Continental Congress until that body ceased to function upon ratification of the Constitution.

In the contemporary debate concerning the extent to which early post-Constitution chaplaincies and prayer proclamations inform the framers' original intent, it thus becomes vitally important to evaluate such practices in the context of traditions that reach at least as far back as the administration of the Continental Congress. These were inherited practices that the First Congress more or less assumed, as a matter of course, to be consistent with the First Amendment. Discernment of the framers' "original intent" as to how such practices influenced the wording of the First Amendment assumes that the framers were attentive to (considered, analyzed, debated) the consequences of their actions. In fact, very little attention seems to have been given to the relationship of these practices to the First Amendment. Thus, one must be careful not to read too much into the framers' purposes by an overemphasis on the early chaplaincy and prayer practices of Congress.

In support of the argument here advanced that emphasizes tradition over principle, annual thanksgiving prayers by presidents in particular must be seen in the context of the long-standing colonial practice (by the states and by the Continental Congress). The practice had such a long tradition that it would have indeed been difficult for members of the First Congress to object to the adoption of the practice, even had they sensed that it might be in conflict with First Amendment strictures. Furthermore, the proposal for reinstatement of the practice in 1789 (after a five-year absence) occurred in the midst of great excitement over the ratification of the new Constitution and the considerable hopes and expectations surrounding the new "republican" form of government that the document embraced. Add to this the realization that Congress's proposal was for the nation's first president, George Washington, already a national hero of mythical proportions, to offer the special prayer of thanks to God for bestowing his blessings on the new nation, and one has the prescription for an event that could hardly have been voted down, no matter what the First Amendment said.

The Declaration of Independence

The Declaration of Independence is arguably the most widely known and influential political document in the history of the world. When the Continental Congress at Philadelphia on July 4, 1776, adopted the Declaration of Independence, it marked an abrupt end to America's acceptance of British authority over the American colonies. The Declaration is important in the present context, however, because, although theologically grounded, it is evidence of progressive thinking that sought to distance divine authority from state affairs.

The Philosophy of the Declaration. The basic philosophy behind the Declaration is that all people are endowed by God with natural rights that are unalienable, and when a government acts to destroy such rights, its subjects are entitled to revolt and establish a new one. This basic philosophy appears in the first part of the second paragraph of the Declaration:

> We hold these truths to be self-evident. That all men are created equal, that they are endowed by their Creator with certain unalienable rights; that among these are life, liberty, and the pursuit of happiness; that to secure these rights governments are instituted among men, deriving their just powers from the consent of the governed; that whenever any form of government becomes destructive of these ends, it is the right of the people to alter or to abolish it, and to institute new government, laying its foundation on such principles and organizing its powers in such form, as to them shall seem most likely to effect their safety and happiness.

The premises of the natural rights philosophy stated in the Declaration were widely held in eighteenth-century America: that there is a "natural order" of things in the universe, expertly designed by God for the guidance of mankind; that the "laws" of this natural order may be discovered by human reason; and that these laws so discovered furnish a reliable and immutable standard for testing the ideas, the conduct, and the institutions of men.[49] An important part of this natural order as it was commonly understood was the notion of a social compact between peoples and governments. Under the theory of the social compact, so thoroughly elaborated by John Locke in his *Second Treatise on Human Government*, governments are formed when people come together and by agreement transfer certain of their "natural rights" to rulers to ensure their safety, protection, and welfare. Some of these natural rights, such as life and liberty, are unalienable and cannot be transferred because they are fundamental to the enjoyment of one's life. When the social compact is violated by the ruler, the compact is dissolved, and the people are thereby free to establish a new government.[50]

But the social compact theory in Locke, Thomas Hobbes, and Jean Jacques Rousseau, among others, rejected the notion of the divine right of kings to rule and posited that social compacts between rulers and subjects were "approved" by God as transactions of "nature." Governments were human institutions, the details of which were worked out by men. God was still involved, but as an approving observer, not as a participating party. In this way, a compact broken by a ruler was automatically dissolved; there was no need to be concerned with violating the will of God by ending an arrangement that God himself had not established in the first place.

It was fundamentally important to Jefferson and the Continental Congress that the colonies' right to independence be grounded in a philosophy that had a theistic framework. Although they did not articulate this position specifically, the delegates undoubtedly knew that without divine sanction, a declaration of independence would never be countenanced by the American people. Thus it is not surprising that there are four references to God in the Declaration— "Nature's God," the "Creator," the "Supreme Judge of the world," and "Divine Providence." These references were enough to place the Declaration in an over-all theistic framework so as to satisfy virtually anyone who held a theistic worldview. Thus in drafting the Declaration, Thomas Jefferson and his congressional colleagues seized upon, and indeed helped to further shape, a bond between Enlightenment latitudinarianism and Christian orthodoxy that made it possible to formally dissolve all bonds with Great Britain and at the same time confidently assert "the protection of Divine Providence."

The status of the Declaration as a Christian or deist document has been much debated. In this author's view, the document is actually neither. The Declaration of Independence was primarily a foreign policy document aimed at England, France, and the rest of Europe, although it was also designed to unify those at home. It was written in a theistic framework primarily because Jefferson, his committee, and indeed the Continental Congress at-large understood the colonists' authority to sever their relationship to Britain as resting upon a theistic, natural rights philosophy. Yet this theistic framework was also adopted because it was broad and general enough to capture the theistic framework in which most colonists understood all earthly events to take place. Thus it was neither specifically deistic (Enlightenment, scientific worldview) nor Christian (biblical worldview) as either position would have excluded those adherents of the other; as a theistic document, it appealed to both.

That said, it should be noted that the Declaration, despite its religious elements, is by no means primarily a religious document, or even a philosophical one. It created no Christian state, or even a religious state. It merely acknowledges that God was a witness and participant, to one degree or another, in the creation of the nation. The document was friendly to what most of the signers wanted: an emerging state that, in the name of religious liberty, would be friendly to all religions. The Declaration was mainly intended as an appeal to public opinion—an attempt to draw favorable attention to the revolutionary cause—among the French, among colonial sympathizers in Britain, and even among waverers in the colonies. Treason is at best an ominous business, and

the Continental Congress was determined that Great Britain and not the colonies revolting should stand condemned before the bar of world public opinion.[51] But the Declaration is a masterpiece of political literature for the primary
reason that it succinctly expresses political ideas widely accepted in 1776.
These political ideas embodied an eighteenth-century philosophy of natural
rights arising out of a philosophy of natural law that reached back to antiquity.
Moreover, this philosophy was stated in a compelling theological framework,
assuring those who would fight and even die for the cause of independence
that their efforts were looked upon with favor from heaven.[52]

Virtue and the Continental Congress

The Continental Congress moved from its truly radical step of the Declaration
of Independence to victory over Great Britain, then pointedly shifted its focus
to establishment of an entirely new government. Even if this were not a state of
nature to which the colonies had reverted, the American situation did offer the
clearest venue yet to create anew. The delegates understood the enormity of the
task and the unparalleled opportunity. "Objects of the most stupendous magnitude," Adams wrote a month before the signing of the Declaration, "and
measures in which the lives and liberties of millions yet unborn are intimately
interested, are now before us. We are in the very midst of a revolution, the
most complete, unexpected, and remarkable, of any in the history of nations."[53]
    But of course the challenge of revolution and government-building for the
millions yet unborn was not straightforward. History offered its litany of governments that flourished, but it could furnish no such list of those that endured.
Describing the attempts to found republics after the fall of Rome, Adams wrote
that these efforts had "foamed, raged, and burst, like so many waterspouts
upon the ocean."[54] That framed the compelling problem for the Continental
Congress as it matured: how to form not just a separate government or an effective government but an enduring one. To do that, the Congress would have
to devise the best of structures *and* ameliorate the worst tendencies of government's practitioners. The founders and the colonists generally recognized that
not only must government restrain injustice and evil, it must itself be restrained.
That is why Madison wrote in the next decade that government itself is "the
greatest of all reflections on human nature." Theory could create the perfect
government on paper, but government still comprises imperfect people, and
that gave the political deliberations of the Congress and, later, the Constitutional Convention its real seriousness. Defiance of the British would prove the
far simpler task.
    It is in this war with the past and the vision for a government that could long
endure that one must approach the Continental Congress and its revolution of
virtue. Talk of virtue was not so much pious cant; it was a serious proposal to

arrest the otherwise inevitable mortality of political society. The success of the body politic would, the Congress held, be dependent on the character of the people it comprised. Adams, writing as "Novanglus" in February 1775, put it succinctly: "Liberty can no more exist without virtue and independence, than the body can live and move without a soul."[55] But how did the Congress regard virtue? How did the delegates employ the ubiquitous term?[56] They began with Aristotle's *Nichomachean Ethics*, and secondarily his *Politics*. To the degree that virtue (Greek *arete*, "excellence") is regarded as "habituated character," the Congress would have concurred.[57] Jefferson certainly emphasized habituation. Writing in 1785 to his fifteen-year-old nephew, Jefferson urged, "Encourage all your virtuous dispositions, and exercise them whenever an opportunity arises, being assured that they will gain strength by exercise as a limb of the body does, and that exercise will make them habitual. From the practice of the purest virtue you may be assured you will derive the most sublime comforts in every moment of life and in the moment of death."[58] And much of Franklin's treatment of virtue in the *Autobiography* also had this Aristotelian emphasis on habituation.

This brings us to the most critical point about virtue and the Continental Congress, and surely the great paradox of their deliberations on republican government. The Congress could agree on the importance of virtue for the health and longevity of the government they were establishing. They could write freely of the merits of promoting it through various avenues. Yet the Congress, as an official assembly, made no direct attempts to establish virtue through the promulgation of religion. The communication of the New York delegates back to their state government illustrates this. The delegation, which included John Jay and Henry Wisner, remarked on the appropriateness of formal resolutions about religion: "This and the former congress have cautiously avoided the least hint on subjects of this kind, all the members concurring in a desire of burrying [*sic*] all disputes on ecclesiastical points, which have for ages had no other tendency than that of banishing peace and charity from the world."[59] Similarly, the Congress refused to compel virtue, just as it chose not to establish religion. Perhaps this is one of the most salient points to emerge from a long, sweltering summer of debate about the new Constitution in 1787. The delegates to the Constitutional Convention met, conscious of the numerous defects of the Articles of Confederation. But the new structure they proposed strengthened only the government; it made no provision to strengthen, or even to inaugurate, a governmental role in improving the people.

In the end, the ideas of Madison prevailed. "If men were angels . . ." he wrote in the most poignant subjunctive of *The Federalist Papers*. But of course men and women are not. His ideas, however, must not be misunderstood. Madison never denigrated virtue even as he never disparaged religion. At the Virginia ratifying convention, Madison declared,

I go on this great republican principle, that the people will have virtue and intelligence to select men of virtue and wisdom. Is there no virtue among us? If there be not, we are in a wretched situation. No theoretical checks, no form of government, can render us secure. To suppose that any form of government will secure liberty or happiness without any virtue in the people, is a chimerical idea.[60]

Similarly, Hamilton observed in *Federalist* No. 76, "The supposition of universal venality in human nature is little less an error in political reasoning than the supposition of universal rectitude. The institution of delegated power implies that there is a portion of virtue and honor among mankind which may be a reasonable foundation of confidence."[61]

An exchange between two long-retired presidents is instructive. In December 1819, Jefferson wrote from Monticello to Adams. He wondered whether virtue, once lost in a nation, might ever be restored. Reflecting on a corrupt Rome, Jefferson decided that Cicero, Cato, and Brutus, working in concert and with unlimited power, probably could not have halted the entropic tide. But what did Adams, his "Apollo," think? Adams answered promptly: "Have you ever found in history one single example of a nation thoroughly corrupted, that was afterwards restored to virtue?, and without virtue there can be no political liberty." But then he added:

Will you tell me how to prevent riches from becoming the effects of temperance and industry? Will you tell me how to prevent riches from producing luxury? Will you tell me how to prevent luxury from producing effeminacy intoxication extravagance vice and folly? When you answer me these questions, I hope I may venture to answer yours. Yet all these ought not to discourage us from exertion, for . . . I believe no effort in favor of virtue is lost, and all good men ought to struggle both by their council and example.[62]

Adams's answer is interesting on several counts. To begin, he dilated Jefferson's question by moving beyond Rome to the present in America. Further, he had the prescience to recognize that the virtues the Puritans and secular Puritans alike so prized (here, industry and frugality) could, paradoxically, lead to the vices they despised. But most important here, Adams—for all his concerns for the nation—did not recommend a government course of action to foster virtue, for as Adams realized, the Constitution was made *for* a moral and religious people, not to *produce* them. The responsibility for virtuous character must rest with the people.[63]

The Continental Congress and Original Intent

We have sought to examine the record of the Continental Congress on religion for the purpose of discovering what that record might contribute toward understanding the original intent of the constitutional framers regarding the interplay of government and religion in the United States. Conclusive statements toward this end do not come easily, due primarily to the fact that the Continental Congress, on the one hand, and the Constitutional Convention and First Congress, on the other, acted at different times and with different ends. The men of the Continental Congress were called upon first and foremost to prosecute a war, whereas those who framed the Constitution and Bill of Rights were charged with prescribing a comprehensive public philosophy that would ensure the success of a new constitution. The former readily put religion to use, whereas the latter had to think more critically about the long-term role of religion in an untested regime.

But it is possible to draw some conclusions, however tentatively. To begin with, it should be noted that the notion of the separation of church and state, at the federal level, was virtually nonexistent in the confederation period. Strict notions of separation were emerging in some of the states—most notably Virginia, following Rhode Island, Delaware, and Pennsylvania in this respect—but these developments had little influence on the Continental Congress. It can therefore be said that the Continental Congress rarely sought to excise religion from its governmental function, unless, of course, the matter at issue was considered to be the domain of the states, in which case Congress painstakingly sought to avoid violating the states' reserved jurisdiction.

Much of the Congress's religiosity, of course, consisted of regular and sincere appeals for divine aid in prosecuting a war against a skillful and powerful military force reputed to be the best on the globe. Its thanksgiving and fast day proclamations would probably not have been promulgated had Congress not been prosecuting a war, although both practices were long-time colonial peacetime traditions, and Congress might have continued the traditions even in the absence of the Revolutionary War. The thanksgiving proclamations that became a regular presidential practice beginning in 1789 were a carryover from the wartime tradition of the Continental Congress and were implemented in the new government virtually as a matter of course. Although the wording of the Establishment Clause persuaded a number of the First Congress's members that the practice was proscribed to any arm of the federal government, the majority of the congressmen, although they were remarkably casual in their consideration of the constitutional issues, apparently did not see it that way. The wartime fast days promulgated by the Continental Congress were discontinued in the post-1789 regime, almost certainly because of the war's end.

The Continental Congress's practice of having daily prayer offered by its official chaplain was another practice that was continued virtually as a matter of course, by the Congress acting under the Constitution. The modern Supreme Court has upheld the practice of legislative prayers on the basis of a historical argument that looks to an unbroken chain of chaplain-led prayers in Congress that began with the Continental Congress and has continued unabated since.[64]

Legislative prayers remain a central part of the American civil religion. As such, they acknowledge generally God's sovereignty over the nation, but without the coercive effects that other governmental religious acts entail, such as programmatic prayer in public schools. In a nation that is profoundly religious and does not wish to be hostile toward religion, legislative prayers are an acceptable way of acknowledging the transcendent dimension of nationhood.

The American tradition of appointing military chaplains to serve the nation's armed forces also began with the Continental Congress. Despite objections by some members of the First Congress, James Madison among them, this practice was resumed by the U.S. government operating under the new Constitution, and has continued without interruption since. If the practice is thought to respect the free exercise rights of servicemen, "establishment" concerns tend to recede so that the military chaplaincy becomes a hallmark of the American tradition of protecting the religious consciences of its citizens.

The absence of religious tests for holding offices in the confederation government might have influenced the framers' decision to proscribe such tests in the Constitution, but Article VI, clause 3 was more likely the product of the framers' realization that a religious test would threaten ratification of the Constitution because the prevailing religious diversity in the nation would render any test unacceptable to all but a few. Still, there were many principled arguments advanced against religious tests for civil office-holding that eventually led most of the states, on the model of the Constitution's religious test ban, to abandon their own religious tests.

There are, of course, other practices that were initiated by the Continental Congress that have not continued to be observed as congressional traditions. The Continental Congress frequently attended sermons as a body, although to avoid favoritism, it made certain to attend the services of a variety of Protestant denominations and, on occasion, Catholic services as well. This did not continue regularly after 1789. The Continental Congress's practice of declaring fast day observances was not resumed by the post-Constitution congresses. Following the adoption of the Constitution, Congress also discontinued the Continental Congress's practice of invoking the name of God in its official documents. Even the Constitution itself, the official charter of the nation, contained no references to God, whereas the document under which the Continental Congress had functioned, the Articles of Confederation, stated that its provisions were aligned with the pleasure and consent of "the Great Governor of the World."

The Declaration of Independence, drafted by Thomas Jefferson and revised to its final form by the Continental Congress, espoused the view that government and law must be in conformity with higher law—the "Laws of nature and Nature's God." The Continental Congress therefore saw its duty to declare American independence from Britain in religious terms: George III was a tyrant precisely because he had perverted his power by overstepping limits imposed by natural law, and the Englishmen in America were therefore free to revolt and form their own government under the same natural law principles. The natural law foundation of the Declaration was couched in broad, generic terms by Jefferson so that it would appeal to Christian pietists and rationalists alike. One goes too far, however, in thinking that this theistic framework created a religious state in America. Actually the Declaration created no state at all; it only separated the colonies from Britain. The "state" was created by the Constitution, and that document intentionally omitted any language that might be construed as formally placing the state under divine authority.

These various actions verify that the Continental Congress operated primarily apart from commitments to church–state separation. But there are at least three pieces of evidences that the separation ideal was beginning to take root and grow into the "nonestablishment" restriction in the First Amendment. The first evidence is the absence of any kind of religious test for holding office in the confederation government. The Continental Congress was respectful of the diversity of religious views across the states, and therefore believed such a test to be repugnant to religious liberty. The gradual disappearance of religious tests for holding public office, both at the federal and state levels, initiated in the founding era, is a sure sign that the meaning of religious liberty in America was progressive, and tended increasingly to "separate" church and state, although a complete separation was probably never in view— nor should it be.

A second evidence is the considerable disagreement that ensued over the question of whether the Continental Congress should play a role in advancing religion in the Northwest Territory. A mild form of advancement (acknowledging that religion, with morality and knowledge, was a goal of the education to take place in the territory) resulted, but it was a far cry from the setting aside of lands for churches that some of the delegates sought.[65] Many of the congressmen were obviously seeking to distance the national government from having too close a hand in religious matters.

A third evidence is the apparent acceptance of the view that virtue and morality cannot be effectively cultivated through government efforts. The classical view of government advancing religion for the production of virtue in the people was first questioned and then rejected by members of the Continental Congress. If we understand the Establishment Clause to have proscribed not only a national religion, but more generally, Congress's advancement and promotion of religion, then we can say that this perspective on virtue was written into the Constitution, thus assigning character-building, insofar as it is dependent upon religion, to personal inquiry, families, churches, and other voluntary associations, but not the federal government. And of course after "incorporation," whereby the majority of the rights set forth in the Bill of Rights became binding on the states and local governments, the same prohibition on religious advocacy would apply to government at every level.

One could add to this list, of course, those occasions in which, despite the reality that the Continental Congress acted in a way that evidenced its firm reliance on a religious worldview, objections ensued. For example, Congressmen Jay and Rutledge objected when the first Continental Congress sought to appoint a chaplain. Madison, in debates on the Northwest Ordinance, objected to Congress providing money to the territories for the purchase of land upon which churches would be constructed. The Continental Congress endorsed an American Bible, but refused, on grounds for which we are uncertain, to pay for the bibles. Were they thinking, presciently, about the "establishment" implications of spending government funds on a patently religious project? In the First Congress, Congressmen Burke and Boudinot objected when the first presidential prayer proclamation was being considered by the First Congress. All of these episodes indicate a budding commitment to church–state separation.

Emerging Separation

The separation of church and state as a political principle is often misunderstood. For many eighteenth-century thinkers, the separation principle was a means of achieving religious liberty. It did not refer to a cultural separation of religion from society, as many today assume, but rather an institutional separation of governmental and ecclesiastical power. The separation of church and state in late eighteenth-century America had three basic components. The primary component was the disestablishment of churches in the various states; the second, the decriminalization of religious activity, thus making real for Americans the free exercise of religion according to the dictates of conscience; and the third, the removal of religious disabilities for civil office-holding. If one attempts a snapshot of the status of religious liberty in, say, 1787, when the Constitution was written, or 1789, when the Bill of Rights was adopted, one gets a very skewed picture of the progress of religious liberty. One cannot gauge the progress of religious liberty at this juncture. The more mature development in the states with respect to disestablishment, the decriminalization of religious behavior, and the removal of religious tests for civil office-holding, was yet in the future. There is no end to the number of books and articles that champion the notion that the separation of church and state is a mere fiction,[66] the supposed proof of which is, unfortunately, a very narrow look at the progress of religious liberty at about the time the Constitution was written. One must look further down the road to see the full ripening of religious liberty, guaranteed by the separation of church and state, as a fundamental American commitment.

The progress in disestablishment was the most notable development in the founding era. Making the churches autonomous resulted in citizens being freed from the requirement of paying taxes for the support of churches with whose doctrines they were not in agreement, and ended the operational and political advantages that some churches maintained over others. These principles of religious voluntarism and equality among sects were believed by separationists such as James Madison, Thomas Jefferson, and Isaac Backus to preserve the integrity of both government and religion. So compelling were these principles in the founding era that the states, one by one, began to "disestablish" their churches. By the time of the Constitutional Convention, seven of the original thirteen states had altogether abandoned governmental support of religion. Those states that had not by 1787 disestablished their churches eventually did so: South Carolina in 1790, Georgia in 1798, Maryland in 1810, Connecticut in 1818, New Hampshire in 1819, and Massachusetts in 1833.

The Constitution with its first set of ten amendments left the issue of church and state firmly located within the framework of limited government. This strategy was part of an amalgam of strategies—including the separation of powers, the system of checks and balances, belief in an informed citizenry, and a theory of reserved powers—that provided the governmental framework for the new nation. For religion, however, the design was that government at the federal level would be conducted without regard to religion. This design, moreover, left the states free to conduct their own governmental affairs with as much attention to religion as they desired. This was essential to the framers' hope of securing ratification of the Constitution, because the states, especially in New England, scrupulously guarded their right to maintain existing religious establishments.

Thus, although all of the states would eventually end their religious establishments, several states had not yet done so when the Constitution was written, and these states were unwilling to consider any arrangement that might jeopardize their jurisdiction over religion. In 1789, when the First Congress was considering amendments to the Constitution, James Madison proposed such an arrangement. His amendment would have imposed on the states the same restrictions against passing laws to create establishments or to prohibit the free exercise of religion that the First Amendment in its final form imposed on Congress.[67] In effect, his proposal would have resulted in the same requirement of the states to abide by the First Amendment that resulted in the twentieth century under the Supreme Court's incorporation doctrine. The House approved of Madison's proposal but the Senate voted it down, thus preserving the various state establishments.

One way to view the founding era is to place it at a critical juncture in a roughly two-hundred-year movement for religious liberty that began in the 1630s with Roger Williams's call for the disestablishment of the Congregational Church in New England and that culminated in the 1830s when the last of the states (Massachusetts was the final state in 1833) disestablished its churches. Seen in this light, the disestablishment of the churches becomes the primary dimension of the religious liberty movement. The framing of the Constitution and the Bill of Rights, then, occurred at a stage in the movement when the conviction that disestablishment was a preserver of religious liberty was not as widely held as it later would be. As a result, the Constitution and First Amendment's provisions on religion, as we have seen, were formulated in terms that might best secure the ratification of the documents of which they were a part, without requiring, as under Madison's rejected proposal, prohibitions on state establishments.

Once disestablishment prevailed across America, however, it found virtually unanimous support among respected churchmen, statesmen, and historians. Philip Schaff, America's leading church historian in the nineteenth century, wrote in 1857 that "the glory of America is a free Christianity, independent of the secular government, and supported by the voluntary contributions of a free people. This is one of the greatest facts in modern history."[68]

The importance of church–state separation for vibrant, authentic religious expression was attested by Alexis de Tocqueville, the French journalist and historian who traveled extensively in the United States in the 1830s. He commented that "the religious atmosphere of the country was the first thing that struck me on my arrival in the United States." He expressed "astonishment" because in his native Europe religion and freedom marched "in opposite directions." After questioning pastors, priests, and laypersons from all of the various churches he visited, he found that "they all agreed with each other except about the details; all thought that the quiet sway of religion over their country was the complete separation of church and state. I have no hesitation in stating that throughout my stay in America I met nobody, lay or cleric, who did not agree about that."[69]

All of these observers had the advantage of witnessing firsthand the growth, spread, and final victory of disestablishment. These developments were a phenomenon that the founding fathers could not totally foresee. The merits of separation, although appreciated by many of the founding fathers, could only be fully verified by the passage of time and the acceptance of the disestablishment principle in the states.

Separation of church and state declares the state to be neutral in matters of religion. Some would say that America is a secular state, which is essentially true, although it is suggested here that the term *secular state* is so commonly associated with the promotion of secularism, which has never been true of the American state, that the term *neutral state* might be preferable. Adherence to the concept of the neutral state,[70] accompanied by the lack of state patronage and support of religion, has unfortunately often been viewed as an attack upon or threat to religion. Such a view is to misunderstand the very nature of the neutral state, which is to be neither hostile nor subservient to the church or the interests of religion. Always in matters of religious faith and ultimate belief, the neutral state is uncommitted. The neutral state is neither religious, nor irreligious.[71] Philip Schaff expressed it pointedly when he wrote that the Constitution "is neither hostile nor friendly to any religion; it is simply silent on the subject, as lying beyond the jurisdiction of the general government."[72]

The neutral state ought not to be regarded as a barrier but as a benefit to religion. Certainly, the phenomenal growth and marked vitality of religion in America—Catholic, Protestant, Jewish, and diverse other minority religions— clearly attests to the fact that religion has not suffered from the American tradition in church and state. This is as one of the founding fathers, Benjamin Franklin, would have wanted it. Franklin, a strong believer in the secular state, wrote of religion: "When a religion is good, I conceive that it will support itself; and, when it cannot support itself, and God does not take care to support it, so that its professors are obliged to call for the help of the civil power, it is a sign, I apprehend, of it being a bad one."[73]

All of the evidence, then, when examined in historical context, supports separation of church and state as that paradigm of church–state thought that best captures the progressively evolving intentions of the founding fathers. Human government functions best when it does not advance, promote, or side with religion, thereby leaving the pursuit of genuine, authentic, and vibrant religious faith to the individual. As government is a human institution, it probably will never escape the attribution to it of the need to conform to religious obligations. Religion, however, is primarily concerned with individuals, not governments, and should therefore be relegated mostly to the individual sphere. During the period of the Continental Congress, this perspective was in its nascent stage of development and only beginning to make an impression on the nation's best political thinkers. It is therefore a mistake to consider that early governmental practices such as congressional chaplaincies and presidential prayer proclamations form the basis of the framers' "original intent." Indeed a closer approximation of the framers' original intent is located in the affirmation of that one who was the principal architect of the Constitution, James Madison, who solemnly declared that "Any alliance or coalition between Government and Religion . . . cannot be too carefully guarded against."[74]

Notes

1. Lord Chatham, Speech to House of Lords, January 20, 1775, quoted in William J. Bacon, *The Continental Congress: Some of Its Actors and Their Doings, With the Results Thereof* (Utica, NY: Ellis H. Roberts, 1881), 3–4.

2. Ibid.

3. Quoted in Ellis Sandoz, "Power and Spirit in the Founding," *This World* 9 (Fall 1984): 67.

4. See further chapter 8 by Carl Esbeck.

5. Richard B. Morris, *The Forging of the Union, 1781–1789* (San Francisco: Harper & Row, 1987), 269. Seven had served in the First Continental Congress, eight had signed the Declaration of Independence, and two had signed the Articles of Confederation.

6. Ibid., 407.

7. *Journals of the Continental Congress, 1774–1789*, 34 vols. (Washington, DC: U.S. Government Printing Office, 1904–37), 2:140–57.

8. Catherine Albanese, *Sons of the Fathers: The Civil Religion of the American Revolution* (Philadelphia: Temple University Press, 1976), 193.

9. Edward Frank Humphrey, *Nationalism and Religion in America, 1774–1789* (Boston: Chipman Law Publishing Company, 1924), 408.

10. *Journals*, 11:592–93, June 12, 1778 (death of Philip Livingston of New York).

11. Ibid., 11:364.

12. Ibid.,1:3, October 20, 1774.

13. *Gaines' New York Gazette*, January 9, 1775, in *The Diary of the American Revolution: From Newspapers and Original Documents*, ed. Frank Moore, 2 vols. (New York: Charles Scribner, 1860), 1:11.

14. John Adams to Abigail Adams, July 23, 1775, in *Familiar Letters of John Adams and His Wife Abigail Adams, During the Revolution*, ed. Charles F. Adams, 2 vols. (Boston: Houghton Mifflin, 1875), 1:84.

15. William Duane, ed., *Extracts from the Diary of Christopher Marshall, Kept in Philadelphia and Lancaster, During the American Revolution, 1774–1781* (Albany, NY: Joel Munsell, 1877), 71.

16. Ibid., 216.

17. *Journals*, 2:81, 87, 192. The members of Congress attended mass on four occasions—two were Te Deums and two were Requiems. On each of these occasions the mass took place at St. Mary's Church, Philadelphia. The Te Deums were the independence commemoration on July 4, 1779, and the celebration for victory at Yorktown, November 4, 1781. The Requiems were September 18, 1777, for General Du Coudray, a French officer, and May 8, 1780, for Don Juan de Miralles, a Spanish agent. See "The Continental Congress at Mass," *American Catholic Historical Researches* 6 (1889): 50–76.

18. Albanese, *Sons of the Fathers*, 199.

19. John Jay to Louis XVI, September 17, 1779, in *The Diplomatic Correspondence of the American Revolution*, ed. Jared Sparks, 12 vols. (Boston: N. Hale and Gray & Bowen, 1829–30), 5:641.

20. John Hanson to Louis XVI, May 20, 1782, in Sparks, *Diplomatic Correspondence*, 6:65.

21. John Adams to Abigail Adams, September 17, 1775, in *Letters of Delegates to Congress, 1774–1789*, ed. Paul H. Smith, 26 vols. (Washington, DC: Library of Congress, 1976–2000), 2:23–24.

22. The states were Maryland, Virginia, North Carolina, South Carolina, Georgia, New York, and Delaware. Leo Pfeffer, *Church, State and Freedom*, 2d ed. (Boston: Beacon Press, 1967), 118.

23. Anson Phelps Stokes, *Church and State in the United States*, 3 vols. (New York: Harper & Brothers, 1950), 1:622. But cf. William M. Hogue, "The Civil Disability of Ministers of Religion in State Constitutions," *Journal of Church and State* 36 (1994): 329. See further chapter 3 by Mark McGarvie and chapter 9 by Daniel Dreisbach.

24. Benjamin Rush to Patrick Henry, July 16, 1776, in Smith, *Letters of Delegates*, 4: 473–75. Rush's letter complained of Virginia's practice of disqualifying clergymen from public office, a practice supported by Patrick Henry.

25. Gaillard Hunt, ed., *The Writings of James Madison*, 9 vols. (New York: G. P. Putnam's Sons, 1900–1910), 5:288.

26. *Journals*, 1:15–16.

27. Charles Turner, Massachusetts Election Sermon, 1773, in *They Preached Liberty*, ed. Franklin P. Cole (Indianapolis, IN: Liberty Press, 1976), 161.

28. Thomas Paine, *Common Sense*, in *Complete Writings of Thomas Paine*, ed. Philip S. Foner, 2 vols. (New York: Harper and Row, 1945), 1:3.

29. *Journals*, 1:26.

30. Adams, *Familiar Letters*, 1:23.

31. John M. Swomley, *Religious Liberty and the Secular State* (Buffalo, NY: Prometheus Books, 1985), 54.

32. P. L. Ford, ed., *The Writings of Thomas Jefferson*, 10 vols. (New York: G. P. Putnam's Sons, 1892–1899), 1:9.

33. Ibid., 1:11.

34. Kate M. Rowland, *Life and Correspondence of George Mason, 1725–1792*, 2 vols. (New York: G. P. Putnam's Sons, 1892), 1:320.

35. Albanese, *Sons of the Fathers*, 199.

36. Pfeffer, *Church, State, and Freedom*, 223.

37. *The Debates and Proceedings in the Congress of the United States*, 42 vols. (Washington, DC: Gales and Seaton, 1834–1856), 1:949, September 25, 1789 [hereafter *Annals*].

38. Ibid.

39. Ibid., 1:950.

40. Ibid.

41. Ibid.

42. Quoted in Pfeffer, *Church, State, and Freedom*, 224.

43. James Madison letter to Edward Livingston, July 10, 1822, reproduced in Hunt, *Writings of James Madison*, 9:100; also reproduced in Philip B. Kurland and Ralph Lerner, eds., *The Founders' Constitution*, 5 vols. (Chicago: University of Chicago Press, 1987), 5:105 (Document 66).

44. Elizabeth Fleet, ed., "Madison's Detached Memoranda," *William and Mary Quarterly* 3 (1946): 554; also reproduced in Philip B. Kurland and Ralph Lerner, eds., *The Founders' Constitution*, 5 vols. (Chicago: University of Chicago Press, 1987), 5:103 (Document 64, circa 1817).

45. Ibid.

46. See Pfeffer, *Church, State and Freedom*, 224.

47. Letter from Andrew Jackson to the Synod of the Reformed Church of North America (refusing to proclaim a national day of fasting and prayer due to outbreak of cholera), June 26, 1832, in John Spencer Bassett, ed., *Correspondence of Andrew Jackson, 7 Volumes* (Washington, D.C., Carnegie Institute, 1926), 4:47.

48. Stephen Botein, "Religious Dimensions of the Early American State Constitutions," in *Beyond Confederation: Origins of the American Constitution and American National Identity*, ed. Richard Beeman, Stephen Botein, and Edward C. Carter II (Chapel Hill: University of North Carolina Press, 1987), 320.

49. Carl Becker, *The Declaration of Independence: A Study in the History of Political Ideas* (New York: Vintage Books, 1958 [1922]), 26.

50. James Madison, during the proceedings of the First Congress in 1789, asserted this view by stating that the colonies in 1776 remained "as a political society, detached from their

former connection with another society, without dissolving into a state of nature; but capable of substituting a new form of government in the place of the old one, which they had, for special considerations, abolished." *Annals*, 1:421–22.

51. Alfred H. Kelly and Winfred A. Harbison, *The American Constitution: Its Origins and Development*, 3d ed. (New York: W. W. Norton, 1963), 89.

52. Ibid.

53. Letter of June 9, 1776, to William Cushing, in Burnett, *Letters*, 1:478.

54. Ibid., 6.

55. In *Papers of John Adams*, ed. Robert Taylor, 15 vols. (Cambridge, MA: Belknap Press, 1977), 2:245.

56. See, e.g., Richard Sinopoli, *The Foundations of American Citizenship: Liberalism, The Constitution, and Civic Virtue* (New York: Oxford University Press, 1992); Gordon Wood, *The Radicalism of the American Revolution* (New York: Random House, 1991); Richard Vetterli and Gary Bryner, *In Search of the Republic* (Totowa, NJ: Rowman and Littlefield, 1987); Ellis Sandoz, *A Government of Laws* (Baton Rouge: Louisiana State University Press, 1991).

57. See Aristotle, *Ethics* Book II, which differentiated "moral" and "intellectual" virtue. In the ensuing discussion, Aristotle held that virtue is not innate but is a matter of choice based on rational principles and which is inculcated through habituation. John Locke, too, made clear that moral formation had primacy, not particular subject matter: "Tis virtue then, direct virtue, which is the hard and valuable part to be aimed at in education. . . . All other considerations and accomplishments should give way and be postponed to this." Aristotle's "habituation" became "good breeding" in Locke. See *The Educational Writings of John Locke*, ed. James Axtell (New York: Cambridge University Press, 1968), 169ff.

58. Letter to Peter Carr, August 19, 1785, in *The Portable Jefferson* ed. Merrill Peterson (New York: Penguin Books, 1975), 381.

59. Burnett, *Letters*, 1:156.

60. Cited in Bernard Bailyn, *The Ideological Origins of the American Revolution* (Cambridge, MA: Belknap Press, 1967), 369.

61. *The Federalist*, ed. Isaac Kramnick (New York: Penguin Books, 1987), 431.

62. Lester J. Cappon, ed., *The Adams–Jefferson Letters* (Chapel Hill: University of North Carolina Press, 1987), 549–51.

63. I am grateful to Mark Long, Baylor University, for assistance in preparing this section on virtue.

64. Marsh v. Chambers, 463 U.S. 783 (1983).

65. For a discussion of this matter, see Derek Davis, *Religion and the Continental Congress, 1774–1789: Contributions to Original Intent* (Oxford: Oxford University Press, 2000), 168–72. Some other portions of this chapter have been partially drawn from the same work.

66. See, e.g., Philip Hamburger, *Separation of Church and State* (Cambridge, MA: Harvard University Press, 2002). For a critique of these arguments against the separation of church and state, see further chapter 1 by T. Jeremy Gunn and chapter 10 by Steven K. Green.

67. *Annals*, 1:783–84.

68. Quoted in Martin E. Marty, "Living with Establishment and Disestablishment in Nineteenth-Century Anglo-America," *Journal of Church and State* 18 (Winter 1976): 72.

69. Alexis de Tocqueville, *Democracy in America*, ed. J. P. Mayer and Max Lerner, trans. George Lawrence (New York: Harper & Row, 1969), 271–72.

70. What constitutes a "neutral" state is, of course, no small problem. For treatments on the meaning of neutrality, see Douglas Laycock, "Formal, Substantive, and Disaggregated Neutrality toward Religion," *DePaul Law Review* 39 (1990): 993; Michael W. McConnell, "Neutrality under the Religion Clauses," *Northwestern Law Review* 81 (1986): 146; Steven D. Smith, *Foreordained Failure: The Quest for a Constitutional Principle of Religious Freedom* (New York: Oxford University Press, 1995), ch. 7; and Stephen V. Monsma, *Positive Neutrality: Letting Religious Freedom Ring* (Westport, CT: Greenwood Press, 1993).

71. James E. Wood Jr., "The Secular State," *Journal of Church and State* 7 (1965): 169.

72. Quoted in ibid., 175.

73. Philip B. Kurland and Ralph Lerner, *The Founders' Constitution*, 5 vols. (Chicago: University of Chicago Press, 1987), 5:48.

74. Hunt, *Writings of James Madison*, 9:100.

8

The First Federal Congress and the Formation of the Establishment Clause of the First Amendment

Carl H. Esbeck

The text and original meaning of the Establishment Clause as drafted by the First Federal Congress was diminished in its importance when the Supreme Court handed down its decision in *Everson v. Board of Education* in 1947. Instead of looking to the record of the debates and minutes of the First Congress, *Everson* adopted the principles animating the disestablishment struggle in Virginia, and somewhat less so the disestablishment experiences in other newly formed states, to give substantive content to the Establishment Clause. The dissenting justices in *Everson* would have taken the matter a step further by generally conflating the beliefs of James Madison of Virginia with the meaning of the Establishment Clause.

The imputation of the disestablishment experience in Virginia to the adoption of the Establishment Clause by the First Congress is open to question as a matter of history. Not only were these two experiences very different law-making events separated by four years, but the Virginia House of Delegates of 1784–1785 and the Congress of 1789 were elected by very different constituencies, composed of quite different legislative officials, bearing different responsibilities, and harboring different ambitions and allegiances.[1] The one common denominator in the two events was the active involvement of James Madison, a highly capable statesman with well-developed and strongly held views on church–government relations. Even Madison, however, was not singularly focused on religious freedom as Congress assembled itself in New York City in the spring of 1789. As a member of the House of Representatives and someone who had the ear of President Washington, Madison was devoted to the implementation of a federated government of robust powers to replace the ineffectual Confederation Congress. When he did focus on a bill of rights, Madison had the good sense to take into account that the First Congress was an altogether different audience than his earlier one in Virginia, and that the rights-declaring task before Congress was the far simpler one of agreeing on what powers to deny to the national government with respect to religion, speech, search and seizure, criminal indictments, and so forth, as opposed to what powers to grant it.

Following the Supreme Court's opinion in *Everson*, a recurring argument has been that the text of the Establishment Clause, as well as the original understanding of the First Congress, which debated and redrafted the phrase from June through most of September 1789, should help shape its modern substantive meaning. Although it has been over sixty years now since *Everson* was decided, these historical arguments show little sign of abating. Moreover, the reliance on the drafting history as well as the text is not exclusive to constitutional conservatives. As the cases and scholarship have unfolded, liberals are just as eager to array the historical record on their side. As often as not, the divide is over which side has the better grasp of the history, as well as which historical events should matter or matter the most.

This chapter sifts through what survives of the debates about religious freedom in the First Congress of 1789 and in the state ratification debates that followed. It also analyzes prominent theories of interpretation of the original understanding of the Establishment Clause, weighing them against this historical evidence.

Drafting the Phrases on Religious Freedom in the First Federal Congress, May to September 1789, and Ensuing State Ratification

The First Federal Congress meeting in New York City was overwhelmingly comprised of Federalists, who had supported ratification of the United States Constitution of 1787, as distinct from the Anti-Federalists who opposed ratification. The House had forty-nine Federalists and ten Anti-Federalists; the Senate had twenty Federalists and only two Anti-Federalists. During the state debates over whether to ratify the Constitution, the Federalists were of the firm conviction that, even in the absence of what became the First Amendment, Congress had no power over religious conscience or to establish a church or multiple churches. No small number of other Americans, though they did not regard themselves as partisan, did not feel so sure, and wanted a bill of rights. Anti-Federalists wanted even more. They sought to reduce the powers vested in the central government, thereby restoring power to the states.

Amendments concerning religious establishment that had been discussed by some of the state ratification conventions for consideration by Congress only confused matters. On the one hand was New Hampshire's proposal that "Congress shall make no laws touching religion, or to infringe the rights of conscience." Maryland's minority proposal was equally direct: "That there be no national religion established by law; but that all persons be equally entitled to protection in their religious liberty." On the other hand, the amendment language recommended by Virginia, North Carolina, and New York did not prohibit the nonpreferential support of organized religion, only the preference of one religion over others. The Virginia ratification convention proposed: "That religion, or the duty which we owe to our creator, and the manner of discharging it, can be directed only by reason and conviction, not by force or violence, and therefore all men have an equal, natural and unalienable right to the free exercise of religion according to the dictates of conscience, and that no particular religious sect or society ought to be favored or established by law in preference to others." With minor changes North Carolina repeated Virginia's language. New York proposed: "That the people have an equal, natural, and unalienable right freely and peaceably to exercise their religion, according to the dictates of conscience; and that no religious sect or society ought to be favored or established by law in preference to others."[2]

Did these latter three states only fear a central government that could favor one religious establishment over others? That is highly unlikely given that by 1788 there was well-documented hostility in Virginia and North Carolina toward the establishment of both exclusive and multiple churches. New York had done away with its establishment in 1777.[3] Accordingly, we will want to examine supplemental evidence with respect to intended limits on the power of the national government over church–government relations. That points us to the drafting and ratification of the First Amendment's two phrases on religious freedom by the First Congress.

Three Lines of First Amendment Interpretation. Before analyzing the House and Senate debates it is helpful to identify three major crosscurrents among scholars with respect to the Establishment Clause. One current comes under the heading of *nonpreferentialism*, another under *specific federalism*, and a third under the *scope* of the power that was denied to the national government. A fourth crosscurrent, which this chapter takes up in a later subpart, is whether the religion clauses of the First Amendment only protect liberty of conscience.

The scope of the text in the proposed amendments from Maryland and New Hampshire would have altogether disempowered Congress from establishing a "national religion" (Maryland) or enacting any law "touching religion" (New Hampshire). The scope of the Maryland disempowerment was very narrow; the New Hampshire disempowerment was very broad. By way of contrast, the scope of the amendments from Virginia, North Carolina, and New York would not prohibit the national government from aiding religion so long as the aid was available to all religions without preference. For example, the national government could aid all religions, without preferring or establishing any, by offering annual $1,000 cash payments to all clerics or other ecclesiastical leaders. The no-preference language from these three states raises the question of whether the Establishment Clause was meant to imply that Congress retained the power to aid religion—delegated to Congress somewhere in the original 1787 Constitution—so long as the national government did so without preferring some religions over others.

This latter claim, called nonpreferentialism, is paradoxical insofar as the amendments from Virginia, North Carolina, and New York were being put forward by Anti-Federalists. Anti-Federalists wanted to reduce the power of Congress, not increase it. Yet, to embody nonpreferentialism in the Establishment Clause would increase national power over religion. Although some Anti-Federalists would have preferred a multiple establishment, they were aware of America's religious pluralism as one moved along the Atlantic seaboard, including large pockets of religious opposition to establishmentarianism of any sort, and thus any such multiple establishment was possible only at a state level. Moreover, from the perspective of the Federalists, nonpreferentialism makes little sense because Federalists were consistent in arguing that nothing in the 1787 Constitution delegated to Congress—even by implication— the power to intermeddle with religion. The larger rule was first stated by James Wilson of Pennsylvania: If the Constitution does not delegate to Congress the power, it is denied. That rule was soon to be made explicit in the Tenth Amendment. The sweep of the Wilsonian argument necessarily included no power to aid all religions without preference. Finally, as we shall see below, there is little in the congressional debates indicating that there was a serious push for permitting nonpreferentialism. Madison's initial draft amendment ignored the no-preference texts from Virginia, North Carolina, and New York. Federalists were entirely in control of the amendment process in both chambers, and when no-preference texts were advanced in the Senate they were eventually voted down.

Nonpreferentialism is problematic for an additional reason. A more obvious solution for Anti-Federalists to achieve their goal of reclaiming state power was a federal amendment that expressly disempowered Congress when it came to the establishment of any or all religions, preferentially or nonpreferentially, thereby confirming relations between church and government remained entirely in the hands of the states. The New England Federalists would have been especially open to such an approach as they did not want the national government intermeddling in the advantages then enjoyed by the Congregational Church in Connecticut, Massachusetts, and New Hampshire.[4] These three states had mandatory religious assessments at the local level, but a taxpayer could designate his assessment to the church of his choice. In practice, this worked to the advantage of the far more numerous Congregationalists. Moreover, such an amendment would serve the interests of those such as James Madison who wanted to keep the national government altogether out of the matter of religious establishments. Once again, Federalists were entirely in control of the parliamentary procedure so what they wanted would hold sway.

But if Anti-Federalists' concerns could be accommodated by the Federalists inserting particular wording into the amendment on religious freedom, then all the better for the eventual success of the upcoming state ratification of the amendments. Thus, there were multiple reasons all around to avoid nonpreferentialism.

Secondly, that the First Amendment, along with all of the other provisions of the Bill of Rights, was meant to bind only the new national government was not a source of contention in 1789.[5] It will be referenced here as the "general federalist" character of the Bill of Rights, and obviously that included the Establishment Clause. What is presently contended among scholars is whether the final text of the Establishment Clause, introduced for the first time by the House-Senate Conference Committee, worked into the interstices of the clause a new participial phrase ("respecting an establishment") that was specifically designed to preserve state sovereignty over the matter of religious establishment. This I call "specific federalism." Specific federalism is a unique claim. The theory attributes to the Establishment Clause alone particular federalist intent, one not present in free exercise, free speech, free press, or other provisions in the first eight amendments. The difference between the general federalist character of the Bill of Rights and specific federalism became important only in 1947 and thereafter when the Supreme Court in *Everson* faced the question of whether to "incorporate" the Establishment Clause through the Fourteenth Amendment, thereby making its restraints binding on state and local governments. Devotees of specific federalism argue that the clause should not have been incorporated because the Court thereby ignored its unique federalist character.

A third crosscurrent is the question with respect to the "scope" of the congressional disempowerment in the Establishment Clause. When Congress (and by extension, the executive or judicial branches) exercised one of its enumerated powers to make law, the more foresighted in the First Congress could envision instances when legislation would have a consequential effect on religion. For example, a congressionally adopted copyright law would raise the question of whether a new translation of the Bible could be copyrighted. Or assume that in formulating legislation to implement the constitutionally required census a decision is made that one item usefully surveyed is the trades and professions. That necessarily would mean counting those Americans who are professional clerics or otherwise in full-time religious service. So the census would incidentally touch on religion. That raises a question whether a census with respect to religious vocations falls within the scope of the no-establishment disempowerment and thus is prohibited as an object of congressional power. The First Federal Congress, as we shall see, finally settled on the scope of disempowerment being laws about "an establishment," the meaning of which is partly—but only partly—revealed by the House and Senate debates.

With these three lines of interpretation in mind, we turn to the surviving debates over the restraints on the national government with respect to religion as developed by the First Federal Congress in 1789.

Before the House of Representatives

JUNE 8, 1789

James Madison, later a leading Republican and ally of Thomas Jefferson, was in the forefront of those Federalists working to report out a bill of rights for state ratification. In preparing a draft of amendments to the Constitution, James Madison had available to him a pamphlet that compiled all of the two hundred-plus state constitutional amendments that were recommended by seven of the eleven states in their ratifying conventions. Madison did not just dispassionately sift through these recommended amendments, selecting those that had merit: He sorted with an eye to retaining all national powers he deemed useful to an energetic central government. He sought to fulfill his promise to safeguard rights that well-meaning Americans believed were at risk, and to avoid a second constitutional convention being earnestly sought by hard-shell Anti-Federalists. Further, he did not hesitate to fashion amendments entirely of his own creation, such as one about certain rights limiting state powers. No one else in the First Federal Congress was as diligent as Madison; thus, his sifting and sorting is equally important with respect to those proposed state amendments he ignored.

On June 8, 1789, Madison addressed the House on the subject of amendments to the Constitution. Madison moved that the House resolve itself as a committee of the whole to consider his amendments. The motion was resisted by both High Federalists, who thought amendments a waste of time, and Anti-Federalists, who wanted a second constitutional convention to consider both a bill of rights and structural amendments that would restore certain state powers.

Madison sought to bring the debate to an end by withdrawing his motion and moving to have the House appoint a select committee to consider the amendments. He continued by remarking on the role the amendments would play "to limit and qualify the powers of the Government, by excepting out of the grant of power those cases in which the Government ought not to act, or to act only in a particular mode."[6] The planned amendments would thus delineate powers that did not lie with Congress as a result of the 1787 Constitution. Agreeing on the powers that Congress should be denied was a much easier task.[7] Accordingly, the amendments take power away from the national government (in the view of Anti-Federalists) or merely clarify the limited delegation of powers in the existing Constitution (in the Wilsonian view of Federalists). Madison stressed that the amendments were to "satisfy the public mind" worried about the lack of a bill of rights, and to thereby gain the peoples' backing for the new government. After all, six states had ratified the Constitution on the promise that amendments would be forthcoming.

Madison next gave the amendments their initial reading, from which we get a glimpse of the provisions addressing religious freedom in their earliest form. Madison's amendments were proposed as interlineations into the text of the 1787 Constitution, as opposed to a list of amendments at the end of the document. By inserting what later became the First Amendment into Article I, Section 9, Madison's clear intent was that the amendment be a disempowerment of national authority, not a new substantive rule on church–government relations. He spoke as follows:

> The amendments which have occurred to me, proper to be recommended by Congress to the State Legislatures, are these:
>
> . . .
>
> Fourthly. That in article 1st, section 9, between clauses 3 and 4, be inserted these clauses, to wit: **The civil rights of none shall be abridged on account of religious belief or worship, nor shall any national religion be established, nor shall the full and equal rights of conscience be in any manner, or on any pretext, infringed.**
>
> . . .
>
> The right of the people to keep and bear arms shall not be infringed; a well armed and well regulated militia being the best security of a free country: but **no person religiously scrupulous of bearing arms shall be compelled to render military service in person.**
>
> . . .
>
> Fifthly. That in article 1st, section 10, between clauses 1 and 2, be inserted this clause, to wit: **No State shall violate the equal rights of conscience**, or the freedom of the press, or the trial by jury in criminal cases.[8]

Madison's Fourth Article does not resemble in the least any of the four state-proposed amendments. In particular, he avoided the no-preference language from Virginia, North Carolina, and New York, and the no-establishment scope of disempowerment was modest ("any national religion"). Part of the amendment was wordy, with the first and last parts addressing the relationship among the government, religion, and the individual, whereas church–government relations occupied a brief middle.

Madison's initial treatment of church-government relations was spare ("nor shall any national religion be established"), with considerable but undefined weight placed on what is meant by the word *established*. Madison made no remarks about its meaning during the June 8 reading. One interpretation is that the text prohibits Congress from establishing one national religion, thereby implying that Congress is open to establishing all religions so long as none is preferred. A more natural reading of Madison's text is that the use of "any" means that the establishment of one or more religions is prohibited. Thus, if Congress had established the Episcopal, Methodist, and Congregational churches, that would constitute three violations of the no-establishment principle in the proffered amendment. Likewise, to establish all religions would be a multiple violation of the amendment.

Those of the nonpreferentialist view, however, argue that the proper reading is that although Congress is prohibited from establishing any religion, there is implied congressional power (stopping short of an establishment) to aid all religions without preference. For example, by implication the amendment does not prohibit Congress from appropriating an annual $1,000 cash supplement to all clerics and ecclesiastical leaders. Such an appropriation would fall short of a full establishment and thus by implication be permitted by Madison's proposed text. However, Madison's text does not require equal treatment, so the nonpreferentialists' argument proves too much because their reading of the text is also open by implication to government aiding some clerics with $1,000 payments, but $500 to others, and nothing at all to yet others.

In Madison's explanation of the other amendments that address religion, he did remark on the proposed Fifth Article that binds *states* with respect to the "equal rights of conscience." This is the only proffered amendment that is binding on the states. It is noteworthy that with respect to religion and the states Madison only attempted an amendment to safeguard conscience, that is, the relationship among government, religion, and the individual. We know that Madison wanted to protect conscience, inclusively defined, because of a letter he had written Jefferson explaining why he opposed a bill of rights. One of his reasons was that in a debate over a bill of rights "the rights of Conscience in particular, if submitted to public definition would be narrowed."[9] Madison feared being unable to protect the non-Christian and the nonreligious, citing as an example the intolerance in New England during the ratification of the Constitution to the Religious Test Clause "open[ing] the door for Jews, Turks, and infidels." Knowing he had a difficult task in advancing an inclusive protection of conscience in public debate, especially protection from states, Madison plunged ahead:

> I wish also, in revising the constitution, we may throw into that section, which interdicts the abuse of certain powers in the State Legislatures, some other provisions of equal, if not greater importance than those already made. The words, "No State shall pass any bill of attainder, *ex post facto* law," &c. were wise and proper restrictions in the constitution. I think there is more danger of those powers being abused by the State Governments than by the Government of the United States. The same may be said of other powers which they possess,

if not controlled by the general principle, that laws are unconstitutional which infringe the rights of the community. I should therefore wish to extend this interdiction, and add, as I have stated in the 5th resolution, that **no State shall violate the equal right of conscience**, freedom of the press, or trial by jury in criminal cases; because it is proper that every Government should be disarmed of powers which trench upon those particular rights.[10]

By seeking to protect the *equal* right of conscience, Madison would extend to the non-Christian and the nonreligious the same safeguards as the conscience of Christians.

After further explanation with respect to his proposed amendments before the House, Madison closed by again moving for the appointment of a select committee. Those seeking delay still resisted. So Madison withdrew that motion and simply moved the adoption of his entire set of proposed amendments. The threat of bringing matters to an immediate head produced quick results. The House promptly voted to refer the amendments to a committee of the whole and then adjourned for the day. The House did not return to the matter of amendments until mid-July, testing Madison's patience.

JULY 21, 1789

That patience finally ran out as Madison "begged" the House to take action on the June 8 amendments. The House responded by referring the matter to a Select Committee of eleven members, one from each state. The Select Committee consisted of Messrs. Vining, Madison, Baldwin, Sherman, Burke, Gilman, Clymer, Benson, Goodhue, Boudinot, and Gale. Each state was represented because eventually each amendment would have to be ratified by three-quarters of the states.

JULY 28, 1789

The Select Committee acted with dispatch by reporting back in just one week. It issued a report to the entire House, where it was tabled without discussion. The phrases on religious freedom, as emerging from the Select Committee, were not just simplified but materially altered with respect to no-establishment and matters of conscience. The amendments read:

> **Fourth. No religion shall be established by law, nor shall the equal rights of conscience be infringed.**[11]
>
> . . .
>
> A well regulated militia, composed of the body of the people, being the best security of a free state, the right of the people to keep and bear arms shall not be infringed; **but no person religiously scrupulous shall be compelled to bear arms.**[12]

. . .

Fifth. No State shall infringe the equal rights of conscience, nor
the freedom of speech or of the press, nor of the right of trial by jury in
criminal cases.[13]

The Fourth Article produced by the Select Committee returned to a clear
pattern of two relationships: first, that of government and organized religion, and, second, that of government, religion, and individual conscience.
With respect to church–government relations, the word *national* was
omitted, probably because it was thought redundant. The article was presented as an amendment to Article I, Section 9, of the Constitution, and
that section spoke to limits only on the national government. The real scope
of national disempowerment still lay with the meaning of *established.* Thus,
the no-establishment alterations by the Select Committee were stylistic.
Not so with respect to the relationship between the national government
and individual conscience. No longer were the "full and equal rights of conscience" protected, but only the "equal rights" thereof. Further, the reference to "religious belief and worship" not being abridged was omitted. The
latter change appears to be for reasons other than mere brevity. "Religious
belief and worship" are easily said to be subsumed into the "full and equal
rights of conscience," but it is less persuasive that they are subsumed into
the narrower "equal rights of conscience."

AUGUST 13–14, 1789

Richard Bland Lee moved for the House to resolve itself into a Committee of
the Whole. Working as a Committee of the Whole permitted House agreement
on the text of each amendment by a mere majority vote. Once the draft amendments were reported by the Committee to the entire House, adoption of each
amendment would require passage by a two-thirds vote.

AUGUST 15, 1789

The debate by the House turned for the first time to the no-establishment provision. This day was the longest discussion of religious freedom in the House.
It unfolded as follows:

> The House again went into a Committee of the whole on the proposed
> amendments to the constitution, Mr. Boudinot in the chair.

> The fourth proposition being under consideration, as follows:

> Article 1. Section 9. Between paragraphs two and three insert **"no religion
> shall be established by law, nor shall the equal rights of conscience be
> infringed."**

Mr. Silvester had some doubts of the propriety of the mode of expression used in this paragraph. He apprehended that it was liable to a construction different from what had been made by the committee. He feared it might be thought to have a tendency to abolish religion altogether.[14]

Peter Silvester's remark is initially puzzling. The Select Committee's amendment is rightly said to "abolish establishment," but it surely did not "abolish religion." Moreover, the amendment unquestionably applied only against the national government given its placement in Section 9 of Article I, whereas all existing religious establishments in America were at the state level. Silvester was a Federalist from New York. New York had completed its disestablishment in 1777, so he could not have been motivated to protect an established church in his home state. Silvester's "apprehensions" and "fears" make sense only if his concern was that the amendment's text ("nor shall the equal rights of conscience be infringed") is understood as "abolishing religion" because it affirmatively protected the nonreligious and even the atheist. This reading fits with Madison's worry earlier expressed in his letter to Jefferson that any attempt to extend in public debate the protection of conscience to the nonreligious would meet with resistance. Today we are quick to regard Silvester as intolerant. But in this period many shared his concern that latitudinarianism and the Enlightenment were on the rise. They thought that traditional religion was instrumental to public morals and thus good government; accordingly, government should not help to further religion's decline by safeguarding its opposite. The debate continued:

Mr. Vining suggested the propriety of transposing the two members of the sentence.

Mr. Gerry said it would read better if it was, that **no religious doctrine shall be established by law[, nor shall the equal rights of conscience be infringed]**.[15]

Elbridge Gerry's suggestion is an attempt by an Anti-Federalist to define *establishment* narrowly, confining it to the legal codification of a religious creed. His proposal went to the scope of the disempowerment of Congress. Gerry was ignored by the Federalists. The debate continued:

Mr. Sherman thought the amendment altogether unnecessary, inasmuch as Congress had no authority whatever delegated to them by the constitution to make religious establishments; he would, therefore, move to have it struck out.

Mr. Carroll.—As the rights of conscience are, in their nature, of peculiar delicacy, and will little bear the gentlest touch of governmental hand; and as many sects have concurred in opinion that they are not well secured under the present constitution, he said he was much in favor of adopting the words. He thought it would tend more towards conciliating the minds of the people to the Government than almost any other amendment that he had heard proposed. He would not contend with gentlemen about phraseology, his object was to secure the substance in such a manner as to satisfy the wishes of the honest part of the community.[16]

Roger Sherman was a Federalist from Connecticut who thought the amendment process a waste of time because the 1787 Constitution delegated no congressional authority to establish religion. Again, this is the Wilsonian argument.

Daniel Carroll was a Federalist as well. However, he was also a Roman Catholic from Maryland. At the time, Catholics were a small minority in America. They were widely discriminated against, albeit less so in Maryland, which at its founding was a refuge for Catholics leaving Great Britain. Perhaps Carroll rose in answer to Sherman. In any event, Carroll spoke in favor of protecting "conscience" but said nothing about "establishment." Carroll reassured the House that many well-meaning Americans, not just a few vocal Baptists in New England and Virginia, were sincerely fearful because the 1787 Constitution lacked a bill of rights, and such was of particular concern to all religious minorities. Everyone in the room would have known that Carroll was one such minority.

Madison responded to the remark by Silvester ("tendency to abolish religion altogether"), as well as that of Sherman ("amendment altogether unnecessary"), as follows:

Mr. Madison said, he apprehended the meaning of the words to be, that Congress should not establish a religion, and enforce the legal observation of it by law, nor compel men to worship God in any manner contrary to their conscience. Whether the words are necessary or not, he did not mean to say, but they had been required by some of the State Conventions, who seemed to entertain an opinion that under the clause of the constitution, which gave power to Congress to make all laws necessary and proper to carry into execution the constitution, and the laws made under it, enabled them to make laws of such a nature as might infringe the rights of conscience, and establish a national religion; to prevent these effects he presumed the amendment was intended, and he thought it well expressed as the nature of the language would admit.[17]

Madison made five points in this reply. The first is that the no-establishment and conscience texts limit only Congress. Thus state establishments or forms of religious coercion with respect to religion were left undisturbed by the amendment. This is the "general federalism" point. Second, as a Federalist Madison was still unwilling to say that the no-establishment and conscience texts were necessary. So he did not contest Roger Sherman's remark. But Madison did note that several states had proposed that a religious freedom amendment was prudent because, as Carroll had confirmed, many Americans needed reassuring. Accordingly, the belief of Sherman notwithstanding, it was prudent to proceed to adopt amendments.

Third, with respect to Silvester's fear, Madison confirmed that the text on conscience was indeed sufficiently broad to protect the nonreligious. Madison said that the amendment would prohibit laws that "compel men to worship God in any manner contrary to their conscience."[18]

Fourth, Madison noted that some of the fears expressed in the state constitutional ratification conventions were not about the abuse of power expressly delegated to the national government but about any consequential "effects" on both no-establishment and conscience that the use of Congress's delegated powers might have. The Necessary and Proper Clause had been singled out by opponents, noted Madison, as one source of possible detrimental "effects." Thus, it can be said that one of the issues expressly thought about by the First Congress is how congressional action pursuant to its enumerated powers of 1787 may have consequential—and indeed detrimental—effects on religious freedom. Whatever Congress's powers to infringe conscience or establish a national religion, real or imagined, Madison argued that the Select Committee's proposal was a corrective.

Madison's fifth point was that the amendment not only restrained a congressional establishment of religion but, in his opinion, also restrained the national government from enforcing the "legal observation of [religion] by law." This helps us to define *establishment* in Madison's thinking. The remark has Madison saying that the scope of the proposed text is not just a bar to a full-fledged establishment, but that the text also disempowers Congress from legislating particular elements ("enforce legal observation . . . by law") of a fully developed establishment. The Church of England, the full religious establishment most familiar to the founders, had multiple elements where particular observances of the Church of England were enforced by law.[19]

In the course of this colloquy, Madison twice said that he apprehended the meaning of the text to be that Congress should not establish "*a* religion." These remarks by Madison are taken by some as narrowing the disempowerment of the no-establishment text. By implication, they claim, Congress is left free to establish multiple religions or all religions without preference. Not only is such a reading inconsistent with Madison's well-known views on church–government relations both before and after this debate, but those of the nonpreferentialist view can claim no solace in this reading because it attributes to the text a disempowerment more narrow than aiding all religions without preference. That is, the reading proves too much to buttress nonpreferentialism because it also allows preferential or multiple establishments that stop short of aiding all.

The debate continued:

Mr. Huntington said that he feared, with the gentleman first up on this subject [Silvester], that the words might be taken in such latitude as to be extremely hurtful to the cause of religion. He understood the amendment to mean what had been expressed by the gentleman from Virginia [Madison]; but others might find it convenient to put another construction upon it. The ministers of their congregations to the Eastward [Huntington's Connecticut] were maintained by the contributions of those who belonged to their society; the expense of building meeting-houses was contributed in the same manner. These things were regulated by bylaws. If an action was brought before a Federal Court on any of these cases, the person who had neglected to perform his engagements could not be compelled to do it; for a support of ministers, or building of places of worship might be construed into a religious establishment.

By the charter of Rhode Island, no religion could be established by law; he could give a history of the effects of such a regulation; indeed the people were now enjoying the blessed fruits of it.[20] He hoped, therefore, the amendment would be made in such a way as to secure the rights of conscience, and a free exercise of the rights of religion, but not to patronize those who professed no religion at all.

Mr. Madison thought, if the word **national** was inserted before **religion**, it would satisfy the minds of honorable gentlemen. He believed that the people feared one sect might obtain a pre-eminence, or two combine together, and establish a religion to which they would compel others to conform. He thought if the word **national** was introduced, it would point the amendment directly to the object it was intended to prevent.[21]

Benjamin Huntington, a Federalist from Connecticut, shared Silvester's concern that the "equal rights of conscience" text could be "hurtful to the cause of religion" by protecting the nonreligious. He favored a rewording so that the amendment secured "a free exercise of the rights of religion, but not to patronize those who professed no religion at all." So neither the nonreligious nor atheist is to be protected.

Huntington also wanted to shield the Connecticut church–state arrangement favoring the Congregational Church. That arrangement was untouched, however, because the proposed amendment was binding only on the national government. Huntington's fear over the no-establishment text makes sense only if he was being overly cautious that it not be misconstrued as being binding on the states. Huntington went on to supply an illustration of such a misconstruction. He thought the text could be read by a federal court to essentially overturn Connecticut's assessment law. The law, like that in Massachusetts and New Hampshire, operated at the local level to provide tax support for churches. The assessment was mandatory, but each taxpayer could direct the amount to the church of his choice. Because each taxpayer could direct the assessment to his own church, Congregationalists such as Huntington did not believe that the tax violated religious conscience. Nor did Congregationalists think such assessments constituted an establishment. Huntington made this clear in his remarks saying he supported the protection of conscience and feared only that the religious assessment "might be construed into a religious establishment" by others.

Baptists in New England disagreed with Huntington, as he was likely aware. First, Baptists believed that church contributions must be voluntary, and thus the mandatory assessment was an affront to religious conscience even when the money was ultimately paid over by the local assessor to the Baptist Church. Second, in practice the assessment law worked to the advantage of the local Congregational Church. The Congregationalists overwhelmingly dominated in the number of followers, and they received assessments from those who were marginally religious but did not want to be viewed as such. Understandably, Baptists argued that this arrangement was not only a violation of conscience but also an establishment of the Congregational Church.

To illustrate his concern over the amendment being misconstrued, Huntington hypothesized a lawsuit in federal court where a claim by the local assessor involved the nonpayment by a citizen of his religious taxes. Huntington wrongly assumed that a federal judge assigned the case would have to follow the bill of rights. But the proposed amendments were not binding on the states. This general federalism, however, was a point on which Huntington was confused.

Of greater interest is Madison's passing contemplation during the foregoing exchange with respect to the scope of the no-establishment text. Madison said that the proposed amendment would bar not just the establishment of a single sect, but also an establishment of multiple sects that combined together to achieve such an objective. Thus, Madison's focus went beyond a single national church. For example, he also sought to prohibit several Protestant churches combining to form a national Protestant establishment. Nonpreferentialists reference Madison's remarks as helping their cause by implying that Congress could aid all religions without favor to any. However, once again there are problems with this claim: their reading would also imply congressional power to aid two or three churches while stopping short of a no-preference rule, and the reading does not take into account Madison's broader and well-known view favoring church–state separation.

Rather than quarrel with Huntington about his mistaken belief that a federal court would apply the amendment to the states, Madison suggested a revision that made it even clearer that the amendment only ran against the federal government. Madison's fix backfired because, as the debate is about to show, it drew the scorn of Elbridge Gerry.

Mr. Gerry did not like the term **national**, proposed by the gentleman from Virginia [Madison], and he hoped it would not be adopted by the House. It brought to his mind some observations that had taken place in the [state] conventions at the time they were considering the present constitution. It had been insisted upon by those who were called antifederalists, that this form of Government consolidated the Union; the honorable gentleman's motion shows that he considers it in the same light. Those who were called antifederalists at that time complained that they had injustice done to them by the title, because they were in favor of a Federal Government, and the others were in favor of a national one; the federalists were for ratifying the constitution as it stood, and the others not until amendments were made. Their names then ought not to have been distinguished by federalists and antifederalists, but rats and antirats.

Mr. Madison withdrew his motion, but observed that the words "**no national religion shall be established by law**," did not imply that the Government was a national one. . . .[22]

Madison repaired the error by quickly withdrawing the motion. The debate continued:

Mr. Livermore was not satisfied with [Madison's] amendment; but he did not wish them to dwell long on the subject. He thought it would be better if it was altered, and made to read in this manner, that **Congress shall make no laws touching religion, or infringing the rights of conscience.**[23]

Like Madison, Samuel Livermore was a Federalist. He hailed from New Hampshire, and moved for the substitution of a text nearly identical to that recommended by the New Hampshire constitutional ratification convention. Livermore's opening phrase ("Congress shall make no laws") unmistakably pointed the object of the amendment to the federal government and not the states, thus meeting the fear of Huntington. Moreover, it achieved what Madison had tried to do by insertion of the word "national," but without angering Anti-Federalists.

Livermore's text also had the effect of preventing Congress from enacting legislation to overturn state laws on religion, which had not been part of the discussion so far. Nor was it a consequence discussed upon introduction of Livermore's amendment. Still, the text's literal effect is to raise the "specific federalism" position: Congress is uniquely disempowered from "mak[ing] . . . laws touching religion." Livermore's text would render ultra vires any congressional law the subject matter of which is a state's manner of dealing with religion. That such an intent was not claimed or disclaimed, or even remarked upon, is perhaps suggestive of no intent along the lines of specific federalism by Livermore, and thus a mild repudiation by silence of the position.

An even more remarkable unknown with Livermore's text came with his use of the word *touching*. This word choice substantially broadened the *scope* of the disempowerment from negating national lawmaking that established religion to one of negating national lawmaking that merely touched religion. All sorts of national legislation could incidentally "touch" religion, such as whether the creation of federal bankruptcy courts meant that financially distressed churches could be discharged of their debts. This broad scope surely would have caused some alert representative in the House to think about congressional legislation's incidental effects on religion, not just about ultra vires actions clearly outside of Congress's enumerated powers. It would have caused attentive representatives to ask themselves whether there were unintended consequences brought on by the sheer breadth of Livermore's amendment. We learned the result five days later.

Finally, in the day's debate Livermore omitted the word *equal* before "rights." Presumably Madison would have preferred to retain "equal" so that it was clearer that the conscience of the nonreligious was protected to the same degree as the religious.

Remarkably, none of the latter three changes in the text drew any discussion on this day. The effect of all of these changes likely took time to be fully realized. For now, there was general relief that Huntington's problem was solved. Matters concluded on that positive note:

> [T]he question was then taken on Mr. Livermore's motion, and passed in the affirmative, thirty-one for, and twenty against it.[24]

At the end of the day the proposed Article of Amendment read: "Article I, Section 9, between paragraphs 2 and 3 insert '**The Congress shall make no laws touching religion, or infringing the rights of conscience.**'"

AUGUST 17, 1789

The House took up the proposed amendments respecting conscientious objectors to war and restricting the states from infringing on "the equal rights of conscience." The debate with respect to the Fifth Article directed against states infringing conscience is reproduced below. It yields an important insight concerning the meaning of the word *conscience*. In complete control of proceedings in the House, Madison and other Federalists were willing to restrain states from infringing the equal rights of conscience but knew they had no chance of restraining states from establishing religion. To attempt the latter would have been futile, of course, because the New England states still had religious assessments and were not about to have the national Constitution order them abolished. Indeed, the New England representatives were High Federalists. Their votes were essential to Madison's efforts at shepherding amendments through the House. Additionally, Maryland, South Carolina, and Georgia retained multiple establishments that they would not have wanted disturbed. The debate follows:

The Committee of the Whole then proceeded to the fifth proposition:

Article 1. section 10. [B]etween the first and second paragraph, insert **"no State shall infringe the equal rights of conscience,** nor the freedom of speech or of the press, nor of the right of trial by jury in criminal cases."

Mr. Tucker.—This is offered, I presume, as an amendment to the constitution of the United States, but it goes only to the alteration of the constitutions of particular States. It would be much better, I apprehend, to leave the State Governments to themselves, and not to interfere with them more than we already do; and that is thought by many to be rather too much. I therefore move, sir, to strike out these words.

Mr. Madison conceived this to be the most valuable amendment in the whole list. If there was any reason to restrain the Government of the United States from infringing upon these essential rights, it was equally necessary that they should be secured against the State Governments. He thought that if they provided against the one, it was as necessary to provide against the other, and was satisfied that it would be equally grateful to the people.

Mr. Livermore had no great objection to the sentiment, but he thought it not well expressed. He wished to make it an affirmative proposition; **"the equal rights of conscience,** the freedom of speech or of the press, and the right of trial by jury in criminal cases, **shall not be infringed by any State."**

This transposition being agreed to, and Mr. Tucker's motion being rejected, the clause was adopted.[25]

The House majority clearly thought they had the votes to pass an amendment restraining states from infringing the rights of conscience, but members knew it was foolhardy to attempt to get past representatives from New England a restraint on state establishments. That means the Federalists in the House regarded liberty of conscience and disestablishment as two different matters, and they did not regard a state establishment as a violation of conscience. This is hardly surprising. Madison and others were aware that in Virginia liberty of conscience was achieved in 1776, but it was not until 1786 that the Anglican Church was disestablished.

At the end of the day the proposed Fifth Article read: "Article I, Section 10, between paragraphs 1 and 2 insert **'Fifthly. The equal rights of conscience,** the freedom of speech or of the press, and the right of trial by jury in criminal cases, **shall not be infringed by any State."** Madison had achieved a material advance. That the amendment passed the House of Representatives was an act of high solicitude for religious conscience in those days. More telling, Madison did not even try for a no-establishment amendment binding on the states. The latter would have created a firestorm in New England where mandatory religious assessments at the parish level were still popular and worked strongly in favor of the Congregational Church.

AUGUST 18, 1789

The House sitting as a Committee of the Whole passed the amendments pro-posed by the Select Committee of eleven, as now amended, and reported them to the entire House.

AUGUST 19, 1789

The full House began consideration. The House decided to place the amend-ments in a "supplement" (or "Bill") at the end of the Constitution. From June 8 forward, Madison had proposed to interlineate the amendments into the existing text of the 1787 Constitution. Those who opposed him sought to keep the 1787 Constitution intact because they were High Federalists who revered the Constitution as a monument to republican government. These Federalists, led by Roger Sherman of Connecticut, sought to deemphasize the amend-ments' importance by placing them at the end. History has shown that the separate listing has had just the opposite effect by giving the Bill of Rights its own revered place as a stand-alone founding document.

AUGUST 20, 1789

Debate continued on other proposed amendments, along with the phrases on religious freedom again being amended. The House also debated the conscien-tious objector language of the Sixth Article on bearing arms. The debate with respect to the no-establishment provision follows:

> The House resumed the consideration of the report of the Committee of the whole on the subject of amendment to the constitution.
>
> Mr. Ames' proposition was taken up. Five or six other members in-troduced propositions on the same point, and the whole were, by mutual consent, laid on the table. After which, the House proceeded to the third amendment,[26] and agreed to the same.
>
> On motion of Mr. Ames, the fourth amendment[27] was altered so as to read **"Congress shall make no law establishing religion, or to prevent the free exercise thereof, or to infringe the rights of conscience."** This being adopted,
>
> The first proposition was agreed to.[28]

Madison, working behind the scenes, is thought by some to have enlisted Fisher Ames of Massachusetts to put forth this version on church–government relations and conscience. The first thing to note is that the text restored the scope of the disempowerment of Congress's authority to "make . . . law establishing religion" and thereby abandoned Livermore's impossibly broad "laws touching" religion. No one can say for certain, but this is likely because during the last five days the House had come to realize that the scope of the amendment's disempowerment needed to be narrowed. Without such narrowing, countless and unavoidable incidental effects of legislation on religion would be swept within the negation of congressional power.

The second matter to note is that the term "free exercise" of religion is introduced for the first time, and it is stated separately from "rights of conscience." The relationship between "free exercise" and "rights of conscience" is not explained. Five days earlier Madison had lost the adjective "equal" modifying "conscience," which diminished the likelihood that the phrase would be interpreted as protecting the nonreligious. The addition of the free exercise text reopened the possibility that "rights of conscience" was broader in meaning and thus protected the nonreligious.[29] This subtlety would typically be how Madison worked, but we cannot know if he was behind it.

AUGUST 21, 1789

The free exercise language appearing in the *House Journal* was slightly altered in style from that of the prior day. No mention is made in the *Annals* of any additional debate over religious freedom. The *House Journal* reads:

> The House proceeded to consider the original report of the [Select] committee of eleven, consisting of seventeen articles, as now amended; whereupon the first, second, third, fourth, fifth, sixth, seventh, eighth, ninth, tenth, eleventh, twelfth, thirteenth, fourteenth, fifteenth, and sixteenth articles being again read and debated, were, upon the question severally put thereupon, agreed to by the House, as follows, two-thirds of the members present concurring, to wit:
>
> . . .
>
> **3. Congress shall make no law establishing religion, or prohibiting the free exercise thereof, nor shall the rights of conscience be infringed.**
>
> . . .
>
> **5.** A well regulated militia, composed of the body of the People, being the best security of a free State, the right of the People to keep and bear arms shall not be infringed; **but no one religiously scrupulous of bearing arms, shall be compelled to render military service in person.**
>
> . . .
>
> **11. No State shall infringe** the right of trial by jury in criminal cases; nor **the rights of conscience;** nor the freedom of speech or of the press.[30]

AUGUST 22, 1789

The House concluded its deliberations on the other amendments and referred arranging the amendments to a Style Committee for presentation to the Senate.

AUGUST 24, 1789

The Style Committee issued its report. The amendment barring states from infringing the rights of conscience was moved from the eleventh to the fourteenth position. Accordingly, religious freedom was addressed in House-proposed amendments Three, Five, and Fourteen. The House ordered the Clerk to deliver an engrossed copy of the Resolve to the Senate. There were a total of seventeen Articles of Amendment proposed by the House.

Before we turn to the record in the Senate, an interim summary is useful about what was debated in the House. Because of their overwhelming numbers the real give-and-take was controlled by the Federalists. There was no discussion reflecting the representatives struggling over a choice between nonpreferential support for religion, on the one hand, and prohibiting the establishment of religion, whether single or multiple, on the other. Only the Federalist Huntington expressed any concern that state establishments might need protection. Huntington did not articulate a concern that the states needed protection from congressional legislation, but that the no-establishment text of its own operation might be used to the detriment of state establishments by the federal courts. However, at the end of the debate of August 15, Huntington was satisfied that the altered text ("Congress shall make no laws") could not be interpreted as binding on the states. At least with respect to the House, that undermines the theory of specific federalism, which claims that additional federalist wording was thought needed.

By way of contrast, the *scope* of the restraint of Congress's disempowerment with respect to "establishment" did receive considerable attention. Most important was on August 20 when the House trimmed back Samuel Livermore's version of "laws touching religion" to the one Fisher Ames introduced, namely "no law establishing religion." A second occasion was on August 15 when the Federalists ignored the Anti-Federalist Elbridge Gerry's attempt to sharply narrow the scope of the restraint on congressional power to "no religious doctrine."

The pattern of two religion phrases—one addressing no-establishment and the other conscience—during the House debate was to be replicated in the Senate.

Before the United States Senate.

AUGUST 24, 1789

The engrossed Resolve of the House was read into the *Senate Journal*.[31] The Senate rejected a motion to put off the subject of amendments to the next congressional session.

SEPTEMBER 3, 1789

The Senate extensively debated the provisions on religious freedom in the Third Article as adopted by the House. The record follows:

> The Senate resumed the consideration of the Resolve of the House of Representatives on the Amendments to the Constitution of the United States.
>
> . . .
>
> On motion, To amend the Article third, and to strike out these words, **"Religion or prohibiting the free Exercise thereof,"** and insert, **"One Religious Sect or Society in preference to others,"** It passed in the Negative.
>
> On motion, For reconsideration, it passed in the Affirmative.[32]

The Third Article now read: **"Congress shall make no law establishing One Religious Sect or Society in preference to others, nor shall the rights of conscience be infringed."** Clearly this version adopted the no-preference position. The nonpreferential terminology likely came from the amendments proposed by Virginia, North Carolina, and New York. Assuming that this text also implied that Congress had among its enumerated powers in the 1787 Constitution the power to legislate about religious establishments,[33] then the only power denied by the scope of this version is when Congress prefers one religion over others. Proceedings continued:

> On motion, That Article the third be stricken out, it passed in the Negative.
>
> On motion, To adopt the following, in lieu of the third Article. **"Congress shall not make any law, infringing the rights of conscience, or establishing any Religious Sect or Society,"** it passed in the Negative.[34]

This rejected version would have dropped explicit use of the no-preference language. Had this version passed it still could be said to align with nonpreferentialism because Congress would have been denied only the power to establish a religion, leaving the no-preference option with respect to lesser support that stops short of a full establishment. Once again, however, there is the problem that this rejected version could also be read to mean that Congress had the power to grant lesser support to just two or three sects—countermanding a no-preference reading. Of course, the nonpreferentialist retort would be that the proposal was voted down for just that reason. Proceedings continued:

> On motion, To amend the third Article, to read thus—**"Congress shall make no law establishing any particular denomination of religion in preference to another, or prohibiting the free exercise thereof, nor shall the rights of conscience be infringed"**—it passed in the Negative.[35]

This rejected version again rejects an explicit no-preference text. Proceedings continued:

On the question upon the third Article as it came from the House of Representatives—it passed in the Negative.

On motion, to adopt the third Article proposed in the Resolve of the House of Representatives, amended by striking out these words—**"Nor shall the rights of conscience be infringed"**—it passed in the Affirmative.[36]

Passage of the latter motion was a major turnabout, and in two respects. First, a no-preference version was rejected in favor of the House's no-establishment language. The Third Article now read: "**Congress shall make no law establishing religion, or prohibiting the free exercise thereof.**" This formulation would not change, thus making for an uphill battle for the proponents of non-preferentialism. Second, the new text dropped "rights of conscience." This narrowed the protection of individual religious liberty. No doubt conscience can be violated by a law whether an individual is religious or nonreligious. But the "free exercise" of religion can only be violated if one first has a religion to exercise. Accordingly, Madison's desire to extend protection from compelled religious observance to the nonreligious continued to slip away just as Silvester and Huntington had advocated during the House debate on August 15.

SEPTEMBER 4, 1789

The Senate adopted an amended version of the Fifth Article on bearing arms that eliminated its religious scruples clause.[37] Although unexplained, the change likely reflected a compromise whereby it was agreed that the matter of a military draft and religious pacifism are best handled by Congress utilizing the greater flexibility of legislation.

SEPTEMBER 7, 1789

The Senate refused to adopt the proposed Fourteenth Article which would bind the states with respect to the rights of conscience (as well as trial by jury, free speech, and free press). The sparse entry appears below:

> The Senate resumed the consideration of the Resolve of the House of Representatives of the 24th of August, on "Articles to be proposed to the Legislatures of the several States as Amendments to the Constitution of the United States."
>
> . . .
>
> On motion, To adopt the fourteenth Article of the Amendments proposed by the House of Representatives—it passed in the Negative.[38]

A possible rationale is that the Senate did not want the Fourteenth Article to disturb the varied state arrangements with respect to even liberty of conscience, a matter on which there was some agreement throughout the states. In a larger sense, however, the First Congress envisioned the Bill of Rights as restraining only the national government. The national government alone presented a new threat and thus the national government alone was in need of restraining by a new Bill of Rights. This thinking underlay what I earlier called general federalism.

SEPTEMBER 9, 1789

The Senate reconsidered its work of September 3 and passed yet another version of the Third Article. For reasons of style, it also combined the Third with the Fourth Article (addressing speech, press, assembly, and petition). The record follows:

> Proceeded in the consideration of the Resolve of the House of Representatives of the 24th of August, "On Articles to be proposed to the Legislatures of the several States as Amendments to the Constitution of the United States"—And,
>
> On motion, To amend Article the third, to read as follows:
>
> **Congress shall make no law establishing articles of faith or a mode of worship, or prohibiting the free exercise of religion,** or abridging the freedom of speech, or the press, or the right of the people peaceably to assemble, and petition the Government for the redress of grievances—it passed in the Affirmative.[39]

This change greatly narrowed the scope of the congressional disempowerment with respect to establishment. Two familiar elements of the Church of England establishment were that the government controlled the church's creed and its liturgy. The scope of the foregoing amendment denying congressional power only with respect to "articles of faith" and "mode of worship" focuses on creeds and liturgy, leaving the implication that Congress arguably retained power over the many other aspects of a full establishment. This was the narrowest scope of congressional disempowerment considered in the Senate. The Senate then passed all of its amendments to the Resolve of the House, which the Senate had reduced from seventeen to twelve in number.

Back to the House of Representatives.

SEPTEMBER 19, 1789

The House considered the Senate's amendments to the Resolve of the House. The House debate at this stage is not recorded.

SEPTEMBER 21, 1789

The House resumed consideration of the amendments proposed by the Senate and requested a Committee of Conference concerning points of disagreement, including those to the Third Article.[40] The House appointed Madison, Sherman, and Vining to serve on the Conference, all Federalists.

Back to the United States Senate.

SEPTEMBER 21, 1789

The message from the House informing the Senate of disagreements and requesting a conference was received. The Senate did "recede" on a minor alteration to the House Resolve, but insisted on all others. It then agreed to the House-Senate Conference. Ellsworth, Carroll, and Paterson were appointed to the Conference, two Federalists and one Anti-Federalist.

The Committee of Conference.

SEPTEMBER 22–24, 1789

Going into the Conference the Senate's version read: "**Congress shall make no law establishing articles of faith or a mode of worship, or prohibiting the free exercise of religion,** or abridging the freedom of speech, or the press, or the right of the people peaceably to assemble, and petition the Government for the redress of grievances." The House version read: "**Congress shall make no law establishing religion, or prohibiting the free exercise thereof, nor shall the rights of conscience be infringed.**"

The Conference was comprised of five Federalists and one Anti-Federalist, so the Federalists were firmly in control. The Conference did not face a choice between a nonpreferentialist Senate version and a no-establishment House version. Nonpreferentialism was not in play. Nor was specific federalism a feature of either of the two choices. Rather, the difference in the no-establishment formulations of the Senate and House was over the *scope* of the disempowerment of Congress. Specifically, the Conference Committee faced a choice between a limited Senate disempowerment ("no law establishing articles of faith or a mode of worship") and a broader House disempowerment ("no law establishing religion").

There is no record of the negotiations by the Committee of Conference. The absence of Madison, Sherman, and Vining from the House roll suggests that the Conference met September 22 and 23. The House members agreed to all of the Senate's amendments to the Resolve of the House, except for the Third and Eighth Articles. These two articles were altered by the Conference, and then the agreement was reported back to the House and Senate. The Third Article now read: "**Congress shall make no law respecting an establishment of Religion, or prohibiting the free exercise thereof;** or abridging the freedom of Speech, or of the Press; or the right of the people peaceably to assemble and petition the Government for a redress of grievances."

With respect to the no-establishment principle, the Conference's text ("no law respecting an establishment of religion") favored the House version more than that of the Senate. So something close to the broader-in-scope House version of Congress's disempowerment prevailed. There also may have been a trade-off. The Conference's text favored the Senate version when it came to adopting the stand-alone "free exercise" text rather than the broader House protection for both "free exercise" and "rights of conscience." That alteration cannot convincingly be dismissed as one of mere style, as if "conscience" was redundant and could be subsumed into "free exercise." So perhaps the broader no-establishment restraint on Congress was secured in return for a free exercise text that does not protect the nonreligious. We know the result but cannot know if it was a conscious trade-off.

What at first seems strangely new to the text is the introduction of the participle "respecting." Then, as now, respecting means "about" or "with regard to." A first reading of the phrase "respecting an establishment of religion" is that in comparison to even the House version, "respecting" broadens the disempowerment of Congress from "establishing religion" to "respecting an establishment of religion." The Conference version seemingly is broader because now Congress cannot establish *or disestablish* religion in the states. Hinging as it does on the first appearance of the word *respecting* and its last-minute introduction said to prevent interference with state establishments, such a reading is the theory of specific federalism.

To one focused only on the text as it emerged from the Conference, the introduction of "respecting" appears to fit with specific federalism. However, recall that a premise underlying the entire debate in both the House and Senate was that all of the Articles of Amendment vested no new power in the national government. This aligns with the Wilsonian argument, made again during the House debate by Roger Sherman on August 15, and the attitude of Federalists generally, that the 1787 Constitution delegated no national power over the matter of religion, including religious establishments in the states. And the Huntington confusion during the House debate of August 15 led to a rewriting of the text so that he was satisfied a federal court could not enforce the Establishment Clause against state religious assessment laws. Finally, whatever the suspicions and objectives of the Anti-Federalists, the Federalists were in firm control of the Conference Committee. These combined factors strongly indicate that in the Conference the manner by which the states (in New England or elsewhere) dealt with their religious establishments was simply not in play. By way of contrast, specific federalism requires there to have been an active concern in the First Congress that the no-establishment text could be construed to imply substantive power in the national government to interfere with state establishments—power that was squelched by the introduction into the text of the participle "respecting." As matters went to Conference, there was no record of any such concern.

Before jumping to the conclusion that a last-minute alteration in the no-establishment text by the Conference Committee was federalist-motivated, there is a simpler grammatical explanation for the textual modification. A straightforward explanation is that the Conference made a stylistic improvement to sharpen the focus of the no-establishment text that started with the House version. Going into conference the House version read: "Congress shall make no law establishing religion, or prohibiting the free exercise thereof, nor shall the rights of conscience be infringed." If first we make the Conference's textual modification dropping "rights of conscience," the House version would read: "*Congress shall make no law establishing religion, or prohibiting the free exercise thereof.*" The desired focus of the Third Article is to emphasize both aspects of religious freedom: no-establishment and free exercise. However, there are two participles ("establishing" and "prohibiting") that bring the focus down on the objects of the participial phrases, namely "religion" and "free exercise." The drafters did not want the focus on "religion" but on "establishment." That meant taking the participle "establishing" and changing it to "establishment," thereby making it the object in a participial phrase. The Conference would need a new participle ("respecting" was selected), leading to a new participial phrase ("respecting an establishment") that brings about the desired focus on the new object ("establishment"). Stylistically this is desirable because the Third Article now begins with two parallel participial phrases ("respecting an establishment" and "prohibiting the free exercise") that bring down the focus on "establishment" and "free exercise," respectively. The focus of the no-establishment text before and after the Conference was the same: assuring Americans that Congress had no power to establish religion. On this reading, the grammatical change improved style but had no substantive impact.

The foregoing explanation is also in line with how committees work when tasked with reconciling competing drafts while being faithful to the duty of making as little change in meaning as possible. Although we cannot know if this is why the Conference introduced "respecting" into the text, the more simple explanation is also the more likely one.

Final Action in the House of Representatives.

SEPTEMBER 24, 1789

The House agreed to the report of the Committee of Conference as follows:

> The House proceeded to consider the report of a Committee of Conference, on the subject matter of the amendments depending between the two Houses to the several articles of amendment to the Constitution of the United States, as proposed by this House: whereupon, it was resolved, that they recede from their disagreement to all the amendments; provided that the two articles, which, by the amendments of the Senate, are now proposed to be inserted as the third and eighth articles, shall be amended to read as follows:

Art. 3. **Congress shall make no law respecting an establishment of religion, or prohibiting** [a or the][41] **free exercise thereof** [, or;][42] or abridging the freedom of speech, or of the press, or the right of the people peaceably to assemble, and to petition the Government for a redress of grievances.

Final Action in the United States Senate.

SEPTEMBER 25, 1789

The Senate concurred in the report of the Conference Committee.[43]

SEPTEMBER 29, 1789

A Preamble explaining the impetus behind their passage, followed by a "Bill" of twelve proposed Articles of Amendment, was inserted in the record of the *Senate Journal*:

> The Conventions of a Number of States having, at the Time of their adopting the Constitution, expressed a Desire, in order to prevent misconstruction or abuse of its Powers, that further declaratory and restrictive Clauses should be added: And as extending the Ground of public Confidence in the Government, will best insure the beneficent Ends of its Institution. . . .[44]

The Preamble makes it clear that the amendments are "restrictive"; thus they do not vest any new powers in the national government. On the contrary, the amendments were to reassure Americans that the national powers delegated in the 1787 Constitution are not misconstrued or abused so as to impute new powers to the national government that it did not have. This is important in rightly interpreting the relationship between the Establishment and Free Exercise Clauses so as not to put them in tension.

Ratification in the States, October 1789 to March 1792. After receiving the proposed amendments, on October 2, 1789, President Washington forwarded them to the states for consideration pursuant to U.S. Constitution Article V. The following table lists the states that ratified the proposed amendments by the date of each state's ratification.

Almost none of the state-by-state debate over the proposed amendments has survived, or indeed was ever recorded. Virginia is the only state where some official record exists of the debate concerning the religion clauses. However, the record is complex and must be situated in its larger context of the Anti-Federalists' struggle to call a second constitutional convention or to secure amendments to the 1787 Constitution that would trim back the powers of the national government with respect to direct taxation and the

TABLE 8.1 Ratification of the Amendments by the States November 20, 1789–March 1, 1792

	Date of Ratification by State	Date Ratification Reported to the Federal Congress	State	Amendments Ratified	Record of Debate?
1	November 20, 1789	August 6, 1790	New Jersey	1, 3–12	No
2	December 19, 1789	January 25, 1790	Maryland	1–12	No
3	December 22, 1789	June 11, 1790	North Carolina	1–12	No
4	January 18, 1790	April 1, 1790	South Carolina	1–12	No
5	January 25, 1790	February 15, 1790	New Hampshire	1, 3–12	No
6	January 28, 1790	March 8, 1790	Delaware	2–12	No
—	February 2, 1790	—	Massachusetts	3–11	Minimal
7	February 27, 1790	April 5, 1790	New York	1, 3–12	No
8	March 10, 1790	March 16, 1790	Pennsylvania	3–12	No
9	June 7, 1790	June 30, 1790	Rhode Island	1, 3–12	No
10	November 3, 1791	January 18, 1792	Vermont	1–12	No
11	December 15, 1791	December 30, 1791	Virginia	1–12	Yes

regulation of commerce. In late September 1789, Virginia's two U.S. Senators, Richard Henry Lee and William Grayson, wrote the Virginia governor and legislature declaring their disappointment with the twelve Articles of Amendment. The letters complained that Virginia's proposed amendments had not been adopted, that the power of the national government remained unchecked, and that civil liberties were endangered. However, neither the Third Article nor religious freedom was explicitly mentioned. The Virginia House, a majority of which were Federalists, approved all the amendments on December 24, 1789.

Dividing by a vote of eight to seven, the Virginia Senate delayed ratification for almost two years, ostensibly because of objections to the Third, Eighth, Eleventh, and Twelfth Articles. One of the claims by the eight Anti-Federalist senators was that the proposed Third Article did not protect the rights of conscience or prohibit certain laws associated with an established church. The eight senators explained their opposition as follows:

> The 3d amendment, recommended by Congress, does not prohibit the rights of conscience from being violated or infringed: and although it goes to restrain Congress from passing laws establishing any national religion, they might, notwithstanding, levy taxes to any amount, for the support of religion or its preachers; and any particular denomination of christians might be so favored and supported by the General Government, as to give it a decided advantage over others, and in process of time render it as powerful and dangerous as if it was established as the national religion of the country.
>
> . . .

This amendment then, when considered as it relates to any of the rights it is pretended to secure, will be found totally inadequate, and betrays an unreasonable, unjustifiable, but a studied departure from the amendment proposed by Virginia and other States, for the protection of these rights. We conceive that this amendment is dangerous and fallacious, as it tends to lull the apprehensions of the people on these important points, without affording them security; and mischievous, because by setting bounds to Congress, it will be considered as the only restriction on their power over these rights; and thus certain powers in the government, which it has been denied to possess, will be recognized without being properly guarded against abuse.[45]

The Establishment Clause could be said to prohibit only the full establishment of a national religion—albeit one familiar with the drafting history would not do so. So construed, however, these eight senators went on to suppose the Third Article thereby left Congress free to impose some practices ("levy taxes") commonly associated with an establishment, while stopping short of creating a national religion. Indeed, the examples given by the senators as consequences to be avoided track those made by James Madison, as well as Presbyterian and Baptist dissenters, when successfully opposing Patrick Henry's General Assessment Bill back in 1784–1785.

What casts suspicion on the eight senators is not just that they were known to be Anti-Federalists, but that they had supported the earlier-established Anglican Church in Virginia and had argued in favor of the General Assessment Bill when it was debated in 1784–1785. Likewise, U.S. Senators Richard Henry Lee and William Grayson had opposed Virginia's ratification of the 1787 Constitution and continued to seek additional amendments restoring power to the states. If the proposed amendments were not ratified, an opportunity would open for another round of amendments more to their liking, or even a second constitutional convention.

In a November 20, 1789, letter to President Washington on Virginia's ratification progress, James Madison questioned these state senators' sincerity and stated his belief that the Anti-Federalists would be unsuccessful in blocking the amendments:

If it be construed by the public into a latent hope of some contingent opportunity for prosecuting the war agst. the Genl. Government, I am of opinion the experiment will recoil on the authors of it. . . . One of the principal leaders of the Baptists lately sent me word that the amendments had entirely satisfied the disaffected of his Sect, and that it would appear in their subsequent conduct.[46]

The referenced letter from Virginia Baptists to Madison is important because it was the Baptists who had, along with the Presbyterians, allied with Madison in Virginia to defeat Henry's General Assessment Bill. And it was the Baptists who are believed to have thrown their votes behind Madison to elect him to the House of Representatives, said to have been in return for Madison's promise to deliver on protecting religious freedom in a national bill of rights.

On January 5, 1790, Madison wrote to President Washington to again express confidence that the tactics of the Anti-Federalists would ultimately backfire:

> You will probably have seen by the papers that the contest in the Assembly on the subject of the amendments ended in the loss of them. The House of Delegates got over the objections to the 11 & 12, but the Senate revived them with an addition of the 3 & 8 articles, and by a vote of adherence prevented a ratification. On some accounts this event is no doubt to be regretted. But it will do no injury to the Genl. Government. On the contrary it will have the effect with many of turning their distrust towards their own Legislature. The miscarriage of the 3d. art. particularly, will have this effect.[47]

The Virginia Senate finally ratified the Articles of Amendment on December 15, 1791. Considered in the context of the Anti-Federalist's goal to reduce the power of the new national government, the lapse of time between eventual ratification and the published interpretation of the religion clauses in the Third Article by the slim majority of Anti-Federalist senators, and these eight senators' earlier opposition to Virginia's disestablishment, there is every reason to fully discount the understanding of the religion clauses that was published back in October 1789 by the senators.

In summary, so far as indicated from the state records that were kept, ratification of the Third Article generated no opposition except in Virginia. Accordingly, it is best said that the official records of state ratifications yield little insight into the original meaning of the Establishment Clause. On March 1, 1792, Secretary of State Jefferson notified the several states that Articles of Amendment Third through Twelfth had been ratified, thus implying the First and Second Articles had so-far failed. A stylist renumbered the successful Articles First through Tenth, and in time they took on the popular appellation "Bill of Rights."

The Text of the Establishment Clause

We are now in a position to pursue more deeply some issues with respect to the plain meaning of the First Amendment that necessarily arose in the first part of this chapter. The text reads, "Congress shall make no law respecting an establishment of religion, or prohibiting the free exercise thereof." Although there is but one clause addressing religious freedom, there are two participial phrases ("respecting an establishment" and "prohibiting the free exercise") modifying the object ("no law") of the verb ("shall make"). Grammatically, each participial phrase is equal to and has a meaning independent of the other phrase. Finally, "of religion" is a prepositional phrase. "Religion" thus modifies "establishment," confirming that the key to the Establishment Clause is the original understanding of the word *establishment*.

The "Specific Federalist" Interpretation of the Establishment Clause. As noted previously, those holding to the theory of specific federalism seize on "respecting" as central to their argument that the Establishment Clause had embedded in it at the last moment by the Conference Committee a federalist principle specifically designed to preserve state sovereignty over how each state handles its church–state affairs.[48] Four observations about this theory need to be made, each of which undermines specific federalism.

First, it is unremarkable that the Conference text had some consequential federalist impact. The earlier House and Senate versions also had participles that worked to incidentally limit congressional power over how each state handled certain of its church–state affairs. For example, the final Senate version said that Congress lacked power to "make . . . law establishing articles of faith or a mode of worship." "Establishing" is a participle, and the participle limited national power over the described subject matter. Consider yourself in a state that had completed its disestablishment by 1789. As a result of this amendment the national government had no power over the subjects of creeds and liturgy in your particular state. It would follow that this Senate version would have had some federalist impact in preserving that state's disestablishment when it came to imposing a creed or particular liturgy. The Conference Committee's substitution of the participle "respecting" for the participle "establishing" did not make the Conference version uniquely federalist. Rather, all of the versions in play had the consequence of restraining some congressional power concerning how states handled their church–state arrangements. What evolved over the various House and Senate versions was not a first-time introduction in Conference of a federalist text, but debate over the *scope* of the congressional disempowerment. In sum, nothing in the final text indicated that the Conference was suddenly seized by an irresistible "state's rights" urge and caused to insert "respecting" into the amendment with the aim to uniquely preserve church–state arrangements.

Second, the Establishment Clause restraint on congressional power works to limit the national government with respect to a given subject matter, namely, the pros and cons of establishmentarianism. This is a jurisdictional restraint: The Establishment Clause limits Congress with respect to *both* the national and state governments. True, the participle "respecting" means that Congress is prohibited from interfering with laws about "an establishment" of religion at the state level. However, the participle "respecting" also means that Congress is prohibited from making laws at the national level about "an establishment" of religion.[49] So the restraint is not just federalist (restraining Congress vis-à-vis the sovereignty of the states) but rather jurisdictional (restraining Congress vis-à-vis church–government relations, be the government national or state). Moreover, the scope of this disempowerment is the *same* with respect to both levels of government, national and state. Accordingly, overblown claims that "respecting" means that the national government can have nothing to do with church–state relations at the state level but that Congress is limited only to establishing a full-blown church at the national level rely on an asymmetry that defies the plain text. The same words ("no law respecting an establishment of religion") grammatically define the same *scope* of congressional disempowerment, whether that disempowerment has the consequence of protecting residual state sovereignty or limiting the national government when acting within its powers such as governing the territories or regulating the armed forces. Specific federalism is not just wrong: it diverts attention narrowly to federalism when the focus should be on the full scope of the congressional disempowerment. I return below to this mischief of confusing state/national federalism with church/government jurisdiction.

Third, the rights with respect to free speech and free press in the First Amendment also have a participle, that is, "abridging." As with the participle "respecting," it can equally be said that the participle "abridging" disempowered Congress with respect to certain subjects within the scope of a participial phrase (that is, "abridging the freedom of speech, or . . . press; or the right . . . to assemble, and to petition"). The Conference's substitution of the participle "respecting" for the participle "establishing" appears unremarkable with respect to federalist restraints on Congress—in contrast to an exotic claim that the Conference reached out and embedded a specific federalist provision uniquely in the Establishment Clause.

Fourth, as the matter went to Conference the record in the House and journal in the Senate are without complaint that states believed their sovereignty over church–state arrangements were in need of additional protection from Congress. The concern voiced earlier by Huntington during the House debate of August 15 was resolved to his satisfaction by Livermore's phrase ("Congress shall make no laws. . . .") that pointed the object of the disempowerment solely at Congress. Neither Connecticut nor Massachusetts asked for an amendment to protect their Congregational Church establishments when they ratified the 1787 Constitution. Additionally, as the foregoing table shows, neither state ratified what became the First Amendment. If citizens in these two states had truly feared for their establishments as claimed by specific federalism, it makes no sense that these states would not have even bothered to ratify a supposed federalist provision meant to protect their Congregational establishments.

The better reading is that the no-establishment text as it emerged from Conference was jurisdictional, not merely federalist. As already indicated, a rejection of the theory of specific federalism is *not* a rejection of the idea that the text of the Establishment Clause had some consequential federalist effect by limiting congressional power to interfere in a state's church–state affairs. That said, the primary focus of the Establishment Clause was to limit the power of Congress, *not* to uniquely protect the states.

The Establishment Clause Does Not Codify a Preexisting Right. The phrasing of many of the first eight amendments in the Bill of Rights is *not* that these rights were being newly created. Rather, the text reads as if many of these rights were already held by Americans. Thus, the rights are merely being made explicit, as a matter of reassurance, and accordingly the preexisting rights were not superseded by the powers delegated to the new national government.

This understanding is suggested by the various participles and verbs chosen by the members of the First Congress. It is most obvious when one reads the phrasing of the Fourth Amendment, which begins by stating an existing right and then negating Congress's power to "violate[]" that right. If one first reads the Fourth and then the First Amendment, that pattern is evident in most of the First Amendment as well. Participles such as "prohibiting" and "abridging" in the First Amendment, the noun "right" characterizing both "assemble" and "petition," as well as the verb "infringed" in the Second Amendment, are all indicative of preexisting rights that the new central government is acknowledging as opposed to creating. The Ninth Amendment even speaks of other rights "retained by the people," further suggesting that many of the rights made explicit in the first eight amendments were already possessed by Americans.

In contrast, the participle "respecting" in the phrase "shall make no law respecting an establishment of religion" stands out as quite different. The difference is that the participial phrase "respecting an establishment" is not describing a right (preexisting or otherwise) but is describing a discrete subject or topic ("an establishment") over which Congress has no power to "make . . . law." In that sense, the Establishment Clause does not read as if it is describing a right (for example, free exercise, free speech, or free press) already held by the people. Rather, it is as if the Establishment Clause is describing a limit on Congress's jurisdiction to legislate on a discrete subject matter. The denied power is that there may be "no . . . law" on the subject described as "an establishment."

The congressional drafters, of course, did not mean to be understood as claiming Congress, in the absence of the Establishment Clause, had the implied power to "establish . . . [a] religion" under the 1787 Constitution. Federalists were in control of the drafting process. And, as we have seen, from James Wilson's speech forward, the Federalists, including Madison, repeatedly denied that the 1787 Constitution vested such power in Congress. Rather, the Establishment Clause meant only that those reading the 1787 Constitution should be reassured that Congress had no implied power concerning the matter of "an establishment." In short, the plain text of the first participial phrase in the First Amendment is different from the balance of the rights-based clauses.

The Establishment Clause reads like part of the structural frame of the national government. Structure concerns delegations and denials of power. As such, the Establishment Clause is a negation of national jurisdiction over a narrow, but nonetheless highly important, subject described as "an establishment," thereby leaving power over that subject to the states or to the people and their houses of worship. This structure limits the national government for in certain respects it may not control the church, and implicitly the text limits the church for in certain respects it may not control the government.

Even beyond the text, it is common sense that free exercise, free speech, free press, freedom to assemble, and freedom to petition were regarded by Americans as preexisting rights. However, in the period 1789–1791 the question of establishment or disestablishment was not everywhere settled. Indeed, in the New England states it was highly disputed terrain with the establishmentarians still in the dominant position. On September 29, 1789, as Congress reported out the amendments for ratification, several states still had tax-supported clergy, whereas other states had recently gone through a disestablishment struggle and placed authority with respect to religion in voluntarily supported societies. That was the situation in the states.

At the national level, the new government never had to choose between keeping an existing establishment or to disestablish, as there had never been a national church. Rather, as a hedge against future abuse, the Establishment Clause denied national power to establish a national church and likely more. Such a limitation on the power of the national government left a jurisdictional restraint on its power with respect to all matters concerning "an establishment."

The Religion Clauses Reduced to Protecting Only Conscience. Another innovation has surfaced that would severely narrow the scope of religious freedom, and this reading too cannot be squared with the historical record. Professor Noah Feldman argues that the Establishment Clause protects only liberty of conscience.[50] His idea is based on the historical claim that in 1789 the only American consensus on religious freedom was that conscience ought to be protected. Feldman thus believes that the protection of conscience is all that could have been agreed to by the First Congress. It follows, Feldman postulates, that protection of conscience in religious matters is the full scope of the Establishment Clause.

Feldman's innovation is problematic at multiple levels. First, we examined earlier the amendments proposed by New Hampshire, Virginia, and New York during their ratification of the Constitution, and North Carolina later copied Virginia's proposal. We also saw a constitutional amendment debated in Maryland, although it did not pass. Each of these amendments addressed conscience and no-establishment separately. Accordingly, these amendments assumed an understanding of religious freedom that entailed more than liberty of conscience. Indeed, one could begin a few years earlier in time by taking note of how Virginia had worked through its struggle for religious freedom. In

Virginia, conscience was protected in the new state constitution of 1776 but disestablishment of the Anglican Church was not achieved until 1786.

Second, the adoption of a Bill of Rights (including the First Amendment) was possible because the focus of the amendments was confined to agreeing on those powers that were *not* delegated to the national government. Historian Thomas Curry has explained that although Americans did disagree over the use of governmental power with respect to the establishment of religion, they could agree on Congress not being vested with any power over the subject.[51] Feldman is thus asking the wrong question, which is not what substantive rule could the Congress of 1789 have agreed to with respect to religious freedom, but what could the Congress have agreed were the powers *not* held by the new national government.

Third, Feldman's argument is at odds with the separate treatment of the Free Exercise and Establishment Clauses as they independently evolved during the 1789 drafting process beginning in the House, then in the Senate, and finally in the Conference Committee. For example, Feldman's claim is contrary to the amendments initially proposed by James Madison. On June 8, 1779, Madison introduced a separate amendment binding on states, which involved only the protection of conscience. That amendment was unlike Madison's amendment binding on the national government, which involved both the concepts of conscience and no-establishment. This not only shows a clear distinction intended by Congress between conscience and no-establishment, but that Madison intended from the very start a no-establishment principle binding on the national government but not the states. The distinction was maintained a week later in the report to the House by the Select Committee, and it remained through the several August drafts in the House. The distinction also continued through the several September drafts in the Senate, albeit conscience was reduced along the way to the more narrow "free exercise of religion." Finally, the distinction was maintained by the Conference Committee, which reported out two independent participial phrases ("respecting an establishment" and "prohibiting the free exercise") clearly bearing two independent legal principles. Thus, the distinction between conscience and no-establishment is not just that of Madison, but it was faithfully maintained by the House and Senate members active in the debate over what came to be the Free Exercise and Establishment Clauses.

Fourth, Feldman's thesis causes him to distort the normative meaning of coercion, for an individual's conscience is violated only when coerced. For example, quite understandably he wants the Establishment Clause to prevent many types of government programs where funding from tax monies is going to religious organizations. Because he limits the Establishment Clause to matters of conscience, he has to claim that such funding constitutes coercion of conscience. But this is rather fanciful when the source of the funding is from general taxes paid into the general treasury, which would mean every taxpayer suffers coercion even when many of those taxpayers are strong supporters of government programs that do not exclude aid recipients on account of religion.

Fifth, as noted in the prior paragraph, for Feldman it is coercive of conscience for a taxpayer to pay taxes into the general treasury from which some money is later appropriated to religious organizations. To Feldman it becomes coercive not when the taxes are initially extracted, but when (and if) the money is later appropriated to organizations some of whom are religious. If that is not illogical enough, one can go on and ask why then is it not coercion of conscience when a taxpayer is forced to pay taxes into the treasury from which some money will certainly be appropriated for causes that directly contradict the taxpayer's sincere religious beliefs? For example, given Feldman's analysis, why is it not actionable coercion to force a religious pacifist to pay federal income taxes when a significant percent will go to military weaponry and fighting wars? If the abstraction of tax-derived money going, inter alia, to pay for education in science and mathematics at a religious school is actionable coercion (and Feldman claims it is), then why is the pacifist's more palpable coercion of conscience not recognized as actionable under the First Amendment? Feldman's privileging of a taxpayer's claim only when the challenge is to a government appropriation where some monies later make their way to a religious organization makes no sense. What does make sense is to say, as the modern Supreme Court has repeatedly said, that an Establishment Clause claim does not require a showing of coercion. And, accordingly, the Supreme Court has protected interests other than liberty of conscience under the Establishment Clause. For example, the Court has found that the government has exceeded its powers as limited by the Establishment Clause when composing voluntary prayers, conducting voluntary devotional Bible reading, resolving intra-church disputes, or involving the judiciary in the meaning of explicitly religious events, beliefs, and practices.

Sixth, if only coercion of conscience is prohibited by the First Amendment, as Feldman claims, then government may favor one or some religions over others. Indeed, as in England today, government may have a full-fledged church establishment while not coercing the faiths of others who choose not to be a member of the Church of England. In order to prevent this result, Feldman once again ends up distorting the meaning of coercion to discover violations of conscience where they do not presently appear, such as equating adolescent peer pressure over unwanted exposure to voluntary prayer as a crisis of conscience.

Finally, this shrinking of the First Amendment to the protection of individual conscience is objectionable because it is altogether inconsistent with the Western legal tradition. The two participial phrases up to the first semicolon of the First Amendment treat the matter of religious freedom as requiring attention to two distinct tasks. One task has to do with the relationship among government, religion, and the individual (free exercise). The second task has to do with the relationship between government and organized religion (no-establishment).

The latter task aligns with over a millennium of Western civilization that envisions the work of religious freedom to be about not merely personal autonomy but also institutional separation of government and church.

It is no happenstance that Feldman's intellectual history bends the historical record toward his preference for liberalism's claim that ultimately only the nation-state and individuals have ontological status, omitting any possibility for autonomy of religious bodies not reducible to the aggregate rights of the body's individual members. From the perspective of the West, however, that historical account is malformed. Feldman's preference fails to account for the dual-authority relationship of church and nation-state that has deeply marked civilization in the West and led to its highest form of religious freedom in the American republic that reject the power of government to instrumentally use organized religion to unify and stabilize the state. The latter step is the rightly celebrated American notion of full religious freedom—not just liberty of conscience—through, inter alia, the institutional separation of church and state.

Incorporating the Establishment Clause: Confusing a Federalist Clause with a Jurisdictional Clause. The incorporation of the Establishment Clause through the Due Process Clause of the Fourteenth Amendment presents an intriguing legal problem, but one that was of interest only to academics until Justice Clarence Thomas took note in 2002 in his concurring opinion in *Zelman v. Simmons-Harris*. The essence of the puzzle is that if the Establishment Clause is structural rather than rights-based, then it makes no sense conceptually to incorporate the clause as a Fourteenth Amendment "liberty" applicable to the states. Of course, there is no chance that *Everson*'s incorporation of the clause in 1947 will be reversed. Aware of that reality, Justice Thomas has taken the less ambitious tack that the Establishment Clause be applied to the states with reduced rigor. For example, one approach is that only when the clause protects conscience from religious coercion would the Establishment Clause bind state and local governments.

The first thing to be sorted when the topic of incorporation of the Establishment Clause arises is the confusion between two concepts. There is a sharp difference between a federalist Establishment Clause and an Establishment Clause that is jurisdictional. A federalist clause tied to the last-minute introduction of "respecting" into the text by the Conference Committee—what I have called "specific federalism"—is not supported by the record in the First Federal Congress. A jurisdictional clause—an Establishment Clause that in certain respects separates church and government, and thereby structures relations between these two centers of authority—is suggested by the text. A jurisdictional Establishment Clause has not only separated organized religion and the national government since 1789–1791, but beginning with *Everson* the clause has separated organized religion from all government (national, state, and local). In summary, a "specific federalist" Establishment Clause is about national/state structure whereas a jurisdictional Establishment Clause is about church/government structure. The former is not supported by the congressional record of 1789 whereas the latter is suggested by it.

Professor Kurt Lash subscribes to the theory of specific federalism.[52] He agrees that the original Establishment Clause was structural and thus could not be incorporated as a "liberty" through the Fourteenth Amendment. However, Lash maintains that between 1789–1791 and 1868 (the year the Fourteenth Amendment was ratified) both the states and Congress came to regard the clause not as federalist but as an individual right. He argues, therefore, that the later incorporation of the Establishment Clause makes sense.

Lash's claim that the Thirty-Ninth Congress had come to regard the Establishment Clause as rights-based has its detractors. Nonetheless, if one assumes, arguendo, that Lash is correct insofar as the Establishment Clause was federalist in 1789–1791 but had lost its federalist character by 1868, it does *not* follow that the Establishment Clause thereby took on the nature of an individual right. Rather, it is probable that the Establishment Clause retained its jurisdictional character as separating church and government. Indeed, many of the sources that Lash cites as evidence that the initial federalist character of the Establishment Clause was supposedly forgotten are more easily understood as evidence that the clause actually increased in the public's mind as guaranteeing the separation of church and government. In Lash's view the incorporation of the Establishment Clause is not a problem because the clause had evolved into a right, and rights (if fundamental) are properly incorporated as "liberty" interests secured by the Fourteenth Amendment. However, to the extent that the post-1868 Establishment Clause separates church and government—that is, it continues to set a jurisdictional limit on government involvement with organized religion—incorporation is still awkward because it is treating church/government structure as a "liberty" interest.

Lash is not the only one to fail to keep distinct the national/state divide (federalist) from the church/government divide (jurisdictional). In an article cataloging individual rights under state constitutions as of 1868, Professor Steven Calabresi and one of his students collected those state constitutions that had adopted a clause similar to the federal Establishment Clause.[53] Calabresi then reasons that if by 1868 a state had adopted such a clause in its own constitution, the state must not have perceived the Establishment Clause as federalist. I agree. Calabresi goes on to assume—as does Lash—that therefore the state must have perceived the Establishment Clause as an individual right. That does *not* follow. Rather, such a state likely presumed that the Establishment Clause separated church and state, the latter being not federalist but a jurisdictional limit separating these two centers of authority.

The question of whether the Establishment Clause—properly understood as jurisdictional—is capable of incorporation as a Fourteenth Amendment "liberty" is one this chapter leaves for the reader to resolve. That said, even if the Supreme Court had never incorporated the Establishment Clause in *Everson*, the clause would still separate organized religion and the national government. Failure to incorporate would mean only that the national government alone would be separated from organized religion. The clause's denial of national power with respect to "an establishment" would still have had substantive consequences in the nature of limiting the national government's jurisdiction. From 1789–1791 forward, this would mean that at the national level Congress alone had no power to "make . . . law respecting an establishment" of religion. However, Congress would remain free to draw on powers enumerated in the 1787 Constitution with respect to enacting laws that may touch on religion. For example, using its power to regulate the armed forces, Congress could provide for military conscription but then could also regulate (that is, touch on) religion by exempting religious pacifists from the draft. Such a statute is within Congress's original enumerated powers, whereas the pacifist exemption, albeit touching on religion, is not a statute about "an establishment" of religion. So the military conscription statute with its pacifist exemption does not run afoul of the limited denial of national power imposed by the Establishment Clause. The draft exemption advances religious freedom rather than advance religion. That was true in 1789–1791, and it is true today.

We thus see that the early Congresses, with an eye to the Establishment Clause, necessarily should have worked out a definable line between when the national government had "jurisdiction" to pass general legislation on a matter that may have incidentally touched on religion and those instances when the legislation was more narrowly about "an establishment" of religion. The former legislation is permitted but the latter is not because it violates the Establishment Clause. Call it jurisdictional, a substantive rule, or a structural restraint, this case-by-case line drawing would have required Congress over time to systematically work out relations between the national government and organized religion. This is another way of saying that the Establishment Clause was intended to police the boundary between organized religion and the national government.

It is certainly true that no fully developed rule of church–government relations was understood by the Federalists in control of Congress in 1789. To that limited extent I agree with Professor Steven Smith that a search for a substantive rule of church–government relations in the congressional debates of 1789 will fail.[54] But from the plain text it cannot be doubted that the amendment prohibited a national establishment. Federalists and Anti-Federalists agreed that Congress should have no power with respect to "an establishment" is a substantive rule—not merely in the sense of federalism, but in the more sweeping sense of limiting national jurisdiction. Moreover, such a substantive rule should have thereafter developed case by case as the three branches of the national government faithfully sought to make general laws that might touch on religion but did not, more narrowly, result in the sort of evils associated with "an establishment."

Because the national government was at first small and for the most part did not focus on day-to-day domestic matters, the occasion for national laws about religion were fewer. The pervasive Protestant ethic of the day reflected in such legislation was often mistaken for merely culture or morals as opposed to being particular to Protestant religion. Accordingly, it would not be until after the Civil War that the Establishment Clause would be called on to do actual work in the federal courts.

Conclusion

Careful attention to the text and original understanding cannot answer all contemporary questions with respect to the current application of the Establishment Clause, but the discipline does eliminate several false paths. The text and originalism do not reveal clearly the definition of *establishment*, but the text and congressional record say much about ersatz theories concerning what the Establishment Clause supposedly means. Nonpreferentialism and specific federalism are mistaken, as is the attempt to limit the religion clauses to liberty of conscience. Rejecting these theories will go far in addressing the uneven character of the much criticized jurisprudence in our federal courts.

From the record of the debate left by the First Federal Congress, we have seen that the overwhelming focus in both houses was on the scope of the limits on national power over religion. Further, because the Bill of Rights was drafted not to grant powers but to clarify what powers the national government was denied, the Free Exercise and Establishment Clauses are negatives. The clauses do have their differences, however, because it fully appears from the text that the Free Exercise Clause sought to acknowledge a preexisting right whereas the Establishment Clause is not rights-based but sets forth a structural limit on the national government's power. That not only harmonizes the clauses, but makes the Establishment Clause jurisdictional in nature. And in the main that is how it has been applied by the post-*Everson* Supreme Court. Some of the rhetoric in *Everson* is problematic, but not its result.

In the vernacular, the Establishment Clause is about church–state separation to the purpose of religious freedom for all. This principle has its roots in the Western legal tradition dating back to the fourth century. There evolved a dual-authority pattern where both church and nation-state had their own center of power. Although the line-dividing authority between them shifted down through the centuries, that there was a line separating these two powers did not change. When both church and government are limited because each has authority only as to the matters within its purview, then separation proved to be good for the body politic and good for organized religion. By good, I mean that the nation-state is not omnicompetent but limited. Such limits liberate the polis to practice religion (or not) as each is led. And, by good, I mean that the institutional integrity of religious organizations is secure, and that the decision to uniquely aid or to interfere in the matters of organized religion is no longer in the jurisdiction of the government. Accordingly, affirmative support for the explicitly religious occurs (if at all) as a voluntary act. In America, however, the dual-pattern relationship developed at the level of the states, where disestablishment took place from 1776 to 1833, not at the national level where the legislative and executive branches of the national government were operating. So it transpired that the modern Supreme Court in *Everson* looked to the dual pattern as it developed in Virginia and other states to give substantive meaning to the text concerning the definition of *establishment*. *Everson*, of course, also extended the Establishment Clause to apply to and bind the states. Whether that discrete act of "incorporation" was within the authority of the Supreme Court, I leave for the reader to decide. But there can be no doubt that a reliance on the disestablishment experience in Virginia and other states is an accurate description of what the Court actually did in *Everson* and in its post-*Everson* cases. Given that there never was a national disestablishment experience, the Court acted properly when it looked to the states to be tutored in the sorts of evils that the struggle to disestablish were meant to remedy.

Notes

An unabridged version of this chapter first appeared in the *Utah Law Review*, vol. 2011: 489–623.

1. On Virginia, see chapter 6 by Ralph Ketcham and chapter 3 by Mark McGarvie.

2. The amendments are collected in John Witte Jr. and Joel A. Nichols, *Religion and the American Constitutional Experiment*, 3d ed. (Boulder, CO: Westview Press, 2011), 295–96.

3. See chapter 3 by Mark McGarvie and chapter 5 by Paul Finkelman.

4. See chapter 2 by Michael McConnell.

5. Barron v. Baltimore, 32 U.S. 243 (1833) (holding that Bill of Rights was not binding on state and local governments).

6. *The Debates and Proceedings in the Congress of the United States*, 42 vols. (Washington, DC: Gales and Seaton, 1834–1856) 1:448 [hereinafter *Annals*].

7. Thomas J. Curry, *The First Freedoms: Church and State in America to the Passage of the First Amendment* (New York: Oxford University Press, 1986), 193–94.

8. *Annals*, 1:451–52 (emphasis added).

9. William Hutchinson et al., eds., *The Papers of James Madison* (Chicago: University of Chicago Press, 1962–1991), 11:297 (letter dated October 17, 1788).

10. *Annals*, 1:450–58 (emphasis added).

11. Ibid., 1:757 (August 15, 1789) (emphasis added).

12. Ibid., 1:778 (August 17, 1789) (emphasis added).

13. Ibid., 1:783 (emphasis added).

14. Ibid., 1:757 (emphasis added).

15. Ibid.

16. Ibid., 1:757–58.

17. Ibid., 1:758.

18. Ibid. From his letter of October 17, 1788, to Jefferson referenced above, we know that Madison desired a level of conscientious protection for all, including the nonreligious, that would prevent compelled religious observance ("worship God in any manner").

19. See chapter 2 by Michael McConnell.

20. This is an unflattering remark directed at Rhode Island about the negative effects of never having had an establishment.

21. *Annals*, 1:758–59 (emphasis added).

22. Ibid., 1:759 (emphasis added).

23. Ibid.

24. Ibid.

25. Ibid., 1:783–84 (emphasis added).

26. The "third amendment" referenced here could be either to the amendments the Committee of the Whole made to the report of the Select Committee of eleven (*see Journal of the House of Representatives of the United States*, 14 vols. (Washington, DC: Gales and Seaton, 1826), 1:82. (May 5, 1789) [hereinafter *House Journal*], or it may be a reference to Madison's original Third Amendment, as proposed to the House on June 8, 1789. Either way, the record in the *House Journal* on the next day, August 21, lists the Third Amendment as having the phrases on religious freedom, reflecting a change in the numbering of the Articles of Amendment. See *House Journal*, 85 (August 21, 1789).

27. The "fourth amendment" referenced here could be either to the amendments the Committee of the Whole made to the report of the Select Committee of eleven (see *House Journal*, 1:82 (August 18, 1789)) or Madison's original Fourth Amendment as proposed to the House on June 8, 1789.

28. *Annals*, 1:795–96.

29. Recall that on August 15 Huntington had suggested the use of the term "free exercise of religion" in place of conscience. *Annals* 1:758. During this period the terms "conscience" and "free exercise" were sometimes used interchangeably in general public discourse. That is likely not the case here. From the many closely drafted iterations of the amendment in the House and Senate it is probable that "conscience" and "free exercise" convey different meanings, specifically with "free exercise" being contingent on the exercise being religiously motivated. The drafters were fully aware it was a constitution they were crafting and that called for a precise use of words.

30. *House Journal*, 1:85.

31. *Journal of the First Session of the Senate of the United States of America, begun and held at the city of New-York, March 4th, 1789, and the thirteenth year of the independence of the said states* (first session, 1789) (New York: Thomas Greenleaf), 103–5 (Early American Imprints, Series I: Evans #22207 reprinted 2002) [hereinafter *Senate Journal*].

32. Ibid., 116 (emphasis added).

33. Such an assumption is unlikely. It would mean rejecting the argument by James Wilson that all powers not delegated are denied. Although Anti-Federalists had reservations about Wilson's argument, the Federalists generally accepted it, and it was the Federalists who were in control of the process in the Senate.

34. *Senate Journal*, 116 (emphasis added).

35. Ibid., 117 (emphasis added).

36. Ibid., 119 (emphasis added).

37. Ibid.

38. Ibid., 121.

39. Ibid., 129 (emphasis added).

40. *Annals*, 1:940.

41. Ibid., 1:948 reads ". . . or prohibiting a free exercise thereof . . .," whereas the *House Journal*, 1:121 reads ". . . or prohibiting the free exercise thereof." The *Senate Journal*, 145, agrees with the *House Journal*.

42. The *Annals* uses a comma, whereas the *House Journal* uses a semicolon. Once again the record in the *Senate Journal* agrees with the *House Journal*. See *Senate Journal*, 145.

43. *Senate Journal*, 150.

44. Ibid., 163.

45. *Journal of the Senate of the Commonwealth of Virginia; Begun and held in the City of Richmond, on Monday, the 19th Day of October, in the Year of Our Lord 1789 and in the Fourteenth Year of the Commonwealth* (Richmond, VA: John Worrick, 1828), 62–63.

46. Hutchinson et al., *Papers of James Madison*, 12:453.

47. Ibid., 467.

48. See, e.g., Vincent Phillip Muñoz, "The Original Meaning of the Establishment Clause and the Impossibility of Its Incorporation," *University of Pennsylvania Journal of Constitutional Law* 8 (2006):585, 628–30.

49. This means Congress would have to be mindful of the Establishment Clause whenever it exercised enumerated national powers. For example, when regulating the territories pursuant to the U.S. Constitution, Article IV, section 3, clause 2, Congress could touch on religion but it could not "make . . . . law respecting an establishment" of religion. Indeed, the Northwest Ordinance of 1787, which the First Congress reenacted, did touch on religion in the Ordinance's Articles 1 and 3, but did so in a manner that was not "an establishment" of religion. See *An Act to Provide for the Government of the Territory Northwest of the River Ohio*, 1st Cong., 1st Sess., ch. 8, 1 Stat. 50, 52 (August 7, 1789).

50. See Noah Feldman, "The Intellectual Origins of the Establishment Clause," *New York University Law Review* 77 (2002):346, 351–52.

51. Curry, *The First Freedoms*, 193–94.

52. Kurt T. Lash, "The Second Adoption of the Establishment Clause: The Rise of the Nonestablishment Principle," *Arizona State Law Journal* 27 (1995):1085, 1090–92.

53. See Steven G. Calabresi and Sarah E. Agudo, "Individual Rights under State Constitutions When the Fourteenth Amendment Was Ratified in 1868: What Rights Are Deeply Rooted in American History and Tradition?" *Texas Law Review* 87 (2008):7, 31–33.

54. See Steven D. Smith, *Foreordained Failure: The Quest for a Constitutional Principle of Religious Freedom* (Oxford: Oxford University Press, 1995), 22–27, 45–48.

{9}

Defining and Testing the Prohibition on Religious Establishments in the Early Republic

Daniel L. Dreisbach

"Congress shall make no law respecting an establishment of religion." What does this phrase mean? There is no easy answer to this question. Indeed, the meaning of these ten words from the First Amendment to the U.S. Constitution has sustained a lively debate for more than two centuries. This question has long plagued church–state policy and jurisprudence. The members of the first federal Congress who drafted these words in the summer of 1789 may have had difficulty answering the question definitively. The ink was barely dry on the Amendment before questions were raised about the scope and application of this prohibition. What makes the interpretation of this phrase so difficult? First, the key words *establishment, religion,* and *respecting* are susceptible to more than one interpretation. The phrase "establishment of religion," in particular, has meant different things to different people in the course of American history. These ten words were written at a time when the definition of religious establishment was in a state of flux. Second, the members of the first Congress were eager to craft a bill of rights quickly in order to move on to the more pressing business of establishing the laws and institutions of the new national government. They may have deliberately settled on language vague in meaning and subject to multiple interpretations and, thus, acceptable to diverse constituencies. These ten words, in short, may have been interpreted in some very different ways by those who framed, adopted, and ratified the First Amendment, each believing it accorded with his or her own construction of "establishment of religion." In this manner, agreement was reached rapidly on a potentially contentious subject. Therefore, the search for a fixed, discernible original understanding of the First Amendment may be an impossible undertaking.

By the time of independence, there was growing disagreement as to what constituted an "establishment of religion," and church–state arrangements in the former colonies were in transition. The definition of *establishment* varied from region to region and from denomination to denomination.[1] There was broad agreement that legal preference for one church, sect, or religion over all others constituted an establishment of religion. So, too, was an arrangement where the civil government imposed articles of faith and forms of worship on all those under its authority. Its antithesis was a state policy that placed all sects on an equal footing before the law. Although this definition was widely accepted, there were disputes about whether specific state policies and practices constituted an establishment. The use of general assessments, which taxed all residents for the support of religion, was an especially contentious policy. Adherents of minority sects, such as the Baptists, were often adamant that anything short of wholly voluntary support of religion, even including a general assessment that permitted taxpayers to designate the church or minister to receive the tax, constituted an offensive religious establishment.

Most of the newly independent states retained laws, institutions, policies, or practices that would be deemed religious establishments by twenty-first-century legal standards. Religious test oaths and laws against Sabbath-breaking, blasphemy, and profane swearing, to give only a few examples, were familiar features in state laws. For many Americans, especially in New England's old Puritan commonwealths, state support for churches and their ministers, as well as religious test oaths, were not necessarily regarded as an establishment of religion or incompatible with the free exercise of religion. Public practices of the time indicate that there was little thought that the First Amendment prohibition on "law respecting an establishment of religion" proscribed all public acknowledgements of God and invocations of divine blessing for the civil polity. Public leaders were encouraged to promote religion through the example of their lives—by being models of moral rectitude, regularly attending church, and acknowledging God in their public pronouncements. There were few public expressions of the view that the civil state could take no action to promote religion and that religion must be encouraged through strictly private, nongovernmental means.

At the end of the colonial era and continuing into the revolutionary period, the Congregationalists enjoyed official favor in much of New England; the Episcopal Church was preferred by law throughout the South. Again, depending on the definition of *establishment*, eight or nine states retained either an established church or something approximating a religious establishment. A few states, such as Rhode Island and Pennsylvania, steadfastly rejected Old World models of an exclusive ecclesiastical establishment and, in so doing, created new models for religious toleration and disestablished polities. These new models would eventually prevail in America.

The lack of consensus on the meaning of important constitutional concepts, such as "establishment," deferred the task of determining the scope and application of the First Amendment. Several important public pronouncements and controversies in the early republic would prove influential in defining the terms and framing the issues in church–state debate in subsequent judicial, scholarly, and popular fora.

This chapter begins with a brief review of the text and legislative history of the Article VI religious test ban, an important but often neglected complement to the First Amendment clauses on the nonestablishment and free exercise of religion. This is followed by a survey of several authoritative pronouncements and church–state controversies, following ratification of the U.S. Constitution and Bill of Rights, which elicited opinions on the prudential and constitutional principles governing church–state relations in the United States. The profiled pronouncements and controversies—all of which garnered national attention— offer insights into how Americans in the early republic came to view the constitutional prohibitions on religious tests and establishments.

The Constitutional Ban on Religious Test Oaths

A constitutional convention that met in Philadelphia in mid-1787 was the culmination of the decade-long quest to create a plan of government conducive to the safety and happiness of the former colonies and the American people. The delegates assembled in May "for the sole and express purpose of revising the Articles of Confederation" and "render[ing] the federal Constitution adequate to the exigencies of Government and the preservation of the Union."[2] The national constitution that emerged from the Convention, together with the First Amendment to it, set forth principles that defined a place and role for religion in American public life.

The constitutional bases for this distinctively American approach to church–state relations are found in Article VI, clause 3—the Constitution's forgotten religion clause—and the First Amendment. Both provisions embodied nonestablishment and free exercise of religion principles. The first states that "no religious Test shall ever be required as a Qualification to any Office or public Trust under the United States," and the second provides that "Congress shall make no law respecting an establishment of religion, or prohibiting the free exercise thereof." The former clause is binding on federal officeholders only. It did not invalidate religious tests that existed under state laws. Similarly, the latter provision initially had no effect on the arrangements and practices at the state and local levels. It was not until the twentieth century that the U.S. Supreme Court incorporated the First Amendment guarantee of religious freedom into the Fourteenth Amendment's Due Process Clause, thereby making this freedom applicable to state and local authorities.[3]

The genesis of the religious test ban was a proposal purportedly offered by Charles Pinckney of South Carolina at the Constitutional Convention in May 1787, which stated that "the Legislature of the United States shall pass no Law on the subject of Religion."[4] Pinckney told convention delegates that "the prevention of Religious Tests, as qualifications to Offices of Trust or Emolument . . . [, is] a provision the world will expect from you, in the establishment of a System founded on Republican Principles, and in an age so liberal and enlightened as the present."[5] Three months later, Pinckney raised the subject again, this time proposing the following clause: "No religious test or qualification shall ever be annexed to any oath of office under the authority of the United States."[6] The proposal was referred to a committee without further recorded deliberation or action. At the end of August, Pinckney once again brought the religious test ban to the delegates' attention. In deference to Quakers and some other sects, the convention discussed adding the words *or affirmation* after the word *oath* in the oath clause. Pinckney then moved to join the test ban with the proposed "oath or affirmation" clause; the motion was debated briefly. Roger Sherman of Connecticut "thought [the ban] unnecessary, the prevailing liberality being a sufficient security against such tests." Gouverneur Morris of Pennsylvania and General Charles Cotesworth Pinckney of South Carolina (Charles Pinckney's second cousin) both voiced support for the motion in unreported speeches. The convention approved Pinckney's amendment before adopting "the whole Article."[7] The article was then forwarded to the Committee on Style, which shaped the final language incorporated into Article VI of the Constitution.

The provision provoked debate among the general public and in the state ratifying conventions. A recurring theme emphasized the role of morality, fostered by the Christian religion, in promoting the civic virtues and social order essential to a system of self-government. Critics said the ban on religious tests suggested inattentiveness to the important task of selecting rulers committed to protecting and nurturing religion and morality. Once it is conceded that not all religions are conducive to good civil government and political order, then there are plausible grounds for excluding adherents of some religions from public office. Accordingly, in the words of Luther Martin of Maryland, "it would be *at least decent* to hold out some distinction between the professors of Christianity and downright infidelity or paganism."[8] Religious tests are one tool, defenders said, for identifying those individuals whose religious beliefs are compatible or incompatible with the interests of good civil government.

Proponents of the religious test ban framed the debate in terms of religious liberty and nonestablishment. Oliver Ellsworth, a Connecticut federalist and delegate at the Constitutional Convention, offered a succinct, vigorous defense of the test ban:

[M]y countrymen, the sole purpose and effect of it is to exclude persecution, and to secure to you the important right of religious liberty. . . . In our country every man has a right to worship God in that way which is most agreeable to his conscience. If he be a good and peaceable citizen, he is liable to no penalties or incapacities on account of his religious sentiments; or in other words, he is no subject to persecution.[9]

Article VI proponents also argued that a test ban was key to preventing a national ecclesiastical establishment. In the Connecticut ratifying convention, Oliver Wolcott described the ban as a useful check against initiatives "to establish one religious sect, and lay all others under legal disabilities."[10] Advocates argued that the test ban provided, in the words of Governor Edmund Randolph of Virginia, the strongest security against religious establishment by placing "all sects on the same footing." "I am a friend to a variety of sects, because they keep one another in order," Randolph continued. "And there are now so many [sects] in the United States, that they will prevent the establishment of any one sect, in prejudice to the rest, and will forever oppose all attempts to infringe religious liberty."[11] In the North Carolina ratifying convention, Judge James Iredell succinctly drew the connection among Article VI, sect equality, and nonestablishment: "This article is calculated to secure universal religious liberty, by putting all sects on a level—the only way to prevent persecution."[12]

Article VI was a departure from the prevailing practices in Europe, as well as most of the states. For centuries, religious test oaths had been a favored instrument for preserving ecclesiastical establishments. Accordingly, modern commentators often describe the test ban as the cornerstone of the secular state and a constitutional expression of church–state separation. The test ban was not strictly a "disestablishment" measure because there was no formal establishment to abolish. However, the test ban practically preempted the prospect of a national ecclesiastical establishment by removing a mechanism for a religious denomination to exert control over the political processes. Moreover, the ban opened the door for members of minority sects to become full and equal participants in the political enterprise.

What was the objective of the religious test ban? Interestingly, religious liberty and nonestablishment provisions coexisted with religious test oaths in many state constitutions of the founding era, indicating that the founding generation did not always or necessarily consider these concepts incompatible.[13] Moreover, the inclusion of religious tests in many state constitutions of the era indicates some measure of support for them. The federal test ban, apparently, was not driven by a general renunciation of religious tests as a matter of principle. Indeed, some delegates at the Constitutional Convention who endorsed the Article VI test ban had previously participated in crafting religious tests for their state constitutions. How can one reconcile this apparent contradiction? Their support for the federal test ban was, perhaps, rooted in the principle of federalism, which denied the national government all jurisdiction in religious matters, including the authority to administer religious tests. (Remember, the Article VI ban was only applicable to offices under the national government.) There was a consensus that religion was a matter best left to individual citizens and to their respective state governments. Some founders arguably supported a federal test ban because they valued religious tests required under state laws, and they feared a federal test might displace existing state test oaths and religious establishments.[14]

Defining and Testing the Public Role of Religion in the Early Republic

The Article VI religious test ban was an important locus of discussion about religious liberty and religious establishment in the early republic. An even more influential constitutional pronouncement was the First Amendment. Drafted by the first federal Congress in 1789, and ratified by the states and added to the Constitution in 1791, the Amendment states: "Congress shall make no law respecting an establishment of religion, or prohibiting the free exercise thereof."[15] The interpretation and application of these sixteen words was, from the start, the source of much debate.

Some of the most divisive conflicts in the early republic addressed lingering questions about religion's place in civic life and the constitutional prohibition on religious tests and establishments. Authoritative pronouncements on these themes from George Washington, Thomas Jefferson, Joseph Story, and others gave further definition to these concepts. These controversies and pronouncements are, arguably, as important to understanding the constitutional principles governing church–state relationships as the state constitutional developments in the years prior to 1787 and the debates surrounding the adoption and ratification of the national Constitution and Bill of Rights.

George Washington's Farewell Address. After eight years as president, George Washington delivered his parting advice to the young republic in a celebrated *Farewell Address* and retired to his home on the south bank of the Potomac River, where he died two years and nine months later. His Address appeared in Philadelphia's *American Daily Advertiser* on September 19, 1796, less than six months before the end of his presidential term. Its reputation as one of the quintessential statements of American political principle grew steadily from its publication onward until it came to be regarded as one of the nation's most important political documents, and it was often studied alongside the Declaration of Independence and the Constitution itself.

The language of this pronouncement, especially two paragraphs on religion, quickly entered the American political vernacular. Americans immediately singled out the passage on religion for special recognition and, within days of the Address's publication, it was being quoted approvingly in pamphlets and newspapers.[16] The famous passage on religion has become the locus classicus of the notion that religion has a vital role to play in American civic life, rejecting by implication the idea that religion must be divorced from civic life and concerns. Washington wrote:

Of all the dispositions and habits which lead to political prosperity, Religion and morality are indispensable supports. In vain would that man claim the tribute of Patriotism, who should labour to subvert these great Pillars of human happiness, these firmest props of the duties of Men and citizens. . . . And let us with caution indulge the supposition, that morality can be maintained without religion. Whatever may be conceded to the influence of refined education on minds of peculiar structure, reason and experience both forbid us to expect that National morality can prevail in exclusion of religious principle.[17]

Three points stand out in this passage, each of which challenges efforts to separate religion from the polity. First, and most obvious, is the bold statement that "Religion and morality are indispensable supports" to "political prosperity." This was a recurring theme in Washington's writings. Years earlier, in a letter to the Synod of the Dutch Reformed Church, he remarked: "True religion affords to government its surest support."[18] Although no one made the argument more famously or succinctly than Washington in the *Farewell Address*, he was certainly not alone among the founders in advancing the notion that religion and morality are essential props for good civil government. The literature of the founding era is replete with this assertion.[19]

Though the founding fathers' religious beliefs ranged from orthodox Christianity to skepticism about Christianity's central claims, there was a consensus among the founders that religion and morality were "indispensable supports" for civic virtue, social order, and political prosperity. Indeed, this was a virtually unchallenged assumption of the age. The challenge the founders confronted was how to nurture personal responsibility and social order in a political system of self-government. Tyrants used the whip and rod to compel subjects to behave as they desired, but this approach was unacceptable for a free, self-governing people. In response to this challenge, the founders looked to religion (and morality informed by religious values) to provide the internal moral compass that would prompt citizens to behave in a disciplined, controlled manner and, thereby, promote social order and political stability. This generation looked to religion to inform public ethics, guide the consciences of ordinary citizens and leaders alike, calm the passions, and soften popular prejudices.

Few, if any, founders doubted that religion—for either genuinely spiritual or strictly utilitarian reasons—was vital to the regime of republican self-government they had created. The question was how best to encourage and promote religion. In this particular passage, Washington was silent about the affirmative steps he thought the civil state should take to promote the religion he believed was essential to social order and political prosperity. He did say that the "mere Politician . . . ought to respect and to cherish" religion and morality, and he drew attention to one vital public role for religion, underscoring the "religious obligation"—arising, presumably, from a belief in God and a future state of rewards and punishments—that buttresses oaths required in "Courts of Justice."[20] This echoed the view of many early Americans who thought oaths and religious tests—at least for state officeholders and voters—would ensure that those who exercised political responsibilities embraced the requisite religious, and attendant moral, values.[21]

Second, Washington discounted the notion that morality can prevail in the absence of religion. He contended, to the contrary, that religion is the wellspring of morality. He conceded that, for rare individuals (perhaps he had Jefferson in mind), "the influence of refined education on minds of peculiar structure" may account for a morality uninformed by religion; however, he went on to say that "reason and experience" forbid us, especially in a large republic such as the United States, from relying on this as sufficient to sustain the popular morality essential to foster the civic virtue vital for social order and political prosperity.

Third, once conceded that religion is indispensable to civic virtue, social order, and political prosperity, it then follows that the enemy of religion is a danger to society. Accordingly, Washington audaciously challenged the patriotism of those in society who sought to undermine or destroy religion's public role. In the sentence immediately following his famous pronouncement that "religion and morality are indispensable supports" to "political prosperity," he warned: "In vain would that man claim the tribute of Patriotism, who should labour to subvert these great Pillars of human happiness, these firmest props of the duties of Men and citizens." These are strong words, indeed, that remind a modern reader of the importance the founders attached to religion's vital place and role in their design for a constitutional republic.[22]

Nothing in this famous passage by Washington would have struck Americans at the end of the eighteenth century as particularly novel or outside the mainstream of political thought. It was an authoritative expression of the prevailing sentiment of the day, confirming a vital public role for religion in the regime of republican self-government so carefully constructed in the national Constitution.

Religion and the Election of 1800. In few, if any, presidential contests has religion played a more divisive and decisive role than in the election of 1800. The campaign was also the first major test, following ratification of the Constitution and the First Amendment, of religion's place on the national political stage. The unpopular incumbent, Federalist John Adams of Massachusetts, faced his longtime rival, Republican Thomas Jefferson of Virginia. The electorate was deeply divided along regional, partisan, and ideological lines, and acrimonious campaign rhetoric punctuated the polarized political landscape.

Jefferson's religion, or the alleged lack thereof, emerged as a critical issue in the campaign. His Federalist opponents vilified him as a Jacobin and atheist. Both charges stemmed, most recently, from his notorious sympathy for the French Revolution, which in the 1790s had turned bloody and, some said, anti-Christian. His statement in the *Notes on the State of Virginia* that "it does me no injury for my neighbor to say there are twenty gods, or no God," published in the mid-1780s, also exacerbated fears that he was a dangerous, demoralizing infidel.[23] The "grand question" posed by the *Gazette of the United States*, a leading Federalist newspaper, in the days before the election was whether Americans should vote for "GOD—AND A RELIGIOUS PRESIDENT [John Adams]; or impiously declare for JEFFERSON—AND NO GOD!!!"[24]

Jefferson's heterodox beliefs, political adversaries contended, raised doubts about his fitness for high office. In 1798, Timothy Dwight, a Congregationalist minister and the president of Yale College, warned that the election of Jeffersonian Republicans might usher in a Jacobin regime in which "we may see the Bible cast into a bonfire, the vessels of the sacramental supper borne by an ass in public procession, and our children . . . chanting mockeries against God . . . [to] the ruin of their religion, and the loss of their souls."[25] In an influential pamphlet published in 1800, the Dutch Reformed clergyman and former chaplain to the U.S. House of Representatives, William Linn, denounced candidate Jefferson, charging him with "disbelief of the Holy Scriptures" and "rejection of the Christian Religion and open profession of Deism."[26] A vote for Jefferson, he warned, "must be construed into no less than rebellion against God." He added ominously that the promotion of an infidel to such high office "by the suffrages of a Christian nation" would encourage public immorality and licentious manners and lead to the "destruction of all social order and happiness."[27] The Presbyterian minister John Mitchell Mason similarly declaimed that it would be "a crime never to be forgiven" for the American people to confer the office of chief magistrate "upon an open enemy to their religion, their Redeemer, and their hope, [and it] would be mischief to themselves and sin against God." Jefferson's "favorite wish," Mitchell charged, is "to see a government administered without any religious principle among either rulers or ruled." He repudiated the notion gaining currency among Jeffersonians that "*Religion has nothing to do with politics.*"[28]

Jeffersonian partisans answered the charges leveled against their candidate for president. They portrayed Jefferson as a leader of uncommon liberality and tolerance—an enlightened man who zealously defended constitutional government, civil and religious liberty, and the separation of religion and politics. Republicans vehemently denied that Jefferson was an atheist or infidel. "[M]y information is that he is a sincere professor of christianity—though not a noisy one," Tunis Wortman wrote.[29] The Jeffersonians also advanced a separationist policy, which would eventually exert much influence on American politics, suggesting that efforts to disqualify candidate Jefferson because of his religious beliefs violated a principle of church–state separation. "Religion and government are equally necessary," Wortman declared in response to the Reverend Linn, "but their interests should be kept separate and distinct. No legitimate connection can ever subsist between them. Upon no plan, no system, can they become united, without endangering the purity and usefulness of both—the church will corrupt the state, and the state pollute the church."[30] In "A Vindication of Thomas Jefferson," the prominent New York politician DeWitt Clinton alleged that Jefferson's clerical critics would "propose a religious test for his subscription, and thereby violate the spirit of that constitution which he has sworn to support." "Has not all experience shewn," Clinton asked, "that tests and subscription articles never interpose obstacles to the wicked, and only serve as snares for the righteous?"[31] (The critics answered that, notwithstanding the religious test ban, "there is nothing in the constitution to restrict our choice" as Christians in voting "our" preference in conformity with "our" consciences.[32])

The perennial debate regarding the prudential and constitutional place of religion in civic life is a legacy of this campaign. Religion, argues one side, is an indispensable support for political prosperity, providing a vital moral compass in a system of self-government. The other side, echoing Jeffersonian partisans, asserts that social cohesion and democratic values are threatened whenever bricks are removed from the wall of separation between religion and politics. The Jeffersonians effectively drew on the principles of the Article VI religious test ban and the First Amendment nonestablishment provision in suggesting that questioning a candidate's fitness for public office because of his or her religious beliefs, or lack thereof, offended fundamental constitutional values.

Religious Proclamations. Official proclamations setting aside days in the public calendar for prayer, fasting, and thanksgiving[33] stirred political controversy in the days leading up to the election of 1800 and, again, in the early days of Jefferson's presidential administration. When, in March 1799, President John Adams recommended a national "day of solemn humiliation, fasting, and prayer," political adversaries depicted him as a tool of establishmentarians intent on formally and legally uniting a specific church with the new federal government.[34] This allegation alarmed religious dissenters, such as the Baptists, who feared persecution by a state church. "A general suspicion prevailed," Adams recounted a decade later, "that the Presbyterian Church [which was presumed to be behind the proclamation] was ambitious and aimed at an establishment as a national church." Although disclaiming any involvement in such a scheme, Adams ruefully reported that he "was represented as a Presbyterian and at the head of this political and ecclesiastical project. The secret whisper ran though all the sects, 'Let us have Jefferson, Madison, Burr, anybody, whether they be philosophers, Deists, or even atheists, rather than a Presbyterian President.'"[35] This reservoir of opposition to "national fasts and thanksgivings," according to Adams, cost him the election in 1800. Jefferson was the political beneficiary, if not the instigator, of this sentiment and, no doubt, was eager to go on the record denouncing presidential religious proclamations.

Once elected, President Jefferson reignited controversy on the issue when he declined to follow the practice of his two presidential predecessors and

virtually all state chief executives in appointing such days for religious observance. To his Federalist detractors, President Jefferson's refusal to issue religious proclamations only confirmed that he was, indeed, an infidel or atheist.
The controversy became so distracting that Jefferson wrote his famous 1802
missive to the Danbury (Connecticut) Baptist Association, in which he
famously remarked that the First Amendment had built a "wall of separation
between church and state," to explain his policy on this delicate matter.[36] Even
though the Baptists had not requested such a proclamation, Jefferson told his
attorney general Levi Lincoln that the Danbury letter "furnishes an occasion
too, which I have long wished to find, of saying why I do not proclaim fastings &
thanksgivings, as my predecessors did."[37]

President Jefferson's stance on religious proclamations is often portrayed
as an example of his principled commitment to church–state separation.[38]
A careful scrutiny of his public record on this practice, however, suggests that
his actions may have been motivated more by politics or his view of federalism
than by a commitment to church–state separation. Significantly, Jefferson's
refusal, as president, to set aside days for religious observances contrasted with
his actions in Virginia where, in the late 1770s, he framed "A Bill for Appointing Days of Public Fasting and Thanksgiving,"[39] and, as governor in 1779, he
designated a day for "publick and solemn thanksgiving and prayer to Almighty
God."[40] The former, far from simply granting the "Governor, or Chief Magistrate [of the Commonwealth]" the authority to appoint "days of public fasting
and humiliation, or thanksgiving," included the following punitive provision:
"Every minister of the gospel shall on each day so to be appointed, attend and
perform divine service and preach a sermon, or discourse, suited to the occasion, in his church, on pain of forfeiting fifty pounds for every failure, not
having a reasonable excuse."[41]

Can Jefferson's conduct in Virginia where he sponsored religious proclamations be reconciled with his refusal to issue such proclamations as president of
the United States? Jefferson maintained that he, as president, could not issue
religious proclamations because the federal government could exercise only
those powers expressly granted to it by the Constitution, and no power to issue
such proclamations was so granted. Insofar as Jefferson invoked the "wall of
separation" to explain why the nation's chief executive could not issue religious
proclamations, the "wall" was erected between the national government and
state governments on matters pertaining to religion, such as religious proclamations, and not, more generally, between religion in all its manifestations
and the civil state at all levels. Jefferson's "wall," in short, affirmed the principle
of federalism. However, the "wall" metaphor, in the course of time, would have
a profound impact on church–state law and policy, straying far from the federalist context in which it was formulated by Jefferson.[42]

The controversy over religious proclamations remerged in the administration of Andrew Jackson. President Jackson's refusal in 1832 to designate a

national day of public fasting, humiliation, and prayer in order to avert a threatening cholera epidemic disappointed many religious traditionalists. In a letter dated June 12, 1832, addressed to the General Synod of the Dutch Reformed Church, the president explained his position. Restating Jefferson's stance in the Danbury Baptist letter of 1802, Jackson argued that, although he believed "in the efficacy of prayer," he thought a presidential fast-day proclamation would be unconstitutional, disturbing "the security which religion now enjoys in this country, in its complete separation from the political concerns of the General Government."[43] Senator Henry Clay, Jackson's political nemesis, introduced a resolution requesting Jackson to reconsider his decision not to designate a fast day.[44] Clay's motion was arguably a cynical political ploy designed to embarrass and discredit Jackson among conservative Protestants and to appeal in the upcoming 1832 election to religious constituents. In any case, by his refusal to recommend a day of national humiliation and prayer, religious traditionalists believed that Jackson was signaling his intent to "carry[] on the business of the commonwealth *professedly* as 'without God in the world.'" The president's religious critics viewed his policy on proclamations as a blatant, arrogant, and dangerous endorsement of "political irreligion." In a widely circulated and influential 1838 tract, an anonymous scribe (who was clearly a religious traditionalist) remarked:

> President Jackson, after Mr. Jefferson's example, refused in 1832 to say a word to the people about humbling themselves before their maker; though it was a time, if ever there was one, that demanded some signal act of religious self-abasement and sorrow at our hands; for it was during the first cholera season, when the angel of destruction was hovering over us with dreadful omen, darkening the heavens with his wings, and scattering unheard-of plagues upon the earth. It was a strange thing to hear from the chief magistrate of a people circumstanced as we were then, that he could lend no countenance to the piety of our wishes, and was even prohibited by the fundamental laws from recommending the slightest public acknowledgment of that deity whose judgements were so visibly abroad.[45]

The consternation of religious traditionalists was heightened when the Democratic governor of New York followed Jackson's lead in declining to proclaim a fast day. The governor's action was especially disconcerting, indeed alarming, to religious traditionalists because it underscored the significant degree to which the political culture had been secularized. Presidents Jefferson and Jackson could plausibly refrain from making such proclamations on the grounds that, as a matter of federalism, the federal chief executive was restrained from taking any action pertaining to religion. The U.S. Constitution deferred to individual citizens and the respective state governments on all matters regarding religion and devotion to God, thereby denying the national government all jurisdiction over religion, including, one could argue, the authority to issue religious proclamations. State chief executives, however, were under no constitutional disability in issuing religious proclamations. In any case, these departures from past practices confirmed the suspicions of many pious citizens that there was a faction in American politics intent on separating religion from the concerns of civil government.

The Sunday Mail Controversy. The transportation and delivery of mail on Sundays were a source of recurring church–state controversy in the early nineteenth century. Sunday postal service heightened conservative Protestant fears about the increasing secularization of public life. It also brought into focus contrasting views of the appropriate relationship between civil government and religion. Religious traditionalists, on the one hand, emphasized the obligation of civil government to preserve and protect fundamental Christian institutions. Defenders of the Sunday mail, on the other hand, warned that acknowledgment by law of religious observance might invade liberty of conscience and foster a dangerous and entangling alliance between religious and political institutions.

Ancient English and colonial laws that imposed restraints on Sunday business were at the root of the Sunday mail controversy. Variant forms of these laws survived well into the nineteenth century, creating problems for the U.S. government in mail delivery. The issue, as it affected postal services, was addressed in a congressional act of April 30, 1810. The statute required postmasters "at all reasonable hours, on every day of the week, to deliver, on demand, any letter, paper or packet, to the person entitled to or authorized to receive the same."[46] Before passage of this legislation, no uniform policy or practice governed Sunday business in U.S. post offices throughout the country. Although no affront to the Christian community was intended, the statute set off an avalanche of protests and petitions from a multitude of religious leaders, denominations, and citizens' committees demanding legislation discontinuing Sunday postal operations. Petitions were generally referred to the postmaster general. Congress, however, was eventually moved to report on the issue. In 1815, both the Senate and the House of Representatives resolved that it would be "inexpedient" to grant the prayer of the petitioners to prohibit postal services on Sunday.[47]

The controversy subsided for a decade and then exploded in the late 1820s. In March 1825, Congress enacted legislation reaffirming postal obligations spelled out in the 1810 law.[48] Once again, Congress was inundated with petitions and counter-petitions revealing strong sentiment on all sides of the issue.[49] On June 19, 1829, Senator Richard M. Johnson of Kentucky, chairman of the Senate Committee on Post Offices and Post Roads, released a report setting forth fundamental reasons why it would be inappropriate for the U.S. government to yield to the demands of religious traditionalists to disallow Sunday mail. Senator Johnson, who later served as vice-president of the United States (1837–1841), argued that proposed legislation to stop the mail on Sunday "was improper, and that nine hundred and ninety-nine in a thousand were opposed to any legislative interference, inasmuch as it would have a tendency to unite religious institutions with the Government." He further opined "that these petitions and memorials in relation to Sunday mails, were but the entering wedge of a scheme to make this Government a religious instead of a social and political institution."[50] Jacksonian democrats and liberal groups embraced the report as a reasoned and eloquent affirmation of religious liberty and church–state separation. Johnson's report stated:

> If kept within its legitimate sphere of action, no injury can result from its [Sunday] observance. It should, however, be kept in mind, that the proper object of government is, to protect all persons in the enjoyment of their religious, as well as civil rights; and not to determine for any, whether they shall esteem one day above another, or esteem all days alike holy.
>
> We are aware, that a variety of sentiment exists among the good citizens of this nation, on the subject of the Sabbath day; and our government is designed for the protection of one, as much as for another. . . . With these different religious views, the committee are of opinion that Congress cannot interfere. It is not the legitimate province of the legislature to determine what religion is true, or what is false. Our government is a civil, and not a religious, institution. Our constitution recognises in every person, the right to choose his own religion, and to enjoy it freely, without molestation. Whatever may be the religious sentiments of citizens, and however variant, they are alike entitled to protection from the government, so long as they do not invade the rights of others. . . .
>
> Extensive religious combinations, to effect a political objective, are, in the opinion of the committee, always dangerous. This first effort of the kind calls for the establishment of a principle, which, in the opinion of the committee, would lay the foundation for dangerous innovations upon the spirit of the constitution, and upon the religious rights of the citizens. . . .[51]

Senator Johnson's report provoked lively debate in congressional chambers. To detractors, it confirmed the triumph of political atheism and secularism. The most ardent opponents of Johnson's secular vision were Senator Theodore Frelinghuysen of New Jersey and Representative William McCreery of Pennsylvania. McCreery drafted a House minority report, released on March 5, 1830, which outlined the themes of the anti-Sunday mail campaign:

> All Christian nations acknowledge the first day of the week, to be the Sabbath. Almost every State in this Union has, by positive legislation, not only recognized this day as sacred, but has forbidden its profanation under penalties imposed by law.
>
> It was never considered, by any of those States, as an encroachment upon the rights of conscience, or as an improper interference with the opinions

of the few, to guard the sacredness of that portion of time acknowledged to be holy by the many.

The petitioners ask not Congress to expound the moral law; they ask not Congress to meddle with theological controversies, much less to interfere with the rights of the Jew or the Sabbatarian, or to treat with the least disrespect the religious feelings of any portion of the inhabitants of the Union; they ask the introduction of no religious coercion into our civil institutions; no blending of religion and civil affairs; but they do ask that the agents of Government, employed in the Post Office Department, may be permitted to enjoy the same opportunities of attending to moral and religious instruction, or intellectual improvement, on that day, which is enjoyed by the rest of their fellow citizens.[52]

Despite these efforts, Senator Johnson's view ultimately prevailed, and the campaign to prevent the Sunday mail failed.[53]

Although much of the debate focused on whether closing post offices on Sunday constituted an impermissible "establishment of religion," both sides claimed their opponent's position threatened "rights of conscience." Legally requiring the suspension of all public business on the Christian "Sabbath," the anti-Sabbatarians argued, would invade the rights of conscience of those who do not observe either the Sabbath or the specific Sabbath day recognized by most Christians. Those opposed to the Sunday mail appealed to the Article VI, clause 3 religious test ban in framing their argument: "Is it not as much an unconstitutional test, to make the violation of the Sabbath the condition of holding an office as it would be to make the keeping of the Sabbath such condition?"[54] An 1830 petition from "citizens of Philadelphia" observed that many pious citizens are "absolutely excluded" under current law from post office employment because they cannot, as a matter of conscience, labor on that day "consecrated by their Maker to a holy rest." The Pennsylvania petitioners, thus, concluded: "A religious, or rather an irreligious, test appears to your memorialists to be in this case imposed, and equal rights to be plainly and injuriously denied to a large portion of the community."[55]

Evangelical conservative Protestants were, for the most part, staunch advocates of laws preserving Sabbath observances. They believed that postal service policy revealed an anti-Christian bias and diminished the role of religion in public life. One religious traditionalist described the Sunday mail legislation as "the first statute enacted by Congress, authorizing and requiring a violation of the religion of the country."[56] Recognition of the Christian Sabbath in the public calendar was important to religious traditionalists because it furnished evidence that the United States was, indeed, a Christian nation. The Sunday mail legislation seemed to confirm a creeping hostility toward traditional Christianity and a movement to strip the public arena of religious influences.

A Christian Party in Politics. The propriety and constitutionality of Christian political activism was the subject of rancorous debate in the late 1820s and early 1830s. The defeat of the anti-Sunday mail campaign strengthened the conviction of many religious citizens that infidelity and radical secularism had gained ascendancy in national politics under a banner of liberal political reform. This was a bitter reversal for religious traditionalists who believed that America was a Christian nation, and it impressed upon them the urgency of mobilizing all their resources, including a potential army of Christian voters, to save the country from political atheism and to reestablish Christian values and morality in public life.

The Reverend Ezra Stiles Ely (1786–1861), an influential Presbyterian clergyman in Philadelphia,[57] addressed the role of Christians in politics in a Fourth of July oration in 1827.[58] In a discourse entitled "The Duty of Christian Freemen to Elect Christian Rulers," Ely proposed "a new sort of union," which he called "*a Christian party in politics.*"[59] The "party" Ely described was an electoral alliance composed of "three or four of the most numerous denominations of Christians in the United States," including Presbyterians, Baptists, Methodists, and Congregationalists. Ely also allowed that the Protestant Episcopal Church, as well as the Lutheran and Dutch Reformed churches, could add to this informal political union.[60] This party was without a strict political or sectarian definition and without membership roles or subscriptions. Rather, Ely envisioned a loose coalition of Christian activists, transcending sectarian lines, united to elect moral candidates for public office and to restore Christian values to a society awash in a sea of infidelity. This was a reform movement, spiritual in its mission and socially conservative in its policies, formed voluntarily by pious citizens "adopting, avowing, and determining to act upon, truly religious principles in all civil matters."[61] The immediate goal was to give a coherent political voice and electoral clout to evangelical conservative Protestants.

Ely's proposal rested on the premise that every citizen—"from the highest to the lowest," both ruler and ruled—"ought to serve the Lord with fear, and yield his sincere homage to the Son of God." He identified the religious criteria that measured fitness for public office: "Every ruler *should be* an avowed and a sincere friend of Christianity. He should know and believe the doctrines of our holy religion, and act in conformity with its precepts. . . . [O]ur civil rulers ought to act a religious part in all the relations which they sustain."[62]

Having established the duty of civil rulers to serve the Lord, Ely argued that righteous citizens had the duty "to honour the Lord Jesus Christ and promote christianity by electing and supporting as public officers the friends of our blessed Saviour."[63] Accordingly, "every Christian who has the right and the opportunity of exercising the elective franchise ought to do it," Ely counseled. He acknowledged that many pious constituents were disillusioned, even disgusted, by politics and, thus, relinquished their right to vote; but "[i]f all *good men* are to absent themselves from elections, then the *bad* will have the entire transaction of our public business."[64] If morality in public life is to be restored, he concluded, then all righteous citizens must be "Christian politicians," and "as conscientiously religious at the polls as in the pulpit, or house of worship."[65] Ely exhorted all who professed to be Christians to "unite and co-operate with *our Christian party*" and, in so doing, to "agree that they will support no man as a candidate for any office, who is not professedly friendly to Christianity, and a believer in divine Revelation." He entreated Christians to "abstain from supporting by their suffrages" candidates given to Sabbath-breaking, intemperance, profane swearing, adultery, debauchery, lewdness, gambling, and profligate living.[66]

> Let us never support by our votes any immoral man, or any known contemner of any of the fundamental doctrines of Christ, for any office: and least of all for the Presidency of these United States. . . . We are a Christian nation: we have a right to demand that all our rulers in their conduct shall conform to Christian morality; and if they do not, it is the duty and privilege of Christian freemen to make a new and a better election.[67]

If pious citizens would unite on voting day, he argued, they could by sheer weight of numbers dominate every public election in America. Significantly, Ely's plan relied not on an imposed theocratic order but on pious citizens acting voluntarily within a democratic framework to elect politicians who would govern in conformity with Christian precepts.

Ely's proposal drew immediate and vehement denunciation from liberal religionists (including Unitarians and Universalists), skeptics, rationalists, and freethinkers.[68] It was attacked as an undemocratic expression of religious intolerance and bigotry that threatened to extinguish civil and religious liberties and to Christianize every aspect of public life. Some critics described it as a Presbyterian plot to organize evangelical sects into a special-interest political bloc that would subject the secular state to ecclesiastical domination.[69] Adversaries of the "Christian Party" were urged to unite in opposition to the "theological tyrants" who "are always studying to extend their influence by seeking alliance with the civil power, and debasing the human mind, in order to accomplish their ends. . . ." Political liberty and the right of suffrage, Universalist minister William Morse declaimed, would be little more than "a name to such as belonged not to the union, if five of the most popular religious sects in this country should unite, and succeed in getting the reins of government into their own hands?"[70] "The cry of war is already sounded by the enemies of our political freedom," a leading Universalist newspaper announced. "It is time the lines were drawn between the friends and the enemies of a national religious establishment."[71] Zelotes Fuller similarly warned of "a deep and artful scheme" that, if consummated, would "tend to infuse the spirit of religious intolerance and persecution into the political institutions of our country, and in the end, completely to annihilate the political and religious liberty of the people." Fuller, a Universalist, raised the alarm:

> Never I beseech of you, encourage a certain *"Christian party in politics,"* which under moral and religious pretences, is officiously and continually interfering with the religious opinions of others, and endeavoring to effect by law and other means, equally exceptionable, a systematic course of measures, evidently calculated, to lead to a union of Church and State. If a union of church and state should be effected, which may God avert, then will the doctrines of the prevailing sect, become the creed of the country, to be enforced by fines, imprisonment, and doubtless death![72]

Ely anticipated and answered the principal criticisms of his proposal. He disavowed, for example, the establishment of any religious sect by law and denied vehemently that his proposal was inconsistent with the rights of conscience, violated the constitutional ban on religious tests, or promoted a union of church and state.[73] "Are Christians," he asked, "the only men in the community who may not be guided by their judgment, conscience, and choice, in electing their rulers?"[74] "Christians have the same rights and privileges in exercising the elective franchise" as are "accorded to Jews and Infidels," he answered.[75] Although he acknowledged that Christianity may not be "a constitutional test of admission to office," Ely argued that Christian citizens retained the right in casting their ballots to "prefer the avowed friends of the Christian religion to Turks, Jews, and Infidels."[76] He saw no constitutional impediment to Christians exercising their political liberty to support Christian candidates and causes by their votes, just as infidels had the political liberty to support anti-Christian candidates and measures.[77]

The national furor sparked by Ely's suggestion did not subside for decades, and it nourished the suspicion of many that Presbyterian clerics were "attempting to control the state to further their own schemes"[78] and to exclude non-Christians from full participation in the political process. The impact of Ely's plan was contrary to that which was intended. Not only did the cohesive electoral bloc Ely envisioned never materialize, but also the proposal unified and energized opponents of conservative Protestant influence in secular politics. In the final analysis, the idea of a "Christian party," ironically, marked the decline of traditional religious influence in society. It confirmed that a Christian ethic was no longer shared by all in public life; rather, Christians were merely one more partisan pressure group competing with others in the political arena for the allegiance of the American electorate.[79] Ely's proposal underscored conservative Protestant consternation with the increasing secularization of public life and tested the constitutional limits of efforts by religious citizens to regain political dominance through the electoral process.

Joseph Story's Commentaries on the Constitution. Few jurists have had a more profound influence on American constitutional law than Joseph Story (1779–1845), a prolific legal commentator, Harvard's first Dane Professor of Law, and associate justice of the U.S. Supreme Court. Story's legal acumen was recognized early, and in 1811, when he was at the tender age of thirty-two, President James Madison appointed him to the high court. His opinions and legal commentaries, written during a distinguished thirty-three-year tenure on the bench, shaped the thinking of generations of lawyers. His three-volume *Commentaries on the Constitution of the United States*, published in 1833, remains a standard treatise on the U.S. Constitution. His treatments of both the Article VI religious test ban and the First Amendment religion guarantees have been frequently cited by courts and commentators as an early authoritative interpretation of these provisions.

The Article VI religious test ban, the great justice opined, was a powerful barrier against religious establishments and intolerance. It was, he wrote,

> not introduced merely for the purpose of satisfying the scruples of many respectable persons, who feel an invincible repugnance to any religious test, or affirmation. It had a higher object; to cut off for ever every pretence of any alliance between church and state in the national government. The framers of the constitution were fully sensible of the dangers from this source, marked out in the history of other ages and countries; and not wholly unknown to our own. They knew, that bigotry was unceasingly vigilant in its stratagems, to secure to itself an exclusive ascendancy over the human mind; and that intolerance was ever ready to arm itself with all the terrors of the civil power to exterminate those, who doubted its dogmas, or resisted its infallibility.... It is easy to foresee, that without some prohibition of religious tests, a successful sect, in our country, might, by once possessing power, pass testlaws, which would secure to themselves a monopoly of all the offices of trust and profit, under the national government.[80]

Turning his attention to the First Amendment religion guarantees, Story noted the importance most Americans attach to religion's public role:

> Now, there will probably be found few persons in this, or any other Christian country, who would deliberately contend, that it was unreasonable, or unjust to foster and encourage the Christian religion generally, as a matter of sound policy, as well as of revealed truth. In fact, every American colony, from its foundation down to the revolution, with the exception of Rhode Island, (if, indeed, that state be an exception,) did openly, by the whole course of its laws and institutions, support and sustain, in some form, the Christian religion; and almost invariably gave a peculiar sanction to some of its fundamental doctrines. And this has continued to be the case in some of the states down to the present period, without the slightest suspicion, that it was against the principles of public law, or republican liberty. Indeed, in a republic, there would seem to be a peculiar propriety in viewing the Christian religion, as the great basis, on which it must rest for its support and permanence, if it be, what it has ever been deemed by its truest friends to be, the religion of liberty.[81]

In two subsequent sections, perhaps the most quoted in the entire *Commentaries*, Story reflected on the role of Christianity in the American constitutional republic.

> Probably at the time of the adoption of the constitution, and of the amendment to it, now under consideration, the general, if not the universal, sentiment in America was, that Christianity ought to receive encouragement from the state, so far as was not incompatible with the private rights of conscience, and the freedom of religious worship. An attempt to level all religions, and to make it a matter of state policy to hold all in utter indifference, would have created universal disapprobation, if not universal indignation. . . .
>
> The real object of the amendment was, not to countenance, much less to advance Mahometanism, or Judaism, or infidelity, by prostrating Christianity; but to exclude all rivalry among Christian sects, and to prevent any national ecclesiastical establishment, which should give to an hierarchy the exclusive patronage of the national government. It thus cut off the means of religious persecution, (the vice and pest of former ages,) and of the subversion of the rights of conscience in matters of religion, which had been trampled upon almost from the days of the Apostles to the present age.[82]

Story concluded by emphasizing that the First Amendment was designed to deny the national regime all jurisdiction over the subject of religion and to preserve state power in this area. The purpose of the First Amendment, he wrote, was "to exclude from the national government all power to act upon the subject [of religion]." He further noted that "the whole power over the subject of religion is left exclusively to the state governments, to be acted upon according to their own sense of justice, and the state constitutions."[83]

Conclusion

There was no national consensus in the days following ratification of the Constitution and Bill of Rights on the scope and application of the Article VI religious test ban and the First Amendment prohibition on laws "respecting an establishment of religion." The public pronouncements and controversies profiled in this chapter cast light on how Americans in the early republic, representing diverse interests and perspectives, were not only interpreting the Article VI and First Amendment prohibitions but also defining key terms and framing the debate on church–state issues. These pronouncements and controversies reveal two distinct and popular views on the appropriate relationship between religion and politics firmly entrenched in American political thought. On the one hand, there was the view endorsed by religious traditionalists that religion provided an indispensable support for civic virtue, social order, and political prosperity. This was a compelling reason, many thought, for civil society to nurture and encourage public assistance for religion and religious institutions. Not all who embraced this view, it should be emphasized, advocated a formal, exclusive ecclesiastical establishment, much less a theocracy, although some religious traditionalists agitated for an official state church. On the other hand, there was a separationist perspective holding that true religion flourished when it relied on the voluntary support of believers and eschewed all corrupting endorsements of the civil state. Neither religion nor the state, it was argued, was dependent on an alliance with the other in order to survive and prosper. Many who held this view denied that they were hostile to religion or thought it unimportant. Rather, they maintained that religion was too important to subject it in any way to governmental control. There were, no doubt, a few extremists who advocated a secular order because they were hostile to traditional orthodox Christianity and thought it incompatible with a rational, enlightened polity.

These very different perspectives informed how early Americans viewed the propriety and constitutionality of religious proclamations, Sunday mail, and the like. Although some liberals and secularists, for example, thought suspending postal business on Sunday constituted a dangerous religious establishment, religious traditionalists thought that requiring Sunday postal service and, thereby, practically excluding the devout Sabbatarian from post office employment, was a de facto religious (or "irreligious") test. And both sides thought the other's position threatened the rights of conscience. The conflicting constitutional claims articulated in this one example foreshadowed how difficult and complex religious disputes would become. Americans were becoming highly sensitive to religion's place in public life and its impact on an increasingly diverse population.

The underlying themes of church–state debate have changed remarkably little in two centuries. Twenty-first-century Americans are struck by how similar church–state debates and themes in the early republic are to those in their own time. This survey of several church–state concerns early in the nation's history casts light not only on the past but also, it is hoped, on the future place of, and role for, religion in the American constitutional regime.

Notes

1. For useful analyses of the meaning of "an establishment of religion" in the late colonial and early national periods, see Thomas J. Curry, *The First Freedoms: Church and State in America to the Passage of the First Amendment* (New York: Oxford University Press, 1986); Donald L. Drakeman, *Church, State and Original Intent* (New York: Cambridge University Press, 2010); Leonard W. Levy, *The Establishment Clause: Religion and the First Amendment*, 2d ed. (Chapel Hill: University of North Carolina Press, 1994).

2. *Journals of the Continental Congress, 1774–1789*, ed. Worthington C. Ford et al. (Washington, DC: U.S. Government Printing Office, 1904–1937), 32:74 (February 21, 1787).

3. The free exercise and nonestablishment of religion provisions were incorporated into the "liberties" protected by the Fourteenth Amendment's Due Process Clause in Cantwell v. Connecticut, 310 U.S. 296, 303 (1940) and Everson v. Board of Education, 330 U.S. 1, 15 (1947), respectively.

4. *The Debates in the Several State Conventions, on the Adoption of the Federal Constitution*, ed. Jonathan Elliot, 2d ed., 5 vols. (Washington, DC: Printed for the Editor, 1836), 1:148; *The Records of the Federal Convention of 1787*, ed. Max Farrand, 3 vols. (New Haven, CT: Yale University Press, 1911), 3:599. This brief history of the religious test ban is adapted from Daniel L. Dreisbach, "The Constitution's Forgotten Religion Clause: Reflections on the Article VI Religious Test Ban," *Journal of Church and State* 38 (1996): 261–95.

5. Farrand, *Records*, 3:122.

6. Ibid., 2:335, 342.

7. Elliot, *Debates*, 5:498; Farrand, *Records*, 2:461, 468.

8. Luther Martin, *Genuine Information* (1787), reprinted in Farrand, *Records*, 3:227; Elliot, *Debates*, 1:385–86.

9. A Landholder [Oliver Ellsworth], To the Landholders and Farmers, Number VII, *Connecticut Courant* (Hartford), December 17, 1787, 1.

10. Speech of Oliver Wolcott (CT), in Elliot, *Debates*, 2:202 (January 9, 1788).

11. Speech of Edmund Randolph (VA), in Elliot, *Debates*, 3:204 (June 10, 1788).

12. See Speech of James Iredell (NC), in Elliot, *Debates*, 4:196 (July 30, 1788). See also Elliot, *Debates*, 4:194 ("Happily, no sect here is superior to another. As long as this is the case, we shall be free from those persecutions and distractions with which other countries have been torn."); Speech of Richard Dobbs Spaight (NC), in Elliot, *Debates*, 4:208 (July 30, 1788) ("No sect is preferred to another. Every man has a right to worship the Supreme Being in the manner he thinks proper. No test is required. All men of equal capacity and integrity, are equally eligible to offices. . . . A test would enable the prevailing sect to persecute the rest.").

13. A number of state constitutions and declarations of rights drafted between the time of independence in 1776 and the framing of the U.S. Constitution in 1787 required religious oaths (or otherwise imposed religious tests) on civic officers while affirming the rights of conscience and religious liberty and prohibiting religious establishments. See, e.g., the North Carolina Constitution of 1776: Declaration of Rights, Article XIX ("That all men have a natural and unalienable right to worship Almighty God according to the dictates of their own consciences."); Constitution, Article XXXIV ("That there shall be no establishment of any one religious church or denomination in this State, in preference to any other; neither shall any person, on any pretence whatsoever, be compelled to attend any place of worship contrary to his own faith or judgment, nor be obliged to pay, for the purchase of any glebe, or the building of any house of worship, or for the maintenance of any minister or ministry, contrary to what he believes right, or has voluntarily and personally engaged to perform; but all persons shall be at liberty to exercise their own mode of worship."); Article XXXII ("That no person who shall deny the being of God, or the truth of the Protestant religion, or the divine authority of either the Old or New Testaments, or who shall hold religious principles incompatible with the freedom and safety of the State, shall be capable of holding any office, or place of trust or profit, in the civil department, within this State."). See also similar provisions in the New Jersey Constitution of 1776, Delaware Constitution of 1776, Massachusetts Constitution of 1780, and New Hampshire Constitution of 1784. See further chapter 3 by Mark McGarvie.

14. For further discussion on the origin and legislative history of the Article VI religious test ban, see Gerard V. Bradley, "The No Religious Test Clause and the Constitution of Religious Liberty: A Machine That Has Gone of Itself," *Case Western Reserve Law Review* 37 (1987): 674–747; Dreisbach, "The Constitution's Forgotten Religion Clause: Reflections on the Article VI Religious Test Ban," 261–95.

15. See the detailed account of its formation in chapter 8 by Carl Esbeck.

16. See, e.g., Anonymous [William Loughton Smith], *The Pretensions of Thomas Jefferson to the Presidency Examined; and the Charges against John Adams Refuted*, Part I (Philadelphia, October 1796), 37–38.

17. George Washington, Farewell Address, September 19, 1796, in *The Writings of George Washington*, ed. John C. Fitzpatrick, 37 vols. (Washington, DC: U.S. Government Printing Office, 1931–1940), 35:229.

18. GW to the Synod of the Dutch Reformed Church in North America, [October 1789], in Fitzpatrick, *Writings of George Washington*, 30:432 n. 33. See also GW to the Clergy of Different Denominations Residing in and near the City of Philadelphia, [March 3, 1797], in Fitzpatrick, *Writings of George Washington*, 35:416.

19. The notion that religion and morality are indispensable to civic virtue, social order, and political prosperity in a system of republican self-government was commonplace in the literature of the founding. It was espoused by Americans from diverse religious and intellectual traditions, walks of life, and regions of the country. See, e.g., John Adams' remark in 1776: "Statesmen, my dear Sir, may plan and speculate for liberty, but it is religion and morality alone, which can establish the principles upon which freedom can securely stand. The only foundation of a free constitution is pure virtue." John Adams to Zabdiel Adams, June 21, 1776, in *The Works of John Adams, Second President of the United States*, ed. Charles Francis Adams (Boston: Little, Brown and Co., 1854), 9:401. On October 11, 1782, the Continental Congress issued a Thanksgiving Day Proclamation, authored by the Presbyterian clergyman and signer of the Declaration of Independence, John Witherspoon, declaring that "the practice of true and undefiled religion . . . is the great foundation of public prosperity and national happiness." Thanksgiving Proclamation of October 11, 1782, in Ford et al., *Journals of the Continental Congress*, 23:647. Benjamin Rush, another venerated signer of the Declaration of Independence, opined in 1786: "the only foundation for a useful education in a republic is to be laid in RELIGION. Without this [religion], there can be no virtue, and without virtue there can be no liberty, and liberty is the object and life of all republican governments." Benjamin Rush, *A Plan for the Establishment of Public Schools and the Diffusion of Knowledge in Pennsylvania* (Philadelphia: Thomas Dobson, 1786), 15. David Ramsay, physician, delegate to the Continental Congress, and the first major historian of the American Revolution, wrote in 1789: "Remember that there can be no political happiness without liberty; that there can be no liberty without morality; and that there can be no morality without religion." David Ramsay, *The History of the American Revolution* (London, 1790), 2:356. In an often-cited 1799 case, the Maryland General Court opined: "Religion is of general and public concern, and on its support depend, in great measure, the peace and good order of government, the safety and happiness of the people." Runkel v. Winemiller, 4 Harris & McHenry, 429, 450 (Gen. Ct. Oct. Term 1799). Writing in 1799 with the anti-Christian impulses of the French Revolution in mind and employing imagery reminiscent of Washington's Farewell Address, the Virginian Patrick Henry stated: "the great pillars of all government and of social life . . . [are] virtue, morality, and religion. This is the armor, my friend, and this alone, that renders us invincible. These are the tactics we should study. If we lose these, we are conquered, fallen indeed." Patrick Henry

to Archibald Blair, January 8, 1799, in *Patrick Henry: Life, Correspondence and Speeches*, ed. William Wirt Henry (New York: Charles Scribner's Sons, 1891), 2:592. Charles Carroll of Maryland, a Roman Catholic and signer of the Declaration of Independence, remarked: "without morals a republic cannot subsist any length of time; they therefore who are decrying the Christian religion, whose morality is so sublime & pure . . . are undermining the solid foundation of morals, the best security for the duration of free governments." Charles Carroll of Carrollton to James McHenry, November 4, 1800, in Bernard C. Steiner, *The Life and Correspondence of James McHenry* (Cleveland, OH: Burrows Bros., 1907), 475. John Adams wrote in an 1811 letter to Benjamin Rush: "religion and virtue are the only foundations, not only of republicanism and of all free government, but of social felicity under all governments and in all the combinations of human society." John Adams to Benjamin Rush, August 28, 1811, in Charles Francis Adams, *Works of John Adams*, 9:636. See further chapter 2 by Michael McConnell and chapter 7 by Derek Davis.

20. Washington, Farewell Address, September 19, 1796, in Fitzpatrick, *Writings of George Washington*, 35:229.

21. See further John Witte Jr., "One Public Religion, Many Private Religions: John Adams and the 1780 Massachusetts Constitution," in *The Founders on God and Government*, ed. Daniel L. Dreisbach, Mark D. Hall, and Jeffry H. Morrison (Lanham, MD: Rowman Littlefield, 2004), 23–52.

22. Washington was not alone in reaching this conclusion. John Witherspoon, signer of the Declaration of Independence and president of the College of New Jersey at Princeton, similarly opined: "That he is the best friend to American liberty, who is most sincere and active in promoting true and undefiled religion, and who sets himself with the greatest firmness to bear down profanity and immorality of every kind. Whoever is an avowed enemy to God, I scruple not to call him an enemy to his country." John Witherspoon, *The Dominion of Providence over the Passions of Men: A Sermon Preached at Princeton, on the 17th of May, 1776, Being the General Fast Appointed by the Congress through the United Colonies* (Philadelphia: R. Aitken, 1776), reprinted in *Political Sermons of the American Founding Era, 1730–1805*, ed. Ellis Sandoz (Indianapolis, IN: Liberty Press, 1991), 554.

23. Jefferson, *Notes on the State of Virginia*, Query XVII, in *The Writings of Thomas Jefferson*, ed. Andrew A. Lipscomb and Albert Ellery Bergh, 20 vols. (Washington, DC: Thomas Jefferson Memorial Association, 1905), 2:221. Critics saw evidence of Jefferson's infidelity and atheism in a host of other statements in the *Notes on Virginia*, including his expressed doubts about the biblical account of a universal deluge (Query VI); reflections on biological differences between the races, thereby allegedly denying the common origin of mankind in Adam (Query XIV); and reservations about placing the Bible in the hands of immature school children (Query XIV).

24. *Gazette of the United States*, September 11, 1800, 2. This question was posed repeatedly by the *Gazette* in the course of the election season.

25. Timothy Dwight, *The Duty of Americans, at the Present Crisis* (New Haven, CT: Thomas and Samuel Green, 1798), in Sandoz, *Political Sermons*, 1382.

26. [William Linn], *Serious Considerations on the Election of a President: Addressed to the Citizens of the United States* (New York: John Furman, 1800), 4.

27. Ibid., 28, 20, 26.

28. [John Mitchell Mason], *The Voice of Warning, to Christians, on the Ensuing Election of a President of the United States* (New York: G. F. Hopkins, 1800), in Sandoz, *Political Sermons*, 1452, 1462, 1465 (emphasis in original).

29. Timoleon [Tunis Wortman], *A Solemn Address, to Christians & Patriots, Upon the Approaching Election of a President of the United States: In Answer to a Pamphlet, Entitled, "Serious Considerations," &c.* (New York: David Denniston, 1800), in Sandoz, *Political Sermons*, 1499.

30. Ibid., 1488.

31. Grotius [DeWitt Clinton], *A Vindication of Thomas Jefferson; against the Charges Contained in a Pamphlet Entitled, "Serious Considerations," &c.* (New York: David Denniston, 1800), 34.

32. [Linn], *Serious Considerations on the Election of a President*, 28. See also [Mason], *The Voice of Warning to Christians*, in Sandoz, *Political Sermons*, 1467 ("It belongs essentially to the freedom of election, to refuse my vote to any candidate for reasons of conscience, of state, of predilection, or for no reason at all but my own choice.").

33. On the genesis of these provisions in the Continental Congress, see chapter 7 by Derek Davis.

34. "Proclamation for a National Fast," March 6, 1799, in Charles Francis Adams, *Works of John Adams*, 9:172–74.

35. John Adams to Benjamin Rush, June 12, 1812, in *The Spur of Fame: Dialogues of John Adams and Benjamin Rush, 1805–1813*, ed. John A. Schutz and Douglass Adair (San Marino, CA: Huntington Library, 1966), 224.

36. Thomas Jefferson to Messrs. Nehemiah Dodge, Ephraim Robbins, and Stephen S. Nelson, a Committee of the Danbury Baptist Association in the State of Connecticut, January 1, 1802, in The Papers of Thomas Jefferson (Manuscript Division, Library of Congress), Series 1, Box 89, December 2, 1801–January 1, 1802.

37. Jefferson to Levi Lincoln, January 1, 1802, in The Papers of Thomas Jefferson (Manuscript Division, Library of Congress), Series 1, Box 89, December 2, 1801–January 1, 1802.

38. See, e.g., Marsh v. Chambers, 463 U.S. 783, 807 (1983) (Brennan, J., dissenting); Lee v. Weisman, 505 U.S. 577, 622–24 (1992) (Souter, J., concurring).

39. *Report of the Committee of Revisors Appointed by the General Assembly of Virginia in MDCCLXXVI* (Richmond, VA: Dixon & Holt, 1784), 59–60; *The Papers of Thomas Jefferson*, ed. Julian P. Boyd et al., 37 vols. to date (Princeton, NJ: Princeton University Press, 1950-), 2:556. This bill was part of a legislative package in Virginia's revised code that included Jefferson's "Bill for Establishing Religious Freedom" and "Bill for Punishing Disturbers of Religious Worship and Sabbath Breakers." All three bills were apparently framed by Jefferson and sponsored in the Virginia legislature by James Madison. See Daniel L. Dreisbach, "A New Perspective on Jefferson's Views on Church–State Relations: The Virginia Statute for Establishing Religious Freedom in Its Legislative Context," *American Journal of Legal History* 35 (1991): 172–204. See further chapter 6 by Ralph Ketcham.

40. "Proclamation Appointing a Day of Thanksgiving and Prayer," November 11, 1779, in Boyd et al., *Papers of Jefferson*, 3:177–79.

41. *Report of the Committee of Revisors*, 60; Boyd et al., *Papers of Jefferson*, 2:556.

42. See generally Daniel L. Dreisbach, *Thomas Jefferson and the Wall of Separation between Church and State* (New York: New York University Press, 2002). The discussion above on the election of 1800 and religious proclamations is adapted from this book. See further chapter 1 by Jeremy Gunn and chapter 12 by Kent Greenawalt.

43. Andrew Jackson to the Synod of the Reformed Church, June 12, 1832, in *Correspondence of Andrew Jackson*, ed. John Spencer Bassett (Washington, DC: Carnegie Institution of Washington, 1929), 4:447.

44. See remarks of Henry Clay in the U.S. Senate on June 27 and 28, 1832, in *The Papers of Henry Clay*, ed. Robert Seager II (Lexington: University Press of Kentucky, 1984), 8:545–46.

45. *An Inquiry into the Moral and Religious Character of the American Government* (New York: Wiley and Putnam, 1838), 10–11.

46. "An Act Regulating the Post-Office Establishment," *Statutes at Large*, II, sec. 9, 592, at 595 (April 30, 1810).

47. William Addison Blakely, ed., *American State Papers Bearing on Sunday Legislation*, rev. ed. (Washington, DC: Religious Liberty Association, 1911), 182–86.

48. "An Act to Reduce into One the Several Acts Establishing and Regulating the Post-Office Department," *Statutes at Large*, IV, sec. 11, 102, at 105 (March 3, 1825).

49. A House committee report on the issue commented: "It is believed that the history of legislation in this country affords no instance in which a stronger expression has been made, if regard be had to the numbers, the wealth or the intelligence of the petitioners." U.S. Congress, House, *Report from the Committee on the Post Office and Post Roads*, 20th Cong., 2d sess., House Rep. No. 65 (February 3, 1829); reprinted in *American State Papers. Documents, Legislative and Executive, of the Congress of the United States*, Class VII, *Post Office Department* (Washington, DC: Gales and Seaton, 1834), 212 [hereinafter *American State Papers*].

50. U.S. Congress, Senate, 20th Cong., 2d sess., *Register of Debates in Congress* (January 19, 1829), 5:42.

51. U.S. Congress, Senate, *Report on Stopping the United States Mail, and Closing the Post-Offices on Sunday, January 19, 1829*, 20th Cong., 2d sess., Senate Doc. No. 46 (January 19, 1829); reprinted in *American State Papers*, Class VII, 211–12.

52. U.S. Congress, House, *Report of the Minority of the Committee on Post Offices and Post Roads, to Whom the Memorials Were Referred for Prohibiting the Transportation of the Mails, and the Opening of Post Offices, on Sundays*, 21st Cong., 1st sess., House Rep. No. 271 (March 5, 1830); reprinted in *American State Papers*, Class VII, 231. See also *Speech of Mr. Frelinghuysen, On the Subject of Sunday Mails*, U.S. Congress, Senate, 21st Cong., 1st sess., *Register of Debates in Congress* (May 8, 1830), vol. 6, Appendix, 1–4. This speech was published and distributed widely throughout the country.

53. For a summary of the arguments in support of and opposition to Sunday mail, see John G. West Jr., *The Politics of Revelation and Reason: Religion and Civic Life in the New Nation* (Lawrence: University Press of Kansas, 1996), 137–70; James R. Rohrer, "Sunday Mails and the Church–State Theme in Jacksonian America," *Journal of the Early Republic* 7 (1987): 53–74. For further discussion on the Sunday mail controversy, see Harmon Kingsbury, *The Sabbath: A Brief History of Laws, Petitions, Remonstrances and Reports, with Facts and Arguments, Relating to the Christian Sabbath* (New York: Robert Carter, 1840); Richard R. John, "Taking Sabbatarianism Seriously: The Postal System, the Sabbath, and the Transformation of American Political Culture," *Journal of the Early Republic* 10 (1990): 517–67.

54. *Western Intelligencer*, February 28, 1829, as quoted in Rohrer, "Sunday Mails and the Church–State Theme," 68.

55. "The Memorial of the Undersigned, Citizens of Philadelphia, in the State of Pennsylvania," reprinted in *American State Papers*, Class VII, 234.

56. Jasper Adams, *The Relation of Christianity to Civil Government in the United States*, 2d ed. (Charleston, SC: A. E. Miller, 1833), 33–34, note D.

57. The Reverend Ely was pastor of Old Pine Street Church in Philadelphia. He also served as moderator of the Presbyterian General Assembly in the United States and was an influential figure in the American Sunday School Union. He wrote several popular theological treatises and for many years edited the weekly publication the *Philadelphian*. See "Notes: The Rev. Dr. Ezra Stiles Ely," *Journal of the Presbyterian Historical Society* 2 (September 1904): 321–24.

58. Ezra Stiles Ely, *The Duty of Christian Freemen to Elect Christian Rulers: A Discourse Delivered on the Fourth of July, 1827, in the Seventh Presbyterian Church, in Philadelphia* (Philadelphia: William F. Geddes, 1828).

59. Ibid., 8 (emphasis in original).

60. Ibid., 11. Ely candidly acknowledged that he would choose to be ruled by "a sound Presbyterian," but he "would prefer a religious and moral man, of any one of the truly Christian sects, to any man destitute of religious principle and morality." "Let a civil ruler, then, be a Christian *of some sort,* . . . rather than not a Christian of any denomination." Ibid., 13 (emphasis in original).

61. Ibid., 8.

62. Ibid., 4 (emphasis in original).

63. Ibid., 6.

64. Ibid., 7 (emphasis in original).

65. Ibid., 14.

66. Ibid., 9, 10 (emphasis in original).

67. Ibid., 14.

68. For a description of the opposition aroused by Ely's proposal, see Joseph L. Blau, "The Christian Party in Politics," *Review of Religion* 11 (1946–47): 26–35; Arthur M. Schlesinger Jr., *The Age of Jackson* (Boston: Little, Brown and Co., 1945), 136–40.

69. This was the theme of Thomas Cooper's compilation of documents and analysis of the "[p]lans and schemes of the orthodox Clergy of the Presbyterian denomination in particular [i.e., the "Christian party in politics"], to acquire a sectarian influence over the political government of the Country and all seminaries of education." [Thomas Cooper], *The Case of Thomas Cooper, M.D. President of the South Carolina College. Submitted to the Legislature and the People of South Carolina. December 1831,* 2d ed. (Columbia, SC: Times and Gazette Office, 1832), Appendix I, 1.

70. William Morse, *An Oration Delivered before the Citizens of Nantucket, July 4, 1829, Being the Fifty-third Anniversary of the Declaration of the Independence of the United States of America* (Boston: Putnam & Hunt, 1829), 12.

71. "Union of Church and State," *The Christian Intelligencer and Eastern Chronicle,* October 5, 1827; *Olive Branch,* October 27, 1827.

72. Zelotes Fuller, *The Tree of Liberty. An Address in Celebration of the Birth of Washington, Delivered at the Second Universalist Church in Philadelphia, Sunday Morning, February 28, 1830,* reprinted in *Cornerstones of Religious Freedom in America,* ed. Joseph L. Blau, rev. ed. (New York: Harper Torchbooks, 1964), 134–36 (emphasis in original).

73. See Ely, *Duty of Christian Freemen,* 5.

74. Ibid., 15.

75. Ibid., 6.

76. Ibid., 10.

77. Ibid., 12.

78. Albert Post, *Popular Freethought in America, 1825–1850* (New York: Columbia University Press, 1943), 213.

79. A number of commentators have noted a connection between the anti-Sunday mail campaign and Ely's "Christian party." See, e.g., Rohrer, "Sunday Mails and the Church–State Theme," 64–65; Bertram Wyatt-Brown, "Prelude to Abolitionism: Sabbatarian Politics and the Rise of the Second Party System," *Journal of American History* 58 (1971): 323–41.

80. Joseph Story, *Commentaries on the Constitution of the United States* (Boston: Hilliard, Gray, and Co., 1833), 3:705, 709, sec. 1841, 1843.

81. Ibid., 3:724–25, sec. 1867.

82. Ibid., 3:726, 728, sec. 1868, 1871.

83. Ibid., 3:730–31, sec. 1873.

10

The "Second Disestablishment"

THE EVOLUTION OF NINETEENTH-CENTURY UNDER-
STANDINGS OF SEPARATION OF CHURCH AND STATE

Steven K. Green

The traditional interpretation of church–state relations in the nineteenth century is ably represented in the work of religious historian Robert T. Handy. Handy entitled his seminal book about the century *A Christian America*, and the book's subtitle—*Protestant Hopes and Historical Realities*—made clear that a "Christian America" during that time meant a "Protestant America." Handy was not alone in this assessment: Religious historians have long documented how an informal "Protestant establishment" existed in nineteenth-century America, one in which a Protestant ethos held sway over the nation's culture and institutions (attributed, in part, to the religious revivals of the Second Great Awakening). The paradox was that this informal establishment occurred despite having followed the nation's political disestablishment of the 1770–1790s. Handy acknowledged the paradox, noting how "[i]n many ways, the middle third of the nineteenth century was more of a 'Protestant Age' than was the colonial period with its established churches." Driving home this thesis, Handy titled a later book about the evolving church–state situation at the close of the century as an "Undermined Establishment." This late century transition helped usher in a "second disestablishment" beginning in the 1930s, one represented by a cultural disestablishment involving the gradual secularization of the society and a constitutional disestablishment brought about by the separationist holdings of the modern Supreme Court.[1]

This accepted accounting of the nineteenth century as an era of Protestant dominance is well-deserved in many ways. American culture and its institutions clearly reflected an evangelical Protestant perspective, and Handy may have been correct that the relations between church and state were never closer than during the nineteenth century. Regrettably, this accounting risks portraying the century as essentially static with respect to popular attitudes and legal interpretations about church–state relationships. An even greater concern about this accounting is that it sets up a conflict between the nineteenth century and the "first disestablishment" of the founding period. Any student of American church and state appreciates the tension between the accepted interpretations of the two eras: By one account, the founders, led by Thomas Jefferson and James Madison, established a regime of church–state separation that abolished religious preferences and establishments. By another account, the nineteenth century was a period of an informal Protestant establishment in which the government and legal system favored and promoted evangelical Protestantism through Sabbath and sumptuary laws and Protestant Bible reading in the public schools.

This dichotomy forces the reader to make a false choice: (1) reconsider the founders' commitment to church–state separation and/or dispute whether it accurately represented contemporary views; (2) explain why later generations turned away from their earlier commitment to church–state separation; or (3) live with the apparent inconsistency by engaging in "law office" historical selectivity. For some fifty years after *Everson v. Board of Education* (1947), the modern U.S. Supreme Court took the last option: emphasizing the founders' commitment to church–state separation while ignoring the later inconsistencies. More recently, revisionist historians have chosen the first option: asserting that the attitudes of the nineteenth century more accurately represent early understandings of church–state relations. Other revisionists have disputed the separationist bona fides of Jefferson and Madison or claimed that the two men were outliers in their views. Sadly, few people have attempted to reconcile the seeming inconsistencies between the first disestablishment and the so-called Protestant establishment of subsequent generations.[2]

There is a way to reconcile the two periods. First, one must resist applying the same thick separationist gloss on the founding period that the Supreme Court painted in its 1947 *Everson v. Board of Education* decision. Justice Hugo Black's opinion was written with the best of historical intentions, seeking to give due recognition of the incomparable contribution of Jefferson and Madison to developing notions of church–state relations.[3] The problem with that analysis was that it failed to give adequate attention to the diversity of views concerning disestablishment and religious liberty that existed during the founding period, views that were dynamic and unfolding. Unquestionably, the changes that occurred between 1775 and 1790 were truly remarkable: In 1775, nine of thirteen colonies maintained religious establishments with assessments systems and legal preferences based on religious affiliation. Only fifteen years later, a majority of states (eleven of fourteen) had either abolished religious assessments or declined to adopt legal mechanisms necessary for their operation, causing the practices to die out. The emerging consensus was that tax assessments for churches and "public worship" were inconsistent with rights of conscience and beyond the authority of government. A majority of states also liberalized their religious prerequisites for civic participation.

However, three or four New England states (depending on the factors one counts) bucked this trend by retaining their "mild and equitable" establishments, insisting that assessments were consistent with republican principles and rights of conscience.[4] For example, in 1795 Connecticut Judge Zephaniah Swift defended his state's system of tax assessments for registered Protestant churches while insisting that:

> yet here is a compleat renunciation of the doctrine, that an ecclesiastical establishment is necessary to the support of civil government. No sect is invested with privileges superior to another. No creed is established, and no test act excluded any person from holding any offices in government.[5]

Judge Swift, like many in New England, saw no inconsistency between religious liberty and the public patronage of religion. In fact, Swift, like most supporters of the New England Standing Order, would have taken umbrage over accusations that their assessment system represented "an establishment," a term people considered to be a form of opprobrium.[6]

As Judge Swift's statement indicates, understandings of disestablishment in the early national period meant something quite different from the concept today. The chief concerns of the period were that one Protestant denomination might receive preferential treatment over another and that people could suffer civil disabilities on account of their religious beliefs. Government regulation and funding of religious and other private entities was practically nonexistent, and public education was in its nascent stage. The issues that defined the church–state conflicts of the twentieth century had yet to materialize. Additionally, people's willingness to support the political disestablishment of the 1770–1790s—including the abolition of religious tax assessments—did not mean that they necessarily surrendered their assumptions about the need for a mutually reinforcing relationship between religion and the government. Noncoercive government acknowledgements of religion, through mechanisms such as thanksgiving proclamations and election-day sermons, remained the common practice, though it is important to recognize that they took place during an era of significantly less religious diversity than today. Also, all states, to varying degrees, retained religious qualifications for office-holding and oath-taking (albeit much less restrictive than under the colonial regimes), and religiously based behavioral laws remained on the books. All of this patronage of religion occurred at the same time as state legislatures were going through the steps of political disestablishment.[7]

In essence, despite the speed of the first disestablishment, understandings of church–state separation developed incrementally during the founding period, not holistically or completely. Few people had the comprehensive and systematic vision of Jefferson and Madison. This does not mean that people of the founding generation considered disestablishment to be an insignificant achievement. On the contrary, people across America viewed religious liberty as an indispensable right, though a still unfolding concept—that the perfect relationship between church and state had yet to be achieved. As the Pennsylvanian "Old Whig" wrote during the debate over constitutional ratification:

> The fact is, that human nature is still the same that ever it was: the fashion indeed changes: but the seeds of superstition, bigotry and enthusiasm, are too deeply implanted in our minds, ever to be eradicated. . . . They are idiots who trust their future security to the whim of the present hour.[8]

In 1790 Pennsylvania revised its revolutionary constitution of 1776, liberalizing its religious test for office-holding, removing previous appeals to God, and adding a provision prohibiting religious establishments and preferences to any modes of worship. Noah Webster predicted that the revision was merely "a prelude to wiser measures; people are just awakening from delusion. The time will come (and may the day be near!) when all test laws, oaths of allegiance, abjuration, and partial exclusions from civil offices will be proscribed from this land of freedom."[9] Georgia, Delaware, and Vermont also underwent revisions of their revolutionary constitutions before the end of the eighteenth century, further liberalizing their church–state provisions. Disestablishment was a dynamic, ongoing process—one that would continue into the nineteenth century.[10]

Nineteenth-Century Background

Just as attitudes during the founding period were neither monolithic nor static, the same can be said for the nineteenth century. Legal, constitutional, and popular attitudes toward church–state relations were varied, dynamic, and evolving throughout the century. On one side, Baptists, deists, freethinkers, and members of the emergent Democratic-Republican party perpetuated the Jeffersonian perspective toward church–state separation, represented by the president's famous letter calling for a "wall of separation between church and state." Early Republican leaders such as New York's DeWitt Clinton and Tunis Wortman and Connecticut's Joel Barlow and Abraham Bishop pushed for greater separation between religious and civil functions.[11] They contested all forms of nonpreferential aid, support, or preferences for religion, with Worthman insisting that "the [general] establishment of christianity, is incompatible with civil freedom." The only arrangement consistent with republican principles, Wortman asserted, was "to maintain religion separate and apart from the powers of this world."[12] A quarter century later during a controversy over whether to halt mail delivery on Sundays, Kentucky senator Richard Johnson would equate Sabbath laws with a religious establishment forbidden by the First Amendment. "The framers of the constitution recognized the eternal principle that man's relation with his God is above human legislation," Johnson wrote in

1830, "and his rights of conscience [are] inalienable." Johnson asserted that "the conclusion is inevitable that the line cannot be too strongly drawn between church and state." Jacksonian Democrats and freethinkers such as Robert Dale Owen and Frances Wright would advance the Jeffersonian separationist impulse through the end of the 1830s.[13]

During this same period, America experienced a surge in evangelical belief and religious piety, facilitated by the revivals of the Second Great Awakening (1801–1830). Church membership tripled, and Protestant evangelicalism quickly became the dominant cultural expression in America, affecting popular attitudes toward church–state relations. As part of this religious transformation, evangelical leaders established moral reform societies to address social issues such as temperance, Biblical literacy, and Sabbath observance. Evangelicals such as Lyman Beecher believed a chief purpose of the reform societies was to assist the government in ensuring public piety. Reform societies would "constitute a sort of moral militia, prepared to act upon every emergency, and repel every encroachment upon the liberties and morals of the State," Beecher insisted. "[I]n a free government, moral suasion and coercion must be united." Even after New England had disestablished religion in 1833, Beecher understood the government and religion to be mutually reinforcing.[14]

At the same time, evangelicals began to redefine popular and legal understandings of disestablishment. Evangelical historians including Robert Baird, Stephen Colwell, and Benjamin Morris created, in the words of historian Jon Butler, "a myth of the American Christian past," which Butler describes as "one of the most powerful myths to inform the history of both American religion and American society." These writers asserted that in drafting the various religious liberty clauses, the nation's founders had not sought to disassociate religion from the state; rather, they had merely intended to avoid rivalry among Protestant denominations while ensuring that America remained a "Christian nation" through government patronage of a general Protestantism.[15] In a widely circulated 1832 sermon, Reverend Jasper Adams claimed that Christianity "was intended by [the founders] to be the corner stone of the social and political structures which they were founding." Adams concluded that "the people of the United states have retained the Christian religion as the foundation of their civil, legal and political institutions." Thus,

> while all others enjoy full protection in the profession of their opinions and practice, Christianity is the established religion of the nation, its institutions and usages are sustained by legal sanctions, and many of them are incorporated with the fundamental law of the country.[16]

These competing visions of church–state separation, and variations thereof, coexisted for the first third of the nineteenth century. As the influence of Protestant evangelism grew, it overpowered alternative understandings of disestablishment in the popular imagination. Evangelicalism became the dominant force in the culture.[17] Yet despite the prominence of evangelical Protestantism and its sway over public institutions and popular attitudes, Americans did not march in theological lockstep. Rather, to borrow Jon Butler's rich phrase, the antebellum period was a "spiritual hothouse" that nourished a cacophony of competing belief systems, including Mormonism, Shakerism, transcendentalism, and spiritualism, as well as less religious forms of expression such as mesmerism and utopian socialism. In later years Protestants faced competition from other faiths, spurred primarily by immigration: Catholicism, Judaism, Eastern Orthodox, and various Asian religions. Dissent from the evangelical mainstream was ever-present, and many objected to the dominant Protestant vision of a Christian nation with its limited understanding of disestablishment. Throughout much of the century, however, those voices were drowned out by the Protestant majority.[18]

Not surprisingly, many judges during the antebellum era shared the emerging evangelical worldview, which in turn affected legal attitudes toward church–state relations. Until the mid-nineteenth century, judges enforced laws prohibiting blasphemy and Sunday activities based on religious grounds while declaring that "Christianity formed part of the common law." This belief that the state had authority over religious matters affected interpretations of constitutional provisions as well. In 1824, the Pennsylvania Supreme Court rejected a claim that a prosecution for blasphemy violated the state constitution. While declaring that "complete liberty of conscience" existed in the state, the court remarked that "[n]o free government now exists in the world, unless where Christianity is acknowledged, and is the religion of the country." The state could regulate those matters that struck at Christianity's favored status. In a different blasphemy case, a New York judge wrote that in disestablishing religion, the framers of the federal and state constitutions "never meant to withdraw religion in general, and with it the best sanctions of moral and social obligation from all consideration and notice of law." Both holdings reflected a narrow view of the constraints disestablishment imposed on state governments to reinforce religious principles through the law.[19]

The most definitive statement offering a narrow interpretation of the meaning of disestablishment came from Supreme Court Justice Joseph Story, who in 1833 wrote:

> The real object of the [First] amendment was not to countenance, much less to advance, Mahometanism, or Judaism, or infidelity, by prostrating Christianity: but to exclude all rivalry among Christian sects, and to prevent any national ecclesiastical establishment which should give to a hierarchy the exclusive patronage of the national government.[20]

Under this view, the government could advance Christianity generally to the exclusion of other religions. "[I]t is impossible for those who believe in the truth of Christianity as a divine revelation to doubt that it is the especial duty of government to foster and encourage it among all the citizens and subjects," Story declared. The prohibitions of the Establishment Clause were thus limited to forbidding the establishment of one sect as the national religion.[21]

Modern-day critics of separation of church and state have frequently pointed to Justice Story as more accurately reflecting both popular and legal perspectives about the original meaning of the First Amendment than Jefferson or Madison. Story, of course, was writing fifty years after the drafting of the religion clauses, and he had no firsthand knowledge of that event. And Story was not without his own church–state proclivities: He supported the assessment system in his home state of Massachusetts to the bitter end. During the 1833 debate over abolishing Massachusetts's general assessment for religion, Story wrote his friend Reverend John Brazer that he opposed the "proposition in our Legislature to destroy the third article on the public maintenance of religion in our constitution," calling the move a "rash experiment[]." Story should not be held up as an unbiased commentator or as reflecting the founding attitudes toward church–state separation. Yet Story likely reflected (and influenced) the views of conservative and evangelical jurists of the antebellum period, many of whom concurred with his narrow view of disestablishment.[22]

Nineteenth-Century Church–State Constitutionalism

With this background in mind, several points are important to remember when considering the constitutional development of church and state during the nineteenth century.

First, nineteenth-century understandings of constitutionalism were not as formal or atomistic as they would become by the mid-twentieth century. When discussing a constitutional right or principle, nineteenth-century judges, lawyers, and public officials often would not identify a particular provision as its source. Instead, they took a more holistic and organic approach, commonly declaring the basis of a right or principle as resting in "our constitutional structure" or as inherent in the nation's "political institutions." This meant when writing or interpreting a constitutional provision, drafters and jurists were less concerned with the particular language than with the overarching principle it would reaffirm. An example of this is seen as far back as the drafting of the national religion clauses by the First Congress. In ushering the religion clauses through the House of Representatives, Madison offered multiple versions of the amendment in an effort to placate recalcitrant representatives. During the ensuing brief debate, Madison and other representatives demonstrated a high degree of flexibility as to the particular phrasing, provided the underlying principles were reinforced. As Samuel Livingston was reported to have said when he sought to cut to the chase, "he did not wish them to dwell long on the subject" of finding the perfect wording so long as the essential principles were affirmed. Still, the House was unwilling to accede to the less rigorous versions of the amendment proposed by the Senate, indicating that some language was viewed as inconsistent with the larger principles at stake. Language mattered, but the principles were of greater importance.[23]

An additional common practice in later state constitution drafting was for delegates to borrow language from the constitutions of other states. This could mean that later drafters simply applied preexisting church–state language unthinkingly; however, the limited data suggests that this was not the prevailing practice—instead, subsequent constitution drafting was purposeful and selective in nature. During the drafting of the Oregon Constitution in 1857, one delegate made the following remark that indicates the drafters gave the issue thoughtful consideration:

> The late constitutions of the western states have, step by step, tended to a more distinct separation of church and state, until the great state of Indiana, whose new constitution has been most recently framed, embraced very nearly the principle contained in this section, as reported, now under consideration.
>
> It is true this constitution goes a step farther than other constitutions on this subject, but if that step is in the right direction, and consistent with the proper development of our institutions, I see no weight in the objection that it is new. Let us take the step farther, and declare a complete divorce of church and state.[24]

Religious liberty provisions in the early state constitutions (1776–1830) commonly fell into four categories. First, all of the state constitutions (including the New England states with establishments) contained a clause protecting the free exercise of religion, usually through a clause guaranteeing a right to worship according to one's conscience. Second, most of the state constitutions outside of New England contained a "no-compelled support" clause preventing officials from assessing taxes for the support of any minister or house of worship. Next, an equal number of constitutions prohibited the state preference of (or discrimination against) any religious society or mode of worship. It was common for these last two prohibitions to appear in the same provision. And finally, a handful of the original states (four of them) prohibited the establishment of any religion or religious society, sometimes stating it was not to be in preference of any other religion. This last "nonestablishment" clause could be seen as being redundant of the second and third clauses, which may explain its less common adoption in state constitutions (though the majority of the original state constitutions preceded the federal Constitution). All of the states of the second generation—Kentucky, Tennessee, Ohio, Indiana, Mississippi, Illinois, Alabama, Maine, and Missouri—incorporated aspects of the first three categories, with approximately half also including a no-establishment clause. The Pennsylvania Constitution of 1790, widely considered to be progressive on church–state issues, was a common model for the new states, and the implication to be drawn is one of a desire to guarantee the utmost degree of religious freedom.[25]

The next generation of state constitutions (1830–1860) commonly included language containing aspects of all four elements. The Iowa Constitution of 1846 offers an example. Article I, section 3 provided that the general assembly could "make no law respecting an establishment of religion, or prohibiting the free exercise thereof; nor shall any person be compelled to attend a place of worship, pay tithes, taxes or other rates for building or repairing places of worship, or the maintenance of any minister or ministry." The succeeding section prohibited any religious test for public office or trust and any legal disqualification on account of religion.[26]

A fifth type of state constitutional provision first appeared with the Michigan Constitution of 1835. In addition to including common language that no person could be compelled to attend, erect, or support any place of worship or to pay taxes to support any teacher of religion, the drafters of the state constitution added a clause: "No money shall be drawn from the treasury for the benefit of religious societies, or theological or religious seminaries." This apparently was the first express constitutional provision prohibiting the public funding of religious institutions, including parochial schools, in any state constitution. Michigan delegates adopted the no-funding provision even though the state lacked a significant number of Catholic parochial schools at the time and had little in the way of Protestant–Catholic conflict.[27] This provision of the Michigan Constitution served as the model for similar no-funding provisions in the new constitutions of Wisconsin (1848), Indiana (1851), Ohio (1851), and Minnesota (1857). The Ohio Constitution in turn served as the model for the no-funding provision of the Kansas Constitution, adopted in 1858, and the Indiana Constitution served as the basis for a similar provision in the 1857 Oregon Constitution.[28] Turning again to the debates over the Oregon Constitution, one delegate articulated his understanding of the constitutional basis for the no-funding provision, stating he did not:

> believe that congress had any right to take the public money, contributed by the people, of all creeds and faith [sic], to pay for religious teachings. It was a violent stretch of power, and an unauthorized one. A man in this country had a right to be a Methodist, Baptist, Roman Catholic, or what else he chose, but no government had the moral right to tax all of these creeds and classes to inculcate directly or indirectly the tenets of any one of them.[29]

The minutes of the Oregon constitutional convention are bereft of statements indicating any controversy over religious school funding; the only religious controversies involved whether to allow for legislative chaplains or acknowledge the deity in the constitution preamble (both rejected). The prevailing sentiment was apparently a desire to achieve "a complete divorce of church and state."[30]

Divining a common understanding of these early constitutional provisions is all but impossible. As stated, the meaning of disestablishment to Americans from 1776 to 1865 was varied and evolving. Each of the original fourteen states (including Vermont) had its own distinct church–state history, so perspectives depended on one's local experience. Settlers of later states, migrating from the eastern states, likely carried their particular experiences with them. Other factors, such as personal religious and political leanings, affected their understandings of church–state separation. For some, disestablishment meant only the uncoupling of formal relationships, including financial support. In Connecticut, following political disestablishment in 1818, Nathaniel Taylor, a stalwart leader of the conservative Standing Order, lectured the state legislature that the abolition of the assessment system did not mean that the state could not patronize religion: "Why should not legislators, judges, magistrates of every description, with every friend of this country, uphold those institutions which are its strength and its glory? . . . Shall clamors about rights of conscience induce us to throw away Heaven's richest legacy to earth?"[31] A similarly narrow view of disestablishment is seen in a passage from the 1824 blasphemy case discussed above. In denying that the legal enforcement of a theological question led to a religious establishment, Pennsylvania Supreme Court Justice Thomas Duncan remarked that the law patronized religion only in a limited sense: "not Christianity founded on any particular religious tenets; not Christianity with an established church, and tithes and spiritual courts; but Christianity with liberty of conscience to all." For Duncan, these were the sine qua non of an establishment, but little else.[32]

For others, disestablishment meant much more. During the hard-fought presidential election of 1800, the New England Standing Order and other orthodox clergy attacked Thomas Jefferson's liberal religious beliefs, calling him a "howling atheist." Republican New York lawyer Tunis Wortman wrote a spirited defense of Jefferson, and in the process provided his understanding of the meaning of disestablishment and church–state separation. Wortman declared:

> Religion and government are equally necessary [for society], but their interests should be kept separate and distinct. No legitimate connection can ever subsist between them. Upon no plan, no system, can they become united, without endangering the purity and usefulness of both—the church will corrupt the state, and the state pollute the church.[33]

This understanding was quite different from that of Connecticut's Nathaniel Taylor. Wortman also used the term "union of church and state" as a condition to be avoided, suggesting that he made no distinction of degree between church–state "unions" and "separations."

Another advocate of an expansive view of disestablishment was Timothy Walker, judge and founder of the law school at Cincinnati College in the 1830s. Walker, an advocate for legal reform through codification, disputed that a higher "natural law" underlay American common law. He also criticized the legal enforcement of religious duties: The law "is not part of religion or ethics," Walker told his students. Those "who consider jurisprudence as looking forward into eternity" commit "an egregious error." Rather, the responsibility of the law "begins and ends with this world. It regards men only as members of civil society." Walker "rejoiced" that the government dared not interfere "between man and his Creator" and that "the blasphemous union between church and state, and the impious usurpation of Almighty jurisdiction" could "never pollute our legal annals." Walker, who had been a student of Story's at Harvard, parted from his mentor. Disestablishment meant more than preventing an official religion or preference of one Christian denomination: It denied the government and legal system all authority to act on religious matters.[34]

Still another understanding of disestablishment is found in two decisions of New York Judge John Duer in 1849 and 1850 involving challenges to testamentary bequests. Under the traditional common law rule, courts refused to uphold bequests to an "impious" entity or for an "impious" use. This practice required judges to determine the religious bona fides of a beneficiary. This had been the issue in the famous *Girard's Will* case where Daniel Webster urged the Supreme Court to overturn a bequest to a school that contained a condition that "no ecclesiastic, missionary, or minister, of any sect whatever" could teach, visit, or be otherwise associated with the school. Webster argued that the rule should be enforced because "the preservation of Christianity is one of the main ends of government. . . . Christianity, is the law of the land." The Court rejected Webster's argument.[35] In later turning back two such challenges in New York, Judge Duer declared that civil courts lacked the authority to determine whether an entity was sufficiently pious. "Under a constitution which extends the same protection to every religion and to every form and sect of religion, which establishes none and gives no preference to any, there is no possible standard by which the validity of a use as pious can be determined." For Duer, the rule conflicted with constitutional principles: To declare what was or was not a valid religion would "violate that equality between different religions and different forms and sects of religion, which the principles of our government and the provisions of our constitution are designed to secure." Disestablishment thus imposed a regime of equality under the law, not solely between Christian sects, but between religion and non-religion, while it prevented government interference in religious matters. Christianity was not "the religion of the state," Duer asserted.[36]

As the century entered its middle years, an increasing number of state judges began to dispute that Christianity formed part of the law or that the government had the authority, if not duty, to promote Christianity, as Justice Story had maintained. This transition came about through the growth of new legal fields such as contract, tort, and corporate law that gradually separated the law from its moral foundations. It also resulted from a growing recognition among judges and lawyers of the nation's expanding religious diversity. In 1853, the

Ohio Supreme Court overturned a Sunday law conviction on the ground the defendant's work activities had not caused a public disturbance. Though leaving the Sunday law in place, Justice Allen Thurman held that it "could not stand for a moment as a law of this state, if its sole foundation was the christian duty of keeping that day holy, and its sole motive to enforce the observance of the day." Drawing from the state constitution, Thurman wrote that "it follows that neither Christianity, nor any other system of religion, is part of the law of the state." "We have no union of church and state," he asserted, "nor has our government ever been vested with authority to enforce any religious observance, simply because it is religious." Separation of church and state thus barred the state from enforcing the Sunday law for religious reasons.[37] Five years later the California Supreme Court went a step further, striking down the state's Sunday law as promoting a religious purpose, the first appellate decision to do so. Chief Justice David Terry wrote that the law conflicted with the state constitution that guaranteed "not only complete toleration, but religious liberty in its largest sense—a complete separation between Church and State, and a perfect equality without distinction between all religious sects."[38] Both decisions reflect the view that church–state separation required more than the abolition of public funding and political preferences, as it also prohibited the government from patronizing Christianity generally through sympathetic legislation.

The most significant judicial examination of the meaning of church–state separation occurred in the 1869 controversy over a decision by the Cincinnati school board to abolish prayer and Bible reading in the public schools. Supporters of the religious exercises had the action nullified by a state trial court, but only over the stinging dissent of Judge Alphonzo Taft, father of the future president and chief justice. Taft wrote that the no-preference clause of the state constitution prohibited the Protestant-oriented religious exercises. To hold that Protestants "are entitled to any control in the schools . . . or that they are entitled to have their mode of worship and their Bible used in the common schools . . . is to hold to the union of Church and State, however we may repudiate and reproach the name." The state constitution afforded "absolute equality before the law, of all religious opinions and sects," he asserted. "No sect can, because it includes a majority of a community or a majority of the citizens of the State, claim any preference whatever." Taft's opinion was a bellwether, though it built on understandings of church–state separation that had been developing over the years. On appeal, the Ohio Supreme Court sided with Taft, reinstating the school board's Bible-ban. Speaking for a unanimous court, Justice John Welch wrote that the national and state constitutions had "at last solved the terrible enigma of 'church and state'" that had plagued other nations. Disestablishment meant more than simply forbidding government tax support of religion or other religious preferences: Welch declared it also meant that religious matters were "not within the purview of human government." Religious instruction in the schools was "eminently one of those interests, lying outside the true and legitimate province of government." Welch also wrote that even if the state supported Christianity only generally through its policies, it would still be "a first step in the direction of an 'establishment of religion;' and I should add, that the first step in that direction is a fatal step, because it logically involves the last step."[39]

This trend continued throughout the remainder of the nineteenth century, with judges and lawyers reading more expansive understandings of church–state separation into their state constitutions. Michigan Supreme Court Justice Thomas M. Cooley, likely the most influential legal commentator of the last quarter of the century, summed up his understanding of the various state constitutional provisions in his treatise *Constitutional Limitations*. First, pursuant to state establishment clauses, legislatures were not "at liberty to effect a union of Church and State, or to establish preferences by law in favor of any one religious persuasion or mode of worship." Even though this statement might suggest the permissibility of nonpreferential assistance for all religions, Cooley made clear that unlike what Story had maintained, this principle prohibited the state from preferring Christianity generally. Second, Cooley noted, state constitutions prohibited "[c]ompulsory support, by taxation or otherwise, of religious instruction." Such authority was "not within the sphere of government." Third, the state constitutions prohibited the compulsory "attendance upon religious worship," which Cooley interpreted broadly to prohibit the imposition of civil disabilities on account of religious belief. Finally, Cooley noted that the state constitutions prohibited restraints upon dictates of conscience and free exercise of belief. Cooley stated that this understanding of disestablishment did not prohibit the government from engaging in the "solemn recognition of a superintending Providence in public transactions," such as days of thanksgiving, but he cautioned that public affirmations were always susceptible to devolve into expressions of religious preference, which was prohibited. In summarizing, Cooley asserted that the state constitutions had "not established religious toleration merely, but religious equality," and, in that sense were "far in advance" of foreign constitutions or even attitudes that had existed at the nation's founding.[40]

These cases and commentaries reveal how, as the century progressed, judges and lawyers were increasingly open to more expansive interpretations of the religion clauses contained in the various state constitutions. As one Wisconsin supreme court justice opined in an 1890 decision striking down Bible reading in the public schools, the religious provisions of the state constitution:

> operate[d] as a perpetual bar to the state . . . from the infringement, control or interference with the individual [religious] rights of every persons. . . . We neither have nor can have in this state, under our present constitution, any statutes of toleration, nor of union, directly or indirectly, between church and state, for the simple reason that the constitution forbids all such preferences and guarantees all such rights.[41]

Understandings of religious liberty, equality, and church–state separation had come a long way since the early nineteenth century.

Separation of Church and State

Despite this expansion in legal attitudes toward disestablishment, critics of church–state separation, led by Philip Hamburger, argue that the concept of *"separation* of church and state" was foreign to most people during the founding period and the first third of the nineteenth century (absent a few die-hard Jeffersonians). Rather, the concept came into being in mid-century chiefly as a rationale for the systemic Protestant domination over Catholics in the culture. Hamburger argues that although characterizations of a "union of church and state" were common, people did not begin speaking about "separation" until the schema benefitted Protestants in their drive to maintain their hegemonic control over the nation's institutions, particularly its public schools. For Hamburger and other critics, interpretations of the federal and state constitutions as prohibiting financial aid to religious schools are based on this tarnished understanding of separation of church and state.[42]

Hamburger is correct that the phrase "separation of church and state" became a more common idiom in mid-century, and that earlier judges and legal commentators often spoke about preventing a "union of church and state." But there is little evidence that judges, lawyers, or public officials were particularly careful in their terminology or understood particular phrases to represent terms of art when they discussed concepts of religious freedom and church–state relations. Judges and commentators of the first half of the century were not conceptual sticklers as they have been accused of being. James Madison, for example, whose extensive thinking and writing on the subject provides ample opportunities for comparison, spoke at times about preventing an "exclusive" establishment, although the context clearly indicated that he was not solely criticizing systems with the preferential treatment of one denomination but also the nonpreferential assistance of religion. In a memorandum written later in his life, Madison spoke about the dangers of a "national establishment" and a "national religion," which again could be interpreted as expressing concern only about the establishing of one church or denomination. We know from his involvement in the Virginia assessment controversy some fifty years earlier that his view of disestablishment was much broader. In the same memorandum Madison went on to criticize the nonsectarian thanksgiving proclamations of George Washington and John Adams, which Madison noted could be "embraced [by] all who believed in a supreme ruler of the Universe."[43] In other writings after his retirement from public life, Madison used different phrasing to represent his understanding of disestablishment: "the total separation of the Church from the State," a "mutual independence," an "alliance or coalition between Government

& Religion," a "perfect separation between ecclesiastical and civil matters," a "direct mixture of Religion & civil Government," and a "union." Each of these phrases could conjure up a slightly different conception of church–state relations. That Madison sometimes spoke about church–state matters in various ways does not indicate an inconsistency of thought but that precise language was less important than the larger principles at stake.[44]

Also, use of the concept of "separation" to describe church and state relationships was more common during the national and antebellum period than Hamburger credits. As John Witte, Douglas Laycock, Kent Greenawalt, and Mark McGarvie have demonstrated, the idea of a "separation" between religious and civic functions and institutions predated the nineteenth century.[45] Equally significant, the phrase/concept was used in contexts not associated with the Protestant–Catholic struggle over common schooling. The above quotations from Tunis Wortman ("to maintain religion separate and apart from [the state]" (1800)), Richard Johnson (a "strongly drawn [line] between church and state" (1830)), and Chief Justice Terry ("a complete separation between Church and State" (1858)) offer three early examples. State judges used other versions of the phrase to demonstrate their understandings of disestablishment as mandated by their respective constitutions. In an 1846 case the Virginia Supreme Court overturned the judicial practice of excluding the testimony of witnesses who could not affirm a belief in God and future accountability. Speaking for the court, Justice John Scott observed that the state constitution "wholly and permanently separated 'religion, or the duty which we owe to our Creator,' from our political and civil government," and placed "all religions on a footing of perfect equality; protecting all; imposing neither burdens nor civil incapacities upon any; conferring privileges upon none."[46] In the same year, a South Carolina trial judge struck down a city Sunday ordinance, noting that "in a community where there is complete severance between Church and State, the observance of any particular day, in a religious sense, is a matter of mere ecclesiastical or religious discipline and authority, and in no way pertain[s] to the civil power or legislative authority of the State."[47] And as discussed above, the Ohio and California supreme courts employed similar language in their respective Sunday-law decisions ("[w]e have no union of church and state") ("complete separation between Church and State").[48] All of this suggests that the notion of a separation between the functions of the two institutions was widely accepted, and that like Madison, people used various terms to explain the concept.

Critics of the notion of church–state "separation" are correct that the concept became popularized during the controversy over religious exercises in public schooling and the funding of religious private schools, called the "School Question" by contemporaries. Where such criticism falls short is with the assumptions drawn from that association. Several points are important to keep in mind. First, the interrelated controversies over public school Bible reading and parochial school funding were the most visible and significant church–state issue of the century, the Mormon Question notwithstanding. The School Question controversy persisted throughout the century and affected communities across America. It should not be surprising that discussions of church–state separation would have occurred most frequently with this issue. Second, as noted above, the idea of a "separation" between religious and civic institutions predated the mid-century influx of Catholic immigrants that served as the catalyst for the ensuing Protestant–Catholic conflicts. The concept of church–state *separation* did not originate with the School Question.[49] That people used the existing concept to rally their opposition to parochial school funding (and, in some instances, legitimate their nativist leanings) does not mean that that issue defined the breadth of the concept, even in the midst of the controversy. The Sunday-law and probate cases discussed above demonstrate that judges used the idiom with various church–state issues. Finally, if one limits consideration of the concept to the nineteenth-century School Question, it is still inaccurate to associate it chiefly with Protestant efforts to subjugate Catholic interests. This last point is illustrated by the following episodes.

One of the first conflicts over the public funding of religious schooling took place in New York City in the 1820s. Two decades earlier, local philanthropists had established the Free School Society, a nonsectarian "charity" school for poor children who could not afford private instruction or attend any of the denominational charity schools. A prototype for public schools (it would later change its name to the "Public School Society"), the Society emphasized a liberal education over religious instruction, though its schools promoted nonsectarian Protestant exercises such as Bible reading, prayers, and hymn singing. Until the mid-1820s, all of the city's charity schools—those of the Free School Society and the denominational schools—received financial assistance from the state, though the Society received the bulk of public funds. Its favored position was challenged in 1822 when a fledgling Baptist school requested additional public funds to pay for a school building. The Society objected to the request in part on the basis that public funding of religious schools violated notions of church–state separation. The Society's memorial to the state legislature articulated several arguments that would serve as the basis for the emergent no-funding principle: that the grant "impose[d] a direct tax on our citizens for the support of religion" in violation of rights of conscience; that funding of religious schools would cause competition and rivalry among faiths; and that the school fund was "purely of a civil character," not to be under the control of a religious institution. "[T]he proposition that such a fund should never go into the hands of an ecclesiastical body or religious society, is presumed to be incontrovertible upon any political principle approved or established in this country, that church and state shall not be united." Although the Society's memorial did not cite directly to the New York Constitution—asserting that its claims were based on "political" principles required by the nature of republican institutions—the Society trustees viewed these principles as having a general constitutional basis. In 1824, the legislative Committee on Colleges, Academies, and Common Schools recommended that the legislature discontinue funding for religious charity schools, with its report opining "whether it is not a violation of a fundamental principle . . . to allow the funds of the State, raised by a tax on the citizens, designed for civil purposes, to be subject to the control of any religious corporation." With this episode, the funding of religious schools became a church–state issue.[50]

In 1831, a new request for a share of the New York state school fund came from two religious institutions: the Roman Catholic Orphan Asylum and the Methodist Charity School. The Public School Society again objected to the petitions, arguing that the allocation would violate notions of church–state separation. This time, the Society relied more directly on the state constitution, stating that public money could not "be diverted from support of the common schools without a *violation* of the Constitution." The purpose of the funding bar was to protect people "of every persuasion, who have conscientious scruples about paying their money for the support of any particular faith," the Society asserted.[51] The Common Council's legislative committee agreed with the Society, writing in its report that "to raise a fund by taxation, for the support of a particular sect, or every sect of Christians, [] would unhesitatingly be declared an infringement of the Constitution, and a violation of our chartered rights." If the council were to approve the funding requests, the report continued, then

> [a] fierce and uncompromising hostility will ensue, which will pave the way for the predominance of religion in political contests. The unnatural union of Church and State will then be easily accomplished—a union destructive of human happiness and subversive of civil liberty.[52]

Consistent with its earlier position, the Common Council rejected the petition of the Methodist Charity School, but then approved the request by the Catholic Orphan Asylum on the theory that the public money primarily supported the *care* of the orphans, not their education.[53]

Several points are significant from the two episodes. First, the various parties equated the funding of religious education with the public support of religious instruction or worship. The Council's committee report stated that its members could not "perceive any marked difference in principle, whether a fund be raised for the support of a particular church, or whether it be raised for the support of a school in which the doctrines of that church are taught as a part of the system of education."[54] Second, the parties perceived the issue of funding the Baptist, Catholic, and Methodist schools in constitutional terms, even though at that time the New York Constitution lacked both a no-establishment clause and a no-compelled support clause.[55] Third and most important, by denying the requests by the Baptist and Methodist schools but approving the request by the Catholic asylum, it is clear that the legislators viewed the prohibition on funding sectarian schools in generic terms. In its earlier memorial, the Society asserted that funding the Baptist school would "promote . . . private and *sectarian* interests," whereas the committee report stated that if the Council approved the funding requests, then:

> Methodist, Episcopalian, Baptist, and every other sectarian school, [would] come in for a share of this fund. . . . If all sectarian schools be admitted to the receipt of a portion of a fund sacredly appropriated to the support of common schools, it will give rise to a religious and anti-religious party, which will call into active exercise the passions and prejudices of men.[56]

The episodes also demonstrate that the origin of the no-funding rule, as a component of church–state separation, was not motivated by anti-Catholic animus. This principle that separation prohibited the funding of religious schools gained momentum as common schools were established during the antebellum period. At the same time, as addressed above, several states adopted express no-funding provisions in their constitutions, many in the absence of significant nativist or anti-Catholic activity.

Ironically—or some might say cynically—Protestant educators and public officials refused to apply the same notion of church–state separation to the public schools where Protestant-oriented values and religious doctrines were taught to children. Despite Catholic complaints about the public schools' Protestant complexion, educators believed they were avoiding indoctrination by teaching only "universal" religious principles upon which all denominations could agree. For most Protestants of the day, church–state separation prohibited the government support of *sectarian* schools, but not of *nonsectarian* ones. Educators were blind (if not hostile) to the fact that unmediated readings from the Protestant King James Bible could be considered sectarian. At least initially, courts agreed that disestablishment did not require the expulsion of nonsectarian religious exercises. In an 1853 Bible reading case arising in Maine, the state supreme court held that nonsectarian instruction was consistent with the state constitution, which mandated "that no subordination nor preference of any sect or denomination to another shall ever by established by law." Instruction into nonsectarian religious principles did not contravene disestablishment.[57]

Over time, the inconsistency in defending nonsectarian education on grounds of church–state separation led moderate Protestants to question whether nonsectarian instruction was consistent with the same principle. Even before Judge Taft's landmark opinion that unmediated Bible reading was "sectarian," some educators and Protestant leaders were calling for a consistent position. In an 1869 article at the height of the Cincinnati Bible controversy, Henry Ward Beecher, the nation's best-known Protestant minister, called for the removal of all religious exercises in the public schools. Constitutional principles required true religious equality, Beecher insisted. "It is too late to adopt the church–state doctrine." Around the same time, influential columnist Samuel Spear, an ordained Presbyterian minister, also asserted that church–state separation meant that public schools should be entirely secular and that no tax money should be used for religious education of any kind. "Those who drew the plan of our National Government built the system upon the principle that religion and civil government were to be kept entirely distinct," Spear wrote.[58] Beecher and Spear were joined by a growing number of educators who insisted that constitutional principles barred the public support of any type of religious instruction, nonsectarian and sectarian alike. William Torrey Harris, superintendent of the St. Louis public schools and later U.S. Commissioner of Education, would write in 1876 that to permit Protestants to control the public schools or to divide the school funds among religious schools would "result in the destruction or injury of political freedom." There was "a widespread conviction" among people, Harris asserted, "that church and state should be separate." Although this broader understanding of separation still represented the minority view among Protestants, it reflected how attitudes were evolving during the second half of the century. An increasing number of people—liberal Protestants, secularists, Jews, and educators—became convinced that disestablishment meant the dismantling of the de-facto Protestant establishment. This progression in attitudes demonstrated, in the words of William Torrey Harris, "a slowly but constantly growing fact in modern history, the separation of church and state."[59]

Still, there can be no denying that an illiberal version of church–state separation emerged in the mid-century in conjunction with Protestant and Catholic clashes over parochial school funding. Nativists and other anti-Catholics embraced constitutional language to advance their bigoted goals. For some nativists, church–state separation meant not only a ban on the funding of Catholic parochial schools; it also justified limits on the legal and civil rights of Catholics and other immigrants. As Hamburger correctly observes, however, many nativists became zealous advocates of church–state separation only after the Catholic leadership began criticizing the common schools and popes condemned the principle in a series of encyclicals. Nativist commitment to church–state separation was chiefly reactive, opportunistic, and one-sided considering the nativists' avid support of Protestant Bible reading. For other Protestants, however, the commitment to the principle was not so reactive or superficial. Nativist misuse of the principle should not be interpreted to represent its broader understanding during the nineteenth century.[60]

Issues of church–state separation received their two most public airings in the events surrounding the Blaine Amendment of 1876 and the Mormon Question of the 1870s–1890s. With the first, controversy over the School Question came to a head following the Cincinnati Bible-reading decision. Republicans, seeking to direct attention away from a failed Reconstruction policy and the corrupt Grant Administration, seized upon the School Question as a way to garner Protestant support. In 1875 President Grant proposed a constitutional amendment to "keep the church and state forever separate" by applying the First Amendment to the states and prohibiting any public appropriation for sectarian education.[61] Protestants, secularists, and nativists rallied behind the amendment, while Democrats and their Catholic supporters generally opposed it. Most observers viewed it as a transparent political ploy. Even the Republican *New York Times* acknowledged that an "appeal to religious passions was worth twenty-five thousand votes to the Republicans." Anti-Catholic rhetoric inflamed the ensuing public debate, although some viewed the controversy as an opportunity to resolve the School Question once and for all. Samuel Spear wrote that although the funding controversy presented "one of the sharpest issues between the Catholic and the Protestant, . . . it manifestly does not cover the whole question in controversy." The "great principles which are involved . . . bring to the surface the whole subject of Church and State, civil government and religion, in their relations to each other." Spear maintained that these were "the principles that lie at the foundation of our political system."[62]

In the end, the Blaine Amendment failed on a strict party-line vote in the Senate. Though the Blaine Amendment was significant as a political event, it had little impact on understandings of church–state separation, either as it related to religious exercises or the public funding of religious institutions. The principle against funding parochial schools had been developing for fifty years and was already installed in the laws and constitutions of many states by the time of the Blaine Amendment (seventeen states had enacted no-funding provisions in their constitutions by 1876). The Amendment had not proposed a new solution to the funding controversy or advanced a novel constitutional theorem on church and state, other than to nationalize the matter. The impact of the Amendment was at best symbolic. In the thirty-five years following the debate over the Amendment, twenty-one states would adopt express no-funding provisions in their constitutions to bolster existing language. That the Blaine Amendment influenced that development is not in doubt. Whether states would not have adopted those provisions but for the events surrounding the Amendment is much less certain. Again, the idea that public funding of religious schooling violated church–state separation went back to at least the 1820s. State legislators may have been motivated by concerns about ensuring the stability of still nascent public schools, preserving the integrity of public school funds, avoiding religious competition, and adhering to the broader principle of church–state separation. Legislators could legitimately have viewed the public funding of parochial schools as a threat to these principles without devolving into anti-Catholic animus. Accordingly, the significance of the Blaine Amendment, and in particular its anti-Catholic connections, on the constitutional development of the no-funding rule at the state level can be overstated.[63]

Unlike the Blaine Amendment, the legal events surrounding the Mormon Question had a significant impact on nineteenth-century understandings of church–state separation. The church–state controversy over Mormonism lasted for approximately fifty years, from the church's announcement regarding polygamy in 1852 until after Utah achieved statehood in 1896. Mainstream Christian abhorrence of the Mormon tenet of "celestial plural marriage" was at the heart of the conflict—polygamy threatened the idea of the monogamous family that had underlain Christian civilization for 1800 years. As the U.S. Supreme Court would remark in 1885, monogamous marriage was "the sure foundation of all that is stable and noble in our civilization; [it was] the best guarantee of that reverent morality which is the source of all beneficent progress in social and political improvement."[64] But the church–state conflict ran much deeper. Mormons were clannish and hierarchical, isolating themselves both theologically and geographically from mainstream Protestantism. The Church of Jesus Christ of Latter-day Saints accumulated massive wealth and property and, critics alleged, exercised absolute political and social control over its adherents. And its leaders or "prophets," Joseph Smith and Brigham Young, possessed enormous religious, political, and even military power in their enclaves of Nauvoo and Salt Lake City. In Mormon settlements, the institutions of church and state were intimately intertwined. These facts and allegations led to charges that the Mormon settlements were effectively "theocracies" operating in violation of republican principles, including the separation of church and state. In the congressional debates surrounding the various federal measures to subdue the church, legislators railed about the need to curb the Mormons' "barbarism" as well as their "theocratic" and "monstrous powers."[65]

Beginning in 1862, Congress enacted a series of laws that outlawed polygamy, restricted the political and civil rights of Mormons, and sought to dismantle the LDS Church by seizing its property and assets. The federal government argued its measures were necessary to preserve church–state separation while, ironically, the Mormon Church defended their practices and actions on the same ground. Mormons, and a few non-Mormons, charged the government's seizure of church property and its persecution of church leaders for teaching a religious tenet exceeded governmental authority while it evinced official disdain for a religion. One brave senator remarked that Congress could not "indirectly legislate for the purpose of destroying any religion, whether false or true." The law seizing control of the church was a "step towards the establishment of religious persecution and intolerance," claimed Senator Wilkinson Call. But the majority in Congress viewed the measures as necessary to dismantle the Mormon theocracy in Utah: "to cut up by the roots this church establishment."[66]

In the most important polygamy case brought under the initial law (the Morrill Act), Brigham Young's personal secretary, George Reynolds, charged his prosecution violated both the establishment and free exercise clauses. On appeal, the Supreme Court dispatched Reynolds's claims, asserting that although Congress lacked authority to regulate religious opinions, it "was left free to reach actions which were in violation of social duties or subversive of good order. . . . Laws are made for the government of actions, and while they cannot interfere with mere religious belief and opinions, they may with practices." This established what became known as the "belief–action" dichotomy, authorizing the government to regulate religious practices closely related to belief.[67] The extent of that government authority over church–state matters became known when the Court considered subsequent legislation that disenfranchised not only practicing polygamists but also Mormons who merely professed a belief in polygamy. In a second seminal decision, *Davis v. Beason*, a monogamous Mormon charged that for the state to deny him his civil rights because of his belief in polygamy amounted to a "law respecting an establishment of religion," imposed a religious test for a public trust, and violated his free exercise rights.[68] The Supreme Court, like Congress, saw the church–state threat differently. Justice Stephen Field reaffirmed the belief–action dichotomy, noting that "[l]aws are made for the government of actions, and while they cannot interfere with mere religious belief and opinions, they may with practices." Field insisted that "[i]t was never intended or supposed that the [First] amendment could be invoked as a protection against legislation for the punishment of acts inimical to the peace, good order, and morals of society. . . . Crime is not the less odious because sanctioned by what any particular sect may designate as 'religion.'"[69] Through these and other Mormon decisions, the Supreme Court not only narrowed the understanding of religious free exercise; it also shrank that aspect of church–state separation that protects the autonomy of religious entities and limits the authority of the government to show disfavor of a despised religious belief. Fortunately, the Mormon decisions were sui generis. The Court's retraction of protections of religious exercise and church–state separation in the Mormon cases stands in contrast with the otherwise gradual expansion of those principles during the nineteenth century.

Conclusion

The nation that emerged from the nineteenth century was dramatically different from the fledgling republic of one hundred years earlier. The nation's boundaries spread from ocean to ocean, and its population had grown almost twenty-fold. The religious situation was also significantly different from before. Even though the majority of Americans in 1900 still professed to be Protestant (and the percentage of church adherence was much higher than in 1800), religious experimentation and immigration had greatly changed the nation's religious complexion. Protestantism's grip on the culture had been ebbing since its apex before the Civil War, and religious pluralism was on the rise.

With that cultural development came changes in attitudes about the relationship between church and state. Understandings of disestablishment and church–state separation broadened, spurred in part by constitutional evolution at the state level, but also by developing attitudes among judges, lawyers, educators, and public officials. Separation now meant more than the formal uncoupling of political and religious institutions. Separation also meant more than prohibiting tax support of religious institutions or preferential treatment of one religion over another. It now embraced religious equality, and it challenged the authority of the government to patronize religion, even generally. Although conceptions of religious liberty and church–state separation still fell short of the understandings that would emerge in the mid-twentieth century with incorporation by the Supreme Court, they were much closer than they were apart. One state judge, writing in 1898, would sum up the change in events:

> The history of the relations of religion and the state shows a continuous evolution. It was not long ago that every government had a system of state religion, calling for the organization and support of churches sustained by a genera tax. This was true in several of the states. . . . As time passed, the injustice of this in a republic was seen, and it also came to be believed that the cause of true religion would lose nothing by the most complete separation of church and state.[70]

The nineteenth century, rather than being a static Protestant empire, was a time of dramatic change in church–state attitudes and relationships. Its developments set the stage for the legal events of the second half of the twentieth century. They also laid the foundation for the Supreme Court's declaration in *Everson* that the Establishment Clause was intended to erect "a wall of separation between Church and State." Whether Justice Black was incorrect in relying on that metaphor, it found its basis in the developments of the nineteenth century as much as in the immortal words of Thomas Jefferson. That century, not the decisions of the Court after 1947, deserves the moniker the "second disestablishment."[71]

Notes

1. Robert T. Handy, *A Christian America*, 2d ed. (New York: Oxford University Press, 1984); Robert T. Handy, "The Protestant Quest for a Christian America, 1830–1930," *Church History* 22 (1953): 8–20, 12; Robert T. Handy, *Undermined Establishment: Church–State Relations in America, 1880–1920* (Princeton, NJ: Princeton University Press, 1991); see Everson v. Board of Education, 330 U.S. 1 (1947); Lemon v. Kurtzman, 403 U.S. 62 (1971); Grand Rapids School District v. Ball, 473 U.S. 373 (1985).

2. Vincent Phillip Muñoz, *God and the Founders* (New York: Cambridge University Press, 2009); Daniel L. Dreisbach, Mark D. Hall and Jeffry H. Morrison, eds., *The Forgotten*

Founders on Religion and Public Life (Notre Dame, IN: University of Notre Dame Press, 2009); Philip Hamburger, *Separation of Church and State* (Cambridge, MA: Harvard University Press, 2002); Daniel L. Driesbach, "'Sowing Useful Truths and Principles': The Danbury Baptists, Thomas Jefferson, and the 'Wall of Separation,'" *Journal of Church and State* 39 (1997): 455–501; Gerard V. Bradley, *Church–State Relationships in America* (Westport, CT: Greenwood Press, 1987).

3. *Everson*, 330 U.S. at 14–16. See further chapter 6 by Ralph Ketcham on Madison and Jefferson.

4. Thomas J. Curry, *The First Freedoms* (New York: Oxford University Press, 1986), 220–22; John Witte Jr., "'A Most Mild and Equitable Establishment of Religion': John Adams and the 1780 Massachusetts Constitution," *Journal of Church and State* 41 (1999): 213–52.

5. Zephaniah Swift, *A System of the Laws of the State of Connecticut* [1795, 1796] (New York: Arno Press, 1972), 1:136, 141.

6. Steven K. Green, *The Second Disestablishment: Church and State in Nineteenth Century America* (New York: Oxford University Press, 2010), 27–31, 43–46, 125–27.

7. Ibid.

8. "An Old Whig, no. 5," (November 1, 1787) in *The Complete Anti-Federalist*, ed. Herbert J. Storing (Chicago: University of Chicago Press, 1981), 3:27–29. See Steven K. Green, "A 'Spacious Conception': Separationism as an Idea," *Oregon Law Review* 85 (2006): 443–80.

9. Noah Webster, "On Test Laws, Oaths of Allegiance and Abjuration, and Partial Exclusions from Office" (March 1787), *The Founders' Constitution*, ed. Philip B. Kurland and Ralph Lerner (Chicago: University of Chicago Press, 1987) 4:636.

10. J. William Frost, *A Perfect Freedom: Religious Liberty in Pennsylvania* (New York: Cambridge University Press, 1990), 74–75; Joel A. Nichols, "Religious Liberty in the Thirteenth Colony: Church–State Relations in Colonial and Early National Georgia," *New York University Law Review* 80 (2005): 1693–1772, 1728–34; Curry, *The First Freedoms*, 159–60, 188–89; Francis Newton Thorpe, ed., *The Federal and State Constitutions*, 7 vols. (Washington, DC: U.S. Government Printing Office, 1909), 568, 785, 800–801, 3100, 3762.

11. See further chapter 9 by Daniel Dreisbach.

12. Tunis Wortman, "A Solemn Address to Christians and Patriots," in *Political Sermons of the Founding Era, 1730–1805*, ed. Ellis Sandoz (Indianapolis, IN: Liberty Fund, 1991), 1489.

13. "Sunday Mails," House Report No. 87, *American State Papers* 27 (March 4 and 5, 1830), 230; Arthur M. Schlesinger Jr., *The Age of Jackson* (New York: Little, Brown & Co., 1945), 136–40, 350–56; Albert Post, *Popular Freethought in America, 1825–1850* (New York: Octagon Books, 1974), passim.

14. Handy, *A Christian America*, 24–56; Lyman Beecher, "A Reformation of Morals Practicable and Indispensable," in *Lyman Beecher and the Reform of Society: Four Sermons, 1804–1828*, ed. Edwin S. Gaustad (New York: Arno Press, 1972), 17–19.

15. Robert Baird, *Religion in the United States of America* (Glasgow: Blackie & Son, 1844); Stephen Colwell, *The Position of Christianity in the United States* (Philadelphia: Lippincott, Grambo & Co., 1854); B. F. Morris, *Christian Life and Character of the Civil Institutions of the United States* (Philadelphia: George W. Childs, 1864); Jon Butler, *Awash in a Sea of Faith: Christianizing the American People* (Cambridge, MA: Harvard University Press, 1990), 285.

16. Jasper Adams, *The Relation of Christianity to Civil Government in the United States* (Charleston, SC: A. E. Miller, 1833), 12–16.

17. Handy, *A Christian America*, 24–56.

18. Butler, *Awash in a Sea of Faith*, 225–88; Alice Felt Tyler, *Freedom's Ferment: Phases of American Social History to 1860* (Minneapolis: University of Minnesota Press, 1944), 47–224; R. Laurence Moore, *Religious Outsiders and the Making of Americans* (New York: Oxford University Press, 1986); James Turner, *Without God, Without Creed: The Origins of Unbelief in America* (Baltimore, MD: The Johns Hopkins University Press, 1985).

19. Updegraph v. Commonwealth, 11 Serg. & Rawl. 394, 406–7 (Pa. 1824); People v. Ruggles, 8 Johns. 290, 295–96 (N.Y. 1811).

20. Joseph Story, *Commentaries on the Constitution of the United States* (Boston: Hilliard, Gray, & Co., 1833), § 1877.

21. Ibid., § 1871.

22. Wallace v. Jaffree, 472 U.S. 38, 104–5 (1985) (Rehnquist, J., dissenting); Robert L. Cord, *Separation of Church and State: Historical Fact and Current Fiction* (Grand Rapids, MI: Baker Book House, 1988), 12–14; Story to Rev. John Brazer, February 16, 1832, in *Life and Letters of Joseph Story*, ed. William W. Story (Boston: Charles C. Little & James Brown, 1851), 2:82–83.

23. Curry, *The First Freedoms*, 216–17. See further chapter 8 by Carl Esbeck.

24. *The Oregon Constitution and Proceedings and Debates of the Constitutional Convention of 1857*, ed. Charles Henry Clay (Salem, OR: State Printing Department, 1926), 302–3 (statement by Mr. Grover).

25. Thorpe, *Federal and State Constitutions*, passim.

26. Ibid., 2:1123–24.

27. Mich. Const. of 1835, Art. I, sec. 5; Thorpe, *Federal and State Constitutions*, 4:1931; Thomas M. Cooley, *Michigan: A History of Governments*, 8th ed. (Boston: Houghton Mifflin and Co., 1897), 306–29. Apparently, Catholic and Presbyterian clergy were instrumental in the movement to establish universal nonsectarian schooling at both the collegiate and common school levels. Cooley, *Michigan*, 309–11.

28. See Thorpe, *Federal and State Constitutions*, 2:1074 (Indiana); 4:1993 (Minnesota); 5:2925 (Ohio); 7:4078–79 (Wisconsin); 2:1232 (Kansas); 5:2998 (Oregon).

29. *The Oregon Constitution*, 305 (statement by Mr. Williams).

30. Ibid., 296–308.

31. Maclear, "'True American Union,'" 51.

32. Updegraph v. Commonwealth, 11 Serg. & Rawl. 394, 400 (Pa. 1824).

33. Tunis Wortman, "A Solemn Address to Christians and Patriots," in *Political Sermons*, 1488. See also "Grotius" (DeWitt Clinton), *A Vindication of Thomas Jefferson* (New York: David Denniston, Printer, 1800).

34. Timothy Walker, "Introductory Lecture on the Dignity of the Law as a Profession, Delivered at the Cincinnati College, November 4, 1837," in *The Legal Mind in America*, ed. Perry Miller (Garden City, NY: Anchor Books, 1962), 240–41.

35. Vidal v. Girard's Executors, 2 How. 127, 133 (1844).

36. Andrew v. N.Y. Bible and Prayer Book Society, 4 Sandf. 156, 181 (N.Y. Super. 1850); Ayers v. The Methodist Church, 3 Sandf. 352, 377 (N.Y. Super. 1849).

37. Bloom v. Richards, 2 Ohio St. 387, 390–92, 404 (1853); accord McGatrick v. Wason, 4 Ohio St. 566, 571 (1855).

38. *Ex parte* Newman, 9 Cal. 502, 506–7, 509 (1858). Three years later a differently constructed state supreme court would uphold a new Sunday law, but solely on the ground that it "enjoins nothing that is not secular, and it commands nothing that is religious; it is purely

a civil regulation, and spends its whole force upon matters of civil government." *Ex parte Andrews*, 18 Cal. 678, 684–85 (1861). For further on the controversies over Sunday mails, see chapter 9 by Daniel Dreisbach.

39. Robert G. McCloskey, ed., *The Bible in the Public Schools: Arguments in the Case of John D. Minor, et al. versus The Board of Education of the City of Cincinnati, et al.* (Cincinnati: Robert Clarke & Co., 1870) (New York: De Capo Press, 1964), 414–16; Board of Education v. Minor, 23 Ohio St. 211, 250–54 (1873).

40. Thomas M. Cooley, *A Treatise on the Constitutional Limitations*, 4th ed. (Boston: Little, Brown & Co., 1878), 581–87.

41. Weiss v. District School Board of Edgerton, 44 N.W. 967, 978 (Wis. 1890) (Cassoday, J., concurring).

42. Hamburger, *Separation of Church and State*, passim.

43. Madison, "Detached Memoranda" (ca. 1832), in *James Madison on Religious Liberty*, ed. Robert S. Alley (Buffalo, NY: Prometheus Books, 1985), 89–94.

44. Madison to Robert Walsh, March 2, 1819, in Alley, *James Madison*, 81; Madison to F. L. Schaeffer, December 3, 1821, in Alley, *James Madison*, 82; Madison to Edward Livingstone, July 10, 1822, in Alley, *James Madison*, 83; Detached Memoranda, in Alley, *James Madison*, 91, 93.

45. John Witte, Jr., "Facts and Fictions about the History of Separation of Church and State," *Journal of Church and State* 48 (2005): 15–45; John Witte Jr., "That Serpentine Wall of Separation," *Michigan Law Review* (2003): 1869–1905; Douglas Laycock, "The Many Meanings of Separation," *University of Chicago Law Review* 70 (Fall 2003): 1667–1701; Kent Greenawalt, "History as Ideology: Philip Hamburger's *Separation of Church and State*," *California Law Review* 93 (2005): 367–96; Mark D. McGarvie, *One Nation under Law: America's Early National Struggles to Separate Church and State* (Dekalb, IL: Northern Illinois University Press, 2004).

46. Perry v. Commonwealth, 44 Va. 632, 641–43 (1846).

47. City Council of Charleston v. Benjamin, 2 Strob. 508, 511 (S.C. 1846). The South Carolina Supreme Court reversed the trial decision on the ground that "christianity is a part of the common law [and] its disturbance is punishable at common law."

48. Bloom v. Richards, 2 Ohio St. 387, 399 (1853); *Ex parte* Newman, 9 Cal. 502, 506–7, 507 (1858).

49. See sources at note 45. For a broader discussion about the evolution of the School Question and its impact on constitutional doctrine, see Steven K. Green, *The Bible, the School, and the Constitution: The Clash That Shaped Modern Church–State Doctrine* (New York: Oxford University Press, 2012).

50. William Oland Bourne, *History of the Public School Society of the City of New York* (New York: William Wood & Co., 1870), 64–67, 70–72. The state legislature authorized the New York Common Council to decide the question, and in 1825 the Council voted to discontinue the funding of religious charity schools.

51. Ibid., 126–29.

52. Ibid., 139–40.

53. Ibid., 145, 148; Lawrence A. Cremin, *The American Common School: A Historic Conception* (New York: Teachers College, Columbia University 1952), 163–64.

54. Bourne, *History of the Public School Society*, 139.

55. Thorpe, *Federal and State Constitutions*, 5:2647–48.

56. Bourne, *History of the Public School Society*, 140.

57. Donahoe v. Richards, 38 Me. 379, 403 (1854); Commonwealth v. Cooke, 7 Am. Law Reg. 417 (Ma. Police Ct. 1859).

58. Henry Ward Beecher, "The School Question," in *The Bible in the Schools* (New York: J. W. Schermerhorn & Co., 1870), 14–19; Samuel T. Spear, *Religion and the State, or the Bible and the Public Schools* (New York: Dodd, Mead & Co., 1876), 55–66, 117.

59. William Torrey Harris, "The Division of School Funds for Religious Purposes," *Atlantic Monthly* (August 1876): 171–84, at 173, 177.

60. Hamburger, *Separation of Church and State*, 229–34, 397. Although it is an overstatement, Hamburger remarks that "[i]ronically, the pope did more than Jefferson to popularize the idea of separation of church and state in America." Ibid., 482.

61. See Steven K. Green, "The Blaine Amendment Reconsidered," *American Journal of Legal History* 36 (1992): 38–69; Steven K. Green, "'Blaming Blaine': Understanding the Blaine Amendment and the 'No-Funding' Principle," *First Amendment Law Review* 2 (2002): 107–52.

62. *New York Times*, October 22, 1875, 1; Spear, *Religion and the State*, 18, 24.

63. See Steven K. Green, "The Insignificance of the Blaine Amendment," *Brigham Young Law Review* (2008): 295–333; Marc D. Stern, "Blaine Amendments, Anti-Catholicism, and Catholic Dogma," *First Amendment Law Review* 2 (2002): 153–78, at 176. See further chapter 1 by T. Jeremy Gunn.

64. Murphy v. Ramsey, 114 U.S. 15, 45 (1885).

65. Orma Linford, "The Mormons and the Law: The Polygamy Cases, Part I," *Utah Law Review* 9 (1964): 308, 314–16; Sarah Barringer Gordon, *The Mormon Question: Polygamy and Constitutional Conflict in Nineteenth-Century America* (Chapel Hill: University of North Carolina Press, 2002), 19–54.

66. H.R. Rep. No. 2735, 49th Cong., 1st sess. 5–8 (1886); 17 Cong. Rec. 507 (1886); Linford, "Mormons and the Law," 326–27.

67. Reynolds v. United States, 98 U.S. 145, 162, 164 (1879).

68. Davis v. Beason, 133 U.S. 333, 338–39 (1890).

69. Ibid., 342–45.

70. Pfeiffer v. Board of Education, 77 N.W. 250, 259 (Mich. 1898) (Moore, J., dissenting).

71. Everson v. Board of Education, 330 U.S. 1, 16 (1947); Green, *The Second Disestablishment*.

11

Disestablishment from Blaine to *Everson*

FEDERALISM, SCHOOL WARS, AND THE EMERGING
MODERN STATE

Thomas C. Berg

With the Supreme Court's 1947 decision in *Everson v. Board of Education*,[1] the history of the First Amendment's Establishment Clause entered its most dramatic and controversial chapter, one that the justices are still writing. Although *Everson* ruled narrowly that states could reimburse parents for the costs of busing their children to and from parochial schools, the opinion took two other, monumental steps. First, it announced that the Establishment Clause—"Congress shall make no law respecting an establishment of religion"—would thereafter apply to state and local government actions as well. Previously the Establishment Clause by its terms had restricted only federal actions, but in *Everson* the Court held (as it eventually would with nearly all of the Bill of Rights) that the no-establishment rule was "incorporated" in the provisions of the Fourteenth Amendment, ratified in 1868 to restrict state actions. Second, the *Everson* Court adopted, as a general approach, a very broad reading of the clause that forbade not only aid or preferences to one religion or denomination, but "aid to [all] religions" or to "religious activities or institutions . . . [in] whatever form"—erecting a "'wall of separation between Church and State.'"[2] The model of strong separation between church and state—applied after *Everson* to every level of government from federal to local—generated numerous decisions over the next forty years striking down practices such as prayers in public schools and funding of religious schools, decisions that in turn sparked heated public controversy.[3]

But as it was embracing the "wall of separation" image, the Court also had to confront counterarguments: that extending a generally available benefit, free busing, to parochial-school students bore little resemblance to historic establishment of a church and would in fact collide with the First Amendment's other religion provision, the Free Exercise Clause, by discriminating against families using parochial schools. Ultimately in *Everson*, five justices accepted the counterarguments. Because a state was also forbidden to "hamper its citizens in the free exercise of their own religion," the Court said it must ensure that in "protecting the citizens of New Jersey against state-established churches, . . . we do not inadvertently prohibit New Jersey from extending its general State law benefits to all its citizens without regard to their religious belief."[4] The bus subsidies survived—barely—because they went to individuals rather than religious schools, were separable from the school's religious instruction, and were available also to families using public schools.

Everson therefore revealed, on its face, a central tension concerning the Establishment Clause in the modern state. It has become customary for government to provide benefits to empower individuals and promote the public welfare in areas such as education and social services. Benefits became pervasive in the "welfare state" created by the New Deal and Great Society, but government aid for education dates back even before the creation of public schools in the mid-1800s. Often government benefits extend to private organizations or the individuals they serve; many of the service providers in education, health, and social welfare are religious organizations. How far can the pervasive pursuit of secular goals through government benefits to private institutions coexist with special restrictions on tax-supported aid to religious institutions? In Everson the justices revealed clearly the tension between the no-aid position and the logic of government educational or welfare assistance. At the same time, they dramatically expanded their own role in resolving that tension by applying First Amendment restrictions to state and local government actions.

This chapter explores the roots of Everson's two crucial holdings in the decades before the opinion. The first two sections examine the incorporation of the Establishment Clause by looking at the evidence in the history surrounding the Fourteenth Amendment and the failed Blaine Amendment of 1876, which would have applied both religion clauses to the states. The remaining sections examine the school-funding controversy from the Blaine Amendment through Everson. The Blaine Amendment debate, I argue, reveals that at a time close to the Fourteenth Amendment's enactment, government aid to religious schools and social services was defended on, among other grounds, the very rationale that the Supreme Court has recently approved: that when properly structured, it allows individuals to choose whether the service they receive will be in a religious or secular setting.[5] But although the Blaine Amendment failed, similar provisions against government aid passed in many states in the second half of the nineteenth century. I briefly summarize these and assess the important role that fear and distrust of Catholicism played in the movement against religious-school funding. Finally, I examine the rise of the welfare state in the early twentieth century and how it strengthened the case that government should assist individuals and families who choose to use religious schooling. In Everson, the logic of the welfare state ran up against the no-funding tradition at a time when the fear and mistrust of Catholicism that helped support that tradition was undergoing another spike in intensity. The result was *Everson's* split personality: broad language about strict church–state separation and no aid, followed by narrow approval of the extension of a safety/welfare benefit to religious-school families.

The Establishment Clause, Incorporation, and the Fourteenth Amendment

The *Everson* opinion disposed of its first great issue, the incorporation of the Establishment Clause, in one sentence: "The First Amendment, as made applicable to the states by the Fourteenth, commands that a state 'shall make no law respecting an establishment of religion, or prohibiting the free exercise thereof.'"[6] Justice Black made no further arguments. He cited previous decisions protecting Jehovah's Witnesses from laws interfering with their preaching and distribution of religious tracts; the relevant guarantees in those cases were free speech and free exercise of religion, rather than nonestablishment, but Black treated incorporation of the entire First Amendment as an accomplished fact.[7]

Given all the implications of incorporating the First Amendment Establishment Clause into the Fourteenth Amendment Due Process Clause and applying them against state and local governments, the Court should have given more careful attention to the issue. The question whether the Fourteenth Amendment was meant in general to incorporate the Bill of Rights raises considerations beyond the Establishment Clause. Recently scholars such as Michael Kent Curtis, Akhil Amar, and Richard Aynes have refined and bolstered the general case for incorporation, primarily under the Fourteenth Amendment's Privileges and Immunities Clause rather than, as the Court has held, the Due Process Clause.[8] They point out that the phrase "[no state shall abridge] the privileges and immunities of citizens of the United States" easily encompasses the substantive personal rights guaranteed by the Constitution's first eight amendments, that is, the Bill of Rights.[9]

Even if incorporation of the Bill of Rights is generally defensible, however, the Establishment Clause presents "special problems," as Professor Amar has put it.[10] He and other scholars have claimed that in 1789 the Establishment Clause primarily guaranteed not the right of an individual to be free from an established church, but rather the rights of states to decide policy toward religion.[11] The argument rests partly on the peculiar textual phrasing, "no law respecting an establishment of religion," which can be read to forbid Congress from taking action concerning the establishment arrangements that existed in several states in 1791. The argument also appeals to historical context: With almost no substantive discussion the first Congress and the ratifying state legislatures agreed on the text even though those states disagreed sharply on whether to have an establishment. Virginia, for example, had decisively rejected tax assessments for clergy in 1786, but New England states steadfastly maintained them, notably Massachusetts in its 1780 Constitution.[12] As Daniel Conkle has put it,

> [t]hese various political actors simply could not have agreed on a general principle governing the relationship of religion and government, whether it be the principle endorsed in *Everson* or any other . . . What united the legislatures was a much more narrow purpose: to make it plain that *Congress* was not to legislate on the subject of religion, thereby leaving the matter of church–state relations to the individual states.[13]

According to this argument, the First Amendment did not adopt a principle of nonestablishment and then exempt the states from it because of federalism concerns. Instead, federalism—the assignment of religion questions to the states—was the "essential" meaning of the provision.[14] This argument has persuaded Supreme Court Justice Clarence Thomas, who wrote that "[t]he text and history of the Establishment Clause strongly suggest that it is a federalism provision intended to prevent Congress from interfering with state establishments."[15] If the clause really meant originally to protect states' rights concerning religion, Thomas said, to incorporate it against states "makes little sense." Incorporation would have, in Steven Smith's words, "effectively repudiated—and hence repealed"—the original decision.[16]

Such complications would not have bothered Justice Black, who believed in wholesale incorporation of the first eight amendments of the Bill of Rights. But the complications would normally have caught the attention of a fellow justice, Felix Frankfurter, for whom the Fourteenth Amendment adopted only those standards "which are 'of the very essence of a scheme of ordered liberty.'"[17] Government establishments of religion can be oppressive, and they certainly may be unwise, but if they are mild in their provisions they can coexist with substantial religious liberty in a state. Great Britain and other European nations offer clear examples of this today, as did several states in 1789 that had establishments (such as tax support for clergy of one or more denominations) yet offered significant freedom of religious exercise to dissenting groups. But Frankfurter never raised such questions. He had intense personal commitments to strict church–state separation and the secular public schools, stemming from his personal experience as a childhood immigrant and a member of a religious minority.[18] These commitments overrode his general attitudes of judicial restraint and of skepticism about incorporation.

There are powerful answers, to be sure, to the federalism-based challenge against the incorporation of the Establishment Clause. One answer is that from its inception the clause included a personal right—an individual freedom from religion imposed or sponsored by the federal government—that made it, as Justice Brennan once argued, "a coguarantor, with the Free Exercise Clause, of religious liberty."[19] There is nothing inconsistent in saying that the founding generation opposed a national church both because it would interfere with states' arrangements on religion and because it would impose on individual liberty. Indeed, one could argue that a national established church would be a greater imposition than state counterparts because it would be more distant from and out of touch with individuals. Thus, the Establishment Clause originally had two components, but with the Fourteenth Amendment the states'-rights component dropped out, leaving the personal right to be applied to the states.

A second response is that even if the Establishment Clause originally reflected no agreed-upon substantive principle against established religion, it came to embody such a principle by the time of the Fourteenth Amendment. Kurt Lash argues that during the nineteenth century, the Establishment Clause's "declaration of 'no [federal] power [over religion]' was reinterpreted to express an aspect of the freedom of conscience," and thus "[b]y 1868, the (Non)Establishment Clause was understood to be a liberty as fully capable of incorporation as any other provision in the first eight amendments to the Constitution."[20]

Several developments in antebellum America, summarized by Lash, cemented the status of nonestablishment as a fundamental liberty. By 1833, every state had eliminated taxes for clergy as well as the official support of any one denomination. By the beginning of the Civil War, several states had their own constitutional provisions prohibiting establishments of religion.[21] Over these same decades, the initiative in American Christianity passed into the hands of populist sects that relied on the zeal of members rather than their standing in society, creating a dominant model of "voluntarist" religion. Other features of legally established churches, such as anti-blasphemy and Sunday-closing laws, were retained but were more and more reinterpreted to rest on secular rather than theological rationales.[22]

Many of these developments occurred in the early 1800s, a period covered by previous chapters in this book. But what does the history surrounding the Fourteenth Amendment indicate concerning that period's understanding of the Establishment Clause? On several occasions, the Amendment's proponents said that it incorporated nonestablishment of religion, along with the rest of the Bill of Rights, as essential liberties of citizens. Representative John Bingham, commenting in 1871 on legislation to enforce the Fourteenth Amendment, said that the "privileges and immunities" in its text were "chiefly defined in the first eight amendments to the Constitution," which he then quoted in full, including the Establishment Clause.[23] Seven years earlier, in a speech on how slavery had trampled federal constitutional rights, Senator Henry Wilson recited the whole First Amendment, including the Establishment Clause, and stated, "With these rights no state may interfere without breach of the bond which holds the Union together."[24]

Wilson and other Republicans focused primarily on how slave states had denied free exercise of religion, not how they had imposed establishments of religion. The persecution of abolitionist preachers and prohibitions on slaves reading the Bible showed that "religion never will be allowed free exercise in any community where slavery dwarfs the consciences of men."[25] But, as already noted, Republican leaders sometimes mentioned the Establishment Clause too.

In short, whatever the understanding of the Establishment Clause was in 1789, there is good reason to believe that by the time of the Fourteenth Amendment, nonestablishment had come to be seen as an essential liberty of citizens. It was no longer, even arguably, a matter on which states disagreed while uniformly endorsing the free exercise of religion; the Establishment Clause was a full partner with the Free Exercise Clause in the dual protection of religious liberty. As a widely accepted liberty, nonestablishment was capable of being incorporated as a liberty in the Fourteenth Amendment—assuming that the Amendment's framers and ratifiers intended such incorporation of the Bill of Rights in general.

A consensus against establishment did not mean the end of government support for religion. As we will see in more detail, nineteenth-century Americans did not see generalized Christian sentiments in government as a form of establishment. Nonestablishment was now fundamental, an essential liberty, but for many citizens it was consistent with such government expressions.

The Blaine Amendment, Issue 1: Incorporation and Federalism

A few years after the Fourteenth Amendment was adopted, Congress turned its full attention to questions about church–state relations and federalism. In December 1875, the former speaker of the House, Republican James G. Blaine, proposed a constitutional amendment reading:

> No state shall make any law respecting an establishment of religion or prohibiting the free exercise thereof; and no money raised by taxation in any state for the support of public schools, or derived from any public fund therefore, shall be under the control of any religious sect, nor shall any money so raised or lands so devoted be divided between religious sects or denominations.[26]

The Blaine Amendment, as it came to be called, passed the House overwhelmingly (180–7), but strict opponents of aid dismissed it as "a fraud and a sham" because it applied only to funds earmarked for public schools.[27] In the Senate, they introduced a much broader version extending the prohibition on sectarian uses to any "public property [or] public revenue." The Senate version—likewise referred to as "the Blaine Amendment" despite its broader scope—failed to receive the necessary two-thirds vote (the tally was 28–16).

The Blaine Amendment episode might seem on its face highly damaging to the case for incorporation, not just of the Establishment Clause, but of the

Free Exercise Clause and indeed the whole Bill of Rights. As many critics have reasoned, if the Fourteenth Amendment had been understood to apply these provisions to the states, why would Congress only seven years later, with many of the same members present, seriously consider the need to adopt an amendment to do the very same thing?[28] Indeed, a number of statements in the Senate debate support the proposition that federal norms on religion still would not apply to states. The Blaine Amendment was defeated in the Senate, after all, and most of the senators who spoke against it appealed at least in part to principles of federalism. William Eaton of Connecticut said he was "opposed to it because it interferes with the rights of the States; that is all," and William Pinkney Whyte of Maryland added that Congress should continue to "leav[e] the whole power for the propagation of [religion] with the States exclusively."[29] His Maryland colleague Lewis Bogy argued, rather tenuously, that if the federal government received the power to prohibit state religious establishments, it would also have the power to create its own.[30] No opponent of the Blaine Amendment argued that the proposal was unnecessary because incorporation had happened in 1868; no proponent argued the proposal was innocuous on that ground.

However, determining the Blaine Amendment's effect on incorporation is complicated, for at least two reasons. First, incorporation could have been intended in 1868 but still needed in 1876 because in the interim the Supreme Court had read the Fourteenth Amendment extremely narrowly in decisions such as *The Slaughterhouse Cases*.[31] More important, the motivating force behind the Blaine Amendment was not the section applying the Religion Clauses to the states, but rather the one prohibiting public funds from being given to "any religious sect." The latter section was primarily intended to restrict government funding for Catholic elementary and secondary schools and others deemed unacceptably "sectarian," and to cement in the Constitution the favored position of state-run schools. Attacking school aid was the dominant purpose of the Blaine Amendment's supporters, and this controversy dominated the congressional debate. The political impetus for the proposal, historian Ward McAfee has shown, came late in Reconstruction when national Republicans sought to deflect Democratic charges that they were "pro-Negro"—"black Republicans"—by appealing to fears of a "foreign invasion of Roman Catholic immigrants" and "a growing Catholic influence within the Democratic party."[32] Accused of betraying the dominant white American culture, Republicans answered by championing a national culture whose key unifying force was the nonsectarian public school. The schooling controversy produced the most heated—and interesting—passages in the Blaine Amendment congressional debate, and I discuss them in the next section.

The Blaine Amendment debate has two features that are hospitable to the idea of incorporation. First, the debate confirms that the Establishment Clause had come to represent a personal liberty against established religions, not an

assignment of the question to the states, and that the liberty was seen as fundamental. Every senator who spoke, including opponents of the Amendment,
agreed that no state should establish a religion. The proponents' position was
summarized by Sen. Oliver Morton of Indiana, who said that "an essential
principle of American liberty [is] that we shall have perfect freedom of religious worship, that there shall be no established church, no religion established
by law that is taught by law," and "the example of one State establishing a religion . . . endangers the perpetuity of the nation."[33] The Democratic opponents
of the Amendment agreed. "Who is in favor of a State establishing a religion or
prohibiting the free exercise thereof? Protestant or Catholic?" asked Bogy. "No;
not one in this broad land of any sect or denomination, or whether he has any
religion at all or not."[34] Francis Kernan of New York said that the nonestablishment principle "has my hearty commendation"; it simply "was not necessary to
put it in the Federal Constitution" because all the states but one already "had
eliminated distinctions on account of religious creeds."[35] Senator Eaton, the
most energetic defender of states' rights, said, "I am opposed to any state
making a law respecting an establishment of religion" and "[i]n my state I will
take care that they do not make any such law," but added: "I do not want the
honorable Senator from Indiana [Morton] to take care of Connecticut."[36]

The federalism principle—let the states decide whether to support religion
or religiously affiliated schools—remained prominent in the Blaine Amendment debate. But no one argued that the Establishment Clause had actually
been intended to protect state establishments, that is, that federalism had been
its "essential" purpose. Instead, the anti–Blaine Amendment side argued that
states could be trusted because all of them had recognized establishments as
wrong. To use Steven Smith's words, federalism had become at most a "side
constraint" on the Establishment Clause—a reason to resist its application to
states—rather than an "essential" part of its meaning. Nonestablishment was a
liberty accepted as appropriate for all levels of government, even if many
people still argued that the federal government need not and should not
impose it upon the states. This change, as Professor Lash argues, removed one
logical barrier to incorporation.

The second feature of the debate hospitable to the idea of incorporation is
that although opponents of the Blaine Amendment did argue against incorporation, they argued more consistently against the clause prohibiting school aid.
The version of the Amendment that overwhelmingly passed the House included the incorporation of the Religion Clauses, together with the narrow
anti-funding provision limited to money earmarked for public schools. Only
when the anti-funding provision greatly expanded in the Senate did Democrats object, and then they raised every argument they could, including objections to incorporation. It is true that the House Democrats accepted
incorporation on essentially tactical grounds; they calculated that allowing a
narrow Amendment would head off the push for a broader one. But Senate

Democrats acted no less on tactical grounds when they criticized incorporation and championed states' rights. Members of Congress were driven less by
their general views on incorporation than by their views on school funding—
which I now examine in the context of the Blaine Amendment debate.

The Blaine Amendment(s), Issue 2: School Aid and the Catholic Question

The crux of the controversy over the Blaine Amendment was not that it prohibited establishments of religion by states, but that it construed "establishments" expansively to forbid evenhanded tax support of religiously affiliated
institutions meeting secular civil needs such as education or social services.
The funding controversy is also the only live one today, as the incorporation
precedents appear irreversible.[37] The Blaine Amendment debate sheds light on
the funding controversy in several interesting ways.

The Amendment arose after more than four decades of bitter debate over
the role of religion in schooling. The vast majority of schools in the colonies
and the early Republic were privately operated; most were religious, and many
of these received support from state or local governments.[38] From the 1820s
on, however, the movement arose for state-sponsored "common schools" that
would instruct children of varying denominations in a shared set of values.
The movement gained support in significant part as a reaction to a wave of
Catholic European immigrants. The proponents of common schools generally
viewed Catholicism as a threat, seeing it as full of theological superstitions
and, because of its hierarchical structure and theology, as antidemocratic. The
common, or public, schools sought to "Americanize" the immigrants and, by
educating children of Protestant denominations together, strengthen values of
democracy and individual freedom to which Protestantism was thought to be
crucial.

Almost no one at the time supported secular public schools; the general
teachings of Christianity were thought to be inextricable from and essential to
public morality. The solution, laid out by public-school pioneer Horace Mann,
was to read the Bible but without "sectarian" comment: to allow the Scripture
"to do what it is allowed to do in no other system—to speak for itself."[39] The
approach contradicted Catholic beliefs that the Bible must be interpreted with
the guidance of the Church. The common-school proponents then com-
pounded the conflict by typically choosing the Protestant translation, the King
James, over the Catholic Douay-Rheims; by following Protestant forms of
prayers; and by including other materials with a Protestant slant. When Catholic children refused to participate in the exercises, they were punished; when
Catholics proposed including their own versions, nativist riots broke out in
Philadelphia and Boston. Finally, when Catholics responded by forming their

own schools and seeking funding for them, they ran into stiff Protestant resistance. New York City set the example in 1844 by barring public aid to any school "in which any religious sectarian doctrine or tenet shall be taught," but continuing to mandate Bible readings without comment in its public schools.[40] As John Jeffries and James Ryan have summarized: "[T]he [nineteenth century] Protestant position was that public schools must be 'nonsectarian' (which was usually understood to allow Bible reading and other Protestant observances) and public money must not support 'sectarian' schools (which in practical terms meant Catholic)."[41]

Scholars such as Steven Green have argued that the no-funding principle developed not only "prior to," but "relatively independent of, Catholic immigration and the resulting Protestant reaction."[42] There were instances of denials of aid to Protestant church-related schools before the Catholic immigration, and some proponents of public schools showed sympathy toward the objections of Catholics. Nevertheless, fear and distrust of Catholicism were important components in the public-school movement, and without them it is highly doubtful that prohibitions on religious-school funding would have become so widespread. Even if some figures in the movement were relatively tolerant, the historical literature on the school wars shows pervasive anti-Catholic statements in public debates and in the press.[43] The positions that funding opponents took revealed not a consistent nonsectarianism, but a "self-interested underside" disfavoring Catholicism:[44] opposition to funding K-12 schools, which almost no Protestants operated, but support for funding colleges and social services, which Protestants frequently operated, and for Protestant-style observances in the public schools. In any event, even figures that Professor Green identifies as open to Catholic interests expressed highly negative views of Catholicism. Horace Mann and leading Congregationalist minister Horace Bushnell may have been receptive to the Douay Bible in some schools—though not to changing the policy of reading without comment—but Mann wrote of "the baneful influence of the Catholic religion upon the human mind," and Bushnell argued that children who were "shut up in" Catholic schools would not learn "the glorious rewards of liberty and the social advancement that follow" but "will be instructed mainly into the foreign prejudices and superstitions of their fathers."[45] These views of Catholicism pervaded the anti-funding movement.

The Federal Blaine Amendment. After a break during the Civil War, the funding controversy resumed during Reconstruction. The Blaine Amendment had precursors that, notably, aimed only to prohibit religious-school funding and not to enforce general norms of nonestablishment. In 1870, Rep. Samuel Burdett of Missouri introduced a constitutional amendment forbidding any state or local government to "appropriate any money, or make any donation from the public funds or property . . . for the support of or aid of any Sectarian, Religious, or Denominational school or educational establishment."[46] Then on September 30, 1875, Republican President Ulysses Grant heated up the issue with a speech to Union Army veterans in Des Moines, Iowa. Grant predicted that the next great national division, if any, would come not between North and South, but "between patriotism and intelligence on one side, and superstition, ambition, and ignorance on the other"—with the set of pejoratives referring, everyone understood, to the Catholic Church. He added:

> Resolve that neither the State or nation, nor both combined, shall support institutions of leaning other than those sufficient to afford every child in the land the opportunity of a good common school education, unmixed with atheistic, pagan, or sectarian tenets. Leave the matter of religion to the family altar, the church, and the private school, supported entirely by private contribution. Keep the Church and State forever separate.

Following Grant's lead, James Blaine introduced his amendment in the House of Representatives two months later.

In the debate over the Senate version of the Amendment, Republicans equated government support of religious schools with establishment of the religion of those schools. Morton stated that "[t]he support of a school by public taxation is the same thing in principle as an established church" because "[t]he power to educate children in a particular faith at the public expense involves the same principle as the support of that church at public expense, and the one inevitably leads to the other."[47] The principle, he argued, was the same: "[R]eligion shall not be taught by law at public expense."[48] Throughout the debate he used the word *establish* to mean "support at public expense," even when the support for a religiously affiliated school came on the same basis as for its state-run counterpart.

Morton argued that not just the principle of nonestablishment, but also the ideal of the nonsectarian public school "has always prevailed in this country" and "has been in the minds of our people for one hundred years." But that was simply false. States continued tax-supported payments for religious primary and secondary schools well after they eliminated payments for clergy and houses of worship. Most funding systems for clergy and church buildings ended before 1820; the Massachusetts system alone survived to 1833. But "'[p]ublic support of private education obtained quite generally until 1850,'" the most comprehensive survey has shown, and after that the "exclusion [of religious schools from funding] was a gradual process" extending over several decades.[49] For example, New York ended public funding for church buildings perhaps by 1738 and at least by 1777,[50] but "until 1850, the voluntary academies"—religious secondary schools—"were looked upon as an integral part of the state system of education, and the policy of the state was to contribute to their support."[51] In the District of Columbia, where the Establishment Clause itself governed, education was provided entirely through private and semipublic schools, including denominational schools, partially at public expense until 1848.[52]

The Senate debate over the Blaine Amendment covered several issues that recurred throughout the nineteenth century and still recur today. The first disagreement was over what would promote equality and harmony in American life. The Amendment's proponents argued that funding religious schools would "give a particular religious sect the advantage of the government and support by public taxation" and that "the principle of equality is gone" when money raised from all taxpayers went to schools operated by particular denominations.[53] Implicitly they argued that such favoritism would create social division. The Amendment's opponents answered that the truly divisive step would be to insert in the Constitution a rule aimed at Catholic institutions. "Instead of allaying strife and dissension," Kernan said, "it will increase them."[54]

There could be little doubt that the Amendment was aimed primarily at Catholic schools, although its proponents emphasized that it would bar aid to Protestant schools too. However, the latter were few in number. For Blaine Amendment proponents such as Oliver Morton and Vermont's George Edmunds, the danger that necessitated amending the Constitution—the "cloud . . . looming above the horizon"—was the existence of "a particular sect" that believed it "the duty of a well-ordered state to teach in its public institutions the particular tenets of a particular denomination," and whose adherents were "utterly opposed to our present system of common schools" and refused to contribute to "any school that does not teach their religion."[55] Both Morton and Edmunds read at length from the 1864 *Syllabus of Errors*, in which Pope Pius IX condemned a long list of ideas and practices such as secular state schools, equality of religions, and the free public worship of non-Catholic faiths in Catholic-majority countries.[56] Edmunds called the Pope's condemnations "at this moment the earnest, effective, dogmas of the most powerful religious sect the world has ever known, or probably ever will know—a church that is universal, ubiquitous, aggressive, restless, and untiring." He concluded from this—and from the fact that "liberty of conscience . . . is universal in every church but one"—that American Catholics must aim ultimately at controlling public institutions, if they were "consistent and true men." Therefore, to protect "the foundation of republican liberty" it was necessary to "preserv[e] public schools from that sort of domination."[57]

As recent scholarship has emphasized, such statements—which echoed those in public debates outside of Congress—reflected colorable fears about Vatican political doctrines and cannot be dismissed as merely anti-Catholic bigotry. The critics feared an "anti-democratic, autocratic Catholic Church which was seeking political power everywhere"; they thought that "core principles of individual freedom and democratic equality were at odds with," among other things, "the church's authoritarian institutional structure," "its insistence on close ties between church and state," and "its rejection of individual rights to freedom of conscience and worship."[58]

But although the fears may have found some basis in formal Catholic doctrine, they undoubtedly were overblown and distorted the attitude of most American Catholics. Senator Whyte, a Maryland Protestant, objected to the virtual "accusation against a large body of fellow-citizens as loyal to republican liberty as we claim ourselves to be," while Bogy added that Catholics were "in favor of perfect religious freedom."[59] Whyte adverted to a letter of Archbishop John Purcell of Cincinnati, who was a frequent defender of Catholicism in public life. In an 1867 exchange of polemical letters with Thomas Vickers, a liberal Congregationalist clergyman in Cincinnati, Purcell had written that "I do not believe the Church has any right to employ force to coerce conscience"; that "I do not want a union of Church and State—I deprecate such a union"; and that "I prefer the condition of the Church in these United States to its condition in" officially or majority-Catholic nations in Europe.[60] Then and in an earlier pastoral letter (to which Senator Whyte may have been referring), Archbishop Purcell had set forth many of the propositions by means of which American Catholics reconciled papal teachings with democracy and religious freedom. He said, for example, that the Church did not support coercing conscience, but merely opposed invoking religious liberty to lift all legal restraints on speech or action; that the Church accepted the existence and freedom of non-Catholic faiths, but refused to regard them as true or to give up efforts "to bring back men to the truth by moral suasion"; and that the state could permit religious freedom while still reflecting religious truths by, for example, enforcing Sabbath laws and refusing to recognize divorce.[61]

Senate opponents of the Blaine Amendment objected most strenuously to the claim that Catholics wanted to take over public schools for Catholic teaching. Kernan emphasized that Catholics were only "opposed to [secular] public schools for their children, not that they would interfere with their neighbors," and that they recognized that "free public schools . . . must be free from any religious teaching at all."[62]

Instead—and this is the third recurring characteristic of the nineteenth century school debates—Blaine opponents objected to the fact that the Amendment ratified supposedly nonsectarian religious practices—prayers and Bible readings—that were actually Protestant in character and assumptions. The Amendment stated that nothing in it "'shall be construed to prohibit the reading of the Bible in any school or institution."[63] Bogy explained that Catholics opposed public schools "for the reason that they were sectarian": "Even the very Bible which was used in the schools was a sectarian book," he said, alluding to the fact that readings typically employed the King James Bible, not the Douay-Rheims, and included no ecclesiastical guidance as the Church taught was necessary.[64] The proponents of the public-school approach may have honestly believed it to be nonsectarian,[65] but it reflected deeply Protestant assumptions about both the content of religious faith and

the means for inculcating it. The opponents pointed out this partiality in tren-
chant ways. Bogy suggested that it was no less sectarian "[t]o tell [a child] that
the Son of God was born and, as God, was crucified for the redemption of a
fallen world" because "the Unitarian would tell you that it is not true."[66] Kernan likewise pressed nonsectarianism to its logical consequence: For the
public schools truly "not to teach any particular creed, . . . they must be like
schools where you send your boy to learn mechanics, and those who want him
taught anything but mechanics must have him taught out of their own expense,
and not out of the public treasury."[67]

In claiming that the public schools of the time were sectarian Protestant in
nature, the Blaine Amendment opponents implied two possible wrongs, and
in turn two kinds of remedy. Sometimes the opponents suggested that the consistently nonsectarian school was possible. Under this approach, the remedy
would be to remove religious elements altogether, including the dominant
Protestant-oriented practices. When pressed by Morton, Senator Kernan said
that Catholics did not want public funding for their own schools—"the thing
is not practicable at all"—and that the Catholic goal with respect to laws was
simply to achieve truly nonsectarian public schools "to which every child in
the State can go and get secular learning without there being anything offensive to the creed of anyone."[68]

At other times, however, the Amendment's opponents said or implied that
all institutions, secular or religious, that provided a service of social value
should be eligible for funding, in order to make options available to benefi-
ciaries of different religious and nonreligious views. The opponents clearly
endorsed the ability of states and municipalities to fund religiously operated
social services—orphanages, hospitals, and juvenile reformatories—and they
objected that the Amendment's text would bar subsidies to institutions that
were often the most effective means of helping their members. Senator Kernan
raised the complaint in terms that echo today's defenses of "charitable choice"
arrangements for funding social services:

> If [the charity] be one created by private benevolence which does a great
> deal of good and relieves the State from a great deal of pauperism, takes care
> of paupers better than they can be elsewhere, you may apply to the State,
> [but under the Senate proposal] if the State gives you aid you must at once
> shut out the ministers of the Gospel of every creed, although your patients
> desire to have their ministrations . . .
>
> These charitable institutions will be founded and they will be managed
> by zealous hands and active feet belonging to one or the other of the Chris-
> tian denominations. They have their faith, and so believing they do not
> want to protrude their views upon others, but they gather up their own
> pauper children, their own pauper sick, their own pauper aged in these
> institutions. Yet you say the State should not encourage them in their need

by aiding [them] from the treasury, because they teach the creed that makes them these ministering angels and zealous workers.[69]

Senator Eaton likewise objected that the Amendment would bar his home city of Hartford from giving "a thousand dollars a year to each" of two children's asylums, Catholic and Protestant, "although by doing it they should save $20,000 a year."[70]

Kernan emphasized that aid should be equal among institutions, given to "each *pro rata* according to the number they supported," a formula corresponding to programs that are familiar today: vouchers given to individuals, or aid given directly to institutions on a per-capita basis (number of individuals who choose to enroll). He applied the argument to education as well as other services:

> Take the ragged school; take any other school that is gotten up by benevolent people. Our state has thought it wise, where so much has been done by these denominations to relieve the State from pauperism and crime, . . . to aid them, and we have done it and done it very cheerfully. . . . But this amendment cuts them off from aid if they teach the child the religious creed of its parents.[71]

This "equal funding" argument by Blaine Amendment opponents was distinct and different from their argument that the ostensibly nonsectarian but actually Protestant religious practices in public institutions should be eliminated. The "equal funding" argument suggested, by contrast, that no service that touched on moral formation and uplift—as education and charity certainly do—could be wholly free of creeds with religious implications. Kernan suggested that to be devoid of a creed, a subject would have to be taught in the manner of mechanics; but most of education is more value-laden than is mechanics. This implicitly more radical critique of nonsectarianism—a critique of what we might call today "value neutrality"—points toward a very different remedy. Because education and charitable work cannot be free of some creed, explicit or implicit, government funding should permit individuals and families to choose from among a variety of ideological options, religious and nonreligious.

Proponents of the Senate Amendment had to answer the objection that it would bar support for religious charities, which was widespread and popular. They made two responses. Some appeared simply to assume that such services, however religiously intense, were a different matter from primary education. Senator Morton, for example, said he would not "be diverted from this great question [of school funding] by what is said in regard to orphan asylums and hospitals."[72] To single out education in this way was highly "self-interested," as John Jeffries and James Ryan have observed; mainline Protestants did not operate elementary or secondary schools but did operate and accept funding for social services. In contrast, Senator Edmunds answered the social-services question by extending his understanding of nonsectarianism to those institutions too: "orphans and prisoners and everybody can be taught religion [in state-funded institutions] without being taught the particular tenets or creed of some denomination."[73] That was the same claim he had made to defend so-called nonsectarian prayers in state-run schools.

In this bevy of arguments over including religious schools and social services in state aid, what role did the concept of nonestablishment play? As already noted, both sides claimed to be supporters of nonestablishment and church–state separation; Blaine Amendment opponents said "not one in this broad land" would disagree with that principle. But they defined the principle differently. Supporters of the Amendment equated the funding of sectarian schools with establishment and the eighteenth-century funding of clergy; they did so even when the funding benefited the civic value of education and was also provided to state-run schools. The Amendment's supporters couched their arguments in terms of "absolute" church–state separation, even though most of them favored government assistance for what they took to be generalized or nonsectarian religious values.

Opponents of the Blaine Amendment countered that funding was not an establishment if it went equally to all religions providing education or other civic services. Sometimes they defended this simply on the ground that government could favor and promote religion if it did so equally among denominations. Today we would call this the nonpreferentialist or nonsectarian interpretation of disestablishment; it remains an alternative to strict church–state separation, although one that has been rejected by the modern Supreme Court.[74] Nonpreferentialism also finds support in other leading materials of the period, such as Thomas Cooley's 1868 *Treatise on Constitutional Limitations*, which stated that American legislatures were forbidden "to establish preferences by law in favor of any one religious persuasion or mode of worship."[75] But nonpreferentialism or nonsectarianism were ambiguous concepts; they meant different things to the Blaine Amendment's opponents than they meant to its proponents. For the opponents, it was nonpreferential or nonsectarian to give equal funding for a given set of services, charitable or educational, provided by any sect. But for Amendment proponents such as Senator Edmunds, nonpreferentialism or nonsectarianism meant that every entity or activity receiving government support should be nonsectarian. Thus Edmunds defended both generalized religious exercises in public schools and funding for social service entities that taught generalized religious values but not "the particular tenets or creed of some denomination."

Other arguments by Blaine Amendment opponents, however, defended funding on grounds different from nonpreferentialism. Sometimes the opponents assumed the existence of state entities in services such as education or child welfare, and argued that the key question was whether the funding

arrangements left it to individuals to decide which service to use, government or private, religious or secular. This argument, effectively, demanded
more than mere nonpreferentialism among religions: it turned on the existence of nonreligious options as well. But this approach also claimed that the
strict "no-funding" version of separation could disfavor and discourage individuals' choices to receive civic services in a religious setting. This argument
therefore resembles the current approach of the Supreme Court, set forth in
Zelman v. Simmons-Harris,[76] that state laws do not violate the Establishment
Clause if they respect or implement the "private choice" of individuals to use
benefits at a particular school among various options public, secular, and
religious.

To reemphasize, the theme of states' rights was strong in the arguments of
those who successfully opposed the Blaine Amendment. But the theme of facil-
itating individual choice through evenhanded government funding also
appeared prominently. Thus, *Zelman's* rule that such funding is consistent with
nonestablishment has a strong historical pedigree from the Reconstruction era.

State Blaine Amendments

Although the broad Senate version of the Blaine Amendment failed, provisions similar to or inspired by it were enacted in numerous states. The states
with specific prohibitions on funding of religious schools can be counted in
varying ways, but one reliable summary puts the number at fifteen by 1876 and
twenty-nine by 1900.[77]

The state Blaine Amendment episodes generally displayed the dominant
features of the federal debate (with the exception, of course, of states-rights
arguments). First, the state provisions' proponents claimed that aid to religious schools would divide society and schoolchildren and would favor
Catholicism over other denominations, whereas opponents claimed that aid
would merely treat Catholic citizens equally, and that the denial of equal aid
would be more divisive. Second, at least some of the state anti-aid campaigns
reflected a fear and distrust of Catholicism, often based on exaggerations and
stereotypes. Third, the Blaine proponents wished to preserve religious observances that they regarded as nonsectarian, but that Catholics and some others
saw as Protestant in nature.

Colorado. These three features were apparent, for example, in Colorado,
which enacted its provision upon entering the Union in 1876, the same year
the federal Blaine Amendment failed. Colorado's provision forbade both state
and local entities, including school districts, to appropriate or pay "anything
in aid of any church or sectarian society, or for any sectarian purpose, or to
help support or sustain any school, academy, seminary, college, university or
other literary or scientific institution, controlled by any church or sectarian

denomination whatsoever."[78] The anti-sectarianism language plainly echoed the federal amendment, and Republicans, who drove the federal campaign, also led the push for Colorado statehood and dominated the constitutional convention.[79]

Colorado's provision was added as a response to perceived Catholic "divisiveness," but in itself it produced substantial "bitterness" and "religious animosity" between Protestants and Catholics.[80] The issue was among the most "hotly debated" at the convention.[81] State constitutional histories describe a "backlash" against comments made by the Catholic bishop of Denver, Monsignor Joseph Machebeuf, who "petitioned [convention] delegates to permit the general assembly to divide the state school fund between public and private schools, threatening to organize a Catholic vote against ratification if his request were denied."[82] The bishop saw himself as simply seeking to preserve equality in "political and religious" rights for Catholics, and he wanted only to leave the matter to future legislatures. But his demand "aroused the Protestant majority" and led to the adoption, verbatim, of constitution language drafted by the new state teachers' union.[83]

Colorado also ended up adopting, indirectly but no less firmly, the Senate Blaine Amendment's provision that Bible reading in the public schools was nonsectarian and therefore permissible. Although the state constitutional provision's ban on payments "for any sectarian purposes" was broad enough to prohibit religious observances in public schools, the delegates rejected a resolution calling for an explicit ban on Bible reading—and in practice, public schoolteachers, the group that had supplied the constitutional language, "saw to it that the constitutional prohibition of 'sectarianism' would not extend to the Bible."[84] A few decades later, the Colorado Supreme Court upheld readings from the King James Bible against a challenge by Catholic families, concluding that it was "logically impossible" for the practice to serve a forbidden "sectarian purpose" as long as it involved reading, "without comment," "those parts which are not sectarian"[85]—that is, as long as it followed the norms of interdenominational Protestantism.

This pattern of results made the targeting of Catholic practices just as clear in Colorado's provision as it had been in the federal Blaine Amendment's Senate version. In addition, the Colorado debate included anti-Catholic accusations, some of them exaggerations and stereotypes. Anti-aid voices suggested that allowing Catholic schools an equal share of educational funding would lead to Catholic oppression: "'[I]s it not enough,' said one newspaper, "that Rome dominates in Mexico and all South America?'"[86] The stereotype that Catholic citizens merely obeyed foreign (Vatican) directives rather than asserting their own rights to equal treatment likewise appeared in the Colorado debate—for example in a Protestant minister's argument that Coloradans could "feel right in 'voting up a constitution which the Pope of Rome . . . [had] ordered voted down.'"[87]

Washington and Other Enabling-Act States. The term *establishment* did not play a significant role in Colorado's debate. But it reemerged in a new form in another set of states, most prominently Washington, that adopted anti-funding provisions in the two decades around 1900.

The 1889 federal Enabling Act for the admission of states in the Dakota Territory—North and South Dakota, Montana, and Washington—included a requirement, irrevocable without the consent of Congress, for "the establishment and maintenance of systems of public schools which shall be open to all children of said States and free from sectarian control."[88] On its face, this language seemed to ban sectarian elements only in state-run schools. But the chief commentator on the provision in Congress, Sen. William Blair, a New Hampshire Republican, explicitly tied it to the anti-parochial-school purposes of the Blaine Amendment, new versions of which he had introduced repeatedly, including in the previous year.[89] Blair opposed admitting the new states, but he called the Enabling Act's public-school section "a feature of redeeming, of saving grace" because it correctly addressed "the leading issue of the immediate future": "Which shall be the survivor, the common school or the parochial, the denominational school in this country?" The Enabling Act section, he said, was a "great precedent for the general adoption of the substance" of his own proposed amendment. His measure tracked the Senate Blaine Amendment in proposing not only to bar the teaching of any sect's "peculiar doctrines . . . or observances" in public schools, but to bar any government money from being "appropriated, applied, or given" to any private school or other institution that taught such doctrines or observances peculiar to a sect. Moreover, Blair's amendment, even more clearly than the Blaine Amendment, would have enforced nonsectarian Christianity, requiring that each state establish public schools educating children "in virtue, morality, and the principles of the Christian religion."[90]

Washington's constitutional convention, meeting immediately thereafter, adopted the congressionally mandated prohibition on sectarianism in public schools.[91] But following the lead of Blair and Blaine, it also included two further provisions explicitly restricting state money for private religious schools. Article I, section 11 stated that "[n]o public money or property shall be appropriated for or applied to any religious worship, exercise or instruction, or the support of any religious establishment"; article IX, section 4 stated that "[a]ll schools maintained or supported wholly or in part by the public funds shall be forever free from sectarian control or influence." Washington's convention, like Colorado's, was dominated by Republicans, in particular the wing of the party that supported James Blaine's presidential campaigns and his views on religion in education.[92] Unsurprisingly, the additional Washington provisions achieved "the basic objective of the Blaine Amendment: preventing state funding for parochial education or activities."[93] Although the Washington record does not show specific anti-Catholic statements, it is no stretch to infer that distrust of

Catholicism characterized the state ratifiers, as it pervaded the anti-funding movement nationally.

Washington's Article I, section 11 also put a twist on the nonestablishment language by barring any state money for "the support of any religious establishment." In this phrasing, the prohibited "religious establishment" could be read simply to mean a state-favored or -endorsed religion. But it also lent itself to a broader reading under which "religious establishment" meant any private religious-affiliated entity itself—parallel to, say, an "eating establishment"— and thus the government could not support it in any way, not even by funds given equally to comparable entities. The provision's first draft, written by a strict-separationist attorney named Lair Hill, forbade appropriations "for the support of any religious establishment or any form of worship," arguably implying that "establishment," like its counterpart "worship," referred to a private institution or activity.[94]

The Washington Supreme Court in 1949 eventually read this textual variation to prohibit the very sort of evenhanded aid to religious-school parents that the U.S. Supreme Court had just approved in *Everson*. The Washington court held not only that busing reimbursements for such families violated article IX, section 4 (supporting sectarian schools "in part . . . by the public funds"), but that each parochial school "constitutes a 'religious establishment,'" barred from state support, "with the meaning of article I, section 11."[95] In the ensuing sixty years, Washington courts have continued to read the clauses, including article I, section 11, in a strict no-funding fashion, citing their distinctive language.[96]

Washington's enactment was not the first time it was suggested that the term *establishment* might refer to the religious institution itself. "Religious establishment" had previously been paired with "mode of worship"—arguably suggesting that both referred to private organizations or activity—in seven state constitutions, beginning with Pennsylvania's in 1790. But those provisions prohibited only a "preference . . . by law" for one establishment or mode of worship,[97] so they still targeted government favoritism rather than all aid whatsoever. To take another example, in 1811 President James Madison had recast the First Amendment's nonestablishment language in vetoing a bill for the incorporation of a church in the District of Columbia that would provide education and charity to the poor. Importing his strict separationist views into the Establishment Clause, Madison (mis)quoted it as saying "Congress shall make no law respecting a religious establishment." He objected that incorporation of the church would blur "the essential distinction between civil and religious functions" by giving "a legal force and sanction . . . to certain articles in [the church's] constitution and administration" and setting "a precedent for giving to religious societies, as such, a legal agency in carrying into effect a public and civil duty."[98] Again, however, Madison's veto might be explained as a means of avoiding government favoritism, as early incorporation laws were special rather than general and thus the incorporation bill would have explicitly written one church's organizational structure into the statute books. By contrast, the Washington State provision, as applied in modern decisions, has struck down truly general, evenhanded aid, singling out religious-school families for exclusion from such a program.

From Washington State, the language banning "support for any religious establishment" spread to other states admitted in the ensuing years. But other courts have not followed Washington's in reading the language to bar all state support by equating the "establishment" with the private institution receiving support as Washington did. Arizona, admitted in 1912, adopted Washington's language verbatim.[99] But in *Kotterman v. Killian*, the Arizona Supreme Court held that a state tax credit for donations to organizations funding private-school tuitions was valid under the clause because "the range of choices reserved" to taxpayers and families among secular and religious tuition-funding organizations made the program neutral and its benefits to religious schools "sufficiently attenuated to foreclose a constitutional breach."[100] Later decisions have taken this to mean that Arizona's no-establishment language simply tracks federal jurisprudence with its principles of neutrality and choice rather than strict non-funding.[101] Restrictions on school funding in Arizona have come instead from the more specific state provision that "No tax shall be laid or appropriation of public money made in aid of any church, or private or sectarian school, or any public service corporation."[102]

In Utah, admitted in 1896, church–state arrangements were deeply influenced by the predominance of the Mormon Church, which took the place of Catholicism as the religion whose power alarmed strict church–state separationists. When the Mormons first petitioned for statehood as Deseret in 1849, their draft constitution provided that "[a]ll men shall have a natural and inalienable right to worship God according to the dictates of their own consciences, and the General Assembly shall make no law respecting an establishment of religion, or prohibiting the free exercise thereof."[103] The second clause, in adopting the First Amendment's language wholesale, confirms that by mid-century the Establishment Clause was not a mere federalism provision, but a model for individual rights at the state level. Another Utah clause, drawn from states further east, abolished religious tests for public office and stated that "no subordination or preference of any one sect or denomination to another shall ever be established by law."[104] The last clause might suggest that forbidden "establishments" were limited to preferences among denominations, although one can imagine a constitution both forbidding denominational preferences in general and forbidding certain specific practices, such as taxes for clergy, even when done nonpreferentially.

In the course of several unsuccessful campaigns for statehood—blocked by the issue of polygamy—Utah modified its religion language.[105] By 1896, when the territory finally achieved admission as a state, its provision read, "No public money or property shall be appropriated for, or applied to any religious worship, exercise, or instruction, or the support of any ecclesiastical establishment."[106] The language, which still governs today, copied Washington's except for the substitution of "ecclesiastical" for "religious." The new anti-funding provision reflected several factors. Desperate for statehood, and hopeful once the Mormon Church renounced polygamy in 1890, Utahns turned to language that had already proved satisfactory in Washington's effort for admission. They also probably felt it necessary to suggest a strict separation of church and state so as to quell the nation's fears of a Mormon theocracy. The Utahns were not directly required to do so by their 1894 federal Enabling Act, which merely contained the familiar clause against sectarian control of public schools and another clause requiring "perfect toleration of religious sentiment."[107] But they likely acted out of an abundance of caution.

Utah's prohibition could be read, like Washington's, to prohibit even neutrally available government support by defining an "establishment" as any ecclesiastical institution itself rather than the government's act of favoring it. But the Utah Supreme Court eventually construed the term more narrowly, holding that public money may indirectly benefit an ecclesiastical establishment if it is "provided on a nondiscriminatory basis" and is "equally accessible to all," "so that each group, religious or secular, has a realistically equal opportunity for the use of the public resource."[108] Although the precise holding of this case was to permit rotating prayers before a city council meeting, the standard the court adopted implies that an evenhanded state voucher program may extend to religious private schools notwithstanding the state's no-support provision.

The (Partial) Decline of Public-School-Sponsored Religion

Between the Blaine Amendment in 1876 and *Everson* in 1947, two further developments affected the application of nonestablishment principles.

The first development was that some state courts concluded that the dominant system of generalized prayers and religious exercise in public schools, endorsed by the Blaine Amendment, was in fact "sectarian" and thus violated their state constitutions. With immigration producing growing numbers of Catholics and (in some places) Jews, generic Protestantism appeared more and more to be one partial view among faiths rather than a neutral baseline constitutive of America's culture and morals. Historian Robert Handy has called this the "second disestablishment" of Protestantism in America: a step beyond the early Republic's formal disestablishment of particular Protestant denominations.[109]

Although the dominant prayers and religious exercises of the public schools might have been characterized as state establishments, the issue under most state constitutions was whether they involved "sectarian" instruction or gave one sect control of state-sponsored schools. The various rationales for invalidating religious exercises are typified by the Illinois Supreme Court decision in *State ex rel. Ring. v. Board of Education of District 24*,[110] where Catholic students in a rural county successfully sued to enjoin readings from the King James Bible and recitations of the Protestant version of the Lord's Prayer. The court held that the prayers violated the state constitution's provision against compulsory worship, while the readings violated the provision against "sectarian instruction" in public schools. The court first noted that Protestants and Catholics each regarded the other side's version of the Bible, Douay-Rheims or King James, as a "sectarian" book, and that the civil government, whether a court or a public school, could not enter the dispute to determine "what religion or what sect is right." But the court also refused to allow the endorsement of generic Christianity, reasoning that "[t]he Bible, in its entirety, is a sectarian book as to the Jew and every believer in any religion other than the Christian religion, and as to those who are heretical or who hold beliefs that are not regarded as orthodox."[111] The court recognized what this logic meant: "[T]he only means of preventing sectarian instruction in the school is to exclude altogether religious instruction, by means of the reading of the Bible or otherwise." Ultimately the court reasoned, in even clearer separationist terms, that "it is no part of the duty of the state to teach religion," because "'all history shows us that the more widely and completely [the two] are separated the better it is for both.'"[112]

The last argument above quoted the Ohio Supreme Court's opinion forty years earlier (1872) in the famous Cincinnati Bible dispute, the first leading decision to suggest that the familiar public-school religious exercises were improper.[113] The school board decided to eliminate the exercises because of objections from Catholics, Jews, and freethinkers. Several citizens sued to force reinstatement of the exercises on the ground that they were mandated by Ohio constitutional provisions—drawn from the Northwest Ordinance of 1787— that grounded the state's duty to maintain public schools on the assertion that "religion, morality, and knowledge" were "essential to good government."[114] Technically, in ruling against the plaintiffs, the court simply upheld the board's discretion to eliminate the practices. But the court's reasoning implied that Bible readings and Christian prayers were actually unconstitutional: They violated the state provision forbidding "control of any part of the school funds" by any "sect or sects," and the state must refrain from providing any religious instruction.[115]

Rulings such as those in Illinois and Ohio adopted the criticism that opponents of the Blaine Amendment had made, namely, that generalized Christian exercises were themselves skewed against non-Christians and against those Christians who could not accept their very abstract, nonspecific content. One might argue, therefore, that these rulings produced a consistent church–state separation—a consistent nonsectarianism—by eliminating even so-called nonsectarian religion from public schools as well as from private schools receiving state funding. But the rejection of public-school prayers and Bible readings did not become common until well after the wave of restrictions on religious-school funding. Writing in 1910, the Illinois court in *Ring* acknowledged that its decision was the minority view; only two other courts had struck down public-school religious exercises, whereas seven had upheld them.[116] Two decades later, as noted above, the Colorado Supreme Court dismissed Catholic parents' suits and held it permissible to read the "non-sectarian" passages of the Bible without comment—that is, to follow the practices of generic Protestantism.[117] As late as 1950—after the U.S. Supreme Court's "wall of separation" pronouncement in *Everson*—the New Jersey Supreme Court upheld readings from the Old Testament and recitations of the Lord's Prayer in *Doremus v. Board of Education.*[118] The nineteenth-century campaigns against funding of Catholic schools were not accompanied by any widespread elimination of Protestant-style practices from public schools; that change did not come until later.

Aid to Religious Organizations in the Welfare State

The second major development in the years between Blaine and *Everson* was the dramatic growth of the welfare state. American government, both federal and state, "underwent a major transformation in the years after 1887": Where it initially had performed only limited functions, it increasingly made efforts to ensure individuals' security and promote social goals.[119] And although the welfare state expanded government's direct provision of services, it also increasingly addressed a "complex, industrialized society" by "funding private—including religious—social services organizations as a means of implementing public social policies."[120]

As already noted, public authorities in the colonies and the early Republic had supported religious educational and social services, but the activity of modern government raised the stakes. Government aid to private social services reached previously unknown levels, and both federal and state governments began to show concern for students' education at whatever school they attended. For example, in 1946 Congress enacted both the federal hot-lunch program, giving food to low-income students, and the G.I. Bill, giving scholarships to veterans attending nearly any college or university, public or private, secular or religious.[121] Likewise, the New Jersey law in *Everson* authorizing bus-fare reimbursements, introduced in 1937 and passed in 1941, was a welfare measure triggered by the Great Depression.[122] A 1945 Kentucky court decision, cited prominently by the school board in *Everson v. Board of Education*, defended bus reimbursements as a public-regarding, secular welfare measure

[i]n this advanced and enlightened age, with all of the progress that has been made in the field of humane and social legislation, and with the hazards and dangers of the highway increased a thousand-fold from what they formerly were, and with our compulsory school attendance laws applying to all children and being rigidly enforced.[123]

As an amicus brief filed in *Everson* by Catholic organizations put it, the modern state acting "as *parens patriae*" took on "an increasingly active role in promoting general education as a principal factor in the general welfare."[124]

This change in the scope of government, the same amicus brief argued, produced a "problem for location of the wall" of separation, a problem "that did not exist in 1791."[125] As state concern for education became more and more comprehensive, it extended to whatever sort of education families chose. As state support for education became more and more the baseline, the no-aid or "absolute" version of church–state separation departed from the baseline more and more by excluding religious-school families from benefits generally available to others.

The U.S. Supreme Court first considered government aid to private religious services under the Establishment Clause at the turn of the twentieth century in *Bradfield v. Roberts*.[126] The District of Columbia government funded the construction of an extra building at a Catholic hospital, requiring two-thirds of the space to be reserved for indigent patients and paying for their care at $250 per patient per year. A District taxpayer filed a complaint challenging the arrangement as a violation of "the article of the Constitution which declares that Congress shall make no law respecting a religious establishment."[127] The complaint altered the constitutional language from "establishment of religion" to imply that the private entity was the "religious establishment" and therefore by law could not receive assistance in any form. This was the same alteration that Washington State had adopted in its constitution just a few years earlier, and that President Madison had made in vetoing the church incorporation in the District of Columbia in 1811. Indeed, the complaint in *Bradfield* relied heavily on the language of Madison's veto message.[128]

The District of Columbia Court of Appeals rejected the plaintiff's argument, noting that Madison had "made the mistake" of misquoting the constitutional language. "In the light of previous English and colonial history, and of the circumstances which led directly to the adoption of the amendment," the court said, "we venture to suggest that 'establishment of religion' . . . can hardly be regarded as altogether synonymous with 'religious establishment.'" Citing Thomas Cooley, Joseph Story, and other authorities, the court concluded that the clause was intended only to secure religious liberty and church–state separation "by the prohibition of any preference, by law, in favor of any one religious persuasion or mode of worship."[129] The District contract, the court said, permissibly funded "actual services" to the poor "without discrimination or preference"; cases under state constitutions were different because they involved "special prohibitions of donations or grants of public money in aid of [sectarian] establishments."[130]

The U.S. Supreme Court affirmed the permissibility of the funding, and it agreed that the wording "a law respecting a religious establishment" "is not synonymous with that used in the Constitution, which prohibits the passage of a law 'respecting an establishment of religion.'" But the Court did not adopt the standard limiting the Establishment Clause to prohibiting preferences among sects; instead it held that, even under a stricter standard by which Congress could make no law respecting a religious institution, the hospital could receive funds because it was secular in nature: "There is no allegation that its hospital work is confined to members of that church or that in its management the hospital has been conducted so as to violate its charter in the smallest degree. It is simply the case of a secular corporation being managed by people who hold to the doctrines of the Roman Catholic Church, but who nevertheless are managing the corporation according to the law under which it exists."[131]

The Court's next pre-*Everson* encounter with government funding cemented another point. Louisiana loaned textbooks for free to children attending private schools, secular and religious, on the premise that this would promote education and "obliterate illiteracy, thereby improving the morals of the children and promoting the general welfare and safety of the people."[132] In the era before the courts applied the Establishment Clause to the states, the only federal ground for challenging the law was that it served a private rather than a public purpose, in violation of the substantive component of the Fourteenth Amendment's Due Process Clause. But the Court rejected this argument, holding that the loan program fundamentally benefitted individual students and therefore society: "Individual interests are aided only as the common good is safeguarded."[133] Although the holding did not specifically apply to the Establishment Clause, it set the stage for the argument in later cases that aid to students served secular rather than religious goals and therefore did not create an establishment.

Everson Revisited: School-Aid and Catholic Disputes in the Modern State

Everson v. Board of Education involved each of the elements discussed in this chapter. It declared the applicability of the Establishment Clause to the states through incorporation in the Fourteenth Amendment. And it was deeply influenced—in conflicting directions—by both the logic of the welfare state and a distrust of Catholicism.

In the end, of course, the Court in *Everson* approved the inclusion of religious-school families in the program of reimbursements for busing costs. The controlling principle was that generated by the logic of the welfare state: New Jersey should not, and certainly need not, exclude any individuals "because of their faith, or lack of it, from receiving the benefits of public welfare legislation." The Establishment Clause did not require a selective exclusion that would effectively "hamper citizens in the free exercise of their religion" and make the state an "adversary" of religion rather than "neutral."[134]

But despite the approval of the bus reimbursements, the opinion's general thrust was against government funding of religiously affiliated education. The Court wrote the "wall of separation" metaphor into the modern case law, together with the strong language prohibiting tax support, "large or small," for "any religious activities or institutions, whatever they may be called." It said that the bus payments approached "the verge" of prohibited action, and it emphasized they were upheld because they benefited children and were "separate [and] indisputably marked off from the [schools'] religious function."[135] Justice Black reportedly told friends that he made approval of the aid "as tight" as possible to render it a "pyrrhic victory" for aid proponents.[136]

The ultimately grudging attitude of *Everson* partly reflected a simple tradition of hostility toward aiding parochial education. But it also certainly stemmed from attitudes of fear and distrust toward Catholicism that were almost as strong as in the nineteenth century. According to one historian, the late 1940s saw a new "nadir" in Protestant–Catholic relations as rancor renewed over the alleged ambition of Catholicism to dominate American life.[137] John McGreevy has detailed how liberal intellectuals around mid-century came to define themselves heavily by their opposition to the Catholic Church, which they viewed as an authoritarian force that threatened reasoned inquiry, democratic politics, and social unity.[138] That view appeared most strongly in Unitarian Paul Blanshard's best-selling 1949 broadside, *American Freedom and Catholic Power*, which compared the Church with Soviet Communism and called for a "'resistance movement' against the 'antidemocratic social policies' of the hierarchy."[139] Blanshard received rave reviews not just from liberals such as John Dewey, but from conservative evangelical voices, such as the Southern Baptist official newspaper that called parochial-aid efforts "part of the world plan whereby the Pope would control the schools, the press, hospitals, government and all matters affecting faith and morals."[140]

Supreme Court justices of this era shared the distrust of Catholicism. Justice Hugo Black, according to his son, read all of Paul Blanshard's books and shared only one view with the Ku Klux Klan: a suspicion of the Catholic Church.[141] Black would later, rather hysterically, label proponents of school aid as "powerful sectarian religious propagandists . . . looking toward complete domination and supremacy of their particular brand of religion." Justice William Douglas's opinions spoke of the Church's "indoctrinati[on]," quoted a rabid anti-Catholic book approvingly, and accused institutional churches (which Catholicism epitomized) of "feeding from the public trough" through charitable tax exemptions.[142] Shortly after *Everson*, four justices attended a

Unitarian-sponsored rally where speakers, in an obvious reference to Catholicism, criticized religions that exercised "autocratic ecclesiastical control over the mind and conscience of [their] individual members."[143]

The fears of Catholicism reasserted themselves in the middle of the twentieth century as a result of a conjunction of factors. On the one hand, American Catholics were increasingly prominent in public life and were beginning to draw even with Protestants in education and economic standing. Yet the Vatican had not yet modified some of its historic objectionable statements, such as those in the *Syllabus of Errors*, on religious freedom.[144] The mid-century distrust of Catholicism found some small justification in those older teachings. But the distrust, and the intense opposition to equal aid for parochial schools that it generated, can be questioned overall because it rested on three flawed premises: (1) an exaggeration of the threat that Catholics posed to the rights of others, (2) a mistaken refusal to acknowledge the denial of equal school aid as a burden on Catholics, and (3) a tendency to oppose the Church for its internal theology and practices rather than its effect on others.[145] Even more so than in the nineteenth century, American Catholics were committed to the moral ideals of religious freedom and the basic separation of church and state. But the official Church as a whole would not affirm these ideals until a decade later, with the Second Vatican Council's Declaration on Religious Freedom.

In short, in the late 1940s the distrust of Catholicism, and the consequent call for a strict no-aid position, hit another one of its spikes in intensity. Just at that moment the Court in *Everson* chose to incorporate the Establishment Clause into the Fourteenth Amendment. In part because of this conjunction, *Everson* set the Court on a forty-year-effort to apply a strong no-aid position to the whole host of state and local benefits touching religion.

More recently, however, the Court has tacked in a different direction, approving programs of aid such as the education vouchers involved in *Zelman v. Simmons-Harris*. *Zelman* and other decisions hold that it is permissible to provide benefits to individuals who can then independently choose whether to use them in religious settings.[146] This newer approach by the Court is an important step, reducing the tension between Establishment Clause case law and the modern state's pervasive provision of benefits to citizens.

Notes

1. Everson v. Board of Education, 330 U.S. 1 (1947).

2. Ibid., 15–16.

3. See, e.g., Robert Cord, *Separation of Church and State: Historical Fact or Current Fiction?* (New York: Lambeth Press, 1982); Robert S. Alley, *School Prayer: The Court, the Congress, and the First Amendment* (Buffalo, NY: Prometheus Books, 1994).

4. *Everson*, 330 U.S. at 16.

5. See Zelman v. Simmons-Harris, 536 U.S. 639 (2002).

6. *Everson*, 330 U.S. at 15.

7. Ibid., 15 & n.22.

8. See, e.g., Michael Kent Curtis, *No State Shall Abridge: The Fourteenth Amendment and the Bill of Rights* (Durham, NC: Duke University Press, 1986); Akhil Reed Amar, "The Bill of Rights and the Fourteenth Amendment," *Yale Law Journal* 101 (1992): 1193; Richard Aynes, "On Misreading John Bingham and the Fourteenth Amendment," *Yale Law Journal* 103 (1993): 57.

9. See, e.g., Lawrence Rosenthal, "The New Originalism Meets the Fourteenth Amendment: Original Public Meaning and the Problem of Incorporation," *Journal of Contemporary Legal Issues* 18 (2009): 361.

10. Amar, "The Bill of Rights and the Fourteenth Amendment," 1263.

11. Ibid.; see also, e.g., Steven D. Smith, *Foreordained Failure: The Quest for a Constitutional Principle of Religious Freedom* (New York: Oxford University Press, 1995), ch. 2; William K. Lietzau, "Rediscovering the Establishment Clause: Federalism and the Rollback of Incorporation," *DePaul Law Review* 39 (1990): 1191; Joseph M. Snee, "Religious Disestablishment and the Fourteenth Amendment," *Washington University Law Quarterly* (1954): 371. See further chapter 8 by Carl Esbeck.

12. See further chapter 6 by Ralph Ketcham; John Witte Jr., "'A Most Mild and Equitable Establishment of Religion': John Adams and the 1780 Massachusetts Constitution," *Journal of Church and State* 41 (1999): 213–52.

13. Daniel O. Conkle, "Toward a General Theory of the Establishment Clause," *Northwestern University Law Review* 82 (1988): 1113, 1133 (emphasis in original).

14. Smith, *Foreordained Failure*, 23–27. See further chapter 8 by Carl Esbeck.

15. Elk Grove Unified School District v. Newdow, 542 U.S. 1, 49 (2004) (Thomas, J., concurring in the judgment).

16. Ibid., 49; Smith, *Foreordained Failure*, 49.

17. Adamson v. California, 332 U.S. 46. 65 (1947) (Frankfurter, J., concurring).

18. See, e.g., McCollum v. Board of Education, 333 U.S. 203, 231 (1948) (Frankfurter, J., concurring) ("Separation means separation, not something less."); *id.* at 216–17 (describing public schools as the "symbol of our secular unity" and "the most powerful agency for promoting cohesion among a heterogeneous democratic people").

19. Abington School District v. Schempp, 374 U.S. 203, 256 (1963) (Brennan, J., concurring).

20. Kurt T. Lash, "The Second Adoption of the Establishment Clause: The Rise of the Nonestablishment Principle," *Arizona State Law Journal* 27 (1995): 1085, 1154.

21. Ibid., 1133 & n.224 (quoting constitutions of Iowa, Alabama, and South Carolina, and proposed constitution for Utah). See further chapter 10 by Steven K. Green.

22. Lash, "Second Adoption," at 1103–11. See further chapter 9 by Daniel Dreisbach.

23. Cong. Globe, 42d Cong., 1st Sess. App. 84 (March 31, 1871) (Rep. Bingham), reprinted in *The Reconstruction Amendments' Debates: The Legislative History and Contemporary Debates in Congress on the 13th, 14th, and 15th Amendments*, Alfred Avins, ed. (Richmond, VA: Virginia Commission on Constitutional Government, 1967), 510–11.

24. Cong. Globe, 38th Cong., 1st Sess. 1202 (March 19, 1864) (Sen. Wilson), reprinted in Avins, *The Reconstruction Amendments' Debates*, 65.

25. Ibid.

26. 4 Cong. Rec. 205 (1875).

27. Ibid., 5593 (Sen. Morton).

28. The argument is noted and sources are collected in Lash, "Second Adoption," 1147; and in Steven K. Green, "The Blaine Amendment Reconsidered," 36 *American Journal of Legal History* (1992): 38, 38–39.

29. 4 Cong. Rec. at 5592 (Sen. Eaton), 5583 (Sen. Whyte).

30. Ibid., 5591 (Sen. Bogy).

31. 83 U.S. (16 Wall.) 36 (1873). See 4 Cong. Rec. at 5585 (Sen. Morton) (complaining that the Fourteenth Amendment had been "in some respects almost destroyed by construction" and urging that the Blaine Amendment be written clearly to avoid the same fate).

32. Ward M. McAfee, "The Historical Context of the Failed Federal Blaine Amendment of 1876," *First Amendment Law Review* 2 (2003): 1, 5–7. See generally Ward M. McAfee, *Religion, Race, and Reconstruction: The Public School in the Politics of the 1870s* (New York: SUNY Press, 1998).

33. 4 Cong. Rec. 5585 (August 14, 1876) (Sen. Morton).

34. Ibid. (Sen. Bogy).

35. Ibid., 5581 (Sen. Kernan). New Hampshire still had a constitutional provision limiting eligibility for governor and the legislature to Protestants.

36. Ibid., 5592.

37. See Wallace v. Jaffree, 472 U.S. 38, 49 (1985) ("This Court has confirmed and endorsed this elementary proposition of law [incorporation] time and time again.").

38. See, e.g., Lloyd P. Jorgenson, *The State and the Non-Public School 1825–1925* (Columbia: University of Missouri Press, 1987), 1–19; for a detailed account of the pluralistic pattern of schools and public funding before the 1830s, see Richard J. Gabel, *Public Funds for Church and Private Schools* (Washington, DC: Catholic University of America, 1937), 147–470.

39. Jorgenson, *The State and the Non-Public School*, 60 (quoting Mann's *Twelfth Annual Report to the [Massachusetts] Board of Education* (1852), 117, 124).

40. Quoted in Jorgenson, *The State and the Non-Public School*, 75.

41. John C. Jeffries Jr. and James E. Ryan, "A Political History of the Establishment Clause," *Michigan Law Review* 100 (2001): 279, 301.

42. Steven K. Green, "The Insignificance of the Blaine Amendment," *Brigham Young University Law Review* 2008: 295, 310. See further chapter 10 by Steven Green.

43. See, e.g., Jorgensen, *The State and the Non-Public School*; Philip Hamburger, *Separation of Church and State* (Cambridge, MA: Harvard University Press, 2002), 217–29 (mid-19th-century statements by public school supporters); Hamburger, *Separation of Church and State*, 405–19 (late-19th-century statements).

44. Jeffries and Ryan, "Political History of the Establishment Clause," 301.

45. On Mann, see Jorgensen, *The State and the Non-Public School*, 37–38; on Bushnell, see Charles Glenn, *The Myth of the Common School* (Amherst, NY: Amherst University Press, 1988), 227–29.

46. H.J. Res. 254, Cong. Globe, 41st Cong., 2d Sess. 2754 (April 18, 1870).

47. 4 Cong. Rec. 5585 (Sen. Morton).

48. Ibid.

49. Gabel, *Public Funds*, 756.

50. See Carl H. Esbeck, "Dissent and Disestablishment: The Church–State Settlement in the Early Republic," *Brigham Young University Law Review* 2004: 1385, 1480–81 & n.319.

51. Jorgensen, *The State and the Non-Public School*, 5.

52. Gabel, *Public Funds*, 173–79.

53. 4 Cong. Rec. at 5584, 5585 (Sen. Morton).

54. Ibid., 5581.

55. Ibid., 5585 (Sen. Morton), 5587 (Sen. Edmunds), 5585 (Sen. Morton).

56. Ibid., 5587–88 (Sen. Edmunds), 5591 (Sen. Morton).

57. Ibid., 5587–88 (Sen. Edmunds).

58. Marc D. Stern, "Blaine Amendments, Anti-Catholicism, and Catholic Dogma," *First Amendment Law Review* 2 (2003): 153, 176; Stephen Macedo, *Diversity and Distrust: Civic Education in a Multicultural Democracy* (Cambridge, MA: Harvard University Press, 2002), 61, 75.

59. 4 Cong. Rec. 5583 (Sen. White), 5590 (Sen. Bogy).

60. *The Roman Catholic Church and Free Thought: A Controversy between Archbishop Purcell, of Cincinnati, and Thomas Vickers* (Cincinnati, OH: The First Congregational Church, 1868), 32.

61. Ibid., 52–55 (quoting 1862 Pastoral Letter published in *Cincinnati Gazette* and *Commercial*).

62. 4 Cong. Rec. at 5586.

63. Ibid., 5580 (Amendment text).

64. Ibid. 5590 (Sen. Bogy).

65. Green, "The Insignificance of the Blaine Amendment," 304–06; Noah Feldman, "Nonsectarianism Reconsidered," *Journal of Law and Politics* 11 (2002): 65, 78–81.

66. 4 Cong. Rec. 5590 (Sen. Bogy).

67. Ibid., 5586 (Sen. Kernan).

68. Ibid.

69. Ibid., 5582–83.

70. Ibid., 5592 (Sen. Eaton).

71. Ibid., 5584, 5583 (Sen. Kernan).

72. Ibid., 5585.

73. Ibid., 5588 (Sen. Edmunds).

74. ACLU v. McCreary County, 545 U.S. 844, 877–80 (2005); Engel v. Vitale, 370 U.S. 421, 430 (1962) ("the fact that [a public-school-sponsored] prayer is 'nondenominational'" cannot "serve to free it from the limitations of the Establishment Clause").

75. Thomas M. Cooley, *A Treatise on the Constitutional Limitations Which Rest upon the Legislative Power of the States of the American Union*, 7th ed. (Boston: Little Brown & Co., 1908), 663–64 ("There is not complete religious liberty where any one sect is favored by the State and given an advantage by law over other sects.").

76. 536 U.S. 639 (2002).

77. See Joseph P. Viteritti, "Davey's Plea: Blaine, Blair, *Witters*, and the Protection of Religious Freedom," *Harvard Journal of Law and Public Policy* 27 (2003): 299, 312–13.

78. Colorado Constitution, Art. IX, § 7.

79. See Dale A. Oesterle and Richard B. Collins, *The Colorado State Constitution: A Reference Guide* (Westport, CT: Greenwood Press, 2002), 5–6.

80. Donald W. Hensel, "Religion and the Writing of the Colorado Constitution," *Church History* 30 (September 1961): 349, 352, 356; see also Oesterle and Collins, *Colorado State Constitution*, 211 & nn.31–34.

81. Oesterle and Collins, *Colorado State Constitution*, 224 & n.31.

82. Ibid.

83. Viteritti, "Davey's Plea," 321.

84. Hensel, "Religion and the Writing of the Colorado Constitution," 354 & n.35; Gabel, *Public Funds*, 475 n.5 (citing Hale, Grove, and Shaddock, *Education in Colorado* (Colorado State Teachers' Association, 1885), 34–52).

85. People *ex rel.* Vollmar v. Stanley, 81 Colo. 276, 286, 255 P. 610, 615 (1927).

86. Hensel, "Religion and the Writing," 354 & n.31.

87. Ibid., 356 & n.50 (ellipsis in original).

88. Act of February 22, 1889, ch. 180, 25 Stat. 676, § 4 (1889).

89. 20 Cong. Rec. 2100 (February 20, 1889) (Sen. Blair).

90. Ibid., 2100–01.

91. Washington Constitution, Art. XXVI ("Provision shall be made for the establishment and maintenance of systems of public schools free from sectarian control which shall be open to all the children of said state.").

92. Robert F. Utter and Edward J. Larson, "Church and State on the Frontier: The History of the Establishment Clauses in the Washington State Constitution," *Hastings Constitutional Law Quarterly* 15 (1988): 451, 468–69.

93. Ibid., 473.

94. Ibid., 472–73.

95. Visser v. Nooksack Valley School District No. 506, 33 Wash. 2d 699, 708, 207 P.2d 198, 203 (1949).

96. Malyon v. Pierce County, 131 Wash. 2d 779, 795 & n.15, 935 P.2d 1272, 1279 & n.15 (1997); Witters v. State Commission for the Blind, 112 Wash. 2d 363, 370, 771 P.2d 1119, 1122 (1989).

97. Pennsylvania Constitution, Art. IX, § 3 ("no preference shall ever be given, by law, to any religious establishment or modes of worship"); see also Arkansas Constitution (1874), Art. II, § 24; Kansas Constitution, Bill of Rights, § 7; Minnesota Constitution, Art. I, § 16; South Dakota Constitution, Art. VI, § 3; Tennessee Constitution, Art. I, § 3; Wisconsin Constitution, Art. I, § 18; Martin v. Beer Board for City of Dickson, 908 S.W.2d 941, 949 (Tenn. App. 1995) (identifying Pennsylvania as origin of the language).

98. *Annals of Congress* 23:982–83 (1811).

99. Arizona Constitution, Art. II, § 12.

100. 193 Ariz. 273, 287, 972 P.2d 606, 620 (1999).

101. Cain v. Horne, 218 Ariz. 301, 306, 183 P.3d 1269, 1274 (App. Div. 2. 2008).

102. Arizona Constitution, Art. IX, § 10.

103. Deseret Constitution (1849), Art. VIII, § 3, reprinted in *Sources and Documents of United States Constitutions*, ed. William F. Swindler (Dobbs Ferry, NY: Oceana, 1979), 9:380.

104. Ibid.

105. See further chapter 10 by Steven Green.

106. Utah Constitution, Art. I, § 4.

107. Ch. 138, 53d Cong., 2d Sess., § 3, 28 Stat. 107, 108 (July 16, 1894).

108. Society of Separationists v. Whitehead, 870 P.2d 916, 937–38 (Utah 1993).

109. See Robert T. Handy, *A Christian America: Protestant Hopes and Historical Realities* (New York: Oxford University Press, 1971). See also Steven K. Green, *The Second Disestablishment of Religion: Church and State in Nineteenth Century America* (New York: Oxford University Press, 2010).

110. 245 Ill. 334 (1910).

111. Ibid., 347–48.

112. Ibid., 349–50.

113. Board of Education of Cincinnati v. Minor, 23 Ohio St. 211 (1872).

114. See Ohio Constitution, Arts. I, §7, VI, § 2.

115. Ibid., Art. VI, § 2; *Minor*, 23 Ohio St. 2d. at 247–48.

116. State *ex rel*. Ring. v. Board of Education of District 24, 245 Ill. 334, 350 (1910).

117. People *ex rel*. Vollmar v. Stanley, 81 Colo. 276, 286 (1927).

118. Doremus v. Board of Education of Borough of Hawthorne, 5 N.J. 435 (1950).

119. Ballard C. Campbell, *The Growth of American Government: Governance from the Cleveland Era to the Present* (Bloomington: Indiana University Press, 1995), 1.

120. Timothy S. Burgett, Note, "Government Aid to Religious Social Service Providers: The Supreme Court's 'Pervasively Sectarian' Standard," *Virginia Law Review* 75 (1989): 1077, 1080.

121. Act of June 4, 1946, c. 281, 60 Stat. 230, 42 U.S.C. §§ 1751–1760 (school lunches); G.I. Bill of Rights, Act of August 8, 1946, c. 886, Public Law 679, 79th Cong., 2d Sess.

122. See Daryl R. Fair, "The *Everson* Case in the Context of New Jersey Politics," in *Everson Revisited: Religion, Education, and Law at the Crossroads*, ed. Jo Renee Formicola and Hubert Morken (Lanham, MD: Rowman & Littlefield, 1997), 1, 3–7.

123. Nichols v. Henry, 301 Ky. 424, 443, 191 S.W.2d 930, 934–35 (1945), quoted in Brief for Appellees, 36, in Philip B. Kurland and Gerhard Casper, eds., *Landmark Briefs and Arguments in the Supreme Court of the United States* (Arlington, VA: University Press of America, 1975), 44:773, 829.

124. Brief Amici Curiae of the National Council of Catholic Men and the National Council of Catholic Women, 35, in Kurland and Casper, *Landmark Briefs and Arguments*, 44:923, 961.

125. Ibid.

126. 175 U.S. 291 (1899).

127. Roberts v. Bradfield, 12 App. D.C. 453, 1898 WL 15628 (D.C. App. 1898).

128. Ibid.

129. Ibid., *8–9.

130. Ibid., *12.

131. *Bradfield*, 175 U.S. at 298–99.

132. Borden v. Louisiana State Board of Education, 168 La. 1005, 1022 (1929).

133. Cochran v. Louisiana State Board of Education, 281 U.S. 370, 375 (1930).

134. *Everson*, 330 U.S. at 16.

135. Ibid., 16, 18.

136. Roger K. Newman, *Hugo Black: A Biography* (New York: Pantheon, 1994), 363–64.

137. Robert S. Ellwood, *The Fifties Spiritual Marketplace: American Religion in a Decade of Conflict* (New Brunswick, NJ: Rutgers University Press, 1997), 17, 51.

138. John T. McGreevy, "Thinking on One's Own: Catholicism in the American Intellectual Imagination, 1928–1960," *Journal of American History* (June 1997): 97; for further elaboration, see John T. McGreevy, *Catholicism and American Freedom: A History* (New York: W.W. Norton, 2003), 166–88, and chapter 1 by T. Jeremy Gunn.

139. Paul Blanshard, *American Freedom and Catholic Power* (Boston: Beacon Press, 1949), 303.

140. McGreevy, "Thinking on One's Own," 97 (quoting Dewey describing Blanshard's "exemplary scholarship, good judgment, and tact"); Hal D. Bennett, "*American Freedom and Catholic Power*: Book Review," *Alabama Baptist* (October 13, 1949): 9.

141. Hugo Black Jr., *My Father, A Remembrance* (New York: Random House, 1975), 104.

142. See Board of Education v. Allen, 392 U.S. 236, 251 (1968) (Black, J., dissenting); Lemon v. Kurtzman, 403 U.S. 602, 636 (1971) (Douglas, J., concurring) (quoting Lorraine Boettner, *Roman Catholicism* (Philadelphia: Presbyterian & Reformed, 1962), 375); Walz v. Tax Commission, 397 U.S. 664, 714 (1970) (Douglas, J., dissenting); *Lemon*, 403 U.S. at 630–31.

143. McGreevy, "Thinking on One's Own," 121–22 (quoting sermon of Frederick May Eliot at the Jefferson Memorial, April 13, 1947).

144. Thomas C. Berg, "Anti-Catholicism and Modern Church-State Relations," *Loyola University Chicago Law Journal* 33 (2001): 121, 131–32.

145. For elaboration of these claims, see ibid., 132, 138–47.

146. See Zelman v. Simmons-Harris, 536 U.S. 639 (2002); Zobrest v. Catalina Foothills School District, 509 U.S. 1 (1993); Witters v. Department of Services, 474 U.S. 481 (1986).

12

Some Reflections on Fundamental Questions about the Original Understanding of the Establishment Clause

Kent Greenawalt

In *Everson v. Board of Education*[1] the Supreme Court unanimously decided that the Establishment Clause of the First Amendment applied to states and localities under the Due Process Clause of the post–Civil War Fourteenth Amendment. The justices were also united in adopting a stringent understanding of the limits set by that clause, partly captured by the phrase "separation of church and state." The justices divided 5–4 on the constitutionality of New Jersey's paying for the bus transportation of students attending parochial schools. Although scholars and subsequent Supreme Court justices have variously characterized the reasons that the majority of the Court was willing to uphold that practice—and indeed passages in Justice Black's opinion for the Court do look in somewhat different directions—a crucial explanation follows from its comment that "No tax in any amount, large or small, can be levied to support any religious activity or institution, whatever they may be called, or whatever form they may adopt to teach or practice religion."[2] Because the opinion goes on the acknowledge that the New Jersey law approached the "verge" of state power,[3] one must conclude that for Justice Black the key was that affording bus transportation to children attending private nonprofit schools did not significantly aid religious education itself.[4]

My interest in this chapter is remote from the exact disposition in *Everson*. Rather, I concentrate on fundamental issues about original intent that the majority and dissenting opinions raise, many of which remain matters of intense controversy. As dominant ideas about these issues change, actual doctrines and results under the Establishment Clause are likely to shift, though there is commonly no neat one-to-one correlation between a position on original intent and a favored result to a specific legal contest.

The related issues I discuss are (1) the basic idea of whether the Establishment Clause should apply to the states; (2) the heavy reliance on the views of Thomas Jefferson and James Madison; (3) the strict concept of nonestablishment, including the idea of separation of church and state; (4) what relevantly should count as the original intent as time from enactment elapses; (5) how much should the "original understanding" now matter; and (6) the relevance of the Establishment Clause for the constitutional permissibility of the so-called "Blaine Amendment" discussed in the last two chapters by Steven Green and Thomas Berg.

The reader should be warned that I am not a historian; I have not conducted independent research to support one position or another. I do believe some apparent claims about the original understanding are hard to sustain, and I do not hesitate to express judgments about these. I also indicate other normative judgments that rest on my sense of our legal traditions and appraisal of what arguments are persuasive. Many of the positions I accept are rejected by other thoughtful analysts whose base of knowledge is at least as great as my own.

Incorporation of the Establishment Clause

In *Everson*, Justice Black's majority opinion assumes without analysis that the Establishment Clause applies against the states as well as the federal government. That proposition is now solidly settled, despite occasional doubts about it expressed in individual opinions of justices.[5] But the virtual certainty that the Supreme Court will not back away from its position that the Establishment Clause applies to the states has not eliminated debate over its soundness.

The decision that the Fourteenth Amendment makes the Establishment Clause applicable against the states depends on the more general proposition that the Due Process Clause of the Fourteenth Amendment rendered the fundamental provisions of the Bill of Rights as limits on state laws. By the time *Everson* was decided in 1947, the Free Speech and Free Exercise Clauses had already been held to limit state activity. Thus, it may have seemed a simple extension to hold that the rest of the First Amendment, which begins "Congress shall make no law," warranted similar treatment. Whether those adopting the Fourteenth Amendment really intended that all or most of the rights in the Bill of Rights apply against the states is uncertain. If they had any intent of this sort, they probably would have conceived the Privileges and Immunities Clause, not the Due Process Clause, as the vehicle, but that clause had earlier received a very narrow construction.[6] I shall leave aside the general question of incorporation. But there are some special concerns about the Establishment Clause.

Two basic arguments against applying this clause to the states are that it was essentially jurisdictional, reserving power to the states, and that it was institutional, not really a matter of individual rights at all.[7] To oversimplify a bit, here is how these contentions support a rejection of incorporation: (1) A provision that kept the federal government out of state business should not be turned around to restrict states, and (2) A provision designed to allocate institutional responsibilities cannot reasonably be incorporated by a provision that is explicitly a protection of individual rights (both the Due Process and Privileges and Immunities Clause of the Fourteenth Amendment concern individual rights).

Debate over the "jurisdictional" point gets fairly convoluted, but here is a spare version of the basic position, followed by the reasons I find it unpersuasive. At the time the Bill of Rights was ratified in 1791, roughly half the states had some forms of favoring religion that are now conceived by many observers as at least weak establishments of religion. Although undoubtedly some influential members of Congress, most notably James Madison, who drafted the Bill of Rights, opposed establishments in principle, other members of Congress were satisfied with the degrees to which their own states favored one or more religions. And, of course, those ratifying the Bill of Rights in their own states had similar views. The manner in which we need to understand the Establishment Clause is as an assurance that the federal government would not interfere with state decisions whether to establish or not. Congress could not create a national church, but states were free to do what they wanted. On this understanding, it was paradoxically wrongheaded for the Court to decide that the Clause actually can restrict the states.

Here is what I take to be unpersuasive about this position. I accept that the clause was partly jurisdictional at the outset, but it was not only jurisdictional, in the sense of leaving states free within their own domains. It says "Congress shall make no law respecting an establishment of religion. . . ." What does that imply for federal domains, areas *not* subject to state authority, such as U.S. embassies abroad, the about-to-be implemented federal enclave of the District of Columbia, and fairly extensive federal territories? Could the national government have created a federal established church for these areas, with relations to government such as those of the Anglican Church in England? The clause's language strongly suggests that the answer is no, and none of the advocates of the jurisdictional view has come up with significant evidence to the contrary. It follows that the original clause was partly jurisdictional, in protecting state determinations, and partly antiestablishment, as it affected federal domains.

By the time that the Fourteenth Amendment was ratified, no state continued to have an established religion, and most states had their own "no establishment" language in their constitutions. By this time, "no establishment" was thought of as a matter of principle, not an allocation of authority between levels of government. If the federal clause was then mainly understood in this way, its antiestablishment coverage might well have been extended to states, along with the rest of the First Amendment.

The argument based on the institutional character of the Establishment Clause cannot be answered so easily; a defense of incorporation against it depends on a more nuanced judgment about the character of the clause and its relations to the First Amendment's Free Exercise Clause and the Equal Protection Clause of the Fourteenth Amendment. The nub of the question is this: If the Establishment Clause is essentially about relations between civil government and institutional religion, how can provisions that protect individual rights be thought to include it?

Part of the answer is that those who have supported nonestablishment in principle have always perceived it as closely related to free exercise. No doubt, a country with an established religion can allow a substantial degree of free exercise, but through the eighteenth century, most countries and principalities with established religions did not grant full privileges to nonadherents. Further, one aspect of nonestablishment is an ideal of nonpreference among adherents of different religions. Such equality might well be encompassed by both the Free Exercise Clause and the Equal Protection Clause. In sum, if the Supreme Court had ruled that the Establishment Clause itself did not apply to the states, it would have had to decide what state measures that would be prohibited to Congress under the Establishment Clause would also violate the Free Exercise or the Equal Protection Clause, and which measures would not violate either of these clauses. Only the latter would be left to states, to determine under their own state provisions on nonestablishment. This position would be coherent, but it would multiply the complexities of Establishment Clause interpretation, with, in all probability, very limited practical consequence for legal outcomes. As a matter of simplicity of judicial administration, acknowledgement that the Establishment Clause bears a sufficient connection to individual rights to be applied against states is preferable.

Reliance on the Views of Thomas Jefferson and James Madison

Justice Black's opinion in *Everson* relied heavily on the views of Thomas Jefferson and James Madison. Subsequent discussions of nonestablishment have paid a great deal of attention to those two founders, although concentration on their views has also been sharply criticized.[8] Our inquiry as to how far their conception of nonestablishment should influence understanding of the Establishment Clause pushes us to come to terms with the kind of original intent that appropriately matters for general clauses of the Constitution that come to us from the founding era.

Why should the views of Madison and Jefferson be of particular weight? Madison, of course, was the original drafter of the Bill of Rights, adopted two years after the Constitution to satisfy those who believed that the power of the federal government was not sufficiently restricted by the original document. A key development toward nonestablishment had been Virginia's earlier rejection of a state tax to support religions, followed by the adoption of Thomas

Jefferson's Bill for Religious Freedom, which, among other things, forbade requiring anyone to support any ministry. Madison had led the fight against the tax, and his *Memorial and Remonstrance* was the clearest, most eloquent public statement of principles of nonestablishment.[9] (The *Memorial and Remonstrance* was printed as an appendix to Justice Rutledge's dissent in *Everson*.) The author of the Virginia bill, Jefferson, was in France when the Bill of Rights was drafted. He was the strictest separationist among the early presidents, and in a now famous (but then obscure) 1802 letter to the Baptists in Danbury, Connecticut, he opined that the Establishment Clause built "a wall of separation between church and state."[10]

One aspect of modern discussions is what Madison and Jefferson really believed. Was Madison's *Memorial and Remonstrance* opposed to all financial assistance to religion or only to preferential assistance? Did Jefferson refuse to authorize national days of prayer because he thought that the government should steer entirely clear of religion or because he did not want implicitly to favor groups that preferred one day of prayer or another?[11] I want here to focus on the prior question of whether their particular views should be accorded disproportionate significance when judges interpret the Constitution.

This requires us to rehearse briefly theories about original intent. In regard to constitutional interpretation as well as statutory interpretation, the place of original intent, and the character of the original intent that should count, are highly contested. Some Supreme Court justices, led by Justice Scalia, believe that original intent should ordinarily be determinative;[12] others accept a historical development of constitutional concepts over time. All justices and scholars agree that original intent is relevant, that it can make at least some difference in how a provision should now be understood. But to say that original intent matters does not tell us what counts as original intent.

At least three questions present themselves. First, should we focus on the actual (subjective) intentions of those who voted to enact or ratify the Bill of Rights, or on what a reasonable participant in that process would likely have had in mind, or on how readers of the time would have understood the provision? Second, should we focus on understood implications for concrete situations or on more abstract principles? Third, should the focus be on what those responsible for, or subject to, a provision conceived, or should we attempt to distill a measure of wisdom about what is just and desirable? For the most part, contentions about relevant original intent concern the first two questions. With respect to those inquiries it is impossible to justify giving so much weight to Jefferson's and Madison's views for interpreting the original Establishment Clause.[13]

We have already identified the main reason this is so. Jefferson and Madison were the strongest proponents of nonestablishment among major political figures in the new republic. But, as we have seen, at least seven states retained various forms of aid to religions.[14] A constitutional amendment must be approved by two-thirds of each house of Congress and by the state legislatures in three-quarters of the states. It is initially implausible to suppose that most of those voting in favor of the First Amendment had specifically in mind a strict separationist approach.

This initial judgment could be countered in one of two ways. It could be shown that various members of Congress and state legislators from states with forms of establishment did advocate a very strict version of nonestablishment for the federal government within federal domains. As far as I am aware, there is virtually no evidence precisely what kind of nonestablishment such legislators understood the Establishment Clause to enact.

The second type of countervailing evidence would be wide publicity that the Establishment Clause embraced the sense of nonestablishment that Jefferson and Madison favored. Such evidence would be analogous to showing that aspects of the original constitution were understood by those ratifying within the states in accord with the explanations provided in The Federalist Papers. Regrettably, the Bill of Rights, as important to American liberties as it has become, was approved by Congress and ratified by state legislatures in a fairly cursory fashion. Because the precise language of "no law respecting an establishment of religion" was novel, not only in the United States but in the world, it is hard to know what exactly a reasonable reader, whether legally trained or not, would have made of it, except to understand that at a minimum a government church, along the lines of the Church of England, was forbidden.[15] If that reader happened to be aware of the preceding Virginia controversy and Madison's position in it, he or she, like ourselves looking back through history, would not have been confident as to whether Madison's own opinions had succeeded within Congress or whether the differences between Madison and others had been compromised, or papered over without resolution. In short, whether one focuses on the subjective intent of most adopters, on how a reasonable adopter would have understood the language, or on what a reasonable reader would have understood, there is little basis simply to accept as decisive the favored positions of Madison and Jefferson.

For the question of what weight to accord Madison and Jefferson, the controversy about "specific intent" and "abstract purpose" may or may not be critical. When one thinks about original understanding, one can focus on people's sense of how a particular provision would apply or the general principles they believe the provision embodies. Thus, it may be that the adopters of the Eighth Amendment did not regard flogging as "cruel and unusual punishment," and we know they did not think the death penalty was barred by that language. Nevertheless, perhaps given our present understanding of what flogging and state-imposed capital punishment entail, these penalties are "cruel" according to the founders' notion of cruelty. Similarly, a practice—such as making blasphemy according to Christian conceptions a crime while allowing comments that would be blasphemy for other religions—might violate notions of nonestablishment, even if the founders failed to recognize that implication.

In deciding whether to look mainly to abstract principle or to concrete applications, one might focus on which inquiry was intended by the adopters or on which approach fulfills an appropriate judicial role. The argument that a shift to abstract purpose does not really make a difference for the status of Jefferson's and Madison's views is that their own broad understandings of nonestablishment was very strict but that others accepted much more moderate abstract understandings. Thus, one should no more rely on *their* sense of abstract purpose than on *their* idea of concrete applications. This argument has force, but we need to consider two possibilities that could point in a different direction.

One, which I shall briefly mention, relates to what I have already said about incorporation of the Establishment Clause. At the time of the Fourteenth Amendment, the idea of "establishment of religion" may have been different than it was three-quarters of a century earlier. Insofar as the enactors and ratifiers of the Fourteenth Amendment were affected by the views of the earlier generation, they were more likely influenced by abstract principles than by specific views about particular practices accepted during the founders' generation. As no state had any formal establishment of religion in the 1860s and virtually all states had their own constitutional nonestablishment clauses, those who wrote and approved the Fourteenth Amendment were probably more consistently antiestablishment, as they understood it, than those who helped adopt the Bill of Rights. Especially if Jefferson's and Madison's views had then maintained prominence, one might conclude that those passing on post–Civil War amendments were particularly influenced by their views. Apart from this nuance about the significance of the subsequent amendment, there is an interpretive issue with deeper significance.

Perhaps I have too quickly treated the relevant abstract principle as something like relatively strict or moderate nonestablishment. Perhaps what is central is a true or sound understanding of what nonestablishment entails. According to this conception of how nonestablishment should be understood, not only may our modern understanding of nonestablishment entail particular *consequences* that would not have been conceived by most people when the Establishment Clause was adopted, the abstract principle now underlying decisions may properly look different from the abstract principle most of them would have understood.

Here is an illustration, crude in its grossly simplistic categorization. Suppose that most of those who voted for the Bill of Rights did not think the government should support any particular church but was free to sponsor particular religious opinions, by, for example, engaging in public prayers, forbidding Christian blasphemy, and using the King James version of the Bible in all government ceremonies and in public schools (once these developed).[16] Their abstract principles, if they thought about them, were that although the government should not favor any specific church, it did operate within a broad Protestant

Christian nation and could reflect that foundation in its actions. A modern understanding of nonestablishment would reject the idea that Protestant Christianity can be afforded degrees of government sponsorship *and* it would perceive a closer connection between government expression of religious ideas and government favoring of particular groups than did most founders. After all, if government expresses particular opinions about religion, this amounts to a kind of implicit, indirect favoring of the churches or other groups that adhere to such opinions.

On an understanding of abstract principles that focuses on the soundest understanding of a basic concept, one *might* turn to Madison and Jefferson as having a truer sense of what nonestablishment entails than most of their contemporaries, a sense that warrants relying heavily on their opinions. Any approach of this sort, in which one takes original abstract principles as those principles that most fully realize the true dimensions of a complex concept such as nonestablishment, can be challenged as no longer really relying on original intent in any straightforward way. I return to this challenge in a section that follows discussion of strict disestablishment.

Strict Disestablishment and Conceptualization

In the *Everson* opinions, closely connected with the reliance on Jefferson and Madison is the conclusion that disestablishment is strict. That understanding is signaled by the use of Jefferson's phrase, a "wall of separation between church and state." Powerful objections have been raised both to the idea that the limits on government practices are as stringent as this strict separationist approach entails and to the very terminology of "separation," a concept that some assert is quite different from "disestablishment." I shall briefly address the claimed gross disparities in substance between the founders' views and those of the modern Supreme Court before tackling the significance of overarching concepts.

This chapter is not the occasion to discuss the details of adjudication under the Establishment Clause, but a brief sketch of where we have come since the *Everson* decision will help provide a sense of how stringent are the presently dominant notions of what are forbidden establishments. In respect to financial assistance to parochial education, the Court for some decades carried forward the implications of *Everson*, striking down financial assistance that held the promise of genuinely aiding religious education, and approving only fringe aids, such as the loan of secular texts and payment for implementation of government tests. That approach has shifted radically. With some preliminary moves toward greater permissiveness, the Court in 2002 approved a voucher plan, according to which private nonprofit schools in Cleveland, the great majority of which were parochial schools, received very substantial financial aid for the education of children from relatively poor families.[17] As far as the federal constitution is concerned, the Establishment Clause is no longer interpreted as a stringent restraint on financial aid to religious institutions engaged in endeavors that serve broader secular purposes.

In regard to government sponsorship of religious beliefs and practices in public schools, however, the underlying theme of *Everson* has been carried forward.[18] Notably, public schools cannot engage in prayers and devotional Bible readings in class, graduation ceremonies, and football games, and they cannot post the Ten Commandments in all classrooms. Nor may public schools teach "creation science" as an alternative to evolution. Similarly, cities and towns cannot erect crèches in a manner that will appear to endorse Christianity. The fundamental principle is that governments, with very limited exceptions,[19] may not themselves endorse or sponsor religious ideas. Justices have strained to explain that "In God We Trust" on coins and "under God" in the Pledge of Allegiance do not really have religious significance, but rather are understood as a reference to historical tradition. At least with respect to "under God," said by young children in school classrooms, such an explanation is wholly lacking in plausibility.

A minority of justices (so far) has proposed that it is entirely appropriate for governments to acknowledge a benign Supreme Being, a belief shared by Christians, Jews, and Muslims. Among the reasons offered by critics of any strict conception of "no endorsement" is that it far exceeds ideas of nonestablishment at the time that the Bill of Rights was adopted. The idea that the United States was a (Protestant) Christian country was widely assumed, and people did not conceive that government had to steer clear of indicating approval of various religious ideas. Chaplains appointed for Congress and state legislatures were one indication; public days of prayer another; laws against Christian blasphemy yet another. And when public schools began to flourish in the early nineteenth century, they were recognizably nondenominationally Protestant, teaching Protestant conceptions of truth and engaging in prayers and in devotional readings from the King James Bible. Not until later were there significant challenges to these practices within public schools, even in the states whose constitutions included prohibitions against establishment.[20]

If one judges the relevant original intent by the types of practice the federal Establishment Clause and the state provisions against establishment of religion were widely considered to preclude, one can hardly resist the conclusion that the prevailing understanding in Supreme Court doctrine is more antiestablishment than the original understanding. For some justices and scholars, that is sufficient to condemn the present approach. They may offer in its stead an interpretation of nonestablishment limited to a bar on preferences for particular churches, or at least a standard more flexible in regard to practices it allows. A considered and honest defense of the present approach must either contend that a different version of original intent is what should matter or that original intent should not prevail over other relevant factors, or both.

Before I engage those subjects directly, I want to turn to the question of conceptualization. Philip Hamburger has argued strongly that the founders did not think of "nonestablishment" as "separation," that the growth of the latter idea has skewed interpretation of the Establishment Clause that both departs from its roots and is unfortunate.[21] I believe this critique substantially overstates the significance and the perils of changes in conceptualization.[22] At the outset, it is worth noting that no one has ever conceived a notion of separation that is truly absolute. Churches receive protection from public police and firefighters, and are subject to regulations about the safety of buildings. Further, despite the language in *Everson* about no tax to support religion (which may be strictly true), churches from the colonial days to today have enjoyed exemptions from property taxes, a huge financial benefit. In modern times, tax deductions for donations also help churches by allowing donors to contribute more generously. It is only the most absolute of separationists, a small number indeed, who think these benefits should be declared unconstitutional. So "wall of separation" must be understood to mean a sharp divide in certain crucial respects, not the absence of all significant contact.

I believe the critique of the concept of separation is exaggerated in two respects, even if one concedes that the concept did not reflect most views when the Bill of Rights was adopted. The critique underestimates the commonness of conceptual shifts, and it overestimates the practical significance of this particular shift.

The ways in which the members of societies conceptualize their experiences and their worlds constantly shift through time. No doubt, these shifts almost always involve some adjustment of perspective, but how significant that adjustment is varies greatly. I will provide one illustration from another realm of constitutional law. I should caution that this illustration by itself proves almost nothing—it could be a peculiar anomaly in social and legal discourse—but it will provide a sense of the distinction that is important.

No one talked about a "right of privacy" in the late eighteenth century. The Fourth Amendment provided a protection of persons, houses, and papers against unreasonable searches and seizures; the Fifth Amendment protected people from being witnesses against themselves in criminal cases. Each of these provisions gives some protection against the government gathering information about one's life that one would prefer to keep secret. The idea that both protections involve a more general right of privacy may seem to connect the two provisions in an illuminating way, but that concept may not alter much, if at all, what exactly the two provisions are thought to cover. In some modern conceptions, and in various legal opinions, the idea of a right of privacy has been regarded as extending to a right to have an abortion, a right to engage privately in sexual relations with other consenting adults, and a right to possess pornography in one's home. In each of these instances, there is some tie to the unseemly means by which the government could seek out forbidden behavior, but the "right of privacy" in these respects reaches engaging in particular behavior, not simply an ability to limit the way information is acquired. "Privacy" in this sense lies very close to "autonomy," and has much broader implications than a restraint of information gathering.

It is from such a perspective that we need to understand the concept of "separation of church and state." Does it, or does it not, radically alter the meaning of "disestablishment" or "nonestablishment"? One measure of comparison is between eighteenth-century ideas of nonestablishment and modern ideas of separation. Given what I have already acknowledged about understandings at the time of the Bill of Rights, we can easily identify substantial discrepancies. But this particular form of comparison is misguided at the outset. That is because it alone tells us almost nothing about the particular influence of the concept of separation. One point about which we can be absolutely certain is that the coverage of "nonestablishment" would have changed over time even if that had remained the exclusive concept for analysis. To draw just two analogies, the ambit of freedom of speech and equal protection has undergone very great adjustments without any substitution of a new terminology for the basic principles they embody.

To estimate the particular significance of "separation," we would need to guess at how "nonestablishment" would have developed absent the parallel concept of separation. Of course, we cannot know what would have happened; but in most respects I do not think "separation" suggests a markedly different approach from "nonestablishment." The one important exception is aid given on a neutral basis to religious institutions performing secular functions. For that issue, "separation" may seem to have greater bite than nonestablishment. As we have seen, the Court has moved away from any stringent limits on such aid.

When one thinks about school prayers or crèches in state buildings, the idea that government should not establish religion seems to have just as much force as any notion of separate spheres, and I believe the same is true for most other issues involving the state's relation to religion. At this stage in history, it is certainly possible that, if the Supreme Court wholly abandons the separation metaphor, the abandonment will accompany greater permissiveness about what governments may do, but I am not persuaded that is because of the differential implications of "separation" and "disestablishment." This leaves me skeptical that the metaphor of "separation" has itself made a great difference in what the Supreme Court has decided up to now.

What Original Intent Should Count and for How Much?

Preliminary Clarifications. I have suggested conclusions that (1) the heavy reliance of the *Everson* Court, and of many later opinions in Establishment Clause cases, on the views of Jefferson and Madison failed to represent the broad range of positions that would have been aspects of an original understanding; and (2) in significant respects modern doctrine is almost certainly more rigorously antiestablishment than were prevailing views among adopters and citizens at the time of the Bill of Rights. For some justices and scholars, these two prepositions are sufficient to condemn a large part of the Court's Establishment Clause jurisprudence, though exactly what they would put in its place varies. For me, these two conclusions are more the beginning rather than the end of an inquiry, raising as they do deep questions about original intent (or understanding) in constitutional interpretation. The fundamental questions are these: What type of original intent should matter, and how greatly should original intent matter? The questions are closely related because concern about the weight of original intent depends considerably on what aspects of that intent are involved.

I shall claim, in sum, that original intent can matter for reasons of political authority, continuity, and wisdom, but that as time passes in the life of a constitution, the political authority reason fades in force. As with all basic constitutional rights, understanding of abstract principles should matter more than beliefs about specific applications, and that for a constitution that is difficult to amend, judges should feel free to treat original intent with diminishing force. Each of these assertions is controversial. None can be shown to be correct by some "knockdown" argument. What I provide here is much less an extended defense than a sketch of considerations, adequate, I hope, to encourage the reader to think carefully about various alternatives.

Prior to engaging the crucial questions head on, I want to put to one side a nuance that should be part of any discussion of these matters but usually is not, and I want to explain why I am omitting analysis of one vital issue for conceptions of "originalism." The nuance involves a subject I have already mentioned: the relevance of the Fourteenth Amendment. According to a doctrine of "incorporation" of virtually all of the Bill of Rights by the Fourteenth Amendment, the visions of the adopters of that amendment, or the understanding of citizens at that time, should be determining factors when the Establishment Clause is applied against states and localities. After all, in 1866, when the Fourteenth Amendment was passed by Congress, people may have had different notions about religion and about what would constitute a law respecting its establishment than did people in 1789 when Congress voted for the Bill of Rights. If we were really to have a *strict* originalist jurisprudence, judges would need to ask for each incorporated right whether conceptions had changed during those seventy-seven years. If they had changed for any particular right, and the Supreme Court recognized this and stuck faithfully to an originalist strategy, it would give the direct federal right (the one provided by the Bill of Rights itself) a different content from the incorporated right (the one provided via the Fourteenth Amendment).

Why do we not see this happening, even when originalist justices are writing their opinions?[23] Partly because, with attention to the original framers, recognition of the relevance of understanding in 1866 has been infrequent (except in regard to parts of the Fourteenth Amendment that were novel, such as the Equal Protection Clause). But the more basic reason we do not see such a division is that a constant splitting of hairs about what a freedom means vis-à-vis the federal government and what it means vis-à-vis the states would be awkward and confusing, if not unmanageable. Whether they admit it or not, judges care about clarity, and they do not aim to make the law much more complicated than it necessarily is. Elaborating separate bodies of Bill of Rights law for the federal government and the states would make the already arduous task of deciding controversies over fundamental right even more so. And such an approach might make citizens feel a sense of injustice that what amounted to an infringement by one political authority would be acceptable coming from another. The Supreme Court has refrained from developing two separate bodies of Bill of Rights law for the same sorts of reason that led it to conclude that the federal government could not maintain racially segregated schools once the states were forbidden to do so—although the original Bill of Rights had no Equal Protection Clause and the founders, having accepted slavery in the original Constitution, would have had no objection to school segregation.

For our purposes, a deeper exploration of the Fourteenth Amendment understanding would not critically affect general conclusions—though it might alter judgments about particular practices—because opinion in 1866 was still less antiestablishment in various respects than present doctrine, as evidenced by the still Protestant flavor of most public schools at the time. But I do believe we should take away one broad lesson from this brief excursion: If the general application of the Bill of Rights depends on the Fourteenth Amendment, and we have no solid basis to credit the views of the adopters of the original amendments more than the views of those who voted for the later amendment, that is a powerful basis to conclude that interpretation should not turn completely on the views held in 1789.

One important question about original understanding is *whose* original understanding, and this question is relevant not only for proclaimed "originalists" but also for those who believe that original understanding is one significant component of constitutional interpretation. On one side are those who say that if a group of people has the authority to adopt a legal rule, it is their understanding of the legal rule that is most important. Difficult as it may be to figure out what most members of a group understand, nevertheless we should credit that understanding to the extent that we can identify it. The competing view is that the critical issue is the understanding of the reader. Legislators and constitution makers have the power to adopt legally binding language, *not* to provide enforcement of their intents. What counts in law is how that language would naturally be understood. Reinforcing the focus on reader understanding is a concern that group intents do not exist (an implausible position in its most extreme form, as sometimes virtually all members of a group do have a common intent) or are rarely present and are nearly impossible to discern. Asking judges to recapture legislative intent is, so the argument goes, a regrettable invitation to them to implement their own opinions about what is right and just. The "reader understanding" stance need not deny the relevance of context, aspects about the background of legislation about which a reader—ordinary or expert—would be aware.

Somewhere between the subjective intent and reader understanding positions is the idea that judges should ask how a reasonable legislator would understand a statute's language. This device appears to focus on legislative intent, but in terms of the factors that it actually takes into account, it may fall closer to reader understanding—because readers, at least knowledgeable ones, would probably understand a piece of legislation nearly as would a "reasonable" legislator.

For many other purposes, I would regard this contest between positions as very important. My own view is that subjective legislator intent and reader understanding both matter. The degree of weight depends partly on the type of legal rule involved *and* on the passage of time—a subject I do address below. But for most of the following analysis, the division is not critical, and I disregard it, referring to intent and understanding without differentiation.

Most of the issues I treat here surface whether one is thinking of adopter intent or reader understanding. Further, in practical terms, when we think about the adoption of the Bill of Rights and of the Fourteenth Amendment (insofar as it is thought to make most of the Bill of Rights applicable against the states), we have little or no basis to distinguish adopter intent from reader understanding. There is slight evidence in the internal debates of the two Congresses about what provisions of the Bill of Rights meant; although we do have alterations of wordings of the Establishment Clause, it is difficult to know exactly why changes were made. In any event, *half* of the process of adoption was ratification within the states. We have no (or only slight) basis to determine what state legislators thought the proposed clauses meant—if they thought about their meaning—apart from what reasonably well informed people of the time would have understood.[24] In short, the evidence for what those legislators intended would be essentially the same as the evidence we would need to comb were we to estimate reader understanding.

Political Authority. The most obvious reason to give great weight, perhaps decisive weight, to original intent or reader understanding is that those who adopted a legal rule had the political authority to do so. They, not judges, had the power to pass a statute or adopt a constitution. The responsibility of judges is to give effect to what the lawmakers did, *not* to implement their personal views or their perceptions of the views of their contemporaries. Within liberal democracies, and indeed in many other forms of government, judges are supposed to interpret and apply laws, not to substitute their views for those of politically superior authorities. It follows they should defer to original intent in some form. Before I suggest other bases to pay attention to original intent, I want to explore an implication and a related reservation about this approach.

What does this basis for settling on original intent tell us about the comparative importance of understood applications and abstract principles? Of course, to some extent, one discerns abstract principles through conceived applications, and one discerns views about specific applications through a sense of the abstract principles thought to govern, but it still can matter greatly if later judges give their primary focus to understood applications or abstract principles, to whether the adopters of the Establishment Clause believed a prohibition of blasphemy (limited to Christian blasphemy) was acceptable for the federal District of Columbia or whether such a prohibition does involve a significant promotion of one religion over others.

The starting point for thought about specific applications versus abstract principle is what those who adopted a rule themselves believed and understood. Should not a faithful originalist judge resolve this issue by his or her originalist premises, asking what the adopters (or readers of the time) would have conceived as central?

According to this approach we have some, hardly conclusive, guides to what was then understood. First, Madison and the other originators of the Bill of Rights chose language that was quite general in its form. Of course, they would not have wanted to clutter a constitution with every specific practice they wanted to forbid, but had they wanted only to reach specific practices, they could have chosen language making direct reference to historical understandings about the limits of legitimate government. In particular, the language about laws "respecting an establishment of religion" could have been replaced by language referring to established churches, along the lines of the Church of England, and to forms of establishment that remained among states when the Bill of Rights was adopted. Second, interpretation of statutes prior to the federal constitution tended to be fairly flexible, not resting on the intents of legislators. Third, the adopters of the Bill of Rights were aware of the demanding process for constitutional amendments. They would not have supposed an amendment could easily be made every time views about appropriate applications of the more general concepts evolved.

I have put this third point in terms of likely understanding at the time, but it also has an independent significance. If a constitution endures over time, *and* parts of its value lie in that endurance as a unifying force for a political society, *and* it is difficult to amend, *and* some of its symbolic value might be lost if frequent amendments made it much longer and less coherent, these are reasons in and of themselves for judges to look to more abstract principles.

Two evident problems with sticking entirely, or mainly, to contemplated applications are technological advances and other changes in the external world and deep shifts in social values. The point about technical advances is most obvious. The adopters of the First, Fourth, and Eighth Amendments imagined oral speech and writing in print, physical intrusions on persons and houses, and various cruel punishments. They did not conceive of electronic media, electronic surveillance, or torture by electric shocks. Does that mean that freedom of speech and of the press has no bearing on electronic communication, that electronic interceptions can never constitute unreasonable searches, or that terrible electric shocks could never be cruel punishments? Does the Constitution need to be amended with each great technological advance or development of an extraordinarily cruel but novel punishment? At the very least, the broad concepts in the Bill of Rights need to be given applications that seem clearly called for but which the adopters never conceived because of the physical environment in which they lived.

The relevance of changes in value is understandably more debatable. At the time of the Constitution, the death penalty was prescribed for a fairly broad range of crimes. The Bill of Rights itself clearly contemplates the death penalty in its Due Process Clause that provides that no one shall be deprived of "*life*, liberty, or property without due process of law." By now, virtually every other liberal democracy has abolished the death penalty, as have some American states. Among those that still retain the penalty, the vast majority of actual executions are within a handful of states. Some justices in past decades have concluded that all death sentences imposed by governments constitute cruel and unusual punishment. But even if one balks at that decision being made by a court, what if a state imposed the death penalty for stealing horses? According to present doctrine about ordinary crimes (that is, not counting treason and espionage) the death penalty can be imposed only for grave crimes such as murder. Can we not say that our understanding of what amounts to cruel punishment has advanced in this respect since 1789? No doubt, our attitudes about the death penalty have altered *partly* because advances in medicine have helped us forestall many of the physical causes of death that visited the human race in centuries past, but the fundamental change concerns a sense of the value of life and disquiet with the idea of the government intentionally terminating it in anything other than war.

In respect to religion and the state, we can perceive a somewhat similar alteration of circumstance and attitude. Among other changes from 1789 are these: The choice of what religion to follow is now regarded much more as an autonomous one for each individual; the number of Roman Catholics has increased dramatically (it is now the largest single denomination in the United States) and, partly because of changes within the Catholic Church, most Protestants now view it as one among many Christian groups, not as a distinctive embodiment of evil or source of tyranny; the number of Jewish, Muslim, Hindu, and Buddhist practitioners has become substantial, and religions dominant in Asia are bound to increase as our immigration laws continue not to impose the decisive discrimination that long favored residents of Europe who wished to immigrate. Although religion within the United States has failed to fade away as many social scientists once assumed, nevertheless the percentage of citizens who profess atheism or agnosticism is much greater than it was in 1789, and most thoughtful citizens do not doubt that nonbelievers are capable of living with justice and virtue.

Because it is very hard to say just what the understanding of free exercise and nonestablishment of religion would have been in 1789, it is also difficult to say exactly what conclusions one would reach now that would not correspond with the original understanding, but most citizens do not now think governments should be able to teach Protestant Christianity as true; the Supreme Court has declared that religious tests of office within states violate the federal establishment clause[25] (although a number of states did once allow such tests); and a prohibition of Christian blasphemy that did not touch what other religions might regard as blasphemy would, in all likelihood, now be regarded as an establishment although it would not have been so in 1789. If one realizes that amendments to the Constitution are difficult and one believes that very frequent amendments to the federal constitution—of the sort that do occur within many states—would be unfortunate, one has good reason to think that constitutional rights formulated in general language may now extend beyond applications conceived by their adopters.

There is one strong argument in the contrary direction: namely, that when judges depart from historically conceived applications they have too much discretion, that judges need to be reined in, and the best way to do this is by insisting that they stick to applications conceived at the time. (One *might* make an exception for novel technologies.) I have said this argument is strong, but I do not think it is nearly strong enough to outweigh all the disadvantages of precluding changes of applications of general principles over time. We need to recognize that for many rights, the injunction to stick with understood applications would not, even if followed seriously, curb discretionary judgment, because it is so hard to figure out what were the historically understood applications, given widespread ignorance and disagreements. But I would find the position unpersuasive even if we imagined that the 1789 range of agreement about applications was extensive and was ascertainable, and we thought judges could identify with considerable confidence what were the historically understood applications.

I have not thus far questioned the premise that the political authority of the original adopters is a reason to follow some sense of original understanding. The force of that premise is simplest for legislation recently adopted by a legislative body that is fairly constructed. It is, after all, the responsibility of such bodies to adopt laws within our system of government. But how should we view political authority when the enacting body, or combination of adopting bodies, acted 220 years ago? These legislators did not *represent us*, and they had only the faintest glimmer of what we would be like. Not only has a passage of time spanned many lifetimes, the country within which the Bill of Rights was adopted had widespread slavery, subjected women to substantial legal disabilities, and often limited voting to property owners. And, of course, as I have already noted, the vast majority of citizens accepted some version of Protestant Christianity. Why should we suppose that those who actually represented white male Protestant holders of property, and themselves fell within that class, would justly reflect the interests of our diverse modern population?

There are a variety of possible answers to this concern about political authority. It might be said that by living in this country and participating politically, we accept the authority of the constitution makers; that, given overlapping generations, the original political authority continues in some way; that for our liberal democracy, this is the constitution and these were its adopters, regardless of fairness of representation and any actual acceptance by present individuals. I shall not here try to address these various proposals, which raise complex issues of political theory. I shall merely report that they do not seem persuasive to me, especially if we focus on the subject that concerns us.

I believe one can fairly say that the actual Constitution is the foundation of our liberal democracy, and that *it* enjoys political authority as a consequence. But that tells us very little about how it should be interpreted. On matters that are not clear from the text itself (such as the minimum age of the president and equal state representation in the Senate), modern citizens have only the vaguest ideas about what the original adopters actually intended and what original readers would have understood. They are much more likely to be aware of recent prominent Supreme Court decisions, which will trouble them only if they have strong objections to the outcome. Many citizens remain outraged that the Supreme Court created a right to have an abortion, and it is contended that the adopters of the Bill of Rights and the Fourteenth Amendment did not have that in mind. By contrast, it is certain that the adopters of the Equal Protection Clause of the Fourteenth Amendment had no inkling that it would be used to guarantee equal rights for women, who then could not vote and were subject to a range of disadvantages that were regarded as objectionable by only a small minority of citizens, yet decisions employing the Equal Protection Clause in that manner have been broadly accepted rather quickly. Indeed one of the principal arguments against ratifying the Equal Rights Amendment was that the Fourteenth Amendment had already solved the problem. If it is the Constitution as a document and as interpreted that *now* has political authority, rather than the adopters, that is a basis to conclude than the intent of the adopters is much less important than it once was, and the understanding of original readers now has even less relevance (unless one theorizes that it shows original intent or simply is what the adopters enacted).

In sum, the political authority argument for following original intent or understanding grows weaker and weaker as time passes. It is particularly weak for issues as to which the adopters would not have fairly represented large swaths of the modern population. That leaves interpreters greater latitude to focus on what aspects of original intent should be given greater weight (whatever the adopters may have believed on that subject) and greater latitude to move beyond original intent in any form to other considerations.

Continuity. I have yet to discuss two other reasons to pay attention to original intent. One is continuity. If original intent figured prominently in earlier interpretations, that is a reason to give it significance as time passes. Particularly if a court is making a new application of a constitutional provision, perhaps reaching an outcome at odds with an earlier case, it is somewhat reassuring if it can show that what it is doing corresponds with the broad principles envisioned by the adopters.

Two comments or qualifications need to be made about continuity in this respect. The first is to draw a distinction between genuine bases of decision and judicial rhetoric. Judges not infrequently overstate some grounds of their decisions and remain silent about or minimize others. Just how far judicial opinions should reflect actual bases of decision is a complicated topic—I am partial to a high degree of candor about that—but realism compels recognition that rhetoric may not reflect true grounds of judgment. Sometimes judges are fully aware of their actual bases of judgment and decide not to reveal them. At other times, they fool themselves as well as many readers. It is arguable that the main reassurance comes from a rhetoric of respect for original intent rather than actual respect. And a fuller analysis than mine might explore in depth the possibility that desirable rhetoric for the Establishment Clause may differ from the desirable weight given to possible bases of decision.

The second qualification is more crucial for our purposes. In legal systems, continuity is desirable but it can take various forms. Within common law systems judges aim for relative continuity in judicially created doctrine. In the context of the common law itself, this means minimizing radical departures from previously decided cases. In the law of statutory interpretation, it entails following earlier decisions about statutory meaning. In both domains, judges follow doctrines of earlier decisions even when they would have (or might have) resolved the earlier cases differently. This kind of continuity also exists in constitutional law, although the Supreme Court regards itself as somewhat freer to depart from prior constitutional case law than prior statutory case law—on the ground that the option of relatively simple correction or change by the legislative branch is not available in constitutional law.

The general lesson here is that we should not suppose that adherence to some form of original intent is the exclusive, or even the main, variety of continuity. And when Supreme Court justices believe that an earlier decision actually departs from original intent, continuity according to original intent actually is in conflict with continuity in the ordinary sense of following precedents.

Wisdom. A third reason to pay attention to original intent is wisdom. The founders, so the argument goes, were an extremely gifted generation. They bequeathed us structures of government that were uniquely suited for American democracy. We can trust the resolutions of these men more than our own less profound judgments. The force of this argument is seriously contested, and it certainly must be narrowed or qualified, but it has important implications for *whose* original understanding matters.

If one thinks about the wisdom of the adopters of the Bill of Rights, it is what they had in mind that should matter, not the manner in which a typical reader would then have understood the language they used. Moreover, when one talks about the wisdom of the founders, one is thinking mainly of political leaders, not ordinary members of the population or representatives in state legislatures. (No doubt, one could conceive that virtually all members of society in the early republic had a wisdom we lack today, but that seems a highly implausible hypothesis in respect to subjects of political organization and fundamental legal rights.) If it is the political leaders whom we deem to be especially wise, those who conceived the Constitution and formulated the Bill of Rights (or similar documents such as the Virginia Bill for Religious Freedom), then we could defend giving weight to the visions of these leaders far out of proportion to what a political authority version of original intent would suggest.

Among the American founders, James Madison's *Memorial and Remonstrance* provided the fullest account of the values of nonestablishment. And in this regard he went well beyond John Locke, whose ideas were greatly influential among the colonists. Locke developed a voluntary conception of religion and religious liberty that may seem to point toward nonestablishment, but he did not actually reach that conclusion. Madison did, and also provided a persuasive explanation of the way nonestablishment carried out an ideal of religious liberty. Especially as he was also the main author of the Bill of Rights, it might well make sense to draw heavily from his understanding—even if we acknowledged that for a political authority version of intent, one would have to take into account all those who accepted his language but did not share his understanding.

This brings us to a critical qualification of the wisdom theory that strongly suggests, if it does not demonstrate, that the theory is only partially originalist. Almost no one today would think the founders were wise about all major subjects. Their views about relations of men and women, about the significance of racial differences, and about appropriate political rights for people who do not hold property, are far out of line with dominant opinion today, not only within the United States but in all liberal democracies. To conclude that the founders' intent should count because of their wisdom, one needs to do some initial screening—a screening that cannot itself rest on original intent.

All this might be conceded, and one still might believe that the main proponents of the Establishment Clause were wise, not only in wanting to keep the federal government away from establishment, but also in believing that nonestablishment was healthy within states. One might think, further, that they were wiser in their general ideas than in respect to practices they may have accepted out of habit, without adequate reflection on how well they conformed with their fundamental abstract principles. One might think, still further, that their wisdom about general ideas has more relevant application to modern conditions than their appraisal of appropriate practices in their time and place. With all these (contestable) assumptions in place, one might think it entirely appropriate to give a place of prominence to the broad ideas of Madison and Jefferson in interpreting and applying the Establishment Clause.

Summary. A summary of this section might be cast in the following way. A political authority basis to accord great significance to original intent fades over time, especially with a constitution designed to last, difficult to amend, and possessed of heavy symbolic significance. The wisdom of the adopters may constitute a reason to follow their intent, but a conclusion about wisdom requires a nonoriginalist judgment about who was wise, what subjects they were wise about, and whether their wisdom was mainly about general principles. Some focus on intent or original understanding may help provide a measure of continuity, but continuity can be achieved in other ways; and in some instances continuity of constitutional decisions may point away from a continuity that emphasizes original intent.

For me, the bottom line is that for the Establishment Clause, interpretations should give some weight, but not determinative weight, to original intent, and the intent that should mainly count is the general principles of those who most fully grasped the values of nonestablishment. The analysis I have provided should leave ample room for readers to disagree with these conclusions, and further to take quite a different view of the values of nonestablishment (and what rigorous nonestablishment may sacrifice) than my own.

Conclusion

I have surveyed a range of questions about original understanding, attempting to develop an analysis that reveals how complex and debatable are many issues that are often treated by advocates as straightforward and one-sided. My fundamental positions are that the original understanding about the Establishment Clause and the Fourteenth Amendment matter but are not determinative; that the political authority and continuity reasons to follow original understanding diminish over time; and that what counts for basic provisions of the Bill of Rights are the abstract principles and wisdom of those who adopted them, not the precise applications conceived by most enactors and ratifiers. According to this approach, giving great weight to the understandings of Jefferson and Madison is warranted, even if their understandings went beyond general conceptions at the time.

Notes

1. Everson v. Board of Education, 330 U.S. 1 (1947).

2. Ibid., 16.

3. Ibid., 17.

4. It does not follow that each of the other four justices joining the opinion took the same view, as justices often join language in majority opinions that does not reflect their precise views.

5. E.g., Elk Grove Unified School District v. Newdow, 542 U.S. 1, 45–46 (2004) (Thomas, J. concurring).

6. See further chapter 11 by Thomas Berg.

7. I consider these arguments in greater depth in Kent Greenawalt, *Religion and the Constitution, Vol. 2, Establishment and Fairness* (Princeton, NJ: Princeton University Press 2008), 26–39.

8. On the relevant roles of Madison and Jefferson, see further chapter 2 by Michael McConnell and chapter 8 by Carl Esbeck.

9. See further chapter 6 by Ralph Ketcham.

10. See further chapter 9 by Daniel Dreisbach.

11. The latter possibility is suggested by Steven D. Smith in "The Establishment Clause and the Problem of the Church," in *Challenges to Religious Liberty in the Twenty-First Century*, ed. Gerard V. Bradley (New York: Cambridge University Press 2012).

12. Scalia does accept the standard doctrine that precedents in constitutional cases are important; thus a justice might appropriately adhere to a well-established precedent even if that deviates from his or her sense of the original intent of a provision.

13. In reaching this conclusion, Donald L. Drakeman, "*Everson v. Board of Education* and the Quest for the Historical Establishment Clause," *The American Journal of Legal History* 46 (2007): 119, refers to other relevant influences. For a balanced account of attitudes during the era of the Bill of Rights, see John Witte Jr., *Religion at the American Constitutional Experiment*, 2d ed. (Boulder, CO: Westview Press 2005), 21–105.

14. See further chapter 2 by Michael McConnell, chapter 3 by Mark McGarvie, and the Introduction by John Witte Jr.

15. Witte, *Religion and the American Constitutional Experiment*, 71–105, describes the origins of the religion clauses.

16. Public schools did not develop until early in the nineteenth century.

17. Zelman v. Simmons-Harris, 536 U.S. 639 (2002).

18. This broad subject is treated in Greenawalt, *Religion and the Constitution, Vol. 2*, 57–121.

19. One exception is chaplains for the military and in prisons, the idea being that in environments in which government controls all of life, it appropriately provides opportunities to worship and receive ministerial assistance. Another exception is legislative chaplains, held to be justified because clearly accepted at the time of the Bill of Rights.

20. See chapter 10 by Steven Green and chapter 11 by Thomas Berg.

21. Philip Hamburger, *Separation of Church and State* (Cambridge, MA: Harvard University Press 2002).

22. Kent Greenawalt, "History as Ideology: Philip Hamburger's Separation of Church and State," *California Law Review* 93 (2005): 367.

23. Justice Thomas in *Elk Grove* would not apply the Establishment Clause against the states, but that is because he is persuaded it should not be regarded as incorporated.

24. See chapter 8 by Carl Esbeck.

25. The original federal Constitution provided that no religious test could be imposed for federal office holders. The case involving a state test is Torcaso v. Watkins, 367 U.S. 488 (1961).

13

Getting Beyond "The Myth of Christian America"

Martin E. Marty

Several chapters in this volume have helped to pierce the many myths and mists that have surrounded American constitutional ideals of separation of church and state. These chapters have exposed the historical caricatures and mythical logics of the story of America the secular nation, with a godless constitution, a naked public square, a privatized religion, and a high and impregnable wall of separation between church and state.

In this final chapter, I take up another persistent myth of American history of church–state relations: "The Myth of Christian America." The rubric that disciplines this inquiry is the single focus of this book, the Establishment Clause in the First Amendment to the U.S. Constitution: "Congress shall make no law respecting an establishment of religion." The phrase "Christian America" of course does not appear there, or indeed anywhere else in the Constitution. Theoretically, the Establishment Clause as it is worded could have been drafted and fostered in societies that represent Buddhist, Hindu, Sikh, or other religious traditions. This is so because it only talks generically about four elements, which could be located in many nations. It refers to a legislative body—in this case, "Congress"; to "law," which is not distinctive to America; to "establishment," a legal term that could be translated to many kinds of jurisdictions; and finally to "religion," here used generically. We shall see later that the claim that America is a Christian nation has shown up very rarely in formal settings, only twice in dicta associated with U.S. Supreme Court decisions. These references have no legal force at all. No one who disagrees with what a judge has said about Christian America will suffer liabilities or penalties. In short, not a molecule of ink on a molecule of paper reproducing the Constitution and the Establishment Clause will give anyone warrant to call the United States "Christian America."

However—and this is an important point—the absence of reference to "Christian America" in the U.S. Constitution does not mean that in nonlegal expressions the concept has to be rejected. Many forms of Christian witness and activity have demonstrably helped shape the moral fabric and on many occasions the policies of the nation. The majority of the citizens have been and are associated with Christianity. Christian norms, motifs, and impetuses merit attention by friend and foe of Christianity alike. All these are often obscured, sometimes perhaps willfully, during debates over the legislative and judicial battles in which Christian America is or is not to be invoked.

To illustrate: If the Christmas crèche is a symbol of some versions of Christianity, it can be freely and flamboyantly featured on tens of thousands of lawns in front of residences in any city. One can picture Jewish neighbors of those who set up such displays coming by to admire and comment on one or another of these, just as Christians might be invited to enjoy a Succoth booth at a Jewish home next door. In the same city, the placement of such a scene creates problems for publics only on the half acre of the courthouse lawn. Similarly the management of a department store may censor the Christmas carols broadcast within the store, fearing that explicit reference to Jesus might alienate some non-Christians, but there is no law against its owners taking that risk. Choral groups at symphony hall or at outdoor concerts may feature gospel or soul songs, spirituals, chorales, or cantatas. Publics who gather to hear any of these in a public park may do so while overlooking the fact that some boisterous witness to Jesus gets shouted and sung on tax-exempt property where, at public expense, police make their rounds for security. Most Americans are quite tolerant about such expressions. Legal problems may occur only when, for example, a public school choir or audience sings distinctively Christian songs. Even there, foreseeing and farseeing high school administrators educate their choirs and audiences to know and show the difference between the performance of great Christian music and singing it as an act of worship.

Further, in the voluntary sector, no one says that advertisers have to shun Christian symbols. Believers, if they wished, could present tasteful advertisements to replace the tasteless and distasteful fare many of them now banner, and they would be perfectly legal in doing so. As for prayer in public, the week has 168 hours, almost all of which can be used for prayer by individuals and voluntary groups. Debate over Christian America ordinarily erupts only when such prayer is even mildly sanctioned and established by public school authorities. Once more: the accent in this chapter is on the *legal* element, not the voluntary scene.

That thoughtful people can be articulate, explicit, and informed Christians and may still reject the idea of Christian America is evident, for example, in a book by three of the most noted evangelical Christian historians of the past half century—Mark A. Noll, Nathan O. Hatch, and George M. Marsden in *The Search for a Christian America*. No one can credibly accuse them of being traitors to the Christian cause or of being less than accomplished as historians. However, having examined the historical evidence and also having posed some theological judgments about their materials, they are brisk and clear: "America is not a Christian country, nor has it ever been one. Failure to recognize this means that Christians rely on the state to do tasks which rightfully belong to Christian institutions but that they are offended when public institutions refuse to follow the advice of the churches."[1] They have listened to their fellow believers who *do* try to witness to Christian America, but are not convinced:

> For those who hold to the "Christian America" view, the situation may be summarized as follows: America was founded as a "Christian nation." But the nation turned from its Christian foundation and in recent decades has been taken over by secular humanism. The goal today is to become a Christian nation once again—by restoring America to its "biblical base," to the "biblical principles of our founding fathers," to a "Christian consensus," etc. (*Typically this biblical heritage is linked directly to America's founding documents, the Declaration of Independence and the Constitution.*) Stated in this way then, the only alternative seems to be an all-out battle between the forces advocating a return to "Christian America" and the ruling forces of "secular humanism"— so that America can become a Christian nation once again.[2]

National Life between the Poles

It can be hazardous for a historian to step into the politicized zones, as the partisans of both wield figurative assault weapons that can catch in crossfire any moderate in the "no-man's-land" between them. Yet it is in that zone where most citizens live and where they invest most of their energies. Thus we do not picture many contemporary Americans waking up in the morning and feeling a need to take a stand on such issues. Yet the issues are there, latent but always potentially vital. And when they do become vital, as is the case in many sessions of the U.S. Supreme Court and in political campaigns, emotions get aroused, research intensifies, and the firing begins. Addressing the issues demands historical inquiry of the sort this book has presented. The authors of the various chapters herein have offered findings and proposed arguments that throw much light on the subject; I do not need to repeat them here.

My own approach is from Abraham Lincoln: "If we could first know where we are, and whither we are tending, we could then better judge what to do, and how to do it."[3] And to know "where we are," in the context of the current inquiry, it is necessary to explore aspects and dimensions of the construct "Christian America." My thesis is modest, anti-Utopian, perhaps frustrating to absolutists, but I think supportable by the evidence. It proposes that efforts to support the concept of Christian America through legal means are doomed to fail, just as efforts to locate the concept of secular America in the founding legal documents has little historical warrant. This means that those who seek a path toward sure and final resolution of controversies in these fields will be frustrated.

They will do better and serve better if they are content with interpreting and acting in a nation that lacks precise or detailed religious definition. This calls for citizens to make decisions on relevant subjects despite some blurring of the lines that distinguish what is represented by the terms "church and state."

In other words, people in neither faction can win, as they and observers usually define winning. Each will have to settle for partial and provisional gains mixed with setbacks. And they may follow invitations or mandates to engage in research and conversation about how to promote the common good without having resolved every issue to their satisfaction. So complex are issues of church and state, so many are the interests, and so frequently do events disturb the peace, that partisans have to learn to live, as their foreparents did, without finding neat resolutions or surefire strategies. At root, their moves will be guided by what they perceive to be the original intentions of those who drafted the documents and the reflections of many of those in the courts who later interpreted such. The original goal was to respect consciences and protect liberties while they were still pursuing the common good.

Why such a thesis? Readers of this book will find that very little has been permanently settled to the satisfaction of the various parties and partisans. A new element for consideration and contention regularly enters the scene and leads to disarray, reflection, and reorganization. For example, a new Congress in a new political climate passes laws that supplant and often contradict those that have been on the books. A differently constituted Supreme Court, changed by as little as one new appointment or one appointee who changed his or her mind, leads to a different outcome, one that resets the legal game. One cultural change that brings about new alliances in the public alters the expectations of voters, and the consequences of their reactions remain for years. To observe this is not to encourage the public to wallow in relativism but only to report on the history of a free, pluralist society through the passing of generations.

The Prehistory of the Christian America Concept

Debates over all these issues go back to the history and memory of church establishment and the efforts to end it via the First Amendment. The pro–Christian Amendment cohort would stake out a different territory and take a different position than would supporters of Christian America. The roots of their argument reach well before 1787 and 1789.

The notion of a Christian America was born with the emergence of the United States among the family of modern nations. Before the sixteenth century in Europe there had been a legally constituted Christian "Holy Roman Empire." Similarly, there had been versions of *Romanitas*, the religious ethos and legal structure on the soil in which Christianity was born and prospered. In both

cases some authorities, central and regional, ruled with religious establishments that wielded power and were intended to enforce some measure of
uniformity. In the Christian case, the eponym "Christendom" carried in its
final syllable, "-dom," the suggestion and the reality of "dominion" or
"domain." Someone who had dominion, rule, authority, and control held this
established power legally and officially in exclusive senses of the term. In a
few instances within Christendom there may have been some barely toler-
ated enclaves of Jews, who were still usually subject to persecution, and at
best only protected. However, the survival of such communities within
Christendom never carried with it the suggestion that these or any other
subcommunities possessed rights to be experienced and expressed beyond
their boundaries. All but the ruling (and thus established) Christians—whether
Eastern Orthodox, Roman Catholic, or later Protestant—were "unestab-
lished" and did not possess legal rights.

Through most of recorded history, whether the governing entity was the
tribe, the council, the city-state, the nation, or the empire, it would not have
occurred to people in power voluntarily to yield some of it to those who did not
share the laws, philosophies, and ethos of the rulers. When outsiders challenged Christendom or its counterparts, often through incursions and military
ventures to upset Christian power and replace it, these invaders were both
experienced and classified as "barbarian" or "infidel." Until modern times,
before legal toleration was invented, supported, and practiced, or its terms
defined, the general rule was the one formulated in the Peace of Augsburg in
1555: *cuius regio, eius religio*. Whoever had the power in a region determined the
religion of the region. Dissenters who resisted were sequestered, exiled, or
killed by the swords of the establishment. In those centuries it made sense to
speak without confusion of the idea of a Christian Empire, Christian Castile, or
Christian Ireland. On the contrary, to speak as many do (or wish to) of Christian America makes little sense and only produces confusion and contention.

The American Experience

Given that prehistory, the American experience was innovative, framed as it
was in a hodgepodge setting of migrant groups who held and practiced different versions of Christian faith—some of them established in Europe, some
of them dissenters. This scene was most complicated within a larger sphere,
namely that of Protestantism, which had taken different and usually competi-
tive forms in the Europe from which all American newcomers but the African
slaves derived. A minority of these Protestants back in Europe—Anabaptists,
Baptists, Quakers, and others—had never held legal domain. They had been
struggling for the disestablishment of official versions of the forms of Christianity in which they did not believe, and which had been mixed with and

empowered by the state. Some of these dissenters, as they settled in Rhode Island or Pennsylvania, immediately opposed church establishment root and branch. But between 1607 when colonists carried the banners of Anglican Establishment to Virginia down to the period of national formation around 1787, establishment prevailed in the majority of colonies and lingered in more than half the states. Most settlers had brought with them the habits and ethos associated with establishment, or at least they were highly aware of the human cost of contesting such establishments, whether, for example, in "Christian Massachusetts" or "Christian Virginia." Those in power who continued to support formal church establishment and its corollaries in the colonies had fourteen centuries of precedent and habit behind them. Religious establishment was the only world they knew, and it was marked by a polity that they patrolled and from which they benefited.

From 1787 on, to speak of an informal establishment as part of Christianity took on various shapes. In the mainline Protestant sphere, first legal and then cultural or habitual experiences with establishment were in part a reflection of the European ecclesiastical ancestry and ethos. Episcopalians carried over from England many habits and practices associated with the Anglican establishment. Even the Methodists as they succeeded in growing quickly became establishmentarian in outlook. For the rest, Presbyterians from Scotland, Lutherans from Scandinavia and much of Germany, the Reformed from the Netherlands and France, and the Congregationalists from their own creation of establishment in earlier New England carried on the benefits of that reminiscence. Only the Baptists and Disciples of Christ among the "big seven" of the old informal establishment had merely tenuous ties to historic establishments.[4] And when by the middle of the twentieth century these mainline groups virtually abdicated and yielded cultural and much political power to Protestants in the complex that came to be called "Evangelicalism," a new set of believers set out to claim power and influence. Among them many came to be the advocates, sometimes in a spirit of nostalgia and more often with an eye on future power, of promoting the idea of a reclaimed Christian America. Most of the literature about attempts to claim cultural hegemony in the recent decades, the impulse to name and rule Christian America, was somehow Evangelical.

Both those who bannered and banner the name and concepts of Christian America and those who were and are opposed to it appeal to the national founders. The founders wrestled with the issue of establishment versus disestablishment and legal privilege (often experienced also in cultural expression) of some citizens as believers versus others who opposed such privileging. They were still dealing with the "-dom" in Christendom when in Article VI of the Constitution and throughout the document they kept religion at a distance, as they did with the First Amendment clauses. They were succinctly addressing urgent issues that never have been dispensed with or dispatched with anything approaching finality.

Producing effective documents that could be ratified was no easy task, and the drafters were wise to do what they could not to raise many religious issues on the federal level. It has been said with some warrant that they solved the religion problem by not solving the religion problem. They and their successors also had a second task: that of dealing with thirteen new state constitutions among legislators who were anything but of one mind in respect to religion and the state. And their third task, one that will receive further attention here, was the matter of addressing the spiritual and moral shape of the federal union as they were participating in what a national motto advertised as a *novus ordo saeclorum*, a new order of the ages—which, on this subject, it was.

Despite efforts stemming from the founding period and continuing into recent history to find an easily applied and universally approved candidate for the name of this polity, all failed. Although the founders included the Latin root (*saeculum*, "of the age") of the word *secular* in their motto, it would not have occurred to them to use such a term to show that they were forming a "secular" state in modern senses of such a term. If not "secular," what else was available for purposes of labeling and designating? Some might have taken a term still present in some state constitutions, namely, "Trinitarian," referring to belief in implied governance by the Holy Trinity of Christian witness. However, there was no chance of this winning as a national label, because some founders were virtual Unitarians and some, such as Thomas Jefferson, vehemently disdained witness to the Trinity. Should they have chosen "Protestant?" Unquestionably, most of the founders were seeking to develop a Protestant ethos in the nation, but the term "Protestant" did not do justice to many of the groups who wanted to be included. "Deist?" Some of the founders held opinions that elsewhere, as in England, were called "Deist," but the constituencies for Deism were too small, too ill-defined, and too readily dismissed by the huge non-Deist majority for it to be useful. "Religious?" That was too broad and too confusing, and many citizens were not sure how to define and demarcate religion. "Pluralist" would have been proper, but the term was unknown and would have been unrecognized.

"Christian," then, is the label that was left, and it became the key term at the birth of the nation just as it lies behind most advocacies today. Later, during the years of World War II and its aftermath, for strategic reasons and in good will some advocacies came to be called "Judeo-Christian,"[5] but the term "Christian" covered more circumstances and appealed to more constituencies. Christian America, then, was the term instinctively and sometimes deliberately advanced, whether the adjective was accurate, appropriate, fair, or wisely applied in the new situation. Obviously and certainly, "Christian" had the prime position in the competition for naming and identity, given the provenance of most colonists and the precedents they knew. Some of the founders were also ready to propose philosophical, moral, and legal claims to demonstrate that they were inheriting and now refashioning Christian America. Often citizens have asked why a nation needed any adjective designed to focus on its religious makeup. They have a point in that the constitutionalists were not called to establish a federal religious sanctuary but a complex state, a union.

After the Civil War, at a time when there were numerous efforts to remake the nation by constitutional amendment, religion inevitably came up. Not all impulses dealt with religion. In 1865 the most important, the Thirteenth Amendment, abolished slavery. The Fourteenth Amendment in 1868 was important in respect to First Amendment cases, as it assured that citizens could not be deprived *by any state* of "life, liberty or property without due process of law." Fatefully, it was this amendment that in the 1940s, through a still-controversial Supreme Court process of "incorporation," stipulated that state and local policies and decisions in matters of religion could now be reviewed by federal courts using the standards of the First Amendment.[6] In 1870, the Fifteenth Amendment set out to assure the right of all to vote. With such a streak of changes going on, it seemed to some the moment to finish the work they thought the founders in 1787 and 1789 had left undone.

Near the beginning of that period, in 1864, a National Association to Secure the Religious Amendment to the Constitution was formed. Its words demonstrate what we spoke of as clarity of purpose, for it paraphrased the existing preamble to the Constitution:

> WE, THE PEOPLE OF THE UNITED STATES, [recognizing the being and attributes of Almighty God, the Divine Authority of the Holy Scriptures, the Law of God as the paramount rule, and Jesus, the Messiah, the Savior and Lord of all,] in order to form a more perfect union, establish justice, ensure domestic tranquility, provide for the common defense, promote the general welfare, and secure the blessings of liberty to ourselves and to our posterity, do ordain and establish the Constitution for the United States of America.[7]

Its successor and still extant organization in 1875 took the name National Reform Association. Its leaders charged that the existing Constitution was a "dishonor . . . to the God of nations." They argued that the "Constitution ought to contain explicit evidence of the Christian character and purpose of the nation which frames it." Congress dismissed the proposals in 1874 and again in 1894, thus signaling to all but the most devoted that no one would be advised to spend much time with promoting an amendment.[8] Yet the ideas behind it, in compromised form, live on. Opponents took the occasion to form the American Secular Union, which opposed the Christian America talk. The issue quickly became appropriated in the politics of the day, where it was considered by Congress in the House Judiciary Committee, but that effort, too, went nowhere.

Efforts to parallel the effect of such an amendment in court decisions have often been sought, and twice have moved to the U.S. Supreme Court. There they included dicta that cheered the Christian America supporters who kept citing it. In one case Justice David Brewer, lifelong a liberal Trinitarian Protestant—many liberal Protestants were at that time leaders in the Christian America cause—wanted to promote the cause. He believed that the genial and congenially beneficent doctrines of such Protestantism, in its devotion to Jesus, could undergird the doings of a nation and its citizens. Brewer's America was God-ordained to sacred purposes.[9] In 1892 he wrote the opinion in a case that assured him a place in the history books, *Church of the Holy Trinity v. United States*. The case had to do with whether a policy of the Catholic Church violated a federal labor law. Brewer recited a long list of examples that, to his mind, spoke to the Christian character of the nation. He then wrote memorably in the face of "this mass of organic utterances that this is a Christian nation, shall it be believed that a Congress of the United States intended to make it a misdemeanor for a church of this country to contract for the services of a Christian minister residing in another nation?"[10] Debates have followed, but most scholars have argued that Brewer's belief that this was a Christian nation was not perfunctory, but that it actually influenced his decision. If so, it was argued then and ever since, the legal notion that this is a Christian nation would have public consequences. Other decisions followed. Brewer argued that "the whole range of service [of chaplains], whether in prayer or preaching, is an official recognition of Christianity." He argued that Christian nations manifested the highest form of civilized life, and that the Bible was "our nation's sacred book." A National Reform Association official seconded such notions: "No nation has ever existed without a religion, and the religion of our nation is Christian."[11]

In a later Supreme Court case, *United States v. Macintosh*, the claim that this is a Christian nation came up one more time. In this case a Canadian theologian, Douglas Macintosh, a Yale Divinity School professor and a pacifist, applied for naturalization as a citizen. Because his pledge to defend America but without taking up arms sounded ambiguous to authorities, his application was denied. Justice George Sutherland, who was ruling in the case, cited Brewer from the *Holy Trinity* case, and wrote: "We are a Christian people . . . according to one another the equal right of religious freedom, and acknowledging with reverence the duty of obedience to the will of God."[12] Justice Charles Evans Hughes in his dissent made no reference to Christianity, but did support theism. Never again did the court identify the United States with Christianity or theism, but the words of Sutherland and Hughes, on opposite sides of the case, often are quoted by advocates of a Christian America.

Still, though amendments have failed and the Supreme Court has largely avoided using any phrase that comes close to defining Christian America, advocates say that there might instead be more frequent references to the Christian (or "Judeo-Christian") base in the legislatures and courts. Privileging Christianity would thus help assure that the spheres of public life had a divine and not merely human and pragmatic base. Therefore legislatures could formulate and courts could judge that all kinds of support for religion can be advanced from year to year. The legal support and judicial monitoring of "faith-based" ventures in recent decades on state and federal levels provide examples of this kind of support. Further, as Christians are in the large majority in the fields of military chaplaincy, and as they benefit most from legal holidays, which match and observe Christian calendars, however reflexively and casually, all that citizens need do, the argument goes, is to take advantage of these. Through public relations efforts they can reinforce in the minds of the public the awareness that Christianity is being favored in the public sphere. The fact that courts all the way up to and including the U.S. Supreme Court will strike down overt efforts financially to support or to privilege Christianity need not be an inhibitor, goes the argument, as during the years when a policy is being debated, or a compromised version of it is proposed, citizens can experience a refreshed sense of the role of religion—and, they hope, Christianity will thus be advanced.

Some citizens with national defense and American exceptionalism in mind advocate a stress on Christian America as an instrument to use against foreign challengers. This was notorious during the Cold War when purportedly "Christian America" faced the "Atheistic Soviet Union." In anticipation of a new "cold war" with Islamicists in our day, in 1979, when the Shi'ite leaders in Iran embarrassed and "defeated" the United States during a hostage crisis, some citizens spoke with envy of Iran, where Islam provided the glue and the propulsion for the attack on the United States. They asked, in effect: "Why can't we be as efficient as the enemy in matters of religious identification and motivation? We are tied up in knots asking who we are and how to mobilize us. It would be simple and efficient just to speak of Christian America, motivated and propelled by devotion as we are to the specific revelation in the Bible, to match Islamdom's single-minded and uncluttered appeal to the Qur'an." Such questions and proposals remained mainly rhetorical, yet there are frequent court cases emerging from aggressive Christian America efforts by some military leaders at academies, such as that of the Air Force in Colorado Springs, Colorado. As elsewhere, such efforts do not survive scrutiny when publicized or adjudicated, but each serves to keep the motion toward Christian America alive in a culture perceived as increasingly secular.

One of the most appealing arguments for Christian America is historical and philosophical. Some of those who oppose ethics that is not grounded in religion, which means moral frameworks that critics consider to be relativistic and merely situational, argue with some warrant that ethical discussion, to be compelling, has to be based somehow in normative texts that make an appeal to divine revelation or to metaphysics, or both. Otherwise, they ask, how can one make truth claims on the basis of which to legislate or adjudicate on important issues? Failing to find or propose such a basis, they argue, reduces ethical discourse to merely emotive appeals. Thus the cry, "Abortion is wrong!" translates to something like "I find abortion unsettling and thus evil; you should find it the same, and we should work to make it simply illegal."[13] Partisans of this view argue positively that if contenders can ground ethical discourse in divine revelation, which scriptural-based Christianity intends to do, they can find absolute or at least quite sure means to provide foundations for particular legal policies.

Less attractive in the eyes of those who criticize Christian America propositions is, in a colloquialism of our day, an "in-your-face" use. Such an attitude or approach often represents attitudes expressed in campaigns to legislate for or, usually, against a policy that is seen to have religious and political implications. Assertions that this is a Christian America and that this fact must be recognized by acts that privilege the Christian story and Christian songs in public school programs, on the courthouse lawn at Christmas, or in invocations at public events, often begin in sincere efforts to gather the faithful and to address their God. In resultant political confrontations both those who support the cause and those who oppose it can take a turn into something that is much more troubling in the public sphere.

This kind of use of Christian America themes is in many cases an effort by supporters of a cause to delineate all others as "outsiders," aliens, strangers, people who do not belong in America or who have or should have status secondary to that of Christians there. "Belongers," as opposed to strangers and aliens on the soil, assert that they should dominate in Christian America because there are more of them than others, that they helped produce many elements of the good in American public life, that they are being obedient to God in their acts of naming, and that they are setting boundaries on the privileges of others. So long as this nation is not designated and self-defined as Christian America, they complain, it is difficult to define and defend the basis of decision.

The Costs of Maintaining the Christian America Myth

If it is potentially profitable for those who do not favor the designation "Christian America," and all the rights and privileges that go with it, to listen to rationales for this naming, so those who advocate Christian America would do well to listen to the arguments of those who oppose this label. Among these are the following:

First, privileging by law or naming rights for one religion will necessarily lead to more intersectarian rivalry, discrimination against the practices of some full citizens, an increase in legislation and litigation, and increasing resentments that unnecessarily upset neighborly and community life, and render official what is already informally a cause for tension among citizens.

Those with Christian America impulses believe that these are small prices to pay when vital Christian teaching and practice is at stake in a pluralist society.

Next, such naming would represent a regression to policies and politics rejected after centuries of mistreatment of minorities and a long process by citizens who seek to realize a society that respects differences and honors the neighbor. Christian America efforts would partly undo an achievement acclaimed by most citizens, including those who may not have thought through the consequences of inventing a privileging Christian America. Critics do not need to conjure up the prospects of holy wars or crusades, but they can help recall the role of religious establishment and privilege in motivating the migration of many from Europe in earlier centuries, or from Asia, Africa, and anywhere else in the world where establishment leads to oppression. The benefits for some who relish the name of a Christian America would not outweigh the losses to everyone else.

A third reason should not concern Jews, Muslims, the nonaffiliated and others—though many of non-Christian faiths on occasion acknowledge benefits of a Christian culture whose faith they cannot accept. It should occur to Christians that with any hint of establishment they would be buying into something detrimental to their own Christian faith and churches. Almost all sociologists of religion, theologians, demographers, and other students of comparative destinies among nations agree that the drastic decline of Christian participation and belief in Europe results in no small measure from the fact that churches were and sometimes even still are favored by the state. One does not have to be a devotee of those schools of sociology that credit American religious vitality to "rational choice theory," "free enterprise rationales," or "the values of competition," to observe what historians of American religion have observed for a century and more. That is, having all religions and non-religion on the same legal and cultural basis has led to energetic activity by church people, and contributes to a self-reforming character among the religions.

In that observation, confirmed by everyone from casual tourists to formal documenters, most churches in the British Isles, along with the Protestant north and the Catholic south of Europe, have tended to "go to seed" because the faith and the churches are taken for granted. Whether or not the clergy are ambitious and active and the laity assertive and devoted, in any particular place the church doors may be open for their single hour on Sunday. A formally Christian America could well lead to a replication of the patterns of Europe. Ironists or cynics who would like to see the place of religion lessened and its vibrancy dimmed might do well to join the Christian America ranks to benefit their ranks and positions.

Another reason many oppose the Christian America moves is that the thinking behind them is perceived as historically inaccurate and, truth be told, untrue. They are unhistorical, because the founders and the drafters of constitutions and covenants were fully aware of what they were doing, and they resisted efforts on the federal level to grant privileges or overt support to Christian churches in the decisive era of the shaping of the nation. Nor need one be an "originalist," a literalist about the original intentions of the founders as being putatively retrievable from their documents, to be wary of this, as if all constitutional creativity ended in 1789. Although the subsequent court cases on the federal level and, since the Fourteenth Amendment has been applied by incorporation to questions of religion and the law at the state and local level, too, the proposals for Christian America have seen ups and downs, forwards and backs, swerves and direct moves; overall and finally these issues were resolved in favor of the courts ruling out Christian nation status.

Often one hears pleas from strategists for Christian America causes to find ways to eliminate incorporation and throw the issue back to the states where, in certain regions, they could sometimes win. Going back and repealing the incorporation ruling, however, presents insuperable difficulties to those who oppose it, so rich and diverse and complex is the history of its use in church–state issues. Therefore to picture going back behind it strikes most legal scholars and historians as a fantasy. It was a very conservative panel of judges who in the *Gitlow v. New York* case in 1925 and the *Cantwell* decision of 1940, set the court on its present course. Incorporation has been invoked or implied too frequently to be overturned now. In the colorful language of constitutional scholar Leonard Levy: "The incorporation doctrine has a history so fixed that overthrowing it is as likely as bagging sharks on the roof of the Court's building." Still, some legal scholars say that an exception could be made in the cases involving the Establishment Clause. Levy argues that to try to circumvent incorporation, even if it were possible, would go against the logic of nonestablishment. He goes on to observe that Madison, so central to reasoning on all sides of this issue, argued that an establishment "violated the free exercise of religion" and therefore would "subvert public liberty." Incorporation, Levy stressed, protects citizens with a "freedom from" religious establishment and thus from legally supported religion.[14]

Conclusion: Back to the Beginnings

Having noticed reasons used by sincere Americans, whether churched or not, and legally informed or not, for supporting or opposing Christian America efforts, we go, as do other authors in this book, "back to the beginnings" to see how the issue of Christian America was debated in the 1780s. It's worth remembering the debates leading up to Article VI of the U.S. Constitution, which ruled out any use of religious tests for holding federal public office. So firm was the judgment that this move was a practical address to the issue of religion and non-religion that James Madison fought the idea of a Bill of Rights. He was so sure that the Constitution without amendments was assuring the rights that the Bill later spelled out that he saw no purpose in spelling out details.

To some it may seem unfair to make the case by reference to Madison, even if he was the most notable, dedicated, and motivated of the Constitutional Convention participants. Unfair, because it is well-known that there were others in the Convention who were less firm about boundaries among claims and practices of church and state, and their understandings deserve to be reckoned with, even if they, in effect, "lost" when it came to voting. The Constitution was intended to be and is a short and undetailed document, whose drafters and assenters could not go into detail or state a philosophical case for every move. Figures as notable as Patrick Henry and George Washington, all through the years of national formation, could be listed as "non-preferentialists." That would mean they were people who thought that religion could be state-supported so long as there was no discrimination among religions when it came to support, providing largesse, or preference. Yet, given the precedence in the earlier acts of the Virginia legislature with its Bill for Religious Freedom, there are reasons to give special notice to Madison, along with the more radical Jefferson, and others who had fought the issues of definition before the doors were closed on the drafters of the Constitution in Philadelphia in the hot summer of 1787.

Mention of the more radical Thomas Jefferson, who was not at the Constitutional Convention, invites a hearing of his views. As is well known, he defined himself as religious in very broad terms, often described as Deist but never atheist, and was polemical about the Christian creeds, the religious authorities, and the claims of religious institutions. He made his position clear when he wrote from a distance that in the American republic there dare be no legal inhibitions against any (law-abiding) form of Christianity, and that the United States must assure that there be no favoritism or privileging of Christianity. After one legislative act Jefferson averred that the vote was "proof" that the legislature "meant to comprehend, within the mantle of its protection, the Jew and Gentile, the Christian and Mahometan, the Hindoo, and infidel of every denomination."[15]

Madison also related this issue to the assurance of equality: that an establishment of religion "violates equality by subjecting some to peculiar burdens," and the result would be "bigotry and persecution" that would "destroy that moderation and harmony which the forbearance of our laws to intermeddle with religion has produced among its several sects."[16] Many of the founders did not share their criticisms of the Christian establishmentarians on the scene, but they were assenting to the contention that non-Christians and nonbelievers should be free to be as at home in the United States as anyone else.

Notes

1. Mark A. Noll, Nathan O. Hatch, George M. Marsden, *The Search for Christian America* (Westchester, Il: Crossway Books, 1981), 102.

2. Ibid. 129 (emphasis added).

3. Abraham Lincoln, The "Cooper Union Speech," in Roy P. Basler, ed., *The Collected Works of Abraham Lincoln*, 9 vols. (Rutgers, NJ: Rutgers University Press, 1953–1955), 2:461–68.

4. William R. Hutchison, ed., *Between the Times: The Travail of the Protestant Establishment in America, 1900–1960* (Cambridge: Cambridge University Press, 1989), esp. p. 4. See also Jackson Carroll and Wade Clark Roof, eds., *Beyond Establishment: Protestant Identity in a Post-Protestant Age* (Louisville, KY: Westminster/John Knox Press, 1993).

5. This is traced and identified best in Mark Silk, *Spiritual Politics: Religion and America since World War II* (New York: Simon & Schuster, 1985), 40–53.

6. A full-length militant attack on incorporation appears in Robert L. Cord, *Separation of Church and State: Historical Fact and Current Fiction* (New York: Lambeth, 1982).

7. David McAllister, Proceedings of the National Convention to Secure the Religious Amendment of the Constitution of the United States (Philadelphia: Christian Statesman Association, 1874), 1.

8. Ibid., 1, with a rationale in ibid., 32.

9. For notice of Judge Brewer's frequently stated views on this subject, see Jay Alan Sekulow, *Witnessing Their Faith: Religious Influence on Supreme Court Justices and Their Opinions* (New York: Rowman and Littlefield, 2006), 134–45.

10. 143 U.S. 457, 471 (1892).

11. Quotations from Brewer are cited by Sekulow, *Witnessing Their Faith.*, 148, 152, by the NRA official in ibid., 152.

12. United States v. Macintosh, 283 U.S. 605, 625 (1931).

13. This case builds on the influential argument by philosopher Alasdair MacIntyre in *After Virtue: A Study in Moral Theory* (Notre Dame, IN: University of Notre Dame Press, 1981) and subsequent books

14. The comments on attempts to remove incorporation appear in Leonard W. Levy, *The Establishment Clause: Religion and the First Amendment* (New York: Macmillan, 1986), 168–69.

15. Quoted in Morton Borden, *Jews, Turks, and Infidels* (Chapel Hill: University of North Carolina Press, 1984), 15.

16. Quoted in ibid.

{ BIBLIOGRAPHY }

Adams, Charles F., ed., *Familiar Letters of John Adams and His Wife Abigail Adams, during the Revolution* (Boston: Houghton Mifflin, 1875)

Adams, Jasper, *The Relation of Christianity to Civil Government in the United States*, 2d ed. (Charleston, SC: A. E. Miller, 1833)

Adams, John, *The Works of John Adams, Second President of the United States*, edited by C. F. Adams, 10 vols. (Boston: Little, Brown, and Co., 1850–1856)

Ahlstrom, Sydney E., *A Religious History of the American People* (New Haven, CT: Yale University Press, 1972)

Albanese, Catherine, *Sons of the Fathers: The Civil Religion of the American Revolution* (Philadelphia: Temple University Press, 1976)

Alley, Robert S. *School Prayer: The Court, the Congress, and the First Amendment* (Buffalo, NY: Prometheus Books, 1994)

———, ed., *James Madison on Religious Liberty* (Buffalo, NY: Prometheus Books, 1985)

Amar, Akhil Reed, "The Bill of Rights and the Fourteenth Amendment," *Yale Law Journal* 101 (1992): 1193

American State Papers, Documents, Legislative and Executive, of the Congress of the United States, 38 vols. (Washington, DC: Gales and Seaton, 1832–1861)

Andrews, John, ed., *A Complete Dictionary of the English Language*, 4th ed. (Philadelphia: William Young, 1789)

Antieau, Chester J., Arthur T. Downey, and Edward C. Roberts, *Freedom from Federal Establishment: Formation and Early History of the First Amendment Religion Clauses* (Milwaukee, WI: Bruce, 1964)

Aristotle, *Nicomachean Ethics* (Chicago: University of Chicago Press, 2011)

Ash, John, *A New and Complete Dictionary of the English Language*, 2 vols. (London: Edward and Charles Dilly, 1775)

Avins, Alfred, ed., *The Reconstruction Amendments' Debates: The Legislative History and Contemporary Debates in Congress on the 13th, 14th, and 15th Amendments* (Richmond: Virginia Commission on Constitutional Government, 1967)

Axtell, James, ed., *The Educational Writings of John Locke* (New York: Cambridge University Press, 1968)

Aynes, Richard, "On Misreading John Bingham and the Fourteenth Amendment," *Yale Law Journal* 103 (1993): 57

Bachman, Van Cleaf, *Peltries or Plantations: The Economic Policies of the Dutch West India Company in New Netherland, 1623–1639* (Baltimore, MD: Johns Hopkins University Press, 1969)

Backus, Isaac, *An Appeal to the Public for Religious Liberty, against the Oppressions of the Present Day* (Boston: John Boyle, 1773)

Bacon, William J., *The Continental Congress: Some of Its Actors and Their Doings, with the Results Thereof* (Utica, NY: Ellis H. Roberts, 1881)

Bailyn, Bernard, *The Ideological Origins of the American Revolution* (Cambridge, MA: Belknap, 1967)

Baird, Robert, *Religion in the United States of America* (Glasgow: Blackie & Son, 1844)

Baker, Robert A., and Paul J. Craven Jr., *Adventure in Faith: The First 300 Years of the First Baptist Church, Charleston, South Carolina* (Nashville, TN: Broadman, 1982)

Bancroft, George, *The History of the United States*, 6 vols. (New York: D. Appleton, 1883–1885)

Banning, Lance, "James Madison, the Statute for Religious Freedom, and the Crisis of Republican Convictions," in *The Virginia Statute of Religious Freedom*, edited by Merrill D. Peterson and Robert Vaughan (New York: Cambridge University Press, 1988)

Basler, Roy P., ed., *The Collected Works of Abraham Lincoln*, 9 vols. (Rutgers, NJ: Rutgers University Press, 1953–1955)

Bassett, John Spencer, ed., *Correspondence of Andrew Jackson*, 7 vols. (Washington, DC: Carnegie Institution of Washington, 1929)

Becker, Carl, *The Declaration of Independence: A Study in the History of Political Ideas* (New York: Vintage Books, 1958)

Beecher, Henry Ward, "The School Question," in *The Bible in the Public Schools: Opinions of Individuals and of the Press, and Judicial Decisions* (New York: J. W. Schermerhorn & Co., 1870), 14

Beecher, Lyman, "A Reformation of Morals Practicable and Indispensable," in *Lyman Beecher and the Reform of Society: Four Sermons, 1804–1828*, edited by Edwin S. Gaustad (New York: Arno, 1972), 17

Beeman, Richard, Stephen Botein, and Edward C. Carter II, eds., *Beyond Confederation: Origins of the American Constitution and American National Identity* (Chapel Hill: University of North Carolina Press, 1987)

Beneke, Chris, *Beyond Toleration: The Religious Origins of American Pluralism* (New York: Oxford University Press, 2006)

Bennett, Hal D., "*American Freedom and Catholic Power*: Book Review," *Alabama Baptist* (1949): 9

Berg, Thomas C., "Anti-Catholicism and Modern Church–State Relations," *Loyola University Chicago Law Journal* 33 (2001): 121

Bernstein, Richard B., with Kym S. Rice, *Are We to Be a Nation? The Making of the Constitution* (Cambridge, MA: Harvard University Press, 1987)

Beverley, Robert, *The History and Present State of Virginia* (Chapel Hill: University of North Carolina Press, 1947)

Black, Hugo, Jr., *My Father, A Remembrance* (New York: Random House, 1975)

Blackstone, William, *Commentaries on the Laws of England*, 4 vols. (Oxford: Clarendon, 1765–1769)

Blakely, William Addison, ed., *American State Papers Bearing on Sunday Legislation*, rev. and enl. ed. (Washington, DC: Religious Liberty Association, 1911)

Blanshard, Paul, *American Freedom and Catholic Power* (Boston: Beacon, 1949)

Blau, Joseph L., "The Christian Party in Politics," *Review of Religion* 11 (1946–47): 26

———, ed., *Cornerstones of Religious Freedom in America* (Boston: Beacon, 1949)

Boettner, Lorraine, *Roman Catholicism* (Phillipsburg, NJ: P & R, 2000)

Boiter, Albert, "Law and Religion in the Soviet Union," *The American Journal of Comparative Law* 35 (Winter, 1987): 97–126

Bonomi, Patricia, *Under the Cope of Heaven: Religion, Society, and Politics in Colonial America* (New York: Oxford University Press, 1986)

Bonomi, Patricia, and Peter Eisenstandt, "Church Adherence in the Eighteenth-Century British American Colonies," *William and Mary Quarterly* 39 (1982): 247

Borden, Morton, *Jews, Turks, and Infidels* (Chapel Hill: University of North Carolina Press, 1984)

Botein, Stephen, "Religious Dimensions of the Early American State Constitutions," in *Beyond Confederation: Origins of the American Constitution and American National Identity*, edited by Richard Beeman, Stephen Botein, and Edward C. Carter II (Chapel Hill: University of North Carolina Press, 1987), 320

Bourne, William Oland, *History of the Public School Society of the City of New York* (New York: William Wood, 1870)

Bowers, J. D., *Joseph Priestley and English Unitarianism in America* (University Park: Pennsylvania State University Press, 2007)

Boxer, C. R., *The Dutch Seaborne Empire, 1600–1800* (New York: A. A. Knopf, 1965)

Bradley, Gerard V., *Church–State Relationships in America* (Westport, CT: Greenwood, 1987)

———. "The No Religious Test Clause and the Constitution of Religious Liberty: A Machine That Has Gone of Itself," *Case Western Reserve Law Review* 37 (1987): 674

Bremer, Francis J., *John Winthrop, America's Forgotten Founding Father* (Oxford: Oxford University Press, 2003)

———. *The Puritan Experiment: New England Society from Bradford to Edwards* (Hanover, NH: University Press of New England, 1995)

Brewer, Holly, "Beyond Education: Republican Revision of the Laws Regarding Children," in *Thomas Jefferson and the Education of a Citizen*, edited by James Gilreath (Washington, DC: Library of Congress, 1999), 49

Brinsfield, John Wesley, *Religion and Politics in Colonial South Carolina* (Easley, SC: Southern Historical, 1983)

Brodhead, John R., Berthold Fernow, and E. B. O'Callaghan, eds., *Documents Relative to the Colonial History of the State of New York*, 15 vols. (Albany, NY: Weed, Parsons, 1853–87)

Brown, Roy M., *Public Poor Relief in North Carolina* (New York: Arno, 1976)

Buckley, Thomas E., *Church and State in Revolutionary Virginia, 1776–1787* (Charlottesville: University Press of Virginia, 1977)

Bugess, Walter H., *John Robinson, Pastor of the Pilgrim Fathers, A Study of His Life and Times* (London: Williams & Norgate, 1920)

Burgett, Timothy S., "Government Aid to Religious Social Service Providers: The Supreme Court's 'Pervasively Sectarian' Standard," *Virginia Law Review* 75 (1989): 1077

Burke, Edmund, *Edmund Burke: Selected Writings and Speeches*, edited by Peter J. Stanlis (Garden City, NY: Anchor Books, 1963)

Burn, Richard, *Ecclesiastical Law*, 3d ed., 4 vols. (London: W. Strahan and M. Woodfall, 1775)

Burnett, Edmund C., ed., *Letters of Members of the Continental Congress*, 8 vols. (Washington, DC: Carnegie Institution of Washington, 1921–1936)

Burrows, Edwin G., and Mike Wallace, *Gotham: A History of New York City to 1898* (New York: Oxford University Press, 1999)

Butler, Jon, *Awash in a Sea of Faith: Christianizing the American People* (Cambridge, MA: Harvard University Press, 1990)

Byrd, James P., Jr., *The Challenges of Roger Williams: Religious Liberty, Violent Persecution and the Bible* (Macon, GA: Mercer University Press, 2002)

Calabresi, Steven G., and Sarah E. Agudo, "Individual Rights under State Constitutions When the Fourteenth Amendment Was Ratified in 1868: What Rights Are Deeply Rooted in American History and Tradition?," *Texas Law Review* 87 (2008): 7

Calvin, John, *Epistles of Paul the Apostle to the Romans and to the Thessalonians*, edited by David W. Torrance and Thomas F. Torrance, translated by Ross Mackenzie (Edinburgh: Oliver and Boyd, 1961)

———. *Institutes of the Christian Religion*, edited by John T. McNeill, translated by Ford Battles, 2 vols. (Philadelphia: Westminster, 1960)

Campbell, Ballard C., *The Growth of American Government: Governance from the Cleveland Era to the Present* (Bloomington: Indiana University Press, 1995)

Capen, Edward Warren, *The Historical Development of the Poor Law of Connecticut* (PhD diss.: Columbia University, 1905)

Cappon, Lester J., ed., *The Adams-Jefferson Letters: The Complete Correspondence between Thomas Jefferson and Abigail and John Adams* (Chapel Hill: University of North Carolina Press, 1959)

Carey, Charles Henry, ed., *The Oregon Constitution and Proceedings and Debates of the Constitutional Convention of 1857* (Salem, OR: State Printing Department, 1926)

Carroll, Jackson, and Wade Clark Roof, eds., *Beyond Establishment: Protestant Identity in a Post-Protestant Age* (Louisville, KY: Westminster/John Knox, 1993)

"The Catholic Church in the United States: 1776–1876," *Catholic World* (July, 1876), 440

Chesterton, G. K., *What I Saw in America* (London: Hodder and Stoughton Limited, 1922)

The Christian Journal, and Literary Register, 14 vols. (New York: T. and J. Swords, 1817–1830)

"Church and State," *Catholic World* (May, 1870): 152

"Church and State in France," *Catholic World* (October, 1889): 16

"The Church Establishment of England," *The Princeton Review* (October, 1834): 523

The City Gazette, and the Daily Advertiser, 18 vols. (Charleston, SC: Haswell & M'Iver, 1787–1803)

Clarke, Erskine, *Our Southern Zion: A History of Calvinism in the South Carolina Low Country, 1690–1900* (Tuscaloosa: University of Alabama Press, 1996)

Clinton, DeWitt, *A Vindication of Thomas Jefferson; against the Charges Contained in a Pamphlet Entitled, "Serious Considerations," &c.* (New York: David Denniston, 1800)

Cobb, Sanford H., *The Rise of Religious Liberty in America: A History* (New York: Macmillan, 1902)

Cole, Franklin P., ed., *They Preached Liberty* (Indianapolis, IN: Liberty, 1976)

Colwell, Stephen, *The Position of Christianity in the United States* (Philadelphia: Lippincott, Grambo & Co., 1854)

Congressional Globe, 46 vols., 3d ed. (Washington, DC: U.S. Government Printing Office, 1789–1909)

Conkle, Daniel O., "Toward a General Theory of the Establishment Clause," *Northwestern University Law Review* 82 (1988): 1113

"The Continental Congress at Mass," *American Catholic Historical Researches* 6 (1889): 50

Cooley, Thomas M., *Michigan: A History of Governments*, 8th ed. (Boston: Houghton Mifflin, 1897)

———. *A Treatise on the Constitutional Limitations Which Rest upon the Legislative Power of the States of the American Union*, 4th ed. (Boston: Little Brown & Co., 1878)

Cooper, Thomas, *The Case of Thomas Cooper, M.D. President of the South Carolina College: Submitted to the Legislature and the People of South Carolina, December 1831*, 2d ed. (Columbia, SC: Times and Gazette Office, 1832)

Cord, Robert L., *Separation of Church and State: Historical Fact and Current Fiction* (New York: Lambeth, 1982)

Corrigan, R., "Book Review," *The Catholic Historical Review* 20 (1934): 199

Cotton, John, *The Bloody Tenent, Washed and Made White in the Bloud of the Lambe* (London: Matthew Symmons, 1647)

Cremin, Lawrence A., *The American Common School: A Historic Conception* (New York: Teachers College, Columbia University, 1952)

Crowley, Weldon S., "Erastianism in England to 1640," *Journal of Church and State* 32 (1990): 549

———. "Erastianism in the Long Parliament, 1640–1646," *Journal of Church and State* 21 (1979): 45

———. "Erastianism in the Westminster Assembly," *Journal of Church and State* 15 (1973): 49

Curry, Thomas J., *The First Freedoms: Church and State in America to the Passage of the First Amendment* (New York: Oxford University Press, 1986)

Curtis, Michael Kent, *No State Shall Abridge: The Fourteenth Amendment and the Bill of Rights* (Durham, NC: Duke University Press, 1986)

Cushing, John D., "Notes on Disestablishment in Massachusetts," *The William and Mary Quarterly* 26 (1969): 185

Dalcho, Frederick, "An Address Delivered in St. Michael's Church before the Charleston Protestant Episcopal Sunday School Society at their Seventh Anniversary, May 16, 1826," *The Christian Journal, and Literary Register* (New York: T. and J. Swords, 1827)

———. *The Evidence from Prophecy for the Truth of Christianity and the Divinity of Christ: In a Course of Catechetical Instruction* (Charleston, SC: n.p., ca. 1818)

Davis, Derek, *Religion and the Continental Congress, 1774–1789: Contributions to Original Intent* (Oxford: Oxford University Press, 2000)

The Debates and Proceedings in the Congress of the United States, 42 vols. (Washington, DC: Gales and Seaton, 1834–1856)

The Declaration of Independence and the Constitution of the United States (Washington, DC: U.S. Government Printing Office, 1956)

De Gurowski, Adam G., *America and Europe* (New York: D. Appleton, 1857)

Diman, J. Lewis, "Religion in America," *The North American Review* (January, 1876): 4

Drakeman, Donald L., *Church, State and Original Intent* (New York: Cambridge University Press, 2010)

———. "*Everson v. Board of Education* and the Quest for the Historical Establishment Clause," *The American Journal of Legal History* 46 (2007): 119

Dreisbach, Daniel L., "The Constitution's Forgotten Religion Clause: Reflections on the Article VI Religious Test Ban," *Journal of Church and State* 38 (1996): 261

———. "A New Perspective on Jefferson's Views on Church-State Relations: The Virginia Statute for Establishing Religious Freedom in Its Legislative Context," *American Journal of Legal History* 35 (1991): 172

———. *Religion and Politics in the Early Republic: Jasper Adams and the Church-State Debate* (Lexington: University Press of Kentucky, 1996)

———. "'Sowing Useful Truths and Principles': The Danbury Baptists, Thomas Jefferson, and the 'Wall of Separation,'" *Journal of Church and State* 39 (1997): 455

———. *Thomas Jefferson and the Wall of Separation between Church and State* (New York: New York University Press, 2002)

Dreisbach, Daniel L., Mark D. Hall, and Jeffry R. Morrison, eds., *The Forgotten Founders on Religion and Public Life* (Notre Dame, IN: University of Notre Dame Press, 2009)

———. eds., *The Founders on God and Government* (Lanham, MD: Rowman and Littlefield, 2004)

Duane, William, ed., *Extracts from the Diary of Christopher Marshall, Kept in Philadelphia and Lancaster, during the American Revolution, 1774–1781* (Albany, NY: Joel Munsell, 1877)

Dwight, Timothy, *The Duty of Americans, at the Present Crisis* (New Haven, CT: Thomas and Samuel Green, 1798)

Eckenrode, H. J., *Separation of Church and State in Virginia* (Richmond, VA: Department of Archives and History, 1910)

Edgar, Walter B., *South Carolina: A History* (Columbia: University of South Carolina Press, 1998)

Elliot, Jonathan, ed., *The Debates in the Several State Conventions, on the Adoption of the Federal Constitution*, 2d ed., 5 vols. (Washington, DC: Printed for the Editor, 1836–1845)

Elliott, Charles W., *The New England History* 2 vols. (New York: Scribner, 1857)

Ellsworth, Oliver, "A Landholder, to the Landholders and Farmers," December 17, 1787, in *Connecticut Courant* (Hartford, 1787), 1

Ellwood, Robert S., *The Fifties Spiritual Marketplace: American Religion in a Decade of Conflict* (New Brunswick, NJ: Rutgers University Press, 1997)

Ely, Ezra Stiles, *The Duty of Christian Freemen to Elect Christian Rulers: A Discourse Delivered on the Fourth of July, 1827, in the Seventh Presbyterian Church, in Philadelphia* (Philadelphia: William F. Geddes, 1828)

Emmanuel, I. S., "New Light on Early American Jewry," *American Jewish Archives* 7 (1955): 5

Esbeck, Carl H., "Dissent and Disestablishment: The Church–State Settlement in the Early Republic," *Brigham Young University Law Review* (2004): 1385

Esbeck, Carl H., "The Establishment Clause as a Structural Restraint on Governmental Power," *Iowa Law Review* (1998): 1

Fair, Daryl R., "The *Everson* Case in the Context of New Jersey Politics," in *Everson Revisited: Religion, Education, and Law at the Crossroads*, edited by Jo Renée Formicola and Hubert Morken (Lanham, MD: Rowman & Littlefield, 1997), 1

Farrand, Max, ed., *The Records of the Federal Convention of 1787*, 3 vols. (New Haven, CT: Yale University Press, 1911)

Feldman, Noah, *Divided by God: America's Church–State Problem and What We Should Do about It* (New York: Farrar, Straus, and Giroux, 2005)

———."The Intellectual Origins of the Establishment Clause," *New York University Law Review* 77 (2002): 346

———. "Nonsectarianism Reconsidered," *Journal of Law and Politics* 11 (2002): 65

Fernow, Berthold, ed., *Documents Relating to the Colonial History of the State of New York* (Albany, NY: Weed, Parsons, 1883)

———, ed., *The Records of New Amsterdam: From 1653 to 1674*, repr. ed. (Baltimore, MD: Genealogical Publishing, 1976)

Feuer, Lewis Samuel, *Spinoza and the Rise of Liberalism* (Boston: Beacon, 1958)

Finkelman, Paul, "A Land That Needs People for Its Increase: How the Jews Won the Right to Remain in New Netherland," in *New Essays in American Jewish History*, edited by Pamela S. Nadell, Jonathan D. Sarna, and Lance J. Sussman (Cincinnati, OH: American Jewish Archives of Hebrew Union College-Jewish Institute of Religion, 2010), 19

———. "School Vouchers, Thomas Jefferson, Roger Williams, and Protecting the Faithful: Warnings from the Eighteenth Century and the Seventeenth Century on the Dangers of Establishments to Religious Communities," *Brigham Young University Law Review* (2008): 525

———, ed., *Religion and American Law: An Encyclopedia* (New York: Garland, 2000)

Fligelman, Jay, *Prodigals and Pilgrims: The American Revolution against Patriarchal Authority* (New York: Cambridge University Press, 1982)

Foner, Philip S., *Complete Writings of Thomas Paine*, 2 vols. (New York: Citadel, 1945)

Foote, William Henry, *Sketches of Virginia: Historical and Biographical* (Richmond, VA: John Knox, 1966)

Ford, P. L., ed., *The New England Primer* (New York: Teachers College, Columbia University, 1962)

Ford, Worthington C. et al., eds., *Journals of the Continental Congress, 1774–1789*, 34 vols. (Washington, DC: U.S. Government Printing Office, 1904–1937)

Formicola, Jo Renée, and Hubert Morken, eds., *Everson Revisited: Religion, Education, and Law at the Crossroads* (Lanham, MD: Rowman & Littlefield, 1997)

Foster, Stephen, *Their Solitary Way: The Puritan Social Ethic in the First Century of Settlement in New England* (New Haven, CT: Yale University Press, 1971)

———. "The French Radicals and the Concordat," *Catholic World* (October, 1885): 135

Friedman, Lawrence J., and Mark D. McGarvie, eds., *Charity, Philanthropy, and Civility in American History* (New York: Cambridge University Press, 2003)

Friedman, Lawrence M., *Crime and Punishment in American History* (New York: Basic Books, 1993)

———. *A History of American Law* (New York: Simon & Shuster, 1973)

Friedman, Saul S., *Jews and the American Slave Trade* (New Brunswick, NJ: Transaction, 1998)

Frost, J. William, *A Perfect Freedom: Religious Liberty in Pennsylvania* (New York: Cambridge University Press, 1990)

Fuller, Zelotes, "The Tree of Liberty. An Address in Celebration of the Birth of Washington, Delivered at the Second Universalist Church in Philadelphia, Sunday Morning, February 28, 1830," in *Cornerstones of Religious Freedom in America*, rev. ed., edited by Joseph L. Blau (New York: Harper Torchbooks, 1964), 134

Gabel, Richard J., *Public Funds for Church and Private Schools* (Washington, DC: The Catholic University of America, 1937)

"*Gaines' New York Gazette*, January 9, 1775," in *The Diary of the American Revolution: From Newspapers and Original Documents*, 2 vols., edited by Frank Moore (New York: Charles Scribner, 1860), 1:11

Gasparin, Agenor de, *The Uprising of a Great People: The United States in 1861* (London: S. Low, 1861)

Gaustad, Edwin Scott, *Historical Atlas of Religion in America* (New York: Harper and Row, 1962)

———., ed., *Lyman Beecher and the Reform of Society: Four Sermons, 1804–1828* (New York: Arno, 1972)

Gibson, William, *James II and the Trial of the Seven Bishops* (New York: Palgrave/Macmillan, 2009)

Gilreath, James, ed., *Thomas Jefferson and the Education of a Citizen* (Washington, DC: Library of Congress, 1999)

Glenn, Charles, *The Myth of the Common School* (Amherst, NY: Amherst University Press, 1988)

Goldman, Shalom, ed., *Hebrew and the Bible in America: The First Two Centuries* (Hanover and London: Brandeis University Press and Dartmouth College, 1993)

Gordon, Sarah Barringer, *The Mormon Question: Polygamy and Constitutional Conflict in Nineteenth-Century America* (Chapel Hill: University of North Carolina Press, 2002)

Green, Fletcher M., *Constitutional Development in the South Atlantic States, 1776–1860; A Study in the Evolution of Democracy* (New York: De Capo, 1971)

Green, Steven K., *The Bible, the School, and the Constitution: The Clash That Shaped Modern Church–State Doctrine* (New York: Oxford University Press, 2012)

———. "The Blaine Amendment Reconsidered," *American Journal of Legal History* 36 (1992): 38

———. "'Blaming Blaine': Understanding the Blaine Amendment and the 'No-Funding' Principle," *First Amendment Law Review* 2 (2002): 107

———. "The Insignificance of the Blaine Amendment," *Brigham Young University Law Review* (2008): 295

———. *The Second Disestablishment: Church and State in Nineteenth Century America* (New York: Oxford University Press, 2010)

———. "A 'Spacious Conception': Separationism as an Idea," *Oregon Law Review* 85 (2006): 443

Greenawalt, Kent, "History as Ideology: Philip Hamburger's Separation of Church and State," *California Law Review* 93 (2005): 367

———. *Religion and the Constitution*, 2 vols. (Princeton, NJ, Princeton University Press, 2008)

Greenberg, Douglas, *Crime in the Colony of New York* (Ithaca, NY: Cornell University Press, 1978)

Gross, Robert A., "Giving in America: From Charity to Philanthropy," in *Charity, Philanthropy, and Civility in American History*, edited by Lawrence J. Friedman and Mark D. McGarvie (New York: Cambridge University Press, 2003), 33

Grossberg, Michael, "Citizens and Families: A Jeffersonian Vision of Domestic Relations and Generational Change," in *Thomas Jefferson and the Education of a Citizen*, edited by James Gilreath (Washington, DC: Library of Congress, 1999), 3

———. *Governing the Hearth: Law and the Family in Nineteenth-Century America* (Chapel Hill: University of North Carolina Press, 1985)

Grossberg, Michael, and Christopher Tomlins, eds., *Cambridge History of Law in America*, 3 vols. (New York: Cambridge University Press, 2008)

Gunn, T. Jeremy, *A Standard for Repair: The Establishment Clause, Equality, and Natural Rights* (New York: Garland, 1992)

Hale, Horace Morrison, Aaron Gove, and Joseph C. Shattuck, *Education in Colorado, 1861–1885* (Denver: News printing company, 1885)

Hall, Timothy, *Separation of Church and State: Roger Williams and Religious Liberty* (Urbana: University of Illinois Press, 1998)

Hamburger, Philip, *Separation of Church and State* (Cambridge, MA: Harvard University Press, 2002)

Handy, Robert T., *A Christian America: Protestant Hopes and Historical Realities*, 2d ed. (New York: Oxford University Press, 1984)

———. "The Protestant Quest for a Christian America, 1830–1930," *Church History* 22 (1953): 8

———. *Undermined Establishment: Church–State Relations in America, 1880–1920* (Princeton, NJ: Princeton University Press, 1991)

Harris, William Torrey, "The Division of School Funds for Religious Purposes," *Atlantic Monthly* 38 (August 1876): 171

Haskins, George L., *Law and Authority in Early Massachusetts: A Study in Tradition and Design* (New York: Macmillan, 1960)

Hastings, Hugh, Edward Tanjore Corwin, and James Austin Holden, eds., *Ecclesiastical Records: State of New York*, 7 vols. (Albany, NY: J. B. Lyon, 1901–1916)

Hening, William Waller, *The Statutes at Large, Being a Collection of All the Laws in Virginia, from the First Session of the Legislature, in the Year 1619*, 13 vols. (New York: R. & W. & G. Bartow, 1819–1823)

Henry, William Wirt, ed., *Patrick Henry: Life, Correspondence and Speeches*, 3 vols. (New York: Charles Scribner's Sons, 1891)

Hensel, Donald W., "Religion and the Writing of the Colorado Constitution," *Church History* 30 (1961): 349

Henson, H. Hensley, *Studies in English Religion in the Seventeenth Century* (London: John Murray, 1903)

Hershkowitz, Leo, "By Chance or Choice: Jews in New Amsterdam 1654," *American Jewish Archives* 57 (2005): 1

———. "New Amsterdam's Twenty-Three Jews—Myth or Reality?" in *Hebrew and the Bible in America: The First Two Centuries*, edited by Shalom Goldman (Hanover and London: Brandeis University Press and Dartmouth College, 1993), 171

———. "Some Aspects of the New York Jewish Merchant and Community, 1654–1820," *American Jewish Historical Quarterly* 66 (1976–1977): 10

Heyrman, Christine Leigh, *Southern Cross: The Beginnings of the Bible Belt* (Chapel Hill: University of North Carolina Press, 1997)

Hobbes, Thomas, *Leviathan*, 2d ed. (London: Ballantine, 1886)

Hoefte, Rosemarijn, and Johanna C. Kardux, eds., *Connecting Cultures: The Netherlands in Five Centuries of Transatlantic Exchange* (Amsterdam: Vrije Universiteit Press, 1994)

Hogue, William M., "The Civil Disability of Ministers of Religion in State Constitutions," *Journal of Church and State* 36 (1994): 329

Holmes, David L., *The Faiths of the Founding Fathers* (New York: Oxford University Press, 2006)

Howe, Mark De Wolfe, *The Garden and the Wilderness: Religion and Government in American Constitutional History* (Chicago: University of Chicago Press, 1965)

Hudson, Rex H., ed., *Brazil: A Country Study* (Washington, DC: Federal Research Division, Library of Congress, 1997)

Hühner, Leon, "Asser Levy: A Noted Jewish Burgher of New Amsterdam," *American Jewish Historical Society Journal* 8 (1900): 99

Humphrey, Edward Frank, *Nationalism and Religion in America: 1774–1789* (New York: Russell, 1965)

Hunter, James Davison, *Culture Wars: The Struggle to Control the Family, Art, Education, Law, and Politics in America* (New York: Basic Books, 1992)

Hutchison, William, ed., *Between the Times: The Travail of the Protestant Establishment in America, 1900–1960* (Cambridge: Cambridge University Press, 1989)

Innes, Stephen, *Creating the Commonwealth: The Economic Culture of Puritan New England* (New York: W. W. Norton, 1995)

Israel, Jonathan, and Reinier Salverda, eds., *Dutch Jewry: Its History and Secular Culture (1500–2000)* (Leiden: Brill, 2002)

Jacobs, Jaap, *New Netherland: A Dutch Colony in Seventeenth-Century America* (Leiden: Brill, 2005)

Jefferson, Thomas, *The Papers of Thomas Jefferson*, 37 vols. to date, edited by Julian P. Boyd (Princeton, NJ: Princeton University Press, 1950)

——. *The Works of Thomas Jefferson*, 12 vols., edited by. P. L. Ford (New York and London: G. P. Putnam's Son, 1904–1905)

——. *The Writings of Thomas Jefferson*, 10 vols., edited by P. L. Ford (New York: G.P. Putnam's Sons, 1892–1899)

——. *The Writings of Thomas Jefferson*, 20 vols., edited by Andrew A. Lipscomb and Albert Ellery Bergh (Washington, DC: Thomas Jefferson Memorial Association, 1905)

Jeffries, John C., Jr., and James E. Ryan, "A Political History of the Establishment Clause," *Michigan Law Review* 100 (2001): 279

Jellinek, Georg, *The Declaration of the Rights of Man and of Citizens: A Contribution to Constitutional History* (Westport, CT: Hyperion, 1979)

John, Richard R., "Taking Sabbatarianism Seriously: The Postal System, the Sabbath, and the Transformation of American Political Culture," *Journal of the Early Republic* 10 (1990): 517

Johnson, Samuel, *A Dictionary of the English Language*, 4th ed., 2 vols. (London: W. Strahan, J. and F. Rivington, 1773)

Jorgenson, Lloyd P., *The State and the Non-Public School 1825–1925* (Columbia: University of Missouri Press, 1987)

Journal of the First Session of the Senate of the United States of America, Begun and Held at the City of New-York, March 4th, 1789, and the Thirteenth Year of the Independence of the Said States (New York: Thomas Greenleaf, 1789)

Journal of the House of Representatives of the United States, 14 vols. (Washington, DC: U.S. Government Printing Office, 1789)

Journal of the Senate of the Commonwealth of Virginia; Begun and Held in the City of Richmond, on Monday, the 19th Day of October, in the Year of Our Lord 1789 and in the Fourteenth Year of the Commonwealth (Richmond, VA: John Worrick, 1828)

Kelly, Alfred H., and Winfred A. Harbison, *The American Constitution: Its Origins and Development*, 3d ed. (New York: W. W. Norton, 1963)

Kelso, Robert W., *The History of Public Poor Relief in Massachusetts, 1620–1920* (Montclair, NJ: Patterson Smith, 1969)

Ketcham, Ralph, "Observing North Atlantic Polities, 1662–1840: Sir William Temple, Voltaire, and Alexis de Tocqueville," in *Connecting Cultures: The Netherlands in Five Centuries of Transatlantic Exchange*, edited by Rosemarijn Hoefte and Johanna C. Kardux (Amsterdam: Vrije Universiteit Press, 1994), 211

———, ed., *Selected Writings of James Madison* (Indianapolis, IN: Hackett, 2006)

Kingsbury, Harmon, *The Sabbath: A Brief History of Laws, Petitions, Remonstrances and Reports, with Facts and Arguments, Relating to the Christian Sabbath* (New York: Robert Carter, 1840)

Koch, Adrienne, and William Peden, eds., *The Life and Selected Writings of Thomas Jefferson* (New York: Modern Library, 1993)

Konig, David Thomas, *Law and Society in Puritan Massachusetts: Essex County, 1629–1692* (Chapel Hill: University of North Carolina Press, 1979)

Kossuth, Louis, *The Future of Nations, In What Consists Its Security: A Lecture Delivered in New York, June 21, 1852* (New York: Fowler and Wells, 1854)

Kramnick, Isaac, ed., *The Federalist* (New York: Penguin Books, 1987)

Kramnick, Isaac, and R. Laurence Moore, *The Godless Constitution: A Moral Defense of the Secular State* (New York: Norton & Co., 2005)

Kurland, Philip B., and Gerhard Casper, eds., *Landmark Briefs and Arguments of the Supreme Court of the United States* (Washington, DC: University Publications of America, 1975)

Kurland, Philip B., and Ralph Lerner, eds., *The Founders' Constitution*, 5 vols. (Chicago: University of Chicago Press, 1987)

Lash, Kurt T., "The Second Adoption of the Establishment Clause: The Rise of the Nonestablishment Principle," *Arizona State Law Journal* 27 (1995): 1085

Laws of the State of New York, Passed at the Sessions of the Legislature Held in the Years 1777–1801 (Albany, NY: Weed, Parsons, 1886–1887)

Laycock, Douglas, "Formal, Substantive, and Disaggregated Neutrality toward Religion," *DePaul Law Review* 39 (1990): 993

———."The Many Meanings of Separation," *University of Chicago Law Review* 70 (2003): 1667

Leland, John, *The Writings of John Leland*, edited by L. F. Greene (New York: Arno, 1969)

Levy, Leonard W., *Blasphemy: Verbal Offense against the Sacred, from Moses to Salman Rushdie* (New York: A. A. Knopf, 1993)

———. *Constitutional Opinions: Aspects of the Bill of Rights* (New York: Oxford University Press, 1986)

———. *The Establishment Clause: Religion and the First Amendment* (New York: Macmillan, 1986)

Library of Education, *The Bible in the Public Schools: Opinions of Individuals and of the Press, and Judicial Decisions* (New York: J. W. Schermerhorn & Co., 1870)

Lietzau, William K., "Rediscovering the Establishment Clause: Federalism and the Rollback of Incorporation," *DePaul Law Review* 39 (1990): 1191

Lincoln, Charles Z., William H. Johnson, and Ansel Judd Northrup, *The Colonial Laws of New York from the Year 1664 to the Revolution* (Albany, NY: J. B. Lyon, 1894)

Linford, Orma, "The Mormons and the Law: The Polygamy Cases, Part I," *Utah Law Review* 9 (1964): 308

Linn, William, *Serious Considerations on the Election of a President: Addressed to the Citizens of the United States* (New York: John Furman, 1800)

Littell, Franklin Hamlin, *From State Church to Pluralism: A Protestant Interpretation of Religion in American History* (Chicago: Aldine, 1962)

Little, David, "Calvin and Natural Rights," *Political Theology* 10.3 (2009): 411

———. "Calvinism, Constitutionalism, and Religious Freedom: An American Dilemma," *Political Theology* (forthcoming)

Lowell, James Russell, *Political Essays* (Boston: Houghton Mifflin, 1888)

Lutz, Donald S., *The Origins of American Constitutionalism* (Baton Rouge: Louisiana State University Press, 1988)

Macedo, Stephen, *Diversity and Distrust: Civic Education in a Multicultural Democracy* (Cambridge, MA: Harvard University Press, 2002)

Machiavelli, Niccolo, *The Discourses*, edited by Bernard R. Crick, translated by Leslie J. Walker (New York: Penguin, 1970)

MacIntyre, Alasdair, C., *After Virtue: A Study in Moral Theory* (Notre Dame, IN: University of Notre Dame Press, 1981)

Maclear, James Fulton, "'The True American Union' of Church and State: The Reconstruction of the Theocratic Tradition," *Church History* 28 (1959): 41

Madison, James, *Letters and Other Writings of James Madison*, 4 vols. (Philadelphia: J. B. Lippincott & Co., 1865)

———. *The Papers of James Madison*, 17 vols., edited by William Hutchinson et al. (Chicago: University of Chicago Press, 1962–1991)

———. *The Writings of James Madison*, 9 vols., edited by Gaillard Hunt (New York: G. P. Putnam's Sons, 1900–1910)

Marcus, Jacob R., *The Colonial American Jew, 1492–1776* (Detroit, MI: Wayne State University Press, 1970)

———. *Early American Jewry: The Jews of New York, New England, and Canada, 1649–1794* (Philadelphia: The Jewish Publication Society of America, 1951)

———. *The Jew in the American World: A Source Book* (Detroit: Wayne State University Press, 1995)

Martin, Luther, *Genuine Information, Delivered to the Legislature of the State of Maryland, Relative to the Proceedings of the General Convention, Lately Held at Philadelphia* (Philadelphia: Printed by Eleazer Oswald, at the Coffee-House, 1788)

Marty, Martin E., "Living with Establishment and Disestablishment in Nineteenth-Century Anglo-America," *Journal of Church and State* 18 (1976): 72

Mason, John M., *The Voice of Warning, to Christians, on the Ensuing Election of a President of the United States* (New York: G. F. Hopkins, 1800)

Masur, Louis B., *Rites of Execution: Capital Punishment and the Transformation of American Culture, 1776–1865* (New York: Oxford University Press, 1989)

McAfee, Ward M., "The Historical Context of the Failed Federal Blaine Amendment of 1876," *First Amendment Law Review* 2 (2003): 1

———. *Religion, Race, and Reconstruction: The Public School in the Politics of the 1870s* (New York: State University of New York Press, 1998)

McAllister, David, *Proceedings of the National Convention to Secure the Religious Amendment of the Constitution of the United States* (Philadelphia: Christian Statesman Association, 1874)

McCloskey, Robert G., ed., *The Bible in the Public Schools: Arguments in the Case of John D. Minor, et al. versus The Board of Education of the City of Cincinnati*, et al. (Cincinnati, OH: Robert Clarke, 1870) (New York: De Capo, 1964)

McConnell, Michael W., "Establishment and Toleration in Edmund Burke's 'Constitution of Freedom,'" *Supreme Court Review* 1995 (1996): 393

———. "Neutrality under the Religion Clauses," *Northwestern Law Review* 81 (1986): 146

McConnell, Michael W., John H. Garvey, and Thomas C. Berg, *Religion and the Constitution*, 2d ed. (New York: Aspen, 2006)

McCurry, Stephanie, *Masters of Small Worlds: Yeoman Households, Gender Relations, and the Political Culture of the Antebellum South Carolina Low Country* (New York: Oxford University Press, 1995)

McGarvie, Mark D., *One Nation under Law: America's Early National Struggles to Separate Church and State* (Dekalb: Northern Illinois University Press, 2004)

McGarvie, Mark D., and Elizabeth Mensch, "Law and Religion in Colonial America," in *Cambridge History of Law in America*, 3 vols., edited by Michael Grossberg and Christopher Tomlins (New York: Cambridge University Press, 2008), 1:324

McGlynn, Edward, "The Pope in Politics: Dr. M'Glynn Talking to the Anti-Poverty People," in *The New York Times* (New York: The New York Times Company, 1888), 9

McGreevy, John T., *Catholicism and American Freedom: A History* (New York: W.W. Norton, 2003)

———. "Thinking on One's Own: Catholicism in the American Intellectual Imagination, 1928–1960," *Journal of American History* 84 (1997): 97

McIlwain, C. H., *Constitutionalism: Ancient and Modern* (Ithaca, NY: Cornell University Press, 1966)

———. *Constitutionalism and Its Changing World* (Cambridge: Cambridge University Press, 1939)

McKinley, Albert E., *The Suffrage Franchise in the Thirteen English Colonies in America* (Philadelphia: University of Pennsylvania Press, 1905)

McLoughlin, William G., *Isaac Backus and the American Pietistic Tradition* (Boston: Little, Brown, 1967)

———. *New England Dissent, 1630–1833: The Baptists and the Separation of Church and State*, 2 vols. (Cambridge, MA: Harvard University Press, 1971)

———, ed., *Isaac Backus on Church, State, and Calvinism: Pamphlets 1754–1789* (Cambridge, MA: Harvard University Press, 1968)

Mead, Sidney E., *The Old Religion in a Brave New World: The Jefferson Memorial Lectures* (Los Angeles: University of California Press, 1977)

Meng, John J., "A Century of American Catholicism as Seen through French Eyes," *The Catholic Historical Review* 27 (1941): 41

Mensch, Elizabeth B., "The Colonial Origins of Liberal Property Rights," *Buffalo Law Review* 31 (1982): 703

———. "Religion Revival, and the Ruling Class: A Colonial History of Trinity Church," *Buffalo Law Review* 36 (1987): 472

Middleton, A. Pierce "The Colonial Virginia Parish," *Historical Magazine of the Protestant Episcopal Church* 40 (1971): 444

Miller, Glenn T., *Religious Liberty in America: History and Prospects* (Philadelphia: Westminster, 1976)

Miller, Perry, *Roger Williams: His Contribution to the American Tradition* (New York: Atheneum, 1962)

———, ed., *The Legal Mind in America* (Garden City, NY: Anchor Books, 1962)

Miller, Perry, and Thomas H. Johnson, eds., *The Puritans: A Sourcebook of Their Writings*, 2 vols. (New York: Harper Torchbook, 1963)

Mines, Flavel S., *A Presbyterian Clergyman Looking for the Church* (New York: General Protestant Episcopal Sunday School Union, 1853)

Monsma, Stephen V., *Positive Neutrality: Letting Religious Freedom Ring* (Westport, CT: Greenwood, 1993)

Mooney, Christopher F., *Public Virtue: Law and the Social Character of Religion* (Notre Dame, IN: University of Notre Dame Press, 1986)

Moore, Frank, ed., *The Diary of the American Revolution: From Newspapers and Original Documents*, 2 vols. (New York: Charles Scribner, 1860)

Moore, R. Laurence, *Religious Outsiders and the Making of Americans* (New York: Oxford University Press, 1986)

Morgan, Edmund S., *American Slavery, American Freedom: The Ordeal of Colonial Virginia* (New York: W. W. Norton, 1975)

———. *Roger Williams: The Church and the State* (New York: Harcourt, Brace & World, 1967)

———, ed., *Puritan Political Ideas, 1558–1794* (Indianapolis: Bobbs-Merrill Co., 1965)

Morris, B. F., *Christian Life and Character of the Civil Institutions of the United States* (Philadelphia: George W. Childs, 1864)

Morris, Richard B., *The Forging of the Union, 1781–1789* (San Francisco: Harper & Row, 1987)

Morrison, Samuel Eliot, *Review of Church and State in Massachusetts, New England Quarterly* (April, 1931): 357

Morse, William, *An Oration Delivered before the Citizens of Nantucket, July 4, 1829, Being the Fifty-third Anniversary of the Declaration of the Independence of the United States of America* (Boston: Putnam & Hunt, 1829)

Muñoz, Vincent Phillip, *God and the Founders* (New York: Cambridge University Press, 2009)

———. "The Original Meaning of the Establishment Clause and the Impossibility of Its Incorporation," *University of Pennsylvania Journal of Constitutional Law* 8 (2006): 585

Nadell, Pamela S., Jonathan D. Sarna, and Lance J. Sussman, eds., *New Essays in American Jewish History* (Cincinnati, OH: American Jewish Archives of Hebrew Union College-Jewish Institute of Religion, 2010)

"A National or a State Church," *Catholic World* (April, 1874): 34

Neem, Johann N., "The Elusive Common Good: Religion and Civil Society in Massachusetts, 1780–1833," *Journal of the Early Republic* 24 (2004): 397

Neuhaus, Richard John, *The Naked Public Square* (Grand Rapids, MI: W. B. Eerdmans, 1984)

Newman, Roger K., *Hugo Black: A Biography* (New York: Pantheon, 1994)

Nichols, Joel A., "Religious Liberty in the Thirteenth Colony: Church–State Relations in Colonial and Early National Georgia," *New York University Law Review* 80 (2005): 1693

Noll, Mark A., Nathan O. Hatch, and George M. Marsden, *The Search for Christian America* (Westchester, IL: Crossway Books, 1981)

Nussbaum, Martha C., *Liberty of Conscience: In Defense of America's Tradition of Religious Equality* (New York: Basic Books, 2008)

Oesterle, Dale A., and Richard B. Collins, *The Colorado State Constitution: A Reference Guide* (Westport, CT: Greenwood, 2002)

Olree, Andy G., "James Madison and Legislative Chaplains," *Northwestern University Law Review* 102 (2008): 145

Oppenheim, Samuel, *The Early History of the Jews in New York, 1654–1664: Some New Matter on the Subject* (New York: American Jewish Historical Society, 1909)

———. "More about Jacob Barsimson, The First Jewish Settler in New York," *Publications of the American Jewish Historical Society* 29 (1925): 39

Padover, Saul K., ed., *The Complete Jefferson, Containing His Major Writings* (New York: Duell, Sloan & Pearce, 1943)

Perry, William, *The Royal Standard English Dictionary*, 1st Amer. ed. (Worcester, MA: Isaiah Thomas, 1788)

Peterson, Merrill, ed., *The Portable Jefferson* (New York: Penguin Books, 1975)

Peterson, Merrill, and Robert Vaughan, eds., *The Virginia Statute of Religious Freedom* (New York: Cambridge University Press, 1988)

Pfeffer, Leo, *Church, State and Freedom*, 2d ed. (Boston: Beacon, 1967)

Pickering, Danby, ed., *The Statutes at Large from Magna Charta*, 46 vols. (Cambridge: Printed by J. Bentham, 1762–1807)

Pincus, Steve, *1688: The First Modern Revolution* (New Haven, CT: Yale University Press, 2009)

Pointer, Richard W., *Protestant Pluralism and the New York Experience: A Study of Eighteenth-Century Religious Diversity* (Bloomington: Indiana University Press, 1988)

Poore, Benjamin Perley, ed., *The Federal and State Constitutions, Colonial Charters, and Other Organic Laws of the United States*, 2d ed., 2 vols. (Union, NJ: The Lawbook Exchange, 2001)

Post, Albert, *Popular Freethought in America, 1825–1850* (New York: Octagon Books, 1974)

Powers, Edwin, *Crime and Punishment in Early Massachusetts, 1620–1692: A Documentary History* (Boston: Beacon, 1966)

Pratt, John Webb, *Religion, Politics, and Diversity: The Church–State Theme in New York History* (Ithaca, NY: Cornell University Press, 1967)

Price, Eli Kirk, *Memoir of Philip and Rachel Price* (Philadelphia: Eli K. Price and Philip M. Price, 1852)

"Prussia and the Church," *Catholic World* (March, 1876): 788

Purcell, John Baptist, and Thomas Vickers, *The Roman Catholic Church and Free Thought* (Cincinnati, OH: The First Congregational Church, 1868)

Quinlivan, Mary Elizabeth, "Ideological Controversy over Religious Establishment in Revolutionary Virginia" (PhD diss.: University of Wisconsin, 1971)

Ramsay, David, *The History of the American Revolution*, 2 vols. (Trenton, NJ: Printed and sold by James J. Wilson, 1811)

Register of Debates in Congress, 14 vols. (Washington, DC: Gales & Seaton, 1824–1837)

"Religion in our State Institutions," *Catholic World* (April, 1875): 1

Rhoden, Nancy L., *Revolutionary Anglicanism: The Colonial Church of England Clergy during the American Revolution* (New York: New York University Press, 1999)

Rhys, Isaac, "Religion and Authority: Problems of the Anglican Establishment in Virginia in the Era of the Great Awakening and the Parsons' Cause," *William & Mary Quarterly* 30 (1973): 4

Rink, Oliver A., *Holland on the Hudson: An Economic and Social History of Dutch New York* (Ithaca, NY: Cornell University Press, 1986)

Roeber, A. G., *Faithful Magistrates and Republican Lawyers: Creators of Virginia Legal Culture, 1680–1810* (Chapel Hill: University of North Carolina Press, 1980)

Rohrer, James R., "Sunday Mails and the Church–State Theme in Jacksonian America," *Journal of the Early Republic* 7 (1987): 53

Rosenthal, Lawrence, "The New Originalism Meets the Fourteenth Amendment: Original Public Meaning and the Problem of Incorporation," *Journal of Contemporary Legal Issues* 18 (2009): 361

Rossiter, Clinton, ed., *The Federalist Papers* (New York: New American Library, 1961)

Rowland, Kate M., *Life and Correspondence of George Mason, 1725–1792*, 2 vols. (New York: G. P. Putnam's Sons, 1892)

Rush, Benjamin, *A Plan for the Establishment of Public Schools and the Diffusion of Knowledge in Pennsylvania* (Philadelphia: Thomas Dobson, 1786)

———. Benjamin Rush to Patrick Henry, July 16, 1776, in *Letters of Delegates to Congress, 1774–1789*, 26 vols., edited by Paul H. Smith (Washington, DC: Library of Congress, 1976–2000), 4:473

Rutland, Robert Allen, *The Birth of the Bill of Rights, 1776–1791* (Chapel Hill: University of North Carolina, 1955)

Sandoz, Ellis, *A Government of Laws* (Baton Rouge: Louisiana State University Press, 1991)

———. "Power and Spirit in the Founding," *This World* 9 (1984): 67

———, ed., *Political Sermons of the American Founding Era, 1730–1805* (Indianapolis: Liberty, 1991)

Saphire, Richard B., "*Torasco v. Watkins* and *McDaniel v. Paty*," in *Religion and American Law: An Encyclopedia*, edited by Paul Finkelman (New York: Garland, 2000), 535

Sarna, Jonathan, *American Judaism: A History* (New Haven, CT: Yale University Press, 2004)

Schaff, Philip, *America: A Sketch of the Political, Social, and Religious Character of the United States of North America* (New York: Scribner, 1855)

———. "Statecraft and Priestcraft," *The North American Review* (November, 1885): 442

Schlesinger, Arthur M., Jr., *The Age of Jackson* (Boston: Little, Brown, 1945)

Schutz, John A., and Douglass Adair, eds., *The Spur of Fame: Dialogues of John Adams and Benjamin Rush, 1805–1813* (San Marino, CA: Huntington Library, 1966)

Seager Robert, II, ed., *The Papers of Henry Clay* (Lexington: University Press of Kentucky, 1984)

Sekulow, Jay Alan, *Witnessing Their Faith: Religious Influence on Supreme Court Justices and Their Opinions* (New York: Rowman and Littlefield, 2006)

"Separation of Church and State in Maryland," *Catholic Historical Review* 21 (July, 1935): 172

Shalhope, Robert E., "Toward a Republican Synthesis: The Emergence of an Understanding of Republicanism in an American Historiography," *William and Mary Quarterly* 29 (1972): 49

Sheridan, Thomas, *A Complete Dictionary of the English Language*, 2d ed. (London: Charles Dilly, 1789)

Silk, Mark, *Spiritual Politics: Religion and America since World War II* (New York: Simon & Schuster, 1985)

Singleton, Marvin K., "Colonial Virginia as the First Amendment Matrix: Henry, Madison, and the Assessment Establishment," in *James Madison on Religious Liberty*, edited by Robert S. Alley (Buffalo, NY: Prometheus Books, 1985), 157

Sinopoli, Richard, *The Foundations of American Citizenship: Liberalism, The Constitution, and Civic Virtue* (New York: Oxford University Press, 1992)

Smith, George L., *Religion and Trade in New Netherland: Dutch Origins and American Development* (Ithaca, NY: Cornell University Press, 1973)

Smith, Paul H., ed., *Letters of Delegates to Congress, 1774–1789*, 26 vols. (Washington, DC: Library of Congress, 1976–2000)

Smith, Steven D., "The Establishment Clause and the Problem of the Church" (Unpublished paper delivered at Princeton University, 2009)

———. *Foreordained Failure: The Quest for a Constitutional Principle of Religious Freedom* (New York: Oxford University Press, 1995)

Smith, William Loughton, *The Pretensions of Thomas Jefferson to the Presidency Examined; and the Charges against John Adams Refuted* (Philadelphia: John Fenno, 1796)

Snee, Joseph M., "Religious Disestablishment and the Fourteenth Amendment," *Washington University Law Quarterly* (1954): 371

Sonnenberg-Stern, Karina, *Emancipation and Poverty: The Ashkenazi Jews of Amsterdam, 1796–1850* (London: Macmillan, 2000)

Sparks, Jared, ed., *The Diplomatic Correspondence of the American Revolution*, 12 vols. (Boston: N. Hale and Gray & Bowen, 1829–1830)

Spear, Samuel T., *Religion and the State, or the Bible and the Public Schools* (New York: Dodd, Mead, 1876)

Stanlis, Peter J., ed., *Selected Writings and Speeches* (Garden City, NY: Anchor Books, 1963)

Stark, Rodney, and Roger Finke, "American Religion in 1776: A Statistical Portrait," *Sociological Analysis* 49 (1988): 39

The Statutes of the Realm, 11 vols. (London: Dawsons, 1963)

Steiner, Bernard C., *The Life and Correspondence of James McHenry, Secretary of War under Washington and Adams* (Cleveland, OH: Burrows Brothers, 1907)

Stephenson, Carl, and Frederick Marcham, eds. and trans., *Sources of English Constitutional History*, 2 vols. (New York: Harper & Row, 1937)

Stern, Marc D., "Blaine Amendments, Anti-Catholicism, and Catholic Dogma," *First Amendment Law Review* 2 (2003): 153

Stokes, Anson P., *Church and State in the United States*, 3 vols. (New York: Harper & Brothers, 1950)

———, and Leo F. Pfeffer, *Church and State in the United States*, rev., 1-vol. ed. (Boston: Beacon, 1967)

Storing, Herbert J., ed., *The Complete Anti-Federalist*, 7 vols. (Chicago: University of Chicago Press, 1981)

Story, Joseph, *Commentaries on the Constitution of the United States*, 3 vols. (Boston: Hilliard, Gray, 1833)

Story, William W., ed., *Life and Letters of Joseph Story* (Boston: Charles C. Little & James Brown, 1851)

Swetschinski, Daniel M., *Reluctant Cosmopolitans: The Portuguese Jews of Seventeenth-Century Amsterdam* (London: Littman Library of Jewish Civilization, 2000)

Swift, Zephaniah, *A System of the Laws of the State of Connecticut*, 2 vols. (New York: Arno, 1972)

Swindler, William F., ed., *Sources and Documents of United States Constitutions*, 11 vols. (Dobbs Ferry, NY: Oceana, 1973–1988)

Swomley, John M., *Religious Liberty and the Secular State* (Buffalo, NY: Prometheus Books, 1985)

Taylor, Robert, ed., *Papers of John Adams*, 15 vols. (Cambridge, MA: Belknap Press of Harvard University Press, 1977)

Tennant, George, "Writings," *South Carolina Historical Magazine* 61.4 (1960): 194

Thomason, John F., *The Foundations of Public Schools of South Carolina* (Columbia, SC: State Co., 1925)

Thorpe, Francis Newton, ed., *The Federal and State Constitutions, Colonial Charters and Other Organic Laws of the State Territories and Colonies Now or Heretofore Forming the United States of America*, 7 vols. (Washington, DC: U.S. Government Printing Office, 1909)

Tierney, Brian, *The Idea of Natural Rights: Studies on Natural Rights, Natural Law, and Church Law, 1150–1625* (Grand Rapids, MI: Wm. B. Eerdmans, 1997)

———. "Religious Rights: An Historical Perspective," in *Religious Human Rights in Global Perspective: Religious Perspectives*, edited by John Witte Jr. and Johan D. van der Vyver (The Hague: Martinus Nijhoff, 1996), 42

Tocqueville, Alexis de, *Democracy in America*, edited by J. P. Mayer and Max Lerner, translated by George Lawrence (New York: Harper & Row, 1969)

Tomlins, Christopher L., *Law, Labor, and Ideology in the Early American Republic* (New York: Cambridge University Press, 1993)

Trattner, Walter I., *From Poor Law to Welfare State: A History of Social Welfare in America* (New York: Macmillan, 1989)

Turner, Charles, "Massachusetts Election Sermon," in *They Preached Liberty*, edited by Franklin P. Cole (Indianapolis, IN: Liberty, 1976), 161

Turner, James, *Without God, Without Creed: The Origins of Unbelief in America* (Baltimore, MD: Johns Hopkins University Press, 1985)

Twiss, Sumner B., "Roger Williams and Freedom of Conscience and Religion as a Natural Right" (unpublished paper delivered at a conference at Harvard Divinity School on November 13–14, 2009)

Tyler, Alice Felt, *Freedom's Ferment: Phases of American Social History to 1860* (Minneapolis: University of Minnesota Press, 1944)

Underwood, James Lowell, *The Constitution of South Carolina*, 4 vols. (Columbia: University of South Carolina Press, 1986–1994)

"Union of Church and State," *The Christian Intelligencer and Eastern Chronicle* (October 5, 1827)

Updegraph, Charles L., *U.S. Marine Corps Special Units of World War II* (Washington, DC: U.S. Government Printing Office, 1977)

Urofsky, Melvin, and Paul Finkelman, *A March of Liberty: A Constitutional History of the United States*, 3d ed., 2 vols. (New York: Oxford University Press, 2011)

Utter, Robert F., and Edward J. Larson, "Church and State on the Frontier: The History of the Establishment Clauses in the Washington State Constitution," *Hastings Constitutional Law Quarterly* 15 (1988): 451

Van der Vyver, Johan D. and John Witte Jr., eds., *Religious Human Rights in Global Perspective: Legal Perspectives* (The Hague: Martinus Nijhoff, 1996)

Van Der Zee, Henri and Barbara, *A Sweet and Alien Land: The Story of Dutch New York* (New York: Viking, 1978)

Vetterli, Richard, and Gary Bryner, *In Search of the Republic* (Totowa, NJ: Rowman and Littlefield, 1987)

Viteritti, Joseph P., "Davey's Plea: Blaine, Blair, Witters, and the Protection of Religious Freedom," *Harvard Journal of Law and Public Policy* 27 (2003): 299

Voltaire, *Lettres Philosophiques* (Paris and Amsterdam: E. Lucas, 1734)

Walker, Timothy, "Introductory Lecture on the Dignity of the Law as a Profession, Delivered at Cincinnati College, November 4, 1837," in *The Legal Mind in America*, edited by Perry Miller (Garden City, NY: Anchor Books, 1962), 240

Walker, Williston, *The Creeds and Platforms of Congregationalism* (Boston: Pilgrim, 1960)

Walters, Kerry S., *The American Deists: Voices of Reason and Dissent in the Early Republic* (Lawrence: University of Kansas Press, 1992)

Warburton, William, *The Alliance between Church and State* (London: Fletcher Gyles, 1736)

Ward, Nathaniel, *The Simple Cobbler of Aggawam in America*, edited by Lawrence C. Wroth (New York: Scholars' Facsimiles & Reprints, 1937)

[Warner, Henry Whiting,] *An Inquiry into the Moral and Religious Character of the American Government* (New York: Wiley and Putnam, 1838)

Washington, George, *The Writings of George Washington*, edited by John C. Fitzpatrick, 39 vols. (Washington, DC: U.S. Government Printing Office, 1931–1944)

West, John G., Jr., *The Politics of Revelation and Reason: Religion and Civic Life in the New Nation* (Lawrence: University Press of Kansas, 1996)

Wiebe, Robert H., *The Opening of American Society: From the Adoption of the Constitution to the Eve of Disunion* (New York: Vintage Books, 1985)

Williams, Elisha, *The Essential Rights and Liberties of Protestants* (Boston: S. Kneeland and T. Green in Queenstreet, 1744)

Williams, Roger, *Complete Writings of Roger Williams*, 7 vols. (New York: Russell & Russell, 1963)

———. *A Key into the Language of America* (Bedford, MA: Applewood Books, 1997)

Wilson, Henry Austin, ed., *Constitutions and Canons Ecclecsiastical, 1604* (Oxford: Clarendon, 1923)

Winchester, Elhanan, "A Century Sermon on the Glorious Revolution (1788)," in *Political Sermons of the American Founding Era, 1730–1805*, edited by Ellis Sandoz (Indianapolis: Liberty Fund, 1991), 969

Witherspoon, John, *The Dominion of Providence over the Passions of Men: A Sermon Preached at Princeton, on the 17th of May, 1776, Being the General Fast Appointed by the Congress through the United Colonies* (Philadelphia: R. Aitken, 1776)

———. *Lectures on Moral Philosophy*, edited by Varnum Collins (Princeton, NJ: Princeton University Press, 1912)

Witte, John, Jr., "'A Most Mild and Equitable Establishment of Religion': John Adams and the 1780 Massachusetts Constitution," *Journal of Church and State* 41 (1999): 213

———. "Facts and Fictions about the History of Separation of Church and State," *Journal of Church and State* 48 (2006): 15

————. "One Public Religion, Many Private Religions: John Adams and the 1780 Massachusetts Constitution," in *The Founders on God and Government*, edited by Daniel L. Dreisbach, Mark D. Hall, and Jeffry R. Morrison (Lanham, MD: Rowman and Littlefield, 2004), 23

————. *The Reformation of Rights: Law, Religion, and Human Rights in Early Modern Calvinism* (Cambridge: Cambridge University Press, 2007)

————. *Religion and the American Constitutional Experiment*, 2d ed. (Boulder, CO: Westview, 2005)

————. "That Serpentine Wall of Separation," *Michigan Law Review* 101 (2003): 1869

Witte, John, Jr., and M. Christian Green, "The American Constitutional Experiment in Religious Human Rights: The Perennial Search for Principles," in *Religious Human Rights in Global Perspective: Legal Perspectives*, edited by Johan D. van der Vyver and John Witte Jr. and (The Hague: Martinus Nijhoff, 1996), 517

Witte, John, Jr., and Joel A. Nichols, *Religion and the American Constitutional Experiment*, 3d ed. (Boulder, CO: Westview, 2011)

Wood, Gordon S., *The Creation of the American Republic, 1776–1787* (Chapel Hill: University of North Carolina Press, 1969)

————. *The Radicalism of the American Revolution* (New York: A. A. Knopf, 1992)

Wood, James E., Jr., "The Secular State," *Journal of Church and State* 7 (1965): 169

Woodhouse, A. S. P., ed., *Puritanism and Liberty: Being the Army Debates (1647–9) from the Clarke Manuscripts with Supplemental Documents*, 2d ed. (Chicago: University of Chicago Press, 1974)

Woolsey, Theodore Dwight, *The Constitution and Government of the United States in Regard to Religion* (New York: Scribner, 1873)

Wortman, Tunis, "A Solemn Address to Christians and Patriots," in *Political Sermons of the American Founding Era, 1730–1805*, 2d ed., edited by Ellis Sandoz (Indianapolis, IN: Liberty Fund, 1998), 1488

Wyatt-Brown, Bertram, "Prelude to Abolitionism: Sabbatarian Politics and the Rise of the Second Party System," *Journal of American History* 58 (1971): 323

Zuckerman, Michael, "Holy Wars, Civil Wars: Religion and Economics in Nineteenth Century America," *Prospects* 16 (1991): 212

Zwierlein, Frederick J., *Religion in New Netherland* (Rochester, NY: John P. Smith, 1910)

{ INDEX }